TRACE METALS IN THE ENVIRONMENT

Volume 2 – SILVER

TRACE METALS
IN THE ENVIRONMENT

Volume 2 – SILVER

by

Ivan C. Smith
Senior Advisor for Environmental Science

Bonnie L. Carson
Associate Chemist

Midwest Research Institute
Kansas City, Missouri

ANN ARBOR SCIENCE
PUBLISHERS INC
P.O. BOX 1425 • ANN ARBOR, MICH. 48106

Published 1977 by Ann Arbor Science Publishers, Inc.
P.O. Box 1425, Ann Arbor, Michigan 48106

Library of Congress Catalog Card Number 77-088486
ISBN 0-250-40215-7
Manufactured in the United States of America

The work upon which this publication is based was
performed pursuant to Contract No. N01-ES-2-2090
with the National Institute of Environmental Health
Sciences, Department of Health, Education, and
Welfare.

PREFACE

        In 1972, the National Institute of Environmental Health Sciences
initiated a program with Midwest Research Institute to assemble information on production, uses, natural environmental levels, anthropogenic
sources, human and animal health effects, and environmental impacts of
selected trace elements. This book on silver is one of several compre-
hensive documents which have resulted from that program. Scientists in
many disciplines should find this work to be of value.

        Bonnie L. Carson compiled the information and was the major author
of this book. Dr. Ivan C. Smith served as the program advisor and technical
editor of the manuscript.

        The authors wish to express their appreciation to consultants
Dr. A. E. Morris, Professor of Metallurgical Engineering at the University
of Missouri at Rolla; Dr. Ernest E. Angino, Department of Geology, Uni-
versity of Kansas; and Dr. A. D. Allen, as well as to our colleagues at
Midwest Research Institute who assisted in the acquisition, compilation,
and editing of the information in this book: Mr. Larry Jennings, Dr. Thomas
W. Lapp, Mr. Kenneth R. Walker, Mr. Greg Morgan, Miss Lynn Reidel, and
Mrs. Maria Luisa Dimagmaliw. Particular thanks are due to the MRI library
staff; Dr. Harold Orel, technical writing consultant; and to Miss Audene
Cook and her staff for typing the manuscript.

        We wish to acknowledge the assistance from various scientists
throughout the world who have offered constructive comments regarding the
scope and organization of these manuscripts and who have encouraged their
continued support and publication.

        Finally, we especially acknowledge the support, encouragement,
and patience of Dr. Warren T. Piver (project officer) and Dr. Hans Falk of
the National Institute of Environmental Health Sciences.

TABLE OF CONTENTS

TABLE OF CONTENTS (Continued)

TABLE OF CONTENTS (Continued)

TABLE OF CONTENTS (Continued)

TABLE OF CONTENTS (Continued)

Page

LIST OF FIGURES

Figure	Title	Page
III-1	Principal Mining Districts From Which Ores and Concentrates of Gold, Silver, Copper, Lead, and Zinc Were Produced in 1957	75
IV-1	Supply-Demand Relationships for Silver, 1968	102
V-1	Silver Cyanidation Flow Sheet.	142
V-2	Flotation Practice, Bunker Hill Company, Kellogg, Idaho. .	149
V-3	Flow Diagram of Copper Smelting and Refining Processes . .	152
V-4	Flow Diagram of Lead Ore Processing Scheme	155
V-5	Flow Diagram of Zinc Ore Processing.	159
V-6	Silver Electrolytic Refining Process	165
V-7	Simplified Flow Sheet for Smelting and Refining of Secondary Precious-Metal Scrap	166
V-8	Eastman Kodak Method for Silver Recovery from Waste Film .	172
VI-1	Weather Modification Projects in the United States-- Fiscal Year 1968	224
VII-1	Silver Flow Based on 6-Months Operation of a Western U.S. Copper Mine-Mill-Smelter.	299
VII-2	Particulate Emissions at Existing Domestic Primary Copper Smelters, Tons/Day.	302

TABLE OF CONTENTS (Continued)

LIST OF TABLES (Continued)

TABLE OF CONTENTS (Continued)

LIST OF TABLES (Continued)

LIST OF TABLES (Continued)

LIST OF TABLES (Continued)

TABLE OF CONTENTS (Concluded)

LIST OF TABLES (Concluded)

SUMMARY

This report, prepared under the sponsorship of the National Institute of Environmental Health Sciences, summarizes available information
on the environmental occurrence (both natural and anthropogenic), processing, uses, and disposal of silver, its alloys, and its compounds. We have
identified sources of losses of silver to the environment, attempted to determine their magnitude and chemical forms, and assessed human health hazards
associated with environmental contamination by silver.

Silver occurs in nature as native silver, natural alloys, and
various minerals. Most silver occurs as argentiferous galena. Principal
silver minerals are argentite, acanthite, argentian tetrahedrite and tennantite, proustite, pyrargyrite, chlorargyrite, and argentojarosite. Silver is frequently recovered as a by-product, for example, from smelting of
Canadian nickel ores and U.S. lead-zinc and porphyry copper ores and from
South African platinum and gold deposits.

The average silver content in crustal rocks and soils is about
0.1 ppm. Ambient air concentrations of silver in rural to highly industrialized urban settings were 0.17 ng/m^3 to 7.0 ng/m^3. (The threshold limit
value for silver is 0.01 mg/m^3.) The highest value recorded in the literature for silver in air is 175 ng/m^3 near a lead smelter which was in the
process of shutting down. The average dissolved silver content in natural
fresh waters is about 0.0002 ppm; an average 0.0026 ppm silver was found
in 6.6% of U.S. surface waters. About 30 to 70% of the silver in surface
waters may be carried on the suspended particulates. The maximum value
found in tapwater was 0.026 ppm silver. Seawater contains about 0.0003 ppm
silver. Higher values in water and soil occur near mineralized zones and
industrial activity. Silver concentrations of 0.00005 to 0.045 ppm have
been found in effluents from municipal sewage treatment plants, and silver
concentrations as high as 900 ppm have been reported in sewage sludge.

Silver is a normal trace constituent of many organisms. A wide
range of silver is found in plant tissues; the ash of terrestrial plants
usually contains about 0.2 ppm silver with the silver concentrations higher
in the seeds, nuts, and fruits than in other plant parts. Enrichment factors as high as 22,000 have been calculated for marine animals, whereas
freshwater animals concentrate silver from the water by a factor of 3,080.
The ash of the vital parts, tissues, and blood of mammals contains up to
50 ppm silver (liver). The human body rarely contains more than 10 ppm
(dry weight) although the body of the sufferer of the worst case of argyria
(tissue pigmentation due to silver ingestion) contained an average 1,300
ppm (wet weight). There are significant unexplained geographical or racial
differences in human tissue silver concentrations, with tissues from persons

1

in the Near East containing the highest concentrations. Silver also occurs
in coal (< 0.1 to 300 ppm) and petroleum (up to 100 ppm in crude oils).
The maximum value found for silver in unused liquid petroleum fractions is
0.117 ppm in residual fuel oil. (Higher amounts occur in used lubricating
oil due to wear of silver bearings.)

Silver ores; copper ores; and complex ores containing copper,
lead, and/or zinc provide approximately equal amounts (about 25 to 32%
each) of U.S. silver mine production. About 12 to 14% of the domestic
silver output is recovered from lead ores and about 4%, from zinc ores.
The silver mines are located chiefly in the Coeur d' Alene mining district
in the northern Idaho panhandle. Following Idaho in rank of production of
silver are Arizona, Utah, Colorado, and Montana. Secondary sources of silver comprise new scrap, which is generated in the manufacture of silver-
containing products; coin and bullion; and old scrap, chiefly comprising,
electrical products, old film and photoprocessing wastes, batteries,
jewelry, silverware, and bearings.

The United States mines and refines about 40 million troy ounces
of new silver annually and refines about the same amount of silver from
foreign ores and concentrates. In addition, the U.S. refines 46.6 to 125.8
million troy ounces (average 78.5 million troy ounces) from secondary sources
in the period 1966 to 1974.

Porphyry copper ores (80% of U.S. copper production), containing
about 0.05 to 0.1 troy oz silver/ton, are mined largely by open-pit methods
in Arizona, Montana, and Utah. Silver ores, including those silver-lead
ores containing less than 5% lead, are mined by a variety of underground
methods, chiefly in the Coeur d' Alene district of Idaho. Gold ores are
mined by placer or underground methods. Lead, lead-zinc, and zinc ores
are generally mined by underground methods. Minor methods for milling
(upgrading) raw ores include amalgamation and cyanidation (gold ores) and
various copper leaching processes (in which little silver is expected to
be recovered). The major process for upgrading base-metal ores containing silver is flotation.

The processing of copper ore follows the sequence of roasting,
smelting to produce matte, converting matte to blister copper, and fire
or electrolytic refining. Fire-refining capacity in the U.S. in 1968 was
365,000 tons, whereas 2.3 million tons of copper was electrolytically refined. There are 15 primary copper smelters in Washington, Arizona, Texas,
New Mexico, Nevada, Utah, Montana, Michigan, and Tennessee. Approximately
60% of the U.S. electrolytic-refining capacity is in six Atlantic Coast
refineries while fire-refining is done in Michigan, New York, New Jersey,
New Mexico, and Texas. In electrolytic refining, blister copper is fur-
naced to produce anodes whose electrolysis leaves anode slimes, which are
treated by silver refineries to recover silver, gold, and other precious
metals.

2

Lead ore concentrates are treated by the sequence of sintering, smelting, drossing, and refining. Most of the silver is recovered
in the lead bullion desilverizing step, wherein silver is recovered in
a top layer of added zinc (Parke's process). In the electrolytic refining of lead, silver is found in the anode slime. Primary lead
smelters operate in Idaho, Montana, Missouri, and Texas.

The major outlet of silver from zinc ore processing is the
residue from the retorting (and reduction) of the zinc oxide produced by
roasting and briquetting, roasting, and sintering, or sintering alone.
The residue is shipped to a lead smelter if the silver, gold, lead, and
copper content warrants recovery. In the electrolytic zinc process, the
roasted zinc is leached with sulfuric acid to leave a silver-containing
residue, which is shipped to a lead plant. There are eight primary U.S.
zinc smelters in Texas, Ohio, Oklahoma, Idaho, and Pennsylvania.

At the primary silver refinery, silver is recovered from the
electrolytic copper refinery slimes or from the dore' metal recovered at
the lead refinery. The slimes are leached and/or roasted to remove impurities, and the treated slimes are smelted to produce dore' metal,
which is electrolytically refined by the Moebius or Balbach-Thum process.
Major U.S. silver producers operated primary silver refineries in 1965
in New Jersey, Maryland, Utah, and Idaho.

Secondary precious-metal refiners smelt low-tenor precious-
metals scrap with scrap lead in a reverberatory furnace to give lead
bullion. This bullion is mixed with clean silver scrap, and the mixture
is cupelled to give dore' metal, which is refined by electrolysis or
acid-parting. Some high-copper scrap containing precious metals is fed
to the blast furnace. High-grade precious-metal scrap and copper anode
slimes are fed to the dore' furnace. Precipitation, ion-exchange, reductive exchange, adsorption by activated carbon, and electrolytic recovery are used to remove silver from wastewater. Processes patented
for removal of silver from photographic solutions include those based
on adsorption, precipitation, and electrolysis. Electrolytic methods
to recover silver from motion-picture waste solutions are preferred because they allow reuse of the fixer and give high-purity silver. The
silver-plate manufacturer collects spills of electrolyte, spent electrolyte, and dilute wash solutions and processes them to precipitate silver
and oxidize cyanide before discharge as plant waste.

Fabrication methods for silver and silver-base alloys include
melting, casting, extruding, rolling, annealing, drawing, and polishing.
Silver powders, which are produced by physical, chemical, and electrochemical processes, are chiefly used for porous electrodes (for primary
batteries and storage cells) and for production of pseudo alloys or

mixtures of metals that cannot be melt-alloyed with silver (used primarily for electrical contacts). More than 95% of all silver utilization in chemicals is for production of silver nitrate with silver cyanide, chloride, and oxide accounting for the remainder. The largest user of silver nitrate products is the photographic industry. Silver nitrate is manufactured by treating 99.9 to 99.99% pure silver with a hot nitric acid solution, precipitating the impurities, crystallizing, and recrystallizing for photographic uses and other uses requiring the highest purity.

The total average net industrial silver consumption in the period 1966 to 1972 was about 150 million troy ounces with the sales distributed among electroplated ware 9.76%, sterling ware 17.05%, jewelry 3.16%, photographic materials 28.03%, dental and medical supplies 1.44%, mirrors 1.15%, brazing alloys and solders 9.88%, batteries 4.91%, contacts and conductors 20.05%, catalysts 2.10%, bearings 0.30%, and miscellaneous 2.18%. Silver in photography probably will not be replaced rapidly, certainly not within the next 10 years, but it may be used more often in only very small catalytic amounts. Since 1970, U.S. subsidiary coinage has not contained silver; although minting of up to 45-million silver-clad subsidiary coins beginning on 4 July 1975, has been authorized.

The chief industrial reactions employing silver catalysts are the dehydration and oxidation of methanol to formaldehyde and the oxidation of ethylene with air or oxygen to ethylene oxide. Silver compounds used to separate mixed hydrocarbon streams in petrochemical refineries may be included in the catalysts category.

The widespread medical use of silver compounds for topical application to mucous membranes and for internal use became nearly obsolete in the past 30 years because of the fear of argyria and the development of sulfonamide and antibiotic antimicrobials. Many new burn dressings containing silver compounds have recently been patented and the medical use of silver may be on the upswing.

Oligodynamic sterilization processes were widely used in the 30s in Europe for treating food, drinking water, and swimming pools. There has been recent renewed interest in silver for water purification of swimming pools and drinking water. Food, drugs, and beverages are frequently processed in silver clad or plated apparatus.

Perhaps as much as 100,000 troy oz silver as silver iodide is used annually in the U.S. at the present time for weather modification purposes including rain and snow-making and hail suppression.

The use of silver as a hair dye has been reported to lead to argyria.

We have identified the chief sources of silver losses to the environment and estimated their annual magnitude: 3.1 million troy ounces in mining and milling (0.042 million troy ounces to the air); 5.5 million troy ounces from primary smelting and refining of copper, lead, zinc, and silver (1.2 to 1.3 million troy ounces to the air); 4 to 8 million troy ounces from secondary smelting and refining of precious-metal scrap (0.8 million troy ounces to the air); 0.15 to 0.26 million troy ounces from fabrication processes (0.097 million troy ounces to the air); 39.1 million troy ounces from use and disposal (0.92 million troy ounces to the air); and at least 26.8 to 28.2 million troy ounces from inadvertent sources (6.0 to 7.4 million troy ounces to the air). Of all the inadvertent sources, only the silver contents of petroleum (fuel oil and gasoline) and coal-burning emissions are well documented so that the estimates of 1.74 million troy ounces lost to the air and 5.7 million troy ounces lost to land (incinerator ashes) from these sources are well founded. If 3.1 million troy ounces silver are emitted by the cement industry, perhaps 15.1 million troy ounces is lost to land (at least 7.8 million troy ounces) and water. Qualitative data and crude calculations indicate that iron and steel-making high temperature operations may emit 1.2 to 2.6 million troy ounces silver annually to the air. (These estimates for iron and steel emissions are modifications of the GCA Corporation estimate of 5.6 million troy ounces.)

Forms of silver in atmospheric emissions are probably silver sulfide, silver sulfate, silver carbonate, silver halides, and metallic silver; only the sulfate is appreciably water soluble.

The chief source of water pollution by silver is the 16 million troy ounces lost annually as silver thiosulfate complexes in photographic developing solutions discarded directly to sewers by small photofinishers. Probably 75% of this silver is eventually trapped in the sewage sludge. Very minor amounts of silver cyanide are expected to be discharged to waters; after treatment at the source, the wastes usually contain silver hydroxide complexes and silver chloride. Silver in sewage treatment plant effluents may be associated with suspended particulates or present as the thiosulfate complex, colloidal silver chloride and sulfide, and soluble organic complexes. In natural waters, silver may be present in these forms and also adsorbed to plankton and present in the tissues of micro-organisms. Silver on suspended matter and in colloidal forms ultimately settles out in the sediments as do insoluble silver salts. At the water-treatment plant, most of the silver is precipitated after lime treatment or adsorbed on the alum flocculent. Chlorination converts some silver to silver chloride or soluble silver chloride complex.

Silver in soils is largely immobilized by precipitation as insoluble salts and by complexation and/or adsorption by organic matter, clays, and manganese and iron oxides. Silver occurring in foods, when due to contamination by processing apparatus or to direct treatment by silver as an antimicrobial, may be ionic silver but more probably is complexed by the organic materials present, probably via sulfur linkages. The forms of silver incorporated into the tissues of edible plants and animals are most probably protein complexes with bonding by sulfide or amino acid residues.

The acute toxic effects of silver and silver compounds in humans--tissue necrosis, hemorrhage, gastrointestinal symptoms, pulmonary edema, and death--have resulted only from accidental or suicidal overdoses of medical forms of silver. Ingestion of 10 g silver nitrate is usually fatal. The most common noticeable effects of chronic human exposure to silver or silver compounds are generalized argyria, localized argyria, and argyrosis (argyria of the eye). Generalized argyria is a slate-gray pigmentation of the skin and hair caused by deposition of silver in the tissues. In localized argyria, only limited areas (usually those to which silver compounds were applied medicinally) are pigmented. Every common silver compound has caused generalized argyria with silver nitrate being the leading cause. Medical and occupational exposure are the two most important routes to argyria; the latter was never common.

Silver may enter the body via the respiratory tract, the gastrointestinal tract, mucous membranes, or broken skin. In most cases of argyria caused by occupational exposure, absorption has taken place via the respiratory tract or at the eyes. Silver is retained by all body tissues and, once deposited, is not liberated. It accumulates in the body with age even if none is administered intentionally. Average human dietary intake is estimated at up to 0.088 mg/day. According to animal experiments, generally, less than 10% of orally ingested silver is absorbed and only about 3 to 10% of the amount absorbed is retained in the tissues. The apparently great variability among individuals in their susceptibility to argyria can probably be explained by the variability in absorption and retention. Most silver reaching the bloodstream by direct injection or from absorption is excreted via the bile into the feces.

Water concentrations as low as 0.004 ppm silver are toxic to some aquatic species (Daphnia, guppies, and sticklebacks). American osyter embryos fail to develop at 0.0037 ppm silver and are killed at 0.0064 ppm silver. The adults of oysters and fish appear more resistant to elevated concentrations of silver than gametes, embryos, and fry.

Silver may retard the growth of freshwater fish and is definitely injurious to them at concentrations 0.1 to 0.5 ppm.

Acute effects from silver in mammals are usually associated with intravenous administration to produce acute pulmonary edema for study. During chronic exposure of birds and mammals to silver, the following effects were observed: lowered immunological activity, altered membrane permeability, enzyme inhibitions including antagonism to copper and selenium metabolism, vascular hypertension, and shortening of the life span.

There is no evidence that terrestrial animals concentrate silver from environmental sources. Fish, mollusks, and crustaceans, especially marine animals, accumulate silver from environmental sources.

Silver is toxic to bacteria and has been used as an antimicrobial in medicine and water purification. For example, water contaminated with 200 to 1,900 microbiological units of microorganisms is completely sterilized in 15 to 20 min with 0.1 to 0.2 ppm silver ion. The toxicity of silver to lower plant life is comparable with that of the very toxic ions of mercury, copper and cadmium. Marine (0.06 ppm silver) and freshwater plants (0.026 ppm) concentrate silver by a factor of 200. Few terrestrial plants serving as human foods, most notably mushrooms, concentrate silver significantly. Aqueous silver ion solutions applied to food crops as a fungicide were toxic. For example, 9.8 ppm silver was fatal to maize, and 100 to 1,000 ppm silver nitrate solutions were toxic to young tomato and bean plants.

Present concentrations of silver found in the environment appear to offer little likelihood for acute or chronic poisoning of humans. The only proven effect of chronic exposure to silver in humans is argyria, which has been caused almost exclusively by occupational or therapeutic exposure to much larger amounts of silver (minimum necessary absorption 0.91 g) than can feasibly be ingested or inhaled from environmental sources. Regular ingestion of food, fish, and plants originating from silver-contaminated waters or soils appears to pose no problem with respect to argyria at present, but no data were found to indicate whether animals pastured or fed grains raised on sewage-sludge-amended soils may have increased silver content in their flesh and milk.

We conclude that of the approximately 80 million troy ounces of silver lost to the environment annually, most will be disposed of onto land, chiefly in the form of the innocuous minerals, metal, or alloys and be largely immobilized. About 9 to 11 million troy ounces silver may be lost to the air, but the estimate of about 4 to 6 million troy ounces from iron, steel, and cement production is highly questionable. The atmospheric silver emissions have yet to produce any reported ambient air concentrations approaching the threshold limit value for occupational exposure of 0.01 mg/m^3.

The most likely silver losses that would enter the food chain are those to surface waters (at least 4.73 million troy ounces from photography, mill tailings, and electroplating) and those to agricultural land (perhaps as much as 2.5 million troy ounces silver from photoprocessing wastes is found in sewage sludges that may be spread on land). Sewage-sludge-amended soil may have 10 times or more silver than normal. However, after mixing the sludge with the soil, most of the silver is immobilized. Little is known about plant uptake of silver from such soils, but it is likely that silver may be incorporated into food crops in greater than normal amounts. Silver levels in mollusks, fish, meats, food crops, and drinking water do not at present pose any threat to the general population with respect to argyria because of the low absorption of silver by humans and its even lower retention by body tissues. In this respect, we conclude that the threshold limit value and the U.S. Public Health Service drinking water standard (1962) for silver (0.05 ppm) misrepresent the relative danger from silver compared with known toxic materials.

Currently, the most likely adverse effect of environmental losses of silver is the toxicity of silver to aquatic plants serving in the food chain and to food fish and mollusks, especially their gametes, embryos, and fry.

We recommend further studies on silver uptake from soils and sediments by plants; on human absorption and retention of silver from food and medicinals; and on emissions from copper, lead, zinc, and silver smelters and refineries and especially those from iron, steel, and cement production.

I. INTRODUCTION

This document summarizes information available from scientific and trade literature and industrial contacts on the environmental occurrence (both natural and anthropogenic), processing from ore to ultimate products, uses, and disposal of silver and its compounds and alloys. The probable losses, distribution pathways, and ecological consequences of silver presented in this report have been based on the best analytical and statistical data, where available, and on subjective evaluations, where reliable data were few or lacking.

The findings of this study are presented in the following nine major sections: Distribution of Silver in the Environment, Domestic Sources of Industrial Silver, Economics of Silver, Primary and Secondary Silver Recovery Processes, Uses of Silver (including a subsection on Fabrication of Silver Intermediate Products), Losses to the Environment, Physiological Effects of Silver and Its Compounds, Human Health Hazard From Environmental Forms of Silver, and Conclusions and Recommendations. Figures appear where first mentioned in the narrative; all tables follow the narrative in each section; and section bibliographies, when included, are found at the end of the sections.

The appendices follow the same general format as the major sections. Appendix A includes tabulations of the physical and mechanical properties of silver and its alloys. Appendix B, Chemistry of Silver, includes the subsections: Oxidation States and Representative Compounds of Silver, Corrosion, Environmental Chemistry of Silver, Alloys, Analysis, and the Photographic Process.

II. DISTRIBUTION OF SILVER IN THE ENVIRONMENT

Silver occurs in nature as native silver, natural alloys, and various compounds, but most silver occurs in the form of argentiferous galena. Domestic silver is obtained chiefly as a by-product from gold, copper, and lead-zinc recovery.

The average silver content in crustal rocks and soil is about 0.1 ppm. The average silver content in natural fresh waters is about 0.2 ppb. Higher values in water and soil occur near mineralized zones and industrial activity. Silver also occurs in trace amounts in plants, animal and human tissues, coal, and petroleum. Coal and petroleum combustion are major sources of atmospheric silver emissions.

A. Silver-Containing Minerals and Deposits

Silver metal occurs worldwide as native silver or associated with other metals.[1] Native silver is widely distributed in small amounts but is more rare than native gold. The silver minerals are listed in Table II-1. Principal silver minerals are argentite, acanthite, argentian tetrahedrite and tennantite, proustite, pyrargyrite, chlorargyrite, and argentojarosite.[2] The silver content of various other minerals is given in Table II-2. Silver is also recovered as a by-product from smelting of Canadian nickel ores and U.S. lead-zinc and porphyry copper ores and from South African platinum and gold deposits.[3]

Silver deposits are classified as copper-silver shale deposits (Kupfershiefer type); disseminations in sandstones ("red bed" type); silver-bearing skarn-type deposits, lodes, veins, etc., usually in sedimentary rocks; silver-gold and gold-silver veins in or associated with volcanic flows, tuffs, etc.; and silver deposits in complex geological environments (sedimentary rocks, volcanic rocks, etc.).[2] See Table II-3, which includes the location and characteristics of the various kinds of deposits.

B. Silver in Rocks

Varying estimates for the terrestrial abundance of silver have been reported in the literature. Goldschmidt (1954) estimated 0.02 ppm silver in the lithosphere; Rankama and Sahama (1950) and Green (1959) estimated 0.10 ppm and 0.2 ppm, respectively, for the average concentration in igneous rocks; and Taylor (1964) calculated 0.07 ppm silver in the continental crust, by averaging the content of basalt

11

(0.1 ppm) and granite (0.04 ppm).[2/] Boyle estimates the terrestrial abundance of silver to be ~ 0.10 ppm, based on hundreds of analyses of various Canadian rocks. The average silver contents of igneous-type rocks are: ultrabasic, 0.08; gabbro, 0.12; diabase, 0.12; diorite, 0.10; and granite, 0.05 ppm, while in sedimentary rocks, the average contents are: sandstone, 0.08; normal shale, 0.10; limestone, 0.07; and anhydrite and gypsum, 0.05 ppm.[2/] The results of silver analysis of numerous U.S. rocks are found in Table II-4.

Silver has been determined incidentally in the analysis of some fertilizers. Except for phosphate rock and a commercial product (Milorganite) made from municipal sewage, most U.S. inorganic fertilizer materials have been found to contain < 5 ppm silver.[4/] See Table II-5.

C. Silver in Soils and Other Weathering Products

Boyle reported the range for silver in normal soils varies from ≤ 0.01 to 5 ppm and estimates an average value of about 0.10 ppm (0.3 ppm in mineralized zones).[2/] Soils, stream sediments, and organic matter near mineralized zones are often high in silver. The silver contents of some normal, enriched, and contaminated soils are given in Table II-6.

Bertine and Goldberg estimated that mobilization of silver by weathering contributes 11×10^9 g/year to river flows and 3×10^7 g/year to sediments.[5/]

D. Silver in Air

Ambient air concentrations of silver found at locations near anthropogenic (man-made) sources range from 0.17 to 7.0 ng/m^3. The concentrations of silver in some atmospheric aerosols are given in Table II-7.

At the Walker Branch Watershed, the major anthropogenic sources of atmospheric metals were three coal-fired steam plants in the Oak Ridge vicinity. The enrichment factor of silver in the aerosol to silver in the soil was 270 (compared with europium).[6/] Bogen calculated an enrichment factor of silver in aerosol to silver in soil at Heidelberg as 9,300.[7/]

12

Bogen also calculated a wash-out factor for silver of 0.76, which is based on the concentration of silver in rainfall divided by the concentration in the atmospheric aerosol. He states that low wash-out factors are characteristic of elements of anthropogenic origin.[7]

Steel mills have been implicated as the major source of aerosol silver, yet the following data[8] did not seem to support this implication. Air particulate samples were collected June 11-12, 1969, at 25 stations in the Northwest Indiana area, including the Hammond-East Chicago-Gary-Whiting metropolitan complex. At that time, the entire sampling area contained three large steel mills as well as four large petroleum refineries, foundries, steel fabricators, chemical plants, a large cement-manufacturing plant, and two large power utilities. The silver concentrations in the area ranged from < 0.5 to 5 ng/m^3. The maximum silver concentration was found at a station downwind from the steel mills. High silver concentrations did not occur at the same stations where maximum iron levels occurred. Therefore, steel manufacturing was not believed to be the major source of silver found in these samples.[9]

At another station, in Gary, near the third steel mill, secondary maxima for iron and eight other metals were associated with a silver concentration < 4 ng/m^3. The direction of the unusually, strong, steady wind prevailing during the sampling was such that most of the shoreline steel and cement plant emissions ($\sim$ 85% and 12.5%, respectively, of the area's industrial particulate emissions) may have been swept directly over the lake so that the observed air concentrations at stations nearest them were much lower than normal.[8] On April 4, 1968, 1 day after general rainfall, with wind blowing at 34 km/hr, the silver concentrations in surface air samples from 22 aerosol-collecting stations in Chicago, Illinois, ranged from 0.18 to 7.0 ng/m^3 (average 4.3 ng/m^3). Correlation coefficients for silver with other elements or dust were not determined.[10]

E. Silver in Waters and Precipitates

1. Silver in surface waters, suspended solids, and precipitates: Natural fresh waters contain an average 0.2 ppb silver and seawater contains 0.25 ppb.[2] Water-analysis data from many sources have been compiled in Table II-8.

Kopp and Kroner found silver in 6.6% of the 1,577 surface water samples collected. Concentrations in samples containing silver varied from 0.1 to 38 ppb with a mean of 2.6 ppb. The maximum silver concentration found by Kopp and Kroner was in the Colorado River at Loma, Colorado. Upstream industries include an oil shale extraction

13

plant at Rifle; uranium plants at Rigle, Grand Junction, and Gunnison; and a gasoline and coke refinery 1 mile from Loma. (The highest vanadium concentrations were also found at Loma.)[11]

Another striking example of water pollution by silver was found in 280 river miles of the Lower North Canadian River (LNCR) Basin of Oklahoma. The range of silver concentrations varied from undetectable to 25 ppb in samples collected during all seasons. Water and sediment samples were collected at eight mainstream stations, eight tributary stream stations, and four Lake Eufaula stations. The LNCR also contained extraordinarily high concentrations of other trace elements and nutrients.[12]

The probable reason for the anomalously high silver concentrations was the low water volume in some of the sampling streams. For example, the maximum concentration of silver was detected on the Soldier Creek Tributary (pH 7), which drained wastes from the northeast corner of Tinker Air Force Base. Silver was never detected at the sampling station closest to the Henryeta zinc smelter, but even the zinc concentration was lowest there.[12]

The silver content of natural precipitates has been discussed by Boyle.[2] The silver content of U.S. natural precipitates ranges from nil to 1,160 ppm. Turekian found 0.4 to 15.0 ppm silver in the suspended matter of 18 U.S. rivers. The Susquehanna River in Pennsylvania, which contained the highest amount of silver, was estimated to be transporting 45 tons of silver per year to the ocean.[13] The estimate is 10 times too high according to the data in the reference. See Table II-9.

In the LNCR, the range of silver content in the ash of total suspended solids (silt plus microorganisms) was from undetected to 0.008 ppm, except at the station where the highest silver concentration was found in the water. Here, the silver content ranged from 15 to 50 ppm in the ash.[12]

Silver concentrations of 0.05 to 45 ppb have been found in effluents from municipal waste treatment plants. Silver concentrations as high as 900 ppm in sewage sludge have been reported. Table II-10 shows the silver content of effluents and sludges from municipal sewage treatment plants.

2. Silver in city water supplies and distribution samples: Of 380 finished waters, 6.1% were found to contain silver at concentrations varying from 0.3 to 5 ppb (mean 2.2 ppb). Table II-11 shows the silver content of water supplies for several U.S. cities. The silver content of these water supplies did not exceed the U.S. drinking water limits for maximum

14

allowable concentration of silver, 0.05 ppm.[14/] In another study, the maximum concentration of silver found in 2,595 distribution samples from 959 public water supply systems was 26 ppb. No silver was found in waters having pH $\leq$ 8, while for those at pH $\geq$ 8.0, the average silver content was 1 ppb. Of Chicago water samples, 15% showed increased concentrations of silver after leaving the water treatment plant.[15/]

In 1935, Braidech and Emery[16/] found 10 to 200 ppb silver (average 80 ppb) in the solid residues of all 24 city water supplies they studied. The highest value was from Denver, Colorado. Although the average copper-silver ratio in all samples was 3.16, the amount of silver in the water of nine cities exceeded that of copper (their ratio in the accessible lithosphere is ~ 1,000:1).[17/]

3. <u>Silver in polluted seawater sediments</u>: Bruland et al.[18/] studied the extent of metal pollution in the Southern California Coastal Zone, which receives Los Angeles area sewage. The average flux of anthropogenic silver into the sediments of the California Coastal Basin was estimated to be 50% greater than the average flux of natural silver (0.09 versus 0.06 $\mu g/cm^2/year$). The flux of anthropogenic silver to the sediments was calculated to be 11 metric tons per year per 12,000 km^2, with the chief source being the municipal wastewaters (15 metric tons per year per 12,000 km^2), rather than the storm water plus dry weather flow or the washout fluxes (1 and 5 metric tons per year per 12,000 km^2, respectively). Extraction studies indicated that the silver in these sediments occurred predominately as sulfides or bound to the organic phase.

The concentrations of silver in the wastewater particulates were 32 to 130 (average 70) ppm compared with about 6 ppm for the sediments in the basins receiving them. (The sediments were collected at 75 to 890 m from the sewage outfalls.)

F. <u>Biogeochemistry of Silver</u>

Silver is a normal trace constituent of many organisms.[2/] Table II-12 reveals the wide range of silver found in plant tissues. The ash of higher plants usually is found to contain < 1 ppm silver, while the ash of terrestrial plants usually contains about 0.2 ppm silver. Higher values occur in trees, shrubs, and other terrestrial plants near regions of silver mineralization although their contents are not correlated with the silver content of the soil. Seeds, nuts, and fruits generally have higher silver contents than other plant parts.

The enrichment factor calculated by Noddacks for silver in marine animals over seawater is 22,000. The dead bodies of animals in reducing environments will contribute their silver to sediments, a major factor in the geochemical cycle of silver.[2] The contents of silver in some marine and freshwater organisms are shown in Table II-13.

Insects, rats, dogs, and cattle have been found to contain traces of silver in their tissues. The ash of the vital parts, tissues, and blood of these mammals generally contains 1 to 10 ppm silver with up to 50 ppm found in the liver and other vital parts.[2] Silver has been found in the ashes of eggs, cow's milk, and animal feces. Fish and plankton were found to concentrate silver from 0.001 ppm in Lake Eufaula water by factors of 4 and 60, respectively.[a] The silver concentrations in the ash of tissues of five fish species ranged from undetectable to 5.31 ppm. The highest values were in the muscle, gastrointestinal tract, and liver of an 18-cm long white crappie, weighing 73 g.[12] The silver levels in fish do not seem to pose a human health hazard. The main problem is the toxicity of the dissolved and suspended silver to the plankton and fish.

In humans, silver is found (0.25 to 10.0 ppm in the ash) in the blood, liver, thyroid, heart, spleen, kidney, brain, hair, skin, and teeth, and 3 to 150 ppm in the ash of urinary calculi.[2] The silver content in tissues of humans from various geographical regions are given in Table II-14. We have found no plausible explanation for the high tissue silver content of Near Easterners.

Silver and many other metals become enriched in humus and humic deposits (peat, bogs, muskegs, and marshes). Humic matter near mineralized zones concentrates silver, e.g., < 1 to 30 ppm silver in the ash. A small part of the silver is adsorbed, but the greater part appears to be tightly bound in the brown humic complexes as silver-organic acid compounds, silver humates, chelated complexes, and organic sulfide complexes.[2]

The silver contents of coals; oil shales, petroleum, and other natural hydrocarbons; and new and used refined oils are given in Tables II-15, II-16, and II-17, respectively.

The silver in coal occurs in many forms: as metal-organic complexes; in pyrite or other minerals (e.g., galena, chalcopyrite, arsenopyrite, bornite, sphalerite, etc.); as native silver and chlorargyrite; or in jarosites and iron oxides from the weathered parts of coal seams, but rarely as argentite or freibergite.[2]

---

a/ See Section II.E.1.

Silver in oil shales, petroleum, etc., probably occurs as a silver-organic acid complex.[2/] Rickard found silver as a metallic coating on black, carbonaceous shale.[19/]

TABLE II-1

SILVER CONTENT OF SILVER MINERALS[2/]

Mineral	Formula	Percent Ag	U.S. Location	Remarks
Native elements and alloys:				
Argentian gold (electrum)	(Au, Ag)	20		"Electrum" used only if Ag content 20%+
Silver[a/]	Ag	100		Rare
Moschellandsbergite	Ag_2Hg_3			
Silver amalgam	(Ag, Hg)			
Sulfides, antimonides, arsenides, tellurides, etc.:				
Dyscrasite	Ag_3Sb		Reese River District, Nevada	
Huntilite[19/]	Ag_3As		Silver Islet Mine, Lake Superior	
Novakite	$(Cu, Ag)_4As_3$			
Argentite	$\alpha\text{-}Ag_2S$	87.1		Most common sulfides of silver
Acanthite[a/]	$\beta\text{-}Ag_2S$			
Aguilarite	Ag_4SeS			
Naumannite	Ag_2Se or $(Ag_2Pb)Se$[20/]	43.0[20/]	Silver City District, Idaho	Comparatively rare
Crookesite	$(Cu, Tl, Ag)_2Se$			
Eucairite	CuAgSe	63	Gold Hill, Colorado	
Hessite	Ag_2Te	42[20/]	Nevada City, California	
Petzite	Ag_3AuTe_2 or $(AuAg)_2Te$		Butte, Montana; Silverton and other places in Colorado	
Stromeyerite	$Ag_{1-x}CuS$			Rare
Mckinstryite	$Cu_{0.8}Ag_{1.2}S$			
Sternbergite	$AgFe_2S_3$			Rare
Argentopyrite	$AgFe_2S_3$		Kerber Creek District, Colorado	
Empressite	AgTe		Several places in Colorado	
Stuetzite	$Ag_{5-x}Te_3$			
Muthmannite	(Ag, Au)Te		Cripple Creek, Colorado	
Sylvanite	$(Au, Ag)Te_4$ or $(AuAg)Te_2$	13.4[20/]	Numerous other places in USA	
Sulfosalts:				
Polybasite	$(Ag, Cu)_{16}Sb_2S_{11}$ or $9Ag_2S\cdot Sb_2S_3$	75.6[20/]	Colorado	
Pearceite	$(Ag, Cu)_{16}As_2S_{11}$			
Polyargyrite	$Ag_{24}Sb_2S_{15}$			
Argyrodite	Ag_8GeS_6	73.5	USA (no specific location given)	Very rare[19/]
Canfieldite	Ag_8SnS_6			
Stephanite	Ag_5SbS_4 or $5Ag_2S\cdot Sb_2S_3$	68.5[20/]		Ruby silver minerals, forming a complete solid-solution series from solidus temperatures down to at least 300°C
Pyrargyrite[a/]	$3Ag_2S\cdot Sb_2S_3$	60[20/]	Silver City District, Idaho	
Proustite[a/]	$3Ag_2S\cdot As_2S_3$	65.5[20/]	Silver City District, Idaho	
Pyrostilpnite	Ag_3SbS_3			
Stylotypite	$(Ag, Cu, Fe)_3SbS_3$			
Xanthoconite	Ag_3AsS_3	Tetrahedrite ≤ 31.3%[19/] Tennantite ≤ 13.65%		

TABLE II-1 (Concluded)

Mineral	Formula	Percent Ag	U.S. Location	Remarks
Sulfosalts:				
Tetrahedrite-tennantite[a]	$(Cu,Fe,Ag)_{12}(Sb,As)_4S_{13}$			
Samsonite	$Ag_4MnSb_2S_6$			
Lengenbachite	$Pb_6(Ag,Cu)_2As_4S_{13}$			
Diaphorite	$Pb_2Ag_3Sb_3S_8$			
Freieslebenite	$Pb_3Ag_5Sb_5S_{12}$			
Owyheeite	$Pb_5Ag_2Sb_6S_{15}$			
Schirmerite	$PbAg_4Bi_4S_9$			
Miargyrite	$AgSbS_2$		Randsburg District, California	
Aramayoite	$Ag(Bi,Sb)S_2$			
Matildite	$AgBiS_2$			
Pavonite	$AgBi_3S_5$			
Smithite	$AgAsS_2$			
Trechmannite	$AgAsS_2(?)$			
Benjaminite	$Pb(Cu,Ag)Bi_2S_4$			
Fizelyite	$Pb_5Ag_2Sb_8S_{18}$			
Ramdohrite	$Pb_3Ag_2Sb_6S_{13}$			
Andorite	$PbAgSb_3S_6$			
Hutchinsonite	$(Pb,Tl)_2(Cu,Ag)As_5S_{10}$			
Betechtinite	$(Cu,Fe)_{11}(Pb,Ag)S_7$			
Marrite	$AgPbAsS_3$			
Halides:				
Chlorargyrite (cerargyrite)[a]	$AgCl$	75.3	Treasure Hill, Nevada; Bullfrog District, Nevada; Leadville, Colorado; Silver City, New Mexico; Tombstone, Arizona; Silver City, Idaho	
Huantajayite	$(Na,Ag)Cl$			
Oetswaldite	Colloidal-like $AgCl$			
Bromargyrite (bromyrite)	$AgBr$		Tombstone, Arizona	
Miersite	$(Ag,Cu)I$			
Iodargyrite (iodyrite)	AgI	46	Tonopah and Goldfield, Nevada; Sierra County, New Mexico; Commonwealth Mine, Cochise County, Arizona	
Bolelte	$Pb(Cu,Ag)Cl_2(OH)_2 \cdot H_2O$		Tintic Standard Mine, Dividend, Utah	
Basic sulfates:				
Argentojarosite[a]	$AgFe_3(SO_4)_2(OH)_6$			
Argentian plumbojarosite	$(Pb,Ag)Fe_{3-6}(SO_4)_{2-4}-$ $(OH)_{6-12}$			

a/ Most common Ag minerals.

19

TABLE II-2

SILVER CONTENT IN OTHER MINERALS[2/]

Mineral	Formula	Ag Content, ppm	U.S. Locations	Remarks
Silicates				
Albite, var., Cleavelandite		0.07 - 0.08	Branchville and Portland, Conn.	
Canadian albites		0.09 - 1.0		Ag present in nearly all silicate minerals.
Other common Canadian silicate minerals		0.05 - 1.0		Other silicates analyzed: Tourmaline, biotite, zircon, garnet, hornblende.
Native Elements				
Iron		1.0 - 10.0		
Copper		1,000 - 40,000		
Gold		1,000 - 200,000		> 200,000 = electrum
Palladium		traces		
Lead		traces to minor amounts		
Osmiridium		traces		
Zinc		traces		
Mercury		traces to minor amounts		
Carbon (diamond)		traces		
Antimony		100 - 10,000		
Arsenic		traces		
Bismuth		traces to 100		
Tellurium		2,000 - 16,900		
Tellurides	$(M)_x(Te)_y$ where M = metal.	770 - 58,700		Ag occurs in almost all tellurides and selenides. Particularly abundant in Au tellurides where it replaces Au.
Selenides	$(M)_x(Se)_y$	traces - 85,000		

TABLE II-2 (Continued)

Mineral	Formula	Ag Content, ppm	U.S. Locations	Remarks
Arsenides and Antimonides				
Niccolite	NiAs	10 - 100 (higher values recorded probably due to impurities)		
Breithauptite	NiSb	No data on pure material		
Loellingite	FeAs$_2$	No data on pure material		
Safflorite	(CoFe)As$_2$	0.5 - 100 (higher values recorded due to impurities)		
Skutterudite	(Co,Ni)As$_3$	Up to 4% Ag but probably due to impurities		
Smaltite-chloanthite	(Co,Ni)As$_{3-x}$	1 - 1,000 (values up to 4% recorded but probably due to impurities)		
Rammelsbergite	NiAs$_2$	1 - 10		
Aurostibite	AuSb$_2$	Up to 1% Ag or greater		
Sulfides and Sulfide-Arsenides				
Digenite	Cu$_{2-x}$S	10 - > 1,000		
Chalcopyrite	CuFeS$_2$	5 - 5,300		In the common sulfides, pyrite, pyrrhotite, and chalcopyrite, Ag is concentrated in chalcopyrite replacing Cu in the lattice.
Pyrite	FeS$_2$	< 1 - 500 (values up to 1,500 ppm have been recorded on isolated samples)		Ag is nearly always a constituent of pyrite.
Arsenopyrite	FeAsS	< 1 - 400		Ag can replace As in pyrite or arsenopyrite or be dispersed particles. Requires roasting for refinement prior to cyanidation.
Galena	PbS	< 1 - 8,000 (values up to 6.4% Ag recorded but probably due to impurities)		Ag may be trapped in interstitial spaces of the lattice or sometimes present in the lattice at low concn. Content varies widely - low in Mississippi Valley type.

21

TABLE II-2 (Continued)

Mineral	Formula	Ag Content, ppm	U.S. Locations	Remarks
Sulfide and Sulfide-Arsenides (Concluded)				
Chalcocite	Cu_2S	< 1 - > 1,000 (contents up to 1% Ag recorded but purity uncertain)		Ag substitutes for Cu in lattice, source of by-product silver. Ag content varies widely.
Bornite	Cu_5FeS_4	< 1 - 1,000		Ag substitutes for Cu in lattice, source of by-product silver. Ag content varies widely.
Covellite	CuS	Traces to 500 ppm		Ag substitutes for Cu in lattice, source of by-product silver. Ag content varies widely.
Sphalerite	ZnS	3 - 3,500 (values up to 1.5% Ag recorded but probably due to impurities)		Strongly adsorbs Ag ion. Ag can substitute for zinc.
Hawleyite	βCdS	~ 50		
Stannite	Cu_2FeSnS_4	Isolated values up to 1% Ag recorded. High values probably due to impurities.		
Pyrrhotite	$Fe_{1-x}S$	1 - 210 (values up to 5,500 ppm recorded but probably due to impurities)		
Pentlandite	$(Fe,Ni)_9S_8$	1 - 50 (average for Sudbury, Ontario, ores - 3.4 ppm) (Hawley, 1962)		
Cinnabar	HgS	< 1 - 10		
Stibnite	Sb_2S_3	Traces to 500 ppm		
Molybdenite	MoS_2	< 1 - > 100		
Molybdenite	MoS_2	0.1 - 100 (Goldschmidt and Peters, 1932)		
Bismuthinite	Bi_2S_3	Traces to 3,000 ppm. Nearly pure materials from Quebec and Bolivia show only < 5 - 70 ppm Ag		
Cobaltite	$(CoFe)AsS$	1 - 100		
Gersdorffite	$NiAsS$	1 - 100		
Ullmannite	$NiSbS$	10 - 1,000		

TABLE II-2 (Continued)

Mineral	Formula	Ag Content, ppm	U.S. Locations	Remarks
Sulfosalts		Traces - 154,000		Ag may be admixed with many sulfosalts in galena.
Halides				Ag content of halides is generally low. Halite, calomel, fluorite and percylite have various sources and Ag concentrations between 0.02 and 89,800 ppm. In sylvite, carnallite, marshite and atacamite from Germany, Nova Scotia, and New South Wales, Ag concn. is from traces to 119,000 ppm and in Italian phosgenite 100 ppm. And Ag may replace Cu in marshite. In percylite, Ag may replace Cu or Pb.
Carbonates				
Azurite	$Cu_3(CO_3)_2(OH)_2$	< 5	Bisbee, Arizona	
Bismutite	$(BiO)_2(CO_3)$	5 - 50	Outpost Mine, Arizona White Picacho, Yavapai County	
Calcites (Canadian)	$CaCO_3$	< 1		Ag may be present in western U.S. calcites bound as silver manganate in Mn oxide.
Siderites (Canadian)	$FeCO_3$	≤ 50		
Smithsonite (Canadian Keno Hill)	$ZnCO_3$	1 - 50		
Cerussite (Canadian Keno Hill)	$PbCO_3$	1 - 50		
Malachites (Canadian)	$Cu_2(CO_3)(OH)_2$	50 - 1,000		
Sulfates				
Chalcanthite, epsomite, copiapite, etc.		0 - 1,160	Tintic District, Utah	Barite, anglesite, anhydrite, gypsum, plumbo-jarosite, and rozenite from Canada and other regions have Ag concn. of 0.05 - 1,000 ppm; 1,600 ppm Ag found in chalcanthite from Tintic Standard Mines; 170 ppm Ag found in other sulfates.
Phosphates, arsenates				
Annabergite	$Ni_3(A_5O_4)_2 \cdot 8H_2O$	< 5	Churchill County, Nevada Keweenaw Co., Michigan	

23

TABLE II-2 (Concluded)

Mineral	Formula	Ag Content, ppm	U.S. Locations	Remarks
Oxides				
Tenorite	CuO	Trace	Algoma mine, Ontonagan, Michigan	
Cuprite	Cu_2O	< 1 - 300	Arizona	
Wad and various manganese oxides		detected 30 - 300 50	USA Ramsdellite, Lake Valley, New Mexico	Wads are those substances whose chief constituent is a hydrous manganese oxide, but whose true identities are unknown.
Various Mn-Ag ores		23 up to 1,000 or more	Polk County, Arkansas	
Hematite	Fe_2O_3	≤ 100		
Limonite	$Fe_2O_3 \cdot 3H_2O$	0-1,000		
Magnetite	$FeFe_2O_4$	1-5		
Chromite	$FeCr_2O_4$	< 1-5		

24

TABLE II-3

CLASSIFICATION OF SILVER DEPOSITS[2/]

Deposit Type	Rock Type	Primary Ore Minerals and Gangue	Secondary Ore Minerals	Ag Content (ppm)	Location	Remarks
Shale: Kupferschiefer type (copper shales)	Deposits occur in sequences of shales, siltstone, argillite, tuffs, and impure calcareous and dolomitic rocks closely associated with sandstones, quartzites, and conglomerates.	Chalcocite, bornite, chalcopyrite	Sometimes pyrite, galena, sphalerite, and other sulfides	0-150	Germany, Northern Rhodesia, Baja California	Ag generally a by-product of Cu mining. Cu content is 1.5-5%. Ag content varies greatly.
	Shales, siltstones, and sandstones	Upper parting shale	Covellite, bornite, chalcopyrite	Up to 150	White Pine, Michigan	Native Ag occurs. Cu is 1-3%. 85% of the Cu is in chalcocite. Remainder is native metal. Parting shale here sometimes has 170 ppm Ag. No evident relationship between Cu and Ag distribution.
	Shales and siltstones	Lower copper bed		1	Creta area, Oklahoma	Up to 4.45% Cu. Average 3.8%. Little Ag; Co enriched over nickel.
Sandstone deposits-- "Red Bed" type. Bedded and vein type copper, lead, silver, vanadium, and uranium deposits.	Arkosic sandstone, conglomerate, and shale of Permocarboniferous, Triassic, Jurassic, or Tertiary age.	Chalcocite, bornite, chalcopyrite, uraninite, covellite, pyrite. Silver sulfides at Silver Reef, Utah.	Malachite, azurite, carnotite, autunite, cerargyrite at Silver Reef, Utah.	Variable. 1,000 at Silver Reef, Utah.	Southwestern U.S. Texas, Oklahoma, New Mexico, Arizona, Colorado, Wyoming, Utah, and Idaho.	Native Ag in sandstones is closely associated with cupriferous shales in some areas such as White Pine. In many deposits, Ag is adsorbed to iron and manganese oxides. Plant remains, porous sandstones or conglomerates may have precipitated Ag. Ore and gangue elements apparently transported by groundwater during weathering.
	Triassic sandstones and shales, extrusive basalt and intrusive diabase sills	Native Cu, chalcocite, bornite, chalcopyrite, pyrite	Malachite, azurite, brochantite, chrysocolla, cuprite, tenorite, and secondary native copper and chalcocite	Very low	New Jersey (Newark series)	Cu content low. Not economically mined.

TABLE II-3 (Continued)

Deposit Type	Rock Type	Primary Ore Minerals and Gangue	Secondary Ore Minerals	Ag Content (ppm)	Location	Remarks
Sandstone (Continued)	Precambrian Copper Harbour conglomerate and sandstone and Noneauch shale and sandstone	Native Ag, native Cu, solid hydrocarbons, chalcocite, etc.		Ag highly variable. 35-2,500 or more.	Michigan	See also White Pine area.
	Jurassic flat-lying sandstones and shales	Argentiferous chalcocite, covellite, bornite, native Cu, argentite, native Ag, kaolin, calcite, barite	Azurite, malachite, cuprite, iron sulfate, argentite, native Ag	Very high grade but small ore shoots up to 17,000.	Montrose County, Colorado	Now exhausted. Worked for Ag and Cu.
	Gently dipping Cambrian (?) calcareous sandstone	Native Ag, chalcocite, and pitchblende; calcite is principal gangue. Some clinozoisite.	Malachite, azurite, native Cu chrysocolla, limonite, gummite, uranophane metatobornite.	High grade Ag. Low grade uranium deposit.	Silver Cliff Mine, Wyoming	Now exhausted.
	Near base of Shinarump conglomerate, upper Triassic conglomerate and sandstones	Uraniferous asphalt and woody fragments	Autunite(?), gummite(?), carnotite, malachite, azurite, chrysocolla, cobalt bloom, native sulfur	Ag uniformly distributed throughout uraniferous zones. Ag 15-60; 21 average.	Emery County, Utah	
	Silver Reef sandstone of Upper Triassic Chinle Formation	Chlorargyrite, silver sulfide	Malachite, azurite, chalcocite, pyrite		Silver Reef, Utah	Now exhausted.
Silver-bearing skarn-type		High-temperature Ca-, Fe-, Mg-silicate and -carbonate compounds such as garnet, epidote, and dolomite. Sulfides include chalcopyrite, pyrite, bornite, pyrrhotite, galena, sphalerite, and molybdenite.		Up to 800 in galena concentrate	Bingham District, Utah; central mining district, New Mexico; Cass District, California	Ag is concentrated in the lead-zinc deposits principally in galena. Contact metamorphic copper types have low Ag.

26

TABLE II-3 (Continued)

Deposit Type	Rock Type	Primary Ore Minerals and Gangue	Secondary Ore Minerals	Ag Content (ppm)	Location	Remarks
Veins, stockworks and tabular bodies, essentially in sedimentary rocks		Argentiferous tetrahedrite-tennantite, argentite, proustite-pyrargyrite, and argentiferous galena. Sometimes native Ag and dyscrasite.	Sphalerite pyrite, chalcopyrite. Sometimes nickel-cobalt arsenides bismuthinite, native bismuth or pitchblende are present.			Some members of this deposit type are among the most productive Ag mines in the world.
Veins in shear zones, faults, and fractures	Quartzite and other more competent rocks	Siderite, quartz, barite, argentiferous, galena, freibergite, sphalerite, chalcopyrite, pyrite, boulangerite, pyrrhotite, marcasite, magnetite, and arsenopyrite. Bornite, chalcocite, stibnite, jamesonite, bournonite, polybasite, proustite, hematite, uraninite, and scheelite occur less frequently.		65-335 (average) 1,000 or more (Sunshine and Polaris Mines)	Coeur d' Alene, Idaho	A leading U.S. silver producing district. Ores average, 3-12% Pb, 3-6% Zn.
Silver-gold and gold-silver veins and lodes in or associated with volcanic flow rocks. Gold deposits	Greenstones	Native gold Quartz	Adhantite, tetrahedrite sulfosalts, ruby silver, etc.	Ag is a by-product of gold mining		Gold is the economic product.
	Tertiary andesites and rhyolites and allied rocks.	Native gold often greatly enriched in Ag (40% or more).	Gold-silver tellurides	Ag is a by-product of gold mining	Mother Lode system (Calif.)	

27

TABLE II-3 (Continued)

Deposit Type	Rock Type	Primary Ore Minerals and Gangue	Secondary Ore Minerals	Ag Content (ppm)	Location	Remarks
Silver-gold-quartz	Tertiary andesites and rhyolites.	Electrum, argentite, tetrahedrite, silver selenides, polybasite, pyrite, chalcopyrite, galena. Quartz, sericite, rhodochrosite, and adularia form the gangue.	Scheelite and wolframite		Tomopah District, Nevada	
	Tertiary volcanic rocks separated by a fault from Mesozoic rocks.	Electrum, gold, pyrite, argentite, polybasite, sulfosalts	Sphalerite and galena		Comstock Lode, Nevada	
Gold-telluride deposits	Calaverite ($AuTe_2$)	Calaverite, quartz, fluorite, carbonate, and roscoelite gangue	Sylvanite, petzite, pyrite, sphalerite, galena, tetrahedrite, stibnite, cinnabar, molybdenite	(Ag content 4% or less of calaverite ore).	Cripple Creek, Colorado	
Gold-selenide		Native gold; electrum; Ag, Pb, and Cu selenides; aguilarite naumannite; berzelianite; pyrite; tetrahedrite; chalcopyrite; galena; sphalerite		Often high Ag	Republic, Washington	Gold-selenide deposits are relatively rare.
Silver deposits in a complex geological environment comprising sediments, volcanic, and igneous or granitized rocks					Canada, Bolivia	
Miscellaneous sources of silver:						
1. Nickel-copper ores		Chalcopyrite		Very low	Sudbury, Canada	

28

TABLE II-3 (Continued)

Deposit Type	Rock Type	Primary Ore Minerals and Gangue	Secondary Ore Minerals	Ag Content (ppm)	Location	Remarks
Miscellaneous sources of silver (continued):						
2. Massive sulfide deposits		Iron, copper, lead, and zinc sulfides. Ag usually in galena or tetrahedrite. Lesser amounts with sphalerite or chalcopyrite. Some deposits bear Ag in electrum, sylvanite, altaite, sulfosalts, tellurides, selenides, etc.		Usually less than 170	Peru	Ag usually found with high-grade lead and copper ores and won as a by-product from treatment of these ores.
		Pyrite, chalcopyrite, sphalerite. Ag occurs as native metal in pyrite, stromeyerite, and digenite.		165	Texas Gulf Kidd Creek Camp, Timmons, Ontario, Canada	World's largest silver mine.
3. Polymetallic deposits		Essentially lead, iron, copper, and zinc sulfides. Ag occurs in galena and tetrahedrite most often.		Very low to 1,300	Various	Ag recovered as a by-product.
4. Lead-zinc deposits	Carbonate	Galena--in southeast Missouri, Ag apparently follows zinc and is concentrated in sphalerite.		Generally low (3.0-330 in concentrates), Crude ore usually < 1.5 ppm	Southeast Missouri	
5. Native copper deposits	Amygdaloidal basalts, sandstones, etc.	Native Ag, small amounts in the native Cu.		0.3	Michigan copper deposits	Irregularly economical.

TABLE II-3 (Concluded)

Deposit Type	Rock Type	Primary Ore Minerals and Gangue	Secondary Ore Minerals	Ag Content (ppm)	Location	Remarks
Miscellaneous sources of silver (continued):						
6. Porphyry copper deposits		Hypogene silver in chalcopyrite, bornite, covellite, enargite, or in specks of tennantite-tetrahedrite, stromeyerite, etc.		35-100 0.3-3.5	Butte, Montana; Bingham, Utah; Ely, Nevada; Ray, Arizona	Yield large amounts of Ag as a by-product of copper mining.
7. Gold deposits						All gold deposits yield some Ag.
8. Eluvial and alluvial fans	Weathered limestones calcareous shales, sandstones, shales, etc.	Argentiferous galena, anglesite, bindheimite, oxidized products of Ag minerals, cassiterite, cinnabar.		Up to 15	Unglaciated countries	Other types rare. Tonnage sometimes large, but not economically mined.
9. The sea				Seawater 0.0002, manganese nodules (see Silver Content in U.S. Rocks), sediments, debris		
10. Gold placers		Native Au				

30

TABLE II-4

SILVER CONTENT OF U.S. ROCKS

Rock Type	Ag Content, ppm (average or range)	Location	Remarks	Reference
Crustal average	0.07			21
Igneous and Sedimentary	0.07			22
Igneous Rocks	-		In most igneous rocks, Ag is present in sulfides or ferro-magnesian minerals. Ag is present at 5 ppm in pyrite and pyrrhotite or several hundred ppm in chalcopyrite. Ferro-magnesian Ag usually ≤ 0.5 ppm. Igneous rocks make up 95% of the earth's crust.	2
Igneous	~ 0.1			23
Igneous	0.07			24
Igneous	0.15			25
Igneous	0.2			26
Ultrabasic (dunites, peridotites, pyroxenites)	0.3			27
Ultramafic	0.3			26
Ultramafic	0.05-0.06			23
Felsic	0.15			26
Diabase	7.44	California		2
Diabase	0.057	Virginia		2
Basic (basalts, gabbros, morites, diabases, etc.)	0.3			27
Mafic	0.3			26
Basalt	0.55	California		2
Basalt	0.1			21
Basalt	0.1			23
Syenite	15.43	Nevada		2
Syenites	0.01-0.09			23
Syenite Rock-1	0.5-1.9	Bancroft, Ontario	Ag in Canadian rocks runs 0.1-2.0 ppm. Others, 0.02-64.9	2
Quartz, monzonite	< 0.4-4.0	Arizona		2
Intermediate rocks (diorites, andesites)	0.07			23

TABLE II-4 (Continued)

Rock Type	Ag Content, ppm (average or range)	Location	Remarks	Reference
Igneous (continued)				
Felsite granites and grandiorites	0.05			23
Granite	0.04	Rhode Island		21
Granite (G-1)	0.042	Nevada		2
Granites	5.59	California		2
Granites	0.94-7.66			2
Granites (high-Ca)	0.051			23
Granites (low-Ca)	0.037			23
Acid Rocks (granites, liparites, rhyolites, etc.)	0.15			27
Sedimentary Rocks			Highest Ag concentration is in black shales, black and sulfide schists, alum shales, and phosphorites. Little Ag occurs in sandstone, quartzites, limestones, and evaporites.	2
Sandstone	0.01-0.09			23
Sandstone	0.05			24
Sandstone	0.4			26
Sandstone (resistates)	0.12			25
Sandstone	0.32-0.54	California		2
Pierre shale	< 0.5	Great Plains Region, USA		2
Black shale and phosphorites	10	Phosphoria Formation, USA		2
Black shales	5-50	Woodford-Chattanooga Shales, Midcontinent area		26
Black shales	< 0.5-10			2
Black shales	0.1-3.0	Oklahoma, Missouri, Kansas		2
Black shales	1-30	Various, Western U.S.		2
Black shales	1-15	Various, Western U.S.		2
Black shales	0.32	Walton area, N.S., Canada	Ag content of Canadian sedimentary rocks ranges from 0.03-4.0 ppm.	2
Shales	0.07			23
Shales	0.05			24
Shales (hydrolyzates)	0.27			25
Clays and shales	0.1			23
Clays and shales	0.9			27

TABLE II-4 (Continued)

Rock Type	Ag Content, ppm (average or range)	Location	Remarks	Reference
Sedimentary (continued)				
Deep sea clays, etc.	0.30-1.9	Atlantic Ocean		2
Deep sea clays	0.11			23
Limestone	0.05			24
Limestone	0.34	Kansas		2
Limestone and dolomite	0.2			26
Manganese oxides (sedimentary)	0 - detected	Arizona		2
Manganese oxides (sedimentary)	30	Nevada		2
Manganese nodules (deep sea)	Not detected	Pacific Ocean	Hewett, 1963	2
Manganese nodules (deep sea)	3.0	Pacific Ocean	Mero, 1961	2
Carbonates	0.19			25
Carbonate rocks	0.01-0.09			23
Carbonate rocks (deep sea)	0.01-0.09			25
Sedimentary			Porphyrin complexes with various heavy metals are found in some petroliferous shales. Such compounds may occur in carbonaceous shales limestones, etc. Ag and other heavy metals are concentrated in skeletal fish debris in sediments of late Pleistocene to recent ages.

In black shales, schists, etc. H_2S produced by bacteria precipitates Ag and other chalcophile elements. Adorption by carbonaceous substances may occur.

Ag traces occur in the salt-dome calcitic and gypsiferous cap rocks of Texas and Louisiana associated with sulfides such as pyrite, hauerite (MnS_2), galena, sphalerite, and sometimes barite, celestite, or native sulfur. | 2 |

33

TABLE II-4 (Concluded)

Rock Type	Ag Content, ppm (average or range)	Location	Remarks	Reference
Argentiferous Sediments			Ag content varies widely from bed to bed and accumulates in Cu-bearing deposits.	2
Cupriferous shale and siltstone	1-160	White Pine, Michigan	High Ag contents occur in beds containing native Cu. Local concentrations of silver ore.	2
Silver Reef sandstone	~ 3	Utah	Cerargyrite above water table, argentine and native silver below.	2
Copper conglomerates and sandstones	0.5-1.0	Keweenaw, Michigan	Estimated. Some sandstones in the area have been mined and similar amounts of Ag occur in Amygdaloidal basalts in the region.	2
Dolomite, limestone, etc., impregnated with galena and sphalerite	6	Mississippi Valley	Very little Ag is found in chalcopyrite. Most is in galena, only traces in sphalerite.	2
	-	Southeast Missouri	Sphalerite may have appreciable silver content.	2
Metamorphic Rocks	0-15	Front Range, Colorado	Thirty samples of vein material and mineralized metamorphic rocks. Ag appears to occur in the same minerals as noted for igneous and sedimentary rocks.	28

SILVER CONTENT OF FERTILIZERS[4/]

Fertilizer	Content (ppm)	USA Source	World
Nitrogen			
$(NH_4)_2SO_4$			
Cal-nitro 16%			
Cyanamide	≤ 0.5	X	
Calurea			
$NaNO_3$			
Urea			
Phosphorus			Various
Marine phosphorite deposits	Present	Western USA	
Phosphate rock	10-1,000	Florida (land pebble phosphate)	
Soft phosphate	Trace (~ 5)	X	
Colloidal phosphate	~ 30	X	
Ground pebble float	~ 80	(one sample) X	
Apatite	1-10	Florida (one sample) X	
Taranakite	Present	Pig Hole Cave, Virginia X	
Di-Ca phosphate	Trace	Made from Florida pebble X	
20% Granulated superphosphate	15	X	
Superphosphate	Trace	X	
Triple superphosphate	~ 30	(one sample) X	
Bone meal steamed	< 4-4 (sic)	X	X
Raw bone meal	≤ 5	X	
	≤	X	

TABLE II-5 (Continued)

Fertilizer	Content (ppm)	USA Source	World[*]
Potassium			
K_2CO_3, K_2SO_4, Kainite, Hardwood ash	$\leqslant 5$	X	X
Mixed and Compound			
Ammophos	$\leqslant 5$		X
Organic			
Milorganite	~ 300	X (one sample)	
Goat manure			
High-grade tankage (dry basis)			
Fish scrap	$\leqslant 5$	X	
Cotton seed meal			
Castor pomace			
Seaweeds	Max. $\leqslant 10$ (in ash) Min. 0.0-0.7	X	X
Dried blood	Trace	X	X
Calcium-Magnesium			
Limestone	$\leqslant 5$ 0.3-4.0 < 0.1-20	Florida Illinois Eastern Kansas Florida and Tennessee	X
Ca-Mg carbonate	$\leqslant 5$		

TABLE II-5 (Concluded)

Fertilizer	Content (ppm)	USA Source	World
Dolomitic limestone	< 0.2-0.5	Missouri	
Kieserite	< 5		X
Miscellaneous			
K-bearing minerals	~ 1		X

TABLE II-6

SILVER CONTENT OF SOILS

Location	Type	Ag Content (ppm)	Remarks	Reference
--	Soils	0.1		27
Scotland	Soils	≤ 2.0		29
Scotland	Soils	< 1-5		27
Missouri (North Central)	Agricultural soils	0.7		29
Missouri (Southeast)	Agricultural soils	0.15-0.7		27
--	Birch-Forest Humus	5.0	Ag content is much higher than the average Ag content of rocks.	27
--	Humus	≤ 5.0	Usually more Ag in humus than in rocks or soils	30
--	Mineral soils	0.1-1.0 (usually) 7.0 (unusual)		31
Soils near a coal-burning plant	Background soils	0.247	Plant discharged 0.5 tons Ag	32
Soils near a coal-burning plant	Enriched soils	0.272	Soil enriched by 0.4 tons Ag. Assumed enrichment confined to upper 2 cm of soil. Plants not enriched in Ag.	32
Florida	Topsoils	detected	Found in 2 of 54 samples	29
Florida	Citrus soils	ND	9 samples	29
Florida	Soils	~ 1	4 of 132 samples	29
California	Soils	0.2-0.7	12 samples	29

TABLE II-6 (Concluded)

Location	Type	Ag Content (ppm)	Remarks	Reference
Grand Rapids, Michigan	Residential	0.13	These samples were classified according to land-use patterns in a 304 sq mile area in and around Grand Rapids.	33
Grand Rapids, Michigan	Agricultural	0.19		
Grand Rapids, Michigan	Industrial	0.37		
Grand Rapids, Michigan	Airport	0.29		
Grand Rapids, Michigan	Industrial-Residential	2.85		
Grand Rapids, Michigan	Airport-Residential	2.24		

39

TABLE II-7

SILVER IN GROUND-LEVEL ATMOSPHERIC AEROSOLS[6,7]/

City	Date	Aerosol Silver Concentration	
		ng/m^3	ppb
Heidelberg, Germany	April - June, 1971	4.2	0.0032
Niles, Michigan	June, 1969	< 1	< 0.00077
East Chicago, Indiana	June, 1969	2.4	0.0019
Oak Ridge, Tennessee Vicinity: Walker Branch Watershed	July, 1974	0.17	0.00013

TABLE II-8

SILVER IN NATURAL U.S. WATERS

Type of Water	pH	Detection Frequency	Ag Content (ppb)	Location	Remarks	Reference
Rainfall	-	-	0.002-0.216	St. Louis, Missouri		34
Precipitation	-	-	< 0.02			35
Precipitation (AgI seeded)	-	-	0.001-4.5		Typically 0.01-0.3 ppb Ag	35
Snowfall (AgI seeded)	-	-	0.11 (0.13 neutron activation anal.)	-		36
Freshwater	-	-	0.01-0.7	-		26
	-	-	0.13	-		22
Springs and surface freshwaters	-	-	0.2	all	Widely diffused, marked regional variations. Surface waters usually have less Ag than springs	2
Hot springs: SO_2, NaCl, HCO_3^-, borate, sulfate carbonate	5.3-9.1	-	up to 43,000 in siliceous	Steamboat Springs, Nevada		2
Steam well: NaCl, $CaCl_2$, KCl	-	-	100-300 in water up to 13,000,000 in residue	Niland, California		2
Spring and well waters	-	36%	> 10	Near Salton Sea, California	Geothermal brines have higher concn. of Ag and other trace metals than municipal or industrial wastewaters. Two of these samples had Ag content in excess of drinking water standards.	37
Desert well brines	-	50%	> 10			37
Oil well brines	-	-	0.1	California		37
Vadose mine waters: SiO_2, Mg, Fe, Al, Ca, Cu, Mn, SO_4	Acid	-	207	Comstock Lode, Nevada		2
Deep mine waters: sulfate, carbonate	Alkaline to neutral	-	3.3	Comstock Lode, Nevada	Temperature, 116-170°F	2
Seawater	-	-	0.15-2.9 (0.29 average)	All	Run-off is of minor importance. Like Ba, Ag concentrates with increasing depth and in areas of high organic productivity. May be less concentrated near shores.	2
Seawater	-	-	0.3	-		38, 22
Seawater	-	-	0.16	Gulf of Mexico		2
Seawater	-	-	0.145	40 miles west of San Francisco		2
Seawater	-	-	0.15-0.3	-		2
Lakes	-	-	< 0.1-3.5	Maine		2
Lakes	-	86%	0.1 (average) 6.0 (maximum)	California	Samples collected from 170 High Sierra Lakes.	39
Lake, ground, and Ottawa River water	-	-	0.006-0.7	Near Chalk River Nuclear Laboratory		40

TABLE II-8 (Continued)

Type of Water	pH	Detection Frequency	Ag Content (ppb)	Location	Remarks	Reference
Agricultural drainage	-	100%	0.8 (1.0 maximum)	Coachella Valley, California		37
Lakes	-	33%	10	Near Sudbury, Ontario	After 60 years of copper smelting	41
Lakes, streams, and rivers	-		10-200 (in residues)	U.S.		2
Surface waters	-	22.4%	0.10-3.0 (0.3 average)	California		28
Stream water	-	-	0.00006-0.0062	St. Louis, Missouri		33
Rivers	-	-	up to 1.0	North America and Norway		2
Large rivers	-	-	0-0.94	North America		2
U.S. river basins	-	6.6%	2.6 (38 maximum)	U.S.	Detection limits for Reference 11 were ppb.	11,42
Northeast River Basin	-	14.3%	1.9 (6.0 maximum)	Northeastern U.S.	Includes New Jersey	11
St. Lawrence River	-	29.6%	2.6 (6.0 maximum)	Massena, New York		11
Hudson River	-		0.13-0.59	Green Island, New York		43
North Atlantic River Basin	-	5.3%	0.9 (2.5 maximum)	U.S.		11
Delaware River	-	11.1%	1.1 (8.2 maximum)	Trenton, New Jersey		44
Delaware River	-	7.03%	3	-		43
Susquehanna River	-	-	0-0.29	Conowingo, Maryland		43
Susquehanna River	-	-	0.39			45
Southeast River Basin	-	5.5%	0.4 (0.7 maximum)	U.S.		11
Apalachicola River	-	-	0.058-0.11	Near Blountstown, Florida		43
Mobile River	-	-	0.085-0.28	Mt. Vernon Landing, Alabama		43
Neuse River	-	-	0.52	North Carolina	Groundwater lithology: Slate	45
Neuse River	-	-	0.56	North Carolina	Shale	45
Neuse River	-	-	0.25	North Carolina	Granite	45
Neuse River	-	-	0.86	North Carolina	Shale and schist	45
Neuse River	-	-	0.30	North Carolina	Cretaceous sand	45
Neuse River	-	-	-	North Carolina	Tertiary lime	45
Neuse River	-	-	0.37 (average)	North Carolina	Standard deviation = 49 based on samples taken at 25 locations.	45
Tennessee River Basin	-	0%	-	Tennessee and adjacent areas		11

42

TABLE II-8 (Continued)

Type of Water	pH	Detection Frequency	Ag Content (ppb)	Location	Remarks	Reference
Ohio River Basin	-	5.4%	2.1 (8.2 maximum)	U.S.		11
Youghiogheny River	-	-	0.05-1.0	West Newton, Pennsylvania	These primary streams receive acid mine drainage, but Ag was not detected 50 miles downstream in Toronto, Ohio	44
Kiskiminitas River	-	-	0.5-1.3	Apollo, Pennsylvania		
Allegheny River	-	5.0%	2.0	Pittsburgh, Pennsylvania		44
Monongahela River	-	8.3%	2.0 (4.7 maximum)	Pittsburgh, Pennsylvania		11
Monongahela River	-	5.0%	4.0	Pittsburgh, Pennsylvania		44
Kanawha River	-	12.9%	1.2 (3.0 maximum)	Winfield Dam, West Virginia		11
Ohio River	-	60%	0.6-1			46
Great Lakes	-	14	1			46
Lake Erie Basin	-	6.4%	5.3 (9.0 maximum)			11
Cuyahoga River	-	0%	ND	Cleveland, Ohio	Receives effluents from automotive, meat-packing, and paper industries	44
Maumee River	-	12.5%	5.3 (9.0 maximum)	Toledo, Ohio	Travels from Ft. Wayne, Indiana through industrial complexes and receives agricultural, petrochemical, and metal working wastes.	11
Maumee River	-	12.5%	3.6 (6.0 maximum)	Toledo, Ohio		
Upper Mississippi River Basin	-	5.4%	3.4 (6.0 maximum)	U.S.		11
Western Great Lakes Basin	-	9.1%	1.4	U.S.		11
Detroit River	-	-	1.0 (3.8 maximum)	Detroit, Michigan		11
Missouri River Basin	-	4.1%	1.2 (1.5 maximum)	U.S.		11
Southwest-Lower Mississippi Basin	-	4.5%	4.3 (9.0 maximum)	U.S.		11
Mississippi River	-	-	0- < 0.22	Baton Rouge, Louisiana		43
Mississippi River	-	-	0.26	-		45
Mississippi River	-	12	0.2-20			46
Missouri River		57	ND-0.33	Krotz Springs, Louisiana		46
Atchafalaya River	-	-				43

43

TABLE 11-8 (Concluded)

Type of Water	pH	Detection Frequency	Ag Content (ppb)	Location	Remarks	Reference
Colorado River Basin	-	18%	5.8 (38 maximum)	U.S.		11
Animas River	-	45%	2.9 (7.0 maximum)	Cedar Hill, New Mexico		11
Colorado River	-	13.6%	16 (38 maximum)	Loma, Colorado		11
Colorado River	-	0	ND			46
Colorado River	-	-	0-1.0	Yuma, Arizona		43
Western Gulf Basin	-	4.3%	3.5 (6.6 maximum)	U.S.		11
Pacific Northwest Basin	-	8.6%	0.9 (3.7 maximum)			11
Columbia River	-	-	0.09-0.15	Near The Dalles, Oregon		43
Columbia River	-	0	0			46
Clearwater River	-	-	0.1	Lewiston, Idaho	1 occurrence	11
Pend Oreille River	-	-	0.2	Albeni Falls Dam, Idaho	1 occurrence	11
Snake River	-	-	0.5-1.3	Payette, Idaho	2 occurrences	11
Snake River	-	-	1.4	Wawawai, Washington	1 occurrence	11
California Basin	-	0	ND	California		11
Sacramento River	-	-	0-0.16	Sacramento, California		43
San Fernando Valley	-	-	20	California	Estimated in wastewater	47
Great Basin	-	5.3%	0.3	Nevada	1 occurence	11
Alaska	-	5.6%	1.1	Alaska		11
Yukon River	-	-	< 0.20-0.31	Mountain Village, Alaska		43

44

TABLE II-9

SILVER COMPOSITION OF SUSPENDED MATERIAL IN RIVERS[13]/

River and State	Suspended Load (mg/ ℓ)	Ag (ppm)	Parts Per Billion Ag Suspended in Water
Brazos, Texas	954	0.4	0.4
Colorado, Texas	150	0.6	0.1
Red, Louisiana	436	0.3	0.1
Mississippi, Arkansas	185	0.7	0.1
Tombigbee, Alabama	25	1.0	0.03
Alabama, Alabama	54	4.0	0.2
Chattahoochie, Georgia	71	7.0	0.5
Flint, Georgia	12	1.0	0.01
Savannah, South Carolina	30	2.0	0.06
Wateree, South Carolina	37	1.5	0.06
Pee Dee, South Carolina	188	0.4	0.08
Cape Fear, North Carolina	61	0.7	0.04
Neuse, North Carolina	36	4.0	0.1
Roanoke, North Carolina	33	4.9	0.2
James, Virginia	41	7.0	0.3
Rappahannock, Virginia	28	1.0	0.03
Potomac, Virginia	34	1.5	0.05
Susquehanna, Pennsylvania	54	15.0	0.81

TABLE II-10

SILVER IN WASTEWATER EFFLUENTS AND SLUDGES AT SEWAGE TREATMENT PLANTS

Location	Date	Ag Content of Influent Wastewater (ppm)	Ag Content of Treated Effluent Wastewater (ppm)	Ag Content of Sewage Sludge (ppm)	Remarks	Reference
United States			0.05 (maximum permissible)			11
Denver, Colorado	After 1969	Not detected	0.04 ppm (0.045 maximum)			48
England and Wales	1972			0.005-0.15 (0.032 mean)		24
Various				100-900		42
California		0.00164	0.00145	0.01-0.30 (0.18 mean)	Six metropolitan sludges	42
		0.00145	0.000048		Sand filtration	42
		0.0546	0.0169		Carbon adsorption	42
					Lime coagulation and recarbonation	42
Southern California:	1971					
Oxnard			≤ 0.01	30		49
Hyperion (Los Angeles)			0.002	130		49
Los Angeles County Joint water pollution control and sanitation districts			0.02	32		49
Terminal Island			0.002	40		49
Orange County			0.02	105		49
Pt. Loma						50
Interstate Sanitation District: New York, New Jersey, Connecticut	1973	Less than 0.05 in 188 of 193 samples	Less than 0.05 in 191 of 193 samples			
Pittsburgh, Pennsylvania	1961		< 0.00012-< 0.00019			51
	1962		< 0.0003-0.0004			51

TABLE II-11

SILVER IN CITY WATER SUPPLIES

Ag Content (ppb)	Location	Remarks	Reference
0.23 (7.0 maximum)			52
50 (maximum)	U.S.	Maximum allowable Ag content of drinking water according to Federal Water Pollution Control Administration.	11
8 (average)	U.S.	2,595 samples of 956	53
30 (maximum observed)		municipal water supplies.	
ND - 0.35	Birmingham, Alabama		54
0.09	Mobile, Alabama		54
ND - < 0.31	Montgomery, Alabama		54
< 0.53 - < 0.92	Phoenix, Arizona		54
ND - < 0.54	Tucson, Arizona		54
ND - < 0.40	Long Beach, California		54
< 0.3	Los Angeles, California		54
< 0.4 - < 0.7	Los Angeles, California		47
< 0.06	Oakland, California		54
< 0.1 - < 0.2	Sacramento, California		54
< 0.78	San Diego, California		54
< 0.06 - < 0.08	San Francisco, California		54
< 0.32	San Jose, California		54
ND - < 0.26	Denver, Colorado		54
0.29	Hartford, Connecticut		54
< 0.14 - 0.30	New Haven, Connecticut		54
< 0.25 - < 0.28	Washington, D.C.		54
ND - < 0.49	Jacksonville, Florida		54
ND - < 0.50	Miami, Florida		54
ND - < 0.21	St. Petersburg, Florida		54
0.55	Tampa, Florida		54
< 0.03 - 0.07	Atlanta, Georgia		54
< 0.05 - < 0.26	Savannah, Georgia		54
< 0.26 - < 0.34	Honolulu, Hawaii		54
0 - 9 (100%)	Chicago, Illinois distribution		55
0 - 1 (74%)	points (maximum 2 ppb at the		
2 - 5 (22%)	treatment plants)		
< 0.2 - < 0.27	Chicago, Illinois		54
< 0.5 - < 0.59	Rockford, Illinois		54
< 0.29	Evansville, Indiana		54
0.2 - < 0.54	Fort Wayne, Indiana		54
< 0.24	Gary-Hobart, Indiana		54
ND - < 0.39	Indianapolis, Indiana		54
< 0.24 - < 0.48	South Bend, Indiana		54

TABLE II-11 (Continued)

Ag Content (ppb)	Location	Remarks	Reference
< 0.30	Des Moines, Iowa		54
< 0.2 - < 0.3	Louisville, Kentucky		54
< 0.30 - 0.80	Baton Rouge, Louisiana		54
< 0.25 - 7.0	New Orleans, Louisiana		54
< 0.18 - 0.24	Shreveport, Louisiana		54
< 0.13 - 0.74	Baltimore, Maryland		54
0.18	Boston, Massachusetts		54
0.14 - 0.49	Springfield, Massachusetts		54
0.06	Worcester, Massachusetts		54
0.21 - 0.22	Detroit, Michigan		54
< 0.25 - < 0.53	Flint, Michigan		54
< 0.23 - < 0.25	Grand Rapids, Michigan		54
< 0.15 - 0.48	Minneapolis, Minnesota		54
< 0.17 - < 0.34	St. Paul, Minnesota		54
0.68	Jackson, Mississippi		54
< 0.28 - < 0.56	Kansas City, Missouri		54
< 0.22 - < 0.23	St. Louis, Missouri		54
0.3	St. Louis, Missouri	Finished water	56
< 0.41	Lincoln, Nebraska		54
< 0.46	Omaha, Nebraska		54
< 0.09	Jersey City (contiguous with Paterson and Newark)		54
0.09 - 0.38	Newark, New Jersey		54
< 0.09 - 0.09	Paterson, New Jersey		54
ND - < 0.5	Albuquerque, New Mexico		54
0.07 - 0.12	Albany, New York		54
< 0.26	Buffalo, New York		54
0.23 - 0.39	New York City, New York		54
< 0.14 - 0.30	Rochester, New York		54
< 0.19	Syracuse, New York		54
0.32 - < 0.41	Yonkers, New York		54
< 0.04 - 0.17	Charlotte, North Carolina		54
< 0.17	Akron, Ohio		54
< 0.29	Cincinnati, Ohio		54
0.23	Cleveland, Ohio		54
ND - < 0.26	Columbus, Ohio		54
1.1	Dayton, Ohio		54
< 0.16	Toledo, Ohio		54
< 0.23	Youngstown, Ohio		54
0.54 - < 0.76	Oklahoma City, Oklahoma		54
< 0.19 - < 0.20	Tulsa, Oklahoma		54
< 0.02	Portland, Oregon		54
< 0.26	Erie, Pennsylvania		54
< 0.15 - < 0.17	Philadelphia, Pennsylvania		54
< 0.12 - < 0.19	Pittsburgh, Pennsylvania		54

TABLE II-11 (Concluded)

Ag Content (ppb)	Location	Remarks	Reference
0.07	Providence, Rhode Island		54
ND - < 0.24	Chattanooga, Tennessee		54
ND - 0.19	Memphis, Tennessee		54
< 0.16	Nashville, Tennessee		54
ND - < 0.29	Austin, Texas		54
0.15 - < 0.29	Dallas, Texas		54
ND - < 0.86	El Paso, Texas		54
ND - < 0.15	Houston, Texas		54
ND - 1.5	Lubbock, Texas	A well	54
< 0.27 - < 0.54	Salt Lake City, Utah		54
< 0.10 - < 0.15	Norfolk, Virginia		54
< 0.10	Richmond, Virginia		54
0.05 - < 0.06	Seattle, Washington		54
0.26 - 0.53	Spokane, Washington		54
< 0.05	Tacoma, Washington		54
< 0.5	Madison, Wisconsin		54
< 0.24 - < 0.25	Milwaukee, Wisconsin		54

TABLE II-12

SILVER CONTENT OF PLANTS

Type or Order	Plant Species	Sample Origin[a]	Ag Content (ppm dry weight)	Ag Content of Soil (ppm)	Other Information	Reference
Average plants		-	1.0	-	Concentration factor = 200	26
Marine plants		-	0.06	-		57
Marine plants		-	0.25	-		38
Plankton	Chaetoceros curvisetus	-	0.25	-		22
Diatom		-	0.2	-		35
Brown Algae		-	0.28	-		22
Algae	Fucus	↓	0.8, 10.0 in ash	-	"Seaweed" and Fucus spp., respectively	35
Algae	Laminaria	-	0.1 to 0.7	-		35
Laminariales	Laminaria saccharina	D	0.18	-		58
Algae	Macrocystis pyrifera	-	0.2	-		35
Gigartinales	Ampheltia plicata	D	0.35	-		58
Freshwater plants		-	0.026	-	Concentration factor = 200	57
Oscillatoriales	Aphanizomenon flos-aquae	E	0.02	-		58
Chroococcales	Anacystis nidulas	E	0.02	-		58
Caulerpales	Caulerpa prolifera	A	10	-		58
Charales	Chara fragilis	A	0.04	-		58
Butomales	Elodea canadensis	A	0.02	-		58
Land plants		E	0.06	-		22
Actinomycetales	Streptomyces arenaea	-	7	-		58
Yeast	Saccaromyces cerevesiae	-	detected	-		35
Fungi		-	0.15	-		22
Fungi		-	high	-		31
Mushrooms		-	up to several hundred	-		35
Lichens		-	0.15	-		35
Lichens	Cladonia retipora	C	4.3	-		58
Pezizales	Aleuria aurantia	C	0.03	-		58
Pezizales	Bulgaria inquinans	C	1.8	-		58
Tuberales	Elaphomyces granulatus	C	0.64	-		58
Spheriales	Hypoxylon fragiforme	C	0.02	-		58
Agaricales	Clavulina cinerea	C	16	-		58
Agaricales	Stereum hirsutum	C	0.01	-		58
Sclerodermatales	Scleroderma verrucosa	-	4.3	-		58
Fungi	Aspergillis niger	-	detected in ash	-		35
Eurotiales	Aspergillis microcysticus	E	0.02	-		58
Bryidae	Hypnum cupressiforme	B	0.03	0.09		58
Sphagnales	Sphagnum acutifolium	C	2.7	-		58
Bryophyte		-	0.1	-		35,22
Bryophyte		-	9.0	-	In 7.9% of Bryophyte samples	35
Marchantiales	Marchantia polymorpha	A	1.6,(0.03)[b]	-		58
Polytrichidae	Polytrichum commune	C	0.07	-		58

50

TABLE II-12 (Concluded)

Type or Order	Plant Species	Sample Origin [a]	Ag Content (ppm dry weight)	Ag Content of Soil (ppm)	Other Information	Reference
Vascular plants			5.0	-	In 1.5% of vascular plants sampled	35
Psilotales	Psilotum triquetrum	B	0.31;0.02[b]	0.04		58
Lycopodiales	Lycopodium circinatum	B	1.0;0.02[b]	0.03		58
Lycoperdales	Lycoperdon pyriforme	C	0.18	-		58
Selaginales	Selaginella willdenowii	A	0.01			58
Equisetales	Equisetum spp.	-	0-2.0 in ash			35
(Horsetails)	Equisetum spp.	-	0.23 (1.0 in ash)			35
	Equisetum giganteum	B	0.05			58
Ophioglossales	Ophioglossum pedunculosum	B	2.3			58
Salviniales	Salvinia auriculata	B	0.10;0.04[b]			58
Ferns		-	0.23			22,35
Gymnosperms		-	0.07			35,22
Gymnosperms		-	0-1.4 (0-30 in ash)			35
Ephedrales	Ephedra geradiana	A	8.0;0.02[b]	0.09		58
Cycadales	Encephalartos lehmanii	B	0.15;0.02[b]	-		58
Ginkgoales	Ginkgo biloba	A	2.0			58
Coniferales	Juniperus communis	A	1.5;0.02[b]	0.09		58
Angiosperms		-	0.9		In grains and cereals	35
Angiosperms		-	0-0.28 (0-3.0 in ash)			35
Angiosperms		-	0.06			22
Cyperales	Carex pendula	A	1.0	0.07		58
Various grasses		-	0.03-0.4		Field grown	29
Graminales	Triticum spp.	-	0.5		Bran contains 1.0 ppm Ag and flour 0.4 ppm	59
Magnoliales	Liriodendron tulipifera	A	0.02			58
Cherimoya	Annona cherimola leaves	-	0.50		Field grown	29
Citrus	Citrus spp. leaves	-	0.03-1.00		Field grown	29
	leaves	-	0.01-0.03		Soln. leaves	29
	fruit	-	0.1-1.0		Field grown fruit	29
Plum	Prunus domestica leaves	-	0.70		Field grown	29
Cherry	Prunus cerasus leaves	-	0.03-0.10		Field grown	29
Apple	Malus spp. leaves	-	0.02-0.3		Garden grown	29
Walnut	Juglans regia leaves	-	0.07-0.3		Field grown	29
Coffee	Coffee spp. beans	-	0.02		Field grown	29
Bur clover	Medicago hispida tops	-	0.20-0.50		Field grown	29
Ladino clover	Trifolium repens tops	-	0.40-0.60		Field grown	29
Alfalfa	Medicago sativa tops	-	0.02-1.30		Field grown	29
Boraginales	Pulmonaria saccharata	A	0.01		Field grown	58
	Tobacco (cigarette)	-	0.27		Neutron activation analysis	60
	Tobacco (cigarette)	-	2.61			60
Tea	Camellia sinensis	-	< 0.20-2.00			29

a/ Source of the plant material: A-exposed land of a botanical garden; B-greenhouse of a botanical garden; C-forest; D-Helgoland, North Sea; E-synthetic media.

b/ Double values for the same species indicate analyses taken in May and September, respectively.

51

TABLE II-13

SILVER IN SOME MARINE AND FRESHWATER ANIMALS

Organism or Phylum	Species	Ag Concentration in Dry Matter (ppm)	Remarks	Reference
Marine animals		3-11	22,000 x water concentration	22
Marine animals				2
Marine animals		1.00 ppm	3,300 x Ag concentration of seawater	57
Freshwater animals		0.4 ppm	3,080 x Ag concentration of freshwater	57
Zooplankton	10 species	Detected		35
Protozoa		Not available	Foraminifera, Radiolaria, etc.	2
Foraminifera		3.0	SiO_2 hard tissues only	35
Porifera		Up to 1.0	Marine sponges	2
Malichondria		1.0	SiO_2 hard tissues only	35
Coelenterata		2.0-6.0	Jellyfishes, anemones, coral, etc.	2
	Cyntcea cappilaton	3.0-5.0	Jellyfish	35
	Metridium dianthus	6.0	Anemone	2
Platyhelminthes-Annelida, Marine worms		Present in some species	Worms	2
	Sabellaria, Owenia, Mellina, Myxicola	Detected		35
	Sagitta	Found in concentrations	Arrow worms	35
Echinodermata		1.0-4.0	Starfishes, sea urchins, sea lilies, etc.	35
	Hard tissues	1.5		
	Brissopsis lyrifera (shell)	1.5	Sea urchin	35
	Stichopus tremulus (eviscerated)	2.6	Sea slug	35
	Asterias rubens (eviscerated)	3.8	Starfish	35
	Blood of Phallusia (tunicate)	Present		2
Mollusca		1.0-10.0	Oysters, clams, snails, etc. (soft parts--concentration is in blood, liver, and kidney most often)	2
		Present	Soft parts of scallop	35
		0.2-2.3	Soft parts of oyster	35
		4.5-7.3	Soft parts of mussel	35
		0.1-0.3		
Crustacea		Up to 2.0	Lobsters, crabs, etc. (tissues and blood contain Ag). (River crustaceans take up Ag through gills.)	2
Crustacea	Maja and Carcimus blood	Present	Crabs	35
	Crab tissue	Present		35

TABLE II-13 (Concluded)

Organism or Phylum	Species	Ag Concentration in Dry Matter (ppm)	Remarks	Reference
Fishes				
Wrasse	Ctenolabrus rupestris	Present in ash		35
		Present in ash		35
Freshwater fish				
Trout	Salvelinus namaycush	0.01-0.1	Aged 1-6 years, Lake Cayuga, New York	61
Trout	Salvelinus namaycush	0.68	7-8 years old	61
Trout	Salvelinus namaycush	0.48	9-11 years old	61
Trout	Salvelinus namaycush	0.58	12 years old	61
Marine fish		0.48		24
		11.0		

TABLE II-14

SILVER CONTENT OF HUMAN TISSUES

Type of Tissue	Observed Ag Concentration	Fraction Observed	Ash % of Wet Tissue Weight	Health Status of Patient or Subject	Age of Patient (years)	Geographical Origin	Remarks	Reference
Human	Rarely > 10.00 ppm	10%						30 (Kehoe, 1940)
Human Body	1300 ppm			Generalized argyria	70	America	Most severe case of general argyria ever reported.	62
Human Tissues	Max. amount 10 ppm dry wt.			Healthy and diseased				63
All Organs	Detected	1/3 (33%)					Unknown reasons for selective absorption.	30 (Fox and Range, 1930)
	Not detected	2/3 (67%)						
Adrenal	0.8 ppm (ash)	10/13 (77%)	0.50			America	Ag was in ~ 0.5 of the samples of every tissue, generally in concentrations near the limit of detection.	64
Alimentary Canal								
Cecum	0.1 ppm (ash)	16/31 (52%)	0.67			America	Values are median.	64
Duodenum	0.1 ppm (ash)	35/68 (51%)	0.81			America	Values are median.	64
Esophagus	< 0.1 ppm (ash)	32/68 (47%)	0.89			America	Values are median.	64
Ileum	0.1 ppm (ash)	49/84 (58%)	0.75			America	Values are median.	65
Intestine	0.02 ppm (wet tissue)	53/104 (51%)	0.92	Normal				64
Jejunum	0.1 ppm (ash)	14/42 (33%)	0.85			America	Values are median.	64
Rectum	< 0.1 ppm (ash)	64/109 (59%)	0.68			America	Values are median.	64
Sigmoid colon	0.1 ppm (ash)	52/130 (40%)	0.82			America	Values are median.	64
Stomach	< 0.1 ppm (ash)					America	Values are median.	64
Stomach	0.00 ppm (wet tissue)a/			Normal				
Aorta	1.59 µg % dry wt.			Atherosclerosis				66
	2.42 µg % dry wt.			Normal				66
	< 0.1 ppm (ash)	6/16 (38%)			≳ 20	Africa		67
	1.2 ppm (ash)	13/13 (100%)			≳ 20	Near East		67
	1.0 ppm (ash)	55/66 (83%)			≳ 20	Far East		67
	< 0.1 ppm	2/5 (40%)				Switzerland		67
	0.1 ppm (ash)	63/105 (60%)	1.70			America		64
	0.008 mg % wet wt.			Atherosclerosis	20-39	Russia		68
	0.01 mg % wet wt.			Atherosclerosis	40-59	Russia		68
	0.004 mg % wet wt.			Atherosclerosis	≳ 60	Russia		68
Bladder	0.1 ppm	46/112 (41%)	0.78			America		64

TABLE II-14 (continued)

Type of Tissue	Observed Ag Concentration	Fraction Observed	Ash % of Wet Tissue Weight	Health Status of Patient or Subject	Age of Patient (years)	Geographical Origin	Remarks	Reference
Blood								
Whole blood	1.58 µg/100 ml			Atherosclerosis		America		66
Whole blood	1.04 µg/100 ml			Normal				66
Plasma	0.77 µg % dry wt.			Atherosclerosis				66
Plasma	0.44 µg % dry wt.			Normal				66
Blood								
Serum	17 ppm			Myocardial infarction				69
Serum	20 ppm			Normal				69
Serum	Present							70
Blood	0.0053 ppm			Otosclerosis			Zn, Ti, Cu, Cr, Mn, and Fe were depressed. Ni and Pb were elevated.	71
Blood	0.0071 ppm			Healthy				71
Blood	0.024 ppm							24
Bone	2100 ppm			Generalized argyria	70	America	Most severe case reported.	62
Bone								
Long bone	0.00 ppm (wet tissue)a/			Normal				65
Rib bone	0.1 ppm (wet tissue)			Normal				65
Brain	100 ppm	6/16 (38%)		Generalized argyria	70	America	Most severe case reported.	62
	< 0.1 ppm (ash)	15/17 (88%)			20-60	Africa		67
	1.7 ppm (ash)	39/51 (76%)			20-60	Near East		67
	0.5 ppm (ash)	5/8 (63%)			20-60	Far East		67
	0.5 ppm (ash)	113/128 (88%)	1.70		20-60	Switzerland		67
	0.6 ppm (ash)				20-60	America		64
Brain	0.03 ppm (wet tissue)			Normal				65
Diaphragm	< 0.1 ppm (ash)	17/91 (19%)	0.98			America		64
Hair	≥ skin < nails			Normal males	15-20			63

55

TABLE II-14 (continued)

Type of Tissue	Observed Ag Concentration	Fraction Observed	Ash % of Wet Tissue Weight	Health Status of Patient or Subject	Age of Patient (years)	Geographical Origin	Remarks	Reference
Kidney	2.07 µg % dry wt.			Atherosclerosis		Russia	Concluded that changes in Ag in the blood have no direct relation to the pathogenesis of the disease.	66
Kidney	1.72 µg % dry wt.		3.30	Normal		Russia		66
Larynx	< 0.1 ppm (ash)	20/50 (40%)		Normal		America		64
Liver	not elevated[b]			Primary carcinoma of liver		Chicago area		74
Liver	Increased or high[b]	10 sampled		Metastatic carcinoma		Chicago area	Primary site: mammary gland or colon.	74
Liver	Increased[b]	1/12 (8.3%)		Nonmetastatic carcinoma of other viscera		Chicago area	Carcinoma of esophagus.	74
Liver	elevated or high[b]	sample of 44		Nonneoplastic diseases		Chicago area	Tubal pregnancy, emphysema, or cirrhosis of the liver.	74
Liver	700 ppm			Generalized argyria		America	Most severe case reported.	62
Liver	elevated or high[a]	(12%)		Nonneoplastic disease		Chicago area		74
Liver	elevated or high[a]	(23%)		Neoplastic disease		Chicago area		74
Liver	< 0.1 ppm (ash)	13/45 (29%)				Africa		67
Liver	1.7 ppm (ash)	30/33 (91%)				Near East		67
Liver	1.4 ppm (ash)	53/67 (79%)				Far East		67
Liver	1.3 ppm (ash)	8/9 (89%)				Switzerland		67
Liver	0.8 ppm (ash)	139/148 (94%)				America		64
Liver	0.96 ppm (ash)		1.30				Analysis of Ag concentrations in 10 regions of the liver showed interhepatic variability to be greater than any intrahepatic variability.	75
Liver	4.66 ppm (dry wt.)	6%		Acute renal failure				73
	7.61 ppm (dry wt.)	7%		Chronic renal failure				73
	0.70 ppm (dry wt.)	13%		Normal (dying of other causes)				73
Liver or Lung, Cancerous	lowered[a]			Cancerous		Chicago area	Ag was lower in cancerous tissue than in surrounding noncancerous tissue. The reverse was true of inflammatory lung lesions.	74

56

TABLE II-14 (continued)

Type of Tissue	Observed Ag Concentration	Fraction Observed	Ash % of Wet Tissue Weight	Health Status of Patient or Subject	Age of Patient (years)	Geographical Origin	Remarks	Reference
Heart	0.00 ppm (wet tissue)[a] / 0.0025 ppm (wet tissue) (range factor: 42)			Normal / Victims of traumatic accidents			Gilmore and Didio (1960) observed far higher concentrations in diseased heart tissue.	65 / 72
	< 0.1 ppm (ash)	2/43 (4.7%)			20-60	Africa		67
	< 0.1 ppm (ash)	9/19 (47%)			20-60	Near East		67
	< 0.1 ppm (ash)	29/63 (46%)			20-60	Far East		67
	< 0.1 ppm (ash)	1/8 (13%)			20-60	Switzerland		67
	< 0.1 ppm (ash)	31/138 (22%)	1.10		20-60	America		64
Heart	1500 ppm			Generalized argyria	70	America	Most severe case reported.	62
Kidneys	0.81 ppm (dry wt.)	(6%)		Acute renal failure			Detection limit 0.2 ppm Ag. Ag, Co, Sr, Ba, Li, and B showed no consistent changes in percent detectability and mean values. Ag was not analyzed in hypertensives.	73
	0.18 ppm (dry wt.)	(5%)		Chronic renal failure				73
	0.36 ppm (dry wt.)	(11%)		Normal (dying of other causes)				
Kidneys	2,400 ppm			Generalized argyria	70	America	Most severe case reported.	62
Kidney	0.00 ppm (wet tissue)[a]			Normal			Ag not detected in normal urine of Mexicans, Americans, Frenchmen, or Germans though traces of Ag were found in their blood.	65
Kidney	< 0.1 ppm (ash)	5/48 (10%)				Africa		67
	< 0.5 ppm	18/31 (58%)				Near East		67
	< 0.1 ppm	24/66 (36%)				Far East		67
	< 0.1 ppm	4/9 (44%)				Switzerland		67
	< 0.1 ppm	67/143 (47%)	1.10			America		64
Kidney	significantly high[b]			Had noncancerous neoplasms		Chicago area		74
Kidney	elevated or high[b]	(4%)		Nonneoplastic disease		Chicago area		74
Kidney	elevated or high[b]	(24%)		Neoplastic disease		Chicago area		74
Kidney	elevated or high[b]	3/25 (12%)		Carcinoma		Chicago area	Healthy kidneys (primary carcinoma of mammary gland or lung).	74

57

TABLE II-14 (continued)

Type of Tissue	Observed Ag Concentration	Fraction Observed	Ash % of Wet Tissue Weight	Health Status of Patient or Subject	Age of Patient (years)	Geographical Origin	Remarks	Reference
Lung	0.04 ppm (wet tissue)			Normal				65
Lung	detected	39%				America		76
Lung	elevated[a]	1/3 (33%)		Died from atherosclerosis		Chicago area		74
Lung	< 0.1 ppm (ash)	23/69 (33%)				Far East		67
	< 0.1 ppm (ash)	1/7 (14%)				Switzerland		67
	< 0.1 ppm (ash)	54/139 (39%)	1.10			America		64
	< 0.1 ppm (ash)	8/44 (18%)				Africa		67
	0.3 ppm (ash)	18/34 (53%)				Near East		67
Lung	increased or high[a]	5/14 (36%)		Had primary carcinoma of lung pavement cells		Chicago area		74
Lung	increased or high[a]	(39%)		Had neoplastic disease		Chicago area		74
Lung	increased or high[a]	(75%)		Inflammatory disease		Chicago area		74
Lung	elevated[a]	2/9 (22%)		Had metastatic carcinoma		Chicago area	Primary site: colon or uterus.	74
Lung	increased or high[a]	4/12 (33%)		Had sarcinoma		Chicago area	Carcinoma of cervix, mammary gland, jejunum, or esophagus.	74
Lung	increased or high[b]	4/8 (50%)		Had inflammatory disease		Chicago area	Had chronic pneumonia, T.B., pneumoconiosis, and chronic emphysema.	74
Lung	higher than normal			Coal miners				77
Muscle	< 0.1 ppm (ash)	27/135 (20%)	1.20			America		64
Muscle	0.00 ppm (wet tissue)[a]							65
Muscle	1,600 ppm			Generalized argyria	70	America	Most severe case reported.	62
Nails	> hair			Normal males	15-20			63
Omentum	0.5 ppm (ash)	61/74 (82%)	0.25			America		64

58

TABLE II-14 (continued)

Type of Tissue	Observed Ag Concentration	Fraction Observed	Ash % of Wet Tissue Weight	Health Status of Patient or Subject	Age of Patient (years)	Geographical Origin	Remarks	Reference
Ovary	0.3 ppm (ash)	2/2 (100%)				Africa		67
	0.5 ppm (ash)	7/11 (64%)				Far East		67
	< 0.1 ppm (ash)	7/16 (44%)	1.00			America		64
Pancreas	< 0.1 ppm (ash)	2/6 (33%)			20-60	Africa		67
	0.5 ppm (ash)	20/26 (77%)			20-60	Near East		67
	0.5 ppm (ash)	34/59 (58%)			20-60	Far East		67
	< 0.1 ppm (ash)	1/4 (25%)			20-60	Switzerland		67
	< 0.1 ppm (ash)	61/137 (45%)	1.10		20-60	America		64
Prostrate	< 0.1 ppm (ash)	24/48 (50%)	1.20			America		64
Skin	1.3 ppm (ash)	21/22 (95%)	0.79			America		64
Skin	≤ hair < nails			Normal males	15-20		Inert metals usually: skin > nails > hair.	63
Spleen	0.00 ppm (wet tissue)a/							65
Spleen	1.02 ppm (dry wt.)	(3%)		Acute renal failure				73
	3.78 ppm (dry wt.)	(7%)		Chronic renal failure				73
	2.68 ppm (dry wt.)	(9%)		Normal (dying of other causes)				73
Spleen	< 0.1 ppm (ash)	1/40 (2.5%)			20-60	Africa		67
	< 0.1 ppm (ash)	14/34 (41%)			20-60	Near East		67
	< 0.1 ppm (ash)	23/62 (37%)			20-60	Far East		67
	< 0.1 ppm (ash)	1/8 (12.5%)			20-60	Switzerland		67
	< 0.1 ppm (ash)	44/141 (31%)	1.40		20-60	America		64
Testis	0.2 ppm (ash)	1/2 (50%)			20-60	Africa		67
	1.3 ppm (ash)	12/17 (71%)			20-60	Near East		67
	0.5 ppm (ash)	27/38 (71%)			20-60	Far East		67
	< 0.1 ppm (ash)	0/4 (0%)				Switzerland		67
	< 0.1 ppm (ash)	24/71 (34%)	1.10			America		64
Thyroid	< 0.1 ppm (ash)	10/20 (50%)	1.40			America		64

TABLE II-14 (concluded)

Type of Tissue	Observed Ag Concentration	Fraction Observed	Ash % of Wet Tissue Weight	Health Status of Patient or Subject	Age of Patient (years)	Geographical Origin	Remarks	Reference
Tooth								
Enamel	0.01-0.77 ppm	56/56 (100%)						78
Enamel	0.0049 ± 0.0012 ppm						Thermal neutron activation analysis.	79
Enamel	0-100 ppm						Chemical analysis.	79
Outer Enamel	97 ppm							79
Body	54 ppm							79
Trachea	0.1 ppm (ash)	32/60 (53%)	1.90			America		64
Uterus	< 0.1 ppm (ash)	10/32 (31%)	1.00			America		64

a/ Concentrations were reported as mg silver/100 g wet tissue.

b/ Silver was reported only in relative amounts because it was precipitated by the chloride ion of the internal standard solution. Analysis was by emission spectrography and the silver values are based on the intensity ratio.

60

TABLE II-15

SILVER IN COAL

Location	Ag Content (ppm)	Remarks	Reference
Western Coals	Max. 1-10	Ash	80
Wyoming, South Dakota	0-34	In coke	2
West Virginia	< 4-27	In ash of bituminous coal	2
West Virginia	5-28, Avg 9	Ash	80
Texas, Colorado, North Dakota, and South Dakota	1-10	Erratically distributed in ash	2
Oklahoma, Kansas, Missouri (Pennsylvania coals)	1.5-15	In ash from beds	2
Various Canadian	0.5-300	-	2
Europe and India	0.1-50	-	2
Unspecified Source(s)	0.5-2		24
	Avg 0.5		5
	< 0.1-< 2		81
Allegheny County, Pennsylvania:			
Float Coal Dust	0.2	Based on whole coal. Determined in ash.	77
	0.5	Dust	77
Pittsburgh Seam	< 0.5	All fractions except the two below:	77
Upper Freeport Seams	1	3.3-5.5 μ and 1.0-2.0 μ fractions	77
	0.5		77
	50	Respirable dust	77

TABLE II-16

SILVER IN OIL SHALES, PETROLEUM AND OTHER NATURAL HYDROCARBONS

Type of Substance	Ag Content (ppm)	Location	Remarks	Reference
Albert shales	< 0.1	New Brunswick, Canada	Compared with other shales, oil shales found to be enriched in Ag	2
Bituminous marks	5-10	-	Ag erratically distributed	2
Western U.S. oils	Up to 100	Western U.S.	Ag in paraffinic compound	2
Anthraxolite	15	Pennsylvania	-	2
Anthraxolite	5	Sudbury area, Canada	-	2

TABLE II-17

SILVER IN REFINED OILS

Type of Application	Ag Content (ppm)	Annual Consumption (gal.)	Estimated Ag Content (troy oz)	Reference
Air Force Jet Engine Lubricating Oil (used)	Avg 1.26			82
Air Force Reciprocating Engine Lubricating Oil (used)	Avg 1.48	15,950,000		82
Diesel Oil (used)	0.1-1.3			83
Reclaimed Oil	0.0314-0.314			84
Distillate Fuel Oil	0.0047-0.013 (avg 0.0088) [a]	4.08×10^{10}	41,400	85
Residual Fuel Oil	0.062-0.117 (avg 0.095) [b]	3.66×10^{10}	438,000	85
	0.0006-0.1 (avg 0.045)			81
Fuel Oil	Avg 0.0001			81
Premium Gasoline	< 0.00073-0.294 (avg 0.124)			81
Low-Lead Gasoline	0.0015-0.060 (avg 0.0707)			81

[a] Based on 1 lb Ag in the particulate/10^6 gal. fuel. Fuel density 7.05 lb/gal.
[b] Based on 1 lb Ag in the particulate/10^6 gal. fuel. Fuel density 7.88 lb/gal.

63

BIBLIOGRAPHY. SECTION II.

1. Wilcox, R. L., "Chapter 2 - Sources of Silver," in Silver Economics, Metallurgy, and Use, A. Butts and C. D. Coxe, Eds., D. Van Nostrand Company, Inc., Princeton, New Jersey, 1967, pp. 16-35.

2. Boyle, R. W., "Geochemistry of Silver and Its Deposits with Notes on Geochemical Prospecting for the Element," Geol. Surv. Can., Bull., No. 160, 1-264 (1968).

3. Ageton, R. W., "Silver," in Minerals Facts and Problems, Bureau of Mines Bulletin 650, U.S. Department of the Interior, U.S. Government Printing Office, Washington, D.C., 1970, pp. 723-737.

4. Swaine, D. J., The Trace-Element Content of Fertilizers, Commonwealth Agr. Bureau, Farnham Royal, Bucks, England, 1962.

5. Bertine, K. K., and E. D. Goldberg, "Fossil Fuel Combustion and the Major Sedimentary Cycle," Science, 173 (3993), 233-235 (1971).

6. Andren, A. W., B. G. Blaylock, E. A. Bondietti, C. W. Francis, S. G. Hildebrand, J. W. Huckabee, D. R. Jackson, S. E. Lindberg, F. H. Sweeton, R. I. Van Hook, and A. P. Watson, "4. Ecological Research," in Ecology and Analysis of Trace Contaminants, Progress Report October 1973 - September 1974, W. Fulkerson, W. D. Schults, and R. I. Van Hook, Eds., Oak Ridge National Laboratory, Oak Ridge, Tennessee, 1974, pp. 61-104.

7. Bogen, J., "Trace Element Concentrations in Atmospheric Aerosols and Rainwater, Measured by Neutron Activation and γ-Ray Spectrometry," in Comparative Studies of Food and Environmental Contamination, Proceedings of a Symposium on Nuclear Techniques in Comparative Studies of Food and Environmental Contamination, Otaniemi, Finland, August 27-31, 1973, International Atomic Energy Agency, Vienna, 1974, pp. 75-90.

8. Harrison, P. R., K. A. Rahn, R. Dams, J. A. Robbins, J. W. Winchester, S. S. Brar, and D. M. Nelson, "Areawide Trace Metal Concentrations Measured by Multielement Neutron Activation Analysis. A One Day Study in Northwest Indiana," J. Air Pollution Control Assoc., 21(9), 563-570 (1971).

9. Dams, R., J. A. Robbins, K. A. Rahn, and J. W. Winchester, "Quantitative Relationships among the Trace Elements Over Industrialized N.W. Indiana," Nucl. Technol. Environ. Pollution, Proc. Symp., 1970, 139-157 (1971).

10. Brar, S. S., D. M. Nelson, J. R. Kline, P. F. Gustafson, E. L. Kanabrocki, C. E. Moore, and D. M. Hattori, "Instrumental Analysis for Trace Elements Present in Chicago Area Surface Air," J. Geophys. Res., 75(15), 2939-2945 (1970).

11. Kopp, J. F., and R. C. Kroner, Trace Metals in Waters of the United States, U.S. Department of the Interior, Federal Water Pollution Control Administration, Cincinnati, Ohio, 1970.

12. Frank, R. H., Jr., Trace Metal Pollution of the Lower North Canadian River Basin, Ph.D. Dissertation, The University of Oklahoma, 1969, Xerox University Microfilms, Ann Arbor, Michigan, 1974.

13. Turekian, K. K., and M. R. Scott, "Concentrations of Cr, Ag, Mo, Ni, Co, and Mn in Suspended Material in Streams," Environ. Sci. Technol., 1, 940-942 (1967).

14. Kopp, J. F., "The Occurrence of Trace Elements in Water," Trace Substances in Environmental Health - III, D. D. Hemphill, Ed., Proceedings of University of Missouri's Third Annual Conference on Trace Substances in Environmental Health, University of Missouri, Columbia, Mo., June 24-26, 1969, pp. 59-73.

15. McCabe, L. J., "Metal Levels Found in Distribution Samples," paper presented at the American Water Works Association Seminar on Corrosion by Soft Water, Washington, D. C., June 21, 1970.

16. Braidech, M. M., and F. H. Emery, "The Spectrographic Determination of Minor Chemical Constituents in Various Water Supplies in the United States," J. Am. Water Works Assoc., 27, 557-580 (1935).

17. Hutchinson, G. E., A Treatise on Limnology. Vol. I. Geography, Physics, and Chemistry, John Wiley and Sons, Inc. New York, N. Y., 1957.

18. Bruland, K. W., K. Bertine, M. Koide, and E. D. Goldberg, "History of Metal Pollution in Southern California Coastal Zone," Environ. Sci. Technol., 8(5), 425-432 (1974).

19. Clarke, F. W., The Data of Geochemistry, Bulletin 770, 5th ed., U.S. Geological Survey, Department of the Interior, Washington, D. C., 1924.

20. Dennis, W. H., Metallurgy of the Nonferrous Metals, Sir Isaac Putnam and Sons, London, 1954, pp. 552-559.

21. Taylor, S. R., "Abundance of Chemical Elements in the Continental Crust: A New Table," _Geochim. Cosmochim. Acta_, $\underline{28}$, 1273 (1964).

22. Bowen, H. J. M., _Trace Elements in Biochemistry_, Academic Press, Inc., New York, N. Y., 1966.

23. Parker, R. L., "Chapter D. Composition of the Earth's Crust," in _Data of Geochemistry_, 6th ed., M. Fleischer, Tech. Ed., Geological Survey Professional Paper 440-D, U.S. Government Printing Office, Washington, D.C., 1967, pp. D1-D19.

24. Lisk, D. J., "Trace Metals in Soils, Plants, and Animals," in _Advances in Agronomy_, Vol. 24, Academic Press, New York, N. Y., 1972, pp. 267-325.

25. Hem, J. D., _Study and Interpretation of the Chemical Characteristics of Natural Water_, 2nd. ed., Geological Survey Water-Supply Paper 1473, U.S. Government Printing Office, Washington, D.C., 1970.

26. Hawkes, H. E., and J. S. Webb, _Geochemistry in Mineral. Exploration_, Harper and Row, Publishers, Inc., New York, N. Y., 1962.

27. Vinogradov, A. P., _The Geochemistry of Rare and Dispersed Chemical Elements in Soils_, 2nd ed., translated from the Russian, Consultants Bureau, Inc., New York, N. Y., 1959.

28. Myers, A. T., R. G. Havens, and P. J. Dunton, "A Spectrochemical Method for the Semiquantitative Analysis of Rocks, Minerals, and Ores," _U.S. Geol. Surv. Bull._, $\underline{1084}$, 207-229 (1958).

29. Vanselow, A. P., "Chapter 26. Silver," in _Diagnostic Criteria for Plants and Soils_, H. D. Chapman, Ed., University of California, Division of Agricultural Sciences, Riverside, California, 1966, pp. 405-408.

30. Browning, E., _Toxicity of Industrial Metals_, Butterworths, London, 1961.

31. Mitchell, R. L., "Chapter 9. Trace Elements," in _Chemistry of the Soil_, F. E. Bear, Ed., Reinhold Publishing Corp., New York, N. Y., 1955, pp. 253-285.

32. Klein, D. H., and P. Russell, "Heavy Metals: Fallout Around a Power Plant," _Environ. Sci. Technol._, $\underline{7}$(4), 357-358 (1973).

33. Klein, D. H., "Mercury and Other Metals in Urban Soils," _Environ. Sci. Technol._, $\underline{6}$(6), 560-562 (1972).

34. Rattonetti, A., "Determination of Soluble Cadmium, Lead, Silver, and Indium in Rainwater and Stream Water with the Use of Flameless Atomic Absorption," Anal. Chem., 46, 739-742 (1974).

35. Cooper, C. F., and W. C. Jolly, "Ecological Effects of Silver Iodide and Other Weather Modification Agents: A Review," Water Resources Res., 6(1), 88-98 (1970).

36. Warburton, J. A., "Trace Silver Detection in Precipitation by Atomic Absorption Spectrophotometry," J. Appl. Meteorol., 8(3), 464-466 (1969); Chem. Abstr., 71, 523-524 (1969).

37. Bradford, G. R., "Trace Elements in the Water Resources of California," Hilgardia, 41(3), 45-53 (1971).

38. Lanford, C., "Effect of Trace Metals on Stream Ecology," Paper presented at the Cooling Tower Institute meeting, January 20, 1969.

39. Bradford, G. R., F. L. Bair, and V. Hunsaker, "Trace and Major Element Content of 170 High Sierra Lakes in California," Limnol. Oceanog., 13(3), 526-530 (1968).

40. Merritt, W. F., "Identification and Measurement of Trace Elements in Fresh Water by Neutron Activation," in International Symposium on Identification and Measurement of Environmental Pollutants, Ottawa, Ontario, Canada, June 14-17, 1971, National Research Council of Canada, Ottawa, Canada, 1971, pp. 358-362.

41. Stokes, P. M., T. C. Hutchins, and K. Krauter, "Heavy-Metal Tolerance in Algae Isolated from Contaminated Lakes near Sudbury, Ontario," Can. J. Botany, 51(11), 2155-2168 (1973).

42. Page, A. L., Fate and Effects of Trace Elements in Sewage Sludge When Applied to Agricultural Lands. A Literature Review Study (Review Copy), Ultimate Disposal Research Program, Environmental Protection Agency, Cincinnati, Ohio, 1974.

43. Durum, W. H., and J. Haffty, Occurrence of Minor Elements in Water, Geological Survey Circular 445, Washington, D.C., 1961.

44. Kopp, J. F., and R. C. Kroner, "Tracing Water Pollution with an Emission Spectrograph," Water Pollution Control Fed., 39(10), 1660-1668 (1967).

45. Andelman, J. B., "Incidence, Variability and Controlling Factors for Trace Elements in Natural, Fresh Waters," in Trace Metals and Metal-Organic Interactions in Natural Waters, P. C. Singer, Ed., Ann Arbor Science Publishers, Inc., Ann Arbor, Mich., 1973.

46. Kroner, R. C., and J. F. Kopp, "Trace Elements in Six Water Systems of the United States," J. Am. Water Works Assoc., 57, 150-156 (1965).

47. Bargman, R. D., and W. F. Garber, "The Control and Removal of Materials of Ecological Importance from Wastewaters in Los Angeles, California, USA" in Advances in Water Pollution Research, Proceedings of the Sixth International Conference held in Jerusalem, June 18-23, 1972, S. H. Jenkins, Ed., Pergamon Press, New York, N. Y., 1973, pp. 773-786.

48. Farnsworth, C. G., Report on the Trace Elements and Their Origin in a Metropolitan Wastewater Effluent, Denver, Colorado, Board of Water Commissioners, Denver, Colorado (undated, 1969 or after).

49. Young, D. R., C. S. Young, and G. E. Hlavka, "Sources of Trace Metals from Highly Urbanized Southern California to the Adjacent Marine Ecosystem" in Cycling and Control of Metals, Proceedings of an Environmental Resources Conference, Columbus, Ohio, October 31 - November 2, 1972, U.S. Environmental Protection Agency, National Environmental Research Center, Cincinnati, Ohio, February 1973, pp. 21-39.

50. Mytelka, A. I., "Heavy Metals in Wastewater and Treatment Plant Effluents," J. Water Pollution Control Federation, 45(9), 1859-1864 (1973).

51. Andelman, J. B., and M. A. Shapiro, "Changes in Trace Element Concentrations in Water Treatment and Distribution Systems" in Trace Substances in Environmental Health - VI, D. D. Hemphill, Ed., Proceedings of University of Missouri's Sixth Annual Conference on Trace Substances in Environmental Health, June 13-15, 1972, Columbia, Mo., University of Missouri, Columbia, Mo., 1973, pp. 87-94.

52. Cannon, H., and H. C. Hopps, Environmental Geochemistry in Health and Disease, The Geological Society of America, Inc., Boulder, Colorado, 1971.

53. Taylor, F. B., "Trace Elements and Compounds in Water," J. Am. Water Works Assoc., 63(11), 728-733 (1971).

54. Durfor, C. N., and E. Becker, Public Water Supplies of the 100 Largest Cities in the United States, 1962, U.S. Geological Survey Water-Supply Paper 1812, U.S. Department of the Interior, U.S. Government Printing Office, Washington, D.C., 1962.

55. McCabe, L. J., "Trace Metals Content of Drinking Water from a Large System," presented at the Symposium on Water Quality in Distribution Systems, Division of Water, Air, and Waste Chemistry, American Chemical Society National Meeting, Minneapolis, Minn., April 13, 1969.

56. Grasso, P., R. Abraham, R. Hendy, A. T. Diplock, L. Goldberg, and J. Green, "The Role of Dietary Silver in the Production of Liver Necrosis in Vitamin-E-Dificient Rats," Exp. Mol. Pathol., 11, 186-199 (1969).

57. Chapman, W. H., H. L. Fisher, and M. W. Pratt, Concentration Factors of Chemical Elements in Edible Aquatic Organisms, UCRL-50564, Lawrence Livermore Laboratory, University of California, Livermore, California, 1968.

58. Horovitz, C. T., H. H. Schock, and L. A. Horovitz-Kisimova, "The Content of Scandium, Thorium, Silver, and Other Trace Elements in Different Plant Species," Plant Soil, 40, 397-403 (1974).

59. Kent-Jones, D. W., and A. J. Amos, Modern Cereal Chemistry, 5th ed., The Northern Publishing Co., Ltd., Liverpool, England, 1957.

60. Nadkarni, R. A., W. D. Ehmann, and D. Burdick, "Investigations on the Relative Transference of Trace Elements from Cigarette Tobacco into Smoke Condensate," Tobacco, 70(11), 25-27 (1970).

61. Tong, S. S. C., W. D. Youngs, W. H. Gutenman, and D. J. Lisk, "Trace Metals in Lake Cayuga Lake Trout (Salvelinus namaycush) in Relation to Age" (Brief Communication), J. Fisheries Res. Board Can., 31(2), 238-239 (1974).

62. Gettler, A. O., C. P. Rhoads, and S. Weiss, "A Contribution to the Pathology of Generalized Argyria with a Discussion of the Fate of Silver in the Human Body," Am. J. Pathol., 3, 631-652 (1927).

63. Romans, I. B., "Chapter 24. Oligodynamic Metals," in Disinfection, Sterilization, and Preservation, C. A. Lawrence and S. S. Block, Eds., Lea and Febiger, Philadelphia, Pa., 1968, pp. 372-400.

64. Tipton, I. H., and M. J. Cook, "Trace Elements in Human Tissue. Part II. Adult Subjects from the United States," Health Phys., 9, 103-145 (1963).

65. Kehoe, R. A., J. Cholak, and R. V. Story, "A Spectrochemical Study of the Normal Ranges of Concentration of Certain Trace Metals in Biological Materials," J. Nutr., 19, 579-592 (1940).

66. Bala, Yu. M., S. A. Plotko, and G. I. Furmenko, "Soderzhanie Margantsa, Nikelya, Tsinka, Medi, Serebra, Svintza v Krovi, Aorte, Pecheni, Poch-kakh i Podzheludochnoi Zheleze u Bol'nykh Aterosklerozom" ("Levels of Manganese, Nickel, Zinc, Copper, Silver, and Lead in the Blood, Aorta, Liver, Kidneys, and Pancreas of Patients with Atherosclerosis"), Ter. Arkh., 39(1), 105-111 (1967); Chem. Abstr., 66, 5054 (1967).

67. Tipton, I. H., H. A. Schroeder, H. M. Perry, Jr., and M. J. Cook, "Trace Elements in Human Tissues. Part III. Subjects from Africa, the Near and Far East and Europe," Health Phys., 11, 403-451 (1965).

68. Avtandilov, G. G., "Vozrastnaya Dinamika Soderzhaniya Mikroelementov Normal'nykh i Izmennykh Aterosklerozom Otdelakh Aorty Cheloveka," ("Trace Element Content in Normal and Atherosclerosis-Affected Portions of the Human Aorta, Connected with Age"), Arkh. Patol., 29(4), 40-42 (1967); Chem. Abstr., 67, 2880 (1967).

69. D'Alonzo, C. A., and S. Pell, "A Study of Trace Metals in Myocardial Infarction," Arch. Environ. Health, 6, 381-385 (1963).

70. Plaut, D., "Timely Topics in Clinical Chemistry: Toxicology and Trace Metals II," Amer. J. Med. Technol., 35(10), 652-658 (1969).

71. Zagarskikh, M. G., "Izmenie Soderzhaniya Mikroelementov v Krovi Bol'nykh Otosklerozom," ("Change in the Content of Trace Elements in the Blood of Patients with Otosclerosis"), Zh. Ushnykh Nosovykh Gorlovykh Boleznei (Kiev), 31, 108-109 (1971).

72. Wester, P. O., "Concentration of 24 Trace Elements in Human Heart Tissue Determined by Neutron Activation Analysis," Scand. J. Clin. Lab. Invest., 17(4), 357-370 (1965).

73. Indraprasit, S., G. V. Alexander, and H. C. Gonick, "Tissue Composition of Major and Trace Elements in Uremia and Hypertension," J. Chronic Diseases, 27(3), 135-161 (1974).

74. Tietz, N. W., E. F. Hirsch, and B. Neyman, "Spectrographic Study of Trace Elements in Cancerous and Noncancerous Human Tissue," J. Am. Med. Assoc., 165(17), 2177-2187 (1957).

75. Perry, H. M., Jr., E. F. Perry, J. E. Purifoy, and J. N. Erlanger, "A Comparison of Intra- and Interhepatic Variability of Trace Metal Concentrations in Normal Men," in Trace Substances in Environmental Health - VII, D. D. Hemphill, Ed., Proceedings of University of Missouri's Seventh Annual Conference on Trace Substances in Environmental Health, June 12, 13, and 14, 1973, Columbia, Mo., University of Missouri, Columbia, Mo., 1973, pp. 281-288.

76. Schroeder, H. A., "Airborne Metals," Scientist and Citizen, 10, 83-88 (1968).

77. Kessler, T., A. G. Sharkey, and R. A. Friedel, Spark-Source Mass Spectrometer Investigation of Coal Particles and Coal Ash, Bureau of Mines Progress Report No. 42, U.S. Department of the Interior, Washington, D.C., 1971.

78. Losee, F., T. W. Cutress, and R. Brown, "Trace Elements in Human Dental Enamel," in Trace Substances in Environmental Health - VII, D. D. Hemphill, Ed., Proceedings of University of Missouri's Seventh Annual Conference on Trace Substances in Environmental Health, June 12, 13, and 14, 1973, Columbia, Mo., University of Missouri, Columbia, Mo., 1973, pp. 19-24.

79. Navia, J. M., "Effect of Minerals on Dental Caries," in Dietary Chemicals versus Dental Caries, Advances in Chemistry Series No. 194, American Chemical Society, Washington, D.C., 1970, pp. 123-160.

80. Abernethy, R. F., and F. H. Gibson, Rare Elements in Coal, Bureau of Mines Information Circular 8163, U.S. Department of the Interior, Washington, D.C., 1963.

81. von Lehmden, D., R. H. Jungers, and R. E. Lee, Jr., "The Determination of Trace Elements in Coal, Fly Ash, Fuel Oil and Gasoline. Part I: A Preliminary Comparison of Selected Analytical Techniques," presented at the American Chemical Society meeting, Dallas, Texas, April, 1973, and submitted to Anal. Chem. for publication, 1973.

82. Reeves, R. D., C. J. Molnar, M. T. Glenn, J. R. Ahlstrom, and J. D. Winefordner, "Determination of Wear Metals in Engine Oils by Atomic Absorption Spectrometry with a Graphite Rod Atomizer," Anal. Chem., 44(13), 2205-2210 (1972).

83. Alder, J. F., and T. S. West, "Atomic Absorption and Fluorescence Spectrophotometry with a Carbon Filament Atom Reservoir," Anal. Chim. Acta, 58(2), 331-337 (1972).

84. National Oil Recovery Corporation, Conversion of Crankcase Waste Oil into Useful Products, Water Pollution Control Research Series, 15080 DBO 03/71, Water Quality Office, Environmental Protection Agency, U.S. Government Printing Office, Washington, D.C., 1971.

85. Levy, A., S. E. Miller, R. E. Barrett, E. J. Schulz, R. H. Melvin, W. H. Axtman, and D. W. Locklin, A Field Investigation of Emissions from Fuel Oil Combustion for Space Heating, American Petroleum Institute Project SS-5, Battelle Columbus Laboratories, Columbus, Ohio, 1971.

III. DOMESTIC SOURCES OF INDUSTRIAL SILVER

In this section are discussed the sources from which primary and secondary silver are produced in the United States for industrial consumption. The locations of the mines producing various silver-containing ores are given. The various types of used materials that can be recycled for their silver contents are described.

A. Primary Sources

About two-thirds of the domestic silver output comes from ores mined chiefly for copper, lead, and zinc; most of the remaining one-third is recovered from ores in which silver is the principal metal. The silver mines are located chiefly in the Coeur d' Alene mining district in the northern Idaho panhandle, which is comprised of a 20 x 30 mile strip in Shoshone County. Following Idaho in rank of production of silver are Arizona, Utah, Colorado, and Montana.[1]

1. Ores: Silver normally occurs in deposits associated with other metals such as copper, lead, zinc, and gold. (Section II.A. is a general discussion of silver-containing minerals and deposits.) In the base-metal ores, silver is found as argentite (Ag_2S); cerargyrite ($AgCl$); proustite (Ag_3AsS_3); pyrargyrite (Ag_3SbS_3); stephanite (Ag_5SbS_4); and more commonly as argentiferous tetrahedrite, tennantite, galena, and their alteration products.[2] Table III-1 describes the kinds of U.S. copper ores. The ore minerals found in lead-zinc ores are shown in Table III-2. Dry ores are those gold, gold-silver, and silver ores with base-metal content too low to be classified as copper, lead, or zinc ores.[2] Silver in dry ores occurs mainly as native silver, argentite, and cerargyrite; as silver-gold alloy; and to a lesser extent, as proustite, pyrargyrite, and stephanite.

The distribution of U.S. silver obtained from ores from 1961 to 1970 was: dry ores, 35.4%; copper ores, 30.4%; lead-zinc ores, 12.3%; and other ores (chiefly lead-copper), 22.0%.[3,4] Silver ores provide 1.6% of the lead, 0.5% of the gold, 0.4% of the zinc, 0.3% of the copper, and 32.1% of the total antimony production.[5]

Table III-3 shows the production of silver in the U.S. in 1971 by state and major ore classes. Some by-product silver is also recovered from uranium, tungsten, fluorspar, and magnetite-pyrite ores.[6]

73

2. **Mines**: The major sources of domestic silver are mines that process silver ores (accounting for 36% of the total silver production in 1971) and porphyry copper ores containing about 0.7 troy oz silver/ton ore (accounting for 32% of the 1971 production). Mines processing lead ores yielded 14% of the 1971 silver production. In the same year, complex ores (copper-lead, lead-zinc, copper-zinc, and copper-lead-zinc) were the source of 17% of the total silver production.[1/]

Principal U.S. mining districts in 1957 are listed in Table III-4 and shown on the map in Figure III-1.

Table III-5 shows the distribution of U.S. mines by state producing silver-bearing ores with a ranking of the nine leading producing states in 1971. The Coeur d' Alene district in the panhandle of Idaho is one of the major silver-lead-zinc producing areas in the world. The major producing mines are clustered in two groups. One group lies north of the Osburn fault in a large triangular-shaped area that extends north and east of the town of Wallace and is called the Mullan-Burke 9-mile area. This group includes such famous old mines as the Hecla, Hercules, Stanford-Mammoth, Tamarack, Tiger-Poorman, Frisco, Star, and Morning. The other group lies on the south side of the Osburn fault, and extends from near Wallace westward beyond Kellogg to near Pine Creek. This group, somewhat more elongate than the Mullan-Burke 9-mile area, includes such famous mines as the Galena, Sunshine, Lucky Friday, Crescent, and Bunker Hill. Numerous other mines and prospects occur in this group, which also include the productive string of mines along the East Fork of Pine Creek. The eastern third of this group is called the Silver Belt of the Coeur d' Alene district because of the silver content of the ore.

The largest single domestic silver mine is the Sunshine mine in the Coeur d' Alene region of Idaho, producing annually about 7.71 million ounces of silver along with substantial quantities of coproducts and by-products. The silver ore contains about 24.9 troy oz silver/ton.

Idaho currently produces 46% of the total U.S. mine production of silver. Silver ores accounted for 60.7% of all Idaho silver production from 1952 to 1961, and for 67.0% in 1971.[7,8/]

Table III-6 lists, by rank, the 25 leading silver-producing mines in the United States in 1971. It should be noted that three of the top five mines produced the silver from silver ores while the remainder obtained the silver primarily from base-metal ores.

The locations and descriptions of the major copper-producing mines in the U.S. can be found in Table III-7. The lead and zinc mines that process silver-containing ores and their locations are shown in Table III-8.

74

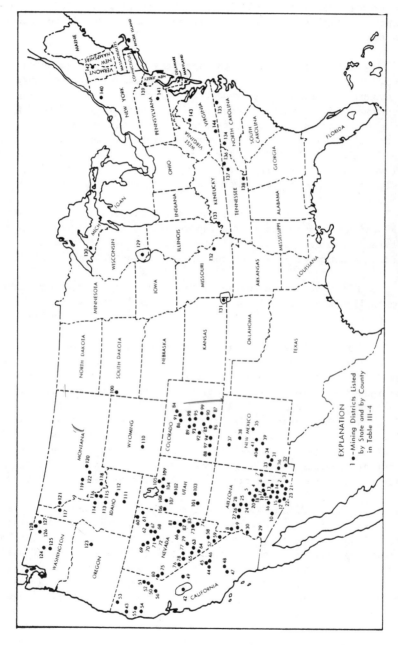

Figure III-1 – Principal Mining Districts From Which Ores and Concentrates of Gold, Silver, Copper, Lead, and Zinc Were Produced in 1957 2/

B. Secondary Sources

Of all 0.999 fine silver bullion produced in U.S. refineries, 39% came from recycled materials in 1972; 40% in 1973; and 38%, in the first 9 months of 1974.[9,10] (In this estimate "new scrap" is not considered as a recycled material.)

Schack and Clemmons consider the data on the amount and nature of new and old scrap created in industry and the arts to be unreliable.[11] The amount of scrap that is reused by the consumer in in-house processing is unknown. For example, anode butts and uncontaminated webbing from silver-clad coin strips and sterling flatware may be remelted by the fabricator.[5] They estimated that new and old scrap generated by the photographic, electrical, and industrial-alloys uses and the arts (sterling, hollowware, plate, jewelry, etc.) comprise 91, 80, 68, and 75%, respectively, of the amounts consumed annually by these applications.[11]

1. New scrap: According to the Silver Institute, "new scrap" means refined production from scrap generated in the manufacture of silver containing products or from silver-containing materials that have not yet moved into commerce as silver-containing products.[10]

"New scrap" in Bureau of Mines statistics, however, refers only to metallic material (bullion). The term excludes sweepings, treasury coinage scrap, and any other material that is normally remelted.[3]

Many silver industries produce a wide range of new scraps, such as blanking scrap, alloys, sweepings, plating solutions, fixing baths, anode ends, and tank scraping and rejected parts.[3] The general cleanup from industrial processing operations may be burned and screened to produce "sweeps" which may go through many hands before reaching the ultimate refiner.[12] New scrap is also generated in the production of solders, brazing, and other alloys; silver-plated bearings, containers, and electrical contacts; and silver-bearing batteries, wire, condensers, and other electronic devices.[11] The general category includes polishings and high-grade precipitates, which are usually handled as separate lots.[12]

About 50% of silverware-industry input becomes new scrap.[3] Silver wastes from production of silver-plated tableware comprise electrolyte spills and spent solutions and dilute wash solutions. The "mill wastes" are processed to reclaim the silver. Sterling silver wastes include defective tableware, trimmings, turnings, punchings, fumes, spillage drosses from melting and casting, and grinding and polishing dusts and abrasives. High-quality materials are processed and reused in-house while lower-quality wastes are processed into impure bullion that is sent to a refiner. No data are available on the amounts of liquid and solid wastes from sterling and silver-plate manufacture.[11]

76

Low-tenor scrap (new or old) may contain silver mixed or alloyed with elements such as cadmium, copper, gold, iron, magnesium, nickel, tin, tungsten, and zinc. Whether silver is recovered or not depends upon the particular base-metal refiner.[3]

2. **Coin and bullion**: In addition to visible stock, meltable hoards of U.S. and foreign coins and private holdings of bullion are large potential sources of secondary silver. Silver coin can be used without refining for about 50% of the silverware uses and perhaps 90% of the brazing-alloy requirement. According to a 1969 estimate, direct melting of coinage would provide 30 million troy ounces of silver.[13]

F. H. Wemple, Vice President and Treasurer of Handy and Harman, Inc., estimated that in 1965 there were 0.37 billion troy ounces of silver in outstanding silver dollars and 1.9 billion troy ounces of silver in outstanding subsidiary coins. Of these coins, many have been lost, destroyed, or otherwise permanently removed from circulation. The remaining hoards constitute a very large potential source of supplies for industry.[14] From 1966 to 1973, 160.1 million troy ounces of silver was used in the coinage of the clad 40% silver half dollars and dollars,[4,15] which will probably not be recycled.

3. **Old scrap**: The principal sources of old scrap are electrical products (chiefly contacts), old film and photoprocessing wastes (especially X-ray and commercial movie), batteries, jewelry, silverware, and bearings. Other sources of used silver-bearing materials include plating wastes, silver-lined bearings, printed circuit boards and other precious metals-containing electronic scrap, timing devices, wave guides, catalysts, chemical salts, dental scrap, silver paint and paste, wiping rags, reproduction paper, contaminated tin-lead alloys, and obsolete electronic and communication apparatus, etc., that are refined chiefly for copper.[3,16,17]

Electronics scrap is an increasing source of silver scrap. Semiconductor scrap, for example, includes multilayered chips, ceramic disks, and complicated piesoelectric disks.[18] The silver content of different electronic components is given in Table III-9.

The source of X-ray film most commonly processed for silver recovery is medical and, to a lesser extent, industries that manufacture castings or pipe and X-ray them to detect fractures. Lithographic film from off-set printing produces an exposed negative with a silver content usually too low to warrant processing.[19]

Silver recovered from hypo solutions used in film development is a major secondary silver source.

The U.S. government is a major source of obsolete silver products. For example, in 1966 to 1968 about 4 million troy ounces annually was recovered from torpedo batteries,[3] which contain silver and cadmium, copper, zinc, or magnesium.[16]

TABLE III-1

U.S. COPPER ORES[20]

Grade	Copper Content (%)	Examples	Remarks	Percent of Primary Copper Production
Concentrating-grade ores	0.6-1% Cu	Porphyry ores of West, Cu sulfide, some oxide.	Most important typical sulfide ores of concentrating grade.	75-80%
Low-grade (leaching-grade) ores	≤ 0.5% Cu	Cu sulfide or oxide. Usually occurs near top of Cu deposits. Sometimes must be removed to reach higher-grade ore.	Not economically concd.	
High-grade sulfide ores		Found underground in vein, pipe, and bedded deposits.		3-10%
Mixed sulfide-oxide ores	0.6-2% (most ≤ 1%)		Require special treatment.	
Native Cu ores	1% Cu	Lake copper from Michigan's northern peninsula.		
Oxide minerals: chrysocolla, malachite, or azurite			Generally leached.	
By-product of ores of Pb, Zn, Ag, Mo, W, and Fe				

TABLE III-2

APPROXIMATE GRADE AND ASSOCIATION OF LEAD-ZINC ORES IN THE UNITED STATES[20]

Region	Approximate Grade							Ore minerals	Gangue Materials
	Cu (%)	Pb (%)	Zn (%)	Mn (%)	CaF_2 (%)	Au (oz/ton)	Ag (oz/ton)		
Virginia	-	1	5	-	-	-	-	Galena, sphalerite	Limestone, dolomite
Kentucky-Illinois	-	0.2	1-2	-	Major	-	-	Fluorite, galena, sphalerite	Limestone
Wisconsin-Illinois	-	0.3-1.0	3-7	-	-	-	-	Sphalerite, galena	Marcasite, limestone, dolomite
New York	-	0.15-0.3	3-9	-	-	-	-	Sphalerite, galena	Limestone
New Jersey	-	-	-	-	-	-	-	Zincite, willemite, franklinite	
Southeast Missouri	-	2-4	Insignificant	-	-	-	-	Galena	Marcasite, siegenite, chalcopyrite, dolomite
Tri-State (Missouri, Kansas, Oklahoma)	-	0.3	2.0	-	-	-	-	Galena, sphalerite	Limestone
Idaho	Tr-0.6	2-10	2-10	-	-	-	1-30	Galena, sphalerite, tetrahedrite, pyrite	Quartz, siderite, calcite dolomite, basite
Utah	0.4	8	5	-	-	0.2	3-7	Galena, sphalerite, chalcopyrite, bornite, tetrahedrite	Quartz, feldspar, shale, limestone
Washington	0.1	1.5	3	-	-	-	0.5	-	-
Colorado	0.7	3	3	-	-	0.1	2-3	Chalcopyrite, galena, sphalerite, tetrahedrite	Limestone
Arizona, New Mexico	0.6	3	7	-	-	0.1	2-3	Chalcopyrite, etc., galena, sphalerite, tetrahedrite	Limestone, etc.
Nevada	-	By-product	By-product	-	-	-	Principal	Tetrahedrite, galena, sphalerite	-
California	-	-	-	-	-	-	-	Galena, sphalerite, cerussite, anglesite	-
Tennessee	-	Low	2-6	-	-	-	-	Sphalerite	Limestone
Montana	Major	a/	a/	Major	-	-	-	Chalcopyrite, etc., sphalerite, galena, rhodocrosite	Quartz, feldspar, etc.

a/ These ores generally contain zinc and lead in minor amounts, usually in the ratio of five parts zinc to one part lead.

TABLE III-3

PRODUCTION OF SILVER IN THE UNITED STATES IN 1971, BY STATE AND BY SOURCES[7]

(troy oz of silver)

| | Lode | | | | | | | Copper-Lead, Lead-Zinc, Copper-Zinc, and Copper-Lead-Zinc Ores | Old Tailings, etc. | Total |
	Placer	Gold Ore	Gold-Silver Ore	Silver Ore	Copper Ore	Lead Ore	Zinc Ore			
Alaska	728	140	-	-	-	-	-	-	-	868
Arizona	-	5,539[a]	-	W	6,106,204	2,253	-	28,265	27,362	6,169,623
California	166	5,521[a]	W	-	-	W	-	390,649[d]	47,425[e]	443,761
Colorado	209	-	-	2,051,236	173,222[d]	W	W	1,164,546	535[e]	3,389,748
Idaho	-	-	-	12,808,269	8,840	3,938,335	936	2,377,873	5,322	19,139,575
Michigan	-	-	-	-	670,052	-	-	-	-	670,052
Missouri	-	-	-	-	-	1,660,879	-	-	-	1,660,879
Montana	2	572	73,166	181,590	2,387,897	50,450	19,924	708	33,248	2,747,557
Nevada	-	-	4,754	2,179	588,202	2,338	W	3,997[d]	-	601,470
New Mexico	-	-	-	89	639,478	-	-	142,874	-	782,441
South Dakota	-	106,785	-	-	-	-	-	-	-	106,785
Utah	-	-	42,632	-	2,566,223	170,020	-	2,514,802	800[e]	5,294,477
Other States[b]	-	286,886	2,328	1,462	34,796	1,172	4,050	202,828	23,384[e]	556,906
Total	1,105	405,443	122,880	15,044,824	13,174,914	5,825,447	24,910	6,826,542	138,076	41,564,142
Percent of Total Silver	[c]	1	[c]	36	32	14	[c]	17	[c]	100

a/ Combined with other dry and siliceous ores to avoid disclosing individual company confidential data.

b/ Includes Illinois, Maine, New York, North Carolina, Oklahoma, Oregon, Pennsylvania, Tennessee, and Washington.

c/ Less than 1/2 unit.

d/ Combined with other base-metal ores to avoid disclosing individual company confidential data.

e/ Includes by-product silver recovered from tungsten ore in California and North Carolina, from fluorspar ore in Colorado and Illinois, from uranium ore in Utah, and from magnetite-pyrite ore in Pennsylvania.

W = Withheld to avoid disclosing individual company confidential data, included with "Other States."

TABLE III-4

PRINCIPAL MINING DISTRICTS OR AREAS FROM WHICH ORES AND
CONCENTRATES OF GOLD, SILVER, COPPER, LEAD, AND ZINC
WERE PRODUCED IN 1957$\underline{2}$/

State	County	Mining District	Figure III-1, Symbol
		Cochise (Dragoon)	1
	Cochise	Turquoise	2
		Warren (Bisbee)	3
	Gila	Banner (Christmas)	4
		Globe-Miami	5
	Graham	Aravaipa	6
	Greenlee	Copper Mountain (Morenci)	7
	Mohave	Owens-Cedar Valley	8
		Wallapai	9
		Ajo	10
		Amole	11
		Baboquivari	12
	Pima	Empire	13
		Helvetia (Rosemont)	14
		Pima	15
Arizona		Silver Bell	16
		Bunker Hill	17
	Pinal	Mineral Creek (Ray)	18
		Old Hat	19
		Pioneer (Superior)	20
		Harshaw	21
	Santa Cruz	Oro Blanco	22
		Patagonia (Duquesne)	23
		Agua Fria	24
		Big Bug, Black Canyon, Hassayampa, and Walker	25
	Yavapai	Copper Basin	26
		Eureka	27
		Verde (Jerome)	28
	Yuma	Castle Dome	29
		Cienega	30
		Central	31
	Grant	Eureka	32
		Pinos Altos	33
		Swartz	34
	Guadalupe	Pintado	35
	Hidalgo	Lordsburg	36
New Mexico	Sandoval	Cuba	37
	Sante Fe	Cerrillos, Cooper, San Pedro, and New Placers	38
	Socorro	Hansonberg	39
		Magdalena	40
	Torrance	Carocito	41

82

TABLE III-4 (continued)

State	County	Mining District	Figure III-1, Symbol
California	Amador, Calaveras, El Dorado, Madera, Mariposa, Tuolumne.	East Belt, Mother Lode, West Belt	42
	Humboldt	Trinity River South (Hoopa)	43
		Darwin	44
	Inyo	Lee	45
		Modoc	46
	Kern	Mojave	47
		Randsburg	48
	Mono	Homer	49
	Nevada	Grass Valley-Nevada City	50
	Plumas	Sawpit Flat	51
	Sierra	Alleghany-Downieville	52
	Siskiyou	Klamath River	53
	Trinity	Hayfork	54
		Trinity River	55
	Yuba	Browns Valley	56
Nevada	Clark	Goodsprings (Yellow Pine)	57
		Las Vegas	58
		Searchlight	59
	Elko	Contact	60
		Delano	61
		Merrimac	62
	Esmeralda	Klondyke	63
		Montezuma	64
		Silver Peak	65
	Eureka	Eureka	66
		Maggie Creek	67
		Railroad	68
	Humboldt	Awakening	69
		Golconda	70
	Lander	Battle Mountain	71
		Bullion	72
	Lincoln	Jack Rabbit (Bristol)	73
		Pioche (Ely)	74
	Lyon	Yerington	75
	Mineral	Aurora	76
		Candelaria	77
		Cedar Mountain	78
	Nye	Tonopah	79
	Storey	Comstock Lode	80
	White Pine	Cherry Creek	81
		Robinson	82
		Tungstonia	83

TABLE III-4 (continued)

State	County	Mining District	Figure III- Symbol
	Boulder	Central, Gold Hill, Grand Island	84
	Chaffee	Monarch	85
	Clear Creek	Alice, Argentine, Empire, Griffith, Idaho Springs, Montana, and Trail Creek.	86
	Custer	Hardscrabble	87
	Dolores	Pioneer	88
	Eagle	Red Cliff (Battle Mountain)	89
	Fremont	Cotopaxi	90
Colorado	Gilpin	Northern, Southern	91
	Gunnison	Domingo, Elk Mountain	92
	Lake	California	93
	Mineral	Creede	94
	Park	Buckskin Gulch, Horseshoe	95
	Saguache	Bonanza	96
	San Juan, San Miguel, and Ouray.	San Juan	97
	Summit	Breckenridge, Montezuma	98
	Teller	Cripple Creek	99
South Dakota	Lawrence	Whitewood (Ida Gray), Portland, and Bald Mountain.	100
	Beaver	Rocky, San Francisco, Star and North Star	101
	Juab and Utah	Tintic	102
	Piute	Gold Mountain, Mount Baldy, Ohio	103
Utah	Salt Lake	West Mountain (Bingham)	104
	Summit	Uintah	105
	Tooele	Clifton	106
		Dugway	107
		Ophir, Rush Valley	108
	Wasatch	Blue Ledge, Snake Creek	109
Wyoming	Fremont	Atlantic City and South Pass	110
	Blaine	Mineral Hill-Camas and Warm Springs	111
	Custer	Alder Creek	112
		Bayhorse	113
		Blackbird	114
Idaho	Lemhi	Blue Wing	115
		McDevitt	116
	Shoshone	Coeur d'Alene (Beaver, Hunter, Evolution, Placer Center, Yreka).	117
	Beaverhead	Argenta	118
	Granite	Flint Creek	119
Montana	Jefferson	Colorado	120
	Sanders	Eagle	121
	Silver Bow	Butte (Summit Valley)	122
Oregon	Grant	Granite	123

TABLE III-4 (concluded)

State	County	Mining District	Figure III-1, Symbol
Washington	Chelan	Railroad Creek (Chelan)	124
		Wenatchee	125
	Ferry	Republic	126
	Pend Oreille	Metaline	127
	Stevens	Northport	128
Illinois, Iowa, Wisconsin	Jo Daviess	Upper Mississippi Valley	129
	Dubuque		
	Grant		
	Iowa		
	Lafayette		
Michigan	Houghton	Lake Superior	130
	Keweenaw		
	Ontonagon		
Kansas, Missouri, Oklahoma	Cherokee	Tri-State	131
	Jasper		
	Newton		
	Ottawa		
Missouri	Madison	Southeastern Missouri	132
	St. Francois		
	Washington		
Illinois	Hardin	Kentucky Fluorspar	133
	Pope		
Kentucky	Caldwell		
	Crittenden		
	Livingston		
North Carolina	Ashe	Ore Knob	134
	Halifax	Enfield	135
Tennessee	Hancock	Treadway	136
	Jefferson	Mascot	137
	Polk	Ducktown	138
New Jersey	Sussex	Franklin Ogdenburg	139
New York	St. Lawrence	St. Lawrence	140
Pennsylvania	Lebanon	Cornwall	141
Vermont	Orange	Stafford	142
Virginia	Rockingham	Timberville	143
	Wythe	Austinville	144

TABLE III-5

DISTRIBUTION OF U.S. MINES PRODUCING SILVER-BEARING ORES

State Producing Silver	Ore Classes[2,21]	Number of Mines Producing Silver[2]	1971 Rank of State in Silver Production[2]
Alaska	Placers, lode gold, copper ore	n.a.[a]	2
Arizona	All classes except placer, Chiefly Cu ore	20	
Arkansas	Lead and zinc ores	n.a.	
California	All classes, little Cu ore	4	4
Colorado	All classes	58	
Idaho	All classes, little placer	50 (60 in 1960[2])	1
Illinois	Pb and Zn ores with Pb and Zn by-products of fluorspar mining	n.a.	
Kansas	Pb and Zn ores	n.a.	
Kentucky	Pb and Zn by-products of fluorspar mining	2	8
Michigan	Cu ore	1	6
Missouri	Pb and Zn ores	5	5
Montana	All classes, chiefly Cu ore	102	9
Nevada	All classes	26	7
New Mexico	All classes except placer, chiefly Pb and Zn ores	32	
New York	Complex base metal ores (Zn and Pb)	1	
North Carolina	Cu and Pb ores	n.a.	
Oklahoma	Pb and Zn ores	1	
Oregon	Placer; Cu, Pb and Zn ores	5	
Pennsylvania	Iron ore (by-product Cu, Au, and Ag)	1	
South Dakota	Gold lode	1	
Tennessee	Complex base-metal ores (Fe, Cu, Zn, Au, Ag, ZnS)	1	
Utah	All classes; little placer, chiefly complex; uranium ore by-product	33	3
Vermont	Cu ore (last mined in 1958)	n.a.	
Virginia	ZnS, Pb and Zn (no silver production reported since 1959)	n.a.	
Washington	Dry, complex ores, little Cu	3	
Wisconsin	(Pb-Zn ores. No silver production reported)	-	
Wyoming	Cu, Ag, and Au; placer Au (very little silver)	n.a.	

a/ n.a. - Not available.

TABLE III-6

TWENTY-FIVE LEADING SILVER-PRODUCING MINES IN THE UNITED STATES IN 1971 [7/]
IN ORDER OF OUTPUT

Rank	Mine	County and State	Operator	Source of Silver
1	Sunshine	Shoshone, Idaho	Sunshine Mining Company	Silver ore.
2	Galena	Shoshone, Idaho	American Smelting and Refining Company	Silver ore
3	Lucky Friday	Shoshone, Idaho	Hecla Mining Company	Lead ore.
4	Utah Copper	Salt Lake, Utah	Kennecott Copper Corporation	Copper, gold-silver ores.
5	Bulldog Mountain	Mineral, Colo.	Homestake Mining Company	Silver ore
6	Berkeley Pit	Silver Bow, Montana	The Anaconda Company	Copper ore
7	Bunker Hill	Shoshone, Idaho	The Bunker Hill Company	Lead-zinc ore, lead-zinc tailings
8	Crescent	Shoshone, Idaho	The Bunker Hill Company	Silver ore
9	Burgin	Utah, Utah	Kennecott Copper Corporation	Lead, lead-zinc ores
10	Copper Queen-Lavender Pit	Cochise, Arizona	Phelps Dodge Corporation	Lead, lead-zinc ores
11	Twin Buttes	Pima, Arizona	The Anaconda Company	Copper ore
12	U.S. and Lark	Salt Lake, Utah	United States Smelting Refining and Mining Company	Lead-zinc ores
13	Pima	Pima, Arizona	Pima Mining Company	Copper ore
14	White Pine	Ontonagon, Michigan	White Pine Copper Company	Copper ore
15	Star Unit	Shoshone, Idaho	The Bunker Hill Company and Hecla Mining Company	Lead-zinc ore
16	Dayrock	Shoshone, Idaho	Day Mines Inc.	Lead ore
17	Buick	Iron, Missouri	Missouri Lead Operating Company	Lead ore
18	Idarado	Ouray and San Miguel, Colorado	Idarado Mining Company	Copper-lead-zinc ore
19	Sierrita	Pima, Arizona	Duval Sierrita Corporation	Copper ore
20	Mayflower	Wasatch, Utah	Hecla Mining Company	Copper-lead-zinc ore

TABLE III-6 (concluded)

Rank	Mine	County and State	Operator	Source of Silver
21	Morenci	Greenlee, Arizona	Phelps Dodge Corporation	Copper ore
22	Mission Unit	Pima, Arizona	American Smelting and Refining Company	Copper ore
23	Copper Canyon	Lander, Nevada	Duval Corporation	Copper ore
24	Tyrone	Grant, New Mexico	Phelps Dodge Corporation	Copper ore
25	Butte Hill Copper Mines	Silver Bow, Montana	The Anaconda Company	Copper ore

TABLE III-7

MAJOR COPPER-PRODUCING MINES IN THE UNITED STATES[20]

Mine	Location	Company and State	Type	Tonnage (ore)
		Arizona		
Bagdad	Bagdad	Bagdad Copper Corporation	Open pit	2,100,000
Christmas	Near Winklemen	Inspiration Consolidated	Open pit	6-7,000,000
Copper Queen[a]	Bisbee	Phelps Dodge	Underground	5,480,000
Esperanza	Sahuarita	Duval Corporation	Open pit	5-6,000,000
Inspiration	Inspiration	Inspiration Consolidated	Open pit	6-7,000,000
Lavender Pit[a]	Bisbee	Phelps Dodge	Open pit	45,000
Magma[b]	Superior	Magma Copper	Underground	
Castle Dome	Miami	Cities Service	Leaching	
Copper Cities	Miami	Cities Service	Open pit	4,000,000
Mineral Park[b]	Kingman	Duval Corporation	Open pit	6,200,000
Mission[a]	Sahuarita	American Smelting and Refining	Open pit	8,000,000
Morenci[a]	Morenci	Phelps Dodge	Open pit	19,000,000
New Cornelia[b]	Ajo	Phelps Dodge	Open pit	11,000,000
Pima[a]	Pima	Pima Mining Company	Open pit	13,000,000
Ray Pit[b]	Hayden	Kennecott Copper	Open pit	12,000,000
San Manuel	San Manuel	Magma Copper Company	Underground	14,000,000
Sierrita[a]	Sahuarita	Duval Corporation	Open pit	20,000,000
Silver Bell	Silver Bell	American Smelting and Refining	Open pit	
Twin Buttes[a]	Anaconda	Anaconda	Open pit	10,000,000
		Michigan		
White Pine[a]	Ontanagon County	Copper Range Company		ca 6,000,000

89

TABLE III-7 (concluded)

Mine	Location	Company	Type	Tonnage (ore)
		Montana		
Butte	Butte	Anaconda	Underground	ca 10,000,000
Berkeley Pit[a/]	Silver Bow	Anaconda	Open pit	ca 10,000,000
Mountain Con	Butte	Anaconda	Underground	ca 10,000,000
Leonard	Butte	Anaconda	Underground	ca 10,000,000
Belmont	Butte	Anaconda	Underground	ca 10,000,000
Steward	Butte	Anaconda	Underground	ca 10,000,000
Kelley	Butte	Anaconda	Underground	ca 10,000,000
		Nevada		
Liberty Pit	Ely	Kennecott Copper Corporation	Open pit	2,000,000
Yerington	Weed Heights	Anaconda	Open pit leaching	
Veteran	Ely	Anaconda	--	--
Copper Canyon		Duval Corporation	--	--
Ruth		Anaconda	Underground	--
		New Mexico		
Chino	Santa Rita	Kennecott	Open pit	8,000,000
Tyrone[a/]	Silver City	Phelps Dodge	Underground	Undetermined
Misens Chest Group	Lordsburg	Banner	Underground	Undetermined
		Tennessee		
Copperhill Group	Copperhill	Cities Service	Underground	2,000,000
		Utah		
Utah Copper[a/]	Bingham	Kennecott Copper	Open pit	40,000,000

a/ One of top 25 silver-producing mines in 1971.[1/]
b/ One of top 25 silver-producing mines in 1967 or 1970 but not 1971.[21,22/]

TABLE III-8

LEAD AND ZINC MINES PROCESSING SILVER-CONTAINING ORES[20]

Mine	Location County and State	Company	Metals Contained in Ore	1968 Ore Production, Short Tons
Page	Idaho	American Smelting and Refining Company	Pb, Zn, Ag	86,560
Bunker Hill[a]	Shoshone, Idaho	Bunker Hill Company	Ag, Pb, Zn	387,120
Crescent[a]	Shoshone, Idaho	Bunker Hill Company	Ag	28,530
Star[a]	Shoshone, Idaho	Bunker Hill Company	Ag, Pb, Zn	189,540
Canyon Silver	Idaho	Canyon Silver Mines	Ag, Pb, Zn	2,310
Dayrock[a]	Shoshone, Idaho	Day Mines, Inc.	Ag, Pb, Zn	26,085
Hand	Montana	Hand, John	Au, Ag, Pb	2,250
Star-Morning	Idaho	Hecla Mining Company	Ag, Pb, Zn	189,540
Silver Summit[b]	Idaho	Hecla Mining Company	Ag, Cu	21,890
Lucky Friday[a]	Idaho	Hecla Mining Company	Ag, Cu, Pb, Zn	95,720
Mayflower[a]	Wasatch, Utah	Hecla Mining Company	Ag, Cu, Pb, Zn	122,100
Burgin[a]	Utah, Utah	Kennecott Copper Corporation	Ag, Pb, Zn	199,580
Iron King[b]	Yavapai, Arizona	McFarland and Hullinger	Ag, Cu, Pb, Zn	101,870
Jubilee	California	Monte Cristo Mining Corporation	Pb, Ag, Au	1,995
Osceola	Colorado	Osceola Metals Corporation	Pb, Zn, Cu, Ag, Au	14,270
United Park City[b]	Summit and Wasatch, Utah	United Park City Mines Company	Pb, Zn, Ag	
Darwin	California	West Hill Exploration Inc.	Ag, Pb, Zn	57,110

a/ One of top 25 silver-producing mines in 1971.[7]
b/ One of top 25 silver-producing mines in 1967 or 1970 but not 1971.[21,22]

91

TABLE III-9

SILVER IN DIFFERENT ELECTRONIC COMPONENTS 23/

	Assay (troy oz/ton)
Circuit Boards	0-60
Connecting Plugs	0-168
Relays	0-665
Wave Guide	421
B-47 Bomber Electronic Scrap	58.6
Recently Generated Scrap	99.8

BIBLIOGRAPHY. SECTION III.

1. Welch, J. R., "Silver," in Minerals Yearbook 1972, Vol. I, Metals,
   Minerals, and Fuels, Bureau of Mines, U.S. Department of the
   Interior, U.S. Government Printing Office, Washington, D.C., 1974,
   pp. 1129-1142.

2. Salsbury, M. H., W. H. Kerns, F. B. Fulkerson, and G. C. Branner,
   Marketing Ores and Concentrates of Gold, Silver, Copper, Lead, and
   Zinc in the United States, Bureau of Mines Information Circular
   8206, Bureau of Mines, U.S. Department of the Interior, U.S.
   Government Printing Office, Washington, D.C., 1964.

3. Charles River Associates, Inc., Economic Analysis of the Silver
   Industry, prepared for Property Management and Disposal Service,
   General Services Administration, Clearinghouse for Federal Scientific
   and Technical Information, Springfield, Virginia, 1969.

4. American Bureau of Metal Statistics, Year Book of the American Bureau
   of Metal Statistics, 51st Annual Issue for the Year 1971, New York,
   New York, 1972.

5. Ageton, R. W., "Silver," in Minerals Facts and Problems, Bureau of
   Mines Bulletin 650, U.S. Department of the Interior, U.S. Government
   Printing Office, Washington, D.C., 1970, pp. 723-737.

6. Hoyt, C. D., "Silver," in Minerals Yearbook 1969, Vol. I, Metals,
   Minerals, and Fuels, Bureau of Mines, U.S. Department of the
   Interior, Washington, D.C., 1971.

7. Welch, J. R., "Silver," in Minerals Yearbook 1971, Vol. I, Metals,
   Minerals, and Fuels, Bureau of Mines, U.S. Department of the
   Interior, U.S. Government Printing Office, Washington, D.C., 1973,
   pp. 1073-1086.

8. Fulkerson, F. B., Economic Aspects of Silver Production in the Coeur
   d' Alene Mining Region, Shoshone County, Idaho, Bureau of Mines
   Information Circular 8207, U.S. Department of the Interior, U.S.
   Government Printing Office, Washington, D.C., 1964.

9. Anonymous, "World Silver Production Rises," The Silver Institute
   Letter, 4 (6), 1-2 (1974).

10. Anonymous, "Latest U.S. Silver Refining Statistics," The Silver
    Institute Letter, 4 (9), 4 (1974).

11. Schack, C. H., and B. H. Clemmons, <u>Review and Evaluation of Silver Production Techniques</u>, Bureau of Mines Information Circular 8266, U.S. Department of Interior, U.S. Government Printing Office, Washington, D.C., 1965.

12. Johnson, O. C., "Chapter 5. Refining Processes," in <u>Silver. Economics, Metallurgy, and Use</u>, A. Butts and C. D. Coxe, Eds., D. Van Nostrand Company, Inc., Princeton, N. J., 1967, pp. 57-77.

13. Materials Advisory Board Committee on Technical Aspects of Critical and Strategic Materials, <u>Trends in Usage of Silver</u>, Publication MAB-241, National Research Council, National Academy of Sciences, National Academy of Engineering, Washington, D.C., 1968.

14. Wemple, F. H., "Chapter 3. The Silver Market," in <u>Silver. Economics, Metallurgy, and Use</u>, A. Butts and C. D. Coxe, Eds., D. Van Nostrand Company, Inc., Princeton, N. J., 1967, pp. 36-56.

15. American Metal Market, <u>Metal Statistics 1974</u>, Fairchild Publications, Inc., New York, New York, 1974.

16. National Association of Recycling Industries, Inc., <u>Standard Classification for Nonferrous Scrap Metals</u>, Circular NF-73, Association Headquarters, New York, New York, 1973.

17. Spitz, A. W., and M. I. Schwab, "New Developments in Smelting Secondary Copper," in <u>Proceedings of the Third Mineral Waste Utilization Symposium</u>, M. A. Schwartz, Ed., Cosponsored by the U.S. Bureau of Mines and IIT Research Institute, Chicago, Illinois, March 14-16, 1972, pp. 265-268.

18. Cohen, B., "Wildberg Operations Geared to Specialization of Recovery," <u>Am. Metal Market</u>, 81 (153), Section 2, 2A (1974).

19. Rosenson, R., "Importance of Precious Metals Recovery," <u>Secondary Raw Materials</u>, 9 (5), 77-9 (1971).

20. Hallowell, J. B., J. F. Shea, G. R. Smithson, Jr., A. B. Tripler, and B. W. Gonser, <u>Water-Pollution Control in the Primary Nonferrous-Metals Industry--Vol. I. Copper, Zinc, and Lead Industries</u>, Battelle Memorial Institute, Prepared for Office of Research and Monitoring, U.S. Environmental Protection Agency, U.S. Government Printing Office, Washington, D.C., 1973.

21. Ryan, J. P., "Silver," in <u>Minerals Yearbook 1967</u>, <u>Vol. I-II</u>, <u>Metals, Minerals, and Fuels</u>, Bureau of Mines, U.S. Department of the Interior, U.S. Government Printing Office, Washington, D.C., 1968, pp. 1037-1056.

22. West, J. M., "Silver," in <u>Minerals Yearbook 1970</u>, <u>Vol. I</u>, <u>Metals, Minerals, and Fuels</u>, Bureau of Mines, U.S. Department of the Interior, U.S. Government Printing Office, Washington, D.C., 1972, pp. 1013-1029.

23. Dannenburg, R. O., and G. M. Potter, "Smelting of Military Electronic Scrap," in <u>Proceedings of the Second Mineral Waste Utilization Symposium</u>, Cosponsored by the U.S. Bureau of Mines and ITT Research Institute, Chicago, Illinois, March 18-19, 1970, pp. 114-117.

IV. ECONOMICS OF SILVER

This section treats silver as an industrial commodity, giving statistics for all industrial transactions from mining to sales to the ultimate consumer. Trends in silver supply, demand, and processing are also discussed.

A. Organization of the Silver Industry

This discussion, which identifies the major producers of primary and secondary silver, is based largely on a similarly titled chapter in Economic Analysis of the Silver Industry, published in 1969 by Charles River Associates, Inc.[1]/

The combined production of the U.S., Mexico, Peru, Canada, Australia, and Japan has accounted for 70 to 80% of the noncommunist-world mine production since 1960. The U.S. silver industry produces at least 50% of the world supply of refined silver.

Whereas new silver in the U.S. is produced from about 350 lode and placer units, 85% of the 1965 output was from 25 mines owned by 14 companies. The eight leading firms, producing more than 2 million troy ounces each, accounted for about 76% of the 1965 production, while the next six largest firms, each producing 450,000 to 700,000 troy ounces, accounted for 9%.

In 1969, ASARCO controlled about 35 to 50% of the noncommunist-world output of refined silver and about 70% of the domestic refinery production. ASARCO, Anaconda, Bunker Hill, Kennecott, Phelps Dodge, and U.S. Smelting and Refining account for 48-50, 12, 12, 9, 8, and 7%, respectively, of the U.S. output of silver contained in smelter products of domestic origin. Practically all imported ores, concentrates, and base bullion are believed to be refined by ASARCO. (International Smelting, an Anaconda subsidiary, treats Chilean imports; and Bunker Hill and International Smelting treat small amounts of Australia and Canada.)

Charles River Associates, Inc., published data for the production of refined silver by AMAX and ASARCO and ASARCO Mexicana in the years 1947 to 1966. They also estimated ASARCO's sources of primary silver in 1965.

ASARCO, AMAX, Engelhard, and Spiral Metals may account for 70 to 80% of the secondary production. In 1967, refining capacities of Engelhard and Spiral Metals were estimated at 50 million and 30 million troy ounces, respectively. Most scrap refining is apparently done on a toll basis.

The largest manufacturer of intermediate products, Engelhard, supplies 50% of the silver market annually. The second largest, Handy and Harman, supplies about 25% of the total silver consumed by industry.[1]

Specific consumers of intermediate silver products are identified in the appropriate subsections of Section VI.

B. U.S. Silver Supply and Demand

The statistical information that has been collected is presented in subsections beginning with the following one entitled World Statistics, and continuing through U.S. Mine Production, Refinery Production, Imports, Exports, Industrial Sales, Coinage, and Supply-and-Demand Relationships 1967-1972. The source of most of the information has been the U.S. Bureau of Mines Minerals Yearbooks.

1. World statistics: Sixty countries produce silver, including eight Eastern Bloc countries.[2] Table IV-1 gives the annual world production of new silver by major geographical regions from 1964 to 1972. A further breakdown by specific countries in Oceania, Asia, Africa, and Europe is found in Reference 3.

Table IV-2 gives Handy and Harman figures for silver consumption by noncommunist countries. The U.S. industrial sales figures given by Handy and Harman do not agree with those of the Bureau of Mines since the former attempts to subtract recycled new scrap.

Table IV-3 gives silver supply data among the noncommunist countries. Even with U.S.S.R. estimates subtracted from the totals of Table IV-1, the latter data do not agree well with the Handy and Harman "Total New Production" figures of Table IV-3. The figures under "Liquidation of...Speculative Holdings and Industrial Inventories" are probably calculated in order to balance the totals of silver "Available for World Consumption" with totals of silver consumption in Table IV-2.

Handy and Harman have attempted to summarize 1972-1973 world stocks of silver in Table IV-4. Where no reliable information was available, the figures they used were conjectural.[4]

2. U.S. mine production: Table IV-5 gives U.S. mine production of silver from 1873 to 1971, except for 1926 to 1930. U.S. production has ranged from 10.61 to 27.65% of the world total between 1931 and 1971. The data from 1873 to 1965 were reported by the Director of the Mint, and those from 1966 to 1971 are attributed to the Bureau of Mines.

Annual silver production by states from 1963 to 1972 is shown in Table IV-6. The states are compared as to total silver production from earliest record to the end of 1972.

The production of silver by state, mine type, and ore class for prior years can be found in Volume I of each annual Minerals Yearbook.

Table IV-7 gives the average troy ounces of silver per ton of ore according to ore class. Table IV-8 shows total U.S. silver production by ore class for each year from 1963 to 1972; data for previous years can be found in the report by Charles River Associates.[1]

Table IV-9 shows the silver produced from ore, ore tailings, etc., in 1972 according to state and method of recovery.

3. U.S. imports: Table IV-10 shows the imports of silver by source country. Ore and bullion constitute a large part of the imports. In addition to ore, concentrates, and bullion, silver is also imported as waste, sweepings, doré, and precipitates. In 1972, 1027 thousand troy ounces were imported as waste and sweepings and 4931 thousand troy ounces, as doré and precipitates.[5]

Coinage silver is not included in the Bureau of Mines import or export data, yet privately owned mints produce small amounts of coins and medals for many small countries such as the Bahamas, Panama, Trinidad, and Tobago.[5,6]

4. U.S. silver exports: The annual amounts of refined silver exported by the U.S. to various countries in the period 1964 to 1973 are given in Table IV-11. In 1972, approximately 90% of the exported silver was in the form of refined bullion, 9.8% as waste and sweepings, and 0.2% as ore and concentrates.[5]

5. U.S. refinery production: In Table IV-12, U.S. silver production by refineries is categorized by source: domestic ores and concentrates, foreign, old scrap, and new scrap for the years 1966 through 1974. In 1974, the Silver Institute predicted that U.S. production of silver in 1975, 1976, and 1977 would be 45.5, 52.0, and 53.1 million troy ounces, respectively.[2]

Statistics on secondary refining of silver are incomplete and unreliable. Until 1966, the only data compiled by the Bureau of the Mint included the recovery of both old and new scrap (excluding "run-around" materials [a/]) as shown in Table IV-13. The Mint canvassed only 15 primary refiners, nine of which did not normally refine scrap. Some of the scrap probably included premelted U.S. and foreign coins. At least 11 other companies not included in the canvass are known to refine silver scrap. In 1969, six of these 11 secondary refiners not canvassed by the Mint produced over 13 million troy ounces from scrap silver. In addition, many major silver consumers recover their own silver waste; e.g., Eastman Kodak may recover 3.5 to 7 million troy ounces silver per year, some of which is from old material. Thus, the Mint's statistics considerably underestimated the recovery of scrap silver. The Mint statistics show the amounts of scrap received, not produced, and therefore do not reflect silver losses during refining. Unless refiners have hoarded significant amounts of silver, the receipts are a reasonable measure of production.

The Bureau of Mines began making its own surveys in 1966. "New scrap" in their statistics refers only to metallic material (bullion) and excludes sweepings, Treasure coinage scrap, and any other scrap that is merely remelted. This newer survey calls for reporting as .999 fine silver so that reporters may either convert their output of lower fineness to this standard or not report this output at all. Almost all silver is refined to .999 fine, but some is sold as alloys. Thus, the Bureau of Mines data may also be underestimated.[1]

Charles River Associates, Inc., in its 1969 _Economic Analysis of the Silver Industry_ [1] states that the data published for 1955 to 1963 in the Bureau of Mines Information Circular No. 8257 are erroneous. The Bureau of Mines indicates the data are for U.S. secondary production; but actually they are worldwide figures. According to the Charles River report, the data source, Handy and Harman, Inc., did not provide actual production statistics but merely a calculated figure to balance supply and demand, which changes in their subsequent annual review to reflect revisions in the estimate of the other items in their table.

Another factor contributing to inaccuracies in scrap statistics is that often the refiner cannot distinguish between old and new scrap, e.g., a used electric contact and one rejected by the manufacturer. Both may be purchased from the large accumulations of scrap-collecting firms.[1]

Schack and Clemmons estimated the amounts of old and new scrap that were generated in 1963 by several categories of end uses; these estimates are shown in Table IV-14.

---

a/ "Run-around" scrap is usually returned within about a 30-day cycle to the fabricator for resmelting.[1]

6. _Industrial sales_: The percentages of total net industrial consumption for the various end uses in 1972 and the average values and percentages for the end uses for the period 1966 to 1972 (derived from Minerals Yearbook statistics[5,7,8,9,10]) are given in Table IV-15. A more detailed compilation of industrial sales, including coinage use, is found in Table VI-1.

7. _Stocks_:

   a. **Treasury stocks and U.S. coins**: The silver in meltable hoards of old U.S. coins may be equal to or greater than that in private holdings of bullion.[11]

   The _Minerals Yearbooks_ give annual data for Treasury stocks and amounts of outstanding coinage silver. However, Charles River Associates, Inc., estimated that the public had withdrawn about 800 million troy ounces silver by December 31, 1968, leaving about 1,020 million troy ounces coinage silver theoretically still in circulation. The Treasury had also withdrawn coins containing about an additional 250 million troy ounces silver, melted them, and sold the melted coin in GSA auctions. When silver was demonetized in the period 1963 to 1967, large amounts of silver were freed for minting and sale to industry in the weekly GSA auctions.[1/a]

   b. **Strategic stockpile**: When the redemption privilege for silver certificates expired on June 14, 1968, 190 million troy ounces silver was released from the monetized reserves. A total of 165 million troy ounces was transferred from the Treasury stocks to the strategic stockpile.[1] In 1970, 25.5 million troy ounces was transferred back to the Treasury to be used to coin one-dollar pieces,[12] which left 139.5 million troy ounces silver in the strategic stockpile at the end of 1973.[4] Defense Department stocks of silver at year end 1972 and 1973 were 8.9 and 6.7 million troy ounces, respectively.[4,13]

8. **Supply and demand relationships**: Figure IV-1 is a chart from _Minerals, Facts, and Problems 1970_ depicting the flow of silver through the economy.

---

a/ Handy and Harman reports government sales at weekly auction were:
        43.6 million troy ounces silver in 1967;
       105.0 million troy ounces silver in 1968;
        89.0 million troy ounces silver in 1969; and
        67.2 million troy ounces silver in 1970.[12]

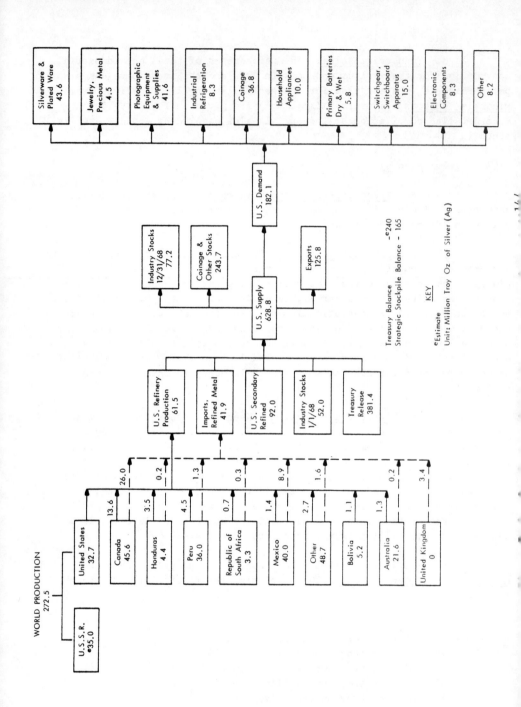

WORLD PRODUCTION 272.5

U.S.S.R. ⁱ35.0		
United States 32.7		26.0
Canada 45.6	13.6	
Honduras 4.4	3.5	0.2
Peru 36.0	4.5	1.3
Republic of South Africa 3.3	0.7	0.3
Mexico 40.0	1.4	8.9
Other 48.7	2.7	1.6
Bolivia 5.2	1.1	
Australia 21.6	1.3	0.2
United Kingdom 0		3.4

U.S. Refinery Production 61.5

Imports, Refined Metal 41.9

U.S. Secondary Refined 92.0

Industry Stocks 1/1/68 52.0

Treasury Release 381.4

U.S. Supply 628.8

Industry Stocks 12/31/68 77.2

Coinage & Other Stocks 243.7

Exports 125.8

U.S. Demand 182.1

Silverware & Plated Ware 43.6

Jewelry, Precious Metal 4.5

Photographic Equipment & Supplies 41.6

Industrial Refrigeration 8.3

Coinage 36.8

Household Appliances 10.0

Primary Batteries Dry & Wet 5.8

Switchgear, Switchboard Apparatus 15.0

Electronic Components 8.3

Other 8.2

Treasury Balance   −ⁱ240
Strategic Stockpile Balance − 165

KEY

ⁱEstimate
Unit: Million Troy Oz of Silver (Ag)

102

Table IV-16 gives accounting statements for the years 1967 to 1972 with respect to silver supply and demand, but the approach is somewhat different from that in Figure IV-1. In Table IV-16, imports of refined bullion and concentrates are combined, and domestic mining production figures are used instead of refining statistics. The degree to which the mining and refining data given in the Minerals Yearbooks agree is shown in Table IV-17.

Table IV-18 shows the distribution of Treasury silver stocks among monetized and free reserves for 1961 to 1968 and stock totals from 1968 to 1973. The annual amounts of monetized stocks transferred to the free reserves can be calculated from this table.

The apparent large excess of silver supply over demand in 1968 includes the 165 million troy ounces silver transferred to the Strategic Stockpile. When the 165 million troy ounces are deducted, the average annual "oversupply" for this period 1967 to 1972 is 50.41 million troy ounces. However, since the average turn-around period for new scrap from the manufacturing user back to the refiner is about 30 days, new scrap refinery totals should probably not be included in the calculation of the new silver supplies of any one year. Deducting "New Scrap" as well as "Demand" from "Supply" figures, therefore, gives an average annual oversupply figure of 22.38 million troy ounces. Standardized bookkeeping procedures are badly needed to resolve many of the problems of developing reliable statistics of metal production and usage.

C. Trends in Silver Supply and Demand

This subsection is a discussion of trends in supply from primary and secondary production and of trends in industrial consumption.

1. Supply trends:

a. Natural sources: Table IV-19 shows the estimate by Charles River Associates, Inc., of U.S. ore reserves of silver based on estimates made in 1965. Recent price increases and exploration activity[a] may have increased this estimate considerably.

Dr. T. P. Mohide, Mineral Resources Director of Ontario, believes that known ore reserves will be exhausted by the year 2000 if

_____

a/ There has been recent exploration for silver in Utah, Montana, Colorado, New Mexico, and Maine. In 1965, new devices were tested by the Geological Survey for detecting small amounts of silver in rocks.[1]

present rates of industrial expansion and population growth continue.[24]/ Since most of the rich silver deposits that have been found were near the earth's surface, mining engineers believe that, like Nevada's famous Comstock Lode, most "epithermal deposits" have already been discovered and exhausted. At the present time, 90% of known silver reserves are located in base-metal deposits.[6]/

Ivor Thompson, managing director of a metal commodities brokerage (Rudolf Wolff and Company), states that only a major silver discovery can avert a silver shortage. "No source is known to be available anywhere. Some of the silver mined with other metals is of too low a content to warrant the expense of recovery." In September 1974, he noted that the recovery rate from all sources is at virtual capacity.[25]/

b. **Mining production:** In 1974, the Silver Institute predicted that world mine production would be up 22.5% in 4 years to 358.6 million troy ounces in 1977. (Current world consumption is about 514 million troy ounces.)[2]/ Louis E. Carabini, founder of the Pacific Coast Coin Exchange, predicted a somewhat slower 5% annual increase, which would result in an annual production of 303 million troy ounces of silver in 1977.[6]/

U.S. mine production is expected to increase from about 39.9 million troy ounces in 1974 to 45.5, 52.0, and 53.1 million troy ounces in 1975, 1976, and 1977, respectively.[2]/

In the past, new silver production has been largely unresponsive to price changes. It requires 5 to 7 years to bring a new mine into production, and during the past 40 years, silver production has risen only 70%. On the other hand, copper production increased 519%; lead, 165%; and zinc, 365%.[6]/

About 30% of new silver produced is recovered as a by-product of copper production. In 1973, Anaconda Company produced 128,000 tons of copper, largely from open-pit operations. Underground mining by Anaconda at Butte, Montana, was curtailed 17 September 1974, and this will reduce their copper production in Butte by about 15,000 or 17,000 tons per year. Anaconda concluded that continued vein mining would impair the mineral potential of the lower-grade underground ore at Butte, which will ultimately be mined by new large-scale, highly mechanized, bulk-mining methods.[26-28]/[a]/ Plans for an additional production

---

a/ Successful bulk-mining methods of the underground deposit (500 million to 1 billion tons), which will require at least 7 years to put into operation, might continue for 50 to 60 years and provide more than 14 billion pounds of copper.[27]/ One method considered is underground nuclear mining combined with leaching.[1]/

cutback of about 18,000 tons of copper per year was reported in February 1975.[28]

John B. M. Place, President of Anaconda, testified at Congressional hearings that the Butte shutdown did not indicate any domestic mining trends, but rather the real trend is away from high-cost, low-productivity methods in underground mining. The Butte underground operations had been unprofitable from 1960 to 1967, and again since 1972 when the pound costs exceeded selling price as the grade of underground ore declined. Ore reserves for Anaconda open-pit operations may last for 15 to 18 years. In addition to the Berkeley and Continental open pits, dump leach and weed concentrator operations will be continued.[27]

Phelps Dodge Corporation's Lavender Pit orebody at Bisbee, Arizona, was finally exhausted--the mine and concentrator were closed 14 December 1974. Copper production from underground mining at Bisbee was expected to be reduced from about 7,000 tons in the last quarter of 1974 to about 2,600 tons in the first quarter of 1975 and will continue only as long as it is profitable. In 1973, the production of the Lavender Pit was 19,387 tons copper and that of the underground mines, 22,628 tons. Dump remining, in process for several months, will also be curtailed at Bisbee.[29]

With higher silver and base-metal prices, mines can afford to work lower grade ore. Efficient mines, however, are already extracting their maximum tonnage. Since less silver is found in the ore as mines go deeper, the level of new silver production from copper ore cannot be maintained.[6]

c. Secondary sources: Dr. T. P. Mohide, Ontario Mineral Resources Director, predicted in 1974 that silver recycling will double by 1979,[30] while Louis E. Carabini of the Pacific Coast Coin Exchange predicted in 1973 that silver salvage will grow at a rate of about 15% per year.[6]

In 1972, 26.9% of all the 99.9% silver bullion produced by U.S. refineries came from old scrap; however, in 1973 and 1974, this value rose to 27.3% and 30.5%, respectively. The amount of silver recycled from old coins in this period increased dramatically from 0.12% of all refinery production in 1972 to 2.0% in 1973 and 8.8% in 1974.[18]

George J. Peer, Group Vice-President of Handy and Harman, Inc., estimated in 1974 that 300 to 400 million troy ounces of U.S. coins "drawn out of hoards" by high silver prices are a potential silver recovery source. He claimed that there is sufficient refining capacity for reclaiming silver from 90% silver coins but not for those containing 40

to 80% silver.[31/] In 1974, some manufacturers of commemoratives, silverware, and solder used silver coin directly.[32/]

Irwin Shishko, Vice-President of Research, J. Aron and
Company, predicted in 1974 that as many as 40% of the Kennedy 90% silver
half-dollars will eventually be melted down. He also felt that lower
prices might not curtail melting of coins or curb East Indian silver
exports.[32/] However, M. W. Harman, Chairman and President of Handy and
Harman, states that "secondary silver supplies tend to dry up" when the
price dips below $4 per troy ounce.[33/]

2. Consumption trends:

a. Future trends in industrial sales: The Minerals Yearbook 1970 forecasts silver consumption for the year 2000 as shown in Table
IV-20. Louis E. Carabini of the Pacific Coast Coin Exchange predicted in
1973 that the average growth in silver consumption through 1977 would be
6%,[6/] while Booz-Allen Applied Research, Inc., has projected a 1.4 to 3.6%
annual growth rate for silver demand from 1968 to 2000.[34/]

b. Past trends: In Table IV-21, silver consumption in
1928 (U.S. population of 123 million) is compared where possible with the
consumption in 1971 (U.S. population of 203 million).[a/] Because of differences in aggregating use categories, we can compare directly only certain areas. The modest per capita increase in sterling ware, electroplating, and dental uses since 1928 can probably be attributed to the
increase in personal disposable income. The dramatic increase in photographic consumption of silver may be partly reduced by a correction factor for scrap and may be partly attributed not only to increased personal
affluence and better health care but also to more leisure time for amateur photography.

The ratio of the total of the 1928 categories of "indus-
trials including silver solder" and "miscellaneous" (1.705 million troy
ounces) to the total of the 1971 categories "electrical and electronic,"
"bearings," "catalysts," "brazing alloys and solders," and "miscellaneous"
is 1:31. Except for photography, these categories represent the largest
potential sources of used silver dissipated to the environment. Silver
items esteemed for their relatively high monetary value and beauty are
much more likely to have been preserved intact. The shift in the principal silver markets away from silverware and jewelry to other industrial
uses and photography occurred during the postwar period.[1/]

---

a/ The ratio of the 1970 population to the 1930 population is 1.65.

106

Table IV-22 lists materials that are already being substituted for silver.

c. Recent trends: The 1974 decrease in silver consumption was especially noticeable in jewelry and brazing alloys as well as silverware. Annual industrial consumption in Europe was expected to be down 10 to 15%.[35] As the world economy slows and silver prices decline, industrial silver consumption may be expected to resume former levels.

(1) Silverware: Piece sales were down about one-third in the silverware industry in late 1974.[36] The International Silver Company, a subsidiary of Insilco Corporation, reported in late 1974 that it plans to sell $14 million worth of finished silverware goods that have been stockpiled for several years and to cut back in production.[37]

(2) Electrical and electronic products: Most of the silver consumed by the electrical and electronics industry goes into electrical control devices of varying sizes, from home wall switches to large control devices that can swith hundreds of amps. The cost rise of silver from $2/troy oz to $5.50/troy oz in 1974 caused the silver cost of large control devices to jump from 1.8 to 5% of the selling price, and of small appliance controls, from 3 to 9%.[38]

Higher silver prices[a] have caused electronic firms to omit silver in some applications, switch from pure silver to combinations of silver with copper, and to decrease amounts of silver used when possible.[30,38,39] According to L. M. Smith, Manager of Electrical Contacts at Texas Instruments, Inc., silver cannot be replaced in high-power applications even if its price were $12/troy oz.[38] Although in many electrical control applications the amount of silver used has been 50% greater than required, it is not economical to effect reductions of less than 20%. Thus, by 1978 or 1979, silver consumption for electrical control is likely to be the same or only slightly less than the amount currently being consumed.[38]

In 1968, the National Research Council Materials Advisory Board predicted that solid-state switching with controlled silicon rectifiers or power transistors would replace many silver contacts but that the use of silver in contacts would increase in spite of the increasing use of solid-state devices.[30]

---

a/ The record price for silver was $6.70 in late February 1974.

Conversion of solar energy into useful forms of energy may utilize silver-backed mirrors or silver connectors.[40] Because silver is more plentiful than other materials previously used in fuel cell electrodes, these electrodes will be used more widely.[40] Research in Japan, Italy, and the U.S.S.R. on economical silver catalytic fuel cell electrodes indicates that silver can be used commercially in alkaline-type fuel cells, while U.S. research gives promise that acid-type fuel cells may also use low-cost silver catalysts.[41] Silver will probably be used also in the new magnetohydrodynamic generation of electric power.[40]

The U.S. government is one of the largest single users of silver, and its consumption will increase with the growth of space and nuclear energy programs. In 1973, the Department of Defense consumed silver in more than 5,000 items.[42]

(3) Photography: High silver prices have encouraged development of photopolymers for use in photography. One to three new photopolymer products are expected to compete with silver in the graphic arts field.[43] Silver in photography probably will not be replaced rapidly, certainly not within the next 10 years, but it may be used more often in only very small amounts as a catalyst. In the future, electrostatic imaging and diazo dyes will also compete with silver-sensitized films.[30,44]

Xonics, Inc., of Van Nuys, California, backed by AGFA-Gavaert, is currently perfecting a silverless X-ray system that might substantially reduce photographic silver consumption.[35] The process called Xonics Radiography (XRG) was developed by Xonics, Inc., and the University of Southern California. Mylar polyester, held in a pressurized metal chamber, substitutes for silver halide film and has a development time of less than 90 sec, compared with 5 to 60 min for ordinary X-ray film. The technique gives sharper, more detailed pictures and reduces patients' X-ray exposure 10 to 30%. XRG is useful in 60% of the diagnostic procedures now done by conventional methods.[45]

The large amount of silver retained annually in conventional X-rays could also be reduced by placing the picture on microfilm so that silver could be recovered from the large X-ray plates.[46]

Table IV-23 shows trends in sales by various segments of the photographic industry. Silver halide product sales usually represent one-third (34.4% in 1972) of total photographic good sales.[47] Handy and Harman, Inc., estimates that 47.0 million troy ounces silver was consumed by the photographic industry in 1974 compared with 52.0 million in 1973.[48]

108

This reduction can probably be attributed to the 1974 recession and the decline of the amateur photography market, which normally accounts for one-third of the photographic industry's dollar business. Another factor reducing silver consumption by the photographic industry is the trend toward amateur use of color film. In 1962, about 43% of the 2.3 billion amateur photophraphs used color; in 1972, about 84% of the 5.6 billion amateur photographs used color. Silver consumption by the photographic industry also fluctuates with silver costs but currently, buying is more closely related to estimates of silver scrap recovery than in past years.[49]

TABLE IV-1

WORLD'S PRODUCTION OF NEW SILVER[3,5,15]/

(By Bureau of Mines and American Bureau of Metal Statistics, in Million Fine Ounces)

Country	1964	1965	1966	1967	1968	1969	1970	1971	1972
North America:									
United States	37.000	39.000	42.500	31.000	31.700	39.675	45.006	41.564	37.233
Canada	29.903	31.917	32.825	37.206	45.389	43.531	44.250	46.024	46.999
Mexico	41.716	40.332	41.984	40.172	40.031	42.904	42.836	36.657	37.483
Total North America	108.619	111.249	117.308	108.378	117.120	126.110	132.093	124.245	121.715
Central America, West Indies	3.654	4.147	4.235	4.415	4.826	4.169	4.204	4.135	4.064
Total South America	46.772	46.606	44.279	42.691	44.805	47.004	49.806	49.308	51.287
Peru	36.818	36.470	32.841	32.704	33.409	35.886	39.836	38.398	40.188
Total Europe	14.313	15.125	15.396	15.172	14.583	15.620	15.278	24.341	24.758
Oceania:									
Australia	18.452	17.312	18.278	19.765	21.618	24.667	26.126	21.703	22.796
Total Oceania	18.536	17.393	18.364	19.844	21.694	25.176	26.186	21.815	23.846
Total Asia	11.579	11.816	13.290	14.021	13.732	14.305	14.925	17.440	16.789
Total Africa	7.908	8.228	8.898	8.440	8.550	7.974	8.070	8.599	8.932
USSR	27.000	27.000	33.000	35.000	35.000	37.000	38.000	39.000	40.000
Estimated World Total	238.381	241.564	254.770	247.961	260.310	277.358	288.562	288.883	291.391

110

TABLE IV-2

WORLD SILVER CONSUMPTION[a]/3,4,15/

(Excluding Iron Curtain Countries)
(In Millions of Troy Ounces)

	1961	1962	1963	1964	1965	1966	1967	1968	1969	1970	1971	1972	1973
Arts and Industries:													
United States	105.0	110.0	110.0	123.0	137.0	150.0	145.0	145.0	142.0	131.0	126.0	151.1	190.0
Canada	4.5	4.6	4.6	5.0	5.3	5.8	5.4	5.1	5.7	6.0	6.0	7.4	8.5
Mexico	3.4	3.3	3.2	4.1	4.7	3.9	5.0	5.0	4.3	5.0	6.6	6.0	11.5
Great Britain	20.0	20.0	20.0	23.0	25.0	25.0	24.0	23.0	25.0	25.0	25.0	27.5	31.5
France	14.0	13.5	13.9	14.8	14.0	14.7	14.7	18.0	18.0	16.0	19.0	20.0	22.5
Italy	20.0	22.0	25.0	25.0	25.0	30.0	28.2	22.5	29.0	32.0	32.0	32.0	33.5
Western Germany	43.5	41.8	40.5	46.3	54.6	48.2	48.2	50.0	50.0	48.2	48.2	60.0	60.0
India [b]/	-	-	-	12.0	16.0	16.0	15.0	16.0	16.0	16.0	16.0	13.0	13.0
Japan	19.1	19.6	20.0	20.0	25.0	31.5	33.2	36.2	41.5	46.5	45.7	54.3	67.5
Other countries	10.0	13.0	20.0	26.0	30.0	30.0	30.0	30.0	35.0	34.0	33.0	20.0	25.0
Total	239.5	247.8	257.2	299.2	336.6	355.1	348.7	350.8	366.5	359.7	357.5	391.3	463.0
Coinage:													
United States	55.9	77.4	111.5	203.0	320.3	53.8	43.9	37.0	19.4	0.7	2.5	2.3	1.5
Canada	6.2	10.9	13.0	13.7	20.4	14.4	14.5	9.9	...	...	0.2	0.1	1.5
France	23.8	13.7	12.2	10.7	7.2	8.7	7.5	2.9	0.6	3.7	0.6	0.8	1.0
Italy	5.6	3.5	0.5	1.4	2.9	4.6	0.7	0.5	...	0.9	0.7	-	-
Japan	1.4	1.4	4.2	17.3	5.8	9.0	...	...	0.7	...	...	-	-
Other countries	44.2	20.7	25.0	21.0	24.5	39.0	38.7	39.0	19.3	15.0	15.0	33.3	16.0
Total	137.1	127.6	166.4	267.1	381.1	129.5	105.3	89.3	40.0	20.3	19.0	36.5	20.0
Total Consumption	376.6	375.4	423.6	566.3	717.7	484.6	454.0	440.1	406.5	380.0	376.5	427.8	483.0

a/ As computed by Handy and Harman.
b/ Included in other countries before 1964.

TABLE IV-3

WORLD SILVER SUPPLIES[4]

(In Millions of Ounces)

	1967[a]	1968[a]	1969	1970	1971	1972	1973
New Production:							
Mexico	38.3	40.0	42.9	42.8	36.7	37.5	38.5
United States	32.1	32.7	41.9	45.0	41.6	37.2	37.5
Canada	36.3	45.0	43.5	44.3	45.9	47.0	48.0
Peru	32.1	36.4	35.9	39.8	38.4	39.0	40.0
Other South and Central American Countries	15.2	16.9	17.0	16.0	19.1	18.0	20.0
Total W. Hemisphere	154.0	171.0	181.2	187.9	181.7	178.7	184.0
Outside the W. Hemisphere[b]	60.0	60.3	60.1	67.7	63.4	65.0	65.0
Total New Production[b]	214.0	231.3	241.3	255.6	245.1	243.7	249.0
Other Supplies:							
U.S. Treasury: New Coinage Sales	43.9	37.0	19.4	0.7	2.5	2.3	1.5
Stocks of Foreign Governments	195.2	179.5	89.0	67.0	-	-	45.0
Demonetized Coin	5.0	15.0	-	10.0	5.0	10.0	15.0
Sales by U.S.S.R.	35.0	50.0	50.0	25.0	20.0	15.0	-
From India and Pakistan	8.0	-	11.3	13.2	-	-	-
Salvage and Other Miscellaneous Sources	20.0	60.0	25.0	16.0	16.0	6.0	26.0
Liquidation of (additions to) Speculative Holdings and	52.9	27.3	14.6	18.3	35.0	55.8	56.5
Industrial Inventories	(120.0)	(160.0)	(60.0)	(40.0)	55.0	95.0	90.0
Total Other Supplies	240.0	208.8	149.3	110.2	133.5	184.1	234.0
Available for World Consumption	454.0	440.1	390.6	365.8	378.6	427.8	483.0

a/ Reference 15.
b/ Excluding communist dominated areas.

TABLE IV-4

SUMMARY OF WORLD STOCKS IN 1972 AND 1973[4]

	(Millions of Ounces)		
	1973	1972	Increase (Decrease)
Reported Private Stocks:			
New York Commodity Exchange	64.4	77.6	(13.3)
Chicago Board of Trade	27.3	22.8	4.5
London Metal Exchange	16.3	7.5	8.8
Industry Stocks in U.S.	39.1[a]	51.9	(12.8)
Total	147.0	159.8	(12.8)
U.S. Government Stocks:			
U.S. Strategic Stockpile	139.5	139.5	-
U.S. Defense Dept.	6.7	8.9	(2.2)
U.S. Treasury (Mint)	44.3	45.8	(1.5)
Total	190.5	194.2	(3.7)
Stocks of Foreign Governments (partial)	50.0	95.0	(45.0)
Conjectural Stocks:			
Unreported Bullion Stocks in the U.S. and abroad	50.0	125.0	(75.0)
U.S. Silver Coins potentially available	300.0	300.0	-
Foreign Silver Coins potentially available	25.0	50.0	(25.0)
Total	375.0	475.0	(100.0)
Total World Silver Stocks	762.5	924.0	(161.5)

a/   As of September 30, 1973.

TABLE IV-5

U.S. MINE PRODUCTION OF SILVER[15/]
(Fine Ounces)

	Production	Percent of World Total
1873-1880	238,738,400	-
1881-1890	414,659,800	-
1891-1900	566,601,300	-
1901-1910	556,131,200	-
1911-1920	664,393,196	-
1921-1925	363,823,269	-
1931	30,932,050	15.75
1932	23,980,773	14.17
1933	23,002,629	13.56
1934	32,725,353	17.56
1935	45,924,454	21.42
1936	63,812,176	24.75
1937	71,941,794	26.10
1938	62,665,335	23.76
1939	65,119,513	25.25
1940	69,585,734	25.45
1941	72,336,029	27.65
1942	56,090,855	22.55
1943	40,900,121	18.84
1944	35,651,049	20.63
1945	29,063,255	18.98
1946	21,103,269	16.09
1947	38,587,069	26.71
1948	39,228,468	22.43
1949	34,944,554	19.83
1950	42,308,739	20.84
1951	39,907,257	20.04
1952	39,840,300	18.36
1953	37,735,500	17.42
1954	35,584,800	16.68
1955	36,469,610	15.89
1956	38,739,400	17.16
1957	38,720,200	16.78
1958	36,800,000	15.43
1959	23,000,000	10.61
1960	36,800,000	15.32
1961	34,900,000	15.06
1962	36,345,000	14.99
1963	35,000,000	14.47
1964	37,000,000	14.83
1965	39,000,000	15.72
1966	43,700,000	16.3
1967	32,100,000	12.3
1968	32,729,000	12.0
1969	41,906,000	14.5
1970	45,005,605	15.1
1971 Est.	40,537,559	13.5

TABLE IV-6

MINE PRODUCTION OF RECOVERABLE SILVER IN THE U.S., 1963-1972, WITH PRODUCTION OF MAXIMUM YEAR AND CUMULATIVE PRODUCTION FROM EARLIEST RECORD TO END OF 1972, BY STATES, IN TROY OUNCES

State	Maximum Production a/ Year	Maximum Production a/ Quantity	Production by Years 1963	1964	1965	1966	1967	1968	1969	1970	1971	1972	Total Production from Earliest Record (Values in parentheses to end of 1965)
Western States:													
Alaska	1916	1,379,171	14,010	7,336	7,673	7,193	5,787	3,900	2,030	2,189	868	288	20,401,095
Arizona	1937	9,422,552	5,373,058	5,810,510	6,095,248	6,338,696	4,588,081	4,958,162	6,141,022	7,330,417	6,169,623	6,652,800	429,344,774
California	1921	3,629,223	156,528	171,621	196,787	189,989	144,515	597,961	491,927	451,150	443,761	175,467	122,169,942
Colorado	1893	25,838,600	2,307,305	2,626,431	2,051,105	2,085,534	1,817,699	1,646,283	2,598,563	2,933,363	3,389,748	3,663,832	795,674,069
Idaho	1937	19,587,766	16,710,725	16,483,495	18,456,809	19,776,785	17,033,330	15,958,715	18,929,697	19,114,829	19,139,575	14,250,725	928,417,710
Montana	1892	19,038,800	4,241,620	5,289,959	5,207,031	5,319,785	2,066,464	2,132,571	3,429,314	4,304,326	2,747,557	3,325,052	875,521,118
Nevada	1913	16,090,083	214,976	172,447	507,113	867,567	565,755	645,192	884,155	718,011	601,470	595,351	610,743,240
New Mexico	1885	2,343,800	256,475	242,405	287,509	242,620	157,495	224,866	465,591	781,952	782,441	1,016,880	77,382,248
Oregon	1941	276,158	58,234	14,372	8,801	343	31	335	4,749	3,594	3,790	2,252	5,478,001
South Dakota	1900	536,200	117,301	132,981	128,971	109,885	121,258	137,668	124,497	119,766	106,785	99,992	12,957,644
Texas	1938	1,433,008	-	-	-	-	-	-	-	-	-	-	
Utah	1925	21,276,689	4,790,511	4,551,960	5,635,570	7,755,411	4,874,640	5,120,772	5,953,567	6,029,737	5,294,477	4,299,604	872,765,690
Washington	1902	721,450	374,373	375,603	358,477	368,788 e/	279,898 e/	371,745 f/	319,718 f/	325,887 e/	362,646 g/	269,262 f/	20,897,709 c/
Wyoming	1901	21,400	-	28	52	-	-	-	-	-	-	-	(75,327)
Total			34,615,116	35,879,148	38,941,146	42,693,808	31,375,055	31,426,425	39,025,112	41,789,334	38,680,095	34,082,243	
West Central States:													
Missouri	1952	517,432	131,664	-	299,522	-	226,168	340,856	1,442,090	1,816,978	1,660,879	1,971,530	15,889,883
States East of the Mississippi:													
Alabama	1936	869	-	-	-	-	-	-	-	-	-	-	(5,239)
Georgia	1904	1,500	-	-	-	-	-	-	-	-	-	-	(10,963)
Illinois	1924	8,891	-	-	-	1,086	568	-	-	-	-	-	(163,707)
Kentucky	1961	2,065	1,515	1,673	1,931	-	-	-	-	-	-	-	(8,855)
Maine	1917	1,092	-	-	-	-	-	-	-	-	-	-	(2,595)
Maryland	1916	716,640	338,997	349,195	457,851	483,000	301,992	472,813	1,009,022	891,579	670,052	785,100	17,705,194
Michigan	1956	84,158	19,544	13,306	11,441	21,590	31,103	27,615	31,755	23,830	17,928	25,070	1,302,752
New York	1960	212,368	26,754	90,539	94,142	100,716	130,078	89,525	78,614	94,770	131,349	83,466	911,721
North Carolina			-	-	-	-	-	-	-	-	-	-	275,126 c/
Oklahoma	1942	15,501	-	-	-	-	-	-	-	-	-	-	(35,325)
Pennsylvania	1940	8,047	b/	b/	-	-	-	-	-	-	-	-	5,002,778
South Carolina	1962	112,251	107,913	-	-	-	-	-	-	-	-	-	(524,585 d/)
Tennessee	1955	50,447	-	-	-	-	-	-	-	-	-	-	
Vermont	1944	18,993	-	-	-	-	-	-	-	-	-	-	(90,689)
Virginia			-	-	-	-	-	-	-	-	-	-	
Total			494,723	454,713	565,365	975,180	743,639	961,698	1,439,109	1,399,293	1,223,168	1,179,149	
Grand Total			35,241,503	36,333,861	39,806,033	43,668,988	32,344,862	32,728,979	41,906,311	45,005,605	41,564,142	37,232,922	(4,575,028,838)

a/ Figures for states east of the Mississippi are peak since 1896, except New York and Pennsylvania, which are peak since 1905. The Illinois figure is the peak since 1907. Alaska, California, Nevada, and Oregon are peaks since 1880.

b/ Pennsylvania included with Vermont in 1956; Pennsylvania included with Washington 1957-1965.

c/ Total production from earliest record to end of 1955; included with Washington 1957-1965.

d/ Includes a small amount from New Hampshire.

e/ Production of Oklahoma, Pennsylvania, and Washington combined to avoid disclosing individual company confidential data.

f/ Production of Maine, Oklahoma, Pennsylvania, Washington, and Wyoming (1969) combined to avoid disclosing individual company confidential data.

g/ Production of Oklahoma, Pennsylvania, Washington, Illinois (1971), and North Carolina (1971) combined to avoid disclosing individual company confidential data.

TABLE IV-7

ORE, OLD TAILINGS, ETC., YIELDING SILVER PRODUCED IN THE UNITED STATES AND AVERAGE RECOVERABLE CONTENT IN 1967, IN TROY OUNCES OF SILVER PER TON 7/

State	Gold		Gold-silver		Silver		Copper	
	Short tons	Average ounces of silver per ton	Short tons	Average ounces of silver per ton	Short tons	Average ounces of silver per ton	Short tons	Average ounces of silver per ton
Alaska	-	-	-	-	-	-	7,604	0.393
Arizona	474	0.222	74,516	0.192	13,551	2.804	72,034,837	0.055
California	408	0.642	1,660	2.180	8	20.750	15	4.200
Colorado	2,520	1.036	1,000	5.611	150,478	0.216	2,109	21.625
Idaho	254	0.307	a/	100.000	704,741	17.224	60,887	0.058
Kentucky	-	-	-	-	-	-	-	-
Michigan	-	-	-	-	-	-	4,979,585	0.061
Montana	239	0.766	3,641	2.995	17,857	4.257	9,014,687	0.202
Nevada	325,339	0.018	-	-	1,460	5.329	6,425,161	0.037
New Mexico	-	-	37,343	0.648	472	.051	4,446,994	0.011
New York	-	-	-	-	-	-	-	-
South Dakota	1,896,311	0.064	-	-	-	-	-	-
Tennessee	-	-	-	-	-	-	-	-
Utah	-	-	39,060	1.239	15,806	0.878	20,864,484	0.084
Other States b/	88,995	2.746	-	-	15	20.133	178,040	0.042
Total	2,314,540	0.162	157,220	0.681	904,388	13.608	118,014,403	0.070

TABLE IV-7 (concluded)

State	Lead		Zinc		Lead-zinc, copper-zinc, and copper-lead-zinc		Total material	
	Short tons	Average ounces of silver	Short tons	Average ounces of silver per ton	Short tons	Average ounces of silver	Short tons	Average ounces of silver per ton
Alaska	-	-	-	-	-	-	7,604	0.393
Arizona	1,451	3.474	69,686	0.462	291,927	1.716	72,486,442	0.063
California	3,620	18.771	-	-	7,860	6.335	13,571	10.502c/
Colorado	1,302	4.690	223,057	0.834	792,227	1.942	1,172,693	1.550
Idaho	239,424	11.917	91,537	0.753	676,589	2.910	1,773,432	9.605
Kentucky	-	-	-	-	-	-	83,575d/	0.007
Michigan	-	-	-	-	-	-	4,979,585	0.061
Montana	4,107	5.582	51,852	2.656	211	7.844	9,092,594	0.227
Nevada	252	26.639	904	0.919	288,509	1.347	6,981,625	0.081
New Mexico	5	2.400	272,058	0.276	44,042	0.248	4,800,914	0.033
New York	-	-	-	-	629,901	0.049	629,901	0.049
South Dakota	-	-	-	-	-	-	1,896,311	0.064
Tennessee	-	-	-	-	1,605,590	0.081	1,605,590	0.081
Utah	253	11.316	16,176	0.197	570,960	5.330	21,506,739	0.227e/
Other States b/	-	-	583,809	0.016	292,628	0.034	1,680,067e/	0.167
Total	250,414	11.839	1,309,079	0.392	5,140,444	1.477	128,710,643	0.250

a/ Less than 1/2 unit.
b/ Includes Oklahoma, Oregon, Pennsylvania, and Washington.
c/ Includes by-product silver recovered from tungsten ore.
d/ Includes by-product silver recovered from uranium ore.
e/ Includes magnetite-pyrite ore from Pennsylvania.

117

TABLE IV-8

PRODUCTION OF SILVER IN THE UNITED STATES, BY SOURCES
1963-1972 1,3,5,8,9,10/

(Thousands of Troy Ounces)

Year	Placers	Dry and Siliceous Ores	Copper Ores	Lead Ores	Zinc Ores	Other a/	Total
1963	18	11,725	10,203	3,802	1,620	7,873	35,242
1964	11	11,746	11,382	5,458		7,737	36,334
1965	8	13,855	12,707	5,342		7,394	39,806
1966	7	14,535	13,130	5,949		10,481	43,669
1967	5	12,504	8,221	3,428		7,959	32,119
1968	3	13,018	9,443	2,964		7,302	32,729
1969	2	15,328	13,588	5,156	273	7,559	41,906
1970	3	15,067	16,022	2,581	46	11,286	45,006
1971	1.1	15,573	13,175	5,825	25	6,965	41,564
1972	0.7	9,230	11,918	5,237	158	10,690	37,233

a/ Includes complex ores, chiefly lead-copper ores.

TABLE IV-9

SILVER PRODUCED IN THE UNITED STATES FROM ORE, OLD TAILINGS, ETC., IN 1972, BY STATE AND METHOD OF RECOVERY, IN TERMS OF RECOVERABLE METAL 5/

| State | Total ore, old tailings etc., treated a/ b/ (thousand short tons) | Ore and old tailings to mills | | | | Crude ore, old tailings, etc., to smelters a/ | |
| | | Recoverable in bullion | | Concentrates smelted and recoverable metal | | | |
		Amalgamation (troy ounces)	Cyanidation (troy ounces)	Concentrates (thousand short tons)	Troy ounces	Thousand short tons	Troy ounces
Alaska	-	-	-	-	-	-	-
Arizona	166.029	165,578	1,050	-	3,296,309	6,507,572	451	145,228
California	18	15	1,440	-	5,056	135,722	3	38,447
Colorado	1,277	1,269	-	-	191,127	3,652,740	8	9,488
Idaho	1,394	1,392	-	-	170,319	14,234,953	2	15,772
Michigan	8,291	8,291	-	-	231,061	785,100	-	-
Missouri	8,486	8,486	-	-	841,174	1,971,530	-	-
Montana	17,201	17,099	-	-	366,990	3,049,841	102	275,211
Nevada	21,336	21,282	-	-	350,804	589,626	54	5,725
New Mexico	20,236	20,127	-	-	702,000	1,004,227	109	12,653
South Dakota	1,467	1,467	-	99,992	-	-	-	-
Utah	36,006	35,846	-	-	852,052	4,096,591	160	203,013
Other States c/	7,019	7,019	-	-	444,080	393,965	d/	2,336
Total	288,760	287,871	2,490	99,992	7,450,972	36,421,867	889	707,873

a/ Includes some nonsilver-bearing ore not separable.
b/ Excludes tonnage of fluorspar and tungsten ores from which silver was recovered as a by-product.
c/ Includes Illinois, Maine, New York, Oklahoma, Oregon, Tennessee, and Washington.
d/ Less than 1/2 unit.

119

TABLE IV-10

SILVER IMPORTS OF THE UNITED STATES (IN TROY OUNCES)[3/]

Country	In Ore and Base Bullion				In Refined Bullion			
	1968	1969	1970[a/]	1971[a/]	1968	1969	1970[b/]	1971[b/]
Canada	13,554,655	13,694,662	12,376,000	15,435,223	26,051,864	33,756,530	24,294,000	16,393,441
Mexico	1,428,922	911,968	992,000	1,206,174	8,916,219	2,657,595	4,269,000	1,986,130
Central America	3,725,452	3,753,084	3,237,000	2,864,756	215,477	99,870	591,000	447,365
Bolivia	1,102,049	514,803	322,000	215,124				
Chile	1,897,227	1,042,387	660,000		297,202			
Peru	4,520,280	9,046,417	8,009,000	8,615,032	1,286,146	2,179,530	3,223,000	4,100,913
Other South America	120,348	480,998	340,000	221,494	322		128,000	64,719
Belgium	86,424				555,272	536,354		45,011
France								158,281
Germany, Federal Republic	2,589	1,341			474	496		1,584
Switzerland		5,875			3,170			8,199
United Kingdom			427,000	895,273	3,379,446			
Other Europe	15,848	75,201	47,000	38,176	351,351	289,981	51,000	2,380
Asia	358,485	300,391	299,000	261,084	271,813	23,239	14,000	480,250
Australia and Oceania	1,266,682	1,589,380	1,769,000	1,026,073	266,213		1,000	
Republic of South Africa	707,181	464,438	768,000	472,881	328,254			
Totals	28,786,142	31,888,945	29,246,000	31,206,290	41,923,223	39,543,595	32,571,000	23,688,273

a/ Ore and concentrates.
b/ Bullion, doré, and precipitates.

120

TABLE IV-11

UNITED STATES EXPORTS OF SILVER (IN TROY OUNCES)[3,4]

Country	1964	1965	1966	1967	1968	1969	1970	1971	1972	1973
Canada	4,719,069	11,503,069	14,042,030	5,014,703	7,177,694	1,509,723	253,300	522,884	900,000	3,000,000
Mexico					10,046,606					
Colombia	5,363	51,895	21,799	50,582	29,347	36,319	30,464	17,959		1,000,000
France	15,480,548	1,793,344	7,129,343	7,681,270	9,160,989	1,888,284	1,202,007	1,500,537	4,600,000	
Germany, Federal Republic	10,612,523	532,046	4,378,467	4,490,800	827,119	667,146	752,089	1,615,175	4,200,000	2,000,000
Italy	3,276,689	40,771	2,940,810	321,614	310,518	429,691	1,462,860			
Switzerland	10,463,319	642,128	11,685,437	13,436,423	15,977,603	10,085,624	8,087,746	1,506,728	4,600,000	
United Kingdom	52,813,535	21,010,568	35,085,500	30,148,685	45,633,327	34,374,845	1,681,136	1,570,035	10,900,000	500,000
Japan	6,618,766	2,544,734	4,882,834	3,023,514	2,038,281	3,030,113	3,182,011	1,303,049		
Other Countries	2,728,683	1,009,253	5,003,044	4,236,333	11,484,154	5,934,782	586,928	460,060	4,400,000	6,000,000
Totals	106,718,495	39,127,835	85,169,264	68,403,924	102,631,638	57,956,527	17,238,541	8,496,427	29,600,000	12,500,000

121

TABLE IV-12

SILVER PRODUCED AT REFINERIES IN THE UNITED STATES BY SOURCE [5,7,8,9,10,17,18]
(Thousand Troy Ounces)

	1966[a]	1967[a]	1968[a]	1969[a]	1970[a]	1971[a]	1972[b]	1973[c]	1974[c]
From Concentrates and Ores:									
Domestic	48,358	30,268	42,052	13,769 [a]	49,451	37,242	38,366		60,697
Foreign	31,080	23,777	31,222	39,723 [d]	31,930	31,449	39,151		
Total	79,437	54,045	73,274	83,492 [d]	81,381	68,691	77,517 (73,215)	70,747	60,697
From Old Scrap [e]	36,629	33,534	57,466	79,798 [d]	56,044	30,075	31,090 (48,350)	47,452	73,239 [f]
From New Scrap	17,033	25,361	34,602	35,873 [d]	23,999	16,524	31,815 (57,100)	43,566	52,583
Total Production	133,100	112,940	165,342	199,163	161,424	115,290	140,423 (178,665)	161,765	186,519

[a]/ U.S. Bureau of Mines
[b]/ U.S. Bureau of Mines (Silver Institute)
[c]/ Silver Institute
[d]/ Revised
[e]/ Includes coin bullion purchased from GSA and refined to commercial grade silver. Also includes coins.
[f]/ Bureau of Mines estimate: 55 Million Troy Oz [19]/

TABLE IV-13

RETURNS OF SECONDARY MATERIALS (SCRAP)
FROM DOMESTIC SOURCES (1938-1966)
AND NET INDUSTRIAL CONSUMPTION (1956-1966) [1,16]/
(Millions of Ounces)

Year	Issued for Industrial Use	Assay Offices	Returns to Private Refiners and Dealers	Total Returns	Net Industrial Consumption
1938				18.4	
1939				25.0	
1940				22.6	
1941				20.4	
1942				30.0	
1943				44.1	
1944				56.2	
1945				58.4	
1946				36.6	
1947				27.9	
1948				23.9	
1949				22.7	
1950				45.3	
1951				46.7	
1952				25.0	
1953				19.4	
1954				18.6	
1955				22.1	
1956				30.0	
1957	Avg 135.8			38.3[a]/	
1958				36.0[a]/	Avg 96.8
1959				42.0[a]/	
1960				49.0[a]/	
1961	155.8			50.3	105.5
1962	180.8	2.2	68.2	70.4	110.4
1963	204.5	2.5	92.0	94.5	110.0
1964	196.6	3.5[b]	72.6	76.1	123.0
1965	198.0	2.8[b]	58.2	61.0	137.0
1966		2.5[b]	57.5	60.0	

---

[a]/ Includes secondary materials to monetary use, jewelry, plate, scrap film, and other forms of scrap.

[b]/ Does not include scrap resulting from coinage operations.

TABLE IV-14

SILVER CONSUMPTION AND SCRAP IN THE
ARTS AND INDUSTRY IN 1963[20]

Use	A. Estimated Net Consumption (millions of troy oz)	B. Estimated New and Old Scrap[a] (millions of troy oz)	(B/A x 100%)
Photography (scrap film, fix and bleach solutions)	33	30	91
Arts (sterling holloware, plate, jewelry, etc.)	25	20	80
Electrical (contacts, wire, batteries, electronic devices, etc.)	22	15	68
Industrial alloy (solders, brazing, and special alloys)	20	15	75
Miscellaneous (catalysts, chemicals, ceramics, special products, etc.)	10	15[b]	–
Total[c]	110	95	Average 86

a/ Charles River Associates, Inc., estimated that about 50% of purchased silver is recovered as primary scrap in the silver industry.[1]

b/ Includes silver in 1942-44 silver nickels processed for silver recovery by private refiners.

c/ Reported by Bureau of the Mint.

124

TABLE IV-15

PERCENTAGE OF TOTAL NET INDUSTRIAL CONSUMPTION
FOR SILVER END USES

	1972, %	Average 1966-1972, troy oz	1966-1972 Avg %
Electroplated ware	8.45	14,633,000	9.76
Sterling ware	18.0	25,544,000	17.04
Jewelry	3.23	4,726,000	3.16
Photographic materials	25.3	42,014,000	28.03
Dental and medical supplies	1.33	2,159,000	1.44
Mirrors	0.81	1,728,000	1.15
Brazing alloys and solders	8.09	14,831,000	9.88
Batteries	3.99	7,357,000	4.91
Contacts and conductors	24.1	30,055,000	20.05
Catalysts	2.27	3,154,000	2.10
Bearings	0.23	455,000	0.30
Miscellaneous	4.22	3,269,000	2.18
Total %	100.02		100.0

Total consumption:
      151,063,000   Avg 149,925,000[a]

---

[a] Excluding 699,000 troy oz for rocket nozzles in 1966.

TABLE IV-16

U.S. SILVER SUPPLY AND DEMAND, 1967-1972[5,7,8,9,10]
(Million Troy Ounces)

Supply	1967	1968	1969	1970	1971	1972
Imports	55.52	70.71	71.88	62.30	57.96	65.41
U.S. Mine Production	32.34	32.73	41.91	45.01	41.56	37.23
U.S. Secondary Production	58.90	92.07	94.47	80.04	46.60	62.91
Release from Treasury Stocks[a]	24.35	381.4[b]	108.4[c]	76.5[d]	2.47	2.28
Release from Industry Stocks[e]	-	-	-	-	24.81	32.88
Total Supply	390.26	576.91	316.66	263.85	173.40	200.71
Total Minus New Scrap	364.90	542.31	280.79	239.85	156.88	168.89

Demand	1967	1968	1969	1970	1971	1972
Exports	70.77	125.76	88.91	27.61	12.22	29.66
Coinage	43.85	36.83	19.41	.71	2.47	2.28
U.S. Industrial Sales	171.03	145.29	141.55	128.40	129.15	151.06
Build-up of Industry Stocks	26.11	83.00	32.43	11.35	-	-
Total Demand	311.76	390.88	282.30	168.07	143.84	183.00
Difference: Supply Minus Demand	78.50	186.03	34.36	95.78	29.56	17.71
Difference: Supply Minus New Scrap Minus Demand	53.14	151.43	-1.51	71.78	13.04	-14.11

a/ Treasury stocks comprise bullion, coin bars, and coinage metal fund silver. The values exclude silver in silver dollars. Treasury releases have included GSA sales, redemption for silver certificates, sales and transfers to other government agencies, and newly minted coins.

b/ The value cannot be reliably calculated from Minerals Yearbook data for year-end holdings. In 1968, Handy and Harman reported Treasury disbursements of 381.4 million troy oz, which can only be accounted for by increased supply within the Treasury. The Coinage Withdrawal Act added 238.2 million troy oz to Treasury free reserves in 1968.

c/ Because of the discrepancy between Bureau of Mines' and Handy and Harman's data for the year-end stocks in 1968 (256 and 210 million troy oz, respectively), the 1969 disbursement values also do not agree. See Table IV-18.

d/ Of the 165 million troy oz silver transferred to the Strategic Stockpile in 1968, 25.5 million troy oz came back to the Treasury, earmarked for coinage use. This amount was considered in calculating the 1970 release.

e/ Industry stocks comprise refiners', fabricators', and dealers' stocks; stocks in COMEX (New York Commodity Exchange) warehouses; and silver registered to the Chicago Board of Trade.

TABLE IV-17

COMPARISON OF BUREAU OF MINES DOMESTIC REFINING AND MINE PRODUCTION STATISTICS

	Domestic Refining Concentrates and Ores (million troy oz)	Domestic Mine Production (million troy oz)	Difference (million troy oz)
1967	30.27	32.34	- 2.07
1968	42.05	32.73	+ 9.32
1969	43.77	41.91	+ 1.86
1970	49.45	45.01	+ 4.44
1971	37.24	41.56	- 4.32
1972	38.37	37.23	+ 1.14
Total	241.15	230.78	+10.37
Yearly Average	40.19	38.46	+ 1.73

127

TABLE IV-18

COMPOSITION OF TREASURY SILVER
(December 31, 1961 - December 31, 1973)[1,12,13,21-23]

	Monetized Stock	Free Reserves	Total	Treasury Release
1961	1,807.0	24.5	1,831.5	
1962	1,712.3	15.8	1,728.1	103.4
1963	1,545.2	9.3	1,554.6	173.5
1964	1,042.2	150.3	1,192.6	362.0
1965	531.7	271.8	803.6	389.0
1966	440.0	154.3	594.3	209.3
1967	289.0	61.8	350.8	243.5
1968[a]			(207.6[b]) 209.9	381.4
1969			101.5	108.4
1970			50.5[c]	76.5
1971			(48.0)	2.5
1972			45.8	2.2
1973			44.3	1.5

a/ Of 188.0 million troy oz remaining on June 24, 1968, 165 million troy
oz was transferred to the Strategic Stockpile and the rest went into
free reserves. Also added to free reserves between 1967 and December
31, 1968 was 238.2 million troy oz silver obtained by the Coinage
Withdrawal Act.[1]

b/ Calculated: 350.8 + 238.2 - 381.4. The value in The Silver Market 1968[2]
is 209.9 million troy oz.

c/ Includes 25.5 million troy oz transferred back to Treasury from Strategic
Stockpile.

TABLE IV-19

1965 ESTIMATE OF SILVER IN ORE DEPOSITS OF THE UNITED STATES [1/]

(Thousands of Ounces)

Predominant Metal in Ore Deposits	Silver Reserves [a/]			Potential Silver Resources [b/]		
	Measured	Indicated	Inferred	Measured	Indicated	Inferred
Straight Silver	52,700	133,000	85,000			
Gold	5,300		4,000			
Tungsten or Iron	700		630			
Total	58,700		89,630			
Copper	203,500		270,000	9,440	16,020	142,000
Lead	10,750	29,980	21,100	250	1,050	15,170
Zinc	100	120	300		100	580
Copper-Zinc	1,610	5,260	640		410	730
Lead-Zinc	11,200	34,800	81,000	1,590	14,000	93,700
Lead-Silver	14,960	15,520	35,000		1,510	1,500
Silver-Lead	60,470	1,370	24,500			
Zinc-Copper	20	1,920	1,670	280	2,660	15,000
Zinc-Lead	43,810	77,470	115,000	1,080	53,480	126,000
Total	346,420	299,440	549,210	12,640	89,230	394,680

Total all Reserves and Potential Resources:

Measured and Indicated: 806,430
Inferred: 1,033,520
1,839,950

a/ "Ore reserves" are those deposits that can be mined, recovered, and marketed at a profit at the time the estimate is made.

b/ "Potential resources" are those deposits that may become exploitable when economic conditions are more favorable or when more economic production methods are available. Reserves and potential resources are classified by the amount and type of exploration on which the estimate is based as measured, indicated, and inferred in descending order.

TABLE IV-20

FORECAST FOR SILVER USE, YEAR 2000 [14]/

	1968 Demand	Demand in Year 2000
	(million troy oz)	
Silverware and plated ware	44	40-80
Jewelry, precious metals	4	5-10
Photographic equipment and supplies	42	100-180
Industrial refrigeration	8	25-40
Coinage	37	-
Household appliances	10	25-50
Primary batteries, dry and wet	6	10-30
Switchgear, switchboard apparatus	15	30-70
Electronic components and accessories	8	25-60
Other	8	20-40
		280-560 (Median 420)

Table IV-21

COMPARISON OF U.S. INDUSTRIAL SILVER CONSUMPTION IN 1928 AND 1971

	Consumption 1928 [50/a/]		Consumption 1971 [10/]		1971/1928
	Troy oz	%	Troy oz	%	Ratio
Sterling	9,429,922	36.4	22,729,000	17.61	2.4
Mirrors			1,112,000	0.86	
Photography	6,560,812	25.4	36,073,000	27.94	5.5
Electroplating	3,840,519	14.9	10,909,000	8.45	2.8
Chemical	1,537,890	6.0			
Jewelry, optical goods, and novelties	2,211,465	8.6	3,447,000	2.68	1.6
Electrical and Electronic			33,585,000	26.02	
Industrials including Silver Solder	1,699,399	6.6			
Brazing Alloys			12,085,000	9.39	
Dental	501,802	1.9	1,485,000	1.15	3.0
Miscellaneous	5,950	0.0	7,721,000[b/]	5.98	
Estimated Losses	38,795	___	_____	_____	
Total	25,787,759	99.8	129,146,000	100.08	
Scrap sent to smelters and refiners	11,412,129				
Total silver turnover	37,238,683				

---

a/ The 1928 figures were adjusted by deducting scrap. The 1971 figures are unadjusted.

b/ Includes catalysts and bearings.

TABLE IV-22

ALTERNATE MATERIALS FOR SILVER[14/]

Silver Use	Substitute	Remarks on Substitute
Photographic paper in office copy work	Xerography	
Flatware and hollowware	stainless steel	Large part of the market for tableware
Reflectors	Al and Rh	Inferior to Ag
Surgical plates, sutures, and pins	Ta	
Coinage	Cupronickel and Ni	Only special minted dollars in U.S. still contain Ag

TABLE IV-23

1973 PHOTOGRAPHIC INDUSTRY SALES[47/]

$ Million Consumed	% Increase over 1972	Use
2,250	10.5	Film, plate, paper, and cloth with Ag halides
4,800	16	Photographic equipment and supplies (economy as whole: 10%)
1,154	15 (over 1971)	Photofinishing
4,876	15 (over 1971)	Offset printing

BIBLIOGRAPHY. SECTION IV.

1. Charles River Associates, Inc., Economic Analysis of the Silver Industry,
    prepared for Property Management and Disposal Service, General Services
    Administration, Clearinghouse for Federal Scientific and Technical
    Information, Springfield, Virginia, 1969.

2. Anonymous, "Mined Silver Output Expected to Gain 22.5% in Four Years,"
    Am. Metal Market, 81 (118), 3 (1974).

3. American Bureau of Metal Statistics, Year Book of the American Bureau
    of Metal Statistics, 51st Annual Issue for the Year 1971, American
    Bureau of Metal Statistics, New York, New York, 1972.

4. Handy and Harman, The Silver Market 1973, 58th Annual Review, Handy
    and Harman, Inc., New York, New York, 1974.

5. Welch, J. R., "Silver," in Minerals Yearbook 1972, Vol. I, Metals,
    Minerals, and Fuels, Bureau of Mines, U.S. Department of the Interior,
    U.S. Government Printing Office, Washington, D.C., 1974, pp. 1129-
    1142.

6. Carabini, L. E., The Case for Silver. How to Protect Your Assets
    Against Inflation, 2nd ed., Pacific Coast Coin Exchange--A Division
    of Monex International, Ltd., Los Angeles, California, 1974.

7. Ryan, J. P., "Silver," in Minerals Yearbook 1967, Vol. I-II, Metals,
    Minerals, and Fuels, Bureau of Mines, U.S. Department of the Interior,
    U.S. Government Printing Office, Washington, D.C., 1968, pp. 1037-
    1056.

8. Hoyt, C. D., "Silver," in Minerals Yearbook 1969, Vol. I, Metals,
    Minerals, and Fuels, Bureau of Mines, U.S. Department of the Interior,
    U.S. Government Printing Office, Washington, D.C., 1971, pp. 997-1011.

9. West, J. M., "Silver," in Minerals Yearbook 1970, Vol. I, Metals,
    Minerals, and Fuels, Bureau of Mines, U.S. Department of the
    Interior, U.S. Government Printing Office, Washington, D.C., 1972,
    pp. 1013-1029.

10. Welch, J. R., "Silver," in Minerals Yearbook 1971, Vol. I, Metals,
    Minerals, and Fuels, Bureau of Mines, U.S. Department of the
    Interior, U.S. Government Printing Office, Washington, D.C., 1973,
    pp. 1073-1086.

133

11. Coyne, H. J., "New Keys to Silver Market Analysis," Scrap Age, 28 (5), 59-66, 84 (1971).

12. Handy and Harman, The Silver Market 1970, 55th Annual Review, Handy and Harman, Inc., New York, New York, 1971.

13. Handy and Harman, The Silver Market 1972, 57th Annual Review, Handy and Harman, Inc., New York, New York, 1973.

14. Ageton, R. W., "Silver," in Minerals Facts and Problems, Bureau of Mines Bulletin 650, U.S. Department of the Interior, U.S. Government Printing Office, Washington, D.C., 1970, pp. 723-737.

15. American Metal Market, Metal Statistics 1972, Fairchild Publications, Inc., New York, New York, 1972.

16. Ryan, J. P., "Silver," in Minerals Yearbook 1965, Vol. I, Metals, Minerals, and Fuels, Bureau of Mines, U.S. Department of the Interior, U.S. Government Printing Office, Washington, D.C., 1967, pp. 829-850.

17. Anonymous, "1973 U.S. Silver Refining Statistics," The Silver Institute Letter, 4 (1), 4 (1974).

18. Anonymous, "Latest U.S. Silver Refining Statistics," The Silver Institute Letter, 5 (1), 4 (1975).

19. Anonymous, "Silver Price Expected Below $4.71 Average of 1974: Frankland," Am. Metal Market, 82 (14), 8 (1975).

20. Schack, C. H., and B. H. Clemmons, "Chapter 4. Extractive Processes," in Silver. Economics, Metallurgy, and Use, A. Butts and C. D. Coxe, Eds., D. Van Nostrand Company, Inc., Princeton, New Jersey, 1967, pp. 57-77.

21. Handy and Harman, The Silver Market 1968, 53rd Annual Review, Handy and Harman, Inc., New York, New York, 1969.

22. Handy and Harman, The Silver Market 1969, 54th Annual Review, Handy and Harman, Inc., New York, New York, 1970.

23. Handy and Harman, The Silver Market 1971, 56th Annual Review, Handy and Harman, Inc., New York, New York, 1972.

24. Anonymous, "World Silver Production Rises," The Silver Institute Letter, 4 (6), 1,2 (1974).

25. Anonymous, "Thompson Urges Conserving, Substitutes as Remedies for World Silver Shortage," Am. Metal Market, 81 (183), 2 (1974).

26. Anonymous, "Anaconda Plans to Close Down Its Underground Copper Mine," Chem. Marketing Reporter, 206 (23), 3, 32 (1974).

27. Wood, J., "Financial, Environmental Reasons Cited by Anaconda for Closing of Butte Mine," Am. Metal Market, 81 (230), 2, 13 (1974).

28. Anonymous, "Anaconda Makes New Montana Cutback," Am. Metal Market, 82 (36), 5 (1975).

29. Anonymous, "Predicted PD Mine Closing Now Real," Am. Metal Market, 81 (233), 29 (1974).

30. Anonymous, "Soaring Prices Put Damper on Silver Use," Chem. Eng. News, 52 (26), 7-8 (1974).

31. Ricter, R., "Coins, Drawn Out by Silver Tags, Called Recovery Source," Am. Metal Market, 81 (116), 2 (1974).

32. Ruth, J., "Forum Told Silver Market May Slip Occasionally, But Metal's Overall Appeal Not Likely to Tarnish. Shishko Sees No Silver Price Drop," Am. Metal Market, 81 (115), 1, 17 (1974).

33. Miller, R., "H & H Chief: Key Silver Markets Show No Sign of Snapping Slump," Am. Metal Market, 82 (31), 1, 7 (1975).

34. Booz-Allen Applied Research, Inc., A Study of Hazardous Waste Materials, Hazardous Effects and Disposal Methods. Vol. II, PB-221, No. 466, U.S. Environmental Protection Agency, National Technical Information Service, Springfield, Virginia, p. 466 , 1973 .

35. Anonymous, "European Observers See Prices Continuing to Decline," Am. Metal Market/Metalworking News, 81 (166), 37 (1974).

36. Miller, R., "Silverware Makers: Metal's Cost Cutting Piece Sales One-Third," Am. Metal Market, 81 (213), 6 (1974).

37. Anonymous, "International Silver Co. to Market $14-Million Worth of Its Inventory," Am. Metal Market, 81 (232), 10 (1974).

38. Adams, C., "Forum Told Silver Market May Slip Occasionally, But Metal's Overall Appeal Not Likely to Tarnish. Silver Use in Electrical Devices Down," Am. Metal Market, 81 (115), 1, 17 (1974).

39. Miller, R., "Silver Market Not Expected to Gleam until Gold's Shining Hour on December 31," _Am. Metal Market_, 81 (230), 9 (1974).

40. Anonymous, "1974 Developments Forecast Future for Silver," _The Silver Institute Letter_, 5 (1), 3 (1975).

41. Anonymous, "Fuel Cell with Silver Makes Direct Electric Power," _The Silver Institute Letter_, 4 (4), 2 (1974).

42. Anonymous, _A Guide to Silver Coin Futures Trading. United States. Canada_, International Monetary Market of the Chicago Mercantile Exchange, Chicago, Illinois, 1973.

43. Anonymous, "Photopolymers Will Challenge Silver-Sensitive Film Mart," _Am. Metal Market_, 81 (116), 1, 12 (1974).

44. Anonymous, "Wingate Says Photopolymers Behind Silver," _Am. Metal Market_, 81 (115), 17 (1974).

45. Anonymous, "X-Rays: A New Look," _Newsweek_, 83 (12), 63 (1974).

46. O'Neil, C., "Silver Industry Warned High Prices May Dull Demand," _Am. Metal Market/Metalworking News_, 81 (53), 31 (1974).

47. Anonymous, "Photographic Industry is Growing," _The Silver Institute Letter_, 4 (4), 3 (1974).

48. Handy and Harman, _The Silver Market 1974_, 59th Annual Review, Handy and Harman, Inc., New York, New York, 1975.

49. Miller, R., "Economic Squeeze Has Negative Effect on Consumption of Photographic Silver," _Am. Metal Market_, 82 (6), 6 (1975).

50. Addicks, L., "Chapter 19. The Statistics of Industrial Consumption," in _Silver in Industry_, L. Addicks, Ed., Reinhold Publishing Company, New York, New York, 1940.

V. PRIMARY AND SECONDARY SILVER RECOVERY PROCESSES

Nearly all commercially produced silver is found associated
with other metals and is produced either as the principal metal of the
ore or as a co-product. In this section, silver is followed from the
mining, milling, and smelting of various silver and silver base-metal
ores to the refining of pure silver. Silver recovery from used silver
products, wastewaters, and photographic and plating wastes is also discussed in this section as well as the disposal of wastes from mining,
milling, and smelting.

A. Mining

Silver and silver-containing ore are obtained by open-pit and
underground mining. Open-pit mining is used when minerals of interest
lie near the surface. Overburden is first removed, leaving the excava-
tion open to the surface. Mining the ore body involves drilling, blasting, loading, and hauling the ore to a mill for processing. Underground
mining is conducted on several levels using stope and pillar methods with
drilling and blasting. The broken ore is raised by hoist and transported
to a mill.

1. Copper ores: The current production of copper ore mined
in the U.S. is 335 million short tons. About 80% of the copper ore has
only a low concentration of copper (0.7 to 1.0%) and silver (0.05 to
0.1 troy oz/ton). The chief regions responsible for by-product silver
from copper ores are Arizona, Montana, New Mexico, Utah, and the Keweenaw
District in Michigan.

Copper is mined by open-pit, underground, or in situ methods.
In open-pit mining, the ore body, comprising disseminated porphyry ore,
host granit porphyry, and mineralized quartzitic rock, is broken up by
drilling and blasting. The ore is loaded by electric shovels into ore
cars or trucks and hauled to the mill for processing. If the copper,
gold, silver, and silica content is high enough, the ore can be shipped
directly to the smelter.[1,2]

2. Silver ores: Silver ores, including those silver-lead ores
containing less than 5% lead, are mined by a variety of underground methods.[3] The methods used for mining silver deposits as well as those for
silver-containing base-metal ores depend on the size, shape, attitude,
and depth of each deposit.[4]

137

The Coeur d'Alene mining district, Idaho, most important domestic silver-producing area in the U.S., is characterized by a steep
terrain. Access to the ore bodies is by adits (horizontal tunnels)
with development in the ore by winzes (short access shafts descending
vertically) or raises (shafts ascending vertically). Mining is almost
exclusively by horizontal slice cut and hydraulic fill stoping. Sand
fill, rock bolting, and various techniques are used to minimize rock
bursts. Development drifts are driven on the veins or, in some mines,
laterals are driven parallel to the vein with crosscuts at regular in-
tervals. It is common practice to hoist from ore pockets below each
working level.[4]

3. <u>Gold ores</u>: Silver, always associated with gold to some
degree in nature, is usually recovered as a by-product in the refining
of gold. However, it is possible with some ores to practice "selective
mining," wherein ore and waste are separated in the actual mining processes. Waste is differentiated from ore by sampling and assaying, and
separated by use of screens, grizzlies, ore washers, and picking belts.

Methods of mining vary considerably and are based on such factors as size and shape of the deposit, physical and mineralogical char-
acter of the ore and surrounding rock, and depth of the deposit. Placer
mining, used for surface or near-surface deposits, involves excavating
and delivering gold-bearing gravel to a washing plant for recovering the
gold it contains. Other methods of placer mining include hydraulic mining, dredging, and drift mining of buried placers too deep to strip.
Lode or vein deposits are mined through shafts or adits, developments on
levels, and the breaking and removal of ore in stopes.

The Homestake Mine in Lead, South Dakota, is the largest domestic producer of gold, practicing cut-and-fill stoping mining methods.
They fill voids caused from mining by hydraulic sand fill, with the addition of cement to top off the fill in the stopes.

Low-grade gold deposits that can be mined by open-pit methods
have recently been developed in the U.S. At the Carlin mine, Eureka,
Nevada, and near Cortez, Nevada, gold occurring in submicron particles
in siltstone and silty dolomitic limestones is mined by trucks and shovels
from 20-ft benches drilled by hammer or rotary drills.[5]

4. <u>Lead ores</u>: Some lead (and zinc) deposits are mined by open-
pit methods in the Tri-State district (Missouri, Kansas, and Oklahoma) and
Washington, but are generally mined by underground methods employing either
open or supported stopes.[6]

138

The methods of underground stoping include timber stoping, cut-and-fill, shrinkage, room-and-pillar, and block caving. Open stoping involves drilling holes up to 150 ft long to facilitate blastings of very large ore tonnage. Shrinkage, cut-and-fill, or square set stoping allow better metal recovery from high-grade ores.[3]

Many ore bodies are characterized by high-back, single-level mines, which are well suited to mechanization. The equipment used includes power shovels, scrapers, and mucking machines for loading. Transportation by motorized trains operating on heavy-gage tracks and trackless mining, which utilizes electric or diesel powered units, are in widespread usage in the lead and lead-zinc mines of Washington, the Tri-State district, the Upper Mississippi Valley, and southeast Missouri. Lightweight percussive and rotary percussive drilling machines with higher efficiencies and metallized explosives are used to disintegrate the ore.[6]

5. Copper-lead-zinc ores: The complex copper-lead-zinc ores are the third largest source of primary by-product silver. The New Lead Belt in southeast Missouri, and the Leadville district, Colorado, recover appreciable amounts of silver as a result of mining their copper-lead-zinc composite ore bodies. The ores are mined from veins filling fractured zones or as replacement deposits in favorable host rocks.[2]

6. Lead-silver ores: Approximately, 12% of the domestic silver production is from lead-silver ores containing an average of 16 troy oz silver per ton and 12% lead.[2] (See Subsections V.A.2 and V.A. 4.)

7. Zinc ores: Zinc ores provide approximately 4% of the domestic primary silver production. Mining is done in the Balmat-Edwards district, New York; Lehigh County, Pennsylvania; and the Mascott-Jefferson City district, Tennessee. The Bureau of Mines reports that Colorado zinc mines also produce silver (about one-fifth of the silver production from zinc ores in 1972).[7]

The underground mining methods include open shrinkage, cut-and-fill, square-set stoping, and open stope and pillar (breast stopes).[2,8] (See Subsection V.A.4.)

B. Milling

According to Bureau of Mines Circular 8206,[1] milling is the upgrading of raw ores to produce a more valuable product by ore dressing or hydrometallurgy. Ore dressing is concentration or beneficiation by physical separation and hydrometallurgy is treatment by leaching or solvent extraction.

Most silver-bearing material is milled, although ore containing more than 20% lead or copper ore with a content of copper, gold, silver, and silica high enough to be profitable can be smelted directly. Extremely low-grade dry ore containing sufficient silica can be used by copper smelters as a flux.[1,3] The major milling method for silver-containing ores is flotation. Other milling methods include amalgamation; cyanidation; leaching of oxidized copper ores; copper segregation; solvent extration; the sink-float and other gravity processes; and magnetic concentration of zinc ores.[1]

The extractive metallurgy of silver is essentially that of copper, lead, and zinc extraction with silver following these metals through the concentrating and smelting processes. The occurrence of silver in high concentrations, independently of these base metals, was once sufficiently widespread to support broad use of direct treatment by cyanidation or amalgamation, processes now used mainly on gold ores. Today less than 1% of the domestic silver and gold-silver ores are treated by the processes of amalgamation or cyanidation to recover silver.[2] The amounts of silver produced in the U.S. at amalgamation and cyanidation mills from 1956 to 1972 are compared with the amounts of silver recoverable by smelting and from placers in Table V-1.

A process of historic interest was the Patio process in which silver minerals were first ground and then treated with salt, copper sulfate, and mercury; mixing and milling were accomplished by driving mules over the flat heap. The silver amalgamated with the mercury and was recovered by retorting the amalgam. Table V-2 outlines the metallurgical history of silver processing.

The minor methods of milling silver-bearing materials are described below followed by a description of flotation, the major milling method.

     1. Amalgamation: The major steps in the amalgamation process are:

     • Grinding (amalgamation is done at as coarse a size as possible).

     • Screening.

     • Beneficiation of fines by gravity to recover a precious-metal-bearing black-sand concentrate.

• Reprocessing of initial concentrate by gravity or, less often, by flotation.

• Usually, amalgamation of the final black-sand concentrate by batch in a barrel amalgamator. (Interfering chemical or greasy films are first removed by grinding, scouring by attrition, and leaching.)

• Recovery:

a. Grinding the amalgam with water to loosen and free entrapped solid impurities; (these are wiped, skimmed, or magnetically removed).

b. Squeezing the amalgam through heavy canvas to remove excess mercury. Often the amalgam is dried by heating in hot water prior to pressing.

c. Retorting pressed dry amalgam (30 to 60% mercury) in cast iron pots or cylinders.

d. After distillation, heating the retort to a bright red heat and then cooling. The sponge residue contains 1 to 2% mercury and other metal impurities. It is mixed with fluxes and melted to give molten gold-silver bullion, which is poured into bars.

Of the free-milling gold-silver ores (about 200,000 troy oz silver per year in 1965), 90% are lode-gold ores, chiefly from the Homestake Mine in South Dakota. Placer gold in Alaska and the western states contribute the other 10%. Silver present in placer ores is usually marketed as gold-silver bullion. Placer gold contains little alloyed silver and is easier to amalgamate than lode gold.[2]/

2. Cyanidation: A process flowsheet for a typical silver cyanidation operation is shown in Figure V-1. In the classifier, 85% of the slime is 150 mesh particulate size with a solution/solid ratio of 2.5:1. At the bullion stage, the cyanidation process provides for a 92-93% overall recovery of the silver in the original ore.

The chemical reactions involved in cyanidation are:

$$2AgCN + 4NaCN + 1/2O_2 + H_2O \longrightarrow 2NaAg(CN)_2 + 2NaOH$$

$$2NaAg(CN)_2 + Zn \longrightarrow Na_2Zn(CN)_4 + 2Ag$$

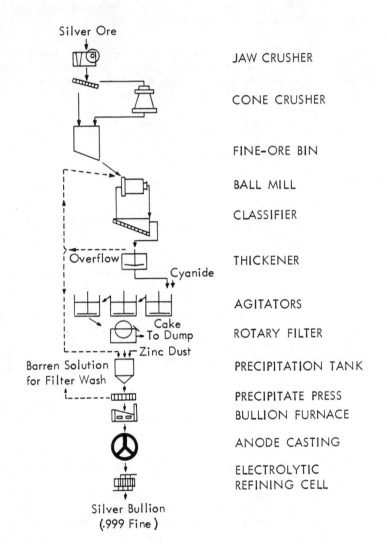

Figure V-1 - Silver Cyanidation Flow Sheet[9/]

Theoretically, about twice as much cyanide is needed for silver (0.2-0.4%) as for gold (0.03-0.1%) and twice as much zinc is needed for precipitation because silver dissolves more slowly.[9] To eliminate cyanicides, refractory ores require roasting, sometimes with water leaching or acid leaching. Ores containing gold and silver as tellurides and sulfides or locked-in pyrite, arsenopyrite, and pyrrhotite must be roasted to facilitate dissolution in cyanide solutions. After very fine grinding, some pyritic ores are leached prior to cyanidation.[1]

Reference 10 describes modern silver cyanidation practice. Homestake Mining Company treats sand and slime products by cyanidation after amalgamation. Knob Hill Mines, Inc., of Republic, Washington, recovers 92.5% of the silver in the gold-silver ore by flotation and cyanidation. (The cyanide precipitate is combined with the base metal sulfide flotation concentrate.) The San Manuel Division of Magma Copper Company, near Tucson, recovers gold and silver from a molybdenum concentrate by cyanidation.

3. Copper leaching: Silver and other valuable by-products of copper smelting are not intentionally recovered when copper oxide minerals and the low-grade sulfides are leached in heaps, vats, or in place with weak or strong sulfuric acid solutions or mixtures of sulfuric acid and ferric sulfate.[1,11/a] Although copper leaching does not constitute a silver recovery process, it does pose a potential threat of contamination to local municipal water and groundwater supplies. The presence of ferric ion may enhance the solubility of silver in the leaching solutions, pushing the equilibrium of the reaction $Ag + Fe^{3+} \rightleftharpoons Fe^{2+} + Ag^+$ to the right.[b] Since a much smaller proportion of the original silver will be leached compared with the proportion of copper recovered, the leached residues will be enriched in silver.

Copper is usually recovered from leach solutions by cementation on scrap iron, e.g., cans. The reactions with respect to copper are:

---

a/ Ferric sulfate is not added since iron minerals are in the ore and bacteria, patented as leaching aids, will produce both ferric sulfate and sulfuric acid.[11]

b/ The ferric sulfate may also be reduced by the reaction $4Fe(SO_4)_3 + CuS + 4H_2O \longrightarrow 8FeSO_4 + CuSO_4 + 4H_2SO_4$.

$$Fe + CuSO_4 \longrightarrow Cu + FeSO_4 \text{ with the side reactions:}$$

$$H_2SO_4 + Fe \longrightarrow FeSO_4 + H_2$$

$$Fe_2(SO_4)_3 + Fe \longrightarrow 3FeSO_4$$

Any ionic silver in the leach solution probably will also be precipitated completely and may be ultimately recovered as a by-product of the cement copper. The loose adherent deposits of cement copper, containing 70 to 90% copper, are removed by washing and fed to reverberatory matte furnaces in smelters or beneficiated by physical and/or chemical processes to an acceptable grade of copper powder for copper metallurgy.[11]

Other methods of copper recovery include solvent extraction and electrowinning. In solvent extraction, leach solutions are contacted with small volumes of an organic solvent that selectively extracts copper into the organic phase. An aqueous stripping solution is added under acidic conditions so that copper enters the aqueous phase to give an electrolyzable solution containing at least 30 g copper/liter. Electrowinning involves depositing copper from leach solutions as cathodes of purity comparable with electrolytically refined copper. The cathodes produced are melted and cast into refinery shapes.[11] The likelihood of by-product silver recovery by these methods of copper recovery is less than with cementation.

Ammoniacal leaching of copper ores containing copper carbonates or native copper, once used in Alaska and the Lake Superior district, may have dissolved significant amounts of silver as $Ag(NH_3)_2^+$ as well as $Cu(NH_3)_4^{2+}$. Boiling the solutions to precipitate cupric oxide would also have precipitated hydrous silver oxide.

The various copper leaching processes are described briefly below:

a. <u>Heap leaching and leaching in place</u>: Very low-grade material is treated by heap leaching and leaching in place. Open-pit mining, while uncovering concentrating grade ores, produces low-grade sulfide or oxide-sulfide ores that are not economical to mill. Ore piles heaped in natural basins or underground are treated with circulating leaching solutions. An improved method of heap leaching insures that the leach solution is not lost by permeation into the ground. The leach solution drains to prepared reservoirs at the base of the pile and is pumped back to the distributing system and then to subsequent copper-recovery operations. Pregnant solutions which contain several grams of copper per liter as $CuSO_4$ are treated by cementation, solvent extraction, etc.

Leaching in place means that the leach solution and air (for oxidizing the sulfide minerals) are circulated intermittently through the depleted or low-grade deposits. The pregnant solution drains into tunnels cut beneath the deposit and is pumped to the surface for copper recovery, usually by cementation.[11]

b. Vat leaching: The concentration grade of mixed sulfide-oxide copper ores contains about 0.8 to 1.0% copper. The oxide minerals are only partly amenable to concentration and their loss in flotation may amount to as much as 50%. Special methods involving leaching are used to treat these ores: vat leaching or leach-precipitation-flotation.

In vat leaching, the crushed ore in concrete vats, whose floors serve as filters to permit the upward and downward flow of leach and wash solutions, is leached with 2 to 5% sulfuric acid solutions to recover 90 to 95% of the oxide copper present. Pregnant and wash solutions, containing copper sulfate, are treated by electrowinning, cementation, or solvent extraction. The leach residue is floated to recover sulfide copper.[11]

c. Leach-precipitation-flotation: This process, which includes dilute sulfuric acid leaching, cementation with sponge iron, and flotation of the leaching residues to recover copper sulfide,[11] will recover silver with the copper.

4. Leaching other ores: Silver refractory minerals are comprised chiefly of silver sulfide, argentojarosite, silver-containing iron oxide, and silver-bearing manganese carbonate-oxide minerals. Such deposits can be found in the Candelaria District of Nevada and the Round Mountain District of Colorado. The Bureau of Mines has developed a method for extracting 80 to 85% of the silver from these ores by leaching with sulfurous acid-sodium chloride, since cyanidation is deterred by mangano-argentojarosites $[Mn-Ag_2Fe_6(OH)_{12}(SO_4)_4]$, manganese oxides and carbonates, and by various oxidized and reduced iron minerals. The sulfurous acid (205-256 lb/ton of ore), conveniently made as a 6% solution by adding sulfur dioxide gas to water, dissolves the iron and manganese to liberate silver from the ore. A 20% sodium chloride solution provides chloride ligands for producing the soluble $AgCl_4^{3-}$ complex.[12]

5. The copper segregation process: The copper segregation process is practiced at the Lake Shore Mine near Casa Grande, Arizona, on ore containing too much iron, calcite, and clay for leaching. Crushed chrysocolla ore containing 2% copper, salt, and pulverized coal or coke are mixed and roasted at about 725°C in a gas-fired rotary kiln to give a calcine containing segregated copper agglomerate. Some silver may be

145

lost in this process as volatilized silver chloride. Calcines are reground and metallic copper is recovered by flotation. Concentrates contain 45 to 50% copper.[1]

6. Gravity concentration: Gravity concentration was used in the period 1860 to 1910. In 1911, flotation was introduced, followed by selective or differential flotation.

An example of ore washing or primitive gravity concentration is the agitation of placer gravels to separate the heavy valuable minerals from the lighter ones. Gravity milling continues in use, although mineral recovery may be lower. While concentrating tables are used for sands and jigs are used for coarser materials, the process is not efficient for finely ground ore. Sulfide and oxide minerals can be separated by simple gravity methods if the differences in the specific gravities of the ore and waste are significant; however, the specific gravity differences are not large enough for copper-iron-zinc ores. To avoid grinding the entire mill feed, gravity milling with flotation jigs and tables is economical for producing low-grade concentrate for later regrinding and flotation.

The sink-float method is used in milling silver containing lead-zinc ores in the Tri-State and Coeur d'Alene districts and the Old Dick copper-zinc mill in Arizona. The method uses a fluid medium of controlled density in which substances of density lower than that of the medium float and heavier substances sink. Commercial mediums include suspensions of quicksand or finely ground magnetite or ferrosilicon. Because the process is efficient on coarse particles, it is used between crushing and grinding.[1]

7. Flotation: Since the first domestic use of froth flotation in 1911, vast tonnages of formerly worthless sulfide-bearing rock have become exploitable sources of nearly all U.S. primary silver, copper, lead, and zinc.[2] At the present time, this is the major process for upgrading base-metal ores containing silver.

Most metal sulfides and many other minerals are wettable, but minerals such as sulfur, graphite, and molybdenite repel water. When air is introduced into a tank (flotation cell) containing finely ground ore in water (the pulp) and agitated, air bubbles become attached to nonwettable particles. Frothing agents are used to improve the stability of the air bubbles. The froth is skimmed and the wettable minerals are removed from the bottom.[2]

Appropriate conditioning agents can be added to the mill pulp to modify the mineral surface (rendering it wettable or nonwettable) so

that different minerals can be floated successively in several stages
to produce separate concentrates of each mineral.[1/]

Flotation agents for silver ores containing silver sulfide
include 15% P_2S_5 in cresylic acid or neutralized solutions; sodium sulfide; and thiocarbanilide solutions, e.g., 15% in hot o-toluidine.[13/]

The largest domestic silver producer is the Sunshine Mine of
the Coeur d'Alene district, Idaho. The silver ore contains about 24.9 oz
silver/ton in argentiferous tetrahedrite and the other sulfide minerals:
tetrahedrite, galena, pyrite, and arsenopyrite. The flotation products
are a concentrate of argentiferous tetrahedrite and a lead-iron concentrate containing 79.1% and 18.7% silver, respectively. The tailings
contain 2.2% silver. Since the recoveries of copper and silver are the
same in the different mill products, it is assumed that silver is chemically combined in the tetrahedrite. The silver concentrate, containing
20% copper, 17% antimony, and 1,115 oz silver/ton, is batch leached with
hot sodium sulfide solution to dissolve the antimony and leave an enriched
silver-copper residue, which is sold to a copper smelter. The lead-iron
concentrate, containing 10% lead and 150 oz silver/ton, is sold to a
lead smelter.[2/]

The silver by-product of copper production is almost entirely
from the low-grade, open-pit-mined ore in Arizona, Utah, Montana,
Nevada, and New Mexico. The largest domestic unit for milling porphyry
copper ores is the Utah Copper Division of Kennecott Copper Corporation.
The Arthur and Magna Mills process 45,000 tons of ore per day. Froth
flotation of an ore containing 0.78% copper and 0.09 troy oz silver/ton
gives a copper concentrate containing 91% of the silver; 9% of the
silver reports in the tailings. The milling process comprises crushing,
grinding, and thickening the pulp to 30% solids. Copper and molybdenum
minerals are collected in rougher and scavenger flotation stages to prepare a tailing for discard.[2/] The rougher concentrate is retreated in
"cleaner" cells without additional flotation reagent.[11/] The cleaner tailing is returned to the rougher circuit and then refloated again to de-
press molybdenite and make a finished copper concentrate. The scavenger
concentrate, after cleaning, is combined with the molybdenum-rich tailing from the rougher copper concentrate. Both are thickened, filtered,
roasted, and repulped.[2/]

Michigan's copper-silver ores rank second to porphyry ores as
a source of by-product silver from copper ores. The largest company in
the Keweenaw district is White Pine Copper Company, which processed 15,000
tons ore/day in the 1960's. Milling of the ore, containing 0.5 troy oz
silver/ton, gives a copper concentrate for copper-silver alloy with 68%
of the silver reporting in it and a copper-silver concentrate, containing

15% of the silver, for separate recovery. Seventeen percent each of the silver and the copper is lost in the tailings.[2]

The Michigan ore comprises chalcocite (75% of the copper), native copper, native silver, and a gangue of shale and siltstone. Since chalcocite oxidizes rapidly during milling and oxide coatings cause sulfide minerals to act like oxides with respect to flotability, flotation is done rapidly to minimize oxidation of the chalcocite. Crushing, grinding, and floating the silver-copper ores give a fine-sized copper concentrate and a crude silver-copper concentrate that contains metallic silver and copper. Refloating the latter produces a tailing containing most of the copper. The froth concentrate is a copper-silver product that is separately smelted in batches. The bullion is processed electrolytically to recover silver.[1,2]

Complex sulfide ores containing two or more base metals are the third largest source of by-product primary silver. Lead-zinc ores predominate with copper-lead, copper-zinc, and lead-zinc-copper ores being less important. The ores, often associated with abundant pyrite, contain 7 to 10% total base metals and 1 to 5 troy oz silver/ton.[2]

Milling at the Bunker Hill Company, Kellogg, Idaho, is representative of most procedures for these ores. The ore comprises galena; sphalerite; argentiferous tetrahedrite; and the gangue minerals pyrite, quartz, siderite, and ankerite. Silver must be recovered with the lead and copper rather than with the zinc because of the low payment made for silver by zinc plants.[a] For an ore containing 4.6 troy oz silver/ton, 7.1% lead, and 2.5% zinc, 92.8% of the silver reports in the lead concentrate, 3.8% in the zinc concentrate, and 3.4% in the tailings.[2] A flow sheet representative of the flotation practices at Bunker Hill Company, Kellogg, Idaho, is shown in Figure V-2.

Contrary to the Bunker Hill practice, most of the recovered silver in Missouri lead-zinc ores, containing 0.4 troy oz silver/ton, is found in the zinc concentrate. After flotation, 42% of the silver is found in the zinc concentrate, 24% in the lead concentrate, 2.0% in the copper concentrate, and 32% in the tailings (7,404,000 tons containing 0.142 troy oz silver/ton).[14]

---

a/ Copper smelters normally will not pay for lead and zinc. Sometimes they penalize for zinc. They pay for a substantial part of the gold and silver. A lead smelter gives partial payment for copper, usually nothing (or a penalty) for more than 5 to 10% zinc, and payment for most of the gold and silver. Zinc smelters give only partial payments for copper, lead, gold, and silver.[1]

148

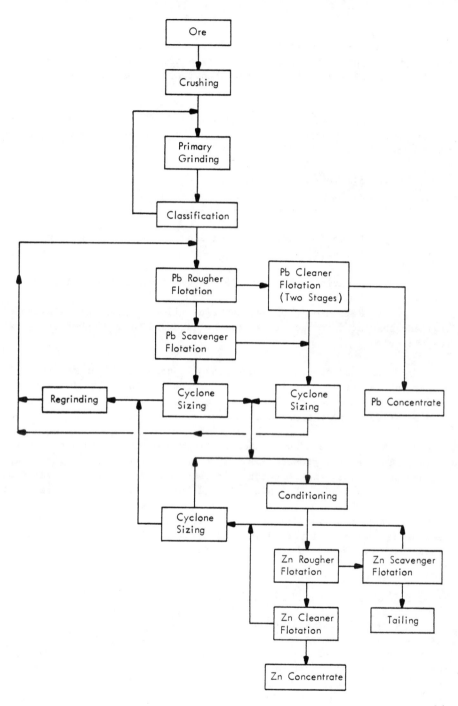

Figure V-2 - Flotation Practice, Bunker Hill Company, Kellogg, Idaho[2]/

Lead-silver ores are the source of about 12% of domestic primary silver production. The ores contain argentiferous galena, perhaps with small amounts of sphalerite and tetrahedrite. Pyrite is common but minor in the gangue.[2]

Typical processing of lead-silver ores containing 21 troy oz silver/ton, 1% zinc, and 12% lead, at the Lucky Friday Mine Company, Wallace, Idaho, are:

1.   Simple-stage grinding.

2.   Screen and cyclone sizing.

3.   Froth floating of the galena and associated silver in rougher, cleaner, and scavenger circuits.

4.   Floating sphalerite in a second, similar circuit.

5.   Returning the lead and zinc middling products (cleaner tailings and scavenger concentrates) to the lead and zinc rougher circuits, respectively.

The lead concentrate contains 120 troy oz silver/ton (98% of the silver in the ore). The distribution of the remaining 2% of the silver between the zinc concentrate (4 troy oz silver/ton) and the tailings (0.1 troy oz silver/ton) was not stated.[2]

Zinc ores are the source of 4% of domestic primary silver production. The largest producer of silver from zinc is the Anaconda Company of Montana. The average ore concentrate contains 1 troy oz silver/ton, 5% zinc, and 1% lead. The chief minerals are sphalerite and argentiferous galena; and a gangue of pyrite, quartz, and feldspar. The zinc concentrate produced contains 25% of the silver; the lead concentrate, 56%. Nineteen percent of the silver is lost in milling. The silver in the zinc concentrate is recovered in an electrolytic zinc plant.[2]

C.   Smelting and Refining of Silver-Containing Ores and Concentrates

Smelting is defined as any process for reducing metals from their ores by some means that includes fusion.[1] The smelting of copper, lead, and zinc concentrates often results in the recovery of silver and may also result in recovery of one or more of the following: gold, platinum, palladium, arsenic, antimony, bismuth, sulfur, selenium, tellurium, nickel, cobalt, indium, thallium, tin, cadmium, germanium, and mercury. Many of

150

these elements, including silver, are circulated between two or more circuits before they are concentrated sufficiently to be recovered profitably if at all. In addition, iron, calcium, manganese, aluminum, chlorine, fluorine, and oxygen must be separated from the valuable elements and discarded, usually as a slag.[15]

Flue dust and fume are separated from furnace gases in scrubbers, settling chambers (flues), cloth filters in baghouses, and electrostatic precipitators and processed to recover silver, gold, lead, zinc, antimony, and arsenic. Slags can be used as a source of iron, in cement manufacture, and for construction materials.[1]

1. The copper circuit: The processing of copper ore follows the sequence of roasting, smelting, converting, and refining as shown in Figure V-3. Silver generally is processed with the copper during all of the procedures up to the electrolytic refining. Although some silver may be lost in the slag resulting from the smelting process, the major concentration of the silver is in the anode slime produced during the final electrolytic refining procedure.

In the roasting process, the ore is treated below the fusion point to drive off uncombined moisture (drying); chemically combined water and carbon dioxide (calcining); or sulfur, arsenic, antimony, tellurium, etc. (roasting). Any flue dust that can be segregated from the fume is normally returned to the charge. The silver present in the copper ore remains with the copper and is not lost during this process.

Smelting of the roasted ore in a blast furnace was once a common practice, but this process of smelting is not suitable for the finely divided sulfide concentrates now available. Therefore, reverberatory furnaces are now generally used to produce matte and sulfur dioxide, which results from excess sulfur. The copper smelter feeds contain 25 to 35% copper, 27 to 33% sulfur, 20 to 30% iron, 10 to 20% gangue constituents, and 2 to 50 troy oz silver/ton.[2] During the smelting process, the bottom and lower walls of the furnace form a hearth or crucible for the molten metallic constituents; and the gas, fuel oil, or powdered coal is burned in the space above the hearth. Fuel and air are introduced at one end, travel the length of the furnace, and are discharged as spent gases through the other end wall.[1] During this process, high-sulfur minerals decompose into sulfur, which burns to SO_2, and matte-forming cuprous and ferrous sulfides. The end result of the smelting process is a molten matte with a slag floating atop the matte. Although small quantities of silver are present in the slag, which is discarded, almost all of the silver is retained in the molten matte.

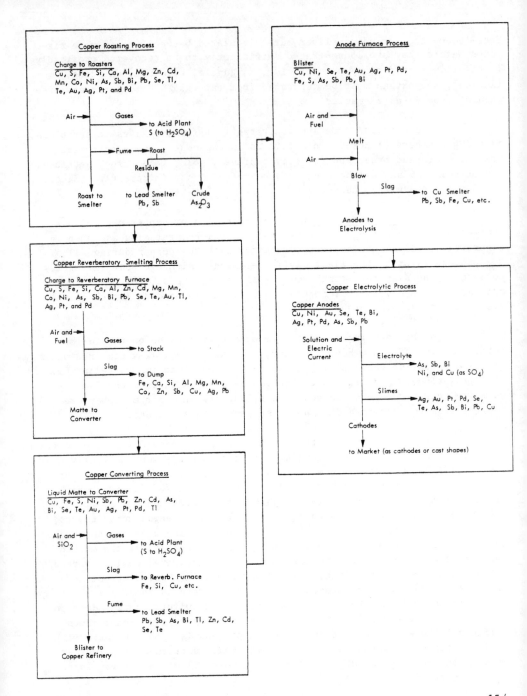

Figure V-3 - Flow Diagram of Copper Smelting and Refining Processes[15/]

During converting, the molten matte is changed to blister copper. The molten matte is periodically removed from the reverberatory furnace and charged to the copper converter with a small amount of silica flux.[16] A copper converter is a cylindrical refractory-lined vessel that can be tilted to discharge its contents and is similar in operation to a Bessemer converter. Air is passed through the matte in two stages to produce the blister copper.[1]

1st stage: $Cu_2S \cdot FeS + O_2 + SiO_2 \longrightarrow FeSiO_3 + Cu_2S + Cu$

$$S + O_2 \longrightarrow SO_2$$

Blister-forming stage: $Cu_2S + O_2 \longrightarrow Cu + SO_2$ [11]

The resultant blister copper, so named due to its rough surface, is transferred to refining furnaces or may be cast into pigs. Throughout the process of converting the copper matte, the silver is retained with the copper and the blister copper product contains $\geq$ 98% copper and 2.5 to 112 troy oz silver/ton.[1,11] Of the 16 U.S. copper smelters, five produce only blister copper while the others fire-refine at least part of the blister copper.[17,18]

The final step in copper refining involves electro- or fire-refining of the blister copper. Fire-refining capacity in the U.S. in 1968 was 365,000 tons, whereas 2.3 million tons of copper was electrolytically refined. Approximately 60% of the U.S. electrolytic-refining capacity is in six Atlantic Coast refineries while fire-refining is done in Michigan, New York, New Jersey, New Mexico, and Texas.

Fire-refining may be done in reverberatory furnaces, which are smaller than those used in matte smelting, or in cylindrical furnaces that can be tilted on trunnions. With the reverberatory furnace, the charge comprises solidified blister copper plus high-grade scrap while the cylindrical furnaces accept molten blister copper directly from the converters.[11] In this process, the molten metal is agitated by compressed air to oxidize sulfur and metal impurities. The metal impurities form oxides which accumulate as slag and are removed by skimming. Silver and gold are not oxidized in the fire-refining process and remain with the copper.[11,18] The copper, containing cuprous oxides, is deoxidized by adding coke and by "poling," in which green wood poles decompose into reducing gases. Natural gas is replacing wood as a purifying agent. If the original material contains insufficient gold or silver to warrant recovery, or if a silver-containing copper is desired, the fire-refined copper is cast directly into forms for industrial use. Fire-refined copper must contain $\geq$ 99.5 to 99.95% copper, but any silver present may be counted as copper. If recovery of the silver and other

153

precious metals is warranted, the refining proceeds only far enough to in-
sure homogeneous anodes for electrolytic refining.[1,11,17,18]

Anode-furnace refining purifies and degases the blister copper
to produce copper anodes containing 2.4 to 9.1 troy oz silver/ton.[11][a]
In the electrolytic copper refining process, the copper anodes are electrolyzed in an electrolyte containing 40 g copper/liter and up to 200 g
free sulfuric acid per liter. The anodes are consumed to 10 to 20% of
their original weight and then returned to the anode furnace for reprocessing into new anodes. Anode slimes comprise 1 to 15% of the original anode
weight and contain all of the silver, gold, lead, selenium, and tellurium
from the anode. This slime may contain 25 to 10,000 troy oz silver/ton
and 0.1 to 500 troy oz gold/ton. A discussion of the recovery of silver
from anode slimes is presented in Section V.D.

The cathode copper, containing 0.05 to 0.5 troy oz silver/ton,
may be sold without further treatment but is usually melted, given a form
of fire-refining, and cast into refinery shapes.[11]

The locations and annual capacities of copper smelters and refineries in 1965 are shown in Table V-3.

2. The lead circuit: The processing of lead ores, containing
copper, silver, gold, and other valuable elements, generally follows a
sequence of sintering, smelting, drossing, and refining as shown in Figure
V-4. Some silver is removed during these processes at several points,
basically in the form of slags or matte, but most of the silver is recovered in the lead bullion desilverizing step. In the electrolytic refining
of lead, silver is found in the anode slime.

In sintering, the roasting temperature is raised to the point
of incipient fusion of the lead ore to give a hard-porous clinker for
blast furnace treatment. The silver content of the sintered product may
range from 30 to 150 troy oz/ton, whereas the silver content of lead concentrates is 0 to 50 troy oz/ton.[1,11]

The silver-containing lead sinter is smelted in a blast furnace
at ~ 1400°C, where the major separation of gangue material is made. The

---

a/ Note that if the silver content of the anode copper is 2.4 to 9.1
troy oz silver/ton and that of blister copper is 2.5 to 112 troy oz/
ton,[11] serious loss of silver has occurred in anode furnacing.
Alternatively, one set of figures may be in error.

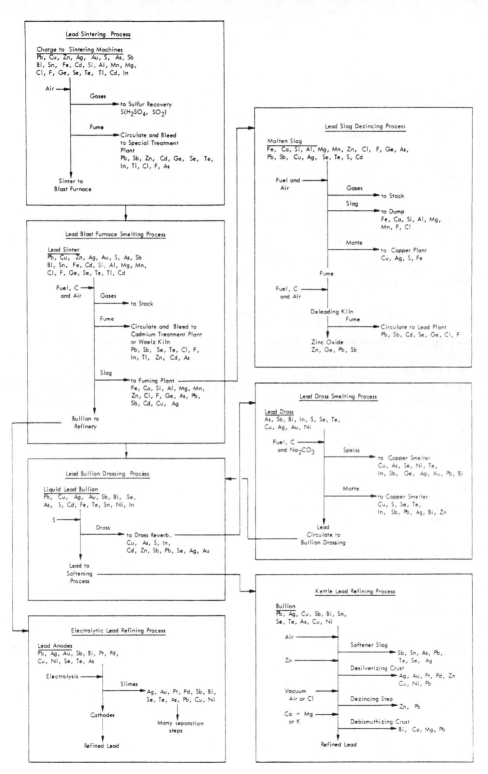

Figure V-4 - Flow Diagram of Lead Ore Processing Scheme[15]/

lead smelter feed contains coke and silica or limestone fluxing materials and may also include secondary products such as lead-bearing dusts, fumes, fines, slags, drosses, and residues shipped from copper and zinc smelters. The slag from the smelting process contains important amounts of silver as well as lead, antimony, and copper and larger concentrations of zinc, chlorine, fluorine, germanium, and arsenic. In addition, the liquid lead as it flows from the blast furnace may contain copper, silver, and other elements; upon cooling, many elements separate from the lead as a dross.[2,6,]

The slag from the lead smelting may undergo a dezincing process and be charged while molten to the zinc-fuming furnace or it may be recycled to the sinter process or totally discarded. In at least one plant, a matte is separated from the slag after fuming and returned to copper smelters to recover the copper and silver from the dezinced slag.[11,15/] The reader is also referred to zinc fuming in Section V.C.3.

Lead bullion, from the smelting process, next undergoes a drossing procedure. The lead bullion drossing process comprises holding molten bullion at a temperature just above the melting point of lead (327.4°C). Copper dross rises to the top and is skimmed off. The last traces of copper are removed by sulfur. Dross can be treated by two processes from which copper, silver, and other elements can be returned to the copper circuit. These processes are silica-matte reverberatory smelting and the soda-matte process, which is preferred if the arsenic content is high or the freight costs for the copper by-product are high. After decopperizing, lead bullion is transferred to the lead refinery circuit.[11,15/]

In soda-matte dross smelting, dross, a small amount of soda ash, and a smaller amount of reducing carbon to balance oxidation are charged into a deep-bath reverberatory furnace. A steep thermal gradient permits separation into three layers:

1. Bottom - Lead, which is circulated back to the drossing kettle.

2. Intermediate - Speiss, containing silver, which is sent to a copper smelter.

3. Top - Matte, containing silver, which is also sent to a copper smelter.

In lead refining, electrolytic and kettle processes are the two most commonly used procedures. Some bullion, especially if high in bismuth, is processed by the Betts electrolytic process,[a/] in which impurities in the bullion (including silver) concentrate in the anode slimes. These impurities are separated and recovered by methods similar to those in the kettle lead refining process.

The first step in kettle lead refining is softening of the drossed lead bullion. Arsenic, antimony, and tin are oxidized into a litharge slag in a reverberatory furnace, or, as in the Harris process, are oxidized in a caustic soda slag in heated steel kettles. The softener slags contain silver. Sometimes, stepwise softening concentrates arsenic, antimony, and tin into separate slags, which are processed into alloys, pure metals, or metal oxides.[15/]

In the desilverizing step, using the Parke's process,[b/] 1 to 2% metallic zinc is added to the softened lead at a temperature above the melting point of zinc (about 420°C) to give, on cooling, a dross or crust of silver-zinc alloy containing noble metals and any copper or nickel present. The residual lead is reheated and scavenged with more zinc to give a zinc crust containing a little silver, which is used as the zinc addition to a new kettle of lead bullion.[16/] Conducting desilverizing in two stages allows isolation of high-gold and high-silver products, which facilitates recovery of these metals.[11/]

Retorting the first zinc crust, which contains usually more than 2,000 troy oz silver/ton at 590.5°C, removes the zinc and leaves residual silver- and gold-rich lead alloy. This lead alloy is cupelled as in copper slimes treatment and may be sent to that circuit at this point. Lead is oxidized in a small reverberatory furnace under strongly oxidizing conditions to litharge (PbO) in the cupel and the litharge dissolves all the less noble impurities and even enough silver and gold to require careful smelting and handling. The residual doré gold-silver alloy is cast into anodes.[11,15,19/]

The location of U.S. lead smelters and refineries is given in Table V-4.

[a/] The Betts process is followed at East Chicago, Indiana. The bismuth can also be removed by the Kroll-Betterton process after desilverization.[6/]

[b/] The Pattinson process has been superceded in the U.S. by the Parke's process. The former is still used elsewhere on low-silver-tenor lead ores. It is based on repeated crystallizations of rather pure lead from a residual melt, whose silver content constantly increases. The enriched lead is cupelled to recover silver and gold.[16/]

3. The zinc circuit: Refined zinc is produced by two methods--
the pyrometallurgical and the hydrometallurgical, which involves leaching
and electrolysis. All new plants coming on stream are electrolytic. If
present in the zinc concentrates, silver will be found, as shown in Figure
V-5, in the products from roasting the zinc concentrates and sintering the
roasted product, in the metal or matte formed from blast furnace processing
of the zinc sinter, in the residue from retorting the zinc sinter, and in
the residue from sulfuric acid leaching of the zinc roast prior to electrolytic zinc refining.[15]

Roasting the zinc concentrates eliminates sulfur and most of the
lead, fluorine, chlorine, and mercury. Zinc sulfide in sphalerite is converted to zinc oxide or sulfate. Common roasting methods are multiple-
hearth roasting, flash roasting (used prior to leaching), and fluidized-
bed roasting.[11]

Zinc sintering removes elements that escaped roasting or were
circulated back. Much of the cadmium reports in the fume and is concentrated enough to be fed directly to a cadmium recovery plant.[15] The chlorides present (salt or chloride solutions from cadmium recovery operations)
help volatilize and remove lead, cadmium, and silver during sintering.[11]

Typical silver concentration in flue dust from sintering zinc
concentrate is 50 troy oz/ton. Such dust has been used as feed to the Amax
cadmium plant at Blackwell, Oklahoma.[a] Here the dust was densified, sul-
fated with 93% sulfuric acid, roasted at ~ 218 to 426°C, water leached,
and filtered to remove the insoluble lead and silver sulfates from soluble
cadmium and zinc sulfates. The lead sulfate residue contained 75 troy oz
silver/ton and 10% of the zinc and 5% of the cadmium in the original dust.[20]
Presumably, the residue was recycled to a lead smelter.

In retorting, the zinc oxide produced by roasting and briquetting,
roasting and sintering, or sintering alone is reduced to zinc vapor by coal
or coke at high temperature (~ 1200°C). The zinc vapor, diluted by carbon
monoxide, is carried out of the retort and condensed. The residue is usually shipped to a lead smelter if the silver, gold, lead, and copper content warrant recovery. It may also be used as a feed for a Waelz kiln or
similar zinc fuming furnace.[1,2,11,15]

---

a/ The Amax Lead and Zinc Division plant was one of the largest U.S. cad-
    mium plants, averaging 50 tons cadmium/month. It is now closed with
    operations shifted to Sauget, Illinois (electrolytic zinc process).

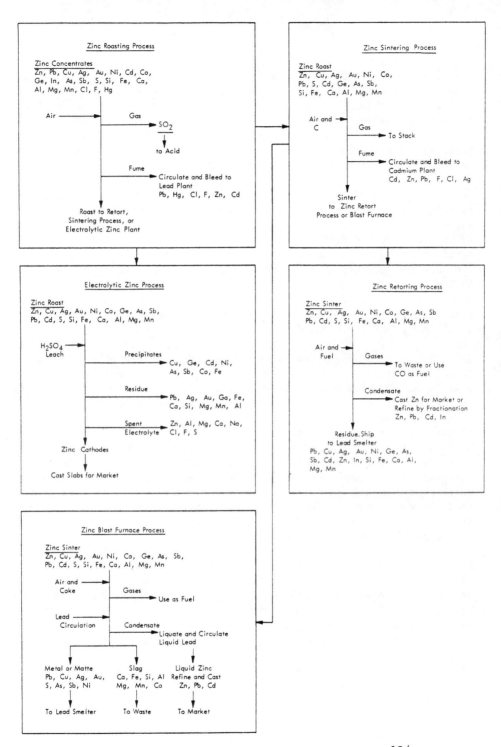

Figure V-5 - Flow Diagram of Zinc Ore Processing[15]/

The zinc blast-furnace process for recovering zinc and lead from the zinc sinter was developed in England since World War II. The sinter is smelted in a special hot-top blast furnace. The gases, which are relatively poor in zinc, are condensed into a large circulating bath of lead by spraying the lead into the gas stream. Zinc is liquated from the cooled bath. The furnace residue is discharged as a liquid that separates into metal and/or matte (containing silver) and a slag, which is discarded. The metal and/or matte is sent to a lead plant.[1,15]

In the electrolytic zinc process, which is now preferred to pyro-metallurgical processes, the roasted zinc is leached with sulfuric acid to leave a residue containing lead, silver, iron, gangue metals, etc., which is shipped to an adjoining lead plant.[a] The copper, nickel, cobalt, arsenic, antimony, germanium, and iron impurities in the zinc sulfate solution are precipitated and shipped to copper or lead smelters to recover at least copper and germanium. Cadmium is precipitated separately and treated in the electrolytic cadmium recovery plant of the electrolytic zinc plant. The purified solution is electrolyzed to give zinc cathodes, from which cast slabs are made.[15]

In zinc fuming processes, any silver in the feed should remain in the residue after zinc recovery. Zinc fuming for the manufacture of zinc oxide once used high-grade oxide ores but now largely uses reasonably lead-free sintered sulfide concentrates and lesser amounts of low-grade oxide ores, residues from zinc retorting and leaching, and lead-smelter slags. In fuming (maximum temperature $< 93°C$), zinc vapor is burned in an oxidizing atmosphere and condensed by cooling from the combustion gases or filtered out in a baghouse. For example, in the Waelz process, calcined or roasted low-grade zinc ore and zinc-retorting or leaching-plant residues are mixed with coal or coke and charged to a rotary kiln fired at the charging end with gas or powdered coal. At the discharge end of the kiln, the zinc vapor is burned to zinc oxide. Electrothermic slag-fuming produces zinc rather than zinc oxide.[1]

Of 13 zinc-producing plants in the U.S. listed by Hallowell et al., only one was reported to produce by-product silver: Matthiessen and Hegeler Zinc Company of LaSalle, Illinois. The plant, which is now closing, used horizontal retorting and Waelz kiln fuming.[11] There were eight existing zinc smelters in the U.S. in mid-1973.

---

a/ Silver is not readily soluble in the sulfate-rich spent electrolyte that is used to leach the calcine. Most of the silver reports in the primary leach residue.[2]

D. Primary Silver Refining

Silver is ultimately recovered from copper, lead, or complex base-metal ores either from the electrolytic copper refinery slimes or from the doré metal recovered at the lead refinery. The silver refinery handles both products. The slimes are leached and/or roasted to remove impurities, and the treated slimes are smelted to produce doré metal, which is electro-lytically refined by the Moebius or Balbach-Thum process. Major U.S. producers of primary (new) silver are shown in Table V-5.

1. <u>Slime treatment</u>: "Slimes" are so-named because of the appearance of the residues from the corroded copper anode when they are still wet. They are collected in the electrolytic copper refining division, known as the tank house; pumped to the precious-metals recovery division; and leached to remove copper. Leaching tanks are normally agitated to provide aeration. Some slimes may be roasted to remove lead, arsenic, antimony, and bismuth.[21]

Copper refinery slimes contain silver in such forms as $CuAgSe$, Ag_2Se, Ag, Ag_2S, Ag_2Te, and $(Au,Ag)Te_2$. In the presence of Ag, CuO, Ag_2O, or Na_2CO_3, Ag_2Se is readily oxidized below 400°C to silver selenite Ag_2SeO_3, which decomposes at 550 to 770°C to silver, SeO_2, and oxygen. During roasting, at 500 to 550°C, $CuAgSe$ also is transformed into silver selenite.[22]

At United States Metals Refining Company (AMAX), the slimes are leached with dilute sulfuric acid at 37 to 54°C to give a solution, free of silver, selenium, or tellurium, that can be returned directly to the tank-house electrolyte system.

The slimes treated by the Raritan Copper, International Smelting and Refining Company (Anaconda) works, contain insufficient silver to combine with all the tellurium and selenium so the slimes are heated at $\geq$ 74°C to decompose the copper compounds, and the tellurium is precipitated with powdered copper at 88°C. Similarly the Baltimore Plant of the American Smelting and Refining Company (ASARCO) heats their slimes and leaching solutions.

Raw slimes containing considerably more selenium than those of the aerating leach type require sulfuric acid digestion at 182 to 204°C.[21] Silver sulfate forms, e.g., by the following reaction:

$$Ag_2Se + 3H_2SO_4 \longrightarrow Ag_2SO_4 + SeSO_3 + SO_2 + 3H_2O.\text{[22]}$$

Roasting at 704°C of the copper and silver sulfates, elemental selenium, and tellurium dioxide or oxysulfate that are produced by acid digestion oxidizes selenium and tellurium to the dioxides. The volatile selenium dioxide, produced by sulfuric acid digestion and roasting, is routed to the collection system; tellurium dioxide remains in the slimes. Counter-current water leaching extracts silver and tellurium as well as copper. The first of a two-stage cementation process precipitates silver on copper. (The second-stage tellurium precipitate is a starting material for tellurium recovery.) The silver precipitate is routed back to the slimes before caustic leaching, which dissolves tellurium dioxide as sodium tellurite. The pressed filtrate is ready for the doré furnace.[21]/

The silver contents of the raw and treated slimes at four silver refineries are given in Table V-6.

2. <u>Furnacing of treated slimes to produce doré metal</u>: Treated slimes are mixed with fluxing materials and smelted in a rever-beratory-type furnace at 1260 to 1649°C. Silicate slags, containing up to 600 troy oz silver per ton, are a small percentage of the doré furnace input. Decreasing the furnace temperature allows the separation of "matte" (actually a mixture of the selenides and tellurides of copper and the precious metals) and impure bullion.

Refining the matte with sodium carbonate and oxidizing with niter (KNO_3) and/or air gives an alkaline slag containing water-soluble sodium selenite and tellurite. Reactions with respect to silver include:

$$Ag_2Se + Na_2CO_3 + O_2 \longrightarrow 2Ag + Na_2SeO_3 + CO_2$$

$$Ag_2Te + Na_2CO_3 + O_2 \longrightarrow 2Ag + Na_2TeO_3 + CO_2$$

The "foul" bullion remaining is refined to doré metal by oxidizing the impurities with niter. Silver refineries may process slimes from other copper refineries as well as industrial scrap and other wastes by adding them to the furnace operation at various points. The doré metal contains copper 3-12, gold 10-50, and silver 940-970 parts per thousand.[21,22]/

3. <u>Electrolytic refining</u>: The doré metal is next electrolyzed by the Moebius or Balbach-Thum process.

a. <u>Balbach-Thum process</u>: In the Balbach-Thum process, the doré metal is cast into anodes about 1 ft square and 0.5 in. thick and weighing 350 to 400 troy oz each. Trays, each containing four or five anodes, are placed horizontally in rectangular earthenware tanks lined with the graphite blocks that form the cathode. During electrolysis, silver dissolves from the anode and deposits as loose crystals on the

cathode. Insolubles, including gold and platinum, remain in a black mud
held by a canvas lining in the trays.

Any copper present in the dore' metal also dissolves and
will precipitate with the silver if allowed to accumulate. To avoid this,
the electrolyte is periodically removed, silver is cemented on sheet
copper, and copper is precipitated by scrap iron.

The silver crystals deposited on the cathode are washed
free of electrolyte, partially dried, and melted to give ≥ .999 fine
silver.[9] Impurities in the silver--copper, lead, iron, bismuth, selenium, tellurium, gold, and palladium--may be present up to several parts
per million.[21]

b. Moebius process: In the Moebius process anodes cast
from dore' metal are vertically suspended and enclosed in canvas bags.
During electrolysis, silver dissolves from the anodes, deposits on the
cathode plates, is continuously removed by mechanical scraping devices,
and falls into trays on the cell bottom.

The Moebius cell has a higher output per square foot of
floor space than the Balbach cell. Although the Balbach cell has no
moving parts and requires less labor, it is much slower and locks up
more silver. A disadvantage of the Moebius cell is the greater risk of
contaminating the cathode with anode slimes.[9]

c. Silver recovery from the anode slimes ("gold mud"):
Slime retained in the anode bags from the above processes contains silver,
gold, and any platinum-group metals present in the original dore' metal.[9]

When the amounts of platinum and palladium are small and,
consequently, the ratio of these metals to gold is low, silver is dissolved by boiling with 60° Be' sulfuric acid,[a] cemented onto copper
anode scrap, and returned to the dore' furnace. After the silver is dissolved, the residue is cast into anodes for use in the Wohlwill process
for gold. The palladium and platinum accumulate in the electrolyte and
are recovered chemically.

Gold mud, high in platinum and palladium, must be digested
with aqua regia. The silver chloride is returned to a furnace operation.
Gold is precipitated and electrolyzed by the Wohlwill process, and the
filtrate is treated chemically to recover platinum and palladium.[21]

---

[a] The presence of appreciable quantities of basic copper nitrate
    requires its decomposition in dilute sulfuric acid before the
    treatment with concentrated sulfuric acid.[21]

An outline of a silver electrolytic refining process is given in Figure V-6.

E. Secondary Silver Recovery (Waste Treatment and Refining)

In this subsection the treatment of silver-containing wastes with respect to silver recovery and/or waste disposal will be discussed. Secondary precious-metal refiners smelt low-tenor precious-metals scrap with scrap lead in a reverberatory furnace to give lead bullion. This bullion is mixed with clean silver scrap, and the mixture is cupelled to give doré metal, which is refined by electrolysis or acid-parting. Some high-copper scrap containing precious metals is fed to the blast furnace. 'High-grade precious-metal scrap and copper anode slimes are fed to the doré furnace. High-aluminum electronic scrap is also a potential source for recovering secondary silver.

Precipitation, ion-exchange, reductive exchange, adsorption, and electrolytic recovery are used to remove silver from wastewater. Silver recovery methods for photographic and plating wastes are described. The types of treatment received by wastes from mining, milling, and smelting are also discussed.

1. Secondary refiners: Table V-7 attempts to identify major domestic secondary silver refiners and their plant locations. Efforts were made to exclude brokers or scrap-collecting firms who merely buy and sell precious-metal residues. The secondary silver industry comprises more than 1,200 companies that process waste and scrap containing silver.[4/]

2. Smelting and refining of secondary silver scrap:

a. Secondary precious-metal refiners: The sources of secondary silver scrap were discussed in Section III.B. Each refiner achieves high recovery of all the precious metals since all dust, fumes, residues, and solutions bearing precious metals are carefully collected, recycled, and re-treated.[2/]

Figure V-7 is a simplified flow sheet for smelting and refining of secondary precious-metal scrap. In secondary refining, the high value of the feed requires accurate sampling and careful feed preparation as well as fast, efficient processing so that the high-value materials are not tied up for long periods. Initially, the scrap is segregated into clean and low-tenor scrap. In the feed-preparation step, low-tenor scrap is mixed with recycled lead, pyrite, and fluxes for smelting in the reverberatory furnace. Alternate procedures from those shown in Figure V-7 may be employed depending upon the type of scrap initially used.[2/]

164

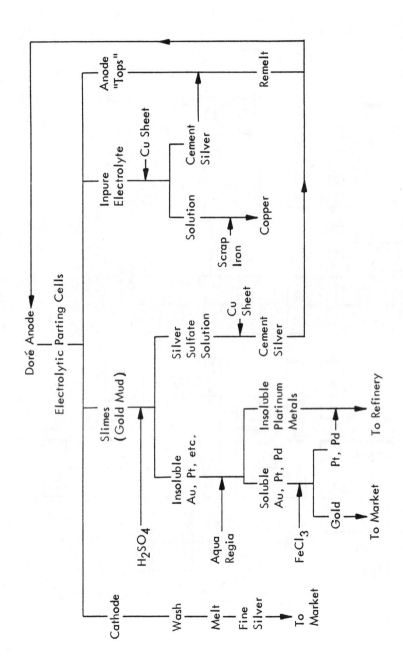

Figure V-6 – Silver Electrolytic Refining Process[9]

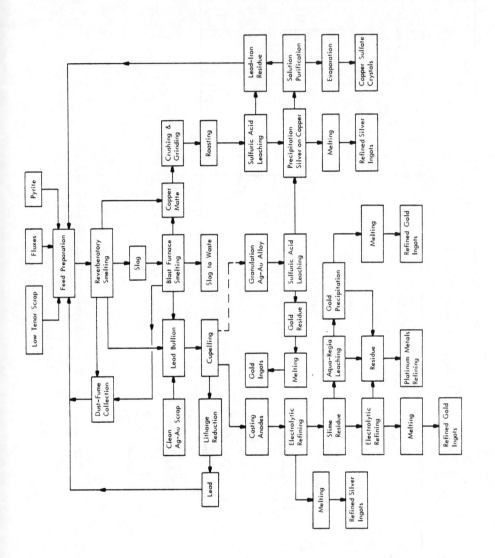

Figure V-7 - Simplified Flow Sheet for Smelting and Refining of Secondary Precious Metal Scrap2/

b. Secondary refiners who are also primary refiners: Some refiners combine scrap material with copper ore in their refining methods. In these instances, high copper-bearing and precious metal-bearing material[a] that contains impurities detrimental to advanced stages of copper refining are fed into a blast furnace to produce "black copper," containing about 70 to 80% metallic copper and 0.73% gold, silver, and platinum. Rotary furnacing of the black copper gives blister copper, which contains the bulk of the precious metals, although some metal may be lost or recovered in smelter by-products. The blister copper is mixed with No. 2 copper scrap and other precious metal secondary materials for casting into anodes in a reverberatory furnace. The anode slimes from electrolysis contain silver and the other precious metals. When the slimes are fed to the doré reverberatory-type furnace, they are mixed with high-grade precious-metal scrap such as bullion. The silver anode produced is treated as described in Section V.D.[23,24]

c. Aluminum sweating: Because of inflexible scrap-processing methods, little military electronic scrap has been recycled. The scrap cannot be accurately sampled and assayed for copper smelter charges. Aluminum and iron have not been sufficiently removed from shredded scrap to produce an easily smelted product. Smelting high-aluminum-content scrap produces a large amount of dross and crude bullion; however, low-aluminum-content scrap can be refined by smelting or electrorefining.[25]

Precious metals and copper are highly soluble in molten aluminum, and serious losses occur if sweated aluminum from electronic scrap is sent to an aluminum smelter (the sweated metal may contain as much as 140 troy oz silver/ton). In research studies, molten salt electrorefining of sweated electronic scrap gave refined aluminum and anode metal containing 94% of the silver. The latter was then suitable for conventional refining.[26]

3. Silver removal from wastewaters: Methods for removing silver from wastewaters, chiefly generated by the photographic and electroplating industries (Sections V.E.4. and V.E.5.), are: (a) precipitation, (b) ion exchange, (c) reductive exchange, (d) adsorption, (e) electrolytic recovery,[27] and (f) borohydride reduction.[28]

---

a/ These materials include obsolete electronic and communication apparatus, small motors, generators, light-gage copper wire wrapped around a steel core, copper-clad steel wire, catalysts, and fabrication wastes. The metals present in these wastes besides copper are zinc, iron, tin, lead, nickel, aluminum, chromium, and frequently, small amounts of sulfur, gold, silver, platinum, and palladium.[23]

a. Precipitation: Dilute plating rinse waters, containing 50 to 250 mg silver/liter, may be treated with chloride to precipitate silver chloride without segregation or precipitation of other metals. Final silver concentrations in the wastes would be low since the water solubility of silver chloride is about 1.4 mg Ag^+/liter.

Cyanide must first be removed by chlorination. When the cyanide concentration is much greater than that of the silver ion, cyanide oxidation with, e.g., sodium hypochlorite, will give high chloride concentrations that reduce the effectiveness of this silver removal process due to formation of soluble chloride complexes.

Coprecipitation with other metal hydroxides under alkaline conditions improves silver removal to < 0.1 mg/liter. Subsequent acid washing removes other metal hydroxides precipitated.

The oldest method for precipitating silver in the photographic film-processing industry uses sulfide ion, but large-scale use of sulfide precipitation leads to problems with respect to solids separation and handling. Treatment with hydrosulfite ion ($S_2O_4{}^{2-}$) yields Ag and Ag_2S in a compact, settleable precipitate; however, the process requires heat and has high chemical costs.[27/]

Recent Canadian studies have shown that ground-up discarded rubber automotive tires plus lime can remove aluminum and many heavy metals, including silver, from wastewater. At pH 6 to 11, the residual silver concentration in treated stock solutions (original concentration ~ 100 ppm) was < 0.1 ppm. Presumably, the metals react with various constituents of commercial rubber, such as sulfur and carbon black.[29/]

In recent studies, a single treatment with a starch xanthate-poly(vinylbenzyltrimethylammonium chloride) complex removed most heavy metals including Ag^+, from effluents to concentrations below Illinois discharge limits. Subsequent treatment with mild acid released the metals.[30/]

b. Ion exchange: Ion-exchange methods are considered uneconomical for silver recovery from photographic wastes but are feasible for low silver concentrations in separated waste streams where the total ionic strength is not much greater than the silver salt concentration. With this procedure, very low residual concentrations are possible.[27/]

The concentration of silver in the effluent from a secondary treatment plant with trickling filters[a] was found to be $\leq$ 4.6 ppb. A lime coagulation-settling process has been shown to remove 97.0% of the silver. Cation exchange alone removed 85.8% of the silver; cation plus anion exchange gave 91.7% silver removal. Sand filtration of sewage effluent, followed in sequence by activated carbon, cation exchange, and anion exchange gave cumulative removals of Ag^+ after each process of 11.6, 97.1, 98.8, and 99.4%, respectively.[31]

c. Reductive exchange (metallic replacement): Reductive exchange involves precipitation of silver onto another metal, usually zinc or iron, which releases zinc or iron ions in solution. The Oneida silverware plant used reductive exchange for silver recovery prior to the cyanide chlorination-silver chloride recovery system presently in use.

Zinc or steel wool in a column can remove 95% of the silver in wastewaters. This method has been recommended for use by small photographic developing plants.[27,32] The Bureau of Mines developed a process that employed steel wool or steel window screen and a smelting process to recover pure silver from sludges containing 27 to 80% silver.[33]

d. Adsorption by carbon: Use of activated carbon would be practical for some heavy-metal ion (including Ag^+) removal from raw-water supplies, either at the treatment plant or the source. Activated carbon shows good adsorption potential for antimony, arsenic, hexavalent chromium, tin, and bismuth. Carbon retains 90% of its weight in silver at pH 2.1 and 12.5% at pH 5.4.[34,35]

e. Electrolytic recovery: Most wastes are not sufficiently concentrated for electrolytic recovery; however, electrolytic recovery is regarded as the best method for the big processors of photographic waste solutions. The electrolytic method of silver recovery requires high initial capital investment and high operating costs since the critical operating conditions must be constantly supervised. The 96% pure silver produced is easily removed from the cathode unit.[27,28,32]

f. Reduction with sodium borohydride: Silver ion is quantitatively reduced to the metal by $NaBH_4$ according to the reaction

$$8Ag^+ + BH_4^- + 2H_2O \longrightarrow 8Ag \downarrow + BO_2^- + 8H^+$$

---

[a] The Boulder, Colorado, White Rocks Treatment Plant. Samples were transported in steel drums whose interiors were painted with epoxy paint.

Bulloch and Thomas hold a 1963 U.S. patent (U.S. Patent 3,082,079) for silver recovery from photographic fixing solutions by the borohydride method.

Whereas costs for electrolytic reduction are high and chemical methods such as silver sulfide precipitation or metal replacement often give products that must be further processed, the borohydride method requires only a pH adjustment, minimal initial investment and offers low operating costs (1.0 lb of $NaBH_4$ can reduce 22 lb Ag^+).[28]

4. Silver recovery from photographic wastes:

a. Extent of silver recycling in the photographic industry: Approximately half of the 40 million troy ounces silver used annually for photography are recovered from hypo solutions, from burning photographic and X-ray film, and from processing emulsions stripped from film.[2,36]

Solid wastes in the photographic industry include scrap trimmings, spoiled or outdated (developed or undeveloped) negative film and print paper, and contaminated emulsion from manufacture of these photo-sensitive papers. Liquid wastes include spent fixing and bleach solutions and wastewater carrying silver-bearing emulsion and compounds from the film manufacturing unit.[2] Other sources of waste film and/or liquid waste include the motion picture industry, government users of black-and-white film, and hospitals. In 1974, P. J. Wingate of Du Pont's Photo Products Department, estimated that about half of the silver in X-ray plates is recovered by most hospitals when film is exposed and developed. Since X-rays are retained for 5 to 7 years at large hospitals before disposal, approximately 50 to 60 million troy ounces silver is present in hospital X-ray files.[37] Few hospitals have facilities for silver recovery from fixing baths.[3]

Few small commercial photofinishers or amateurs attempt to recover silver. Most refiners feel that there is not enough silver in amateur film to justify refining even though the amateur market accounts for approximately one-third of the industry's total dollar business.[2,3,38]

Because of pollution laws and the monetary gains,[a] silver recovery from photographic processes is expected to increase, especially in the areas of engineering, graphic arts, and computer-output microfilm.[32]

---

a/ Since recovered silver must be shipped, assayed, and refined, the seller of recovered silver received only about 40 to 70% of the silver value when its price was $2 50 to $3.00/troy oz.[32]

Moderate-sized and most major film users sell silver precipitated from solutions and ashes from solid wastes to custom refiners. Many refining companies offer truck pickup service and shipping containers. Small firms may sell used fixer as well as reclaimed silver to refiners.[2,39] Commercial solution services may install special apparatus to recover photographic silver, supply new reagents to the user as necessary, and remove the spent ones for silver recovery.[40]

b. <u>Silver recovery from and waste treatment of photographic</u> <u>solutions</u>: Processes patented for removal of silver from photographic solutions include those based on adsorption (by ion-exchange resin or by colloid sludges), precipitation, and electrolysis.[2]

Figure V-8 shows the Eastman Kodak method for processing waste film and photographic wash solutions (U.S. Patent 2,131,072; September 27, 1938). The silver-containing products of this process are refined silver, an essentially "silver-free" slag, and an electrolytic slime that is sent to a custom smelter.[2]

Much of the silver (60 to 80%) in exposed black-and-white film and print paper, and nearly all from color pictures, dissolves in the hypo solution fixing bath. Table V-8 shows the silver content of unprocessed motion-picture films. MacWilliam[40] states that films often contain 5 to 15 g (0.16 to 0.48 troy oz) silver per square meter. Spent-fixing baths contain up to 12 g silver/liter, and well-seasoned bleach solutions contain < 1 g/liter. Schack and Clemmons estimate that two-thirds of the silver recovered from photographic wastes is derived from processing fixing and bleach solutions. Fixing baths (usually containing hypo--$Na_2S_2O_3$--or $(NH_4)_2S_2O_3$ as fixing compound) solubilize the unwanted silver halide of the developed film by forming silver complexes such as $AgS_2O_3^-$.[2,33,39]

Bleaches are used in black-and-white reversal processing (where silver instead of the silver halide is removed). For example,

$$6Ag + K_2Cr_2O_7 + 7H_2SO_4 \longrightarrow 3Ag_2SO_4 + K_2SO_4 + Cr_2(SO_4)_3 + 7H_2O.$$

At the price of silver in the middle 1960's, silver recovery from black-and-white reversal films and processes was uneconomical. In color reversal processes, the soluble silver salt produced by bleaching is available for recovery.[39]

Chemical methods for precipitating silver from motion-picture photographic waste solutions include addition of sodium sulfide (40 to 70% silver in the dry sludge), sodium hydrosulfite ($Na_2S_2O_4$) (the sludge contains 85% Ag as Ag and Ag_2S), magnesium sulfate or calcium hydroxide, hydrolyzed sugar solutions, sodium hydroxide, or exhausted developer or boiling to

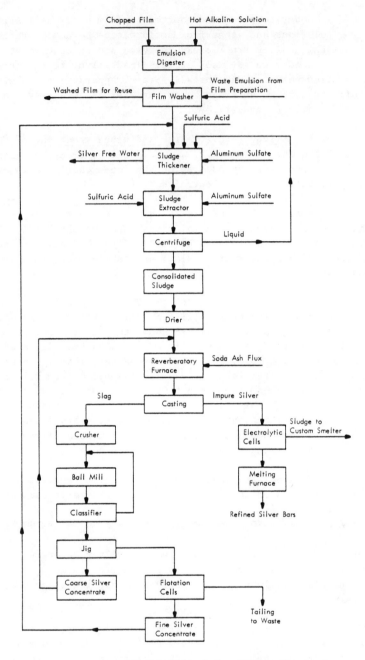

Figure V-8 - Eastman Kodak Method for Silver Recovery
from Waste Film[2]/

172

precipitate silver sulfide.[39] Eastman Kodak holds a 1950 patent (U.S. Patent 2,507,175), employing precipitation of silver from waste photographic solutions containing high levels of organic acids. Adding magnesium sulfate and lime probably precipitates silver as a mixed sulfate-oxide. Silver is recovered from the sludge. Solutions that contain silver thiosulfate complex, such as exhausted thiosulfate fixing solutions, are chlorinated with Cl_2 or NaOCl under alkaline conditions to precipitate a silver-bearing sludge from which silver can be separated. This process is described in a 1971 Eastman Kodak patent (U.S. Patent 3,594,157).[27] Kodak Australia Proprietary, Limited, holds a 1973 German patent (German Patent 2,242,700) for precipitating silver from wastes, such as emulsion washwater containing up to 130 ppm silver, and film-waste dispersions by use of an enzyme (from Bacillus subtilis or pancreatin) that hydrolyzes the gelatin to soluble peptides at pH 8. At pH 3.5 to 4.2, the peptides precipitate along with silver and other metals. After settling, the supernatant liquid contains < 2 ppm silver.[41]

Permutit Company, Limited, holds a 1949 British patent (Brit. 626,081) that uses basic ion-exchange resins to remove silver from dilute photographic washwaters. The silver is recovered by elution or incineration. A combination of ion exchange plus electrolysis was suggested by Arden in 1968 for thiosulfate developer baths. An ion-exchange resin accumulates the silver in the electroplating washout waste and the resin regenerant is electrolyzed to remove silver and provide developer bath makeup water.[27]

Electrolytic methods to recover silver from motion-picture waste solutions are preferred because they allow reuse of the fixer and give high-purity silver.[39] Several companies produce commercial apparatus to regenerate hypo solutions.[40] Two types of electrolytic recovery systems allow reuse of hypo solution. In the batch process, the silver content decreases from 5 g/liter to 0.5 g/liter and the desilvered fixer solution is augmented with the necessary chemicals for reuse. Since the silver content of the used fixer is allowed to become fairly high, a significant amount of silver is lost in the solution carried out with the film. A more efficient electrolytic process involves a recirculation system. Since the silver content in the bath can be less than 0.5 g/liter, silver carry-out by the film is minimal. Commonly, a tailing cell removes the last traces of silver with less than 0.1 g silver/liter remaining after electrolysis. Three motion-picture silver recovery firms, using electrolytic methods, recovered over 200,000 troy oz 95 to 96% pure silver/year (over-all recovery 80 to 85%).[39]

Eastman Kodak uses a recently patented apparatus for electrolytic recovery of silver from photographic fixer liquid. The apparatus comprises a cylindrical cathode (the outer wall) and an inner suspended anode. An impeller forces fluid through a central passage at lower pressure and discharges through an outer passage at higher pressure.[27]

Eastman Kodak has operated a primary waste-treatment plant on the Genesee River at Rochester, New York, since 1957 and a secondary waste-treatment plant was begun in early 1968 to remove more than 90% of the impurities in the industrial wastewater from Kodak Park.

Eastman Kodak claims that silver ions in fixing baths discarded to a waste line by a small processor will precipitate as the chloride, sulfide, or a complex compound. The concentration of all chemicals in processing solutions, including washwater overflows, is generally less than 0.005% and the processing effluent is further diluted by other plant waters.

Large-scale processors continuously replenish systems and do not normally discard solutions. If an occasion arises which necessitates dumping, the solution should be slowly bled from holding tanks to the waste line. Kodak cautions against the use of storm sewers for disposal, which might contaminate surface waters and seep into water supplies.[42]/

   c. Silver recovery from solid photographic wastes: Chopped waste film can be processed as described in the preceding section. Burning can also be used to remove the silver remaining on black-and-white films or ion-exchange resins.[33]/ High-purity silver can be recovered from waste film by combustion of film at 700 to 1100°C with air blowing in a melt containing 20 to 80% sodium sulfate and the rest sodium carbonate or a eutectic of sodium, lithium, and potassium carbonates containing 10% sulfates. (Rockwell International Corporation holds a new German patent for the process.[43]/) Recent Indian Patent 126,988 describes another incineration method for recovering silver from waste photographic film.[12]/

   5. Silver recovery from plating wastes: Plating wastes comprise spills of electrolyte, spent electrolyte, and dilute wash solutions. The silver-plate manufacturer collects these solutions as "mill wastes" and processes them to precipitate silver and oxidize cyanide before discharge as plant waste.[3]/ In the batch treatment of mixed plating wastes, chlorine oxidizes CN^-; $FeSO_4$, $NaHSO_3$, or SO_2 is added to reduce Cr^{6+}; and lime precipitates the heavy metals. Lancy's integrated treatment of cyanide and chromium wastes is suitable for plating processes that can be split into several operations. Toxic contaminants are destroyed by countercurrent rinsing before they can enter the rinse water.[44]/

   A typical plating mill-waste solution may contain 250 ppm Ag^+ and about 150 ppm CN^- and the rinse water alone may contain as much as 50 to 250 ppm silver. Silver may be recovered by precipitating with chloride or zinc dust or by ion-exchange.[2,44]/

Before 1953, Oneida, Limited, Oneida, New York, recovered the silver in its electroplating wastes by zinc precipitation, but since that time, they have used the chlorination-oxidation process. Treatment of these wastes by chlorination-oxidation reduced the silver content from 130 to 585 ppm silver in the raw waste to 0 to 8.2 ppm in the supernatant.[45/] As of the late 1960's at Western Electric in Indianapolis, cyanide wastes were treated by the two-stage alkaline chlorination-oxidation process, whereby cyanide was oxidized to cyanate at pH 10.0, and cyanate was oxidized to carbon dioxide and nitrogen at pH 8.5. After heavy metal ion removal and coagulant addition, the effluent was released to the sewer or partly reclaimed for reuse; the sludge was stored, dehydrated, and used as landfill. The discharged effluent contained less than 10 mg hydrous metallic suspended solids per liter.[46/]

The Bureau of Mines developed a method for treating electroplating wastes by the "waste-plus-waste method" wherein slow addition of acidic rack-stripping or chromium solution wastes to alkaline electroplating wastes allows precipitation of the metals as cyanides. Silver recovery was optimum at pH 5.5 to 6 when chromium waste was added to two electroplating waste solutions containing 0.9 to 2.2 and 5.5 to 29 g Ag^+/liter.[47/]

During the 1950's, the Sperry Rand electronics plant at Gainesville, Florida, discharged about 2,000 gal. of waste per week, containing about 1.4 ppm silver, after treatment of the plating wastes by ion-exchange coupled with cyanide oxidation. Acid regenerate waste from the cation units was pumped to the alkali regenerate tank (after cyanide oxidation); more caustic was added to increase the pH to 10.5, where copper and nickel precipitated as the hydroxides and silver, as the chloride. Wastes were pumped to a sludge drying bed.[48/]

Small and medium-sized metal processing and plating operations widely practice lagooning of the wastes after precious metals such as silver are first removed. For example, a Los Angeles plant discharges its wastes into an abandoned rock quarry.[49/]

All waste solutions containing silver nitrate plus ammonium hydroxide are explosion hazards and should be treated with hydrochloric acid to precipitate silver chloride for recovery.[50/]

In small plating shops, countercurrent rinsing reduces the water volume. (Two or three still rinse tanks are also used and the concentrated (first) tank can usually be returned to the plating solution.[51/]) Where no wastewater discharge is permitted from cyanide silver plating, the Handbook of Practical Electroplating[50/] recommends that the rinses be evaporated and the solution returned to the plating bath after treatment with a slight

excess of calcium or barium hydroxide to precipitate the carbonates formed
by cyanide decomposition during evaporation and after filtration. Where a
municipal sewer is used, cyanide-bearing rinse waters should be collected
in a tank and batch-treated with calcium hypochlorite or sodium hypochlorite
before releasing to the sewer.

6. Other used silver wastes:

a. Electric and electronic scrap: The chief sources of old
silver scrap are silver-rich bearing, wires, solders, brazing and special
alloys, and batteries. Approximately 40% of the total silver used in the
production of alloys and electrical products is recycled.[2] According to
the National Materials Advisory Board, salvage of installed electrical contacts is "a fairly long-cycle proposition." Silver is recovered if the
scrap goes to copper smelters but not if the scrap goes into steel.[36]

The Bureau of Mines claims that only a small part of electronic scrap has been recycled and has recently studied the economic feasi-
bility of collection and recovering silver and other precious metals in
electronic scrap.[4] The precious metals recovered by Martin Metals of Los
Angeles chiefly comprise 60% gold, 30% silver, and 10% platinum-group
metals.[52]

b. Analytical chemicals: Silver used in analytical and
clinical laboratories is probably largely unrecovered because so little is
used at any one site. A survey of metropolitan Buffalo hospital laboratories indicated a total of 90 g (< 3 troy oz) silver was discharged in
1972.[53/a] Further figures from this study indicate that the silver content
of the wastewater discharge by a theoretical 1,000-bed hospital would be
≤ 66 ppb.

7. Trends in secondary refining: Changes expected by nonferrous
metals refiners include higher refining charges; larger lots of materials
which will necessitate other facilities and systems for handling; larger
volumes of material with lower precious-metal content as values increase;
better segregation practices; and specialized processing for specific types
of material, e.g., cyanide stripping of gold from nickel electronic scrap.[5]
Handy and Harman is developing specialized processing lines to handle specific types of material, e.g., stripping silver alloys from Kovar of Alloy
42.[55]

---

a/ Silver is used in the Cotlove chloridometer.

176

Silver recycling is becoming more expensive with its increased safety and environmental requirements, higher operating costs, and expenses and inventory taxes directly related to silver price.[56/]

The refining cost for 90% silver coins in 1974 was 2 to 3% of the silver content per troy oz not including interest.[55/]

8. Treatment of mining, milling, and smelting wastes: Wastewater treatment and disposal practice in the primary production of copper, lead, and/or zinc has been summarized by J. B. Hallowell et al.[11/] In addition, Hallowell assesses the current wastewater practices for mining, milling, roasting, and smelting operations for each of these base metals, and waste-treatment improvements under study. The chief sources of silver loss in water from mining and milling operations are flotation mediums and acid mine drainage. These are discussed in Section VII.A. The occurrence of silver as a by-product of the production of these base metals was discussed previously in Sections V.A., V.B., and V.C.

Table V-9 shows that 77.7% of all discharged waters have received some type of treatment, mostly by holding in tailings ponds.

Tailings ponds are made by depositing tailings behind earth dams as in water reservoirs or by using the tailings themselves to build the dams. Most ponds are built by a combination of the two methods. Dried tailings can be stabilized to prevent blowing dust by chemical stabilization, coatings of asphalt or clay, or reseeding with native vegetation.[57/]

Some copper mine tailings dumps are currently being reprocessed. In some cases, the copper yield from the mine tailings dumps is nearly as much as from the mine itself. Kennecott recovers copper and perhaps some silver from mine tailings via precipitation. Water that has percolated through the dump goes into a precipitator cone filled with iron onto which copper is cemented. The red precipitate, containing 80% copper and any extracted silver, is used as smelter feed. The water is recirculated to the dump.[44/] Improved milling procedures, coupled with the basic cyanide silver-gold recovery process, are being used to treat mine dumps and tailings from operations in Arizona and Montana.[58/]

Bureau of Mines studies found percolation or tank cyanide leaching effective for recovering soluble silver from mine waste and mill tailings. Subsequently, the silver is recovered as the sulfide upon sodium sulfide addition, and gold is adsorbed by activated carbon. Carbon-cyanidation methods were also studied for slimy materials. Alkaline alcohol elution followed by electrowinning recovers 98% of the adsorbed silver from carbon (300 troy oz silver/ton) and recovers 99% of the silver from the strip solution.[59/] Carbon-in-pulp cyanidation, tested by the Bureau

177

of Mines on a bench scale, recovered 70 to 80% of the 3 to 5 troy oz silver ton of flotation tailings at the Homestake Mining Company's mill at Creede, Colorado, in the first step (cyanide agitation leaching). Activated carbon adsorbed about 500 troy oz silver/ton from the leach solution. Stripping the carbon with hot alkaline cyanide solution and electrodeposition from the latter recovered the silver.[60/]

The Bureau of Mines has studied electrooxidation on a bench scale and has been successful in recovering 77 to 90% of the silver (3 to 5 troy oz/ton average) and 90 to 95% of the mercury (from mechanical loss during amalgamation) from Nevada and Mexico mill tailings. Some of the silver and mercury in the tailings are combined as amalgam. In the electrooxidation technique, the tailings are pulped with brine solution. The brine solution is electrolyzed to dissolve the silver and mercury as chloride complexes. Silver and mercury are recovered by precipitation on iron powder followed by distillation and fire refining.[61/]

The Bureau of Mines research has also studied recovery of silver, indium, molybdenum, and vanadium from vanadium-extraction-plant wastes.[62/]

Copper- and lead-smelting slags are generally dumped wherever it is most economical. Because of transportation costs, slags used in making concrete and for road metal are only utilized in the smelter area.[57/] The fate of water used in copper smelter gas scrubbing is largely unknown. Water from copper slag granulation is usually settled and recycled for the same use.[11/]

TABLE V-1

SILVER PRODUCED AT AMALGAMATION AND CYANIDATION MILLS IN THE UNITED STATES AND
PERCENTAGE OF SILVER RECOVERABLE FROM ALL SOURCES /63-65/

Year	Bullion and precipitates recoverable (troy ounces)		Silver recoverable from all sources (percent)			
	Amalgamation	Cyanidation	Amalgamation	Cyanidation	Smelting a/	Placers
1956-60 (average)	90,582	394,883	0.3	1.1	98.5	0.1
1961	90,527	214,956	0.3	0.6	99.0	0.1
1962	89,203	101,887	0.2	0.3	99.4	0.1
1963	89,777	99,289	0.26	0.28	99.41	0.05
1964	91,401	120,894	0.25	0.33	99.39	0.1
1965	167,331	48,632	0.42	0.12	99.44	0.02
1966	80,033	41,098	0.18	0.09	99.71	0.02
1967	84,290	47,054	0.26	0.15	99.57	0.02
1968	92,021	53,666	0.28	0.16	99.55	0.01
1969	83,775	49,312	0.20	0.11	99.68	0.01
1970	95,287	24,892	0.21 b/	0.05	99.73	0.01
1971	993	106,785		0.26	99.74	b/
1972	2,490	99,992	0.01	0.27	99.74	b/

a/ Crude ores and concentrates.
b/ Less than 1/2 unit.

179

TABLE V-2

SILVER METALLURGY[4,9,61]

Process Name	Process Description	Place	Recovery (%)	Dates
- ·	Washing the ores and smelting the concentrate or directly smelting the ores. Refining the Pb bullion produced by cupellation to recover the Ag.	Laurium, Greece		~ 1000 B.C.
Amalgamation	Metallic Ag is wetted by and alloyed with Hg. The Ag is formed by treating Ag minerals with NaCl and $CuSO_4$.			From 1540
Augustin	Roasting the ore with NaCl to convert to AgCl, leaching with hot brine, and precipitating the Ag with metallic Cu.			~1850
Patio	Chloridizing roast, brine leaching, and amalgamation: NaCl + Cu pyrite $\longrightarrow$ Cu chlorides. Cu chlorides in salt solution + Ag_2S $\longrightarrow$ AgCl. AgCl + Hg $\xrightarrow{Hg}$ AgI; $\longrightarrow$ Ag-Hg.	Pachuca, Mexico	75	From 1557 to start of 20th century
Washoe (pan amalgamation)	Grinding crushed Ag ore in cast-Fe pans; adding Hg, $CuSO_4$, H_2SO_4, and NaCl to the steam-heated pulp; and retorting to recover the Ag from the amalgam.	Comstock Mines, Washoe County, Nevada	≤ 85	1861
Reese River	Salt roast prior to Washoe process for more complex ores.	Austin, Nevada		Late 19th century
von Patera	Roasting with NaCl; leaching AgCl with $Na_2S_2O_3$, and precipitating Ag_2S by adding Na_2S. Dissolving Ag_2S in acid and precipitating Ag on Cu or roasting and then mixing and cupelling to recover Ag.	Joachimsthal, Bohemia		Replaced in 1900's by cyanide process
Cazo (Cu pan)	Similar to Patio process. Ore, salt, and water heated in a Cu vessel over a wood fire.	Bolivia		
Cyanidation	See text.		92-93	Since 1900
Flotation	See text.			Since 1911
Parkes	Separation of Pb from Ag by skimming off a Ag-Zn alloy, which is retorted to distill off the Zn. Cupelling of the residue recovers Ag and Au as doré metal and Pb as litharge.			
-	Ag in Cu ores separates out into the anode slimes and is recovered as Ag bullion by smelting.			
-	Ag produced with Au (gold-placer or lode-gold mining) is recovered in electrolytic refining of the Au bullion.			

TABLE V-3

COPPER SMELTERS AND REFINERIES[11]

State	City	Smelters Company	Smelters Annual Capacity[a] Charge (short tons)	Electrolytic Refineries Company	Electrolytic Refineries Annual Capacity[a] Charge (short tons)	Fire Refineries Company	Fire Refineries Annual Capacity, Tons of Product
Arizona	Hayden	ASARCO	360,000				
	Hayden	Kennecott	400,000				
	Miami	Inspiration	360,000	Inspiration	63,000		
	Superior	Magma	150,000				
	San Manuel	Magma	360,000				
	Morenci	Phelps Dodge	900,000				
	Ajo	Phelps Dodge	300,000				
	Douglas	Phelps Dodge	1,250,000				
Maryland	Ann Arundel			Kennecott	198,000		
	Baltimore			ASARCO	198,000		
Michigan	White Pine	White Pine	65,000[b]			White Pine	65,000
	Hancock	Quincy	12,000[b]			Quincy	12,000
Missouri	St. Louis			Cerro	42,000		
Montana	Anaconda	Anaconda	1,000,000	Anaconda	150,000		
	Great Falls						
Nevada	McGill	Nevada	440,000				
New Jersey	Carteret			U.S. Metals	150,000	U.S. Metals	125,000
	Perth Amboy			ASARCO	168,000		
	Raritan			International Smelting	240,000		
New Mexico	Hurley	Kennecott	400,000			Kennecott	84,000
Tennessee	Copperhill	Cities Service	300 tons/day				
Texas	El Paso	ASARCO	420,000	Phelps Dodge	290,000	Phelps Dodge	25,000
Utah	Garfield	Kennecott	1,225,000	Kennecott	204,000		
Washington	Tacoma	ASARCO	1,200 tons/day				

a/ Data from U.S. Bureau of Mines Information Circular 8225, published in 1965. Additional data from EPA Publication EPA-450/2-74-002a.
b/ Production capacity.

181

TABLE V-4

LEAD SMELTERS AND REFINERIES IN THE UNITED STATES[11]

Company	Smelters		Refineries			
	Location	Annual Capacity (Lead Bullion), short tons	Location	Type of Refining	Annual Capacity (Refined Lead), short tons	By-Product
American Smelting & Refining Co.	East Helena, Montana	107,770	--	--	--	--
American Smelting & Refining Co.	El Paso, Texas	107,770	--	--	--	--
American Smelting & Refining Co.	Glover, Missouri	89,815	Glover, Missouri	Pyro	89,815	Au, Ag
American Smelting & Refining Co.	--	--	Omaha, Nebraska	Pyro	179,630	Au, Ag, Bi, Sb
Bunker Hill Co.	Kellogg, Idaho	124,340	Bunker Hill, Idaho	Pyro	122,340	Au, Ag, Cd, Cu, Sb
International Smelting & Refining Co.[a]	Tooele, Utah	65,860	--	--	--	--
Missouri Lead Operating Co.	Boss, Missouri	99,790	Boss, Missouri	Pyro	99,790	Ag, Cu
St. Joseph Lead Co.	Herculaneum, Missouri	224,525	Herculaneum, Missouri	Pyro	220,125	Ag
U.S. Smelting, Refining & Mining Co.	--	--	East Chicago, Indiana	Electro	39,915	--

a/ Not included with existing U.S. lead smelters in EPA Publication No. EPA-450/2-74-002a.

TABLE V-5

BASE METAL AND SILVER REFINING PLANTS OF MAJOR U.S. SILVER PRODUCERS, 1965[3]

	Copper Capacity (Thousands of Short Tons)	Lead Capacity (Thousands of Short Tons)	Silver Capacity (Millions of Ounces)	1965 Production of Ag From Own Refineries (Millions of Ounces)			Origin of Silver-Bearing Material Treated
				New	Scrap	Total	
ASARCO	Σ 468	Σ 530	[80-100][a]	61.4	7.0	68.4	U.S., Peru, Canada, Australia, South Africa, South America, Honduras
Perth Amboy, N.J.	168						
Baltimore, Md.	200						
Tacoma, Wash.	100						
Omaha, Nebraska		180					
Selby, Calif.		72					
AMAX							
Carteret, N.J.	275		N.A. [b]	< 5[c]		15.4	
Anaconda	Σ 725		N.A.	11.8	-	11.8	U.S., Chile
Great Falls, Mont.	190						
Perth Amboy, N.J.	216						
Kennecott	Σ 667			< 5			U.S.
Garfield, Utah	192		N.A.				
Ann Arundel, Md.	192		N.A.				
Bunker Hill							
Kellogg, Idaho	110		N.A.	4.6	-	4.6	U.S., Canada

a/ Estimated.
b/ N.A. = Not available.
c/ Only 5% of AMAX output is derived from new material (1965).

TABLE V-6

SILVER CONTENT OF RAW AND TREATED SLIMES[21]

Refinery	Silver Content, Troy Oz Per Ton	
	Raw Slimes	Treated Slimes
Raritan Copper Works, Anaconda Co.	3,750	6,500
Great Falls Copper Works, Anaconda Co.		10,000
American Smelting and Refining Co., Baltimore	2,800	7,000
U.S. Metals Refining Co.	5,500	6,200

TABLE V-7

SECONDARY (SCRAP) SILVER REFINERS[a]

Company	Location	Activity
Ag-Met, Inc.	Hazleton, Pennsylvania	Secondary refining.[b,c] 1974 silver production estimate: 7.5 to 8 million troy ounces. Leases Ag recycling app. to hospitals and graphic arts industries.[74]
Alpha-IRC Co. (Joint venture between Alpha Metals, Inc., and International Recycling)[75]	Sayreville, New Jersey	Refines precious-metal-bearing solder and other Sn-Pb alloys. Uses a newly developed proprietary electrochemical process.
American Chemical and Refining Co.	Waterbury, Connecticut	Secondary refining.
American Metal Climax, Inc. (AMAX) (See United States Metals Refining Co.)		Primary and secondary refining. Refined 40 million troy ounces Ag in 1970.
American Smelting and Refining Co. (ASARCO)	Baltimore, Maryland	Primary and secondary Ag refining. Cu electro refining.
The Anaconda Co. (See International Smelting and Refining Co.)	--	--
Attleboro Refining Co.	Attleboro, Massachusetts	Secondary refining.
Baker Film Salvage[76]	Chicago, Illinois	Consumers of scrap X-ray film and litho precious metal.
Behr and Sons, Inc.	Rockford, Illinois	Primary and secondary refining.[b,c]
Cincinnati Gold and Silver Refining Co.	Cincinnati, Ohio	Secondary refining.[c,d] (Ag for jewelers, dentists, platers).[77]
Ciner Chem. Refining Co., Inc.[78]	Brooklyn, New York	Purchases Ag in any form.
Commonwealth General Limited	South Plainfield, New Jersey	Secondary refining.[b,c] One of the largest recyclers of photographic wastes (capacity 100 tons/month). Full capacity 5 million troy ounces Ag. Plans to double capacity.[79]
Denron, Limited	Oak Creek, Wisconsin	Secondary refining.[c,e]
Dentalloy, Inc.	Costa Mesa, California	Recovers and refines secondary precious metals (chiefly from electronics scrap) to produce gold alloys for dentistry.[80]
Eastern Smelting and Refining Corp.	Boston, Massachusetts	Refining from all types precious metal-bearing material.
Eastman Kodak Co.	Rochester, New York	Recovery from photographic wastes.

185

TABLE V-7 (Continued)

Company	Location	Activity
Engelhard Industries, Inc.	Murray Hill, New Jersey	Secondary refining.c,e/
Garfield Smelting and Refining Co.	Philadelphia, Pennsylvania	Secondary refining.
Gerald Metals, Inc.	Chicago, Illinois	Secondary refining.
Goldsmith Division, NL Industries, Inc.	Chicago, Illinois	Secondary refining.b/
Handy and Harman	Fairfield, Connecticut Los Angeles, California	Secondary refining.b/ Fabrication alloys, powders, flakes, anodes, wire, bars, solders, etc.
Hudsar, Inc. (formerly Hudson Smelting and Refining Co.)	Newark, New Jersey	Smelts residues containing Ag.
International Recycling Corp. 81/	Sayreville, New Jersey	Smelting, refining, recycling, merchant banking.
International Smelting and Refining Co. (Anaconda)	Perth Amboy, New Jersey	Electrolytic Cu refining f/ (blister Cu and scrap). Primary and secondary Ag refining.
Martin Hannum Refining Co.	Los Angeles, California	Secondary refining.
Martin Metals, Inc.	Los Angeles, California	Secondary refining.b,g/
McAlpine, Edward B.	Providence, Rhode Island	Secondary refining.
Metal Bank of America (formerly L. Goldstein and Sons, Inc.)	Philadelphia, Pennsylvania	Secondary refining.b/ Electrolytic Cu refining. Refining of Cu scrap and residues.
Metallic Development Corp. 82/	Wichita Falls, Texas	Secondary refining.
Metal Industries, Inc.	Detroit, Michigan	Buys any amount of scrap X-ray film.
Metz Metallurgical Co.	South Plainfield, New Jersey	Secondary refining.
Midland Processing Co. 83/	Pomona, New York	Recycling Ag and plastic from surplus photographic film.
Nassau Recycle Corp. (formerly Nassau Smelting and Refining Co., Inc.) 84/	Tottenville, Staten Island, New York	Refining Western Electric telephone scrap.
Noblemet Refining. 85/	Mapleville, Rhode Island	Buys precious-metal scrap. (Buys, sells, and converts Ag). 86/
Pease and Curren, Inc.	Warwick, Rhode Island	Secondary refining.b,c/ (Ag scrap and residues from elec., electronic, mirror, film, dental, and other manufacturers, mostly on toll.)

186

TABLE V-7 (Concluded)

Company	Location	Activity
Phister Manufacturing Co. [87]	Wenonah, New Jersey	Burning of X-ray films and precious-metal residues.
Sabin Metal Corp.	Brooklyn, New Jersey	Secondary refining. [b,c]
Sel-Rex Co., The [88]	Nutley, New Jersey; Chatsworth, California	Secondary refining.
Silvachem Corp. [89]	Linden, New Jersey	Hydrometallurgical extraction of Ag from Ag-bearing residues such as film.
Simmons Refining, Inc.	Chicago, Illinois	Secondary refining. [b]
SiPi Metals Corp.	Chicago, Illinois	Secondary refining. [b,c]
Sitkin-Midland, Inc.	Detroit, Michigan	Secondary refining (Ag residues). [90]
Sitkin Smelting and Refining Co.	Lewistown, Pennsylvania	Secondary refining. [b] Material handled includes electronic scrap, jewelry residues, catalysts, and power source residue. Sitkin has recently quadrupled its capacity for precious metals. [91]
Spiral Metals Co.	South Amboy, New Jersey	Secondary refining.
Suppo Smelting and Refining Co., Inc. [92]	Chicago, Illinois	Secondary refining (electronic components, plating solns., etc.)
Troy Metals	N. Hollywood, California	Secondary refining. Buys jewelry, residues, solutions, etc. Sells bars, chlorides, rods of Ag and other precious metals.
United States Metals Refining Co. (AMAX)	Carteret, New Jersey	Primary and secondary Cu and Ag refining. Handles high-grade materials such as bullion and sweeps. [93]
Wildburg Bros.	San Francisco, California	Secondary refining.

a/ Compiled chiefly from data in References 3 and 66-73.
b/ Accepts small lots of scrap photo and X-ray film, metal parts, silverware, and coins except where noted.
c/ Sells .999 fine (99.9% pure) Ag bars weighing ≤ 100 oz.
d/ Buys sterling or coins in commercial lots.
e/ No films.
f/ Ag not indicated as a product.
g/ No untreated film.

TABLE V-8

SILVER CONTENT OF UNPROCESSED AND PROCESSED MOTION-PICTURE FILMS[39]

Film Type	Negative or Positive	Unprocessed Film Silver Content troy oz/ 1,000 ft (305 m)	Percent of Original Amounts of Silver Retained after Processing
Black-and-White (35 mm)	Negative	3.0 ($\sim$ 0.2 troy oz/m^2) (0.02 oz/ft^2)	10-20
Black-and-White (35 mm)	Positive[a]	1.3	$\sim$ 25
Black-and-White Reversal (16 mm)	--	0.42	
Color (35 mm)	Negative	2.5	$\sim$ 0
Color (35 mm)	Positive	1.1	$\sim$ 0
Color Reversal (16 mm)	--	0.70	

a/ Major source of recyclable photographic silver. As a rule of thumb, it is assumed that one can recover 1 troy oz silver/1,000 ft 35 mm film.

TABLE V-9

SUMMARY OF WASTEWATER TREATMENT PRACTICES[11]/

Treatment Method	Amount Treated, MGY	Percent of Total
Tailings pond	37,984	69.2
Other settling	2,043	3.7
Dilution	2,016	3.7
Neutralization	25	0.1
No treatment	12,798	23.3
Total Discharge	54,866	100.0
Evaporated	248	

BIBLIOGRAPHY. SECTION V.

1. Salsbury, M. H., W. H. Kerns, F. B. Fulkerson, and G. C. Branner, <u>Marketing Ores and Concentrates of Gold, Silver, Copper, Lead, and Zinc in the United States</u>, Bureau of Mines Information Circular 8206, U.S. Department of the Interior, Bureau of Mines, U.S. Government Printing Office, Washington, D.C., 1964.

2. Schack, C. H., and B. H. Clemmons, <u>Review and Evaluation of Silver-Production Techniques</u>, U.S. Bureau of Mines Information Circular 8266, U.S. Government Printing Office, Washington, D.C., 1965.

3. Charles River Associates, Inc., <u>Economic Analysis of the Silver Industry</u>, prepared for Property Management and Disposal Service, General Services Administration, Clearinghouse for Federal Scientific and Technical Information, Springfield, Virginia, 1969.

4. Ageton, R. W., "Silver" in <u>Minerals Facts and Problems</u>, Bureau of Mines Bulletin 650, U.S. Department of the Interior, U.S. Government Printing Office, Washington, D.C., 1970, pp. 723-737.

5. Ageton, R. W., "Gold" in <u>Minerals Facts and Problems</u>, Bureau of Mines Bulletin 650, U.S. Department of the Interior, U.S. Government Printing Office, Washington, D.C., 1970, pp. 573-586.

6. Paone, J., "Lead" in <u>Minerals Facts and Problems</u>, Bureau of Mines Bulletin 650, U.S. Department of the Interior, U.S. Government Printing Office, Washington, D.C., 1970, pp. 603-620.

7. Welch, J. R., "Silver" in <u>Minerals Yearbook 1972, Vol. I, Metals, Minerals, and Fuels</u>, Bureau of Mines, United States Department of the Interior, U.S. Government Printing Office, Washington, D.C., 1974, pp. 1129-1142.

8. Heindl, R. A., "Zinc" in <u>Minerals Facts and Problems</u>, Bureau of Mines Bulletin 650, U.S. Department of the Interior, U.S. Government Printing Office, Washington, D.C., 1970, pp. 805-824.

9. Dennis, W. H., <u>Metallurgy of the Nonferrous Metals</u>, 2nd ed., Sir Isaac Putnam and Sons, London, 1961.

10. McQuiston, F. W., Jr., and R. S. Shoemaker, <u>Gold and Silver Cyanidation Plant Practice</u>, The American Institute of Mining, Metallurgical, and Petroleum Engineers, Inc., New York, New York, 1975.

11. Hallowell, J. B., J. F. Shea, G. R. Smithson, Jr., A. B. Tripler, and
    B. W. Gonser, Water-Pollution Control in the Primary Nonferrous-
    Metals Industry. Vol. I. Copper, Zinc, and Lead Industries,
    Battelle Memorial Institute, Prepared for Office of Research and
    Monitoring, U.S. Environmental Protection Agency, U.S. Government
    Printing Office, Washington, D.C., 1973.

12. Anonymous, New Silver Technology. Silver Abstracts from the Current
    World Literature, The Silver Institute, Washington, D.C., January
    1975, pp. 54-55.

13. Anonymous, "Flotation Reagents," Eng. Mining J., 156 (3a), 66-69 (1955).

14. Morris, A. E., Associate Professor of Metallurgical Engineering,
    University of Missouri, Rolla, personal communication, June 1975.

15. Phillips, A. J., "The World's Most Complex Metallurgy (Copper, Lead
    and Zinc)," Transactions of the Metallurgical Society of AIME,
    224, 657-668 (1962).

16. Schack, C. H., and B. H. Clemmons, "Chapter 4. Extractive Processes"
    in Silver. Economics, Metallurgy, and Use, A. Butts and C. D. Coxe,
    Eds., D. Van Nostrand Co., Inc., Princeton, New Jersey, 1967, pp. 57-
    77.

17. Ageton, R. W., and G. N. Greenspoon, "Copper" in Minerals Facts and
    Problems, Bureau of Mines Bulletin 650, U.S. Department of the In-
    terior, U.S. Government Printing Office, Washington, D.C., 1970,
    pp. 535-554.

18. Arthur G. McKee and Company, "Va. Copper, Zinc, and Lead Smelting
    Practice," Systems Study for Control of Emissions. Primary Non-
    ferrous Smelting Industry, Vol. I, National Air Pollution Control
    Administration, Public Health Service, U.S. Department of Health,
    Education, and Welfare, 1969, pp. Va-1 to Vb-5.

19. Anonymous, "Lead Refining," ASARCO News, 12 (1), 7-11 (1972).

20. Nauert, R. L., "Cadmium Preparation at Blackwell," J. Metals, 1, 15-
    17 (1966).

21. Johnson, O. C., "Chapter 5. Refining Processes" in Silver. Economics,
    Metallurgy, and Use, A. Butts and C. D. Coxe, Eds., D. Van Nostrand
    Co., Inc., Princeton, New Jersey, 1967, pp. 57-77.

22. Jennings, P. H., and J. C. Yannopoulos, "Recovery and Refining of Selenium" in Selenium, R. A. Zingaro and W. C. Cooper, Eds., Van Nostrand Reinhold Company, New York, New York, 1974, pp. 31-86.

23. Spitz, A. W., and M. I. Schwab, "New Developments in Smelting Secondary Copper" in Proceedings of the Third Mineral Waste Utilization Symposium, M. A. Schwartz, Ed., Cosponsored by the U.S. Bureau of Mines and IIT Research Institute, Chicago, Illinois, March 14-16, 1972, pp. 265-268.

24. Schmidt-Fellner, A., "Role of Refiner in Precious Metals," Secondary Raw Materials, 9 (5), 64-70 (1971).

25. Dannenburg, R. O., and G. M. Potter, "Smelting of Military Electronic Scrap" in Proceedings of the Second Mineral Waste Utilization Symposium, March 18-19, 1970, Chicago, Illinois, U. S. Bureau of Mines and IIT Research Institute, Chicago, Illinois, 1970, pp. 114-117.

26. Singleton, E. L., and T. A. Sullivan, "Electronic Scrap Reclamation," J. Metals, 25 (6), 31-34 (1973).

27. Sittig, M., Pollutant Removal Handbook, Noyes Data Corporation, Park Ridge, New Jersey, 1973.

28. Anonymous, Inorganic Reductions with Sodium Borohydride. Principles and Practices, Ventron Corp., Beverly, Massachusetts, 1974.

29. Netzer, A., P. Wilkinson, and S. Beszedits, "Removal of Trace Metals from Wastewater by Treatment with Lime and Discarded Automotive Tires," Water Res., 8 (10), 813-817 (1974).

30. Wing, R. E., C. L. Swanson, W. M. Doane, and C. R. Russell, "Heavy Metal Removal with Starch Xanthate-Cationic Polymer Complex," J. Water Pollution Control Federation, 46 (8), 2043-2047 (1974).

31. Linstedt, K. D., C. P. Houck, and J. T. O'Connor, "Trace Element Removals in Advanced Wastewater Treatment Processes," J. Water Pollution Control Federation, 43 (7), 1507-1513 (1971).

32. Yaeger, D., "See Silver Reclamation from Photo Process Up," Am. Metal Market/Metalworking News, 80 (205), 28 (1973).

33. Hoyt, C. D., "Silver" in Minerals Yearbook 1969, Vol. I. Metals, Minerals, and Fuels, U.S. Department of the Interior, Washington, D.C., 1971, pp. 997-1011.

34. Sigworth, E. A., and S. B. Smith, "Adsorption of Inorganic Compounds by Activated Carbon," Water Technol./Quality, 64 (6), 386-391 (1972).

35. Patterson, J. W., and R. A. Minear, Waste Water Treatment Technology, 2nd ed., Illinois Institute for Environmental Quality, Chicago, Illinois, PB-216 162, National Technical Information Service, Springfield, Virginia, 1973.

36. Materials Advisory Board Committee on Technical Aspects of Critical and Strategic Materials, Trends in Usage of Silver, Publication MAB-241, National Research Council, National Academy of Sciences, National Academy of Engineering, Washington, D.C., 1968.

37. Anonymous, "Photopolymers Will Challenge Silver-Sensitive Film Mart," Am. Metal Market, 81 (116), 1, 12 (1974).

38. Miller, R., "Economic Squeeze Has Negative Effect on Consumption of Photographic Silver," Am. Metal Market, 82 (6), 6 (1975).

39. Schreiber, M. L., "Present Status of Silver Recovery in Motion Picture Laboratories," J. Soc. Motion Picture Television Engrs., 74, 505-513 (1965).

40. MacWilliam, E. A., "Chapter 14. Silver in Photography" in Silver. Economics, Metallurgy, and Use, A. Butts and C. D. Coxe, Eds., D. Van Nostrand Co., Inc., Princeton, New Jersey, 1967, pp. 200-217.

41. Anonymous, New Silver Technology. Silver Abstracts from the Current World Literature, The Silver Institute, Inc., Washington, D.C., January 1974.

42. Anonymous, Disposal of Photographic-Processing Wastes, Kodak Publication No. J-28, Eastman Kodak Company, Rochester, New York, 1969.

43. Anonymous, New Silver Technology. Silver Abstracts from the Current World Literature, The Silver Institute, Washington, D.C., July 1974.

44. Resource Engineering Associates, State of the Art Review on Product Recovery, Water Pollution Control Research Series, 17070DJW 11/69, Federal Water Pollution Control Administration, U.S. Department of the Interior, Washington, D.C., 1969.

45. Eichenlaub, P. W., and J. Cox, "Disposal of Electroplating Wastes by Oneida, Ltd. V. Plant Operation," Sew. Ind. Wastes, 26, 1130-1135 (1954).

46. O'Connor, S., B. W. Mountjoy, Jr., and N. S. Chamberlin, "Western Electric Builds Modern Plant for Treating Metal Finishing Wastes," Water Wastes Eng., 6 (7), D-16 to D-19 (1969).

47. George, L. C., and A. A. Cochran, Recovery of Metals from Electroplating Wastes by the Waste-Plus-Waste Method, Bureau of Mines Solid Waste Research Program, Technical Progress Report 27, U.S. Department of the Interior, Washington, D.C., 1970.

48. Eidsness, F. A., and P. B. Bergman, "The Treatment of Metal Plating Wastes at Sperry's Gainesville, Florida, Plant," Plating, 43, 1005-1007 (1956).

49. Ottinger, R. S., J. L. Blumenthal, D. F. Dal Porto, G. I. Gruber, M. J. Santy, and C. C. Shih, Recommended Methods of Reduction, Neutralization, Recovery, or Disposal of Hazardous Waste. Vol. V. National Disposal Site Candidate Waste Stream Constituent Profile Reports. Pesticides and Cyanide Compounds, TRW Systems Group for the U.S. Environmental Protection Agency, PB-224 584, National Technical Information Service, U.S. Department of Commerce, Springfield, Virginia, 1973.

50. Rodgers, T. M., Handbook of Practical Electroplating, The MacMillan Co., New York, New York, 1959.

51. Orr, M. A., "Chapter 11. Electroplating" in Silver. Economics, Metallurgy, and Use, A. Butts and C. D. Coxe, Eds., D. Van Nostrand Co., Inc., Princeton, New Jersey, 1967, pp. 180-189.

52. Haflich, F., "Coast Gold, Silver Scrap Supplies Falling, But Pick Up Expected," Am. Metal Market, 81 (119), 15A (1974).

53. Pragay, D. A., "Pollution Control and Suggested Disposal Guidelines for Clinical Chemistry Laboratories," Am. Lab., 6 (12), 9-10, 12-16, 19-20, 22-23 (1974).

54. Anonymous, "Rising Costs of Refining Gold and Silver Changing Our Industry, Peer Tells NARI," Am. Metal Market/Metalworking News, 81 (53), 27 (1974).

55. Ricter, R., "Coins, Drawn Out by Silver Tags, Called Recovery Source," Am Metal Market, 81 (116), 2 (1974).

56. Anonymous, "Soaring Prices Put Damper on Silver Use," Chem. Eng. News, 52 (26), 7-8 (1974).

57. Ottinger, R. S., J. L. Blumenthal, D. F. Dal Porto, G. I. Gruber, M. J. Santy, and C. C. Shih, Recommended Methods of Reduction, Neutralization, Recovery, or Disposal of Hazardous Waste. Vol. XIII. Industrial and Municipal Disposal Candidate Waste Stream Constituent Profile Reports. Inorganic Compounds (Continued), TRW Systems Group for the U.S. Environmental Protection Agency, PB-224 592, National Technical Information Service, U.S. Department of Commerce, Springfield, Virginia, 1973.

58. White, J. B., Jr., "Silver-Gold Recovery Practices from Dumps and Tailings" (abstr.), J. Metals, 26 (12), 42 (1974).

59. Heinen, H. J., D. G. Peterson, and R. D. Lindstrom, "Silver Extraction from Marginal Resources" (abstr.), J. Metals, 26 (12), 42 (1974).

60. Salisbury, H. B., S. J. Hussey, F. M. Howell, Jr., and G. M. Potter, "Silver Recovery from Flotation Trails (sic) by Carbon-in-Pulp Cyanidation" (abstr.), J. Metals, 26 (12), 42 (1974).

61. Scheiner, B. J., D. L. Pool, and R. E. Lindstrom, Recovery of Silver and Mercury from Mill Tailings by Electrooxidation, Report of Investigations 7660, Bureau of Mines, U.S. Department of the Interior, Washington, D.C., 1972.

62. Smithsonian Science Information Exchange, Environmental Protection Research Catalog, U.S. Environmental Protection Agency Office of Research and Monitoring, U.S. Government Printing Office, Washington, D.C., 1972.

63. Ryan, J. P., "Silver" in Minerals Yearbook 1967, Vol. I-II, Metals, Minerals, and Fuels, Bureau of Mines, U.S. Department of the Interior, U.S. Government Printing Office, Washington, D.C., 1968, pp. 1037-1056.

64. Welch, J. R., "Silver" in Minerals Yearbook 1971, Vol. I, Metals, Minerals, and Fuels, Bureau of Mines, U.S. Department of the Interior, U.S. Government Printing Office, Washington, D.C., 1973, pp. 1073-1086.

65. Ryan, J. P., "Silver" in Minerals Yearbook 1965, Vol. I, Metals, Minerals, and Fuels, U.S. Department of the Interior, Washington, D.C., 1967, pp. 829-850.

66. Anonymous, "New Members of the Silver Institute," The Silver Institute Letter, 3 (2), 3 (1974).

67. Anonymous, "1972 U.S. Silver Refining Statistics," The Silver Institute Letter, 3 (2), 3-4 (1973).

68. Anonymous, "Silver Available in Less Than 1,000-Ounce Bars," The Silver Institute Letter, 3 (11), 3 (1973).

69. Anonymous, "What Can I Do with Old Silver?--A Question Frequently Being Asked the Institute," The Silver Institute Letter, 3 (11), 3-4 (1973).

70. Anonymous, "Refining Firms That Buy Old Silver, Sell Ingots," The Silver Institute Letter, 4 (1), 3 (1974).

71. Anonymous, "Four New Members of Silver Institute," The Silver Institute Letter, 4 (4), 3 (1974).

72. American Metal Market, Metal Statistics 1972, Fairchild Publications, Inc., New York, New York, 1972.

73. Cordero, H. G., and T. J. Tarring, Eds., Non-Ferrous Metal Works of the World, 1st ed., Metal Bulletin Books, Ltd., London, 1967.

74. Anonymous, "Ag-Met Credits Reverse Marketing for Record Net Income Earnings," Am. Metal Market, 81 (212), 14 (1974).

75. Anonymous, "Form Joint Refining Venture," Am. Metal Market, 81 (121), 15 (1974).

76. Baker Film Salvage, Advertisement, Am. Metal Market, 81 (113), 22 (1974).

77. Cincinnati Gold and Silver Refining Company, Advertisement, Am. Metal Market, 81 (119), 16A (1974).

78. Ciner Chem. Refining Co., Inc., Advertisement, Am. Metal Market, 81 (116), 13 (1974).

79. Miller, R., "Commonwealth Aims to Double Capacity of N. J. Gold, Silver Recycling Plant," Am. Metal Market, 81 (212), 10 (1974).

80. Haflich, F., "Semiconductors Rich 'Vein' for Refiners of Gold Scrap," Am. Metal Market, 81 (105), 1 (1974).

81. International Recycling Corporation, Advertisement, Am. Metal Market, 81 (104), 11 (1974).

82. Metallic Development Corp., Advertisement, Am. Metal Market, 81 (119), 16A (1974).

83. Midland Processing Inc., Advertisement, Am. Metal Market, 81 (116), 10A (1974).

84. Anonymous, "Change Company Name to Reflect Its Activities," Am. Metal Market, 81 (241), 12 (1974).

85. Anonymous, "Precious Metals and Who Supplies Them," Am. Metal Market, 81 (119), 22A-24A (1974).

86. Refinemet International Co., Advertisement, Am. Metal Market, 81 (119), 20A (1974).

87. Phister Manufacturing Co., Advertisement, Am. Metal Market/Metalworking News, 81 (171), 59 (1974).

88. Sel-Rex Co., The, Advertisement, Am. Metal Market, 81 (119), 21A (1974).

89. Anonymous, "Silvachem Completes New Scrap Plant," Am. Metal Market, 82 (63), 8 (1975).

90. Sitkin-Midland, Inc., Advertisement, Secondary Raw Materials, 9 (3), 6 (1971).

91. Anonymous, "Sitkin Quadruples Capacity in Precious Metal Refinery," Scrap Age, 31 (2), 146 (1974).

92. Suppo Smelting and Refining Co., Inc., Advertisement, Am. Metal Market, 81 (119), 16A (1974).

93. MacGregor, I., "The Future for Copper," Secondary Raw Materials, 8 (4) 52, 54-55, 57, 59, 61, 63, 65-66 (1970).

VI. USES OF SILVER

In this section, the general methods for the fabrication of silver intermediate products (metal and alloy forms, powders, and chemicals) are summarized. Following the general introduction to fabrication, each of the major uses of silver will be discussed in descending order, beginning with the largest consumption. Statistics for silver consumption by end use are found in Tables IV-15 and VI-1.

A. Fabrication of Silver Intermediate Products

1. _Silver and silver-base alloys_: "Silver can be melted, cast, hammered, rolled, punched, stamped, drilled, engraved, polished, drawn, tapped, carved, tooled, welded, brazed, soldered, and ground."[1] This subsection describes most of the mechanical and some of the major chemical transformations that silver undergoes during the fabrication and manufacture of silver-containing products.

Engelhard and Handy and Harman carry out the bulk of intermediate production. In 1969, they were virtually the only firms producing silver in sheet, strip, and coil. In 1966, the total annual production of intermediate products was over 170 million troy ounces. Since industrial use in that year was only 150 million troy ounces, much of the intermediate production probably includes secondary scrap.[2]

a. _Melting_: Charges to the diverse melting apparatus comprise carefully weighed alloying elements and deoxidizers (e.g., P, Li, Na-Zn, CaB). Volatile alloy components are provided in excess to compensate for their loss during melting.

Smaller melts are produced in clay-graphite or silicon carbide crucibles in gas- or oil-fired furnaces. Medium-sized melts (1,000 to 12,000 troy oz) are produced in gas- or oil-fired furnaces or high-frequency furnaces. The charges is often covered with a carbonaceous material that sacrificially protects it from oxygen in the atmosphere. The melt in the crucible is carried by tongs to the mold. Larger charges are handled in trunnion-mounted furnaces, which can be tilted for pouring into molds. Some are fuel-fired, but most are high-frequency furnaces.[3]

b. _Casting_: The melt is poured into molds to form a flat bar for sheet, or a wire bar or extrusion bar for wire. Cast-iron or more modern copper, water-cooled molds are used to produce flat bars;

graphite molds also have limited use. When the alloy contains highly oxidizable dross formers such as Mg, Mn, Li, or Al, Durville molds are used.

Continuous casting is used by American Smelting and Refining
Company to make round bars for wire, flat bars for strip, and shells for
tube drawing. The bar is slowly withdrawn from a cooled graphite die,
which is attached to and continuously fed from a holding crucible.

Where oxidizable elements are involved or improved soundness
is required, vacuum melting with induction heating is used. Because of
the relatively high volatility of silver, manganese, and lithium, partial
backfilling with argon is necessary in later stages to avoid excessive
evaporation.[3/]

c. Extruding: Extrusion is used for materials that are
hard and brittle when cold, such as many of the brazing alloys. Silver
and many high-silver alloys for electrical contacts are preferentially
extruded. Powder metal mixtures of granular materials can be consolidated
by extrusion into full-density wire, and composite billets can be extruded
into well-bonded bimetal wires.[3/]

d. Rolling:

(1) Wire: Wire bars from cannon molds or from con-
tinuous casting machines can be cold- or hot-rolled by passing the casting
through a series of progressively smaller grooves to reduce the cross
section and increase the length. Cold-worked materials require interrup-
tions for annealing. Round, square, or rectangular wire is flat rolled
(and edge rolled to control shape) or rolled on shaped rolls to produce a
cross section other than rectangular.

(2) Sheet and strip: Rectangular castings are quickly
reduced to sheet by passes through large, rough rollers. Alloys that are
malleable at room temperature are cold rolled. Reduction is usually followed by annealing (often in molten salt), a flattening, and an "overhaul."
The latter involves milling to improve surface quality. High-production
horizontal machines are used with the cutter working against the bottom
face, while some older factories use a fly cutter on a boring mill.

Cleaned, annealed slabs are "run-down" with light
passes on a smooth, slightly lubricated two-high roll. After such rolling,
heavy sheets are cut to dimension and bright annealed. Metal for light-
gage strip is trimmed, coiled, bright annealed, and rolled on two-high,
four-high, or cluster mills with annealing as required.[3/]

e. Bright annealing: Rolls and dies routinely impart good, bright finishes to the mill products, which are not purposely polished or buffed. Buffing should be done after fabrication of the finished articles. Sterling silver is preferably bright annealed in oxygen-free atmospheres although many shops use open furnaces or torches, which can oxidize the copper in the alloy. The oxidation may be too extensive to remove by buffing or pickling acid.[3/]

f. Drawing: Castings, extrusions, and rolled wire can be reduced further by drawing through carbide or diamond dies. The reduction by drawing involves cold working interrupted by annealing. Wires intended for cold heading into rivet-type contacts must be "scalped" to remove any minor defects that act as stress raisers in the heading process. In scalping, the cast or extruded surface is removed by pulling the rod through a sharp-edged die.[3/]

g. Chemical machining: Chemical machining involves selective or overall removal of metal by controlled chemical attack to produce desired shapes and dimensions. Areas where metal is not to be removed are masked by photoresist coatings, screening, off-set printing, or scribe-and-peel. Solutions used for etching silver are 50 to 90 vol. % nitric acid at 38 to 49°C or ferric nitrate solutions (4 lb/gal) at about 50°C.

In general, chemical blanking is for cutting or stamping out parts from thin material, whereas chemical contour machining or chemical milling is for metal removal from thicker material. Chemical blanking gives intricate, burr-free shapes better than by conventional punch-press or press-brake blanking. Typical chemically blanked parts that may contain silver are electrical contacts and terminals.[4/]

2. Silver powders: Silver powders can be produced by physical, chemical, and electrochemical processes. The most common physical method for producing silver powders is atomization of a molten stream of silver with a high-velocity jet of gas or air. The atomized powder is spherical and has the highest "poured, or apparent density" of the kinds of powdered silver: about 6.0 g/cm^3. (The density of silver metal is 10.49 g/cm^3.)

The numerous chemical processes used to produce powders can be divided into two general classes: (a) those in which silver ions are replaced from solution by another more anodic metal and (b) those in which silver ion is reduced by an organic reducing agent, usually in the presence of caustic.

Replacement processes give dendritic, irregularly shaped powder with a poured density of about 1.2 to 2.4 g/cm^3. These are also called galvanic or cemented powders.

201

Chemically reduced powders are usually dusts of particle size 0.5 to 2 μ. Clumps 40 μ in diameter can be produced in the galvanic powder size range. The poured density of fine powders is 0.61 to 1.1 g/cm^3; of coarser powders, 1.8 to 2.4 g/cm^3. Finer chemical powders are used in conductive coatings and adhesives. They may be converted into silver flake for some use by ball milling with a polar, long-chain aliphatic compound, which prevents cold welding of the silver particles.

Electrolytic powders, which are used for catalysts and pigments in conductive coatings and in powder metallurgy, are produced by electrolyzing a silver salt such as silver sulfate, usually with free acid, at a current density high enough to liberate hydrogen vigorously and simultaneously with the silver. Depending on electrolysis conditions, powders resemble either cemented or chemical powder. The process is relatively unimportant commercially.

Some catalytic silver is produced from screened fines of electrolytic "needle" silver produced in the Moebius or Balbach-Thum refining processes.

The two most important metallurgical uses of silver powder are for porous electrodes (for primary batteries and for storage cells) and for production of pseudo alloys or mixtures of metals that cannot be melt-alloyed with silver. The latter are used primarily for electrical contacts. Both cemented and chemical powders are used. Powder metallurgy "alloys" include Ag-10% CdO, Ag-10% W, Ag-10% Fe, and Ag-40% Ni. They may be produced in wrought form from sintered powder billets or by rolling and drawing, or they may be used as pressed, shaped, and sintered parts.[5/]

3. Silver compounds:

a. Silver nitrate: Silver nitrate production comprises more than 95% of all silver utilization in chemicals with silver cyanide, chloride, and oxide accounting for the remainder. Almost all other silver chemicals are derived from silver nitrate. The silver content of the silver nitrate produced was about one-third of the 1966 U.S. industrial silver consumption. The major producers of silver nitrate are shown in Table VI-2; in addition, both General Aniline and Du Pont may also produce silver nitrate.[2/] In 1963 and 1967, over half of the silver nitrate production was used at the same plant as its manufacture.[6/] The largest user of silver nitrate products is the photographic industry.[2,7/]

Classically, silver nitrate is manufactured by treating 99.9 to 99.99% pure silver with a hot nitric acid solution prepared from equal volumes of water and 42°Be' acid. The fume (NO and NO$_2$), mixed with entrained air, is scrubbed in an absorption tower with an alkaline solution to take up the nitrogen dioxide before venting to the atmosphere.

A slight excess of Ag_2O is added to the nitrate solution to give pH ~5.9; subsequent boiling precipitates most of the copper, lead, bismuth, iron, and gold impurities. The filtered solution can be used directly to produce other silver chemicals.

Silver nitrate is crystallized and then recrystallized for photographic uses and other uses requiring the highest purity. Silver nitrate crystals form when the reacidified solution is evaporated to 85% $AgNO_3$ and cooled.

The Kestner-Johnson Process (U.S. Patents 2,581,518 and 2,581,519) developed by Johnson and Sons' Smelting Works, Ltd., facilitates the dissolution of silver in nitric acid. Many plants use the process to produce solutions for direct use and for crystallizing. In this process, silver bars are leached with 45% nitric acid in a pure oxygen atmosphere; the nitric oxide is continuously oxidized to nitrogen dioxide, which reacts with water to form more nitric acid and nitric oxide. The nitric acid solution is then passed over a bed of granulated silver in the presence of oxygen to exhaust most of the acid. The resulting solution contains about 84 troy oz silver per gallon.

The Eastman Kodak process gives 85% silver nitrate solutions by dissolving 99.97% pure silver in 65% nitric acid. Du Pont holds patents for the precrystallization purification of silver nitrate solutions using high-surface adsorbers and UV-radiation-induced reduction of noble-metal impurities. Certain Du Pont processes and the Kestner-Johnson process are used by Engelhard's New Jersey plant, with a silver nitrate capacity of 62,500 lb/year.[7]

        b. Silver cyanide: Silver cyanide is usually precipitated from silver nitrate solutions by adding sodium or potassium cyanide. The product is packed in cardboard tubes or fiber containers and shipped express since silver cyanide is not mailable.[8]

        c. Other silver chemical products: Battery manufacturers are among the largest users of other silver chemicals. Materials used in this industry include silver chloride, silver iodide, Ag oxides, and silver powder. The major producers of silver batteries are shown in Table VI-3. Silver for batteries is processed for most companies (except Yardney) into sheet silver and silver powder.[2]

        Producers of silver chemicals for laboratory and industrial uses are identified in Table VI-4.

B. Silver Use Categories

Following is a discussion of the major uses of silver and silver compounds.

1. Photographic uses: The photographic industry consumed an average of 42,014,000 troy oz silver per year in the period 1966 to 1972, which was 28.03% of the total industrial consumption.

One can calculate from the U.S. Bureau of Census data in Table VI-5 that about 7% of the value of manufacturer's shipments of silver-containing photographic products represents the net difference between exports and imports. Thus it appears that 7% of the silver sold to the photographic industry industry is not consumed in this country. Average annual U.S. consumption of silver for photographic purposes would then be reduced from about 42 million troy ounces to 39 million troy ounces.

During the 1960's, Eastman Kodak consumed about 50% of the silver used annually for photographic products; the next three largest consumers, in approximate order of consumption, were General Aniline and Film (GAF), Du Pont, and 3M. Smaller silver consumers (less than 1 million troy ounces per year) were Xerox, Bell and Howell, Powers Chemco, Polaroid, Killborn Photo Paper Co., and Agfa-Gavaert Inc. Eastman Kodak and Du Pont, who produce X-ray film, manufacture their own silver nitrate while 3M (industrial film) manufactures some of its silver nitrate but purchases the majority of it from other producers.

In 1965, Eastman Kodak may have accounted for over 90% of the positive and negative industrial film sales, 95% of the 35 mm movie film sales, 50% of the X-ray film market, and 75% of the film used by the motion picture industry.[2/]

Table VI-6 shows the forms of silver used in certain photographic uses and Table VI-7 shows the silver forms in office copying systems.

2. Electrical uses: Uses of silver in electrical contacts and conductors, conductive coatings, electronics, and batteries are discussed in this section.

a. Electrical contacts and conductors: Average annual sales of 30,055,000 troy oz silver for contacts and conductors comprise one-fifth of total industrial sales. In 1929, silver was not used at all for electrical contacts and conductors. The consumption of silver in this use area grew rapidly in the period 1935 to 1940, and now silver is the most common material in make-and-break contacts. Primary uses of silver contacts are automotive, appliances, motor controls, communications, and electronics.[2,9]

Several ultimate contact users make their own contacts, but the nine principal fabricators of electrical contacts are:

> Deringer Metallurgical Corporation
> Fansteel
> Texas Instruments
> H. A. Wilson Company (subsidiary of Engelhard)
> C. S. Branen
> Gibson Electric
> R. P. Mallory
> Contacts, Incorporated
> Precision Metallurgical Company

H. A. Wilson, Texas Instruments, C. S. Branen, and R. P. Mallory process their own silver from silver bullion. The others purchase the wire and strip from either American Platinum (Engelhard) or Handy and Harman, Inc.[2]

Typical classes of silver contacts are (a) pure silver and silver alloys, (b) silver with semirefractory elements, and (c) silver with a refractory constituent.[9] Tables VI-8, VI-9, and VI-10 provide examples of these three classes.

Typical contact alloys contain 75 to 99.9% silver. Most semirefractory materials[a] contain more than 80% silver (range: 40.0 to 99.3%) with the most used silver semirefractory contact material being 85 to 97.5% Ag-CdO. Tungsten, tungsten carbide, nickel, carbon, magnesium, iron, cadmium oxide, or molybdenum improve silver's resistance to electrical erosion and "welding" or sticking. Refractory materials Ag-WC and Ag-W contain 40 to 65% and 27.5 to 90% silver, respectively.[2,9]

Table VI-11 gives the uses of silver contact materials in telecommunications apparatus. Miscellaneous electrical uses of silver other than electrical contacts are shown in Table VI-12.

---

[a] Semirefractory materials are mixtures of silver with other elements, metalloids, or metallic oxides. They are fabricated by powder metallurgy techniques because the components do not have compatible melting temperatures or are not mutually soluble.

b. Conductive coatings (other than electroplate): Silver used in ceramic paints is included in the Minerals Yearbook miscellaneous consumption category. The total miscellaneous consumption of silver increased from 2,564,000 troy oz in 1966 to 6,381,000 troy oz in 1972. Conductive coatings include electrically conductive coatings produced with silver paint, protective coatings, and others; examples of these applications are shown in Table VI-13.

c. Electronics: R. W. Ageton estimated that 8 million troy ounces silver was used in electronic components and accessories in 1968 and that 30 million troy ounces would be used in the year 2000.[10]

Electronic components that may use silver include relays, resistors, switches, integrated circuits, hearing aids, and lasers. Automotive electronic systems include voltage regulators, anti-pollution systems, electronic ignition systems, fuel-injection systems, and safety systems such as seat-belt interlocks.[11] Specific electronic uses of silver are shown in Table VI-14.

d. Batteries: The average annual amount used for batteries in the period 1966 to 1972 was 7,357,000 troy oz or 4.91% of total industrial consumption. Silver batteries were first used on a large scale in World War II. In 1967, about 90% of the amount of silver used for batteries was still in defense and space applications: torpedoes, missiles, helicopters, target and reconnaissance drones, sounding balloons, satellites space vehicles, and transceivers (at least 13% of total annual silver battery sales in the sixties). Thus, the amount of silver used for batteries is linked to defense spending.

Silver-containing batteries are also used in portable and industrial equipment, portable electronics, photographic equipment, small appliances, and portable television sets. Silver competes with mercury for some hearing aid batteries. The silver-cadmium battery competes directly with more common batteries in consumer appliances and has a longer life than the silver-zinc battery.

Industry experts in the late sixties did not expect that silver would be a serious contender as a battery component for electric cars. The Yardney model electric car battery contained 1,000 troy oz silver. At that rate, 150,000 cars would require an amount of silver comparable with the entire U.S. industrial consumption.[2]

Table VI-15 shows the uses of silver oxide-zinc, silver oxide cadmium, silver chloride-magnesium, and other silver batteries.

3. <u>Sterling and coinage silver</u>: This section describes uses of silver in sterling flatware and hollowware, jewelry, collector arts, and coinage.

a. <u>Sterling flatware and hollowware</u>: The average annual silver sales to industry for sterling ware production in the period 1966 to 1972 was 25,544,000 troy oz (17.04% of the total industrial sales). Most sterling silver is used in the manufacture of sterling silver flatware and hollowware. Sterling ware also includes other items for home, office, and personal use, such as collector arts.

Silverware firms are the principal purchasers of silver sheet, strip, and coil. Gorham, Samuel Kirk and Son, Tiffany, and possibly International Silver, however, roll their own silver, which is purchased from primary producers or the government. All four purchase 20 to 50% of their silver from Handy and Harman and Engelhard. Other silverware firms purchase from these same two sources and return all scrap to them for processing on a toll basis. In the 1960's, International Silver consumed 5 million troy ounces silver per year. Gorham, Oneida, Towle, Reed and Barton, and Wallace purchased 1 to 5 million troy ounces each. Lunt Silversmiths, Kirk, Stieff, and Tiffany each purchased less than 1 million troy ounces per year.[2]

b. <u>Jewelry</u>: The average annual consumption of silver for jewelry purposes in the period 1966 to 1972 was 4,726,000 troy oz or 3.16% of total consumption.

Silver jewelry can be manufactured either by electroplating base metals or plastics or by fabrication from refinery forms.

Silver can also be incorporated into jewelry via jewelry solders (silver binary alloys with gold, nickel, platinum, or copper),[12] colored golds (gold-silver-copper alloys),[13] cladding aluminum,[14] and the Niello inlaying process (silver sulfide).[15]

Silver used by U.S. Indians comes through the usual commercial channels to white traders in the Southwest, who often stake silversmiths to a supply of slug, sheet, and wire. Silver jewelry by the Zuni, Navajo, and Hopi tribes are commonly retailed items.[16]

c. <u>Collector arts</u>: Table VI-16 gives the amounts of silver in the category "Commemorative and Collector Arts" since 1969 when Handy and Harman first estimated silver consumption for this purpose. The category includes commemorative medals and medallions, souvenir plates, 1-oz .999 fine bars, small souvenir bars, etc. Previously, this type of use was distributed between sterling ware and miscellaneous.[17]

d. <u>Coinage</u>: The Coinage Act of 1965 eliminated silver from dimes and quarters and reduced the silver content of half-dollars to 40%. Legislation in 1970 curtailed the use of silver in half-dollars. Since that time U.S. subsidiary coinage has not contained silver.[18]/

In 1975, beginning on July 4, minting of up to 45 million silver-clad quarters, half-dollars, and dollars has been authorized. They will probably be three-layer composites with the same silver content as the dollars presently being minted: outer layers 80% silver and 20% copper, and the core 21.5% silver and 78.5% copper.[19]/

Use of 47.4 million troy ounces silver for minting 150 million Eisenhower memorial dollars was authorized in 1970.[20]/ Little of this amount has been so used to date. Coinage consumption of silver in the U.S. in 1970, 1971, 1972 was 0.709, 2.474, and 2.284 million troy ounces silver, respectively.[21]/

4. <u>Brazing alloys and solders</u>: Brazing alloys and solders accounted for 9.88% of the annual industrial sales in the period 1966 to 1972; this is an average of 14,831,000 troy oz/year.

a. <u>Brazing alloys</u>: Brazing, according to Merriam Webster, means soldering with relatively infusible alloys compared with common solder. The American Welding Society uses the term "Brazing Filler Metals" as the correct term referring to metals used to fill a braze--a weld produced by distributing a molten filler metal, above 421°C but below the melting temperature of the base metals, by capillary flow into the joint between them. "Brazing alloys" is the commonly used term for "brazing filler metals."[22]/

Leach, in 1940, divided the silver alloys used for joining metals according to their melting temperatures: (a) those alloys (and pure silver) melting above 870°C, (b) those melting from 630.5 to 870°C, and (c) those melting below 630.5°C. Fine silver rod is used to join silver-clad iron or nickel. Alloys in Group 2 had been called "silver solders" for many years and comprised chiefly silver-copper and -zinc alloys with or without cadmium; they contained 5 to 80% silver. The switch to the term "silver brazing alloys" was prompted by confusion with tin-lead alloys or soft solders. The third group comprises lead or cadmium-based alloys containing typically 2.5 to 6% silver. They melt above common soft solders (> 200°C).[23]/

Silver brazing alloys came into wide use in the 1930's. Silver alloys are now the most widely used material for brazing in all metalworking industries. The approximate order of importance of uses of silver brazing alloys are:

       (1) Air conditioning and refrigeration.[a]

       (2) Plumbing and heating (industrial and commercial piping).

       (3) Automotive parts.

       (4) Aircraft and aircraft engines.

       (5) Electrical appliances.

       (6) Shipbuilding.

       (7) Motors and generators.

       (8) Electronic components.

       (9) Space and missiles.

     (10) Silverware and jewelry.[2,18,22,24]

Brazing alloys are also used in bicycle manufacture and manufacture of military goods such as artillery shells, firearms parts, and rocket tubing.[18]

Silver brazing alloys are used for joining steel, stainless steel, iron, copper, brass, bronze, nickel and its alloys, and silver-base alloys but are not used for aluminum and magnesium.[22] Most are silver-copper alloys modified with zinc, cadmium, tin, indium, nickel, manganese, phosphorus, and/or lithium. The BAg alloys contain 39 to 93% silver; BCuP-3 and BCuP-5 alloys contain 5 and 15% silver, respectively, and the rest copper. Typical cadmium-based alloys contain 4 to 5% silver and 78.4 to 95.0% cadmium with or without zinc and copper. Most of the commercial alloys have flow points of 593 to 871°C.[24]

The advantages of silver brazing alloys over cheaper base-metal and tin-lead alloys are (a) the ability to wet a variety of base metals at temperatures much below the melting points of the base metals, (b) lower melting points than the "soft" alloys, (c) noncorrosiveness to steels in normal usage, (d) malleability and ductility, (e) corrosion resistance, (f) high electrical conductivity, (g) usefulness in step-brazing,

---

[a] Most copper tubing in refrigeration systems is brazed or soldered with silver alloys.

and (h) ability to join dissimilar combinations, e.g., stainless steels to nonferrous metals and cermets.[2,24]/

Their disadvantages include (a) melting at temperatures too high for some types of bonding (e.g., bonding of lead pipes), (b) their high cost for many applications, (c) lower electrical conductivity than certain copper-intensive brazing alloys, and (d) their weakening at high temperatures with strength declining rapidly above 200°C.[2]/

Specific brazing uses of silver are given in Table VI-17.

b. Solders: According to The Silver Institute, soldering temperatures are generally 175 to 315°C as compared with brazing temperatures of 315 to 815°C. As a manufacturing step, soldering is somewhat easier, faster, and cheaper than brazing.[25]/

The Silver Institute states that silver solders are used in plumbing, heating, refrigeration, air conditioning, food service and processing utensils, hollowware, and electronics.[25]/ These applications approximate those mentioned above for silver brazing alloys. The solders listed in Table VI-18 are based on tin, lead, gold, or cadmium and contain 35.0% or less silver.

5. Electroplate and other coatings:

a. Electroplate: Although electroplating is a manufacturing procedure used in fabrication of various end-use items, the Bureau of Mines classifies electroplated ware as a major use category. The average annual industrial consumption of silver for electroplated ware during the period 1966 to 1972 was 14,633,000 troy oz or 9.76% of total industrial consumption.

The major products where silver electroplating is used include: silverware, bearings, chemical and food processing equipment, electrical apparatus, jewelry, and decorative art. See Table VI-19.

The Metals Handbook states that a conventional silver-plating bath contains 3.4 to 4.4 oz of AgCN, 4 to 6 oz of KCN, and 3 to 12 oz of K_2CO_3 per gallon of bath although in some special silver-plating operations higher silver concentrations are used.[26,27]/

Alloys of silver are also electrodeposited. Binary alloys of silver with antimony, bismuth, cadmium, cobalt, copper, gold, indium, iron, lead, nickel, palladium, platinum, rhodium, ruthenium, selenium, thallium, tin, and zinc had been electrodeposited from aqueous solution by 1960. Between 1960 and 1972, techniques for depositing binary alloys with molybdenum, rhenium, and tungsten were developed.

210

Production of a silver-rhenium alloy, first reported in 1965, is by a patented industrial process in which the alloy is plated from solutions containing silver cyanide, sodium perrhenate, potassium carbonate, and potassium cyanide. The alloys are used for solid-film lubrication, grease retention-secondary lubrications, swaged _in situ_ bearings, electrical rotary switches, and fretting corrosion-resistant coatings. Silver-rhenium is superior to other silver or gold alloys in wear life and lubrication properties. Substituting sodium molybdate in the bath gives a silver-molybdenum alloy.

Several patents have recently been given on electrochemical production of bright, high-carat alloys of gold with silver. Gold coatings containing 5 to 20% silver can be applied to electrical components from EDTA-containing cyanide baths. Bright white cadmium-silver-nickel alloys electroplated on jewelry, instruments, automobile trim, etc., give adherent rhodium-like coatings. They resist ordinary wear, abrasion, scuffing, and tarnishing.

Electrodeposition gives a Ag-3% Sb alloy suitable for contact components. Electrodeposited silver-antimony and silver-tin possess hardness and wear resistance. An electrodeposited silver-tungsten alloy meets precision resistance requirements.

The production of ternary alloys of gold and silver with antimony, copper, or indium by electrodeposition has been studied recently.[28/]

   b. Conductive coatings (paints): Silver paints are used for solder bonding to nonconductors and nonmetallic surfaces, decorating porcelains and glass, and producing electrically conductive surfaces on nonconductors. The paints used for bonding to ceramics and other refractory materials contain a fusible ground-glass flux. Paints for wood, paper, and plastics, all of which cannot be subjected to high temperatures, contain no glass flux and may be air-dried or baked at about 150°C. A typical air-drying paint contains 50% silver flake, lacquer or 5 to 15% varnish resin plasticizer, other nonvolatiles, and the rest solvents.

   After applying and low-temperature baking, the solvent is driven from the flux-containing silver paint. Heating the pieces to the glass-fusion temperature ($\sim$ 500 to 700°C) melts and wets the refractory substrate, burns off the organic binder, and sinters the silver particles to give a $\leq$ 0.001-in. porous, sintered silver film penetrated by a bonding glass phase. The surface appearance is matte or satin-like. Single applications of paints containing 60% silver give 0.0029 to 0.006 g silver/cm^2 when wet, 0.0022 to 0.0045 g/cm^2 baked, and 0.0019 to 0.0039 g/cm^2 fired.[29/]

211

c. <u>Vacuum coatings</u>: Vacuum-deposited silver coatings are
used for decorations applied to plastics, ceramics, glass, etc.; mirrors,
especially those in optical instruments; thin-film conductors; and electric
light bulb reflectors.[30/] The function of the soft, optical coatings is
to give high reflection of visible and infrared light. The evaporant is
in the form of silver wire or shot. For decorative coatings, the evaporant
is silver wire, chunks, or pellets.[26/]

In the vacuum evaporation process, silver is placed in contact with a refractory-metal (tungsten or molybdenum) filament or boat
inside a bell jar. The object to be coated is placed near the filament.
A vacuum of $\leq 10^{-4}$ Torr is applied and the filament is heated electrically
until the silver melts (20 to 60 sec) and deposits by evaporation on the
substrate (at 1049°C, the silver vapor pressure is 10^{-2} Torr). The total
exposure time is 1 to 3 min.[26,30/]

Silver may be applied to the refractory metal vaporizer by
electroplating; applied as a slurry containing finely powdered silver,
nitrocellulose binder, and solvent; or applied as an alloy in the form of
rolled strip or wire. The latter method is the only one adaptable for mass
production. The alloy is made by vacuum melting to avoid degassing during
vaporization; the amounts of the alloying elements, silicon and lithium,
are too small to affect the reflectivity of the silver surface produced.

d. <u>Electrolessly deposited coatings</u>: Electroless silver
plating (chemical reduction plating) is used to render nonconductors conductive for subsequent plating operations. This procedure, as applied to
mirror production, will be described in Section IV.E.1. Silver, copper,
and nickel are the most common metals for plating nonconductors with
stannous chloride being the normal sensitizer. Electroless plating is
usually followed by an intermediate copper plating, followed by the desired
plating.[31/] Four recent patents, summarized below, illustrate some uses
for silver in this process.

Water-sensitive surfaces are coated by immersion in anhydrous
solution of a silver-pyridine complex, followed by the addition of dextrose
to reduce the silver ions and produce the silver coating.[32/]

Copper and other metals less noble than silver can be coated
by immersion or swabbing with aqueous solutions of silver nitrate and sodium cyanide. This process is useful for electric circuit components.[32/]

Copper and brass objects may be dipped in solutions containing silver nitrate, sodium cyanide, triethanolamine, and hydrazine at
room temperature to produce 0.4-μ-thick silver coatings.[32/]

212

After 6 months, a complex aqueous solution, containing 1% AgBr, BeO, $Si_2H_5Cl_3$, and kerosene, deposited a 10-μ silver alloy film on a polished mild-steel plate. This solution may be useful as a water treatment to prevent corrosion of steel tanks, pipes, heaters, and boilers.[32/]

6. Catalysis and petrochemicals separation: This subsection is concerned primarily with the utilization of silver in two important industrial applications: catalysis and petrochemicals separation.

a. Catalysis: Reactions catalyzed by silver or silver compounds can be classified as oxidation, reduction or decomposition, petroleum refining, and polymerization. Specific examples of these uses are shown in Tables VI-20, VI-21, VI-22, and VI-23.

(1) Oxidation catalysts:

(a) Formaldehyde production: The silver catalyst used in production of formaldehyde by dehydration and oxidation of methanol at 450 to 600°C comprises ≥ 99.95% twice-electrodeposited silver crystals and/or silver screens. (The only allowable impurity is 0.05% copper.)[33,34/] The catalyst, whose life is 0.5 to 1 year, is regenerated by burning off carbon, treating in concentrated hydrochloric acid, removing silver chloride with ammonia, and electrolyzing twice to restore the original catalytic effectiveness.[33/]

With plants at 53 sites, the total U.S. formaldehyde capacity is 7.873 billion pounds.[35/] The Silver Institute claims that most of the U.S. formaldehyde production is made by passing methanol and air over pure silver meedles and gauze.[36/]

(b) Ethylene oxide manufacture: The catalytic oxidation of ethylene with air or oxygen to ethylene oxide in the presence of a silver catalyst is used in more recently built plants, replacing the production of ethylene oxide via ethylene chlorohydrin.[37/] Total installed ethylene oxide plants in the U.S. and Puerto Rico in 1972 might have required 7.4 million troy ounces silver, based on the calculation that 1.2 billion pound oxygen plant capacity required only 1/2 lb catalyst for each 1,000 lb/year of oxide capacity. Silver use in catalysts in 1966 was 2.7 million troy ounces; in 1967, 5.8 million troy ounces; in 1968, 2.2 million troy ounces; in 1969, 4.1 million troy ounces; in 1970, 2.1 million troy ounces; and in 1971, 1.7 million troy ounces. The average in the period 1966 to 1972 was 3.2 million troy ounces per year or 2.10% of total industrial consumption. Total installed ethylene oxide capacity in the U.S. and Puerto Rico in 1972 was about 4.8 billion pounds,[a/] 75% of which was

―――――――――――――――――――

a/ Actual annual U.S. production has been closer to 4 billion pounds. For example, it was 4.08 billion pounds in 1972.[36/]

based on air and 25% on oxygen.[38/]   The locations of these plants can be found in Reference 35.

The reaction is

$$CH_2:CH_2 + 1/2O_2 \xrightarrow{\text{Ag}} \triangledown + CO_2 + H_2O$$

The catalyst (10 to 15% silver) usually comprises silver oxide deposited on an inert carrier, e.g., corundum. Faith, Keyes, and Clark's 1965 edition of <u>Industrial Chemicals</u> states that the catalyst in the air oxidation process is replaced every 18 months and that the catalyst charge is 3.4 lb/ton ethylene oxide capacity. In oxygen plants, the catalyst charge is two to three times larger, but its life is prolonged.[37/]

Burke in <u>Chemical Week</u> in 1972 stated that since use of oxygen doubles the capacity of a reactor, the catalyst cost of an oxygen plant should be half that of an air plant.[38/]   Commercial plants using the Shell Development Company process[a/] continuously for 12 years claim to still be using the original silver catalyst charge with no change in pressure drop, activity, or selectivity.[39/] Burke gave the average life of an air plant catalyst as about 3 years and the catalyst charge as 1 lb/ 1,000 lb oxide capacity per year. He calculated that a modern oxide plant (air) with a minimum size of 300 million pounds ethylene oxide capacity would use catalyst containing about 525,000 troy oz silver. It was further stated that the annual market for replacement of silver catalysts for ethylene oxidation was 1.3 million pounds which at a 12% silver content would contain 2.3 million troy ounces of silver.[38/]

Union Carbide, the biggest ethylene oxide producer, makes its own silver catalyst. Scientific Design's Catalyst Development Corporation supplies catalysts for its licensees and has its silver activity boosted by gold, copper, or barium.[33/] Harshaw custom makes catalyst for Shell for plants using the Shell process. Dow makes its own catalysts for domestic consumption.[38/]

The 100 to 1,500:1 silver-beryllium catalyst used in Du Pont's vortex-layer process is metallic silver, containing beryllium oxide reduced <u>in situ</u> on kieselguhr or α-Al_2O_3. The catalyst contains 5 to 12% silver. Brittle alloys of silver with 20 to 60% calcium, aluminum,

---

a/   In November 1973, there were 25 in worldwide operation and 4 in design
        or construction.[39/]   At that time, there were 49 plants in 15 coun-
        tries using the Scientific Design Company, Inc., process that had
        been built or were being designed.[40/]

magnesium, antimony, zinc, or barium can be crushed and extracted to give catalysts similar to Raney-nickel. For example, the ground alloy 84% Ag-10% Al-6% Ca is extracted with 4 $\underline{N}$ hydrochloric acid and used to catalyze the oxidation of ethylene to ethylene oxide.[33] Most ethylene oxide is converted to other chemicals, e.g., ethylene glycol,[a] in the plant where it is produced.[37]

(c) Glyoxal: Ethylene glycol can be oxidized in the vapor phase to glyoxal (CHOCHO) with an air-nitrogen mixture in the presence of a catalyst comprising finely divided silver and/or silver oxide on a carrier. Glyoxal is used for producing synthetic fibers (glyoxal-HCHO resins) and for increasing the crease resistance of textiles made of synthetic fibers.[33]

(2) Reduction and/or decomposition catalysts: "Hydrogenation reactions using silver catalysts, as illustrated by Raney metals and platinum metals, are unknown" according to Paul Pickhardt of DEGUSSA and the University of Mainz, Germany.[33] The hydrogenation catalysts included in Table VI-21 include silver as the sulfide or alloyed with palladium.

Among "organic name reactions" appearing in The Merck Index,[41] only the Bart reaction employs silver as a catalyst. Reactions such as the Hofmann degradation and the Hunsdiecker reaction employ silver compounds as reactants. As judged by references to it, the decomposition of hydrogen peroxide is a well-known silver-catalyzed reaction.[2,33]

(3) Petroleum refining catalyst: Catalysts containing silver have been patented or studied for petroleum refining processes such as hydrocracking, desulfurization, reforming, and isomerization. See Table VI-22.

(4) Polymerization catalysts: Some studied or patented uses of silver compounds as polymerization catalysts are given in Table VI-23.

Cosmetic firms or their suppliers may use 0.1 to 100 ppm silver salts (or cupric, ferric, or chromic salts) to catalyze vinyl polymerization. The polymers are used for fingernail elongators. The formulations, which do not contain silver catalyst but usually methyl methacrylate or its low polymer and benzoyl peroxide, polymerize when applied to the fingernails.[42,43]

---

a/ Major markets for ethylene glycol include antifreeze and polyesters such as terephthalates.

b. <u>Petrochemicals separation</u>: Silver compounds have been patented for separation of gases in petrochemical refinery mixed hydrocarbon streams since at least 1959.[33/] Since three of the processes described in Table VI-24 have been patented within the last 2 years, this use of silver is probably widespread and undergoing constant improvements.

7. <u>Dental, medical, and nonmedicinal antimicrobial uses</u>: The various dental, medical, and nonmedicinal antimicrobial uses of silver, as well as certain preparative methods, are presented in this discussion.

a. <u>Dental uses</u>: The principal supplier of amalgam alloy in the 1960's was L. D. Caulk and Company. Other suppliers included S. S. White Company, Engelhard's Baker Artist Alloy, General Refineries, and Karr Company.[2/]

Procedures for manufacturing amalgam alloy comprise (a) melting, (b) casting, (c) reduction of ingots to filings, (d) magnetic removal of iron particles and screening, (e) annealing, and (f) cleaning of the filings with hydrochloric acid.[44/] Typically, alloys for dental amalgam comprise silver, 67 to 70%; tin, 25.3 to 27.7%; copper, 0 to 5.2%; and zinc, 0 to 1.7%. Amalgam alloys are alloyed without oxidation, cast into cylindrical ingots, cooled, comminuted into filings, heat treated to "age" the filings, and delivered to the dentist.

The dentist or his assistant triturates the alloy filings with mercury in a definite proportion, generally 5:8, and quickly introduces the amalgam into the prepared cavity.[45/]

Silver is not only used in amalgam alloy for dental restorations of decayed teeth but also for solders, wires, casting alloys, and prophylactic treatment. See Table VI-25.

The average annual combined sales to the dental and medical supply industries was 2,159,000 troy oz during the years 1966 to 1972; this corresponds to 1.44% of the total industrial sales. Listings of the major U.S. silver fabricators and their plant locations may be found in References 46 and 47. Among these are primary refiners, tabulated in Section V.D. and secondary refiners, Section V.E.

b. <u>Medical uses</u>: The use of silver compounds for topical application to mucous membranes and for internal use has become nearly obsolete because of the fear of argyria and the advent of quaternary ammonium, sulfonamide, and antibiotic antimicrobials. Hill and Pillsbury's <u>Argyria: The Pharmacology of Silver</u>[48/] should be consulted for an in-depth picture of silver in medical practice prior to 1939. Table VI-26 lists the proprietary silver compounds in use in 1939. Much of the literature with respect to the physiology of silver makes use of these terms.

Silver nitrate is a broad spectrum antimicrobial compared with antibiotics and sulfonamides. Sensitization with silver compounds is rare or nonexistent and development of resistant strains of organisms is relatively unknown.[45/] Laws in many states still require that a few drops of a 1 or 2% silver nitrate solution be applied to the conjunctiva of the eyes of newborn infants to prevent ophthalmia neonatorum.[49/]

Dr. Harry Margraf, inventor of many of the new ointments and dressings containing silver compounds for treating burn patients, believes that medical use of silver will increase and that silver will again be used to treat stomach ulcers, bladder infections, and venereal diseases.[50/]

Silver surgical prostheses and/or splints have been used since at least 1804. When silver wires and other metal prostheses and splints were used to bind bone fragments, they were removed after healing because of corrosion in the body. With the advent of Vitallium and stainless steel prostheses, this is no longer necessary. Silver lacks structural strength and has caused bone erosion as well as discoloration and excessive scar in tissue.[51/]

Medical uses of silver, both those current and those falling into obsolescence, are given in Table VI-27. The significance of the widespread long-term medical use of silver compounds in relation to the potential hazards of environmental exposure to silver will be discussed in Section IX.

c. Nonmedicinal antimicrobial uses: Oligodynamic sterilization processes such as that employing Katadyn quartz sand were widely used in the thirties in Europe for treating food, drinking water, and swimming pools.[52,53/] The oligodynamic effect is that lethal effect of metals in concentrations as low as 1 ppb in small populations of a given organism. The approximate descending order of oligodynamic activity of metals is Cu, Ag, Hg, Cd, Zn, Mg, Pb, Sn, and Pd.[52/]

"Katadyn" silver, developed by Krause in 1928, comprised a spongy, lamellar, metallic form of pure silver to which was added an activating metal below silver in the electrochemical series, such as palladium or gold. The silver was used as a coating on sand or as container linings or was impregnated into filters.[45/] The "Katadyn-Electro" process brought active silver in high concentrations into solution by electrolysis in aqueous liquids.[52/]

Other products that utilize the oligodynamic effect of silver include U-glow Black Silver Sand (sand coated with Ag-Mn), Fissan-Silver Powder (silver with milk albumin and a colloid), Movidyn, and O-silver.[45]/

Between approximately 1900 and 1915, soluble silver salts as sprays with wetting agents were field tested as fungicides but fell into disrepute. Silver nitrate was used in many tobacco-growing areas to protect tobacco seed against *Bacterium tabacum*.[53]/

There has been recent renewed interest in silver for water purification of swimming pools and drinking water. Adding small amounts of silver compounds to swimming pools cuts down the dosage of other chemicals, which irritate swimmers' eyes and mucous membranes.[54]/

Several nonmedicinal antimicrobial uses of silver are shown in Table VI-28. See also Section VI.B.10, which includes antimicrobial applications of silver in food processing.

8. Mirrors and other glass applications:

a. Mirrors: Metallized glass, first produced in the 7th century, had used lead and tin until the 14th century when mercury use began. Justus von Liebig in 1835 first suggested the possible use of silver in making mirrors.

In mirror production, two separate solutions are prepared, one containing ammonia-complexed silver ion and the other containing a reducing agent, usually formaldehyde, Rochelle salts, invert sugar, or hydrazine.

Since World War II, all major mirror manufacturers have used proprietary conveyerized operations including spraying the polished glass with stannous chloride to prepare for an even deposit; rinsing; duel spraying with the silvering and reducing solutions, which almost instantaneously reduces the silver; rinsing; and, usually, copper plating. Spent solutions contain considerable amounts of silver and residues should be acidified prior to recovery processes because Ag^+ and NH_3 in alkaline solutions form "fulminating silver" (Ag_3N or possibly Ag_2NH[55]/), which is very shock-sensitive and violently explosive.

A typical mirror has a silver coating of 0.15 g/ft^2. The film thickness is 1.2 to 7.9 x 10^{-6} in. Protective silicone coatings are baked on at 115°C.[56]/

In the 1960's, the mirror industry comprised 19 firms with Hilan Company in North Carolina and Century Engineering in New Jersey supplying 90 to 95% of the silver used.[2/]

Industrial sales of silver for mirrors averaged 1,728,000 troy oz per year in the period 1966 to 1972, or 1.15% of total industrial consumption.

Mirrors, containing chemically or vacuum-deposited silver, are used for decorative purposes and also for optical instruments.[57/]

Silver mirrors are used as the reflecting surface of visible and infrared reflectors.[13/] Vacuum-deposited aluminum-silver systems are used for optical mirrors in laser-Raman spectrophotometers and commercial mirrors.[58/]

Spacecraft temperatures are controlled by second surface mirrors comprising silver-metallized fluorocarbon Type-A film adhesive, which is bonded to the aluminum surface of the spacecraft.[59/]

b. Glass: A recent development of silver use in glass has been photochromic glass for eyeglass lenses. Uses in connection with glass include automobile rear window defrosting, polishing and coloring glass, and glazing materials that reflect sunlight. See Table VI-29.

9. Bearings: In the period 1966 to 1972, an average of 455,000 troy oz/year (0.30% of the total industrial consumption) was sold to industries for bearings manufacture.

In the manufacture of bearings, silver is plated or bonded to a backing material, usually a low-carbon steel, and the final bearing configuration is machined to size.

The current principal method of bearings manufacture is electroplating. Steel with a microlayer of nickel or copper is plated with silver from a silver cyanide solution and machined prior to flash plating a lead-tin overlay.

In thermal bonding, the heating of a three-layer composite of silver, intermediate flux, and steel under pressure with subsequent rolling is successful for producing uncomplicated or off-round bearing parts.

The original method for producing bearings was casting. Silver is cast into steel shells much as is done with conventional bearing materials. Since silver will not alloy with steel to form a diffusion layer or adequate bond in this process, the steel is first bonded to copper.[60/]

219

Table VI-30 shows several applications for silver as a bearing material.

10. Silver in processing equipment: In this subsection, the variety of uses of silver are discussed with respect to chemical process and laboratory equipment and apparatus and additives for beverages, food, and drug processing.

a. Food and drug processing apparatus: The quantities of silver utilized for these purposes are distributed between the electroplated ware and the sterling silver statistics in the Minerals Yearbook.

In Table VI-31, we have attempted to segregate uses of silver apparatus that might ultimately contribute traces of silver to drinking water or other beverages, food, and drugs. See also Section VI.B.7., Nonmedicinal antimicrobials.

A recent patent [U.S. Patent 3,725,202 (April 3, 1973), Standard Brands Incorporated] describes the use of silver nitrate in enzyme preparations to inactivate transglucosidase and glucoamylase and render the preparation more useful for making dextrose from starch.[19/]

Other applications of silver in foods and beverages have been recommended (e.g., the use of finely divided silver chloride to remove off flavors in wine)[57/] but do not appear to have been employed industrially.

b. Other process and laboratory equipment: Due to its corrosion resistance, silver has many applications in chemical process and laboratory equipment. Examples of these uses are presented in Table VI-32.

11. Cloud seeding:

a. Cloud-seeding agents and their mode of action: In 1947, Bernard Vonnegut, in General Electric laboratory experiments, showed that silver iodide crystals can initiate ice crystal formation. (Solid carbon dioxide had proved successful in 1946.) Since then, cloud seeding has been used in attempts to increase or decrease precipitation, spread heavy snowfall over larger areas, dissipate fogs, reduce the size of hailstones, and suppress hurricanes and lightning.[61/]

Silver iodide crystals belong to the same hexagonal crystallographic system as ice crystals and can form nuclei for the condensation and crystallization of water in a supercooled ($\leq -4°C$), and therefore supersaturated, moisture-laden atmosphere.[62/] Optimum conditions must be such that precipitation is incipient but lacks only the nuclei to trigger it. Clouds and down currents are needed to induce precipitation. Although some natural rain would fall, the amount can be increased because the nuclei are effective at much lower altitudes in a cloud than are the natural nuclei.[63,64]

Lead iodide, phloroglucinol, 1,5-dihydroxynaphthalene, and metaldehyde are possible substitutes for silver iodide. The latter three require warmer temperatures to induce nucleii, there are sublimation losses when they are finely divided, and they cannot be dispensed efficiently from the ground. Metaldehyde is known to be toxic. (It is used as a snail and slug poison.)[62,65]

A 1968 report stated that silver iodide and lead iodide (for pyrotechnic devices) were still the most practical nucleants.[66]

The advantages of silver iodide with respect to substitutes are that it induces ice crystal formation at relatively high temperatures, it is easily finely subdivided, it is readily carried in updrafts to cloud bases, and small amounts initiate nucleation.[65] Ten to 1,000 times the weight of other substances is required to produce the same number of ice crystals.

Violent winds may be reduced by seeding when the latent heat that is released (as water droplets change to ice crystals) causes air expansion within the cloud and fall of atmospheric pressure below the cloud.[61]

Research in dispersing fog over airports and highways seldom employs silver iodide. Warm fog may be dissipated by hygroscopic nucleators such as sodium chloride, calcium chloride, polyelectrolytes, or surfactants. Dry ice is used to dissipate cold fog. The use of seeding to suppress lightning was still experimental in 1968.[66]

Silver iodide may become a less important cloud-seeding agent as more reliance is placed on pyrotechnic devices, aircraft, and other aerial delivery schemes rather than on ground generators.[65]

b. Methods of silver iodide dispersion and delivery:
There are two variations of silver iodide dispersion. Either the iodides are dispersed by a mixture of the composite-propellant type, or the iodide is produced chemically; e.g., silver iodate is used as an oxidizer with a gas-forming binder and a heat-producing fuel metal.[62]

Five methods of dispersion of silver iodide smokes were described in 1964[67]:

(1) Evaporating powdered silver iodide from electrically heated wire to give pure silver iodide particles.

(2) Burning silver iodide in acetone to give an aircraft-type aerosol.

(3) Burning silver iodide in a ground-based liquid petroleum-gas burner.

(4) Burning a silver iodide-impregnated string in a liquid petroleum-gas flame.

(5) Impregnating a mealy pyrotechnic mixture with silver iodide complex in acetone.

Aerosol particles from Methods (1) and (2) also contain potassium iodide.

It was stated in a 1951 publication that the usual practice of dispersing silver iodide was from ground generators.[63/] Most silver iodide released in 1968 was still from ground-based generators.

The reported silver iodide output of 12 steady-state generators in 1968 ranged from 6 to 1,589 g/hr (average 255 g/hr). The average silver output would be 3.8 troy oz/hr. One generator is usually required per 100 sq miles target area.[65/] On this basis, 980 generators would have been required in 1965 to cover the 98,000 sq miles treated that year. Thus, in 1 hr of operation, the 980 generators would produce 3,700 troy oz silver. One commercial operator (North American Weather Consultants of Utah) operated silver iodide generators for "some 18,000 hr" in 36 months of 1959 to 1964.[68/]

Cooper has reported that the typical silver content of seeded precipitation ranges from 0.01 to 0.03 ppb.[65/] A 1968 NSF report states that fresh, seeded precipitation may contain 1 to 10 ppb silver and that the silver concentration of precipitation when no seeding has been done is 0.01 ppb.[66/] Reports in 1963 indicated that silver iodide nuclei are carried over and redistributed from one day to the next.[69/]

A 1972 report by Stanford Research Institute (SRI) and sponsored by the National Science Foundation has concluded that increasing snowfall in the Upper Colorado River Basin by cloud seeding would increase the annual water supply by nearly 17%. About 3,700 lb or 54,000 troy oz silver would be released to the environment per winter season. The silver content of the seeded snow would be about 0.038 ppb. A pilot project has been conducted for the past four winter seasons in the southwestern Colorado San Juan Mountains. Additional water is needed in the arid regions for strip-mining the coal deposits in the Four Corners Region of Colorado, Utah, Airzona, and New Mexico and for mining the oil shale deposits in Colorado and Wyoming.[70]

The use of pyrotechnic devices (usually flares that burn for 5 to 10 min) instead of steady-state burners to disperse nucleating agents is growing.

Almost all hail suppression attempts have favored pyro-technic flares. Hail modification attempts have been made in the U.S., U.S.S.R., Switzerland, and Argentina with silver iodide. In Soviet exper-iments, a bursting artillery shell releases 100 g silver iodide ($\sim$ 1.5 troy oz silver), which produces 10^{15} nuclei that are assumed to spread rapidly through 1 km^3 of cloud. In the Soviet experiments, many rockets carrying 0.5 to 2 lb silver iodide ($\sim$ 3.5 to 14 troy oz silver) were launched into a single hailstorm. In U.S. experiments to modify severe storms, "massive quantities" of silver iodide are periodically released over an 8- to 10-hr period.[66,69]

   c. Extent of use:

      (1) Commercial operations: By the early 1950's, 10% of U.S. land area was being treated by cloud seeding. Annual investments by ranchers, resort owners, towns, etc., rose to $3 to $5 million although the potential benefits of the process had not been scientifically evalu-ated. Commercial results were such that by the early 1960's, cloud-seeding operations were only 10% what they had been at their peak. In 1965, only 3% of the U.S. land area was covered by commercial operations. An esti-mate for private expenditures in fiscal year 1972 was $750,000.[61]

      Figure VI-1 shows the approximate locations of seeding projects operated in the U.S. in 1968. None of the 1963 to 1968 NSF reports gave the quantities of seeding agents used, although from December 29, 1965, to September 1, 1968, every organization engaged in weather modification activity was required to maintain a log stating the types of material dis-persed, rate of material release, and total quantity released during opera-tion, of each generator.[71] Operators were also required to give NSF 30 days' notice of any weather modification operation. After September 1, 1968, reporting became voluntary and data for areas treated by seeding de-clined sharply in fiscal 1968. Either reporting declined or operators had become more conservative in estimating the affected areas from seeding.[66] Table VI-33 from the 1968 NSF report summarizes field operators' reports for fiscal years 1966 to 1968.

      (2) Government-sponsored operations: In 1957, the President's Advisory Committee on Weather Control reported that winter

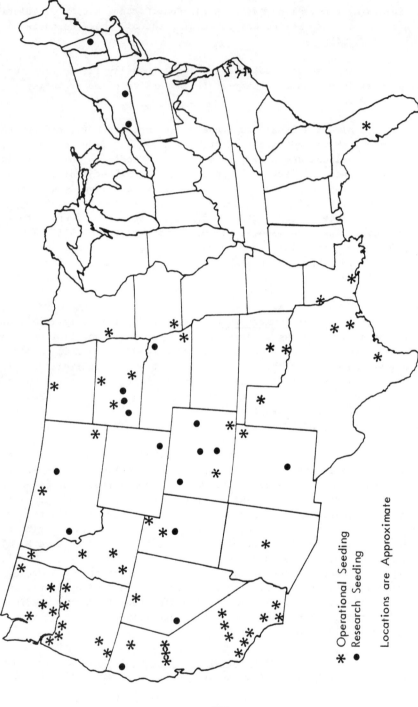

Figure VI-1 - Weather Modification Projects in the United States--Fiscal Year 1968 [66/]

* Operational Seeding

● Research Seeding

Locations are Approximate

seeding in the western mountains increased precipitation 10 to 15%. Responsibility for coordination of weather modification was shifted in 1968 from the National Science Foundation (NSF) to the Interdepartmental Committee for Atmospheric Sciences (ICAS).[61]

The ICAS in June 1971, designated seven national projects for: (a) augmenting the Colorado River Basin snowpack; (b) reducing hurricane winds; (c) reducing lightning-caused fires; (d) increasing cumulus-cloud rainfall; (e) reducing hail damage; (f) spreading snowfall inland from the Great Lakes; and (g) improving visibility in fog. Total government agency support for weather modification in the period 1965 to 1974 was about $141 million. A summary of federal weather modification projects may be found in Reference 61.

The Colorado River Basin Project has been directed and supported by the Bureau of Reclamation of the Department of the Interior. To judge from funding statistics,[a] this is the largest government weather modification project and, possibly, the largest or second largest use of silver iodide for cloud seeding. Silver output by extensive cloud seeding in this region may increase to 54,000 troy oz silver per winter season.[70]

12. Miscellaneous uses: The Bureau of Mines "miscellaneous" category includes silver-bearing copper, silver-bearing lead anodes, ceramic paints, etc. The "miscellaneous" category of the Silver Users Association, accounting for about 6 million troy ounces per year or about 4% of the total end uses in the sixties, includes rocket nozzles; bearings; catalysts; decorative coatings on plastics, ceramics, and glass; thin-film conductors; and high-quality electric light bulbs.[2] The miscellaneous uses appearing in Table VI-34 include those uses not readily classifiable according to those categories discussed in the preceding subsections.

An ingredient survey by The Cosmetic, Toiletry and Fragrance Association, Inc., in 1972 revealed that silver is an ingredient used by the cosmetic industry. Data on amounts were not requested in the survey.[72] The use of silver nitrate in hair dyes is the major use of silver in this industry.

---

a/ In fiscal year 1972, for example, the Bureau of Reclamation funding for precipitation augmentation and redistribution was $6.1 million (3.8 million for universities and nonprofit research institutions) compared with $3.6 million for hail suppression funding, and $19.9 million for total weather modification funding.[61]

225

TABLE VI-1

U.S. CONSUMPTION OF SILVER BY END USE 2,21,73-78/

(Thousand troy oz)

	1961 a/	1962 a/	1963 a/	1964 a/	1965 a/	1966	1967	1968	1969	1970	1971	1972	1973 79/	1974 80/
Electroplated ware						21,486	17,897	15,279	12,706	11,437	10,909	12,716	15,000	
Sterling ware	25,000	22,000	22,000	22,500	25,000	30,894	30,269	28,349	20,291	19,116	22,729	27,163	28,000	27,000
Jewelry						6,349	5,751	4,538	3,011	5,119	3,447	4,870	6,000	
Photog. materials	32,300	33,300	33,300	40,300	45,000	48,435	50,306	41,607	41,380	38,044	36,073	38,251	48,000	46,000
Dental and med. supplies	4,900	5,000	5,100	5,200	5,000	2,457	2,690	3,094	1,591	1,804	1,485	1,991		
Mirrors	3,100	3,100	3,100	3,100	3,000	2,946	2,174	1,744	1,510	1,386	1,112	1,225		
Brazing alloys and solders	11,000	13,000	13,000	15,800	17,000	18,419	15,390	15,124	16,549	14,035	12,085	12,214	14,000	
Commemorative & Collector arts b/											[6,000]	[11,500]	[23,000]	
Elec. & electronic products:														
Batteries	5,000	6,000	6,200	9,000	10,000	12,517	11,404	5,764	3,799	6,342	5,631	6,044		
Contacts & conductors	24,000	25,000	26,000	30,300	35,000	33,676	26,777	25,805	34,555	25,183	27,954	36,434	47,000	37,000
Rocket nozzles	-	1,000		1,000	1,000	699								
Catalysts						2,683	5,847	2,310	4,081	1,999	1,730	3,430		
Bearings						569	600	451	481	383	355	344		
Misc.(includes Ag-bearing Cu, Ag-bearing Pb anodes, ceramic paints,etc.	200	2,000	1,100			2,564	1,925	1,228	1,590	3,556	5,636	6,381	9,000	
Total net ind. consumption	105,500 c/	110,400 c/	110,000 c/ (110,000) d/	127,100 (123,000) d/	140,000 (137,000) d/	183,696	171,032	145,293	141,544	128,404	129,146	151,063	190,000	
Coinage	56,000	78,000	112,000	203,000	320,000	53,852	43,851	36,833	19,407	709	2,474	2,284	1,500	
Total consumption						237,548	214,883	182,126	160,951	129,113	131,620	153,347	191,500	

a/ 1961-1965 are U.S. Department of Commerce estimates. Estimates for 1966-1967 do not agree well with Bureau of Mines figures.

b/ Bureau of Mines distributes these partly in sterling ware and partly in miscellaneous.

c/ See Table IV-13.

d/ Reference 74.

TABLE VI-2

COMPANIES PRODUCING SILVER NITRATE
AND THEIR ESTIMATED 1966 OUTPUT[2]

Company	Silver Nitrate Production (Millions of Ounces)	Silver Content (Millions of Ounces)
Eastman Kodak	52	33
M. Ames Chemical Co.	19	12
Engelhard	10	6
Goldsmith Division, National Lead	6	4
Mallinckrodt	4	3
Phillips and Jacobs	3	2
Total	94	60

TABLE VI-3

MAJOR PRODUCERS OF SILVER BATTERIES[2]

Firm	Principal Silver Battery Products
ESB (Electronic Storage Battery)	Silver-zinc, secondary and primary
Gould-National[a]	Silver-zinc, secondary and primary
Delco Remy	Silver-zinc, secondary
Yardney[b]	Silver-cadmium, secondary; silver-zinc, primary
Gulton Industries[c]	Silver-cadmium (very small volume)
Eagle Picher	Silver-zinc, secondary and primary
Whittaker	Silver-zinc, secondary and primary
Electrochemics	Silver-zinc, secondary
Union Carbide[c]	Silver-zinc, primary (hearing aid)
P. R. Mallory[c]	Silver-zinc, primary (hearing aid)

a/ Second largest producer
b/ Largest producer
c/ Fairly small producers

TABLE VI-4

SILVER CHEMICAL PRODUCERS[81]/

Company	Location	Products
Allied Chem. Corp. Specialty Chems. Div.	Marcus Hook, Pa.	AgF_2, Ag fluoborate, $AgNO_3$, Ag_2SO_4
M. Ames Chem. Works	Glens Falls, N. Y.	AgCl, AgCN, $AgNO_3$, Ag oxide
Apache Chems., Inc.	Rockford, Ill.	AgBr, Ag_2CO_3, AgCl, AgI, $AgNO_3$
City Chem. Corp.	Jersey City, N. J.	AgOAc, Ag arsenate, Ag arsenite, Ag bichromate, $AgBrO_3$, AgBr, $AgClO_3$, AgCl, Ag_2CrO_4, AgF, AgI, Ag lactat Ag mercuriiodide, Ag metaborate, Ag metaphosphate, Ag molybdate, $AgNO_2$ Ag_3PO_4, Ag orthovanadate, $AgMnO_4$, Ag peroxide, Ag_2S, Ag tungstate
Deepwater Chem., Co., Ltd.	Compton, Calif.	$AgIO_3$, AgI
Wilbur B. Driver, Co., Subsidiary of Western Gold and Platinum Co.	Belmont, Calif.	AgCN
Eastern Chem. Corp.	Pequannock, N. J.	Ag diethyldithiocarbamate
Eastman Kodak Co., Eastman Org. Chems.	Rochester, N. Y.	$AgNO_3$
Engelhard Minerals & Chems. Corp., Engelhard Industries Div., Silver Products Dept.	Newark, N. J.	AgBr, Ag_2CO_3, AgCl, AgCN, $AgIO_3$, AgI $AgNO_3$, Ag oxide, Ag_2S
D. F. Goldsmith Chem. & Metal Corp.[a]/	Evanston, Ill.	AgOAc, AgCl, AgCN, $AgNO_3$, Ag oxide, Ag_2S, Ag_2SO_4, and 14 other Ag salts
Kewanee Oil Co., Harshaw Chem. Co., Div. Crystal-Solid State Dept.	Elyria, Ohio Solon, Ohio	AgBr, AgCl
Mallinkrodt Chem. Works Industrial Chems. Div.	St. Louis, Mo	AgOAc, Ag_2CO_3, AgCl, AgCN, AgI, $AgNO$ Ag oxide, Ag_2SO_4
Mooney Chems. Inc.	Franklin, Pa.	Ag neodecanoate
NL Industries Inc., Goldsmith Div.	Chicago, Ill.	AgCN, $AgNO_3$
Ozark-Mahoning Co.	Tulsa, Okla	AgF_2, Ag fluoborate, $AgPF_6$, AgF, AgI
Phillips and Jacobs, Inc.	Philadelphia, Pa.	$AgNO_3$
R.S.A. Corp.	Arsdley, N. Y.	AgOAc, AgBr, Ag_2CO_3, $AgIO_3$, AgI, Ag picrate, Ag propionate, Ag_2S
The Shepherd Chem. Co.	Cincinnati, Ohio	Ag acetylacetonate, Ag 2-ethylhexoate (Ag octoate)
G. Frederick Smith Chem. Co.	Columbus, Ohio	Ag diethyldithiocarbamate, $AgIO_3$, AgM Ag perchlorate
Ventron Corp., Alfa Products Div.	Beverly, Mass.	Ag fluoborate

_____

[a]/ Also supplies powder, alloys, bars, sheets, granules; buys scrap and residues.[82]/

TABLE VI-5

VALUE OF OUTPUT, EXPORTS, AND IMPORTS OF SILVER-CONTAINING PHOTOGRAPHIC PRODUCTS[83]/

	Photographic Sensitized Plate and Film[a]/		Sensitized Photographic Paper and Cloth, Ag Halide	
	1970	1971	1970	1971
Manufacturer's shipments, millions of dollars	1,409.6	1,547.3	285.7	310.4
Exports, millions of dollars	183.2	202.1	32.6	39.9
Exports, as percent of manufacturers' shipments	13	13	11	13
Imports for consumption, millions of dollars	78.9	89.3	18.2	21.2
Imports, as percent of new supply (output plus imports)	5	5	6	6
Net exports (exports-imports), as percent of manufacturers' shipments	7.4	7.3	5.0	6.0

a/ Includes X-ray.

229

TABLE VI-6

PHOTOGRAPHIC USES

Use	Form of Silver	Remarks	References
Photo prints, motion picture film, microfilms, X-rays, lithographic printing (films and typesetting), papers, glass plates, cloth	Ag halides	30 to 40% of the emulsion weight. Lithographic printing is one of the fastest growing consumers of Ag halide film.	84 57
Photographic papers and other low-sensitivity emulsions	AgCl, Ag chlorobromide, or AgBr		57
High-sensitivity emulsions	AgBr plus $\leq$ 5 mole % AgI	Pure AgI emulsions not commercially important. AgF not used.	57
Transmission of photographs by telephone	12% Ag behenate-suspension as coating on polyester	The Ag is stable to light until heat (127°C) is applied. German Patent 2,302,462 (July 19, 1973), Minnesota Mining and Manufacturing Company	85 86
Collodion emulsions	Ag_3PO_4		41

230

TABLE VI-7

OFFICE COPYING SYSTEMS 57/

Use	Form of Silver	Remarks
Office-copying systems	Light-sensitive Ag halides in diffusion-transfer, gelatin-transfer, or stabilization processes	
Thermographic systems	Ag salts of fatty acids combined with organic reducing agents	Belgian Patent 663,112 (October 27, 1965), 3M Company; British Patent 954,198 (April 21, 1960), 3M Company
Print-out coatings	Ag benzenesulfinate	U.S. Patent 3,152,904 (June 29, 1964), 3M Company
Photoconductographic developers for Ag- and Ni-image products	Ag-ethylenethiourea complex; a soluble Ni salt plus a trace of AgOAc as an initiator, respectively	U.S. Patents 3,165,456 and 3,076,752, respectively, 3M Company

TABLE VI-8

SILVER AND SILVER-ALLOY CONTACTS AND CONDUCTORS

Use	Form of Silver	Remarks	References
Relays (AC and DC) handling current < 0.5 A.	90.0% Ag-10.0% Au (Alloy 11)		9
Other Ag alloys frequently used as elec. contacts	92.5% Ag-7.5% Cu (sterling), 90.0% Ag-10.0% Cu (coin Ag), 72.0% Ag-28.0% Cu (Alloy 1), 75.0% Ag-24.5% Cu-0.5% Ni (Alloy 2), 99.55% Ag-0.25% Mg-0.20% Ni (Alloy 6), 97.0% Ag-3.0% Pt (Alloy 7), 90.0% Ag-10.0% Pd (Alloy 8), 97.0% Ag-3.0% Pd (Alloy 9), 99.0% Ag-1.0% Pd (Alloy 10), Ag-Cu-Cd-Au (Alloy 12)		9
Elec. gages, automotive voltage regulators, relays, as a pos. contact against 97.0% Ag-3.0% Pd (Alloy 9).	77.0% Ag-22.6% Cd-0.4% Ni (Alloy 3)	Ag-Cd alloys have good arc-quenching characteristics and high resistance to material transfer, mech. wear, welding, and arc erosion	9
Current-carrying spring contacts; TV tuners, collector rings, and switches where RF signals are carried.	86.8% Ag-5.5% Cd-0.2% Ni-7.5% Cu (Alloy 4)		9
Cladding for contacts, conductors, waveguides	Ag-clad Cu, brass, Al, Ni, beryllium Cu, Invar, Monel, phosphor bronze		14
Low- and medium-current switching devices used by appliance, industrial, and automotive industries.	Fine (99.9%) Ag	Fabricated into solid tubular, and composite rivets, solid welding buttons; steel-backed welding buttons; and composite Ag-faced screws. Elec. vehicles use more Ag contacts, switches, and conductors than gasoline-powered vehicles.	9 87
For uses where low contact resistance must be combined with greater hardness.	Ag-base alloys with 7.5-28.0% Cu		9
Line starters, solenoid relays for automotive and aircraft starters, other devices subjected to high-surge currents.	85.0% Ag-15.0% Cd (Alloy 5)		9

TABLE VI-8 (continued)

Use	Form of Silver	Remarks	References
Thermomech. thermostats in household heating and cooling, cooking, and elec. blankets	Ag, Ag-Pd alloys, 90% Ag-10% Cd, Ag-CdO		13
Precision snap-action switches in heat thermostats	35% Pd-30% Ag-14% Cu-10% Pt-10% Au-1% Zn alloy, Ag-CdO, Ag	Hg-Mo or Hg-Pt alloy preferred	13
Micropotentiometer brushes	69% Au-25% Ag-6% Pt, Au-Ag-Pt, 35% Pd-30% Ag-14% Cu-10% Pt-10% Au-1% Zn alloy		13
Wire of micro slip rings	70% Au-16% Cu-7% Ag-5% Pt-1% Pd-1% Zn alloy	Pt-Rh alloy preferred	13
Brush rings (micro slip rings)	35% Pd-30% Ag-14% Cu-10% Au-1% Zn, 69% Au-25% Ag-6% Pt		13
British Post Office miniature relays for portable app., printed circuit boards, app. formerly using std. 3000-type relay mounting plates.	60% Pd-Ag	Relays handle ≤ 1 amp at 100 V with a max. resistive load of 50 W and contact force ≥ 10 g.	88
Thick-film resistors, capacitors	Fired Ag-Pd and Ag-PdO resistor pastes	Ag pastes are used in the fabrication of potentiometer and resistor terminations, transducers, crystal oscillators, automobile heated windshields and demister panels, thick-film units, and the mounting of semiconductor dice.	89, 90
Thermistor leads	Pt and Ag + binder		13
Ceramic-condenser electrodes	Ag with bonding agent		13
Air-condenser electrodes, printed-circuit conductors, terminals, lugs, tabs, and other connectors	Ag		13
Computers and telephone and aviation equipment	Ag wire contact relays		91

TABLE VI-8 (continued)

Use	Form of Silver	Remarks	References
Conductors, resistors, dielectrics, multi-layer chip capacitors used in computers, calculators, automobiles, and TV's	Ag Micro-circuit compns.		91
Anti-static carpets	Ag-coated nylon yarn	Now being used by several carpet manufacturers	92
High-strength, high-cond. wire	93% Cu-7% Ag	Ag raises the softening or annealing temp. of Cu.	93
Precision resistance wires	60% Pd-40% Ag		13
High-temp wire or strip	Solid Ag, Ag-Mg-Ni		13
Fuses: Steel mills, chem. plants, and utility companies	Ag-Au Ag-plated fuses	Ag helps prevent over-heating in enclosed switches and panel boards	91
High-temperature coils, high-frequency conductors, braiding for radar cables, lead wire	Ag-clad Cu, Ni, or steel		14
Elec. relays such as in telephone equipment for low-noise contact service with extreme reliability.	40% Ag-60% Pd Alloy	Ag-Pd alloys contg. > 50% Pd have max. resistance to sulfidation or ozone oxidn., but those with ~ 40% Ag have max. hardness and resistivity. Alloys contg. > 60% Pd are used for contacts operating at low-contact forces.	94-97
Ford Motor Co. automobile alternator regulators having 2 sets of precious-metal contacts.	Pt-Pd-Ag alloy and Ag alloy contacts for high speeds.	A Pt-W contact is for low speeds	98, 99
Electromagnetic vibrators for auto-motive voltage regulators, bells, buzzers, horns, and radio vibrators.	Pd-Ag-Ni-W Ag-Mo	2nd choice; W-0.5% Mo preferred	13

TABLE VI-8 (concluded)

Use	Form of Silver	Remarks	References
Electromagnetic relays in control systems, engineering equipment, lighting, and appliances.	Ag and Ag alloys. Ag-CdO, Ag, Ag-Cu, Ag-Cu-Ni		13
Wedge-action relays for advanced electronic systems in aircraft, missiles, space vehicles, and computers.	Fine Ag and 24-carat Au electroplated contacts	The device has the highest confidence level ever achieved in an electromech. relay: one failure in 10^7 operations. Manufactured by Electro-Tec Corp.	99
High-current-carrying elec. contacts	Mo- $\geq$ 20% Ag	Properties remain unaltered by current-generated heat. Produced by powder-metallurgical techniques.	100
Conductive lubricant, e.g., for sliding elec. contacts	Ag-Re alloy developed by General Dynamics Corp.	Useful temp. range -62 to 760°C.	101
Contact-point material in the manufacture of the Western Electric multicontact wire spring relay.	Ag bimetal tape	The contact points were built up from a precious-metal cap and a common metal base.	101
Make-and-break contacts for choppers, tape-readers, and automotive signal flashers; sliding contacts for switching disks, cermet trimmer pots, and potentiometer windings; telephone spring wire relays; brushes for switches and wires in brush assemblies; video slip rings; and/or ductile raw material for parts with severe forming.	Pt-Pd-Ag-(Au) alloys, Au-Ag-(Pt) alloys containing 4.5 to 25% Ag		102
Potentiometers	40% Ag-60% Pd	This alloy has an unusually low coeff. of resistivity	95, 100
Contact surfaces that make and break intermediate and heavy electric currents.	Ag and Ag alloys	Generally, a Ag button or a silver rivet is attached to a copper or other base metal switch arm or conductor	103
Light contactor blades	Ag-Mg-Ni alloy		101

235

TABLE VI-9

SILVER CONTACTS WITH SEMIREFRACTORY CONSTITUENTS

Use	Form of Silver	Remarks	References
Materials having relatively high elec. cond., low stable contact resistance, and excellent resistance to sticking and welding.	Mixtures of Ag with 2.5-15.0% CdO, 5-60% Ni, 0.25-10% C, Mg, 10 & 50% Fe, or other elements or compds.	Produced by powder-metallurgy techniques because the components do not have compatible m.p.'s or are not mutually sol. Ag-CdO most widely used of type; most popular contain 10 and 15% CdO.	9
Heat-resistant elec. contact material for use in low-power-factor ($\geq$ 0.45) circuits.	0.05% MgO)-0.13% SnO_2-12% CdO-87.82% Ag, 0.29% MgO-2.5% SnO_2-14.7% CdO-82.51% Ag	Japanese patent 73 23,764 (July 16, 1973).	86
Contactors and relays to make high-surge currents of several hundred amps such as aircraft relays, motor-truck relays, and line motor starters.	Ag-CdO		9
Contacts operated against Ag in some lower-rating line starters; main contacts in circuit breakers and switching devices where auxiliary arcing contacts are used.	Ag-$\leq$ 10% Ni compns.	Better wear resistance than fine Ag. Compns. contg. $\leq$ 10% Ni are ductile and fabricated into wire, strip, rivets, disks, or solid welding buttons.	9
Circuit breakers and disconnect switches.	Ag-10-40% Ni compns.	Fabricated in special molded shapes by powder metallurgy. Frequently operated against a Ag-graphite material.	9
Brush contacts; used in ac and dc circuits primarily to reduce sticking.	Ag-$\leq$ 1.5% C	The lubrication by graphite reduces the tendency to gall or score in sliding contacts, hinge joints, and slip-rings. Can be fabricated into wire and headed into rivets.	9
Make-and-break contacts usually operating in conjunction with Ag-Ni or other Ag-base alloys.	Ag-2-10% C	Materials contg. 5 and 10% graphite are fabricated into round or rectangular disks or as pressed shapes.	9

TABLE VI-9 (concluded)

Use	Form of Silver	Remarks	References
Contact systems with currents ranging from a few amperes to a few thousand amperes.	Ag-CdO prepd. by compacting and sintering Ad-CdO powder blends, internally oxidizing a cast Ag-Cd alloy, or internally oxidizing a Ag-Cd powder blend followed by compacting and sintering.	Bulk elec. cond. and thermal properties of Ag-CdO similar to those of Ag, but its hardness and wear resistance are better.	104
Modifications of the basic binary 40% Ag-60% Mo contact patented by Westinghouse in 1934.	Mo and Ag with Cd; C; Cu; Mn; Ni; Si; S; Zn; Zr; Sb and Cu; and C, Fe, and Ni.		100
Contact buttons	Ag-CdO		101

TABLE VI-10

SILVER CONTACTS WITH REFRACTORY-METAL CONSTITUENTS[9]

Use	Form of Silver	Remarks
Elec. switchgear of the type used in the generation and distribution of elec. energy having good elec. and thermal conductivities, resistance to arc erosion, high strength, and resistance to welding and sticking.	Materials (not alloys) contg. 27.5-50.0% Ag; 0-1.0% C; and 10.0-72.5% W, 35.0-60.0% WC, or 50 or 60% Mo.	Fabricated by special powder-metallurgy techniques.
Arcing or shorting contacts in multistage circuit breakers or high-voltage switches. Used in both air-and oil-type devices.	27.5% Ag-72.5%W	Prime function to break high-energy arcs and protect main contacts.
Molded-case household and industrial-type circuit breakers and aircraft circuit breakers as a single pair of contacts.	35.0% Ag-65.0% W	
Current-carrying contacts such as main contacts in power circuit breakers and switches, where the contacts are subjected to momentary current of several thousand amperes.	46.0-50% Ag-50.0-53.0% W-0-1.0% C	
Industrial-type molded-case circuit breakers and high-speed teletype relays.	40.0% Ag-60.0% WC	
Molded-case and metal-clad industrial-type circuit breakers, used in combination with Ag-CdO. Sliding applications such as aircraft-generator slip rings	50.0% Ag-50.0% WC	
Arcing contacts in power circuit breakers in both oil-and air-type devices; contactors that control high inrush currents.	40.0% Ag-60.0% Mo	Ag-Mo preferred to Ag-W compns. where mass and acceleration are critical factors.
Arcing contact in high-voltage oil circuit breakers. Molded-case household-type breakers to carry rated current as well as to interrupt short-circuit current.	50.0% Ag-50.0% Mo	

TABLE VI-11

CONTACT MATERIALS FOR TELECOMMUNICATIONS APPARATUS[13/]

Use	Form of Silver
Sliding Contacts	
Electromech. rotary switches (telephone type) 10^6 max. operations	69% Au-25% Ag-6% Pt overlay on phosphor bronze terminal
Manual rotary switches 10^6 max. operations	Ag-plated brass. 90% Ag-10% Cu rotor blades against 90% Ag-5% Cu-5% Zn or 90% Ag-5% Cu-5% Cd clips. 69% Au-25% Ag-6% Pt overlay on brass for both blades and and clips.
Slip rings and brushes	Ag, 90% Ag-10% Cu, 70% Au-30% Ag, Pd-Ag-Cu, coin Ag, Au-Ag-Pt
Butting Contacts	
Sensitive relays	69% Au-25% Ag-6% Pt
General purpose relays	69% Au-25% Ag-6% Pt, Ag
Switches	69% Au-25% Ag-6% Pt

TABLE VI-12

MISCELLANEOUS ELECTRICAL USES OF SILVER

Use	Form of Silver	Remarks	References
High-quality light bulbs	Ag applied by vacuum evaporation	The greatest use of Ag for vacuum evaporation. Ag's reflectivity in the visible and IR spectra is higher than that of any other available metal coating.	30
Controlling the use of Cl in the pulp bleaching process with a sensing device, Inserta-probe, which measures the redox potential of the pulp chlorination solution.	Pt-Ag electrode	The sensing portion of the probe contains two epoxy-bonded Pt-Ag electrodes at the end of the probe.	99
Anodes for electrolyzing seawater (electrolytic antifouling devices for ships)	Pb-Ag-As alloys	Japanese Kokai patent 73 29,681 (April 19, 1973), Hitachi Cable, Ltd.	19
Electric heating device that defrosts auto rear windshields	Ag suspension paste	~ 10 to 20% of U.S. cars and most imported cars are so equipped.	91
Insol. anodes in electrolytic Zn refining	99% Pb-1% Ag		93

Table VI-13

COATINGS OTHER THAN MIRRORS AND ELECTROPLATE

Use	Form	Remarks	References
Paint that conducts electricity, suppresses static in radios and other electronic devices, and shields industrial equipment against electromagnetic and radio frequency interferences. The paint can also be used as a reflector in painting plastic antenna forms, nonconductive surfaces, and inflatables. It can be used to elec. ground insulators.	Ag acrylic aerosol spray paint and similar coatings	Technical Wire Products, Inc., and Chomerics, Inc.	105
Metallic meshes for deployable spacecraft antennas	Ag-metallized fabrics of metal, polyester, or fiberglass yarns		86
Paints for producing elec. conductive surfaces on nonconductors, for solder bonding to nonconductors or nonmetallic surfaces, and for applying Ag decorations on porcelains and glass. Used, e.g., for painting mica capacitor electrodes.	Typical air-drying paint contains 50% Ag flake, lacquer or varnish resin, plasticizer, solvents, etc.		29
	Paints for application to ceramics, mica, quartz, glass, and other refractory materials also contain a low-melting glass powder. Fired films are $\leq$ 0.001 in-thick porous, sintered Ag interpenetrated by a glass phase bonding the Ag to the substrate.	Glass and ceramics can also be metallized by vacuum sublimation.	13
Paint for high-temp. applications requiring elec. conductance	Dynaloy 2510, a Ag-filled polymer-in-solvent paint		101
Protective coatings for Nb and its alloys	Spray-coated slurry containing 60-96% Ag, 3-30% Si, and 1-10% Al in lacquer	Nb and alloys are protected from oxidation at 2000°C (3632°F)	86

241

Table VI-13 (Concluded)

Use	Form	Remarks	References
Flame-sprayed coatings for rotating components in aircraft engines to assure accurate fit between mating parts, anti-seizure characteristics, and an air-tight seal.	Ag alloy	Flame spraying is effective for economical maintenance operations during engine overhauls.	99
Colored films on Al and Al alloys	Ag deposited from 0.01-0.03% dispersions of colloidal Ag, Ag_2O, or AgOH in water-sol. resin liquids by adjusting the pH	Color produced (white, yellow, brown red, or green) depends on the colloidal Ag solution used.	86
Prevention of galling of high-temp. bolts at $\leq 641°C$	Finely divided Ag in a paste		13
Preparation of plastic condensers prior to Zn application by vacuum metallizing		Nucleation with Ag required	13

TABLE VI-14

ELECTRONICS

Use	Form of Silver	Remarks	References
Thick-film composites: Ag microcircuit compns. for conductors, resistors, and dielecs. and for multilayer chip capacitors. The compns. are used for making conductive circuitry for computers, calculators, automobile, and television units.	Ag with glass frit and org. binders and thinners	General Motors and Zenith are big customers of Du Pont's new thick-film composites for silk-screening onto substrates.	106
Bonding all types of semiconductor chips to substrates in hybrid circuit fabrication. Also used in optoelectronics.	Ag-filed, elec. conducting epoxy bonding materials	Produced by Epoxy Technology, Inc.	106
Pocket-calculator digital display	Ag metallizing prepn. silk-screened on the glass panel and fired.	The Ag pattern is an elec. conductor track. A gas such as neon or argon in a partial vacuum under the glass lights up when elec. current is applied.	90
Electron-tube secondary emitters	1.7% Mg-Ag		13
Electron-tube base pins	30% Ag-70% Au		13

243

TABLE VI-15

SILVER-CONTAINING BATTERIES

Use	Form	Remarks	References
Silver Oxide-Zinc Batteries			
Main or auxiliary power source for torpedoes, missiles, manpack radios, aircraft, submarines, sounding balloons, satellites, and electric and space vehicles.	$Ag(I)$ and $Ag(II)$ oxides-Zn secondary batteries. Ag wire, cloth, and powder used in manufacturing.	KOH-electrolyte Ag batteries cost more than lead acid (industrial type) batteries. Maximum life of Ag-Zn and Ag-Cd batteries is 1.5 and 2.5 years, respectively. Short life and high cost (because of small volume and lack of automation in production) preclude use in most applications except military (90% of output) and aerospace. The energy storage capacity per unit weight or per unit volume is larger than that of any other present practical system. Secondary batteries can deliver 100 cycles of charge-discharge.	57 87 103 107 108
Ranger, Mariner, and Surveyor space programs.	Ag oxide-Zn sealed batteries.	Overcharge and gassing are prevented by control of the charge.	107 57
Military applications requiring the ability to deliver instantaneously full wattage and capacity, e.g., in torpedoes, missiles, and rockets.	Ag oxide-Zn primary batteries (Ag-plated Cu can be used for grids. Grids can be pasted with AgO.)	Battery cells are filled at the time of use by a self-contained activating device. Primary-type batteries are capable of only one discharge.	107
Power for Nike Hercules Missiles and torpedo drones.	Ag-Ag oxide-Zn battery with pure Ag wire connectors.	Missiles require Ag batteries for guidance control, separation of stages, and hydraulic and ignition systems. Batteries for new torpedo targets are 3 to 4 times more powerful than former models and contain 3 to 4 times more Ag ($\sim 5,000$ troy oz each). These super batteries create the greatest possible energy unit of weight and volume. Produced by Yardney Elec. Corp., Pawcatuck, Connecticut.	109
Button cells to power hearing aids and electric watches.	Ag_2O cathode and Zn anode.	Cells deliver 15 to 20% more energy than the Hg-type cell. Excellent capacity retention after storage.	107
Power new Pulsar watch manufactured by HMW Industries, Inc. (Hamilton Watch Company).	Minuscule, wafer-thin Ag-Zn batteries weighing 0.13 oz each.	Battery produced by Ray-O-Vac Division of ESB, Inc., Philadelphia, Pennsylvania.	110
Power Defense Department devices.	0.055-in. thick Ag oxide-Zn battery.	Developed by Harry Diamond Laboratory.	111
Goodyear auto racing engines.	Ag-Zn batteries.		108
Prototype commuter vehicle.	Ag oxide-Zn batteries.	Skylab and vehicle batteries built by Eagle-Picher Industries. The Ag can be re-used indefinitely. All Ag recyclable.	112

TABLE VI-15 (concluded)

Use	Form	Remarks	References
Silver Oxide-Cadmium Batteries			
Limited military uses; developed for torpedoes and aircraft. Some used for satellites and spacecraft. Tried commercially in cordless appliances.	Ag_2O and AgO-Cd.	Overcoming short life and maintenance problems. Should broaden commercial applications. KOH is the electrolyte. Batteries have moderate current densities and life.	107 57
Sealed silver oxide-cadmium batteries.		Recent development.	107
Silver Chloride-Magnesium Batteries			
Power for torpedoes and sonobuoys. Emergency lights aboard boats.	AgCl-Mg battery. (Negative plate usually Al-Zn-Mg alloy.) Powdered AgCl and Ag foil used in manufacturing.	A primary battery that is activated at the time of use by immersion in seawater or fresh water, which serves as the electrolyte. Heavy production almost entirely for military uses.	107
Other Silver Batteries			
Civilian alarm when linked to sensors.	Ag-iodide battery.	Can respond to a national defense alarm to fire missiles. The battery's self-heating feature has to be activated before it operates, so it lasts indefinitely without deterioration, prior to activation.	113
Possible use in space systems.	Li-AgCl.		57
Rechargeable solar-energy cells to power spacecraft, recharge electric-vehicle batteries, and operate small home appliances.	AgCl membrane. Ag bar conductors.		57 114
Thin, flexible power sources to conform to almost any shape of equipment in communications, computers, and electronics.	Solid electrolyte batteries of metallic Ag and Ag-Rb iodide, < 1/16 in.	Batteries by Gould, Inc.	111
Composite electrodes.	0.1 to 10% powdered Ag-remainder powdered Pb.	Japanese Patent 73 26,578	115

TABLE VI-16

SILVER CONSUMPTION IN COMMEMORATIVE
AND COLLECTOR ARTS[115-119]

Year	Handy and Harman Estimates (million troy ounces)	Silver Institute[a] Estimates	Handy and Harman % of Total
1969	4.0		3
1970	5.0		4
1971	8.0	6	6
1972	10.0	11.5	7
1973	22.0	> 15	11.2
1974	21.0	≥ 24	12.2

---

a/ November, 1973

TABLE VI-17

BRAZING ALLOYS

Use	Form of Silver	Remarks	References
Low-temp. joining of Fe-, Cu-, Ni-, and Ag-base alloys, refractory and rare metals, powder-metal parts, cermets, graphite, and ceramics. Useful in step-brazing. For applications where environmental temps. are $\leq 427°C$ such as in wing structures and forward engine sections.	Ag-Cu alloys modified with Zn, Cd, Sn, In, Ni, Mn, P, and/or Li or special Cd-based alloys containing 4.0 to 5.0% Ag	Most commercial Ag brazing alloys have flow points 593 to 871°C. Joint thickness generally recommended: 0.001-0.005 in.	24
Joining alloys based on Fe, Co, or Ni.	Ag-Cu-Zn alone or with Cd or Sn	Zn is the most helpful wetting promoter for joining Fe-, Co-, and Ni-based alloys.	24
Self-fluxing brazing alloys for Cu.	E.g., 15% Ag-80% Cu-5% P	Cu-Ag-P alloys are widely used for brazing Cu tubing and electrical connections. Some P oxidizes to P_2O_5 while it reduces Cu oxides and forms a protective layer of flux.	22 24
Brazing stainless steels and sterling Ag. Brazing food handling equipment.	E.g., 56% Ag-22% Cu-17% Zn-5% Sn		22
Brazing Ag and Ag alloys.	Ag-Cu; 59 to 81% Ag-15 to 26% Cu-2 to 17% Zn		120 22
Brazing brass where color match is important, e.g., band instruments.	E.g., 9% Ag-53% Cu-38% Zn		22
Brazing W carbide tool tips and tool blades.	Ag-Cu-Zn-Ni alloys		22

TABLE VI-17 (continued)

Use	Form of Silver	Remarks	Reference
Brazing stainless steels and other alloys that form refractory oxides in reducing (pure, dry H_2) or inert atms. without flux.	Ag brazing alloys containing 0.15 to 0.3% Li as the wetting agent		24
Brazing stainless steel honeycomb structures; other aircraft and missile assembly brazing.	92.5% Ag-0.2% Li-7.3% Cu; Ag-Pd-Mn alloy; or, e.g., 54% Ag-40% Cu-5% Zn-1% Ni		120 22
Brazing Be.	Ag, 72% Ag-28% Cu, Ag-Al eutectic		120
Brazing Pd.	Cu-Ag eutectic, Ag-Cu-Pd		120
Brazing Cu in vacuum devices.	Cu-Ag eutectic, Pd-Ag-Cu, Ag-Cu-In	Brazing alloys used in vacuum-tube industry where high v.p. of Zn intolerable.	121
Brazing alloy product com. for joining metals to ceramics. Ti used as a wetting agent.	Ag-Cu eutectic	Composite wire Ti core surrounded by Ag-Cu eutectic brazing alloy.	121
Brazing Au.	Au-Cu-Ag		120
Brazing Cu to itself or to other metals.	Ag-Cu-Pd alloys	Cu brazing alloys are used in vacuum devices and for brazing components where Cd and Zn brazing alloys are unsuitable.	120
Brazing in the assembly of internal components of large electronic valves.	Ag-Cu-Pd alloy		120
Brazing radio-valve components.	Ag-Cu-Pd alloy		120
Brazing Nb or Ta.	Ag-Cu-Pd		120

TABLE VI-17 (continued)

Use	Form of Silver	Remarks	References
Brazing joints between Be and Monel or Cu-plated mild steel.	Ag-Cu-Pd		120
Brazing Ti.	52% Ag-28% Cu-20% Pd alloy		120
Brazing joints on low-expansion alloys based on Ni-Fe or Ni-Fe-Co, e.g., in glass-to-metal seals in vacuum-tube devices.	Pd-Ag-Cu alloy	The low-expansion alloys are first Ni plated.	120
Brazing ceramic insulators to metal sheaths to protect thermocouples used in the nuclear field.	Ag-Cu-Pd and other Pd-containing alloys		120
Brazing stellites, cemented carbides, and Mo- or W-rich refractory alloys.	50 to 85% Ag alloy with 3 to 15% Mn and Ni, Cu, and/or Sn	Mn and/or Ni is the wetting agent.	24
Brazing W carbide tips to drill shanks for geol. or mining operations.	Ag-Pd-Mn alloy, Ag-Cu-Zn-Ni alloys		120 22
Brazing Mo to itself, to W, and to other metals.	Ag-Pd-Mn alloy	Used commercially	120
Brazing Mo electrodes for elec. heated glass-melting furnaces.	Ag-Pd-Mn alloy		120
Brazing stainless steels used for high-temp. service, chiefly the austenitic Ni-Cr type.	Ag-Pd-Mn alloy	Many nonsilver alloys proposed.	120
Brazing gas-turbine blades of Ni and Ni alloys.	Ag-Pd-Mn alloy		120

TABLE VI-17 (concluded)

Use	Form of Silver	Remarks	Reference
Joining the thin-walled Ni-alloy tubing in the F-1 liquid-propellant rocket engine that was used in the 1st stage of the Saturn V lunar space rocket.	20% Pd-75% Ag-5% Mn alloy		122 123
Brazing stainless steel, Inconel, and other heat-resistant alloys.	Pd-Ag		13
Brazing without flux in atm. or vacuum furnaces or for assemblies to be used under high vacuum at intermediate temps.	Ag alloys with In or Sn replacing Zn or Cd		24
Brazing Zr	Molten Ag		120

TABLE VI-18

SILVER SOLDERS

Use	Form of Silver	Remarks	References
For soldering components subjected to stress and heat, e.g., radiator headers and tanks. Similar solders are used in the electronics industry.	Low Sn-Ag-Pb solders containing ~ 0.4 to 0.6% Ag and ~ 2.5% Sn	All Big Three car manufacturers use this type of solder.	124
Proposed for soldering food cans instead of Pb and Sn.	Ag-Sn		125
Apparatus to freeze and store ice cubes.	Sn-Ag	Manitowoc Equipment	25
Soldering the base to the body of the West Bend 18-cup percolator.	95% Sn-5% Ag		25
Soldering copper water pipes into the brass manifold beneath the control knobs in American Standard kitchen and bathroom appliances.	Sn-Ag		25
Soft Ag solder for soldering Al and Al alloys to Cu, brass, and other metals more noble than Al.	2 to 3% Ag - 3 to 5% Sn - $\leq$ 0.1% Sb - $\leq$ 2% Cd and Bi - remainder Pb	U.S. Patent 3,768,141 (October 30, 1973), Ford Motor Company used with a $ZnCl_2$ flux. A 75% Ag-25% Zn layer forms, which gives a noncorroding bond for the metals.	86
Solders for karat golds.	Au 33.3 to 66.7%, Ag 15.0 to 35.0%, Cu 12.0 to 28.0%, Zn 1.5 to 11.7%, Cd 0 to 9.0%		126
Precious metal solders Low-karat solder General-purpose solder High-karat solder	45% Au-30 to 35% Ag-15 to 20% Cu 60% Au-12 to 22% Ag-12 to 22% Cu 80% Au-3 to 8% Ag-8 to 12% Cu	Plus 2 to 3% Sn and 2 to 4% Zn	126
Fine instrument work.	96.5% Sn-3.5% Ag, 95% Sn-5% Ag		14
On Cu, brass, and similar metals with torch heating.	97.5% Pb-2.5% Ag, 94.5% Pb-5.5% Ag, 97.5% Pb-1.5% Ag-1.0% Sn		14
Joining Al to itself or dissimilar metals.	95% Cd-5% Ag		14
Low temperature Sn-free Ag solders for soldering electrically conductive elements of heated aircraft and automobile windows to the tinned Cu wires connecting them to the current source.	2 to 5% Ag - 45 to 65% In - 30 to 50% Pb	U.S. Patent 3,771,221 (November 13, 1973), PPG Industries, Inc.	86

TABLE VI-19

ELECTROPLATED WARE

Use	Form of Silver	Remarks	References
Ag coatings for plastic buttons, beads, buckles, costume jewelry, clock cases, brooches, wall plaques, etc.	Ag plate on polyesters, acrylonitrile-butadiene-styrene copolymers, polypropylene, and poly(phenylene oxide)	Cu, Au, and Ni are also used.	127
Sulfide-corrosion-resistant Ag coatings for pure metals or alloys.	0.1 to 0.12% In-0.2 to 0.3% Zn-4 to 10% Sn-89.6 to 95.7% Ag	Ag, Zn, In, and Sn are electroplated in that order and heated for mutual thermal diffusion to form the alloy.	86
Coatings on Al products such as busbars, switchgears.	Ag plated on Cu		26
Silver-plated tableware, jewelry, casket hardware, etc.	Ag plated on nickel silver (Cu-Ni-Zn) common for tableware.		13 31
Surfacing UHF conductors for radar.	Ag plate		13

252

TABLE VI-20

OXIDATION CATALYSTS

Reaction	Form of Silver	Remarks	References
Producing H_2O_2 from H_2 and O_2 in a liquid medium inhibiting decompn.	Pd-Ag (Pd-Au)/SiO_2	U.S. Patent 3,361,533 (1968), ICI, Ltd.	128
Oxidation of chloride with Ce(IV).	Ag^+		57
Improved Deacon process for making Cl_2 from HCl with air and a catalyst.	Catalyst: 1 part by wt. Ag with 4 parts Cu and 1 part Ca on a Silica Gel B carrier.	East German research. Process does not use elec. energy. HCl is increasingly available as a by-product of many Cl_2 uses and from treating NaCl with H_2SO_4 (produced in pollution control of SO_2).	129
$HCl + O_2 \longrightarrow Cl_2$ without use of elec. power.	Ag_3PO_4-$Cu_3(PO_4)_2$/SiO_2-Al_2O_3	U.S. Patent 3,760,867 (September 18, 1973), Velsicol Chemical Corp.	86
Oxidation of SO_2 to SO_3.	Ag_2SO_4 and silica	German Patent 1,133,350 (July 19, 1962), Badische Anilin- und Soda-Fabrik A.G.	57
Oxidation of Mn^{+2} with peroxysulfate.	Ag^+		57
(Amm)oxidation of propylene to acrylonitrile or acrolein.	Dried and activated coprecipitate of ammonium paramolybdate and silver nitrate	German Patent 2,359,546 (June 12, 1974), S.I.R. Societa Italiana Resine. Com. ammoxidn. catalysts are not based on silver.	32 38
Gas masks to prevent CO poisoning.	Hopcalite, a 1:6:10:3 mixture of the oxides of Ag, Cu, Mn, and Co; $AgMnO_4$	Used since World War I.	57
Engine exhaust-gas combustion catalysts; e.g., oxidation of CO in engine exhaust.	Ag porous powdered glass	British Patent 1,040,295 (August 24, 1966), Peter Spence and Sons, Ltd.; German (East) Patent 94,607 (December 20, 1972).	19
Air purifiers.	Ag and Cu oxides	U.S. Patent 3,034,947 (April 25, 1956), U.S. Army.	57
Production of aldehydes.	Ag oxide	Belgian Patent 657,746 (April 30, 1965), Dynamit Nobel A.G.	57
Preparation of unsaturated aldehydes and acids from olefins.	Solid catalyst containing Mo, Te, O, and $\geq$ 1 metal from the group Cd, Tl, Cu, Ni, Mn, Zn, Bi, Sn, Sb, Pb, W, V, Cr, Ag	French Patent 1,447, 982 (August 5, 1966) Mitsubishi Rayon Co., Ltd.	130
Vapor-phase oxidation of anthracene to anthraquinone.	Ag or Cu vanadate with Mo or W oxide	Japanese Patent 4,627 (July 26, 1954).	131

253

TABLE VI-20 (concluded)

Reaction	Form of Silver	Remarks	References
Oxidation of ethylene to ethylene oxide at 200 to 250°C.	Ag/Al_2O_3, Ag/pumice, Ag thiocyanate, $Pd-Ag/Al_2O_3$, Ag/ceramics, "Raney" Ag prepd. from Ag-Al or Ag-Ca alloys	Supported Ag (4 to 12% Ag) may contain Au, Cu, Ba (Process by Scientific Design Co., N.Y.) or BeO (Du Pont); U.S. 1972 production of ethylene oxide 4.08 billion pounds.	33 132, 128 36
Oxidation of other olefins.	Ag/pumice, MgO, Zr-Si oxide, Mg-Al oxide, BeO, or magnetite	U.S. Patent 2,593,098 (April 15, 1953), Ethyl Corp.	33
Oxidation of MeOH to HCHO.	$AgNO_3$, Ag needles and gauze	U.S.S.R. Patent 175,043 (September 21, 1965). Most of U.S. HCHO production (5.5 billion pounds in 1972) is made by passing MeOH and air over pure Ag needles and gauze at 500 to 600°C. Catalyst life 0.5 to 1 year.	57 36 33
Vapor-phase oxidation of ethylene glycol, $HOCH_2CH_2OH$, to glyoxal, OHCCHO, in an air-N_2 mixture.	Finely dispersed Ag and/or oxide on a carrier		33
Air oxidation of water suspensions of starch or cellulose to produce a nonphosphate detergent.	Powdered Ag oxide and powdered Ag	Netherlands research.	133
Oxidation of benzene at 460 to 505°C to maleic acid in 95 to 99.8% yield.	Two catalysts: V_2O_5-MoO_3-UO_2-Ag_3PO_4, V_2O_5-MoO_3-UO_2-$AgNO_3$-Ag_3PO_4	British Patent 944,494 (December 18, 1963), Allied Chem. Corp. Ag_3PO_4 serves as a promoter.	130 131
Preparation of vinyl acetate from ethylene, AcOH, and O_2.	Pd-Ag (Pd-Au)/SiO_2	Catalysts containing 10 to 50% Ag prepared by NH_2NH_2 redn. and modified by NaOAc treatment. Regenerated by NH_3 treatment. Pd-Au preferred. Four British and U.S. Patents, 1968, 1969, 1971, by Knapsack Aktiengesellschaft.	128
Production of phthalic anhydride.	Ag oxide	Belgian Patent 661,854 (September 30, 1965), Badische Anilin- und Soda-Fabrik A.G.	57
Synthesis of nitriles from aldehydes and ammonia: $RCHO + NH_3 \longrightarrow RCH:NH \longrightarrow RCN + H_2$	Ag-Zn	U.S. Patent 2,786,867 (March 26, 1957), Eastman Kodak Co.	33
Chlorination oxidation of complex metal cyanides in wastewater.	$AgNO_3$, AgCl	U.S. Patent 3,772,194 (November 3, 1973), Eastman Kodak Co.	86

TABLE VI-21

REDUCTION AND/OR DECOMPOSITION CATALYSTS

Reaction	Form of Silver	Remarks	References
Conversion of NH_4NO_3 to N_2O.	$AgNO_3$	British Patent 510,889 (1939), E. I. du Pont de Nemours and Co., Inc.	57
Preparation of silanes by heating Si and (H) under pressure.	H_2S plus Ag_2S and other metal sulfides	Japanese Patent 21,507 (November 9, 1961).	57 131
Preparation of ethylene from CO and H_2 (a Fischer-Tropsch Synthesis)	Cd, Cu, Zn and/or Ag plus Cr, V, Nb, Mo, or W oxides	British Patent 833,976 (May 19, 1960).	131
Catalytic decomposition of CO to C and other products.	Ag (or other metal) single crystals	Research study, 1954.	131
Bart Reaction: Formation of aromatic arsonic acids by treating aromatic diazonium compounds with alkali arsenites.	Powdered silver (or copper or cupric salts)	German Patent 250,264 (1910).	41
Hydrogenation of acetylene to ethylene at 60 to 200°C.	Diatomaceous-earth-supported Pd-Ag containing 1 to 40% Ag	U.S. Patent 2,802,889 (1957), The Dow Chemical Co.; the catalyst is regenerated by oxidation at 400°C followed by reduction with H_2 at 200°C.	128
Disintegration of highly concentrated H_2O_2, used as an energy source.	Sintered Ag powder containing 5 to 20% Cu oxide	Catalyst must be stable at ≤ 700°C and moisture resistant. British Patent 893,987 (D. Napier and Son, Ltd.)	33

TABLE VI-22

PETROLEUM REFINING CATALYSTS

Reaction	Form of Silver	Remarks	References
Hydrocracking.	Ag associated with W, Ru, or Rh.	Used by Shell Oil Company.	101
Desulfurization of benzene by oxidation.	Mixture containing Ag_2O_3, pumice, and oxides of Al, V, Fe, and Mo.	Russian study, 1963.	130
Desulfurization of petroleum distillates.	Ag/Al_2O_3		33
Hydrogenation, dehydrocyclization, and hydrodealkylation reactions related to treatment of petroleum and natural-gas hydrocarbons, e.g., n-hexane to benzene and olefins to dienes.	Unsupported Pd-Ag alloy.	British Patent 1,199,683 (1970), Institute of Petrochem. Synthesis, Academy of Science, U.S.S.R.	128
Reforming.	$Pd-Ag/SiO_2$ or Al_2O_3 among other catalysts. (0.5 to 50% Ag).	U.S. Patent 2,911,357 (1959), Phillips Petroleum Co. Catalysts more sintering resistant than the usual Pt-type catalysts.	128
Isomerization of $\underline{n}-C_4$ to C_8 paraffins.	Pd-Ag (or Pd-Au)/Al_2O_3	U.S. Patent 3,442,973 (1969), Esso Research and Engineering Co. Catalysts were more selective than the pure metals, while cracking was minimized.	128
Desulfurization of gases from decomposition of asphalts or heavy oils.	Ag (or Cu)	Japanese Kokai, Patent 73 74,504, Nippon Kokan Kabushiki Kaisha. Ag can be used at lower temperatures than Cu.	86

256

TABLE VI-23

POLYMERIZATION CATALYSTS

Reaction	Form of Silver	Remarks	References
Production of poly-(tetrafluoroethylene).	$AgNO_3$	Belgian Patent 629,806 (October 21, 1963).	57
Polymerization of acrylonitrile in DMF.	$AgNO_3$ + a combination of amines.		33
Condensation of HCHO to polyoxo compounds.	Ag_2O or other metal oxide.	Polish study, 1962.	131
Condensation of HCHO to polyoxo compounds.	Pt metal promoted by Ag or other low-valence metals.	French Patent 1,371,111, Asaki Chem. Industry Co., Ltd.	131
Olefin polymerization.	Moist $AgC\colon CH$	Cu acetylide is preferred since it is less sensitive to shock.	33

TABLE VI-24

SEPARATION OF PETROCHEMICALS

Use	Form of Silver	Remarks	References
Separation of specific olefin isomers desired for chemical manuf. from refinery streams of mixed hydrocarbons.	Ag zeolite	Ag zeolite selectively dequesters the desired olefins, which are later eluted with pentane and ether. French Patent 2,148,999 (1973), Universal Oil Products.	134
Separation of olefins from saturated hydrocarbons in mixed gas streams.	Membranes satd. with $AgNO_3$ solns.	The $AgNO_3$ solns. are inert to satd. hydrocarbons but will complex with and dissolve olefins at elevated pressures. U.S. Patent 3,800,506 (April 2, 1974), Standard Oil of Indiana.	32
Extraction of olefins from cracking gases (partially hydrogenated to avoid formation of Ag acetylide, a detonator).	Ag salts such as $AgBF_4$ and Ag fluosilicate in aqueous solution.	Olefins absorbed as complexes while CO, CO_2, N_2, and H_2 are not absorbed. Absorbed olefins are driven off by heating. The $AgBF_4$ soln. contains ~650 g Ag/liter. In use since at least 1959.	33
Purification of olefins by removing acetylenes and aromatic hydrocarbons.	$AgBF_4$		57
Separation of hydrocarbons such as styrene and ethylbenzene, xylene isomers, ethylene and propylene, etc.	Ag trihalomethane sulfonates: F_3CSO_3Ag and Cl_3CSO_3Ag; $(AgSO_3R)_m L_n$ where R = perfluoroalkyl, L = ligand, $\underline{M}$ = 1 or 2, and $\underline{n}$ = 1-4	German Patent 2,317,396 (October 25, 1973), Mitsubishi Chem. Industries, Inc.; U.S. Patent, Esso.	86

TABLE VI-25

DENTAL USES

Use	Form	Remarks	References
Ag solders for constructing orthodontic appliances for stainless steel or Ni-Ag parts.	10 to 80% Ag-16 to 52% Cu-4 to 38% Zn-0 to 5% Cd alloys.		44
Amalgam alloys.	67 to 70% Ag-25.3 to 27.7% Sn-0 to 5.2% Cu-0 to 1.7% Zn	Amalgam alloys are mixed in 5:8 ratio with Hg. Excess Hg is squeezed out prior to filling the prepared cavity. The nominal composition of the restoration is 33% Ag-52% Hg-12.5% Sn-2% Cu-0.5% Zn.	126 45 135
Dental solders: Low-karat General purpose High-karat	45% Au-30 to 35% Ag-15 to 20% Cu 60% Au-12 to 22% Ag-12 to 22% Cu 80% Au-3 to 8% Ag-8 to 12% Cu (All three solders contain 2 to 3% Sn and 2 to 4% Zn.)		126
Casting alloys for partial dentures, saddles, arches, bars, clasps, etc.	Au, Pt, Pd, Ag, Cu, and Zn.	Yellow golds 3 to 26% Ag; white golds 7 to 26% Ag; substitution alloys (low Au content) require high-cost skills for fabricating; new Ni-based alloy promising.	13 126 136 44
Precious-metal wires.	0 to 41% Ag-Au		126
Local application to teeth to arrest dental decay.	Ammoniacal $AgNO_3$		57
Dental-inlay casting golds: all types of inlays, 3/4 crowns.	Type A alloys: Au-Ag-Cu with minor amounts of Zn or other modifiers. Type B alloys Type C alloys	Brinell hardness 40-75; 20-22 carat golds. Brinell hardness 70-100 Brinell hardness 90-140	44
Wrought Au alloys for wires, bars, clasps, etc.	5 to 41% Ag with 5 to 7 other metals from the group Au, Cu, Pt, Pd, Ni, Zn, Fe, Ir, Mn, Sn.		44 126
Au solders for joining wrought Au alloys to cast Au structures or to join parts of wrought Au into a single appliance.	65 to 80% Au-8 to 17% Ag-6 to 17% Cu-1 to 3% Sn.		44

Table VI-26

Proprietary Name	Chemical Description
Actol	silver lactate
Alb-Argentum	silver iodide with a soluble, hydrolyzed gelati base containing 18-22% silver iodide in collo dal combination
Albargin	compound of silver nitrate with gelatose
Anticilloid	dosage form of Protargol
Argaldin	silver-formaldehyde-albumin combination
Argental	mild silver protein
Argentamin	10% solution of silver nitrate in a 10% aqueous solution of ethylene diamine
Argentellin	silver nucleinate containing about 25% silver
Argentide	concentrated solution of silver iodide
Argentiform	silver methenamine
Argentol	silver-oxyguino-linsulfonic acid combination
Argobol	silver phosphate preparation
Argochrome	compound of methylene blue and silver repre- senting about 20% of the metal
Argocol	colloidal silver preparation representing 20-25% of the metal
Argoferment	colloidal solution of silver 0.02%
Argoflavine	silver trypaflavine
Argoid	combination of metallic silver with a substance a proteoid--closely allied to the constituent of the mucous membrane
Argolaval	silver methenamine nitrate
Argonin	silver caseinate
Argyn	mild protein silver--U.S.P.
Argyrol	mild silver protein
Arox	colloidal dispersion of silver oxide suspended in a mixture of paraffin hydrocarbons
Arvitin	20% silver with egg yolk protein
Cargel	emulsion of lanolin in an aqueous solution of mild silver protein and casein
Cargentos	mild protein silver--U.S.P., a colloidal prepa- ration of silver oxide and modified casein
Choleval	combination of colloidal silver and sodium cholate
Collargol	colloidal silver and silver oxide
Collene	solution in distilled water of 0.05% colloidal silver, in the metallic state

Table VI-26 (Continued)

Proprietary Name	Chemical Description
Collosol Argentum	colloidal suspension claimed to contain 0.05% metallic silver
Cryptargol	silver derivative of thioglycerin sulfonate of sodium containing 35% Ag
Cuprocollargol	electrocolloid copper silver solution containing 0.05% Cu and 0.05% Ag
Delegon	dosage form of Protargol
Dispargan	colloidal silver 30%
Electrargol	electric colloidal silver, marketed in the form of a very dilute (0.04%) solution
Fulmargin	colloidal solution of silver 0.1%
Hegonon	silver nitrate ammonio-albumose
Ichthargan	silver sulfoichthyolate
Ichtargol	silver sulfoichthyolate preparation containing about 12% silver
Io-Dargin	solution silver iodide, concentrated
I-O-Sil	aqueous solution of silver iodide containing 20 g silver iodide per 100 cc
Isotachiol	silver silicofluoride
Itrol	silver citrate
Jalon	solution containing 0.1% collargol
Jodcollargol	colloidal silver iodide preparation
Lunargen	mild protein silver preparation
Lunosol	preparation of colloidal silver chloride containing silver chloride, 10%, and sucrose, 90%
Lysargin	colloidal silver protein preparation
Methargyl	compound of methylene blue and silver representing about 20% of the metal
Microsil 1-500	colloidal suspension containing in each cc 0.002 g of metallic silver
Nargol	silver nucleinate
Necaron	somewhat similar to Silvogon but containing 35% silver
Neo-Protosil	colloidal silver iodide compound containing about 20% silver iodide
Neo-Reargon	chemically combined Anthrachinonglucoside with silver nitrate of about 15% Ag content
Neo-Silvol	compound of silver iodide with a soluble gelatin base
Novargan	silver proteinate
Omorol	silver protein preparation containing about 10% Ag

Table VI-26 (Continued)

Proprietary Name	Chemical Description
Orargol	colloidal suspension of Ag and Au prepared electrically from an alloy composed of Au, 10%, and Ag, 90%
Picrotol	silver picrate
Proganol	strong silver protein type
Protargentum	strong silver protein type
Prophylactol	dosage form of Protargol
Protargol	strong protein silver--U.S.P., a compound of silver-albumose
Protosyl	colloidal silver iodide preparation
Pyelon	colloidal silver iodide preparation
Silberol	silver phenol-sulfonate
Silloid	preparation of the mild silver protein type
Sil-Mer-Caine	ophthalmic ointment containing silver nucleinate 10% plus benzocaine and yellow mercury oxide
Silver Arsphenamine	contains not less than 19% arsenic and 12-14% Ag
Silver Lactate-Merck	brand of silver lactate
Silver Picrate-Wyeth's	brand of silver picrate
Silver Protein Mild	mild silver protein--U.S.P.
Silver Protein Strong--Merck	strong protein silver--U.S.P.
Silversal	contains approximately 20% Ag in colloidal diffusion
Silvocaine	1% silver proteinate and 0.1% procaine in a water soluble base
Silvogon	organic compound of silver potassium cyanide with potassium choleate, representing 16.7% Ag
Silvol	mild protein silver--U.S.P., a compound of colloidal silver with an alkaline proteid
Siocol	colloidal silver iodide preparation
Skiargen	sterile solution of collargol containing 9% Ag
Solargentum	mild protein silver--U.S.P., a compound of Ag and gelatin, containing 19-23% Ag in colloidal form
Solargyl	silver protein preparation containing about 30% silver
Sophol	silver-formaldehyde-nucleinic acid combination
Special Caustic Applicators	silver nitrate 75%
Stagophor	dosage form of Protargol
Syrgol	silver protein preparation containing about 20% Ag
Tachiol	silver fluoride

Table VI-26 (Concluded)

Proprietary Name	Chemical Description
Talisman	dosage form of Protargol
Tanargentan	silver and tannin albuminate combination previously called "Tanargan"
Targesin	combination of Ag with diacetyl tannin-protein, representing about 6% Ag
Toxogon	silver bound in colloidal form upon Ricinic acid
Urosanol	dosage form of Protargol
Vargol	mild silver protein, 21.8%
Ventrase	10% colloidal silver solution
Viro	dosage form of Protargol
Zinc-Iodin Co.	mixture of zinc sulfate, iodine, and silver proteinate in extract of witch hazel

TABLE VI-27

MEDICAL USES

Use	Form	Remarks	References
Topical Application			
Mucous membrane antiseptics and germicides:		See Reference 48 for use of Ag in medicine prior to 1939.	
Local antibacterial in conjunctivitis, cystitis, gonorrhea, nose and throat infections.	Lunosol (colloidal AgCl containing 10% AgNO₃ stabilized by sucrose or other protective colloid).	Hille Labs.	57
Treatment of conjunctivitis, cystitis, nose and throat infections, prophylaxis of gonorrhea (Armed Forces).	Mild Silver Proteins (19 to 23% Ag, prepared by treating Ag oxide with a casein, alk. gelatin, or serum albumin solution): Argyn (Abbott); Argyrol (Barnes); Cargentos (MSD); Lunargin (Lilly); Silvol (Parke, Davis); Solargentum (Squibb).	Solutions decompose with time and become increasingly astringent. Dose 0.1 to 50% solution. Nearly obsolete.	45 49 57
Local antibacterial in conjunctivitis, cystitis, gonorrhea, nose and throat infections.	Neo-Silvol (18 to 22% colloidal AgI in gelatin).	Parke, Davis and Co. Dose 0.05 to 10% solution. Obsolete. Most widely used of the Ag halide compounds. Doesn't stain linens as the proteinates do.	45 49 57
Veterinary ointment or solution for general germicidal and parasiticidal purposes.	Ag₂O	Formerly used internally in medical practice for chorea and epilepsy and topically for venereal infections.	41
Mastitis and as antiseptic ointment in superficial infected lesions of the skin and mucous membranes.	5% Ag₂O colloidal dispersion.		41
Treatment of conjunctivitis, cystitis, nose and throat infections, prophylaxis of gonorrhea (Armed Forces).	Strong Silver Proteins, e.g., Protargol, contain 7.5 to 8.5% Ag and are prepared by treating a Ag salt with a purified protein.	Winthrop Labs. Dose 0.05 to 10% solution. Intermediate in activity between mild proteins and AgNO₃ solutions. Strong silver proteins release a higher Ag‡ concentration and are more germicidal and irritating. Protargol is about 0.1 as irritant as AgNO₃. Obsolete.	45 49 57
	Colsargen, an aqueous colloidal suspension containing 0.5% metallic Ag.	Crooke Labs.	57
Applied to conjunctiva of newborn infants for the prophylaxis of ophthalmia nionatorium (a conjunctivitis of infants born to mothers afflicted with gonorrhea; frequently leads to blindness).	Silver nitrate ophthalmic solution: 0.95 to 1.05% AgNO₃, possibly buffered by NaOAc.	Dose: a few drops of solution, ~ 0.1 ml. Use required by law in many states. In others, it has been replaced by treatment with antibiotics, sulfa drugs, or mild silver protein (2%).	45 49

264

TABLE VI-27 (Continued)

Use	Form	Remarks	References
Topical Application			
Mucous membrane antiseptics and germicides:			
Painting posterior pharynx or rinsing after meals.	10% AgNO$_3$ or 0.5% AgNO$_3$ solution, respectively.	Smoking causes a disagreeable irritating taste. Too cumbersome for widespread use.	45
Antiseptic and astringent for irrigation of bladder and urethra.	0.01% AgNO$_3$		49
Local treatment of infected mouth ulcers.	10% solution or pencils containing 94.5% AgNO$_3$ and the rest AgCl.	Pencils and sticks of "lunar caustic" also used for removal of granulation tissue, warts, etc.	49
Applied to infected areas in tooth cavities.	Ammoniacal silver nitrate solution 28.5 to 30.5% Ag, 9.0 to 9.7% NH$_3$ per 100 g of solution.	Mixed with a reducing agent such as HCHO (1:10) to be applied topically. Pptd. Ag sterilizes the dentin. Within a month, the ppt. is carried into the pulp.	45 49
Veterinary: locally in inflammations, wounds, and ulcers of mucous membranes; otorrhea of dogs; infectious sinusitis of turkeys; intramammary to destroy mucous membranes.	AgNO$_3$ solutions.	Dose: horses and cattle, 0.5 to 2.0 g; dogs, 10 to 50 mg.	41
Insufflations for treating vaginitis of humans and cattle.	1% Ag picrate in powdered talc. (Picragol) or kaolin (Picrotol).	Dose in cattle 5 g of 1% dispersion.	41 57
Replacement of F in mouth hygiene.	(See ammoniacal AgNO$_3$)	Currently studied.	54
Urethral injection.	0.01% Ag citrate solution.	Obsolete. Powdered Ag citrate used as Crede's antiseptic from 1897.	45 49
Mouthwashes and gargles.	0.05 to 1% Ag lactate solutions.	Obsolete.	49
Topical disinfectant.	A silver β-cycloheptylamylose inclusion designated as $(C_6H_{10}O_5)_7 \cdot 0.2$ Ag.	German Patent 2,260,536 (July 4, 1974).	32
Burns and other nonintact skin:			
Compresses, etc., for treating severe burns on ≤ 70% of the body.	0.05 to 0.5% aqueous AgNO$_3$ solutions.	Besides the germicidal effect, esp. on Pseudomonas aeruginosa, a membrane is formed that protects against fluid loss and reduces scar formation. AgNO$_3$ disturbs the balance of body salts and must be discontinued periodically.	50 57

TABLE VI-27 (Continued)

Use	Form	Remarks	References
Burns and other nonintact skin:			
Burns, open wounds.	Katadyn silver powder or spray (particles 2 μ by 0.01 μ containing 10% Ag); O-Silver gauze (an aqueous solution of Ag, Cu, and Zn nitrates and dextrose);		45 137
	Ag sulfadiazine; ointments containing Ag_2O, neomycin, and bacitracin; creams containing Ag lactate or acetate; Ag phosphanilamido-pyrimidine.	Approved by FDA for medical use. Analog of Ag sulfadiazine that can be used safely on patients with sulfonamide sensitivity.	19 50,138 86
	Ointment containing 0.3% Ag as Ag allantoinate.	British Patent 1,346,544 (February 13, 1974).	32
Emergency burn kit.	Ag lacto allantoinate.	Polyethylene sheets and bags are treated with 1% Ag powder that adheres by electrostatic action.	50 139
Wet dressings for treating acute eczema and athlete's foot.	0.1 to 0.25% $AgNO_3$.		57
Healing skin ulcers refractory to penicillin and sulfa drugs.	Ag-Zn allantoin.	Used in clinical trials. Effective 120/130 times.	50
Other Modes of Application			
Oral:			
Peptic ulcers, gastrointestinal disturbances, epilepsy, tabes, multiple sclerosis, pernicious anemia.	$AgNO_3$ solutions or pills, Argyrol, Ag_2O.	Obsolete. $AgNO_3$ and Ag_2O were used as pills containing 10 to 20 mg in kaolin and petrolatum for gastric ulcer and hyperacidity. Great risks of argyria. Ag foil, filings, and salts were used up through the 19th century as a caustic, purgative, and a treatment for epilepsy, other nervous disorders, and insanity.	45 48
Pulmonary TB	Collargol pills.	Obsolete.	48
Injection:			
Immunosuppressive agent after organ transplants.	Ag chelates.	Animal experiments by H. W. Margraf. The chelates prevent cell proliferation.	140
Former treatment of syphilis.	0.5% Ag arsphenamine solution, Ag neoarsphenamine.		57

266

TABLE VI-27 (Concluded)

Use	Form	Remarks	References
Other Modes of Application			
Inhalation:			
Aerosol bactericide.	200 ppm Ag^+ in H_2O.	Two 1/2-hr treatments at 0.4 mg Ag^+/min (max. 10 ppb in the air) cured baby chicks infected with Escherichia coli and Salmonella pullorum-gallinarum. Results similar to those given by neomycin, but the Ag treatment was cheaper.	141
Surgical implants, sutures, etc.:			
Grafting heart valves or other graft materials to a damaged body.	Ag-heparin complex.	Research by H. W. Margraf. Application of the complex creates nonthrombogenic and antimicrobial surfaces.	50 140
Sutures.	Ag wire.	Alleged to have some antiseptic action but definitely irritating to some tissues. Use is somewhat limited.	49
Sutures.	Plastic surgical sutures treated with Ag compounds.	First use of silver sutures was the use by Bell in 1804 of Ag-tipped pins to close lacerations. The body reacted unfavorably to the Ag-steel combination.	50 51
Prosthetic devices and/or splints. Plates to repair skull injuries. Other devices for internal bone fixation.	Metallic Ag.	Bone plates, first used in 1886 by Hansmann, slowly replaced the silver wires used since 1827 to hold bone fragments together. (Wire for redn. of long bone fractures was accepted surgical practice by 1860). Original steel plates replaced by Al, Ag, and brass. Silver used for bolts, screws, and pegs since early 1900's.	50 51
Bearings to repair human bone joints and sockets.	Ag coatings.		50
Other Medical Uses			
Antimicrobial filter agent.	Ag-coated silica gel.	Research by H. W. Margraf. Organisms are adsorbed, but the Ag is not dissolved.	140
Recording brain, heart, and other bodily actions.	Ag electrodes.	Electrode developed by NASA, U.S. Patent 3,669,110, is a pre-filled disposable, electrolyte-satd. silicone rubber sponge containing a chlorided Ag disk with a wire leading to a monitor.	142
Flexible electrodes to monitor and register heart beats, etc., suitable for implantation.	Powdered Ag-coated knit fabric; silicone rubber loaded with Ag-plated particles.	Technical Wire Products, Inc.	143

267

TABLE VI-28

NONMEDICINAL ANTIMICROBIALS

Use	Form	Remarks	References
Water purification:			
To remove odors and tastes of drinking water and swimming pools, algicides.	Katadyn quartz sand.	Cannot kill pathogenic spores. Katadyn-treated swimming pools were tried in the thirties.	137
	Filtering systems with activated carbon of very high surface area coated with pure metallic Ag. Release 10 to 50 ppm Ag^+.	Several swimming pools in U.S. such as the North Severna Park Community Association installation near Annapolis, Maryland, and the Denver Hilton pool. Swimming pool filters are manufactured by American Water Purification, Inc. (The Silverator System™) and Ionics, Inc.	144 145 146
Algicide.	Ag metharsonate.		57
Slimicides for industrial water (and antifouling paints).	Ag compounds.	British Patent 953,753 (April 2, 1964).	54 57
Sterilization.	AgBr crystals.	U.S. Patent 3,257,315 (June 21, 1966), Pall Corp.	57
Soft drinks.		Currently studied. Ag eliminates unpleasant odors and tastes.	54
Soviet space ship and orbiting station program.	100 to 200 ppb Ag^+.	The Russians found Ag safe, stable, and long-lasting.	147
Sea or brackish water deionization and purification.	Ag oxide mixed with Ag zeolite.	Provided in survival kits for astronauts, airmen, and sailors.	57 134
Other antimicrobial uses:			
Brewery and perfumery.	≥ 0.015 mg Ag/liter.	Prevents cloudiness due to growth of microorganisms in vinegar, cider, and wine. Improves taste and odor of alcoholic liquids by affecting the acid-ester ratio.	137
Microbiocides in hydrocarbon fuels.	10 ppm salts such as Ag oleate, butyrate, and caproate or Ag dimethylbenzenesulfonate, $AgBu_2PO_4$, and Ag toluenesulfonate.	1965 patent by W. R. Grace and Co.	148

268

TABLE VI-29

GLASS

Use	Form of Silver	Remarks	References
Electrically heated glass (e.g., automobile rear windows).	E.g., pastes containing Ag and low-melting fritted glass powder fired onto glass.	U.S. Patent 3,723,080 (March 27, 1973), Corning Glass Works.	19
Polishing and coloring glass yellow.	Ag_2O		41
Sunlight-reflecting window glazing material.	5- to 43-μ Ag platelets dispersed in poly(vinylbutyral) sheet between two glass layers.	German Patent 2,313,278 (September 27, 1973), E. I. du Pont de Nemours and Company.	58
Prevent daylight glare through auto glass, yet give normal light vision.	0.05 to 0.3% AgCl plus a reducing agent.	Belgian Patent 643,613 (August 10, 1964), Corning Glass Works.	57
Other photosensitive glasses.	AgCl or Ag molybdate.	U.S. Patent 3,252,374 and Belgian Patent 644,989, Corning Glass Works.	57

269

TABLE VI-30

SILVER BEARINGS

Use	Form	Remarks	References
Self-lubricated bearings for continuous operation at >> 400°C.	Ag powder compacted with $AlPO_4$; BaF_2; CaF_2 and Al_2O_3, Si_3N_4, or $MoSi_2$.	U.S. Patent 3,755,164 (August 28, 1973), Boeing Co.	86
Rotor bearings.	Ag-impregnated graphite.	Ag-impregnated graphite also useful for motor brushes.	86
Critical master rod and other bearings of reciprocating aircraft engines and wrist-pin bushings in high-performance diesel railroad locomotives.	Ag plated or bonded in 0.020- to 0.030-in. layers to a suitable backing material with an overlay of 0.0005 to 0.003 in. Pb, Pb-Sn, Pb-In, etc.	Lubricating oils in these applications contain little or no Zn dialkyl dithiophosphate or other antiwear and antioxidant additives that are extremely corrosive to Ag.	60
Conventional bearings with improved fatigue properties.	Cu-Pb-1% Ag.		60
Plating of rolling element or antifriction bearing cages in main-shaft gas-turbine engine bearings.	Ag.		60
Bearing cage materials for NASA liquid rocket engine turboprop bearings.	Ag-plated iron, silicon bronze, or Ag-plated 4130 or 6414 steel.	The liquid rocket engines are for installation in future space shuttles with a life of 100 round trips.	149
High-temperature bearings.	Ag-coated Si nitride.	Currently studied.	54
Proposed for dry bearings. Efficient at high temperatures.	Ag alloy-plastic composites.	Studied in cooperation with British labs.	125 54

TABLE VI-31

USE OF SILVER IN WATER, FOOD, AND DRUG PROCESSING

Item	Silver Processing Equipment	Corrosion Resistance	Remarks	References
Beverages	Pipelines, siphons, tops, nozzles, containers, pasteurizing coils.	Ag stable to all beverages that do not contain S.	Ag used com. in Europe on a fairly large scale by 1940 to preserve certain fruit juices, vinegar, wine, and beer. (Oligo-dynamic processes such as Katadyn and Matzka.)	150
Beer		No discoloration nor flavor change after long storage of beer in con-tact with Ag-lined containers.		52
Cider				
Fruit juices and extracts.	Pure Ag and Ag-lined stills, con-densers, pipelines.			150
Fruit syrups	Sterling Ag cooling coils where a slight contamination would occur if some other metal, such as Cu or Ni, were used.			150
See also Brewery fluids, Wines.				150
Brewery fluids	Ag valve disks for special fittings in the brewery.		Use of Ag favored for its ability to keep container surfaces free of bacteria.	150
Dairy products	Ag-plated cooling coils in common use.			150
Essential oils	Ag-lined pans, coils, and taps used by distillers.	No catalytic effect that would de-compose an oil and its characteris-tic flavor.		150
Foodstuffs	Ag used especially where Cu, Ni, or some other metal would contaminate or discolor the food.	Unattacked by almost all common foods except those containing S.		150
Formaldehyde	Ag-lined containers to produce HCHO free of contamination for production of pharmaceuticals and formaldehyde resins.			150
Glycerol	Ag-lined steel barrels have been used to transport pharmaceutical glycerin (glycerol).	Glycerol does not attack Ag.		150

271

TABLE VI-31 (Concluded)

Item	Silver Processing Equipment	Corrosion Resistance	Remarks	References
Hormones	Generally Ag.			13
Pectin	Ag apparatus used in handling jellies and gelatin.			150
Pharmaceuticals	Ag coatings for boiling vessels, heating coils, distillation app., and columns.	Ag or its surface decompn. products resistant to the halogens.		150
Vinegar		Condensing coils used in contact with all strengths of acetic acid showed no deterioration in 15 years.	Ag used in making white vinegar to prevent discoloration.	150
		A strip of 999.3 fine Ag had a corrosion loss of 1.19 mg/cm^2 when immersed in boiling glacial acetic acid for 27 hr.	Katadyn processes were used as anti-bacterials in vinegar, cider, and to prevent fermentation in fruit juices.	52
Vitamins	Generally Ag, e.g., Ag-plated centrifuges.			
Water	Ag or Ag-alloy application common for handling wet or dry Cl_2 in filtration plants employing chlorination.	Dry Cl_2 forms protective AgCl film, which is destroyed in the presence of moisture.	Katadyn processes were used for steriliz-ing water in military campaigns, swimming pools, etc.	52 150
		Ag wholly insoluble in pure water at all temperatures from the stand-point of corrosion. Pure leaf Ag in pure water for 21 days in total darkness dissolved to the extent 0.000035 g/liter (0.000036 g/liter after 180 days). Ag not attacked appreciably by water vapor at any temperature.	(New processes employ Ag for sterilizing swimming pool water.)	
Wines	Bottle caps or crowns containing a spot of pure Ag foil to seal high-pressure wines (usually too expensive for ordinary bottling).		Matzka method was used to produce oligo-dynamic Ag in liquids such as wines and fruit juices.	52 150

TABLE VI-32   PROCESS AND LABORATORY EQUIPMENT

Use	Form of Silver	Remarks	References
Joining Al thermal conditioning panels for the Saturn program.	Ultrathin Ag layers.	Components are bonded by eutectic diffusion under heat and pressure.	101
Cladding on Cu, brass, Ni, Fe.	Ag-Au-Pd alloys; fine Ag.	Clad metals also used in contacts and conductors.	13 95
Electroplate over Cu, Ni, C-steel plate.	Fine Ag; ≥ 0.15 mil on internal surfaces; ≥ 0.5 mil on external surfaces + 0.007 mil Rh plate.	Ag-clad, -lined, or -plated app. used for chem. and food production.	13
Diffusion units to produce ultrapure H_2, e.g., from cracked NH_3, for gas chromatog., and for metallurgical atms.; to remove the H_2 carrier gas from the gas stream of gas chromatographs; to admit H_2 into vacuum lab. app.; and to reduce the H_2 content of synthesis gas in preparation for chem. processing.	23 to 27% Ag-Pd alloys.	H_2 diffusors operate preferably at ~450°C.	94 123 151-153
Rupture disks where pressure relief is required.	Fine Ag.		12
Engraved scales on surveying equipment.	Ag-Zn, Ag-Cd.	More tarnish resistant than pure Ag or its common alloys.	93
Apparatus for handling caustics:			
Immersion pumps for caustic potash melts.		Erosion of Ag 0.086 mm/year at 400°C.	154
Evaporator for formation of anhyd. NaOH or KOH at ~ 615°F (320°C).	Ag-lined Ni or Inconel evaporator tubes.	Erosion of Ag 0.014 mm/year at 400°C.	13 154
Apparatus for handling strong and/or boiling mineral acids.	E.g., 99.98% Ag; ≤ 33% Ag-Au alloys plated on Ag, Cu, or Cu alloys; 30% Au-30% Pd-40% Ag.		154
Ag reactors to prep. fluorophosphoric acid from P_2O_5 and anhyd. or concd. HF.			13
Ag vessels to fuse fluophosphoric acid with the desired base to give fluophosphates.			13
Ag-lined evaporators to prepare Na_2HPO_4 and NaH_2PO_4.			13
Pressure vessels and process app. in handling aqueous HCl, especially in association with organic hydrocarbon liquids.			13
Handling HF without S compounds:			13
Condensers for condensing 70% HF from hot HF vapors formed in the hydrofluorination of U compounds.	Bonded Ag linings or solid Ag inner pans.		
Open or closed vessels for evaporating F⁻ solutions and preparing F compounds.			13
Vacuum pans, evaporators, condensers, and storage vats for evaporating and concentrating organic acids and phenol.			13
Handling wet Cl_2 gas in water-purifications installations (control and metering apparatus, tubing).	Fine Ag or 7.5% Cu-Ag alloy often in association with plastics.		13
Autoclaves for urea synthesis from CO_2 and NH_3 at ≤ 191°C and ≤ 3,000 psi.	Ag linings.		13

TABLE VI-33

SUMMARY OF WEATHER MODIFICATION FIELD OPERATORS' REPORTS
FISCAL YEARS 1966, 1967, AND 1968[a]

Purpose	Area Treated (square miles)			Number of Projects			Number of States[b]			Number of Operators[b]		
	1966	1967	1968	1966	1967	1968	1966	1967	1968	1966	1967	1968
Rain augmentation and snowpack increase	61,429	62,021	53,369	35	41	37	21	20	21	22	25	23
Hail suppression	20,566	20,556	13,510	3	4	4	3	3	5	3	4	4
Fog dissipation	100	118	145	22	15	15	15	13	9	17	15	10
Cloud modification	19,345	28,300	18,600	9	18	8	8	12	7	8	14	6
Lightning suppression	314	314	314	1	1	1	1	1	1	1	1	1
Totals	101,744	111,383	85,938	70	79	65	30	23	25	46	44	37

a/ Data for fiscal year 1968 include reports received to September 1, 1968.
b/ Totals are not the sum of the items since many States and operators are involved in more than one type of activity.

TABLE VI-34

MISCELLANEOUS USES OF SILVER

Use	Form of Silver	Remarks	References
Hair colorings. The 5% $AgNO_3$ solution with $Na_2S_2O_3$ developers is widely used to dye eyebrows and eyelashes (only colorant commonly used for this purpose in the U.S.). [Ag powder was briefly used in France ~ 1853 in ladies' hair.]	0.5 to 15% $AgNO_3$ solutions containing various amounts of NH_3 to give gradations of shade. [$Na_2S_2O_3$ developers are added to the hair first.] Formerly used with Na, K, or NH_4 bisulfide or pyrogallol as the developer.	Silver darkens on light exposure and stains proteins brown. Incompatible with permanent waving and oxidn. dyes. Still used by men as a hair coloring. Ag dyes regularly used for hair since ~ 1800. $CuSO_4$ or $CuCl_2$ are occasionally sold for a final rinse to cover the iridescent effect of Ag-dyed hair. Combinations with Ni are used to give dark brown.	155 156
Ag polish.	0 to 1% $AgNO_3$.		15
Nuclear reactor control rods.	80% Ag-5% Cd-15% In alloy.	Of growing importance. The use is of the order of hundreds of thousands of ounces. After 3,000 hr in a high-flux region, the alloy becomes 76% Ag-10% Cd.	103 126
Clutch	Preferably 61% Mo and 39% Ag.	British Patent 575,929 (1946).	100
Special-purpose lubricants.	Ag_2S, AgI, $AgBrO_3$.	Ag compds. are added to oils used for high-temperature applications.	57 157
Additive to lubricating oils for extreme-pressure lubricants.	Organic Ag compounds.	Currently being studied.	54
Removal of radioactive iodine from cooling air in some nuclear power plants.	Ag zeolites. New: Ag-impregnated SiO_2-based porous material.	German Patent 2,236,223 (February 7, 1974).	134 32
Ionization detector for cosmic rays, radar screens, and IR radiation windows.	AgCl.		57
Personal dosimeters for detecting toxic propellants, e.g., N_2O_4, F_2, and Me_2NNH_2.	Ag films coated with appropriate salts.	Magna Corporation, Redondo Beach, California.	158
Detection of H_2S in air of oil refineries, sewage systems, natural gas operations.	Ag-impregnated paper tapes.		58
Seals for aerospace applications, e.g., seals in liquid O_2 pumps.	Ag strengthened with 20 and 40 vol. % Mo fibers; sterling Ag.	The composites remain resilient after repeated deformations.	100 159
Caulking compound for caulking seams in shielded rooms or filling imperfections in castings that are to be electroplated.	Epoxy Products, Inc.; Ag-filled E-Kote No. 3202.		101
Accelerant in rocket propellants.	Ag perchlorate.	$AgClO_4$ explodes when struck.	57 41

TABLE VI-34 (Concluded)

Use	Form of Silver	Remarks	References
Noisemakers called "torpedoes", trick cigars and matches.	Ag fulminate.		62
Sheath for explosive cord used in high-performance aircraft and the space program to sever straps, bolts, rings, and supports, and to activate emergency escape systems. Has also been used in the metallurgical industry. Now available com., the explosive-cord products may have application for quick-release mechanisms for floodgates, etc.; emergency-escape systems in mines; and precise demolition of large structures.	99.9% Ag. X-Cord and Jetcord use 0.2 to 3.3 troy oz. Ag/linear foot.	The sheath precisely confines the small amount of explosive (e.g., hexanitrostilbene) for a satisfactory detonation.	32
Temp. indicator for measuring pellet-bed temps. in a shaft furnace treating Fe concs.	Ag-Pd alloy wire having specific m.p.'s 1090 to 1370°C.	The condition of the wires after the firing cycle reveals the max. temp. attained.	101
To detect overheating in journal bearings, etc.	Ag_2HgI_4.	Becomes blood red at 40 to 50°C; yellows again on cooling.	41
Heating element for producing high temperatures without combustion and the resulting pollution from stack gases.	Metallic Ag resist layer on a ceramic-coated heat-resistant metal base.	Operates at 400 to 700 °F (200 to 370°C). Patent assigned to Whirlpool Corp.	160
Economic fuel cells.	Ag-Pd alloys.		36
"Permanent" magnet.	87% Ag-9% Mn-4% Al, Ag_5MnAl.	The alloy can be magnetized in any direction and stays that way. A magnetic Ag alloy has a potential use for elec. contacts.	145 161
Low-temp. alloy that is light, ductile, and strong.	72% Mg-7% Li-6% Ag-6% Zn-5% Cd-3% Cd-3% Th-1% Zr.	Wellman Dynamics Corp.	162
Strengthening Al-Mg alloys.	Al-10% Mg-0.1 to 0.8% Ag alloy.	Stronger and more durable as construction materials than Al-Mg.	86
To introduce small amts. of Zr into Mg to give Zr-Mg alloys of good tensile strength and corrosion resistance.	≤ 85% Ag-Zr.	Zr-Mg alloys difficult to make with the use of $ZrCl_4$. Japanese Patent 7,409,286 (March 4, 1974), Honda Motor Company.	32
Semiconductor laser.	Ag-doped $CdSnP_2$.	U.S. Patent 3,750,046 (July 31, 1973), Bell Telephone Labs., Inc.	19

BIBLIOGRAPHY. SECTION VI.

1. Anonymous, Constitution Mint, Constitution Mint, Provo, Utah, 1974.

2. Charles River Associates, Inc., Economic Analysis of the Silver
   Industry, prepared for Property Management and Disposal Service,
   General Services Administration, Clearinghouse for Federal
   Scientific and Technical Information, Springfield, Virginia, 1969.

3. Marsland, C. R., "Chapter 21. The Fabrication of Silver and Silver-
   Base Alloys," in Silver. Economics, Metallurgy, and Use, A. Butts
   and C. D. Coxe, Eds., D. Van Nostrand Company, Inc., Princeton,
   New Jersey, 1967, pp. 310-321.

4. Lyman, T., H. E. Boyer, W. J. Carnes, L. Carr, M. W. Chevalier, E. A.
   Durand, P. D. Harvey, H. Lawton, T. M. Leach, C. H. Willer, I. A.
   Anderson, H. V. Bukovics, B. A. Caldwell, and J. S. Elliot, Eds.,
   Metals Handbook, Vol. 3, Machining, 8th ed., American Society for
   Metals, Metals Park, Ohio, 1967.

5. Coxe, C. D., "Chapter 31. Manufacture and Uses of Silver Powder," in
   Silver. Economics, Metallurgy, and Use, A. Butts and C. D. Coxe,
   Eds., D. Van Nostrand Company, Inc., Princeton, New Jersey, 1967,
   pp. 446-454.

6. Bureau of the Census, 1967 Census of Manufacturers. Vol. II, Industry
   Statistics. Part 2 Major Groups 25-33, U.S. Department of Commerce,
   Washington, D.C., 1971.

7. Coxe, C. D., "Chapter 16. Silver Nitrate," in Silver. Economics,
   Metallurgy, and Use, A. Butts and C. D. Coxe, Eds., D. Van Nostrand
   Company, Inc., Princeton, New Jersey, 1967, pp. 221-226.

8. Ottinger, R. S., J. L. Blumenthal, D. F. Dal Porto, G. I. Gruber,
   M. J. Santy, and C. C. Shih, Vol. V. National Disposal Site Candi-
   date Waste Stream Constituent Profile Reports. Pesticides and
   Cyanide Compounds, TRW Systems Group for the U.S. Environmental
   Protection Agency, PB-224 584, National Technical Information
   Service, U.S. Department of Commerce, Springfield, Virginia, 1973.

9. Larsen, E. I., and R. H. Imes, "Chapter 26. Electrical Contacts--
   Applications," in Silver. Economics, Metallurgy, and Use, A. Butts
   and C. D. Coxe, Eds., D. Van Nostrand Company, Inc., Princeton,
   New Jersey, 1967, pp. 372-385.

10. Ageton, R. W., "Silver," in Minerals Facts and Problems, Bureau of
    Mines Bulletin 650, U.S. Department of the Interior, U.S. Government
    Printing Office, Washington, D.C., 1970, pp. 723-737.

11. Anonymous, "U.S. Markets 1974," Electronics, 47 (1), 94-120 (1974).

12. Weglein, E. B., "Chapter 9. Mechanical Properties and Uses of Fine
    Silver," in Silver. Economics, Metallurgy, and Use, A. Butts and
    C. D. Coxe, Eds., D. Van Nostrand Company, Inc., Princeton,
    New Jersey, 1967, pp. 137-152.

13. Lyman, T., H. E. Boyer, P. M. Unterweiser, J. E. Foster, J. P. Hontas,
    and H. Lawton, Eds., Metals Handbook, Vol. I., Properties and
    Selections of Metals, 8th ed., American Society for Metals, Novelty,
    Ohio, 1961.

14. Anonymous, "1974 Materials Selector," Mater. Eng., 78 (4), 1-484 (1973).

15. Berkowitz, J. B., G. R. Schimke, and V. R. Valeri, Water Pollution
    Potential of Manufactured Products. Catalog Section II - Product
    Listing, EPA-R2-73-179c, Office of Research and Monitoring, U.S.
    Environmental Protection Agency, U.S. Government Printing Office,
    Washington, D.C., 1973.

16. Anonymous, "Miners Produce for Silver Art," The Silver Institute
    Letter, 3 (7), 1 (1973).

17. Handy and Harman, The Silver Market 1970, 55th Annual Review, Handy
    and Harman, Inc., New York, New York, 1971.

18. Coxe, C. D., "Silver and Silver Alloys," in Kirk-Othmer Encyclopedia
    of Chemical Technology, Vol. 18, 2nd completely revised ed., Inter-
    science Publishers, Division of John Wiley and Sons, Inc., New York
    New York, 1969, pp. 279-294.

19. Anonymous, New Silver Technology. Silver Abstracts from the Current
    World Literature, The Silver Institute, Inc., Washington, D.C.,
    January 1974, pp. 4, 9, 13, 16-18.

20. Anonymous, "Silver--Salient Statistics," in Chemical Enconomics Handbook
    Stanford Research Institute, Menlo Park, California, February 1972.

21. Welch, J. R., "Silver," in Minerals Yearbook 1972, Vol. I, Metals,
    Minerals, and Fuels, Bureau of Mines, U.S. Department of the Interior,
    U.S. Government Printing Office, Washington, D.C., 1974, pp. 1129-
    1142.

22. Anonymous, Silvaloy Brazing Alloys for Industry, Engelhard Industries Division, Engelhard Minerals and Chemicals Corporation, Plainville, Massachusetts [undated].

23. Leach, R. H., "Chapter 7. High-Temperature Bonding of Silver," in Silver in Industry, L. Addicks, Ed., Reinhold Publishing Corporation, New York, New York, 1940, pp. 199-219.

24. Chamer, E. S., "Chapter 27. The Use of Silver Brazing Alloys," in Silver. Economics, Metallurgy, and Use, A. Butts and C. D. Coxe, Eds., D. Van Nostrand Company, Inc., Princeton, New Jersey, 1967, pp. 386-408.

25. Anonymous, "Tin-Silver Solders Make Quality Products," The Silver Institute Letter, 5 (2), 2, 3 (1975).

26. Lyman, T., H. E. Boyer, P. M. Unterweiser, J. P. Hontas, L. R. Mehlman, W. J. Carnes, and H. Lawton, Eds., Metals Handbook, Vol. 2, Heat Treating, Cleaning and Finishing, 8th ed., American Society for Metals, Metals Park, Ohio, 1964.

27. Orr, M. A., "Chapter 11. Electroplating," in Silver. Economics, Metallurgy, and Use, A. Butts and C. D. Coxe, Eds., D. Van Nostrand Company, Inc., Princeton, New Jersey, 1967, pp. 180-189.

28. Krohn, A., and C. W. Bohn, "Electrodeposition of Alloys: Present State of the Art," Electrodeposition and Surface Treatment, 1 (3), 199-211 (1973).

29. Coxe, C. D., "Chapter 15. Conductive Coatings," in Silver. Economics, Metallurgy, and Use, A. Butts and C. D. Coxe, Eds., D. Van Nostrand Company, Inc., Princeton, New Jersey, 1967, pp. 218-220.

30. Pertwee, K. S. G., "Chapter 3. Vacuum Evaporation of Silver," in Silver. Economics, Metallurgy, and Use, A. Butts and C. D. Coxe, Eds., D. Van Nostrand Company, Inc., Princeton, New Jersey, 1967, pp. 455-457.

31. Rodgers, T. M., Handbook of Practical Electroplating, The Macmillan Company, New York, New York, 1959.

32. Anonymous, New Silver Technology. Silver Abstracts from the Current World Literature, The Silver Institute, Washington, D.C., January 1975, pp. 3, 12, 18, 21, 22, 39, 40, 45, 47.

33. Pickhart, P., "Chapter 12. Silver Catalysts," in Silver. Economics
    Metallurgy, and Use, A. Butts and C. D. Coxe, Eds., D. Van Nostrand
    Company, Inc., Princeton, New Jersey, 1967, pp. 190-192.

34. Faith, W. L., D. B. Keyes, and R. L. Clark, "Formaldehyde," in Industrial
    Chemicals, 3rd ed., John Wiley and Sons, Inc., Somerset, New Jersey,
    1965, pp. 390-396.

35. Chemical Information Services, 1974 Directory of Chemical Producers.
    United States of America, Stanford Research Institute, Menlo Park,
    California, 1974.

36. Anonymous, "The Power of Silver Catalysts," The Silver Institute Letter,
    3 (5), 2 (1973).

37. Faith, W. L., D. B. Keyes, and R. L. Clark, "Ethylene Oxide," in
    Industrial Chemicals, 3rd ed., John Wiley and Sons, Inc., New York,
    New York, 1965, pp. 380-385.

38. Burke, D. P., "Catalysts. Part 1: Chemical Catalysts," Chem. Week,
    111 (9), 35-45 (1972).

39. Anonymous, "Ethylene Oxide--Shell Development Company," Hydrocarbon
    Process., 52 (11), 130 (1973).

40. Anonymous, "Ethylene Oxide--Scientific Design Company, Inc.,"
    Hydrocarbon Process., 52 (11), 129 (1973).

41. Stecher, P. G., Ed., The Merck Index, 8th ed., Merck and Company, Inc.,
    Rahway, New Jersey, 1968.

42. Viola, L. J., "Chapter 31. Fingernail Elongators and Accessory Nail
    Preparations," in Cosmetics: Science and Technology, E. Sagarin,
    Ed., Interscience Publishers, Inc., New York, New York, 1957, pp.
    693-716.

43. Viola, L. J., "Chapter 30. Fingernail Elongators and Accessory Nail
    Preparations," in Cosmetics: Science and Technology, Vol. 2, 2nd ed.,
    M. S. Balsam, E. Sagarin, S. D. Gershon, S. J. Strianse, and M. M.
    Rieger, Eds., Wiley-Interscience, Division of John Wiley and Sons,
    Inc., New York, New York, 1972, pp. 543-580.

280

44. Freeman, F. H., "Dental Materials," in <u>Kirk-Othmer Encyclopedia of Chemical Technology</u>, Vol. 62, 2nd revised ed., A. Standen, Executive Ed., Interscience Publishers, Division of John Wiley and Sons, Inc., New York, New York, 1965, pp. 777-847.

45. Crannell, M. Y., "Chapter 17. Silver in Medicine," in <u>Silver. Economics, Metallurgy, and Use</u>, A. Butts and C. D. Coxe, Eds., D. Van Nostrand Company, Inc., Princeton, New Jersey, 1967, pp. 227-234.

46. Anonymous, "Precious Metals and Who Supplies Them," <u>Am. Metal Market</u>, <u>81</u> (119), 22A-24A (1974).

47. Anonymous, "Silver," in <u>Thomas Register of American Manufacturers and Thomas Register Catalog File 1973, Vol. 5, Products and Services</u>, 63rd ed., Thomas Publishing Company, New York, New York, 1973, pp. 7911-7915.

48. Hill, W. R., and D. M. Pillsbury, <u>Argyria, the Pharmacology of Silver</u>, The Williams and Wilkins Company, Baltimore, Maryland, 1939.

49. Martin, E. W., Ed.-in-Chief, <u>Remington's Pharmaceutical Sciences</u>, 13th ed., Mack Publishing Company, Easton, Pennsylvania, 1965.

50. Margraf, H., "The Story of Silver in Medicine. How Silver is Used to Relieve Suffering and Save Lives," <u>Pacific Coast Coin Exchange Gold and Silver Newsletter</u>, September 1-4, 1974.

51. Ludwigson, D. C., "Today's Prosthetic Metals," <u>J. Metals</u>, <u>16</u> (3), 226-229 (1964).

52. Goetz, A., R. L. Tracy, and F. S. Harris, Jr., "Chapter 16. The Oligodynamic Effect of Silver," in <u>Silver in Industry</u>, L. Addicks, Ed., Reinhold Publishing Company, New York, New York, 1940.

53. Nielsen, L. W., and L. M. Massey, "Chapter 17. Silver as a Fungicide," in <u>Silver in Industry</u>, L. Addicks, Ed., Reinhold Publishing Company, New York, New York, 1940.

54. Anonymous, "New Markets for Silver," <u>The Silver Institute Letter</u>, <u>3</u> (11), 1-2 (1973).

55. Kleinberg, J., W. J. Argersinger, Jr., and E. Griswold, <u>Inorganic Chemistry</u>, D. C. Heath and Company, Boston, Massachusetts, 1960.

56. Pohl, R. D., "Chapter 13. Mirrors," in <u>Silver. Economics, Metallurgy, and Use</u>, A. Butts and C. D. Coxe, Eds., D. Van Nostrand Company, Inc., Princeton, New Jersey, 1967, pp. 193-199.

57. Tischer, T. H., "Silver Compounds," in the <u>Kirk-Othmer Encyclopedia of Chemical Technology</u>, Vol. 18, 2nd completely revised ed., Interscience Publishers, Division of John Wiley and Sons, Inc., New York, New York, 1969, pp. 295-309.

58. Anonymous, <u>New Silver Technology. Silver Abstracts from the Current World Literature</u>, The Silver Institute, Washington, D.C., July 1974, pp. 5, 14, 35.

59. Vaccari, J. A., "What's Ahead in Aircraft and Aerospace Materials," <u>Mater. Eng.</u>, 80 (6), 45-56 (1974).

60. DeBruyne, N., "Chapter 32. Silver Bearings," in <u>Silver. Economics, Metallurgy, and Use</u>, A. Butts and C. D. Coxe, Eds., D. Van Nostrand Company, Inc., Princeton, New Jersey, 1967, pp. 446-454.

61. Fleagle, R. G., J. A. Crutchfield, R. W. Johnson, and M. F. Abdo, <u>Weather Modification in the Public Interest</u>, American Meteorological Society and the University of Washington Press, Seattle, Washington, 1974.

62. Ellern, H., <u>Military and Civilian Pyrotechnics</u>, Chemical Publishing Company, Inc., New York, New York, 1968.

63. Evans, T. H., "Problems in Rain Making," <u>Public Works</u>, 82, 36-38, 76-78 (1951).

64. Bowers, N. A., "Planes Make Heavy Rains; Lawyers Study Legal Aspects," <u>Eng. News-Record</u>, 142 (3), 57, 59 (1949).

65. Cooper, C. F., and W. C. Jolly, "Ecological Effects of Silver Iodide and Other Weather Modification Agents: A Review," <u>Water Resources Res.</u>, 6 (1), 88-98 (1970).

66. National Science Foundation, <u>Weather Modification. Tenth Annual Report 1968</u>, U.S. Government Printing Office, Washington, D.C., 1969.

67. Koenig, L. R., "Some Chemical and Physical Properties of Silver-Iodide Smokes," <u>J. Appl. Meteorol.</u>, 3, 307-310 (1964).

68. Taubenfeld, H. J., <u>Weather Modification. Law, Controls, Operations</u>, NSF 66-7, National Science Foundation, Washington, D.C., 1966.

69. National Science Foundation, Weather Modification. Fifth Annual Report, 1963, U.S. Government Printing Office, Washington, D.C., 1964.

70. Anonymous, "Cloud Seeding Studied for Colorado Basin," Chem. Eng. News, 52 (45), 12 (1974).

71. National Science Foundation, Weather Modification. Eighth Annual Report, 1966, U.S. Government Printing Office, Washington, D.C., 1967.

72. Estrin, N. F., Cosmetic, Toiletry, and Fragrance Association, Inc., personal communication, August 15, 1972.

73. Anonymous, "Silver," in Minerals Yearbook 1966, Vol. I-II, Metals, Minerals, and Fuels, Bureau of Mines, U.S. Department of the Interior, U.S. Government Printing Office, Washington, D.C., 1967, pp. 352-361.

74. Ryan, J. P., "Silver," in Minerals Yearbook 1967, Vol. I-II, Metals, Minerals, and Fuels, Bureau of Mines, U.S. Department of the Interior, U.S. Government Printing Office, Washington, D.C., 1968, pp. 1037-1056.

75. Hoyt, C. D., "Silver," in Minerals Yearbook 1969, Vol. I, Metals, Minerals, and Fuels, Bureau of Mines, U.S. Department of the Interior, U.S. Government Printing Office, Washington, D.C., 1971, pp. 997-1011.

76. West, J. M., "Silver," in Minerals Yearbook 1970, Vol. I, Metals, Minerals, and Fuels, Bureau of Mines, U.S. Department of the Interior, U.S. Government Printing Office, Washington, D.C., 1972, pp. 1013-1029.

77. Welch, J. R., "Silver," in Minerals Yearbook 1971, Vol. I, Metals, Minerals, and Fuels, Bureau of Mines, U.S. Department of the Interior, U.S. Government Printing Office, Washington, D.C., 1973, pp. 1073-1086.

78. Anonymous, "Soaring Prices Put Damper on Silver Use," Chem. Eng. News, 52 (26), 7-8 (1974).

79. Handy and Harman, The Silver Market 1973, 58th Annual Review, Handy and Harman, Inc., New York, New York, 1974.

80. Anonymous, "Latest U.S. Silver Refining Statistics," The Silver Institute Letter, 5 (1), 4 (1975).

81. Chemical Information Services, 1972 Directory of Chemical Producers. United States of America, Stanford Research Institute, Menlo Park, California, 1972.

82. D. F. Goldsmith Chemical and Metal Corporation, Advertisement, Am. Metal Market, 81 (119), 18A (1974).

83. U.S. Bureau of the Census, U.S. Commodity Exports and Imports as Related to Output, 1971 and 1970, ES2-14, U.S. Department of Commerce, U.S. Government Printing Office, Washington, D.C., 1974.

84. Anonymous, "'Smile, Please': The $4 Billion Industry," The Silver Institute Letter, 3 (4), 1-2 (1973).

85. Anonymous, "Dry Silver Used in 'Photos by Phone,'" The Silver Institute Letter, 4 (5), 3 (1974).

86. Anonymous, New Silver Technology. Silver Abstracts from the Current World Literature, The Silver Institute, Washington, D.C., April 1974, pp. 2, 9, 11, 13, 15, 17, 25, 27, 28, 31, 32, 36, 37.

87. Anonymous, "Silver Components Used in Electric Vehicles," The Silver Institute Letter, 4 (3), 2 (1974).

88. Anonymous, "The New Post Office Relay (The Reliability of Palladium-Silver Contacts)," Platinum Metals Rev., 15 (4), 141 (1971).

89. Anonymous, "Palladium-Silver Resistor Pastes," Platinum Metals Rev., 14 (2), 53 (1970).

90. Anonymous, "Silver Metallizing in Digital Display," The Silver Institut Letter, 4 (1), 3 (1974).

91. Carabini, L. E., The Case for Silver. How to Protect Your Assets Against Inflation, 2nd ed., Pacific Coast Coin Exchange/A Division of Monex International, Ltd., Los Angeles, California, 1974.

92. Anonymous, "Silver-Coated Yarn in Anti-Static Carpets," The Silver Institute Letter, 4 (8), 3 (1974).

93. Gillett, H. W., The Behavior of Engineering Metals, John Wiley and Sons, Inc., New York, New York, 1951.

94. Hampel, C. A., "Chapter 17. Platinum Metal," in Rare Metals Handbook, Vol. 2, 2nd ed., Reinhold Publishing Corp., London, 1961, pp. 304-334.

95. Wise, E. M., Palladium. Recovery, Properties and Uses, Academic Press, New York, New York, 1968.

96. World Health Organization, Report of a Meeting of Investigators on Trace Elements in Relation to Cardiovascular Diseases, Joint WHO/IAEA Research Project, Geneva, Switzerland, 1971.

97. Anonymous, The Platinum Group Metals in Industry, The International Nickel Company, Inc., New York, New York [undated, ca. 1963].

98. Anonymous, "The Story of the Platinum Metals," Engelhard Industries, Inc., Newark, New Jersey [undated].

99. Cohn, J. G., "Precious Metals Withstand Tough Environments," Mater. Design Eng., 64 (3), 100-105 (1966).

100. Manzone, M. G., and J. Z. Briggs, Mo. Less-Common Alloys of Molybdenum, Climax Molybdenum Company, New York, New York, 1962.

101. Ryan, J. P., "Silver," in Minerals Yearbook 1965, Vol. I, Metals, Minerals, and Fuels, U.S. Bureau of Mines, U.S. Department of the Interior, U.S. Government Printing Office, Washington, D.C., 1967, pp. 829-850.

102. Anonymous, Precious Metals, Electrical Contacts, and Contact Components, The J. M. Ney Co., Bloomfield, Connecticut [undated, ca. 1972].

103. Materials Advisory Board Committee on Technical Aspects of Critical and Strategic Materials, Trends in Usage of Silver, Publication MAB-241, National Research Council, National Academy of Sciences, National Academy of Engineering, Washington, D.C., 1968.

104. Kossowsky, R., and P. G. Slade, "Effect of Arcing on the Microstructure and Morphology of Ag-CdO Contacts," IEEE Transactions on Parts, Hybrids, Packaging, PHP-9 (1), 39-44 (1973).

105. Anonymous, "Silver Paint Conducts Electricity, Cuts Static," The Silver Institute Letter, 3 (3), 1 (1973).

106. Anonymous, "New Electronics Technology Uses Silver," The Silver Institute Letter, 3 (7), 2 (1973).

107. Donahue, J. F., "Chapter 10. Silver Batteries," in Silver. Economics, Metallurgy, and Use, A. Butts and C. D. Coxe, Eds., D. Van Nostrand Company, Inc., Princeton, New Jersey, 1967, pp. 153-179.

108. Anonymous, "Racing Engines Use Silver Zinc Batteries," The Silver Institute Letter, 3 (11), 3-4 (1973).

109. Anonymous, "More Silver Needed by New Strategic Defense Systems," The Silver Institute Letter, 3 (4), 3 (1973).

110. Anonymous, "Silver Batteries Power Solid State Wristwatch," The Silver Institute Letter, 3 (4), 3 (1973).

111. Anonymous, "Thin, Supple Flexible Power Source with Silver," The Silver Institute Letter, 3 (8), 2-3 (1973).

112. Anonymous, "One-Cent-a-Mile Energy for Commuter Vehicle," The Silver Institute Letter, 3 (11), 1-2 (1973).

113. Anonymous, "When Alarm Sounds, Silver Battery Responds," The Silver Institute Letter, 4 (1), 2 (1974).

114. Anonymous, "Silver Can Help Relieve Energy Crisis," The Silver Institute Letter, 4 (3), 3 (1974).

115. Anonymous, New Silver Technology. Silver Abstracts from the Current World Literature, The Silver Institute, Washington, D.C., April 1975, p. 6.

116. Handy and Harman, The Silver Market 1972, 57th Annual Review, Handy and Harman, Inc., New York, New York, 1973.

117. Handy and Harman, The Silver Market 1974, 59th Annual Review, Handy and Harman, Inc., New York, New York, 1975.

118. Sibbet, J. H., "Let's Talk...Silver," in Independence Enterprises Newsletter, No. 3, T. J. Weir, Representing Constitution Mint, Manchester, Missouri, May 20, 1974.

119. Anonymous, "Booming Trade in Silver 'Collectibles' and Gifts," The Silver Institute Letter, 3 (10), 1 (1973).

120. Rhys, D. W., and W. Betteridge, "Brazing for Elevated Temperature Service," Metal Ind., 101 (2), 2-4, 27-30, 45-46 (1962).

121. McDonald, A. S., B. R. Price, and G. H. Sistare, "Chapter 18. Alloying Behavior of Silver and Its Principal Alloys," in Silver. Economics, Metallurgy, and Use, A. Butts and C. D. Coxe, Eds., D. Van Nostrand Company, Inc., Princeton, New Jersey, 1967, pp. 235-271.

122. Tugwell, G. L., "Industrial Applications for the Noble Metlas," Metal Progr., 88, 73-78 (1965).

123. Anonymous, Palladium. The Metal, Its Properties and Application, The International Nickel Company, Inc., New York, New York [undated, ca. 1965].

124. Anonymous, "Silver in Tin-Lead Solders Does More for Less Money," The Silver Institute Letter, 3 (4), 3-4 (1973).

125. Anonymous, "Committee Finds New Uses for Silver," The Silver Institute Letter, 3 (9), 2 (1973).

126. McDonald, A. S., B. R. Price, and G. H. Sistare, "Chapter 19. Ternary and Higher-Order Alloys of Silver," in Silver. Economics, Metallurgy, and Use, A. Butts and C. D. Coxe, Eds., D. Van Nostrand Company, Inc., Princeton, New Jersey, 1967, pp. 272-303.

127. Shaddock, A. W., "Printing on Plastics: An Art Form," Ind. Finishing Surface Coatings, 25 (302), 9, 20 (1973).

128. Allison, E. G., and G. C. Bond, "Structure and Catalytic Properties of Palladium-Silver and Palladium-Gold Alloys," Catal. Rev., 7 (2), 233-289 (1972); Chem. Abstr., 78 (14), 317 (1973).

129. Anonymous, "Silver Can Make Chlorine without Electric Power," The Silver Institute Letter, 4 (2), 2 (1974).

130. Losey, E. N., and D. K. Means, Molybdenum Catalyst Bibliography (1964-1967), Supplement No. 1, Climax Molybdenum Company, Inc., an AMAX Subsidiary, New York, New York, 1969.

131. Warner, P. O., and H. F. Barry, Molybdenum Catalyst Bibliography (1950-1964), Climax Molybdenum Company, Inc., an AMAX Subsidiary, New York, New York, 1967.

132. Anonymous, Harshaw Catalysts for Industry, The Harshaw Chemical Company, Division of Kewanee Oil Company, Cleveland, Ohio [undated, ca. 1971].

133. Anonymous, "Non-Phosphate Detergents from Silver," The Silver Institute Letter, 3 (8), 2 (1973).

134. Anonymous, "Ready-Unmix...with Silver Zeolite," The Silver Institute Letter, 3 (10), 2-3 (1973).

135. Wolf, D. F., (to Dentsply Research and Development Corporation), "Dental Alloys," U.S. Patent 3,841,860, October 15, 1974.

136. Anonymous, "Training in Use Called Main Problem for Dental Alloys," Am. Metal Market/Metalworking News, 80 (73), 27 (1973).

137. Romans, I. B., "Chapter 24. Oligodynamic Metals," in Disinfection, Sterilization, and Preservation, C. A. Lawrence and S. S. Block, Eds., Lea and Febiger, Philadelphia, Pennsylvania, 1968, pp. 372-400.

138. Anonymous, "Silver Sulfadiazine Analogue Treats Burns," The Silver Institute Letter, 3 (10), 2 (1973).

139. Anonymous, "Silver in First-Aid for Burns," The Silver Institute Letter, 3 (10), 2 (1973).

140. Anonymous, "Silver Plays Medical Role," The Silver Institute Letter, 3 (2), 3 (1973).

141. Anonymous, "Worldwide Silver Technology in New Publication," The Silver Institute Letter, 4 (5), 1-2 (1974).

142. Anonymous, "Silver in Space-Age Medical Applications," The Silver Institute Letter, 4 (2), 3 (1974).

143. Anonymous, "Flexible Silver Electrode Stretches," The Silver Institute Letter, 3 (10), 3 (1973).

144. Anonymous, "Silver Carbon Filter Purifies Swimming Pool," The Silver Institute Letter, 3 (5), 1-2 (1973).

145. Anonymous, "Silver Institute Board Hears of New Silver Market," The Silver Institute Letter, 3 (8), 1-2 (1973).

146. Anonymous, "Silver Purifiers at Swimming Pool Show," The Silver Institute Letter, 4 (2), 2 (1974).

147. Anonymous, "Silver Cleans Up Polluted Water," The Silver Institute Letter, 3 (7), 3 (1973).

148. Baptist, J. N., P. R. Steyermark, and P. L. Veltman (to W. R. Grace and Co.), "Microbiocides in Hydrocarbon Fuel Compositions," U.S. Patent 3,226,210, December 28, 1965, 4 pages; Chem. Abstr., 64, 7953a (1966).

149. Anonymous, "Silver Bearings for NASA," The Silver Institute Letter, 3 (11), 3 (1973).

150. Butts, A., and J. M. Thomas, "Chapter 15. Corrosion Resistance of Silver and Silver Alloys," in Silver in Industry, L. Addicks, Ed., Reinhold Publishing Company, New York, New York, 1940.

151. Stiles, D. A., and P. H. Wells, "The Production of Ultra-Pure Hydrogen," Platinum Metals Rev., 16 (4), 124-128 (1972).

152. Anonymous, "Miniature Palladium Diffusion Tubes for Chromatography," Platinum Metals Rev., 15 (4), 131 (1971).

153. Uhlig, H. H., Ed., The Corrosion Handbook, John Wiley and Sons, Inc., New York, New York, 1948.

154. Lehrnickel, W., "Edelmetalle in Apparatebau," Dechema Monograph., 39 (600-615), 239-253 (1961).

155. Wall, F. E., "Chapter 21. Bleaches, Hair Colorings, and Dye Removers," in Cosmetics: Science and Technology, E. Sagarin, Ed., Interscience Publishers, Inc., New York, New York, 1957, pp. 479-530.

156. Wall, F. E., "Chapter 23. Bleaches, Hair Colorings, and Dye Removers," in Cosmetics: Science and Technology, Vol. 2, 2nd ed., M. S. Balsam, E. Sagarin, S. D. Gershon, S. J. Strianse, and M. M. Rieger, Eds., Wiley-Interscience, Division of John Wiley and Sons, Inc., New York, New York, 1972, pp. 279-343.

157. Craft, A. H., "Prospects for Precious Metals," Secondary Raw Materials, 10 (7), 77-78 (1972).

158. Defense Documentation Center, Trace Metal Effects, A Report Bibliography, Search Control No. 083144, Defense Supply Agency, Alexandria, Virginia, 1972.

159. Anonymous, "Silver Creates Perfect Seal," The Silver Institute Letter, 4 (8), 2-3 (1974).

160. Anonymous, "Non-Polluting, High-Temperature Heater Uses Silver," The Silver Institute Letter, 3 (7), 2 (1973).

161. Anonymous, "Magnetic Silver Developed," The Silver Institute Letter, 3 (2), 1 (1973).

162. Anonymous, "Six Percent Silver in New Low Temperature Alloy," The Silver Institute Letter, 3 (9), 3 (1973).

VII. LOSSES TO THE ENVIRONMENT

More silver may be lost from inadvertent sources such as iron and steel production, cement manufacture, and fossil fuel combustion than is lost during primary and secondary silver recovery or fabrication processes, at least with respect to atmospheric emissions. However, the chief losses of silver to the environment are those incurred during use and disposal, especially of photoprocessing wastes, which may contain about 16 million troy ounces silver annually. This section attempts to assess the magnitude of these losses and to judge the probable chemical forms of environmental silver contaminants. The best estimates for these losses are summarized in Table X-1.

A. Production and Fabrication Losses of Silver

In this subsection, the losses of silver resulting from production and fabrication processes will be discussed with respect to the mining and milling processes, smelting and other ore-refinement processes, fabrication of metallic silver products, and the manufacture of chemical compounds.

1. _Mining and milling losses_: Concentrations of silver in various mining and milling wastes are reported with any other pertinent information that might indicate the chemical form of the silver. Where no information for silver content has been reported, the concentrations of the other metals whose chemistry and/or physical properties are similar to silver's are used as an indication of the silver pollution potential of the wastes.

The greatest production source of silver loss to the environment is apparently the Coeur d'Alene mining district in Idaho, where up until 1968, concentrator tailings from the flotation process were largely discharged directly to the Coeur d'Alene River. However, leaching of the old tailings, such as those from which Cataldo Mission Flats was built, by the river apparently does not result in silver concentrations in the river which are in excess of the drinking water standard (0.05 ppm). An even lesser problem is acid mine drainage. The concentrations of silver in acid drainage from abandoned mines in the Pacific Northwest ranged from 1 to 8 ppb.

a. _Magnitude of losses_: A crude estimate for milling losses might be made on the basis of Bureau of Mines data for amounts of recoverable silver in the various ores and estimates of silver recoveries in typical milling operations as shown in Table VII-1 for 1971. However, the Bureau of Mines data do not indicate the large loss of silver in Missouri lead ore tailings, which was about 1 million troy ounces in 1974 or 32% of the silver in the ore.[1] In 1971, over 8.6 million tons of the total 8.9 million tons of silver-containing lead ores was produced in Missouri, but only 28% of silver production from lead ores came from Missouri. We calculate that in 1971 losses of silver in Missouri were a "nonstatistical" 780,000 troy oz. Thus, to the difference between Bureau of Mines data for 1971 domestic mining and domestic primary refining production of 4.4 million troy ounces silver (41.6 minus 37.2 million troy ounces)[a] should be added 0.8 million troy ounces for a total loss from ore to refined silver of 5.2 million troy ounces. Of the 5.2 million troy ounces, 3.1 million troy ounces is estimated to be lost in milling.[b]

Using W. E. Davis estimates for copper and zinc emissions, GCA Corporation estimates that nonferrous mining and milling operations produce 200 lb of silver emissions per 1,000 tons of silver mined.[2-4] Thus, on the basis of an annual silver production of 45 million troy ounces, 4,500 troy oz silver is emitted in dust each year.[2]

The MRI Handbook of Emission Properties,[5] however, estimates that crushing operations in the processing of copper, zinc, and lead ore produce 2 lb dust/ton ore. In 1971, the 234.2 million tons of silver-containing ores produced had an average silver content of 0.18 troy oz/ton. On the basis of these figures, the silver emitted as dust would have been 42,000 troy oz.

Thus, of the 3.1 million troy ounces silver in milling wastes, 0.04 million troy ounces is lost to the air, 0.70 million troy ounces (23%)[c] is lost directly to water (neglecting mine drainage or leaching from tailings), and about 2.4 million troy ounces is held in tailings ponds. We presume silver is still in its original mineral forms but in a much finer state of subdivision. Much of the tailings pond materials settle out before

---

a/ The merit of this procedure is highly questionable since the difference between domestic mining production and domestic primary refining production of silver fluctuates widely and is sometimes even negative. See Table IV-17.

b/ The Bureau of Mines total for recoverable silver, 41.6 million troy ounces, can still be used to calculate the smelting loss of 5% or 2.1 million troy ounces.

c/ In Section V.E.8., wastewater treatment practices for mining, milling, roasting, and smelting operations for production of copper, lead, and/or zinc were discussed. Tailings ponds receive 69.2% of the wastewater; 23.3% of the wastewater receives no treatment before direct discharge.[6]

discharge so that their water pollution potential is reduced. Evaporation and seepage in desert climates may lead to no tailings pond discharge.[7] However, dried unstabilized tailings may be a source of water pollution by leaching and of air pollution by blowing.

Table VII-2 gives the accumulated wastes for copper and lead-zinc-silver production. Booz Allen Associates[8] subdivides the lead-zinc-silver values further into mine waste (700 million tons covering 15,000 acres), mill tailings (740 million tons, 13,000 acres), and smelter slag, (32 million tons, 2,500 acres).

b. <u>Silver losses from specific processes, places, and types of wastes</u>: Before cyanidation, flotation, and improved gravity concentration methods, recovery of valuable minerals was less than 50 to 60%. Since 1890, recoveries of 90 to 95% have been attainable with flotation and cyanidation. Recoveries with modern gravity equipment are not as good as with flotation.[9]

Since very little silver is recovered by cyanidation and/or amalgamation procedures, silver losses from these recovery processes will be negligible. Only 99,992 troy oz silver was recovered by cyanidation in 1972 (0.27% of production).

In cyanidation, some silver is lost in discarded solutions as water-soluble $NaAg(CN)_2$. Any refractory ores that require roasting prior to cyanidation may give wastes containing silver as the oxide rather than the original mineral species.

Homestake Mine in South Dakota is the chief user of amalgamation-cyanidation. It recovers 72% of the gold in the ore by amalgamation and 25% by cyanidation.[10] If the recovery of silver is comparable with that of gold, the annual silver loss would be 3% of its silver production. Cyanidation losses are generally 7 to 8%,[9] so the total U.S. loss may be about 24,000 troy oz/year.

Ammoniacal leaching of refractory copper ores may have produced some wastewaters containing $Ag(NH_3)_2^+$. The practice is not used in the U.S. presently, although it was once used both in Alaska and the Lake Superior district.[9]

Leaching of copper ores and tailings with dilute sulfuric acid will dissolve little of the silver. Loss of leachate to the environment probably contributes little silver sulfate to natural water courses. Most of the dissolved silver is probably recovered along with the recovered copper by cementation or electrowinning.

At the White Pine Copper Company, the largest copper-silver mine in the Keweenaw District of Michigan, 17% of the silver and copper in the ore is lost in the tailings ($\sim$ 470,000 troy oz silver/year). Silver occurs as the native metal, and some of the chalcocite is oxidized. White Pine markets fire-refined blister copper containing about 25 troy oz silver/ ton copper. Smaller producers in the area market copper containing 15 troy oz silver/ton.[10]

At Bunker Hill Company, Kellogg, Idaho, 3.4% of the silver (4.6 troy oz silver/ton lead-zinc ore) reports in the tailings. However, silver loss from lead-zinc selective flotation may be as high as 29%.[9] For example, in 1974, Missouri lead mills discarded tailings containing about 1 million troy ounces silver--32% of the silver in the ore.[1]

Milling losses from porphyry copper ores (0.05 to 0.1 troy oz silver/ton) in Arizona, Utah, Montana, Nevada, and New Mexico are about 10%.[11]

Utah Copper Division of Kennecott Copper Corporation, the largest domestic copper producer, loses 9% of the silver in the tailings. At 45,000 tons ore/day, the annual silver loss might be 0.14 million troy oz. Improved concentrating processes instituted in May 1971, at Arthur and in April 1974, at Magna may have improved silver recoveries.[12]

Silver losses at the Sunshine Mine, Idaho, are about 2% with 79.1% of the silver in the silver ore reporting in the silver concentrate and 18.7% reporting in the lead-iron concentrate. Since copper recoveries are the same, it is assumed that silver is still chemically combined in the tetrahedrite.[10]

Lucky Friday Mine Company in Wallace, Idaho, processes lead-silver ore containing 21 troy oz silver/ton and recovers 98% of the lead and silver. The relative distribution of the remaining 2% silver between the zinc concentrate and the tailings is not known. The tailings are reported to contain 0.1 troy oz silver/ton.[10]

Most wastes from Idaho silver operations were discharged directly into streams leading into the Coeur d'Alene River and Lake from 1890 to 1968. Recent programs have been instituted for impounding mine drainage and mill tailings so that only clear water is discharged to the rivers. These programs resulted in a 99% reduction in suspended solids, greatly enhancing the establishment of benthic life in the South Fork of the Coeur d'Alene River.[13,14] Of the metals antimony, arsenic, cadmium, chromium, copper, iron, mercury, and zinc, only zinc concentrations in the groundwater of the Coeur d'Alene River Valley exceed the drinking water standards.[15]

Table VII-3 summarizes the fate of mine drainage and mill waste effluents from several large silver producers in the Northwest. The South Fork of the Coeur d'Alene River receives most of the effluents.

The Lucky Friday Mine and the Crescent Mine, ranking third and eighth among the largest silver-producing mines, discharge their mine drainage directly to streams. The Lucky Friday mine drainage contains 0.03 ppm copper and 0.7 to 0.87 ppm zinc; the drainage from the Crescent Mine contains 0.19 to 0.47 ppm copper and 0.07 ppm zinc.[15]

Table VII-4 gives the range of silver concentrations in mine drainage from several abandoned mines in the Pacific Northwest.[15]

In the San Juan Mountains of Colorado, the location of the mining towns Telluride, Silverton, and Ouray, the mine drainage is intensely sulfuric. Although gold, silver, and lead are extensively mined, very little silver or lead and no gold are found in the drainage.[16]

Primary lead-zinc ore production, largely in Missouri, is more than 5.5 million tons/year, leaving a residue of more than 5 million tons. In Southeast Missouri, primary crushing is underground so that air pollution would not be a major factor. Most mines must pump 3,000 to 7,000 gal. water/min to prevent flooding. The mine water contains fine galena, associated trace metals, and spillage. Part of the mine water is used in the flotation process. Mine water and tailing wastes are discharged to settlement and treatment lagoons. Before mining activity, the concentrations of copper, zinc, and cadmium in the streams were 1 to 20 ppb; now they range up to 0.237 ppm. Aquatic vegetation near the tailings dams and tall fescue on the gondola-car route to the smelter are found to concentrate trace metals.[17]

Lead-zinc mine concentrator effluents at pH 5.0 to 8.0 are reported to contain 0.004 to 0.3 ppm copper and 0 to 0.18 ppm lead.[6] Heavy-metal values reported for an effluent-receiving stream in southeast Missouri are 0 to 0.040 ppm lead, 0.003 to 0.140 ppm zinc, and 0 to 0.015 ppm copper.[18] No data are reported for silver.

At the Galena Mine in Idaho, which produces silver ore, concentrations of dissolved lead, zinc, cadmium, and copper (< 0.05 ppm) in seepage water from tailings ponds are not deemed to be a pollution problem. Tailings discharged to the tailings ponds contain about 0.02% copper. (The pH of tailings ponds is usually 7.4 to 10.1.) The dissolved copper content ranges from < 0.09 to 0.7 ppm copper compared with < 0.05 ppm copper in Lake Creek above and below the pond system.[19] If the silver loss in

295

the tailings is proportional to that of copper,[a/] the maximum dissolved silver concentration in the milling effluent would be 0.165 ppm silver (1.1 ppm copper). At 0.7 ppm copper in the pond outflow, the silver concentration would be 0.105 ppm; and at 0.05 ppm copper, 0.008 ppm silver. Only the latter concentration would not exceed the drinking water standard for silver.

At Magna, Utah; Hayden, Arizona; and San Manuel, Arizona, tailings contained 0.10, 0.115, and 0.06% copper, respectively.[20/] Silver losses would be lower than those assumed above because of lower silver values in the ore.

Other analyses of wastewaters from copper mine and concentrator operations are 0.10 ppm copper in a concentrator discharge, 0.33 and 0.28 ppm copper in plant drain wastewaters, and 0.01 ppm copper in a tailings pond effluent.[6/]

Leaching of old mine tailings by groundwater is caused by oxidation of sulfides by microorganisms to sulfuric acid. Sulfate-reducing bacteria reduce sulfate to sulfide so that metals will be precipitated at about pH 6.6. Decrease in pH with depth destroys sulfate-reducing bacteria so that dissolution and leaching increase.[21/]

Cataldo Mission Flats, lying about 14 miles southeast of Coeur d'Alene, Idaho, was built up from tailings deposited by or dredged from the South Fork of the Coeur d'Alene River from about 1875 to 1930. The tailings were discharged to the river at several points 8 to 26 miles upstream. No difference was found between the river metal concentrations 2.5 miles above and 2 miles below Cataldo Flats. Contributions of trace metals by groundwater from the tailings may be masked by high concentrations of elements already contributed from the Flats upstream. The average concentration of the silver in tailings samples is 10.7 ppm at depths 2 to 6 ft. Most samples were collected at the depth of 3 ft. The average surface concentration is 7.4 ppm silver at pH 6.6 to 7.25, but by depths of 5 to 6 ft, the silver concentration has decreased to 0.5 to 0.6 ppm. During spring runoff and groundwater flow peak, more leaching occurs and at higher levels in the tailing as the groundwater level rises. During warm weather, salts precipitate on the surface. The silver concentration in the concretions and salt is 3 ppm.[21/]

---

a/ Copper may have been added as a flotation reagent and, thus, no relationship would exist between copper and silver.

In laboratory experiments, at pH 4, 5, 7, or 8, 0.02 ppm silver dissolved from the tailings. At pH 6, the dissolved silver concentration was 0.01 ppm. (The concentration of copper at all pH's was 0.01 ppm.)[21] These values would be consistent with Boyle's statement that the background dissolved silver in spring and stream waters associated with silver-bearing areas is rarely more than 0.10 ppm.[22]

Normal background silver concentration in stream sediments is about 0.1 ppm, but stream sediments in the Keno Hill silver belt of Canada contain 10 ppm silver. Known mineralized zones usually are associated with stream sediments containing 0.5 to 2.0 ppm silver.[22]

Polluted sediments are not uniformly extended over the whole southern portion of Coeur d'Alene Lake. The metal content in the sediments decreases from the mouth of the Coeur d'Alene River to the mouth of the St. Joe River. The maximum metal contents of the sediment are about 5,000 ppm zinc, 3,500 ppm lead, 110 ppm copper, and 80 ppm cadmium.[23]

The top layer of dry sediments comprising the fine silt typical of mine tailings was collected from the Coeur d'Alene River delta and analyzed. The average metal contents were 10 ppm silver (range 6 to 15 ppm), 115 ppm copper, 3,700 ppm lead, and 8,000 ppm manganese. There was no decrease in metal content with depth. The whole bay area in the delta appeared to be covered by polluted sediments within a 900-m radius from the river mouth.[24] Mining activities do not appear to have raised the silver content in these sediments by even an order of magnitude greater than normal background levels.

2. Losses from smelting and refining silver-containing ores and concentrates: We have calculated that the magnitude of these smelting losses in 1971 from domestic ores was about 2.1 million troy ounces silver, based on an estimated overall recovery rate of 95% in smelting and refining. The estimated 3.1 million troy ounces silver loss in milling represents 92% recovery so that the overall recovery of silver from ore to refined metal is about 87%. Schack and Clemmons conclude the overall recovery of silver is 85 to 90%.[10] The overall recovery rate can be verified from data for several Canadian mining companies, which included the grade of the ore (average 0.48 troy oz/ton), the 1967 ore production, and the silver produced by refineries. The data represented 19% of the ores which produced 69% of the silver.[25] The calculated average overall recovery rate from these data is 84%.

U.S. base-metal smelters and refineries also treat ores and concentrates from foreign sources, chiefly Canada, Peru, and Mexico, to produce refined silver in amounts approximately the same as refined production from domestic sources. Since the tonnage of imported ores and concentrates

297

containing silver are not reported, the silver content of the foreign materials cannot be estimated. For primary copper and lead, foreign materials comprise about 15% of total U.S. production. Apparently the imported materials are very high in silver content and are probably chiefly from silver and gold ores. If we estimate losses from smelting and refining of imported ores and concentrates to be equal to losses from processing domestic ores and concentrates, a total loss of about 4 million troy ounces is probably the correct order of magnitude.

In this subsection, we estimate that about 4.8 million troy ounces silver is lost during the smelting and refining of copper, lead, and zinc ores and concentrates, about 600,000 troy oz of which is lost to the air.

a. <u>Primary copper smelting and refining wastes</u>: Schack and Clemmons estimate that the recovery in the smelting of copper, silver, and gold is about 95%. Cleaned smelter gases and reverberatory slag are the only silver-containing waste products in copper smelting. The loss of silver in the slag is 1 to 2%, the same as that of copper.[a/] Miscellaneous losses from spillage and water streams comprise 2 to 3%.[10/] Schack and Clemmons do not estimate any silver loss in stack gases.

Some silver is found as an impurity in by-product metals. For example, palladium sponge was found to contain an average of 11 ppm silver.[27/] Silver-bearing copper is intentionally manufactured to contain from 8 to 30 troy oz silver/ton copper (0.0274 to 0.103%).[28/]

Hallowell et al. give wastewater data for some unidentified copper smelting operations.[6/] Silver is not included in the analyses.

Figure VII-1 shows the silver flow at a western U.S. copper mine-mill-smelter. The tailings loss is very high compared with the milling data given in Section VII.A. The total copper smelting-refining loss is about 6% based on the smelter's estimate of about 68% overall silver recovery from the ore. Silver in the reverberatory slag may be recovered when the furnace is rebuilt. As much as 20,000 troy oz silver may be found in the furnace bottom. Silver recovery from the recirculated slags and

---

a/ The wasted sesquisilicate slags contain about 0.5% copper[10/] (0.4%).[26/]
    Copper losses from oxide ores may be higher since some copper enters
    the slag before it is reduced to metal or matte. Matte is slightly
    soluble, but its mechanical entrainment is more important. Slags
    may be used as a source of iron, for cement manufacture, and for con-
    struction materials; however, the slag from reverberatory smelting
    usually goes to the dump.[9/]

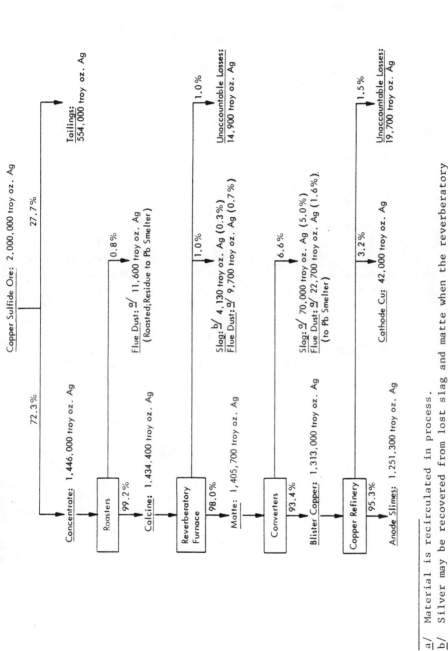

Figure VII-1 - Silver Flow Based on 6-Months Operation of a
Western U.S. Copper Mine-Mill-Smelter[29/]

a/ Material is recirculated in process.
b/ Silver may be recovered from lost slag and matte when the reverberatory
furnace is shut down and rebuilt.

299

flue dusts may be poor since the apparent 6% smelting-refining loss of 87,000 troy oz is not accounted for by only the reverberatory slag loss plus the "unaccountable losses" (38,700 troy oz), which are presumably the losses to air and water (or to sulfuric acid when recovered by acid plants). Thus, an additional 48,000 troy oz silver may be lost to the environment.

Estimates of silver losses as air emissions from the smelting of all silver-containing ores, from emissions data for a few smelters, are not very reliable since smelter feed content can vary widely and emissions contents can even vary widely on the same day.[30/]

We have been unable to formulate a very reliable estimate for atmospheric silver emissions from copper smelting. GCA Corporation estimated that primary copper smelting and associated processes emit 90,000 troy oz silver annually. This calculation is based on the 1970 copper production of 1,765,000 tons, 1,000 lb dust emitted per ton of copper production before controls, 99% control efficiency, and silver content in the emissions of 10.1 troy oz/ton (0.035% silver).[2/] Note that the GCA estimate of the silver emission before control is more than half the amount of silver ultimately recovered from copper ores.

The MRI Handbook of Emission Properties, however, estimates 68,000 tons of particulate emissions after controls in the primary copper industry from the roaster (85% control), reverberatory furnace (81% control), and converter (81% control), plus 5,000 tons (32% control) from materials handling based on 1968 copper production of 1.437 million tons. If the MRI dust emission estimate is scaled up to 1970 production, the emissions after controls in primary copper smelting would be 84,000 tons compared with the 8,800 tons in the GCA Corporation estimate. A silver emissions estimate on the basis of this higher dust estimate would be 860,000 troy oz silver/ year.

W. E. Davis estimated that 8,700 tons of copper was emitted to the atmosphere in 1969 by primary metallurgical operations on the basis of 10 lb copper emitted/ton copper produced from six operations. A typical copper smelter effluent is reported to contain 1.03% copper and 0.035% silver.[3/] These data would lead to a value of about 1,000 lb dust emitted per ton of copper production after control and a value of 9 million troy ounces silver in the emissions. This would be more than 50% of the silver in the ore.

The amount of silver in the emitted dusts of the W. E. Davis data may not be typical. The silver contents of emissions from the INCO smelter stacks at Copper Cliff, Ontario, in 1973, were 0.0469% from the Orford Stack (2.8 tons dust/day) and 0.0291% from the Copper Stack (4.6 tons dust/day). However, the Coniston Smelter Stack (6.4 tons dust/day) emitted only 0.0022% silver in the dusts.[31/]

300

A better estimate of silver emissions from copper smelting can probably be made from recent EPA data[32] regarding particulate emissions from 14 of 15 U.S. copper smelters. These are shown in Figure VII-2 with estimates of silver emissions in troy ounces per day given in parentheses. These estimates are based only on the 0.035% silver value given in Ref. 3 and are given only to establish a relative order of magnitude of silver in copper smelter emissions for a particular geographical region. Based on these data, the total annual silver emission from copper smelting may be about 480,000 troy oz/year. As a further check on the magnitude of these losses, we might assume that the unaccountable copper-smelting losses in Figure VII-1 of 34,600 troy oz were losses only to air and represent about 10% of domestic copper-smelting atmospheric silver emissions (based on total U.S. silver production from copper ores of about 14 million troy ounces). Thus, a value of 350,000 to 480,000 troy oz silver is probably the best estimate that can be made at this time. This represents about a 3% loss of silver in copper smelting stack gases.

b. Primary lead smelting and refining wastes: Smelting losses of silver from argentiferous lead concentrates are estimated at 5%. Again, most wastes are carefully recycled so that the chief sources of loss are the smelter stack gases and the residual slag from the slag fuming furnace.[10]/[a] J. B. Hallowell et al. report data on water pollution by lead smelters and refineries but give no silver concentrations.[6]

In 1974, smelting and refining of Missouri lead concentrates containing 1.3 troy oz silver/ton (781,000 troy oz silver) produced lead containing 7.8% of the silver. Approximately 13% of the silver (105,000 troy oz) was lost to the environment[b] including 8.8% in the slag.

Since most silver recovered from domestic ores is associated with lead and we have estimated below a minimum 58,000 troy oz silver loss from zinc sintering operations alone, the estimate by the GCA Corporation of 45,000 troy oz silver for air emissions from primary smelting and re- fining of silver-containing ores other than copper seems very low. MRI had estimated that primary lead furnacing operations produce 29,000 tons of particulates per year,[5] but a recent EPA report states that U.S. lead smelters emit only 3.52 tons of particulates/day with current control tech- nology.[32] (See Figure VII-3.) At 1,285 tons of particulates/year and

---

a/ Primary lead smelters, equipped with efficient dust and fume collection systems, recover about 97 to 99% of the lead in the ore.[33]

b/ Part of the residual figure 4.6% might merely have been unrecovered silver in increased concentrate inventory.

301

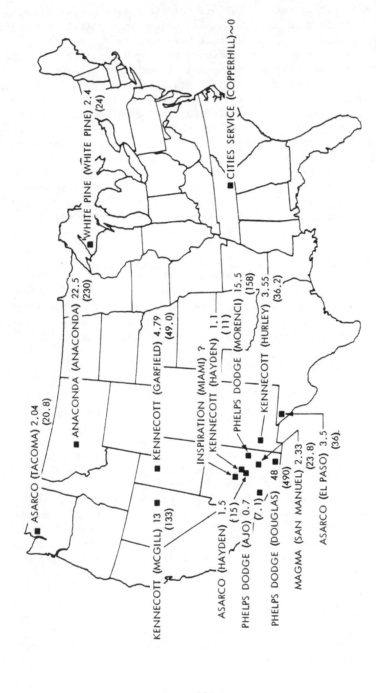

ASARCO (TACOMA) 2.04 (20.8)

ANACONDA (ANACONDA) 22.5 (230)

WHITE PINE (WHITE PINE) 2.4 (24)

CITIES SERVICE (COPPERHILL) ~0

KENNECOTT (GARFIELD) 4.79 (49.0)

INSPIRATION (MIAMI) ?

KENNECOTT (HAYDEN) 1.1 (11)

PHELPS DODGE (MORENCI) 15.5 (158)

KENNECOTT (HURLEY) 3.55 (36.2)

KENNECOTT (MCGILL) 13 (133)

ASARCO (HAYDEN) 1.5 (15)

PHELPS DODGE (AJO) 0.7 (7.1)

PHELPS DODGE (DOUGLAS) 48 (490)

MAGMA (SAN MANUEL) 2.33 (23.8)

ASARCO (EL PASO) 3.5 (36)

Figure VII-2 – Particulate Emissions at Existing Domestic
Primary Copper Smelters, Tons/Day[32]

Note: Values in parentheses are estimates of silver
       emissions in troy oz/day based on data for one
       smelter: 10.2 troy oz silver/ton particulate
       emissions.

302

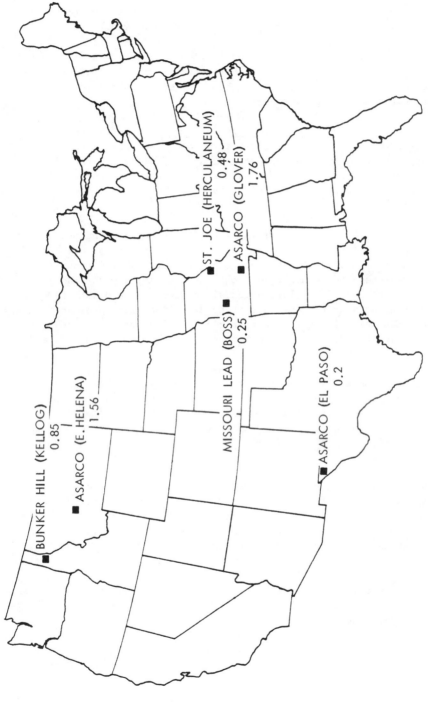

Figure VII-3 – Particulate Emissions at Existing
Domestic Primary Lead Smelters, Tons/Day[32/]

BUNKER HILL (KELLOG)
0.85

■ ASARCO (E.HELENA)
1.56

MISSOURI LEAD (BOSS)
0.25

■ ASARCO (EL PASO)
0.2

ST. JOE (HERCULANEUM)
0.48

■ ASARCO (GLOVER)
1.76

0.175% silver in the particulates,[a] the atmospheric silver emissions from primary lead smelting would be about 70,000 troy oz/year.

If we assume that about 45% of silver production passes through lead smelters (lead and silver ores), then a 5% smelting loss would be 1.6 million troy ounces. Thus, about 1.5 million troy ounces would be lost to water and solid wastes.[b]

c. <u>Primary zinc recovery wastes</u>: Zinc recovery at a zinc plant is 88 to 96%. The older, retort method for recovering zinc is inefficient for recovering precious metals, and any silver in the zinc concentrate is retained in the retort residue. The latter is not retreated unless the content of silver, lead, and copper warrants shipment to a lead smelter.[9,10]

The Bureau of Mines has developed a smelting process for recovering all of the silver from the magnetic fraction of waste from horizontal retort distillation furnaces. Perhaps 200,000 tons of zinc smelter residues are accumulated each year containing more than 2.5 million troy ounces silver (13 to 14 troy oz silver/ton). One plant has about 200,000 tons of such residue in storage.[35] Since zinc ores and complex ores (copper-lead, lead-zinc, copper-zinc, and copper-lead-zinc) were the source of about 6.85 million troy ounces domestic silver in 1971 and most lead ores also contain zinc,[c] it is quite probable that zinc smelter residues are a major trap for silver losses in nonferrous smelting processes; however, horizontal retort furnaces are currently being replaced with more productive systems. Currently, of the eight existing domestic primary zinc plants, three use horizontal retorts, two use vertical retorts, two use the electrolytic technique, and the eighth produces zinc calcine for zinc oxide production.[32] (See Figure VII-4.)

Zinc blast-furnace slag is discarded after zinc or matte (containing silver) have separated.[36] Silver concentrations of zinc smelter wastewater effluents were not found.[6] Typical silver content of flue dust from sintering zinc concentrate is 50 troy oz/ton (1,700 ppm). Such dust was once treated at the AMAX cadmium plant at Blackwell, Oklahoma, to recover cadmium, zinc, and silver in a lead sulfate residue.[37]

---

a/ The GCA Corporation report[2] assumes that emissions from other non-ferrous smelters would contain five times as much silver as those from a copper smelter.

b/ The maximum amount of silver in various refined loads is 15 to 200 ppm,[34] but the content may be much less (e.g., 4.8 ppm in Missouri lead[1]).

c/ The zinc concentrate from Missouri lead ores alone in 1974 contained almost 1.4 million troy ounces silver.[1]

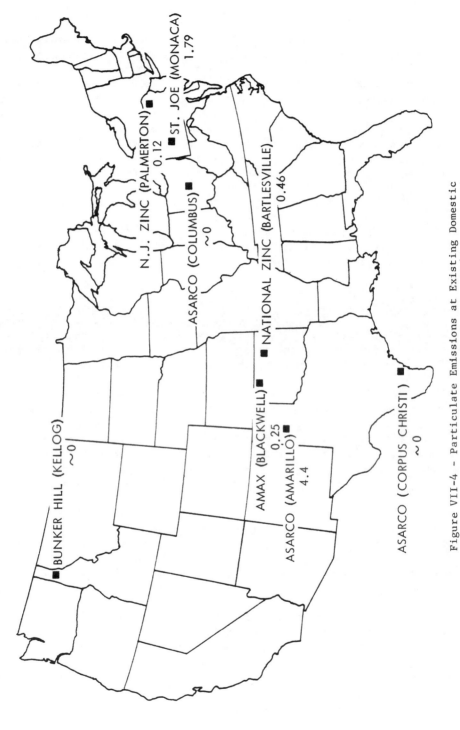

BUNKER HILL (KELLOG)
~0

N.J. ZINC (PALMERTON)
0.12

ST. JOE (MONACA)
1.79

ASARCO (COLUMBUS)
~0

NATIONAL ZINC (BARTLESVILLE)
0.46

AMAX (BLACKWELL)
0.25

ASARCO (AMARILLO)
4.4

ASARCO (CORPUS CHRISTI)
~0

Figure VII-4 - Particulate Emissions at Existing Domestic
Primary Zinc Smelters, Tons/Day[32]/

305

Recent EPA data indicate that the domestic primary zinc smelting operations of roasting and sintering produce 7.56 tons of particulates/day, 4.4 tons of which being emitted by the only smelter that does not employ acid plants as control for roaster gases.[32] Thus, the sintering emissions may be 3.16 to 7.56 tons/day. If all sintering emissions contain 50 troy oz silver/ton, the annual silver emission from zinc smelting would be at least 58,000 troy oz. The losses may be considerably higher, since 26% of domestic zinc production involves horizontal retorts, whose emissions are not controlled. MRI estimated that 15,000 tons of particulates/year are emitted in zinc distillation procedures.[5]

In the electrolytic method for recovering zinc, most of the silver remains in the primary leach residue since silver is not readily soluble in the sulfate-rich spent electrolyte. This residue is processed in the lead smelter operated with the electrolytic zinc plant. Schack and Clemmons state there are no silver losses.[10]

3. Silver refining losses:

a. Primary silver refining losses: No data were found on actual silver losses during refining starting with the copper anode slimes through electrolysis of the silver anode and recovery from the "gold mud." While silver recovery in copper smelting from ore containing as little as 0.07 troy oz silver/ton up to anode copper is about 87%, recovery from anode slimes containing at least 2,800 troy oz silver/ton[38] is considerably better Once the silver is concentrated to these high levels, all wastes are carefully retreated to extract the precious metals. Based on primary silver refinery production (domestic plus foreign) of about 70 million troy ounces and overall losses of 1%, the silver loss would be about 0.7 million troy ounces distributed among particulate emissions to the air (probably the major loss), discarded leach and electrolyte solutions, and slags. Some of the silver lost to water will be in the form of the sulfate and the nitrate.

b. Secondary silver refining losses: Secondary precious metals refineries treat low-grade scrap in a reverberatory furnace with lead metal scrap to give impure lead bullion, matte, and slag with the bullion and matte containing most of the precious metals. The slag is treated in a blast furnace to give a barren slag and additional bullion and matte.

Perhaps as much as 4 to 8 million troy ounces is lost altogether from processing all types of silver-containing scrap based on a 90 to 95% estimate of platinum-group metals recovery.[39] Howard Martin of Martin Metals secondary refinery estimated that there are no losses of palladium (whose vapor pressure is about one order of magnitude less than silver's) when Western Electric recovers precious metals from used telephone equipment. Martin stated that ordinarily 95% palladium is recovered from

306

the copper scrap anode furnace and 96 to 97% from the silver doré furnace or cupel.[40/] Silver, being more volatile is probably lost at a somewhat higher rate.

No data were found for atmospheric silver emissions from secondary silver recovery from precious metal scrap involving lead scrap reverberatory smelting and blast furnacing at a precious metals refinery. Controls would probably be 100% applied and 99% efficient since metals much more precious than silver are involved. Since an average 81 million troy ounces are recovered from old and new scrap and coins each year (1966 to 1974), atmospheric losses of silver as high as 1% would be 810,000 troy oz.

GCA Corporation based its estimate for atmospheric emissions of 19,000 troy oz silver from secondary silver refining after control (1,280,000 troy oz before control) on the assumption that all secondary silver is refined via reverberatory furnaces (30 lb silver emissions/ton of metal) and electrolysis (2 lb emissions/ton) controlled at an estimated 98.5%. The source cited for the emissions[3/] contains no such estimate.

The GCA Corporation calculated that only 0.05 tons (1,460 troy oz) silver is generated in secondary lead refining "before control" based on an average precontrol emission factor of about 15 lb/ton, postcontrol assays of 0.01%, and about 75,000 tons of scrap lead refined.[2/a/] Since the recovery of secondary lead according to the Minerals Yearbook is about 550,000 to 620,000 tons/year, the GCA estimate is low. On this basis, precontrol silver emissions would be about 13,000 troy oz or about 200 troy oz after 98.5% control.

There is little useful information on which to base a reliable estimate for silver emissions from secondary copper smelting. The GCA Corporation based its estimate of 5,250 troy oz silver emissions from secondary copper refining on the W. E. Davis estimate of 210 tons copper emitted after controls and the ratio of electrical silver to electrical copper sales (25 troy oz silver/ton copper).[2,3/] Since most secondary copper comes from nonelectrical uses, the 25 troy oz silver/ton copper ratio is probably inapplicable.

---

a/ The GCA Corporation cites unspecified EPA reports as stating that one secondary lead blast furnace produced 1.14 lb emissions/ton of scrap after controls (90% efficiency). The emissions contained 30 ppm silver. Another operation produced 0.17 lb particulate/ton, containing about 170 ppm silver, after controls (99% efficiency).

4. <u>Silver losses in manufacturing products containing metallic</u>
<u>silver</u>: Addicks estimated that about 0.2% of industrially consumed silver
is lost in manufacturing processes.$\underline{41}/$ Based on 1971 total net industrial
consumption of 129,146,000 troy oz silver, the manufacturing loss would be
260,000 troy oz. We identify sources for at least 150,000 troy oz of these
losses below. Of these, about 120,000 troy oz are atmospheric losses.

a. <u>Silver and silver-alloy items</u>: Alloying and shaping
processes, weighing, charging, melting, pouring and casting, rolling,
slitting, and drawing are well controlled with respect to silver losses.
Aerosol losses would be only an occupational hazard since the silver would
settle out in the plant dust. Shavings, dust, etc., are probably recycled
as "sweeps."

Sterling and jewelry manufacture with their buffing and pol-
ishing operations are estimated to emit 200 troy oz of aerosol silver.$\underline{2}/$
Addicks estimated that silversmiths lost 0.2% of silver consumed in manufacturing in 1928. Based on 1966 to 1972 consumption for sterling ware
after scrap return, the loss would be 25,000 troy oz.

Production of brazing alloys and solders are estimated to
lose 150 troy oz/year to the air. Preparation of materials for medicine
and dentistry may annually produce 100 troy oz aerosol silver.$\underline{2}/$

GCA Corporation estimates that negligible silver losses occur
when powdered silver is made by combining a jet of molten silver with a
high velocity air jet.$\underline{2}/$

b. <u>Coatings, including electroplate</u>: GCA estimates the
following atmospheric emissions: spray painting of conductors, 10,000;
spraying of mirroring solutions, 1,500; and electroplating, chemical and
liquid spills, 250 troy oz.$\underline{2}/$

Addicks estimated that 0.1% silver consumed by silver elec-
troplaters is lost in manufacturing.$\underline{41}/$ On the basis of the average amount
of silver consumed for electroplated ware in 1966 to 1972, the electroplating
loss might be only about 15,000 troy oz. However, consumption for electrical contacts and bearings includes electroplated items which would increase
the loss estimate. We estimate that at least 30,000 troy oz silver is lost
annually by electroplaters, some of which is contained in sewage sludge.

There are an estimated 15,000 to 20,000 metal-finishing facilities in the U.S., and less than 0.5% of the total wastewater is treated
before discharge.$\underline{33}/$ Perhaps as many as 12,500 of these metal-finishing
facilities are involved in silver plating.$\underline{42}/$ Obviously, silver platers as
a subgroup will be more inclined to treat their wastewaters to recover the
more valuable silver. In a survey response by 191 members of the National

Association of Metal Finishers, 75% reported that they discharged their wastewaters to municipal sanitary sewers: 12% to storm sewers, 3% to land, 2% to lagoons, 5% to natural bodies of water, and 3% to "others." Small and medium-sized platers widely practice lagooning after silver and other precious metals are removed.[43]/

Table VII-5 depicts the relative magnitude of waste from electroplating operations that probably involve the use of silver. Copper, cadmium, and zinc are also plated from cyanide solutions.[44]/

Waste plating solutions typically contain 250 ppm Ag^+ and about 150 ppm CN^-, and the rinse water may contain 50 to 250 ppm silver. Oneida Ltd. at Oneida, New York, reduces the silver content in its wastewater from 130-585 ppm to 0-8.2 ppm by zinc precipitation.[45]/ In the 1950's, Sperry Rand in Gainesville, Florida, discharged wastes containing 1.4 ppm silver (as silver chloride) after ion exchange and cyanide oxidation to a sludge-drying bed.[46]/ Another estimate of silver content in cyanide wastes after treatment by ion exchange is about 2.6 ppm silver.[44]/ A discharge of 165,000 gal/day containing 4 ppm silver from silverware electroplaters would result in an annual loss of 28,000 troy oz. However, one plating company has reported that it lost almost 11,000 troy oz silver in electroplating wastes.[47]/ If these treated wastes are typical of silver-plating discharges, then the silver content is probably sufficient to cause disturbances among life forms in natural bodies of water in the vicinity of the discharge point.

Treated wastes will usually contain silver as the chloride or hydrous oxide. If cyanide is present in the discharge, it will complex some of the silver. If the wastes are ultimately treated in a sewage disposal plant, silver will be an expected component of the sewage sludge. One analysis of Denver sewage sludge ash found 0.011% silver.[48]/ Sludge may be disposed of to land (possibly as fertilizer) or incinerated at the sewage-treatment site or with municipal refuse.

5. <u>Losses in manufacturing silver compounds</u>: Although fumes escape when silver is dissolved in enclosed vessels by hot nitric acid, they are scrubbed to remove nitrogen oxides and probably little silver escapes. With hydrogen evolution during the electrochemical conversion of silver to the sulfate, some silver sulfate may be entrained. If losses from silver nitrate production are assumed to be very small, losses from production of silver cyanide and other compounds should be much smaller, based on their relative production.[2]/

Manufacture of silver catalysts and their regeneration and erosion are estimated to emit 250 troy oz aerosol silver.[2]/

Addicks estimated that the silver loss in manufacturing photographic products in 1928 was 0.2%.[41/] On the basis of 1966 to 1972 average photographic silver consumption, losses would be 84,000 troy oz silver.

One Russian source described significant losses of the silver halide used to sensitize photochromic glasses during their founding. For example, a glass containing 0.4 wt % silver and 1.6% chloride was founded in a Silit furnace in a quartz crucible at 1500°C for 2.5 hr. Silver was added as a 50% silver nitrate solution. During fusion of the batch, 55% of the silver was lost; ≤ 10% was lost during clarification.[49/] Even if such losses are common to all founding of silver-containing glasses, they would not be an appreciable source of air pollution by silver since the use of silver in glass is not large enough to be reported separately in statistics.

B. Losses From Use and Disposal

Information is developed in this subsection that indicates that about 39 million troy ounces silver are lost to the environment annually during use and disposal, less than 2 million troy ounces of which is lost to the air.

1. Photography losses: GCA Corporation estimated that of the 38 million troy ounces used in photographic materials, 14 million troy ounces are recovered by precipitation and 6.5 million troy ounces by incineration.[2/] In 1963, Schack and Clemmons estimated that if two-thirds of silver recovered from new and old photographic wastes are from processing, fixing and bleach bath solutions, the amount of silver would be about 20 million troy ounces annually.[10/]

Recovery of silver from silver precipitates or silver reduced from solution by replacement reactions is 75 to 90%. Silver recovery by electrolytic methods is ≤ 90%. (The 1 to 1.5 g Ag/liter remaining in solution does not impair reuse of the solution for the fixing bath.[10/])

Since there are no estimates of the amounts of silver in undeveloped film, etc., we will base our calculation on the assumption that all of the silver sold annually for photographic purposes is incinerated or is processed in fixing or bleach baths. If the net difference between exports and imports (7%) is subtracted from the average 42 million troy ounces of photographic silver, our estimate of 39 million troy ounces per year of domestic silver used in photography agrees well with the GCA Corporation value of 38 million. If 20.5 million troy ounces are recovered, then 17.5 million troy ounces times the percentage of silver that goes into the fixing baths are potentially lost. If we assume this value is 90% (60 to 80% for black-and-white film and ~ 100% for color), then the amount of silver that may be lost as soluble $Ag_2S_2O_4$, etc., is up to 16 million troy ounces. This silver will be discarded by small processors and amateurs as spent fixing baths containing ≤ 12 g silver/liter or as bleach solutions containing about 1 g/liter.

GCA Corporation estimated that 70,000 troy oz of silver is lost to the air in the incineration process for silver recovery.[2/]

2. **Attrition of electrical contacts**: GCA Corporation estimated that 600,000 troy oz silver is emitted annually as an aerosol from attrition of contacts in appliances, automobiles, telephones, etc., based on a 5% consumption rate (20 year lifetime) and an annual use of 12 million troy ounces for contacts.[2/] Obviously, if all contacts in use are eroding at that rate and the average lifetime of the contacts is 20 years, this estimate should be 5% of all silver contacts in use. However, it cannot be assumed that silver contacts are even 50% consumed at the end of their lifetimes.

The Metals Handbook discusses attrition of silver contact materials.[28/] Silver is used most widely for medium-current make-and-break contacts (1 to 20 amp, often up to 30 amp) and is widely used in contacts that remain closed for long time periods. Other uses are as contacts subject to occasional sliding (e.g., rotary switches) and, to a limited extent, for low-resistance sliding contacts such as slip rings.

Loss of silver from the contact may occur by several methods: migration through the insulation, arcing of silver(I) oxide (produced by ozone exposure), metal transfer from one electrode to another, flow discharge in air (where silver nitrite forms), and erosion via silver sulfide formation. Thus, the attrition rate of a contact not only depends on its type of use but also on its environment. In a dust-free IBM computer room in New York City, the major contaminants were sulfur dioxide and hydrogen sulfide which formed a black, tenacious silver sulfide film 204 Å thick on the contacts. In an East Coast chemical plant, with a high concentration of organics and free exchange of outside air, a 490 Å-silver sulfide film and a 38 Å-silver chloride or silver oxide film formed on the silver contacts. The film was fluffy and nonadherent. In the boiler shop of an East Coast oil refinery where heavy apparatus welding was done, a film comprising 348 Å silver sulfide and 214 Å silver oxide formed. After 9 months, the film was 2000 Å thick.[50/]

Whatever the amounts, the silver in the aerosol and dust emitted from eroded contacts is very probably silver sulfide, silver oxide, etc., not metallic silver.

3. Losses of brazing alloys in manufacturing: The GCA Corporation
report estimates that 1% of the silver used for brazing alloys and solders is
emitted as fume and that emissions are 50% controlled so that the annual emission (based on 14 million troy ounces silver in brazing alloys) would be 70,000
troy oz silver.[2] Since silver brazing is most often done with fluxes (e.g.,
for resistance brazing) and most contact brazing is done in controlled atmosphere furnaces,[51,52] it can be concluded that there is little uncontrolled
silver emitted during brazing. Whatever the amount of silver emitted, it
would be strictly an occupational hazard as an aerosol. Silver metal settling out in the shop dust should be innocuous whatever the ultimate disposal.

4. Silver losses from other uses: GCA Corporation estimated silver emissions from the following uses: "bearings and lubricants, loss of
flake silver lubricant in use"[a] (2,000 troy oz); "batteries,[b] sintering,
electrolytic processes, chemical losses" (900 troy oz); and catalysts, preparation, regeneration, and erosion" (250 troy oz).

Discarded solutions of silver compounds used in analytical chemistry should be in such small amounts that they would be adequately diluted by
other wastewaters.

Acid sludge and spent clay generated in acid/clay waste oil re-
refining plants might contain significant amounts of silver sulfate (14 ppm
silver from diesel oil sludge; 0 ppm silver from crankcase oil sludge). The
acid sludge is disposed of to landfills or lagoons, usually without neutralization. The spent clay usually goes to landfills, but some clay-containing
oil has been used to surface stable floors and unpaved raods.[53]

GCA Corporation estimated that emissions from cloud seeding and
coinage wear are "negligible."[2] We do not concur with the cloud-seeding
estimate. The silver iodide produced from ground-based generators is first
of all an air pollutant and definitely remains one if the seeding attempt
fails to induce precipitation, as many commercial ones have done. Teller
and Cameron report that one ground-based generator in the upper Colorado

---

a/ Silver is often determined in used jet engine lubricating oils. The
    amounts of metals are criteria for changing the oils. See Table
    II-17.
b/ When batteries are recycled for their silver content, other components
    besides the positive plate should be treated. For example, silver
    losses from the positive plate of a silver-zinc storage cell may
    reach 13% after 90 cycles. Ninety percent of the silver accumulates
    in the film separator and ~ 5% in the alkaline electrolyte.[54]

project when burned "only eight times during the seeding season" produced 35.2 troy oz silver.[55]/ On the basis of 30 generators for the 1,130 sq mi target area, a total U.S. target area of about 100,000 sq mi would require about 100,000 troy oz silver.

Junked automobiles (8×10^6/year weighing 7.2×10^6 tons[56]/) probably represent a large pool of dissipated silver. Less than 7 million autos are recycled per year. Silver is used, for example, in solder, window-defrosting systems, electronic ignitions, voltage regulators, and stereos.[57,58]/ Based on 0.5% average copper content of dismantled auto scrap,[59]/ about 6 million tons scrap steel from autos, and 25 troy oz electrical silver to 1 ton electrical copper sales, the auto scrap reprocessed into steel per year may contain 750,000 troy oz silver; this amount plus the 1.7 million troy ounces from recycled household appliances (see Subsection VII.B.5) is not enough to account for the silver content ascribed to steel-making emissions. It is assumed that most silver used in automobiles, when recovered, will be refined with secondary copper. Any silver remaining in automobile "graveyards" is not likely to pose any environmental threat.

5. Land disposal of silver: With the use of Table VII-6, we have calculated that about 34 million troy ounce silver is disposed of on land annually. Of this value, some silver may be maintained in situ. For example, much of the silver represented would be in construction uses (brazing in air-conditioning and electrical switches), and most of that would not be returned to the land for many decades until demolition. (Metals recovery from demolition of houses and buildings is no longer considered economical.[58]/)

For purposes of the calculation, use of silver in coinage was not considered since little of it will be lost to the environment except in secondary refining. Recycling from old coins was not significant during 1966 to 1972, so that "old scrap" in Table VII-6 largely represents used products. Of the remaining sales categories not mentioned in the table, batteries and catalysts are probably included in the "old scrap" value. A small amount of silver-containing dental scrap is recycled. The remaining major sales figures are brazing alloys and solders, 14.8 million troy ounces, and contacts and conductors, 20.055 million troy ounces. Contacts and brazing alloys in discarded home appliances account for a large fraction of silver disposal onto land. We have calculated 6.7 million troy ounces silver dissipated annually in this way, with another 1.7 million troy ounces probably being recycled in steel scrap.[a/] After new electrical scrap and discarded household appliance figures are subtracted, the remaining brazing and electrical silver totals about 13 million troy ounces.

We assumed that 70 to 80% of the industrial silver originally disposed of to water, such as photographic and electroplating wastes, would be disposed of with the sewage sludge to landfills ($\sim$ 50%) and lagoons ($\sim$ 25%) at treatment plants and to agricultural landspreading operations ($\sim$ 20%).[60/] For purposes of the calculation, the fate of the residue from sewage sludge incineration ($\sim$ 5%) was assumed to be distributed among the former three methods.

We have calculated that "combustible" refuse may contain at least 14 million troy ounces silver.[b/] This figure probably does not include all of the remaining 13 million troy ounces brazing and electrical silver, which may largely remain in situ; but the figure may represent silver never appearing in industrial statistics such as paper[c/] (51% of municipal refuse), food waste (8.0%), dirt (5.5%), grass and leaves (5%), plastics (3%), textiles (3%), wood (3%), and rubber and leather (1%).[64/] Silver in urban refuse may also occur as an impurity in other metals, especially electrical copper. Another source of "nonstatistical" silver would be incinerator ashes.

Typically, a leachate from an urban refuse landfill contains 0.10 to 9.0 ppm copper. If one assumes that silver leaches out at the same rate

---

a/ The calculation is based on 10 million troy ounces silver in household appliances in 1968,[14/] $\sim$ 25 million household appliances sold per year (1964 to 1974), and 21 million discarded appliances per year.[56/] If 80% of the appliances discarded are disposed of to land, 6.7 million troy ounces silver will be involved. If only 2% of the copper in appliances is recovered, most of the silver in recycled scrap appliances will report in the steel the scrap is used to produce.[58/]

b/ If there is 0.01% silver in the bottom ash of incinerated municipal refuse,[61/] ash content of refuse is 3.7%,[62/] and total municipal refuse is 125 x 10^6 tons/year, the residual silver content of combustible, or at least incineratable, refuse may be as high as 14 x 10^6 troy oz. Many discarded appliances would obviously be too bulky to be fed into an incinerator. Since some small discarded appliances and appliance parts are amenable to grinding prior to incineration, there could be overlap between the discarded appliance figure and that for combustible refuse.

c/ Pinta reports that paper of different types contains 0.05 to 4 ppm silver; thus, paper may contribute at least 90,000 troy oz silver to urban refuse.[63/]

314

as copper[a/] and that the ratio of the annual increments of copper and silver to urban solid waste ($\sim$ 250,000[58/]:760[b/]) is proportional to their total contents in landfills, then the possible concentration of silver in the leachate would be 0.3 to 27 ppb. The chloride ion concentration of 100 to 2,400 ppm in the leachate[66/] may keep silver ions immobile as silver chloride or mobilize it as the $AgCl_2^-$ complex. High concentrations of Fe(II) and Mn(II) forms in the leachate, produced by reduction of insoluble forms or Fe(III) and Mn(IV) under anaerobic conditions,[67/] would probably tend to tie up any mobilized silver species.

6. Losses of silver in incineration: GCA Corporation estimated that 1.1 million troy ounces silver are emitted before controls during municipal waste incineration (0.037% silver in the emissions) and 0.68 million troy ounces after control.[2/] Since only about 10% of collected municipal refuse is incinerated,[68/] a figure of 11 million troy ounces silver as potentially emittable from combustion of municipal refuse seems quite high since in Section VII.B.5., we have calculated that only 14 million troy ounces of silver is expected to be retained.

On the basis of the temperatures involved,[c/] we might expect little, if any, silver would be emitted during municipal or industrial incineration. However, one source gave a silver content in fly ash from municipal incineration < 0.01 to > 0.10%.[61/] Another source gave 0.01 to 0.07% (average of eight fractions 0.02%).[69/] On the basis of 12.5 million tons solid waste incinerated,[70/] 32 lb fly ash per ton waste incinerated,[68/] and 0.02% silver, we calculate silver emissions, before controls, of 1.16 million troy ounces silver, which agrees with the GCA estimate.

GCA Corporation estimated a 70,000 troy oz silver loss from incineration of solid photographic wastes in recovery operations.[2/]

---

a/ Another source gives the silver concentration of a landfill leachate into groundwater at a municipal refuse disposal site near Austin, Texas, as < 10 ppb and the copper concentrations is 108 times that of silver. However, analyses at northern Illinois sites showed < 100 ppb silver and only 50 ppb copper.[65/]

b/ Based on the estimate 22.2 million troy ounces (760 tons).

c/ Municipal incinerator combustion chambers, 1031 to 1370°C; incinerator gases, 980 to 1090°C; flue gas temperatures, 649 to 980°C (cooled to 200 to 311°C before discharge); and industrial incinerator combustion chambers, 811 to 871°C.[68/]

C. Losses From Inadvertent Sources

The largest sources of silver emitted to the atmosphere are allegedly not those related to the silver industry itself or to the use and disposal of products manufactured by the silver industry but are attributed to some inadvertent sources. Losses to the atmosphere by inadvertent sources-- iron and steel-making operations, cement production, and burning of fossil fuels--have been estimated by the GCA Corporation. These estimates are excerpted from Reference 2 in Table VII-7 and the geographical distribution of these sources is found in Table VII-8.

Burning of hydrocarbon fuels containing trace amounts of silver is a large source, contributing at least 1 to 2 million troy ounces silver/ year to the atmosphere. Cement manufacture'and the iron and steel industry are alleged to be even larger emitters of aerosol silver. Few data regarding silver emissions from these sources are available, but we conclude that the emissions are about one-half to two-thirds those estimated by GCA Corporation and are possibly considerably smaller. If air emissions from these industries are ultimately shown to be so large, losses of silver in solid and liquid wastes are probably comparably large and should be identified.

1. Iron production and steelmaking: The GCA Corporation estimates of silver in iron and steel emissions are based on very few data: The Air Pollution Engineering Manual[71] reported that the particulate emissions from an open hearth furnace contained ~ 0.05% silver, 0.5% copper, and 10 to 15% zinc, and that the average content of two samples of baghouse dust collected from a gray iron cupola was 0.0091% silver, 0.35% copper, and 6.5% zinc (qualitative spectrographic analyses only). The GCA Corporation assumed that the silver-zinc ratio, 0.003, and silver-copper ratio, 0.1, in these open hearth furnace emissions would be the same for all iron and steel emissions, apparently not considering that the zinc content of the emissions varies with the content of galvanized scrap in the charge.[2] Iron foundries also use considerably more iron scrap than pig iron. The other reference regarding iron and steel-making emissions[72] cited by the GCA Corporation reported 0.08 to 0.16% copper and 0 to 3.0% zinc in particulate emissions from three oxygen-lanced open hearth furnaces and 0.48% zinc in dry blast-furnace flue dust. In addition, emissions from an electric arc furnace contained 0.16% copper.[71]

a. Iron production

(1) Sinter production: Sintering fuses collected dusts, fine ore, coke fines, and mill scale into a stable mass suitable for blast furnace use. Particulates discharged include unreacted ore, coke, and ash with 4 to 19% of the particulates being smaller than 10 μ.[73] Collected dusts are recycled.

316

Since coking involves the destructive distillation of coal at temperatures above 1000°C, most silver in the coal would have been emitted prior to sintering. Therefore, the major source of the silver emitted would have to be the ore. Of the iron ore minerals, Boyle reports values of "detected" to 300 ppm silver in hematite (Fe_2O_3), 0 to 1,000 ppm in limonite, and 1 to 5 ppm in magnetite ($FeFe_2O_4$). In 1972, about 70% of iron ore was magnetite, 29% hematite, and 1% limonite.[74] Taconite is an iron silicate, and Boyle states that the silver content in most silicates is rarely greater than 0.5 ppm. Canadian silicates range from < 0.05 to < 1 ppm silver.[22]

The GCA Corporation estimate for sintering losses appears to be based on the iron foundry emissions containing about 0.01% silver. A crude estimate of the silver content of the material(s) that might give emissions containing 0.01% silver may be made by comparing the smelting of copper ore concentrates. Copper smelter feeds contain 2 to 50 troy oz silver/ton of concentrate.[10] If material containing only 2 troy oz silver/ton (from roasting, smelting, and converting) produces emissions containing 0.035% silver,[3] then the silver source might contain up to about 0.6 troy oz/ton or about 20 ppm. Porphyry copper ore contains only about 0.07 troy oz/ton or 2.4 ppm.

At only $2/troy oz, the silver content of the sinter furnace charge would be worth $1.20/ton or about 10% of the value of the iron ore per ton.[75] At 100 ppm (0.01%) silver and $2/troy oz, the collected dust would contain $6 worth of silver per ton, and at silver prices greater than $4/troy oz the silver value would exceed its value as iron ore.

Pellet sinter stacks at INCO's Canadian iron ore recovery plant, operated in connection with a copper smelter, produce dust containing 0.50 to 0.85 troy oz silver/ton (17 to 29 ppm or 0.0017 to 0.0029%).[31] We conclude that the estimate of 0.01% silver in sintering emissions is high by at least a factor of 5 to 10.

(2) Blast furnace iron production: According to the GCA Corporation, iron ore blast furnaces generate 16.8 million troy ounces silver before control.[2/a] This is more silver than is produced from concentrates of domestic porphyry copper ores! (The GCA Corporation estimated that copper smelters emit 9 million troy ounces silver before control.)

---

a/ The iron ore blast furnaces process at least 10 times the amount of material that primary copper smelters do. (The iron ore is not appreciably concentrated.) Both blast furnace and sinter plant solid emissions that are recovered are used as blast furnace burden if there are sintering facilities.

Limestone[73]/ and dolomite are common fluxes in blast furnace iron production. The average silver content of all limestone is 0.07 ppm, although Kansas limestone contains 0.1 to 20 ppm. Dolomite, containing galena and sphalerite, from the Northwest Territories, Canada, contains 6 ppm silver. Nova Scotian dolomite plus argillaceous dolomite contain about 4 ppm silver.[22]/ There seems to be nothing in the iron blast furnace charge (iron ore, sintered dusts, flux, and coke) that would contribute sufficient silver to give emissions (0.01% silver) approaching those (0.035% silver) from smelting copper concentrates, which contain more than 68 ppm silver.[a]/

b. Steelmaking:

(1) Open hearth steelmaking: The major air pollution source of silver according to the GCA Corporation is open hearth steelmaking, allegedly emitting 4.90 million troy ounces silver per year, based on a production level of 65.8 million tons raw steel in 1968.[2]/ The use of open hearths in steelmaking, however, has been rapidly diminishing since the peak year in 1964 when over 98 million tons raw steel was produced in open hearth furnaces. The 1974 production of open hearth furnaces was only about 35.5 million tons raw steel, which would have decreased any silver emissions by about 45%. In addition, some major steelmakers are reported to have installed electrostatic precipitators and other equipment to control 99% of the emissions from open hearth stacks, a definite improvement over the 40% emission control estimated by GCA Corporation.[2,77]/

At least a quarter of U.S. open hearth steel-making capacity is to be replaced in the next 2 to 3 years. Much of the remainder will probably operate sporadically and will be phased out in about 10 years. Currently, the remaining open hearth furnaces are operating at less than 90% capacity.[77]/ The locations of these furnaces are given in Table VII-9. From the information presented in the table, one is able to predict that the available open hearth capacity at the end of 1975 may be only 27 million tons/year and open hearth production may be only 24 million tons/year. Silver emissions from this source would be reduced to 1.8 million troy ounces on the basis of the original GCA estimate if reported controls have been implemented and 1975 production figures are used.

There may be more silver in steel-making emissions than in iron-making emissions because of the high scrap content. Presumably some increase in the silver content of steel will occur as more of this metal is

_____

a/ Ingot iron NBS-SRM 1165 contains only 5 ppm silver and 172 ppm copper.[76]/

318

recycled and because of the difficulty of separating electrical components from, for example, automobile scrap.[a/]

Some ambient air sampling in the vicinity of three steel mills suggests that they may not be much greater sources of atmospheric silver than other industrial processes[79-81/] (see Section II). The emissions figure of 0.05% silver is based on only one qualitative measurement, which the GCA Corporation admits is of "questionable reliability."[2,71/] The metals content of these emissions varies widely during the furnace operation.[b/] Clearly, many more silver analyses of open hearth steel-making emissions must be made before their contribution to atmospheric silver pollution can be reliably estimated.

(2) Basic oxygen steelmaking: Basic oxygen furnaces accounted for 56% of the steel production in 1974.[77/] The charge to the basic oxygen furnace includes burnt lime, fluorspar, ore, limestone, dolomite, and scrap. Steel leaves the furnace at 1560°C.[82/]

GCA Corporation stated that the silver-zinc ratio and the silver-copper ratio in the steel emissions data they consulted were about 0.003 and 0.10, respectively. However, the source of zinc is largely galvanized material in the scrap while copper could come from copper-plated material and alloy copper. Since silver may be an impurity in copper, there could be a correlation with the copper content of scrap. Carrillo et al., of the Bureau of Mines, have estimated that the basic oxygen furnace produces 20 lb dust/ton steel (0.05% copper and 3% zinc), the open hearth furnace produces 25 lb dust/ton steel (0.1% copper and 5% zinc), and the electric arc furnace produces 20 lb dust/ton steel (0.27% copper and an average of 16% zinc).[58/] The percent scrap used in each of these processes is 29.1% in the oxygen furnace, 4.40% in the open hearth, and 97.4% in the electric arc furnace.[83/] Note that the zinc-copper ratio is 50 or 60 to 1 for each of the three processes. There appear to be too few data to explain the trend in the GCA Corporation estimates for silver content in emissions from the basic oxygen furnace (0.004%), open hearth furnace (0.05%), and electric

---

a/ All of the copper, nickel, and molybdenum in the open hearth charge report in the steel as do most of the tin, arsenic, antimony, and vanadium. With increasing use of nickel-bearing steel in the period 1930 to 1945, the nickel content of open hearth charge increased from 0.043 to 0.084%. In the same period, when not much copper-alloy steel was made, the copper content increased from 0.099 to 0.108%.[78/]

b/ For example, the iron content of the particulates averages 50% over most cycles but is greater than 60% during the working period and ore boil and 80% during oxygen-lancing.[73/]

arc furnace (0.05%).2/ If the silver-copper ratio 0.1 is correct, then the estimate of the silver content of the open hearth emission is out of line with the foregoing information and should be about 0.01% rather than 0.05%. If the GCA estimate is correct, then the emissions from basic oxygen furnaces in 1974 would have been approximately 15,000 troy oz.

Wet gas-cleaning methods in steelmaking cause water pollution by suspended solids. Wastewater from the basic oxygen furnace may be treated with chemical coagulants or by magnetic agglomeration. High zinc concentrations in the solid wastes recovered have been thought to make the material unsuitable for reuse in the furnace.84/ No data were found on the silver content of these materials.

(3) <u>Electric arc furnace steelmaking</u>: Electric furnaces produced 17.5% of the raw steel in 1973 and an estimated 20% in 1974.77/ The composition of the particulate emissions from the electric arc furnace, which uses almost entirely scrap as the iron source,a/ may vary widely. Three sources reported zinc emissions of 0 to 44% and copper emissions of 0.2 to 1.18%. About 70% of the particles are less than 5 μ in size with poundage estimates (per ton of steel) of 20 lb/ton,58/ 10 lb/ton,5/ and 13.8 lb/ton.85/

Because of the greater use of electric arc furnaces in 1974, silver emissions from them would have been about 400,000 troy oz if the GCA estimate is correct.

c. <u>Iron foundries</u>: The GCA Corporation report estimated that iron foundries emit about 130,000 troy oz silver annually based on a production level of 22 million tons/year, 75% control, and 0.008% silver in the emissions.2/ This amount is greater than that attributed to copper smelter emissions.

The foundry cupola is the major source of molten iron for producing castings. The charge comprises iron scrap, coke, limestone, dolomite, fluorspar, and silica sand. The ratio of the charge materials varies widely.51/ Particulates < 5 μ in size in the emissions range from 1 to 23.6% of the total. The amount of emissions varies with the amount of coke in the charge. The source of zinc in the emissions is chiefly from galvanized scrap and of copper, copper-plated scrap.73,86/

---

a/ The charge contains per ton of ingots produced: limestone 35 to 55, burnt lime 40 to 70, fluorspar 10 to 20, burnt dolomite 35 to 50, magnesite 4 to 8, silica sand 3 to 5, and coke 8 to 12 lb. The heating time may be about 8 hr with a maximum furnace temperature of 3100°C.78/

MRI has concluded that "no simple accurate estimate can be made of the nature and quantity of pollutants emitted from foundry cupolas."[5] The level of 75% control is probably erroneous. MRI estimates that the net control (80% efficient, but only 33% applied) is 27% for foundry furnaces, whereas an American Foundryman's Society source[87] states that 90% of the gray iron melting furnaces are cupolas and only 18% of these had air pollution devices installed in 1970. Another estimate is that melting operations emitted 75% of the particulates generated to the atmosphere by cupolas and electric arc furnaces.[85] Emissions from electric-arc (5 to 10 lb/ton metal charged) and electric-induction furnaces (about 2 lb/ton metal charged) are "cleaner," comprising primary metallic fumes.[5] It would be expected that the concentrations of silver would be higher in such emissions, but we have not found any such data.

If the cupola net controls are as high currently as 27%, the silver emissions from foundries would be approximately 380,000 troy oz. However, the trend in iron foundry closings[a] and the use of electric arc and induction melting will tend to reduce this value annually.

2. Cement manufacture: GCA Corporation estimated that the cement industry is the second largest producer of silver aerosol emissions with 3.1 million troy ounces, based on assays of 0.015% silver in three cement plant clinker coolers and of 0.008% silver in dust from three air separators (EPA data).[2]

Tables VII-10 and VII-11 show the materials used in the cement industry and the relative amounts used in the years 1944 to 1946. About 1.6 lb raw material and 0.27 lb coal are required in a kiln operation to produce 1 lb of cement.[88] The maximum temperature attained by the raw materials is about 1600°C.[89] Combustion gases leave the kiln at about 150 to 980°C.[5] The average silver content of limestone is 0.07 ppm; of clay and shale, 0.1 ppm; and of gypsum, < 1 ppm.[22] Processes have been patented to recover silver, copper, lead, zinc, and gold from pyrite cinders and steel-making converter slags. These materials are, at times, used as cement raw materials and would increase the silver content in kiln emissions.[90,91] It does not appear, however, that cement kiln emissions would contain 100 ppm silver, as has been estimated. We hesitate to impugn cement-making operations as significant air polluters by silver until more data are found.

---

a/ Foundries producing gray, malleable, and ductile iron have decreased at the rate of about 70 per year since 1947 so that by 1969 there were only 1,670. In the past 25 years, the number of cupola furnaces, probably the major source of silver emission, has declined by 2,500 to 1,970 in the year 1970.

About 34% of 80 cement plants surveyed reported that they returned all dust to the kiln. About the same number practiced dry surface piling. The remainder said that they returned the dust to the quarry (dry), leached it, slurried and discarded it, sold it, and/or had it hauled away by the contractor.[89]

3. Fossil fuels combustion as a silver source: GCA Corporation[2] estimated that coal and fuel oil combustion contributes 13.6% to U.S. silver emissions, basing the estimate on silver contents of the ashes of coal and fuel oil, 7 ppm and 50 ppm, respectively. The fuel oil silver content was based on oil-ash analyses by Levy et al.,[92] and by Walsh, who found 18 ppm and 300 ppm silver, respectively.

Bertine and Goldberg estimated that annual world-wide mobilizations of silver into the atmosphere from coal and fuel oil are 7×10^7 g (2×10^6 troy oz) and 2×10^4 g/year (640 troy oz), respectively.[93] GCA's U.S. fuel oil emissions estimate of about 13 million grams (0.41 million troy ounces) silver is about 650 times larger than the world-wide estimates above by Bertine and Goldberg, who used the average value of 0.001 ppm silver in fuel oil. Our own calculation, based on the data of Levy et al.[92] gives 0.4 million troy ounces silver in fuel oil consumed in the U.S. (see Table II-17)

If the U.S. accounts for 22% of annual world coal consumption, Bertine and Goldberg's calculations are comparable with those of the GCA: 0.75×10^6 troy oz compared with 1.24×10^6 troy oz, respectively. If coal is considered a significant source of atmospheric pollution by silver, calculations should include emissions from ignited coal refuse disposal areas, dust from refuse and coal storage piles, etc. A 1964 Bureau of Mines study indicated that there were 500 burning piles, some containing millions of tons of refuse, in 15 states, mostly in Pennsylvania and West Virginia.[88]

D. Chemical Form of Environmental Contaminants

1. Air: The forms of silver emitted to the air by human actities depend on the particular process, the temperatures, and the other chemical elements present. Mining and milling activities emit forms of silver normally found in the ore, and the concentrations of silver in the particulates are no higher than those found in the ores. Since the particles in the dust are relatively large and settle quickly, only mining and milling personnel in the low-population areas where these activities occur are likely to be subject to any risk of argyria.

High-temperature fabrication methods employing silver or silver alloys and furnacing during silver refining emit aerosol metallic silver or possibly, during cooling, submicron-sized particulates coated with argentous oxides.[a/] The hazard again is almost entirely occupational.

The chemical forms of emissions from smelting lead, lead-zinc, silver, and copper ores have not been identified but are likely to be particulates of metallic silver, silver sulfide, and silver sulfate. (Zinc sintering emissions may contain silver chloride.[6/]) As the particles cool, some silver oxide may form, but silver oxide should react with sulfide-containing species to form silver sulfide or with atmospheric carbon dioxide to form silver carbonate. Such silver compounds are likely to form during all high-temperature base-metal refining and iron and steel-making processes as long as sulfur is present. Emissions due to entrainment from these processes may also contain silver in the chemical form found in the ore.

Some evidence[2/] has implicated cement making as the second largest source of aerosol silver. We have not been able to ascertain what raw materials could possibly be the source of so much silver. Kiln emissions of any silver would likely be in the form of metallic silver coated with silver oxide and/or carbonate.

Burning of fossil fuels and municipal refuse, the next largest source of aerosol silver, probably emits metallic silver, whose particles become coated with silver oxide, silver sulfide, and/or carbonate as they cool. Burning of solid photographic waste (at about 811 to 980°C) to recover silver produces emissions containing the vaporized silver halides and silver carbonate.

The other obvious source of atmospheric silver emissions is cloud seeding with silver iodide from ground-based generators or airplanes, where up to 150 troy oz silver/hr/storm may be released to the atmosphere.[94/]

Silver which vaporizes when electrical contacts arc probably trapped in the electrical device and does not seem to pose an occupational or environmental hazard.

---

a/ Values of the decomposition temperature of argentous oxide are reported in the range 100 to 300°C.

2. <u>Water</u>: The chief human activity leading to water pollution is the disposal of developing solutions by small photofinishers directly to municipal sewers. The solutions contain silver as thiosulfate complexes, chiefly $[Ag(S_2O_3)_2]^-$ and $[Ag(S_2O_3)_2]^{3-}$.[a/] Sedimentation treatment of the sewage probably removes at least 50%,[b/] perhaps as much as 70% or more, of the silver in the form of silver adsorbed to organic matter. More sophisticated treatments may remove 90% or more of the silver present. For example, anaerobic digestion may remove considerable amounts of silver as the sulfide. Table II-9 shows that effluents from sewage-treatment plants contain 0.000048 to 0.04 ppm while sewage sludges have been reported containing 0.005 to 900 ppm silver. Probably less than 30% of the estimated 16 million troy ounces silver discharged to wastewater annually as thiosulfate complexes ultimately reaches natural watercourses. Silver in municipal treatment effluent is probably present as thiosulfate complexes, as colloidal silver chloride and sulfide, or as soluble organic complexes. Little soluble silver is in the form of complexes with dissolved organic matter according to Stumm and Bilinski.[96/] Much silver in natural water is associated with suspended particulates.

Very little silver cyanide is discharged to sewers because of the toxicity of cyanide and the regulations regarding its treatment. The usual treatment of cyanide wastes is chlorination-oxidation; the silver species in the discharges are probably $Ag(OH)_2^-$ and silver chloride or silver chloride complex. The effluents from sewage treatment of these wastes again would contain predominately silver chloride and silver sulfide.

In natural waters, silver occurs as the free ion, possibly as soluble AgSH, $Ag(SH)_2^-$, and $Ag_2S_3H_2^{2-}$;[96/] as soluble and colloidal complexes; in the tissues of microorganisms; and in forms adsorbed to suspended particulates such as plankton, carbon, soil, and clay.[c/]

---

a/ The stability constant of $[Ag(S_2O_3)_2]^{3-}$ is 6 x 10^14. The former complex is stable in alkaline or neutral solutions. Acids decompose thiosulfate to sulfur, hydrogen sulfide, and H_2S_2. Mild oxidizing agents convert it to $S_4O_6^{2-}$ and stronger ones to SO_4^{2-}. Thiosulfate also forms complexes with Cd^{2+} which might be present in higher concentrations than silver.[95/]

b/ Sedimentation for the normal 12-hr period reduces the copper content by 45%; for 18 hr, 62%.

c/ We calculate from data in References 97 and 98 that the percent of the silver content carried by suspended material in the Susquehanna River is 69%; Brazos River, 50%; Neuse River, 27%; and the Rhone River, 36%.

The soluble species are precipitated by colloid coagulation; adsorption to carbon compounds, metal hydroxides, and iron and manganese oxides; death of organisms; and sulfide and humate formation in the presence of decaying organic matter or under strongly reducing conditions.

Some silver may be redissolved from sediments or suspended matter when the ammonia content of the water is high from agricultural runoff (fertilizer and animal wastes) but will become insoluble again when the ammonia is ultimately oxidized to nitrate.

Minor amounts of silver are added to natural waters from acid mine drainage, leaching of ore deposits and base-metal tailings, and tailings-pond discharge (chiefly silver sulfate); atmospheric fall-out and wash-out (silver sulfide, silver sulfate, silver carbonate, silver oxide, silver chloride, and silver iodide); urban stormwater runoff; and leaching and erosion of silver associated with the soil, e.g., urban refuse landfill, sewage-sludge-amended agricultural soil, and mineralized zones enriched in silver. The suspended matter in the natural waters should ultimately adsorb and/or complex much of the dissolved silver.

Data for heavy-metal concentration in drinking water-treatment-plant influents are higher than values in U.S. source waters because of the bias toward sampling at plants known to have high trace-metal levels. Thus, the average silver concentration in 956 municipal water supplies was 8 ppb[99] compared with the average value 2.6 ppb silver found in 6.6% of U.S. source waters.[100]

The average percentage silver removal by drinking water-treatment plants is probably at least as good as the removals of copper (49%) or iron and manganese (65%)[101] with hydrous silver oxide precipitating after the treatment with lime or being adsorbed to the alum flocculent. Smaller particles are probably removed by sand filtration. Use of activated carbon would tend to increase the efficiency of silver removal.[a] Chlorination with elemental chlorine will convert the soluble silver and possibly some of the silver in the suspended matter to silver chloride or the soluble silver chloride complex.

---

a/ Lime coagulation and recarbonation of a sewage-sludge effluent containing 0.0546 ppm silver reduced the silver concentration to 0.0164 ppm (70% removal). Treating the latter effluent by sand filtration removed 11.6% of the remaining silver and carbon adsorption removed over 96% of the silver from the filtration effluent. Overall removal of silver was 99.4%.[102]

Silver has been found in tap-water samples in higher concentrations than those in water leaving the treatment plant. For example, 26% of the samples collected from the Chicago distribution system contained 2 to 9 ppb silver when the maximum at the water-treatment plant was 2 ppb.[103]/

3. Soil: Silver may reach the soil via atmospheric fallout; irrigation by sewage effluent; application of sewage sludge; landfilling with household refuse, sewage sludge, or industrial solid wastes; and leaching of tailings dumps; mobilization from mineral deposits; and tailings ponds and lagoons of industrial liquid wastes.

The silver metal and alloys present in household and industrial solid wastes are already inert. The forms of silver in tailings ponds are probably the innocuous mineral forms found in nature. Plating-waste lagoons contain silver cyanide, hydroxide, and/or chloride. The forms of silver, or any other heavy metal for that matter, in the products of sewage treatment (i.e., sludge and effluent) are unknown and probably depend on the particular sewage plant.[104]/

Silver in contaminated soils may be complexed and/or adsorbed by organic matter, clays, and manganese and iron oxides. Insoluble inorganic forms may remain unchanged or be converted to the least soluble form, silver sulfide, in anaerobic soils. Some silver is undoubtedly incorporated into the tissues of or at least adsorbed by soil-dwelling organisms. Factors promoting mobilization from soils are good drainage, acidity, and formation of soluble organic complexes, e.g., via oxidation of humic complexes or decay of organic matter.

The most probable source of soil contamination by silver and one of the most likely points of entry into the food chain is the use of sewage sludge to fertilize cropland or sludge effluent for irrigation. See Table II-9 for typical silver concentrations in sewage sludges and effluents. Page estimated that 100 metric tons domestic sewage sludge containing 10 ppm silver when applied to 1 ha of soil at a depth of 15 cm (equivalent to a low application rate: 10 metric tons/ha/year for 10 years) would give 1 kg silver/ha as compared with 0.02 to 10 kg silver/ha normally present in soil (a typical level in soil is 0.2 kg/ha).[104]/ Since sewage sludges may contain up to 900 ppm silver and often contain about 100 ppm, soils can be significantly enriched by amendment with sewage sludge.

Although after mixing the sludge with the soil, most of the silver is immobilized, some is still water-soluble and available for plant uptake. For example, the long-term experiments by Rohde, who applied sewage sludge to land, showed that higher amounts (concentrations not reported) of silver, lead, barium, and cadmium were found in the soil beneath unhealthy plants. Trace elements in sludge-amended soils usually remain chiefly in the surface soil to the depth of tillage and are available for plant uptake for at least 6 years.[104]/

The availability of silver to plants will depend on the soil solution pH. At about pH 7, silver ion concentration in soil solution is less than 0.05 ppm. At pH 5 to 6, the concentration increases and at pH 7.5 to 8.5, decreases.[104]

That silver remains immobilized at the soil surface is supported by analyses of soils near a silver iodide ground generator at Steamboat Springs, Colorado. The deposited silver was retained chiefly in the upper 2 cm of soil with silver levels as high as 1,400 ppm 4 years after the last seeding. Soils with high silver concentrations exhibited lower pH; higher water content, respiration rates, and concentrations of organic matter with increasing silver iodide content up to 50 ppm; and greater numbers of microorganisms. Adsorption and complexing of silver by the soil humates would tend to inhibit their decomposition and lessen the toxic effect of silver on soil microorganisms.[a] Higher moisture retention by organic matter would also promote greater numbers of microorganisms.

The effects of accumulated silver in soils around generators are likely to continue for long periods because of silver's immobility; however, continuous seeding for several thousand years would not produce as much as 1 ppm silver in the soils of target areas.[94]

4. Food: Silver has been detected in some food crops, meats, and fish and mollusks (see Tables II-12, VIII-5, and II-13, respectively). Kehoe estimated the daily intake of silver from food to be 0.088 mg.[105] An experiment is described in Section VIII., Physiology of Silver, in which a man ingested only 0.035 mg silver/day and his wife 0.044 mg/day.[106]

Silver appearing in foods due to contamination or direct treatment by silver during processing may be ionic $Ag+$, but more probably is complexed by the organic species present, probably via sulfur linkages. The forms of silver in the tissues of plants and animals are most probably protein complexes with bonding via sulfide and/or histidine or other amino acid residues. Ionic silver (Ag^+) or any metallic silver ingested orally (e.g., from corrosion or mechanical degradation of silver in tableware or dental restorations or prostheses) will ordinarily be in such low concentrations that the hydrochloric acid of the stomach will convert it (very little of it in the case of metallic silver) to the soluble silver chloride complex. In the intestine, where most metal absorption into the blood stream occurs, the silver is primarily complexed or adsorbed on organic matter. Some small fraction of the silver in the intestine will be present as soluble complexes

---

a/ For example, in laboratory experiments, 100 ppm silver iodide retarded cellulose decomposition in mud 10% by inhibiting the growth of the soil microorganism Arthrobacter.

with amino acids, etc., and may be absorbed in those forms. Silver may compete with copper for binding sites on proteins in the intestinal mucosa that are involved in copper absorption,[107] and thus may be released slowly into the plasma transport mechanisms as is copper. The relative contributions of absorbed and unabsorbed dietary silver to the feces, the major excretory route, have not been determined, but laboratory mammals were found to absorb less than 10% of orally ingested $^{110}AgNO_3$.[108/a] Possibly, absorption of silver from food as compared with therapeutic silver nitrate would be higher because of the presence of organic material, although Hill and Pillsbury stat that the presence of food in the digestive tract has no effect on absorption.[109]

---

a/ Silver chloride and nitrate are absorbed more rapidly than colloidal
    silver compounds.[109]

TABLE VII-1

ESTIMATED MILLING LOSSES OF SILVER

Type of Ore	1971 Ore Production, tons [10]	% of Total Domestic Production	Amounts of Recoverable Silver in the Ore, troy oz	% Silver Recovery for Typical Milling Operation [10]	Estimated Milling Loss, troy oz
Ag	673,116	36	15,044,825	98	300,000
Cu	217,245,002	32[a]	13,174,914	91	1,200,000
Pb	8,925,109[b]	14	5,825,447[c]	Mo., 68; other, 98	860,000
Zn	102,299	< 0.5	24,910	81	5,000
Cu-Pb-Zn, Pb-Zn, Cu-Pb, Zn-Pb	5,115,314	17	6,826,542	Cu-Pb-Zn, 97 [10] (all 3: 85-95%)	620,000 (10%)
Old tailings, etc.	100,809	< 0.5	138,076	90	120,000
Au, Au-Ag, and placer	2,049,298	< 2	529,428	98	11,000
	234,210,947		41,564,142	Average 92[c]	3,116,000[d]

_____

a/ Includes a small amount of Michigan Cu-Ag ores. Silver recovery 15%. 68% of the silver is recovered as Cu-Ag alloy. Thus, milling loss of silver for these ores would be 17%.

b/ Over 96% of the silver-containing lead ore production is attributed by the Bureau of Mines to Missouri.

c/ Bureau of Mines statistics for recoverable silver on Missouri lead ores apparently do not account for the 32% loss of silver in the tailings.[1]

d/ Reference 10 estimates average loss in milling 5%. Here the loss would be 2,080,000 troy oz silver.

329

TABLE VII-2

ACCUMULATED WASTES FROM MINING, MILLING, AND SMELTING BASE-METAL ORES[8/]

State	Lead-Zinc-Silver		Copper	
	Million Tons	Acres	Million Tons	Acres
Alaska	640.0	2,000	13.6	302
Arizona	-	-	4,764.0	20,500
California	9.3	85	30.0	1,100
Colorado	330.0	5,500	-	-
Idaho	153.5	3,160	90	-
Illinois	17.1	349	-	-
Kansas	25.0	2,250	-	-
Maine	-	-	1.5	7
Michigan	-	-	431.0	1,150
Missouri	42.0	4,600	-	-
Montana	45.9	2,160	930.0	5,600
Nevada	-	-	1,346.0	9,000
New Mexico	16.2	485	867.0	4,035
North Carolina	-	-	0.8	15
Oklahoma	101.8	5,210	-	-
Oregon	-	-	0.4	35
Tennessee	7.2	148	3.0	100
Texas	12.0	70	-	-
Utah	53.8	2,385	2,930.5	10,732
Washington	22.5	250	12.5	140

MINE DRAINAGE AND MILL WASTE DISPOSAL PRACTICES[15/]

Mine	Ore	1971 Silver[1/] Production, troy oz	Mine Drainage Disposal Practice	Mill Waste Disposal Practice
Bunker Hill Mine	Pb-Zn	1,614,417	Mine drainage is discharged along with mill wastes into a large tailings pond. Decant pipe discharges effluent to South Fork Coeur d'Alene River. (Wastes also include smelter and sewage wastes.)	Waste discharged to large tailings pond. Effluent to South Fork Coeur d'Alene River.
Clayton Silver Mine				Waste discharged to tailings pond. Effluent to Kinnikinic Creek, a tributary to the Salmon River.
Crescent Mine	Ag	1,663,417	Mine drainage is discharged directly into Big Creek, a tributary of the South Fork Coeur d'Alene River.	
Day Rock Mine	Pb		Mine drainage is discharged directly to Ninemile Creek, a tributary to the South Fork Coeur d'Alene River.	Waste discharged to small tailings pond. Effluent to Ninemile Creek.
Galena Mine	Ag	3,900,797	Mine drainage is discharged along with mill waste into a series of tailings ponds. Effluent from tailings ponds is either pumped for industrial use at the mill or discharged to Lake Creek, a tributary to the South Fork Coeur d'Alene River. Combined discharge is about 0.7 MGD.	Waste discharged to a series of four small tailings ponds and two clarifying ponds. Effluent is either recycled back to the mill or discharged to Lake Creek.
Lucky Friday Mine	Pb	3,343,075	Mine drainage is discharged directly to Gold Hunter Creek, a small tributary to the South Fork Coeur d'Alene River.	Waste pumped across the town of Mullan and discharged into a tailings pond. Effluent to South Fork, Coeur d'Alene River.
Knob Hill Mine			Mine drainage is pumped to a small pond near the No. 1 shaft. Pond discharges to Eureka Creek by subsurface percolation.	Waste is pumped to a tailings pond. Effluent from pond is discharged to Eureka Creek.
Pend Oreille Mine[a/]	Pb-Zn-Cu		Mine drainage is discharged directly into the Pend Oreille River.	Mill wastes are discharged to a tailings pond prior to discharge to the Pend Oreille River.
Star-Morning Mine (Star Unit)	Pb-Zn		Mine water is discharged directly to Slaughterhouse Gulch Creek, a tributary to the South Fork Coeur d'Alene River, and part is discharged to the Star Tailings Pond.	Mill wastes are piped some 6 miles down the Canyon Creek Valley from Burke to three large tailings ponds. Effluent from the ponds is discharged into Canyon Creek.
Sunshine Mine	Ag	7,047,463[b/]	Mine drainage is combined with mill waste and discharged to a large tailings pond. Effluent from pond discharged to Big Creek, a tributary to the South Fork Coeur d'Alene River.	Mill effluent treated with a flocculating agent and piped several miles down the Big Creek Valley to a large tailings pond. Effluent from pond discharges to Big Creek, a tributary to the South Fork of the Coeur d'Alene River.

a/ The Pend Oreille Mine has been absorbed into the Knob Hill mine.
b/ Includes production for outside companies as well as Hecla.

TABLE VII-4

MINE DRAINAGE FROM ABANDONED MINES[15/]

Mine Name	Location	Concentration of Silver, ppb	Drainage Basin
California Gulch	Ninemile Creek, Idaho	1	Coeur d'Alene
Duncan Gulch	West of Murray, Idaho	1	Coeur d'Alene
Golconda	Along South Fork near Mullan, Idaho	1	Coeur d'Alene
Monitor	Near Wallace, Idaho	1	Coeur d'Alene
Murray	Murray, Idaho	1	Coeur d'Alene
Placer Gulch	South of Wallace, Idaho	1	Coeur d'Alene
Silver Beaver	On Deer Creek, North of Wallace, Idaho	1	Coeur d'Alene
Snowstorm Peak	East of Mullan, Idaho	1	Coeur d'Alene
Sunset Peak	North of Wallace, Idaho	1	Coeur d'Alene
Ajax	Near Granite, Oregon	2	-
Al Sarena	Near Prospect, Oregon	1	Rogue River
Argonaut	Near Bourne, Oregon	1	-
Ashland	Near Ashland, Oregon	1	Rogue River
Benton	Near Gahce, Oregon	2	Rogue River
Blackjack	Near Granite, Oregon	1	John Day
Buckeye	Near Bourne, Oregon	1	Powder
Buffalo	Near Granite, Oregon	2	Powder
Cougar	Near Granite, Oregon	3	Powder
Magnolia	Near Granite, Oregon	2	John Day
N. Pole	Near Bourne, Oregon	1	Powder
Silver Peak	Near Canyonville, Oregon	1	Rogue River
Chloride Queen	Near Colville, Washington	8	Colville
Eureka	Washington	5	Colville
Gold Hill	Near Darrington, Washington	1	Stillaguamish
Holden	Along Railroad Creek and above Lake Chelan, Washington	2	Lake Chelan
Triune	Near Groville, Washington	2	Okanogan

TABLE VII-5

VOLUMES OF CYANIDE-BEARING WASTES FROM TYPICAL
ELECTROPLATING OPERATIONS[44/]

Type of Work Plated	Volume (gal.)	CN⁻ (ppm)
Aircraft engines and parts	293,760/day	-
Missile parts	32,000/day	80
Instrumentation and control equipment	13,000/day	-
Electronic hardware	259,200/day	200-1,500
Home appliances	108,000/day	-
TV antenna	11,000/day	-
Silverware	165,000/day	172
Instrument motors and electrical clocks		-

TABLE VII-6

MASS BALANCE OF SILVER SOLD ANNUALLY TO INDUSTRY

Disposition		Annual Average, 1966-1972 (million troy ounces)
Annual sales		149.9
	New scrap[a]/	- 26.5
Silver fabricated into products		123.4
	Exports (7% of photog. silver)	- 2.9
Silver in new U.S. products		120.5
	Old scrap[b]/	- 46.4
Increment of silver to silver products in use[c]/		74.1

Products likely to be preserved as wealth			
Electroplate		14.6	
Sterling[d]/		12.7	
Jewelry		4.7	
Preserved photog. materials		1.5	- 33.5
Silver in products that may be buried, incinerated, or lost directly to water (or maintained in situ)			40.6
Unrecycled photog. silver lost to water[e]/			- 4.0
Incineration loss			- 0.7
Photog. silver in sewage sludge			
Lagooned		3.2	
Landfilled at treatment plant		6.3	
Landspreading		2.5	- 12.0
Silver potentially available for urban landfill disposal			23.9
Combustible refuse		14.0	
Discarded household appliances			
Landfill		6.7	
Recycled in steel scrap		1.7	
Other noncombustible refuse[f]/		1.5	- 23.9
			0

---

a/ Estimated amount of new sterling silver scrap 12.8 million troy ounces; the rest is chiefly electrical scrap.

b/ Assumed that this value includes all recovered photog. silver, ~ 20 million troy ounces.[10]/

c/ This assumes that the recycling rate will not change appreciably so that the silver that will eventually be recycled is included.

d/ Estimated amount of sterling into new products if ~ 50% of sales is scrap.

e/ About 75% is estimated to be trapped in sewage sludge.

f/ This is merely a residual number.

Table VII-7

SOURCES AND SILVER-CONTAINING EMISSIONS
ESTIMATED BY GCA CORPORATION[2]

Source	Uncontrolled Particulate Emission Factor lb/ton[2831]	Production Level (tons/yr)[2831]	% Ag in Emissions	Ag Emissions Before Controls 10⁶ oz/yr	Estimated Level of Emission Control (%)	Ag Emissions After Controls 10⁶ oz/yr
Iron and Steel						
Sinter Process	20 Sinter	51,000,000	0.01	1.5	90	0.15
Blast Furnace	130 Pig Iron	88,800,000	0.01	16.8	99	0.17
Open Hearth	17 Steel	65,800,000	0.05	8.2	40	4.90
Basic Oxygen	40 Steel	48,000,000	0.004	1.1	99	0.01
Electric Arc	10 Steel	16,800,000	0.05	1.2	78	0.27
Iron Foundry	20	22,000,000	0.008	0.5	75	0.13
Coal	NA	33,800,000[a]	0.0007	6.9	82	1.24
Oil	NA	287,000[a]	0.005	0.41	0	0.41
Gasoline, etc.	NA	450,000,000	0.000001[b]	0.13	0	0.13
Cement	NA	7,790,000[c]	(0.008-0.0I5) 0.01[e]	26.0[d]	88	3.1[d]

NA = Not applicable.
a/ Uncontrolled emission.
b/ % Ag in fuel.

c/ Particulate emissions before control.
d/ Intermediate value.
e/ GCA estimate.

335

TABLE VII-8

GEOGRAPHICAL DISTRIBUTION OF
EMISSION SOURCE AND EMISSIONS
ESTIMATED BY GCA CORPORATION2/

EPA Region	States	Open Hearth Steel		Iron and Steel, Other		Cement Production		Oil Burning		Coal Burning	
		No. of Plants	tons/yr	No. of Plants	tons/yr	No. of Plants	tons/yr	% Oil	tons/yr	% Coal	tons/yr
I	Conn., Maine, Mass., N.H., R.I., Vt.	1	3.7	23	1.4	1	0.6	18.0	2.5	0.7	0.3
II	N.J., N.Y., Puerto Rico, Virgin Is.	1	3.7	33	2.0	13	7.7	29.1	4.1	5.7	2.4
III	Del., Md., Penn., Va., W.Va., District of Columbia	18	65.7	111	6.7	28	16.8	15.0	2.1	21.8	9.3
IV	Ala., Fla., Ga., Ky., Miss., N.C., S.C., Tenn.	2	7.3	39	2.4	27	15.8	9.6	1.3	21.1	9.1
V	Ill., Ind., Mich., Minn., O., Wis.	17	62.3	146	8.8	30	17.9	7.6	1.1	41.3	17.6
VI	Ark., La., N.M., Ok., Tex.	2	7.3	20	1.2	27	15.8	3.7	0.5	1.4	0.6
VII	Iowa, Ks., Mo., Neb.	0	0	5	0.3	20	11.8	0.9	0.1	4.1	1.7
VIII	Colo., Montana, N.D., S.D., Utah, Wyoming	2	7.3	2	0.1	9	5.3	1.8	0.3	3.3	1.4
IX	Ariz., Calif., Nev., Hawaii, the South Pacific	3	11.0	29	1.7	19	11.2	11.6	1.6	0.7	0.3
X	Alaska, Idaho, Or., Wash.	0	0	10	0.4	7	4.1	2.7	0.4	0.3	0.1
	Totals	46	168	415	42.5	181	107	100	14	100	4.5

TABLE VII-9

OPEN HEARTH STEEL-MAKING FURNACES STILL IN OPERATION, 1975[77]

Location	No. of Furnaces	Annual Capacity, million tons/year	Operator	Remarks
Fairless Works	9	> 4	U.S. Steel	
Homestead Works, Pittsburgh, Pennsylvania	11	3.5	U.S. Steel	Furnaces equipped with oxygen lances to speed up steelmaking. Two to be rebuilt in 1975.
Youngstown, Ohio	14	~ 1.5	U.S. Steel	
Geneva, Utah	10	~ 2.5	U.S. Steel	
Sparrows Point Plant near Baltimore, Maryland	7	>> 3	Bethlehem Steel	
Fairfield Works	9	~ 2	U.S. Steel	All replaced by bottom-blown oxygen converters (Q-BOPs) and shut down by May 1975.
Lackawanna, New York	6	~ 1.5	Bethlehem Steel	Eight smaller furnaces inoperative for several months.
Johnstown, Pennsylvania	8	~ 2.2	Bethlehem Steel	Will be shut down and replaced with oxygen converters.
Indiana Harbor plant near Chicago	7	~ 2	Inland Steel	Mostly cold-charged.
Indiana Harbor	7	1.5	Youngstown Sheet and Tube Company	Supplement oxygen converters.
Youngstown area: Campbell Works	10	2.6	Youngstown Steel	Open hearths of Campbell Works to be replaced by mid-1978.
Brier Hill Works	10		Youngstown Steel	
East Texas	5	~ 1	Lone Star Steel	
Cleveland, Ohio	4	~ 1	Republic Steel	Oxygen-lanced. Supplement oxygen converters.
East Chicago	4	~ 1	Republic Steel	To be replaced by Q-BOP oxygen converters.
Pittsburgh Works	5	1.5	Jones and Laughlin Steel Corporation	Oxygen-lanced.
Mansfield, Ohio	6	0.5	Empire-Detroit Steel Division, Cyclops Corp.	
Portsmouth, Pennsylvania	5	1 (potential)	Empire-Detroit Steel Division, Cyclops Corp.	
Fontana, California	8	~ 1.5	Kaiser Steel Corp.	

337

TABLE VII-10

MATERIALS USED IN CEMENT INDUSTRY[112]/

Source of CaO	Source of Al_2O_3	Source of SiO_2	Source of Fe
Cement rock	Clay	Clay	Limestones
Limestone	Shale	Shale	Clay
Marl	Ash from coal	Ash	Shale
Fossil shell	Slag	Slag	Iron ores
Recent shell	Igneous rocks	Sand	Slag
Alkali waste		Sandstones	Pyrite cinders
Blast-furnace slag			Mill scale

TABLE VII-11

RAW MATERIALS USED IN PRODUCING PORTLAND CEMENT
IN THE UNITED STATES, 1944-1946[112]
(short tons)

Raw Material	1944	1945	1946
Cement Rock	5,119,318	5,656,390	10,781,078
Limestone	19,958,151	22,747,654	34,579,673
Marl	643,412	646,391	860,798
Clay and shale	2,822,881	3,162,458	4,845,224
Blast-furnace slag	278,998	380,970	706,986
Gypsum	597,297	683,158	1,157,324
Sand and sandstone	230,288	272,077	460,910
Iron materials	123,079	128,312	218,634
Miscellaneous	22,442	36,100	144,139
Total	29,795,866	33,713,510	53,754,766
Average total weight required per barrel (376 lb) of finished cement	Pounds 656	Pounds 656	Pounds 655

BIBLIOGRAPHY. SECTION VII.

1. Morris, A. E., Professor of Metallurgical Engineering, University of Missouri, Rolla, personal communication, June 15, 1975.

2. GCA Corporation, GCA Technology Division, National Emissions Inventory of Sources and Emissions of Silver, Contract No. 68-02-0601, prepared for the Monitoring and Data Analysis Division, Office of Air Quality Planning and Standards, U.S. Environmental Protection Agency, Washington, D.C., 1973.

3. W. E. Davis and Associates, National Inventory of Sources and Emissions. Barium, Boron, Copper, Selenium, and Zinc. Copper, Section III, Environmental Protection Agency, Research Triangle Park, North Carolina, 1972.

4. W. E. Davis and Associates, National Inventory of Sources and Emissions. Barium, Boron, Copper, Selenium, and Zinc. Zinc, Section V, Environmental Protection Agency, Research Triangle Park, North Carolina, 1972.

5. Vandegrift, A. E., and L. J. Shannon, Handbook of Emissions, Effluents, and Control Practices for Stationary Particulate Pollution Sources, prepared by Midwest Research Institute for Division of Process Control Administration, U.S. Department of Health, Education, and Welfare, Cincinnati, Ohio, 1970.

6. Hallowell, J. B., J. F. Shea, G. R. Smithson, Jr., A. B. Tripler, and B. W. Gonser, Water-Pollution Control in the Primary Nonferrous-Metals Industry. Vol. I. Copper, Zinc, and Lead Industries, Battelle Memorial Institute, prepared for Office of Research and Monitoring, U.S. Environmental Protection Agency, U.S. Government Printing Offices, Washington, D.C., 1973.

7. Hallowell, J. B., J. F. Shea, G. R. Smithson, Jr., A. B. Tripler, and B. W. Gonser, Water-Pollution Control in the Primary Nonferrous-Metals Industry. Vol. II. Aluminum, Mercury, Gold, Silver, Molybdenum, and Tungsten, Battelle Memorial Institute, prepared for Office of Research and Monitoring, U.S. Environmental Protection Agency, U.S. Government Printing Office, Washington, D.C., 1973.

8. Booz Allen Applied Research, Inc., A Study of Hazardous Waste Materials, Hazardous Effects and Disposal Methods. Vol. II, PB-221 466, U.S. Environmental Protection Agency, National Technical Information Service, Springfield, Virginia, 1973.

9. Salsbury, M. H., W. H. Kerns, F. B. Fulkerson, and G. C. Branner, Marketing Ores and Concentrates of Gold, Silver, Copper, Lead and Zinc in the United States, Bureau of Mines Information Circular 8206, U.S. Department of the Interior, Bureau of Mines, U.S. Government Printing Office, Washington, D.C., 1964.

10. Schack, C. H., and B. H. Clemmons, Review and Evaluation of Silver-Production Techniques, U.S. Bureau of Mines Information Circular 8266, U.S. Government Printing Office, Washington, D.C., 1965.

11. Schack, C. H., and B. H. Clemmons, "Chapter 4. Extractive Processes," in Silver. Economics, Metallurgy, and Use, A. Butts and C. D. Coxe, Eds., D. Van Nostrand Co., Inc., Princeton, New Jersey, 1967, pp. 57-77.

12. Anonymous, "New Tailings Retreatment Facilities Produce 110 TPD of Concentrate at Kennecott Operation," Eng. Mining J., 172(8), 26 (1971).

13. Mink, L. L., R. E. Williams, A. T. Wallace, and L. M. McNay, "Renovation of Wastes by Mine Tailings Ponds," Mining Eng., 25(7), 81-88 (1973).

14. Ageton, R. W., "Silver," in Minerals Facts and Problems, Bureau of Mines Bulletin 650, U.S. Department of the Interior, U.S. Government Printing Office, Washington, D.C., 1970, pp. 723-737.

15. Sceva, J. E., Water Quality Considerations for the Metal Mining Industry in the Pacific Northwest, Draft Copy, Environmental Protection Agency, Region 10, Seattle, Washington (undated, after 1972).

16. Larsen, H. P., J. K. P. Shou, and L. W. Ross, "Chemical Treatment of Metal-Bearing Mine Drainage," J. Water Pollution Control Federation, 45, 1682-1695 (1973).

17. Wixson, B. G., E. Bolter, N. L. Gale, J. C. Jennett, and K. Purushothaman, "The Lead Industry as a Source of Trace Metals in the Environment," in Cycling and Control of Metals, Proceedings of an Environmental Resources Conference, Columbus, Ohio, October 31-November 2, 1972, U.S. Environmental Protection Agency, National Environmental Research Center, Cincinnati, Ohio, February 1973, pp. 11-19.

18. Jennett, J. C., and B. G. Wixson, "Treatment and Control of Lead Mining Wastes in S.E. Missouri," Paper presented at the 26th Purdue Industrial Waste Conference, Lafayette, Indiana, May 4-6, 1971.

19. Williams, R. E., A. T. Wallace, and L. L. Mink, "Impact of a Well Managed Tailings Pond System on a Stream," Mining Congr. J., 57, 48-56 (1971).

20. Ottinger, R. S., J. L. Blumenthal, D. F. Dal Porto, G. I. Gruber, M. J. Santy, and C. C. Shih, Recommended Methods of Reduction, Neutralization, Recovery, or Disposal of Hazardous Waste. Vol. XIII. Industrial and Municipal Disposal Candidate Waste Stream Constituent Profile Reports. Inorganic Compounds (Continued), TRW Systems Group for the U.S. Environmental Protection Agency, PB-224 592, National Technical Information Service, U.S. Department of Commerce, Springfield, Virginia, 1973.

21. Galbraith, J. H., and R. E. Williams, "Migration and Leaching of Metals from Old Mine Tailings Deposits," Groundwater, 10, 33-44 (1972).

22. Boyle, R. W., "Geochemistry of Silver and Its Deposits with Notes on Geochemical Prospecting for the Element," Geol. Surv. Can., Bull., No. 160, 1-264 (1968).

23. Maxfield, D., J. M. Rodriguez, M. Buettner, J. Davis, L. Forbes, R. Kovacs, W. Russel, L. Schultz, R. Smith, J. Stanton, and C. M. Wai, "Heavy Metal Content in Sediments of Southern Part of Coeur d'Alene Lake," Environ. Pollution, 6(4), 263-266 (1974).

24. Maxfield, D., J. M. Rodriguez, M. Buettner, J. Davis, L. Forbes, R. Kovacs, W. Russel, L. Schultz, R. Smith, J. Stanton, and C. M. Wai, "Heavy Metal Pollution in Sediments of Coeur d'Alene River Delta," Environ. Pollution, 7(1), 1-6 (1974).

25. George, J. G., "Silver," Can. Mining J., 90(2), 101-105 (1969).

26. Gomes, J. M., K. Uchida, and M. M. Wong, "Recovery of Metal Values from Industrial Slags by the Use of a Two-Phase Molten Electrolyte System," in Proceeding of the Third Mineral Waste Utilization Symposium, M. A. Schwartz, Ed., Cosponsored by the U.S. Bureau of Mines and IIT Research Institute, Chicago, Illinois, March 14-16, 1972, pp. 55-61.

27. Kohler, J. C., and A. J. Lincoln, "Spectrographic Method for the Quantitative Determination of 28 Elements in Palladium Sponge," Engelhard Ind. Tech. Bull., 10(3), 92-98 (1969).

28. Lyman, T., H. E. Boyer, P. M. Unterweiser, J. E. Foster, J. P. Hontas, and H. Lawton, Eds., Metals Handbook, Vol. I., Properties and Selections of Metals, 8th ed., American Society for Metals, Novelty, Ohio, 1961.

29. Morris, A. E., Professor of Metallurgical Engineering, University of Missouri, Rolla, personal communication, June 23, 1975.

30. Wesolowski, J. J., W. John, and R. Kaifer, "Lead Source Identification by Multi-Element Analysis of Diurnal Samples of Ambient Air," in Trace Elements in the Environment, Advances in Chemistry Series 123, E. L. Kothny, Ed., American Chemical Society, Washington, D.C., 1973, pp. 1-16.

31. Anonymous, Internal Report 1973 (on emissions from copper smelters and the Iron Ore Recovery Plant), International Nickel Company, Sudbury, Ontario, 1973.

32. Environmental Protection Agency Office of Air and Waste Management, Office of Air Quality Planning and Standards, Background Information for New Source Performance Standards: Primary Copper, Zinc, and Lead Smelters. Vol. 1. Proposed Standards, EPA-450/2-74-002a, National Technical Information Service, U.S. Department of Commerce, Springfield, Virginia, 1974.

33. Booz Allen Applied Research, Inc., A Study of Hazardous Waste Materials, Hazardous Effects and Disposal Methods. Vol. III, PB-221 467, U.S. Environmental Protection Agency, National Technical Information Service, Springfield, Virginia, 1973.

34. Nance, J. T., and K. D. Luedtke, "Lead Refining," in Air Pollution Engineering Manual, J. A. Danielson, Ed., Public Health Service Publication No. 999-AP-40, U.S. Department of Health, Education, and Welfare, Cincinnati, Ohio, 1967, pp. 300-305.

35. Powell, H. E., and L. W. Higley, Recovery of Zinc, Copper, Silver, and Iron from Zinc Smelter Residue, Report of Investigations 7754, Bureau of Mines, U.S. Department of the Interior, Washington, D.C., 1973.

36. Phillips, A. J., "The World's Most Complex Metallurgy (Copper, Lead and Zinc)," Transactions of the Metallurgical Society of AIME, 224, 657-668 (1962).

37. Nauert, R. L., "Cadmium Preparation at Blackwell," J. Metals, 1, 15-17 (1966).

38. Johnson, O. C., "Chapter 5. Refining Processes," in Silver. Economics, Metallurgy, and Use, A. Butts and C. D. Coxe, Eds., D. Van Nostrand Co., Inc., Princeton, New Jersey, 1967, pp. 78-94.

39. Carsillo, N. F., Manager Purchases and Sales Platinum-Group Metals, Engelhard Industries, personal communication, December 1973.

40. Martin, H., Martin Metals, Member of Precious Metals Commission of National Association of Secondary Metal Industries, personal communication, December 1973.

41. Addicks, L., "Chapter 19. The Statistics of Industrial Consumption," in Silver in Industry, L. Addicks, Ed., Reinhold Publishing Co., New York, New York, 1940.

42. U.S. Bureau of the Census, Census of Manufactures, 1972 INDUSTRY SERIES: Jewelry, Silverware, and Plated Ware, MC 72(2)-39A, U.S. Government Printing Office, Washington, D.C., 1974.

43. Ottinger, R. S., J. L. Blumenthal, D. F. Dal Porto, G. I. Gruber, M. J. Santy, and C. C. Shih, Recommended Methods of Reduction, Neutralization, Recovery, or Disposal of Hazardous Waste. Vol. V. National Disposal Site Candidate Waste Stream Constituent Profile Reports. Pesticides and Cyanide Compounds, TRW Systems Group for the U.S. Environmental Protection Agency, PB-224 584, National Technical Information Service, U.S. Department of Commerce, Springfield, Virginia, 1973.

44. Watson, M. R., Pollution Control in Metal Finishing, Noyes Data Corp., Park Ridge, New Jersey, 1973.

45. Eichenlaub, P. W., and J. Cox, "Disposal of Electroplating Wastes by Oneida, Ltd. V. Plant Operation," Sew. Ind. Wastes, 26, 1130-1135 (1954).

46. Eidsness, F. A., and P. B. Bergman, "The Treatment of Metal Plating Wastes at Sperry's Gainesville, Florida, Plant," Plating, 43, 1005-1007 (1956).

47. George, L. C., and A. A. Cochran, Recovery of Metals from Electroplating Wastes by the Waste-plus-waste Method, Bureau of Mines Solid Waste Research Program, Technical Progress Report 27, U.S. Department of the Interior, Washington, D.C., 1970.

48. Farnsworth, C. G., Report on the Trace Elements and Their Origin in a Metropolitan Waste Water Effluent, Board of Water Commissioners, Denver, Colorado (undated, 1969 or after).

49. Pavlovskii, V. K., I. V. Tunimanova, and V. A. Tsekhomskii, "Use of Radioactive Isotopes to Determine Silver Losses During the Founding of Glasses," Izv. Akad. Nauk SSSR, Neorg. Mater., 5(8), 1480-1481 (1969); Chem. Abstr., 71, 236-237 (1969).

50. Chiarenzelli, R. V., and E. L. Joba, "The Effects of Air Pollution on Electrical Contact Materials: A Field Study," J. Air Pollution Control, 16(3), 123- 127 (1966).

51. Duell, J. P., Jr., and K. H. Koeneke, "Chapter 25. Electrical Contacts Manufacture," in Silver. Economics, Metallurgy, and Use, A. Butts and C. D. Coxe, Eds., D. Van Nostrand Company, Inc., Princeton, New Jersey, 1967, pp. 354-371.

52. Chamer, E. S., "Chapter 27. The Use of Silver Brazing Alloys," in Silver. Economics, Metallurgy, and Use, A. Butts and C. D. Coxe, Eds., D. Van Nostrand Company, Inc., Princeton, New Jersey, 1967, pp. 386-408.

53. Weinstein, N. J., Waste Oil Recycling and Disposal, EPA-670/2-74-052, National Environmental Research Center, Office of Research and Development, U.S. Environmental Protection Agency, U.S. Government Printing Office, Washington, D.C., 1974.

54. Dmitrenko, V. E., V. S. Levinson, and V. V. Belostotskaya, "Distribution of Silver in Silver-Zinc Storage Cells," Elektrotekhnika, 1967 (8), 3 (1967); Chem. Abstr., 68, 3413 (1968).

55. Teller, H. L., and D. R. Cameron, "Preliminary Studies in the Disposition of Silver from Cloud Seeding," Water Resour. Bull., 8, 715-723 (1972).

56. Cannon, J., "Steel: The Recyclable Material," Environment, 15(9), 11-20 (1974).

57. Anonymous, "Coatings and Finishes News. Silk Screening Process Makes Auto Circuitry," Materials Eng., 80(4), 34 (1974).

58. Carrillo, F. V., M. H. Hibpshman, and R. D. Rosenkranz, Recovery of Secondary Copper and Zinc in the United States, Bureau of Mines Information Circular 8622, U.S. Department of the Interior, U.S. Government Printing Office, Washington, D.C., 1974.

59. Makar, H. V., P. J. Gallagher, and R. E. Brown, "Removal of Copper from Molten Ferrous Scrap," in Proceedings of the Third Mineral Waste Utilization Symposium, M. A. Schwartz, Ed., Cosponsored by the U.S. Bureau of Mines and IIT Research Institute, Chicago, Illinois, March 14-16, 1972, pp. 249-253.

60. Aleti, A., Senior Environmental Engineer, Midwest Research Institute, personal communication, June 1975.

61. Wilson, E. B., and D. J. Akers, "Chemical and Physical Characterization of Metropolitan Incinerator Refuse and Flyash," in Proceedings of the Second Mineral Waste Utilization Symposium, U.S. Bureau of Mines and IIT Research Institute, Chicago, Illinois, March 18-19, 1970, pp. 313-326.

62. Greco, J. R., "Analyzing by Categories U.S. Urban Refuse," Solid Wastes Management/Refuse Removal J., 17(11), 60, 62 (1974).

63. Pinta, M., Detection and Determination of Trace Elements, Distributor Daniel Davey and Co., Inc., New York, New York, 1966.

64. Cannon, H. S., and M. L. Smith, "Chapter 10. Recycling of Glass and Metals: Container Materials," in Recycling and Disposal of Solid Wastes. Industrial, Agricultural, Domestic, Ann Arbor Science Publishers Inc., Ann Arbor, Michigan, 1974, pp. 301-334.

65. Clark, T. P., "Determination of Trace Element Levels in Landfill Leachate by Ion-Exchange, X-Ray Spectrography," in Trace Substances in Environmental Health - VII, D. D. Hemphill, Ed., Proceedings of University of Missouri's 7th Annual Conference on Trace Substances in Environmental Health, June 12-14, 1973, Columbia, Missouri, University of Missouri, Columbia, Missouri, 1973, pp. 401-408.

66. Boyle, W. C., and R. K. Ham, "Biological Treatability of Landfill Leachate," J. Water Pollution Control Federation, 46(5), 860-872 (1974).

67. Chen, K. Y., and F. R. Bowerman, "Chapter 12. Mechanisms of Leachate Formation in Sanitary Landfills," in Recycling and Disposal of Solid Wastes. Industrial, Agricultural, Domestic, Ann Arbor Science Publishers Inc., Ann Arbor, Michigan, 1974, pp. 349-367.

68. Baum, B., and C. H. Parker, Solid Waste Disposal. Vol 1: Incineration and Landfill, Ann Arbor Science Publishers Inc., Ann Arbor, Michigan, 1974.

69. Buttermore, W. H., W. F. Lawrence, and R. B. Muter, "Characterization, Beneficiation and Utilization of Municipal Incinerator Flyash," in Proceedings of the Third Mineral Waste Utilization Symposium, M. A. Schwartz, Ed., Cosponsored by the U.S. Bureau of Mines and IIT Research Institute, Chicago, Illinois, March 14-16, 1972, pp. 397-410.

70. Parker, C. H., and B. Baum, "Chapter 5. Future for Solid Waste Utilization," in Solid Waste Disposal. Vol 2: Reuse/Recycle and Pyrolysis, Ann Arbor Science Publishers Inc., Ann Arbor, Michigan, 1974, pp. 133-173.

71. Hammond, W. F., J. T. Nance, and K. D. Luedtke, "Steel-Manufacturing Processes," in Air Pollution Engineering Manual, J. A. Danielson, Ed., Public Health Service Publication No. 999-AP-40, U.S. Department of Health, Education, and Welfare, Cincinnati, Ohio, 1967, pp. 241-270.

72. Varga, J., Jr., and H. W. Lownie, Final Technological Report on A System Analysis Study of the Integrated Iron and Steel Industry to Division of Process Control Engineering, National Air Pollution Control Administration, Department of Health, Education, and Welfare, Battelle Memorial Institute, Columbus Laboratories, Columbus, Ohio, 1969.

73. Sebesta, W., "Ferrous Metallurgical Processes," in Air Pollution, Vol. 3, 2nd ed., A. C. Stern, Ed., Academic Press, New York, New York, 1968, pp. 143-169.

74. Klinger, F. L., "Iron Ore," in Minerals Yearbook 1972, Vol. I, Metals, Minerals, and Fuels, Bureau of Mines, U. S. Department of the Interior, U.S. Government Printing Office, Washington, D.C., 1974, pp. 611-639.

75. American Metal Market, Metal Statistics 1974, Fairchild Publications, Inc., New York, New York, 1974.

76. Paulsen, P. J., R. Alvarez, and C. W. Mueller, "Spark Source Mass Spectrographic Analysis of Ingot Iron for Silver, Copper, Molybdenum, and Nickel by Isotope Dilution and for Cobalt by an Internal Standard Technique," Anal. Chem., 42(6), 673-675 (1970).

77. Howard, H., "Side Lights. America's Changing Steel Scene," Am. Metal Market, 82(19), 22, 24 (1975).

78. Bray, J. L., Ferrous Process Metallurgy, John Wiley and Sons, Inc., New York, New York, 1954.

79. Brar, S. S., D. M. Nelson, J. R. Kline, P. F. Gustafson, E. L. Kanabrocki, C. E. Moore, and D. M. Hattori, "Instrumental Analysis for Trace Elements Present in Chicago Area Surface Air," <u>J. Geophys. Res.</u>, <u>75</u>(15), 2939-2945 (1970).

80. Harrison, P. R., K. A. Rahn, R. Dams, J. A. Robbins, J. W. Winchester, S. S. Brar, and D. M. Nelson, "Areawide Trace Metal Concentrations Measured by Multielement Neutron Activation Analysis. A One Day Study in Northwest Indiana," <u>J. Air Pollution Control Assoc.</u>, <u>21</u>(9), 563-570 (1971).

81. Dams, R., J. A. Robbins, K. A. Rahn, and J. W. Winchester, "Quantitative Relationships among the Trace Elements over Industrialized N. W. Indiana," <u>Nucl. Technol. Environ. Pollution, Proc. Symp.</u>, <u>1970</u>, 139-157 (1971).

82. Effluent Guidelines Division, Office of Air and Water Programs, <u>Development Document for Proposed Effluent Limitations Guidelines and New Source Performance Standards for the Steel Making Segmentof the Iron and Steel Manufacturing Point Source Category</u>, U.S. Environmental Protection Agency, Washington, D.C., 1974.

83. Reno, H. T., and F. E. Brantley, "Iron," in <u>Minerals Facts and Problems</u>, Bureau of Mines Bulletin 650, U.S. Department of the Interior, U.S. Government Printing Office, Washington, D. C., 1970, pp. 291-314.

84. Bramer, H. C., "Pollution Control in the Steel Industry," <u>Environ. Sci. Technol.</u>, <u>5</u>(10), 1004-1008 (1971).

85. Gutow, B. S., "An Inventory of Iron Foundry Emissions," <u>Mod. Casting</u>, 61(1), 46-48 (1972).

86. Greenberg, J. H., "Systems Analysis of Emissions--The Iron Foundry Industry," <u>Chem. Technol.</u>, <u>1</u>(12), 728-736 (1971).

87. Giever, P. M., "Characteristics of Foundry Effluents," Preprint, American Foundrymen's Society, Presented at the Total Environmental Control Conference, Ann Arbor, Michigan, November 16-19, 1970; <u>Air Pollution Aspects of Emission Sources. Ferrous Foundries. A Bibliography with Abstracts</u>, EPA-450/1-74-004, U.S. Environmental Protection Agency, U.S. Government Printing Office, Washington, D.C., 1974, p. 2.

88. Sussman, V. H., "Nonmetallic Mineral Products Industries," in <u>Air Pollution</u>, Vol. 3, 2nd ed., A. C. Stern, Ed., Academic Press, New York, New York, 1968, pp. 123-142.

89. Effluent Guidelines Division, Office of Air and Water Programs, Development Document for Effluent Limitations Guidelines and New Source Performance Standards for the Cement Manufacturing Category, U.S. Environmental Protection Agency, U.S. Government Printing Office, Washington, D.C., 1974.

90. Resource Engineering Associates, State of the Art Review on Product Recovery, Water Pollution Control Research Series, 17070DJW11/69, Federal Water Pollution Control Administration, Department of the Interior, Washington, D.C., 1969.

91. Anonymous, New Silver Technology. Silver Abstracts from the Current World Literature, The Silver Institute, Washington, D:C., July 1974.

92. Levy, A., S. E. Miller, R. E. Barrett, E. J. Schulz, R. H. Melvin, W. H. Axtman, and D. W. Locklin, A Field Investigation of Emissions from Fuel Oil Combustion for Space Heating, American Petroleum Institute Project SS-5, Battelle Columbus Laboratories, Columbus, Ohio, 1971.

93. Bertine, K. K., and E. D. Goldberg, "Fossil Fuel Combustion and the Major Sedimentary Cycle," Science, 173(3993), 233-235 (1971).

94. Sokol, R. A., and D. A. Klein, "Responses of Soils and Soil Microorganisms to Silver Iodide Weather Modification Agents," J. Environ. Quality, 4(2), 211-214 (1975).

95. Kleinberg, J., W. J. Argersinger, Jr., and E. Griswold, Inorganic Chemistry, D. C. Heath and Company, Boston, Massachusetts, 1960.

96. Stumm, W., and H. Bilinski, "Trace Metals in Natural Waters; Difficulties of Interpretation Arising from Our Ignorance on Their Speciation," in Advances in Water Pollution Research, Proceedings of the Sixth International Conference held in Jerusalem, June 18-23, 1972, S. H. Jenkins, Ed., Pergamon Press, New York, New York, 1973, pp. 39-52.

97. Kharkar, K., K. Turekian, and K. Bertine, "Stream Supply of Dissolved Ag, Mo, Sb, Se, Cr, Co, Rb, and Cs to the Oceans," Geochim. Cosmochim. Acta, 32, 285-298 (1968).

98. Turekian, K. K., and M. R. Scott, "Concentrations of Cr, Ag, Mo, Ni, Co, and Mn in Suspended Material in Streams," Environ. Sci. Technol., 1, 940-942 (1967).

99. Taylor, F. B., "Trace Elements and Compounds in Waters," J. Am. Water Works Assoc., 63(11), 728-733 (1971).

100. Kopp, J. F., and R. C. Kroner, Trace Metals in Waters of the United States, U.S. Department of the Interior, Federal Water Pollution Control Administration, Cincinnati, Ohio, 1970.

101. Zemansky, G. M., "Removal of Trace Metals During Conventional Water Treatment," J. Am. Water Works Assoc., 66, 606-609 (1974).

102. Linstedt, K. D., C. P. Houck, and J. T. O'Connor, "Trace Element Removals in Advanced Wastewater Treatment Processes," J. Water Pollution Control Federation, 43(7), 1507-1513 (1971).

103. McCabe, L. J., "Trace Metals Content of Drinking Water from a Large System," presented at the Symposium on Water Quality in Distribution Systems, Division of Water, Air, and Waste Chemistry, American Chemical Society National Meeting, Minneapolis, Minnesota, April 13, 1969.

104. Page, A. L., Fate and Effects of Trace Elements in Sewage Sludge When Applied to Agricultural Lands. A Literature Review Study (Review Copy), Ultimate Disposal Research Program, Environmental Protection Agency, Cincinnati, Ohio, 1974.

105. Kehoe, R. A., J. Cholak, and R. V. Story, "A Spectrochemical Study of the Normal Ranges of Concentration of Certain Trace Metals in Biological Materials," J. Nutr., 19, 579-592 (1940).

106. Tipton, I. H., P. L. Stewart, and P. G. Martin, "Trace Elements in Diets and Excreta," Health Phys., 12(12), 1683-1689 (1966).

107. Burch, R. E., H. K. J. Hahn, and J. F. Sullivan, "Newer Aspects of the Roles of Zinc, Manganese, and Copper in Human Nutrition," Clin. Chem., 21(4), 501-520 (1975).

108. Furchner, J. E., C. R. Richmond, and G. A. Drake, "Comparative Metabolism of Radionuclides in Mammals. IV. Retention of Silver-110m in the Mouse, Rat, Monkey, and Dog," Health Phys., 15(6), 505-514 (1968).

109. Hill, W. R., and D. M. Pillsbury, Argyria, the Pharmacology of Silver, The Williams and Wilkins Co., Baltimore, Maryland, 1939.

110. Welch, J. R., "Silver," in <u>Minerals Yearbook 1971, Vol. I, Metals,</u> <u>Minerals, and Fuels</u>, Bureau of Mines, U.S. Department of the Interior, U.S. Government Printing Office, Washington, D.C., 1973, pp. 1073-1086.

111. <u>Year Book of the American Bureau of Metal Statistics</u>, 51st Annual Issue for the Year 1971, American Bureau of Metal Statistics, New York, New York, 1972.

112. Myers, W. M., "Cement Materials," in <u>Industrial Minerals and Rocks</u> <u>(Nonmetallics Other Than Fuels)</u>, The Committee on the Industrial Minerals Volume, Ed., The American Institute of Mining and Metallurgical Engineers, New York, New York, 1949, pp. 158-181.

VIII. PHYSIOLOGICAL EFFECTS OF SILVER AND ITS COMPOUNDS

Silver and silver compounds apparently do not pose serious environmental health problems in spite of the toxicity expected from threshold limit values established at 0.05 ppm in water and 0.01 mg/m^3 in air.[1/] Argyria in humans has resulted from medicinal applications and occupational exposure, and silver nitrate pencils have caused death in humans when taken orally.[2/]

Silver ion is very toxic to microorganisms and has been used as a water treatment procedure and antimicrobial medicinal. The action of silver ions at low concentrations seems to involve reversible bonding with sulfhydryl groups of enzymes or other active compounds at the cell surface.[3/]

Comenge and Guelbenzu are the only workers reporting an essential metabolic role for silver. They found that mulberry leaves which did not contain silver "failed to serve as food for the silkworm."[4/]

The physiological effects of silver on humans, animals, plants, and enzymes are discussed more fully in the following subsections.

A. Human Effects

Acute toxic effects of silver and silver compounds in humans, summarized in Table VIII-1, have resulted only from accidental or suicidal overdoses of medical forms of silver.

The most common noticeable effects of chronic human exposure to silver or silver compounds are generalized argyria, localized argyria, and argyrosis (argyria of the eye unless stated otherwise). The two most important causes of argyria are medicinal application of silver compounds and occupational exposure. Numerous case histories are summarized in Table VIII-2. Generalized argyria is a slate-gray pigmentation of the skin and hair caused by deposition of silver in the tissues. Additional manifestations of generalized argyria include: silver coloration of hair and fingernails, and blue halo around the cornea and in the conjunctiva. In localized argyria, only limited areas are pigmented.

1. Generalized argyria, localized argyria, and argyrosis:

a. Iatrogenic: Every silver compound in common chemical use has caused generalized argyria. Of 239 recorded cases of generalized therapeutic argyria analyzed by Hill and Pillsbury,[2/] 118 were caused by

353

silver nitrate and 28 by Argyrol (mild silver protein), the second most frequent causative agent. Only 19 were caused by intravenous injection of silver arsphenamine. Of 178 cases, in which the route was other than intravenous, 89 were caused by oral intake of silver and another 75 by administration to the nose and throat.

In cases of argyria, discoloration predominates about the face (especially the conjunctiva), hands, and fingernails. The concentration of silver in the skin from various parts of the body is the same, regardless of degree of pigmentation. In cases of argyria, silver is deposited in most body structures with the possible exception of nerve tissues and muscles. Silver accumulates in the blood vessels and connective tissue, as well as the skin, possibly as deposits of metallic silver or silver oxide.

There is no convincing evidence of central nervous system changes in humans receiving therapeutic silver. The two reports of true dermatitis resulting from medicinal silver compounds may have been a reaction to the complex molecules with which the silver was combined. Silver compounds, with the possible exception of silver oxide, are not absorbed through unbroken skin in significant amounts. Localized argyria of therapeutic origin is relatively rare, usually resulting from parenteral administration into a saccular appendage of the skin or repeated application to an ulcer.

Urethral application of Protargol for treatment of gonorrhea resulted in argyria after 2 days, the most sudden onset of argyria reported. Silver nitrate-impregnated compresses applied to abraded skin caused argyria 14 days after the treatment. In only two other cases did argyria result in less than 6 weeks after treatment.

Colloidal silver compounds have been widely used to treat upper respiratory infections, but the amount of silver absorbed and permanently retained by the respiratory tract has not been determined. The total safe period for nasal instillation of colloidal silver compounds is believed to be 3 to 6 months. Colloidal silver compounds in the nose interfere with normal ciliary activity.

Argyrosis involves all eye tissues except the optic nerve. Instillation of 0.25% silver nitrate for 3 weeks and instillation of 3 to 5% silver colloidal compounds for 5 to 10 weeks have produced argyrosis.[2/] An Italian physician who dyed his eyebrows, moustache, beard, and eyelashes with a silver dye for 25 years developed argyria in the conjunctiva of both eyes.[5/]

The gastrointestinal tract, especially the duodenal portion of the small intestine, is the most important site of absorption of silver.

b. Occupational exposure: Generalized argyria as an occupational disease was never common. It occurred almost exclusively among silver nitrate makers and is now disappearing due to improved work conditions. Some workers involved in mirror plating, glass bead silvering, silver Christmas cracker manufacturing, photographic plate manufacturing, silver mining, and packaging silver nitrate have developed argyria as a result of ingestion or inhalation of silver fulminate, nitrate, albuminate, and cyanide.[6] Bronchitis and emphysema have been described in workers with pulmonary argyria, but a cause-and-effect relationship has not been established.[7]

Argyrosis occurred in all cases of argyria caused by occupational exposure and was generally more pronounced than therapeutically produced argyrosis. Localized argyria is rare, usually resulting when silver compounds contact broken skin or mucous membranes.[2] It has occurred in workers who handle metallic silver in filing, drilling, polishing, turning, engraving, forging, soldering, or smelting operations. Local argyrosis has occurred in galvanizers, firecracker makers, silver mirror manufacturers, etc. Silver polishers exposed over long periods sometimes exhibit increased densities in their lung X-rays due to silver impregnation of the elastic membranes of the pulmonary vessels. Pigmentation occurs slowly in workers who develop localized argyria--50% of the workers have been employed 25 years or more. The time of the onset of pigmentation has varied from 2 to 38 years.[1,2]

In three cases, post-mortem examination showed that the distribution of silver in the tissues of persons having argyria resulting from occupational exposure was the same as the distribution of silver in tissues of those having therapeutic argyria.[2]

2. Toxicity:

a. Acute: No systemic pathology has been directly attributable to silver among workers occupationally exposed to it.[1] However, large doses of silver compounds may have serious effects (see Table VIII-1). For example, ingestion of 10 g silver nitrate is usually fatal.[2] Silver nitrate taken orally causes necrosis in the gastrointestinal tract. In the body, it may be precipitated by protein or chloride ion. Table salt (sodium chloride) is an antidote for silver nitrate poisoning. There is little likelihood of systemic effects, but it may cause degenerative liver changes.[8]

b. **Chronic**: Argyria or argyrosis is the most common effect
of chronic exposure to silver. Table VIII-2 summarizes many cases. Argyrosis of the cornea in workers who handle silver nitrate may be accompanied
by turbidity of the anterior lens capsule and a disturbance of dark adapta-
tion. Deposition of silver in the eye does not usually result in loss of
vision. Two silver nitrate workers afflicted with argyrosis of the lung
showed mild chronic bronchitis with silver impregnation in the walls of the
middle and upper region of the nasal mucosa. In a more severe case, the
bronchial mucous membrane also showed basal membrane deposits and some
squamous metaplasia. There was less evidence of phagocytosis than in the
nasal mucosa and no hazard of fibrosis. Pigmentation was comparable with
that of anthracosis and siderosis.[9]/

3. **Absorption, deposition and excretion of silver**:

a. **Absorption and deposition**: Silver found in the human
body has no known function and is suspected of being a contaminant.[10]/ Silve
may enter the body via the respiratory tract, the gastrointestinal tract,
mucous membranes, or broken skin. In most cases of argyria caused by occupational exposure, absorption has taken place via the respiratory tract or
at the eyes. Once deposited, silver is not liberated in amounts detectable
by spectrochemical methods.[1]/ Experimental evidence shows that radiosilver
particles are retained mainly by the reticulo-endothelial system.[9,11]/
Silver is transported within the body chiefly via the blood plasma, presumably in the form of silver chloride or silver albuminate,[2]/ and as expected is also found in the blood serum.[12]/ The amount of silver, its
chemical form, and the route by which it is administered affect the tissue
content and distribution of silver within the body.[13]/

Body absorption of silver resembles whole-body retention.
It is retained by all body tissues (see Table II-14). The primary sites
of deposition in persons who have never taken silver therapeutically are
the liver, skin, adrenals, lungs, muscle, pancreas, kidney, heart, and
spleen. Silver is also deposited in blood vessel walls, kidneys, testes,
pituitary, nasal mucous membrane, maxillary antra, trachea, and bronchi.[14]/
Although silver does not accumulate in the lungs with age, it was present
in 39% of the lungs from Americans analyzed by Tipton.[15]/ Examinations
of accidental death victims indicated that the silver content of the myo-
cardium, aorta, and pancreas tended to decrease with age.[16]/ Silver
accumulates in the body with age, however, even if none is administered
intentionally.[2]/

A striking feature of argyria is the regular deposition of silver
in blood vessels and connective tissue, especially around the face, conjunctiva, hands, and fingernails.[2]/ The silver-bearing particles in one
case of localized argyria of a photoprocessor were found to be silver

356

sulfide (Ag_2S), possibly contained in the mitochondria.[17] The silver-containing particles were sparsely distributed at the dermoepidermal junction of the papillary bodies adjacent to the epidermal portion of the sweat ducts. The silver had entered the skin via the sweat glands.[18]

In argyria, aside from the blood vessels and connective tissues, the skin, glomeruli of the kidney, choroid plexus, mesenteric glands, and thyroid contain the greatest amounts of deposited silver. The epitheleum is free of silver. Other tissues where deposition may occur include: bone marrow, pancreas, liver, spleen, testes, and ovaries.[2,14,19] The adrenals, lungs, dura mater, bones, cartilage, muscles, and nervous tissue are minimally or never involved as deposition sites for silver.[2]

Average human intake from the diet is estimated at up to 0.088 mg/day.[20] At that rate if 100% of the silver ingested is retained in the body, 31 years would be required to accumulate 1 g of silver. Based on the data of Tipton et al.[15] in Table II-14, the average silver content in wet tissue of normal Americans is about 0.05 ppm. The body of a 150-lb human, whose tissue content was 0.05 ppm would contain only 32 mg silver or 3.2% of a 31-year ingestion total. It would appear that very little of the silver ingested from nontherapeutic sources is actually retained in the body.

b. Excretion: Kehoe found only 0.06 mg/day eliminated in the feces, which was less than the 0.088 mg/day dietary intake of silver. Although silver was detected in the blood of normal Americans, Frenchmen, Mexicans, and Germans, it was not detected in their urine (see Table II-14).[20] Browning reports that almost all silver is excreted in the feces with only traces in the urine.[9] However, silver may be detected in urine in cases of silver poisoning.[21] Silver has also been detected in nasal and vaginal secretions.[22]

Analyses for silver were made on diets and excreta of a man (Subject B) and wife (Subject A) for 30 days. Subject B had a mean intake of 0.035 mg silver/day and Subject A 0.04 mg silver/day. Subject A drank five cups of coffee (not analyzed for silver content) per day, had a fecal/urinary silver excretion ratio of 3, and a positive average silver daily balance of 0.007 mg/day (2.6 mg/yr). Subject B drank three glasses of milk per day (analyzed for silver content), had a fecal/urinary excretion ratio of 8, and a negative average daily silver balance of 0.054 mg after 30 days.[23][a]

---

[a] Subject A retained 16% of the dietary silver she ingested, but Subject B excreted 2.5 times more silver than he ingested from his diet. (Both A and B excreted about the same amounts of silver in their urine.) Subject B was also in negative balance for copper, barium, and nickel. His medicine intake and occupation were not mentioned nor was the state of his dental restorations.

In a case of generalized argyria, there was very little excretion of silver over three different 7-day periods. Food intake included 0.7 mg silver/week. Fecal excretion was 1.3 to 2.3 mg silver/week. The negative balance was possibly due to desquamation of the silver pigmented alimentary tract cells.[9]

Administration of Ca EDTA, a common metal chelating agent, reportedly increases urinary excretion of silver. Ligating the bile duct in laboratory animals increased renal excretion while reducing fecal excretion by a factor of 10 thereby further demonstrating the biliary nature of silver excretion.[13] Radiosilver (^{110}Ag) iodide was removed from the blood 2 hr after intravenous administration and was slowly excreted through the bile and urine in a nonionic form.[11]

B. Animal Effects

1. Toxicity:

a. Acute: Table VIII-3 summarizes the effects of silver on aquatic animals, and Table VIII-4 summarizes effects on terrestrial animals. Concentrations as low as 0.004 ppm silver are toxic to some aquatic species (e.g., Daphnia, guppies, and sticklebacks). A gold-silver-cyanide complex proved more toxic to the fish Orizias latipes than hydrogen cyanide alone, perhaps causing a layer of mucous to cover the gill surfaces and resultant asphyxiation.[24] Swelling and breakdown of gill epithelium, possibly due to enzyme inhibition, have also been proposed as the mode of action.[13]

Silver affects aquatic species at many stages of development and affects behavior as well. For example, American oyster embryos fail to develop at silver nitrate concentration 0.0058 ppm and are killed at 0.01 ppm silver nitrate. Metallic silver has a toxic effect on sea urchin sperm and larvae. The cytolytic effect of metallic silver on Convoluta in a drop of water appears to be ameliorated by positioning the silver foil on tin.[25] The snails, Taphius glabratus and Australorbis glabratus, suffer distress--the inability to attach their feet, to feed, or to breathe atmospheric air at silver concentrations between 0.03 and 0.1 ppm.[26,27] Silver may retard the growth of fish in fresh water.[28] At concentrations of 0.1 to 0.5 ppm in soft water, silver is definitely injurious; however, it is less toxic in hard, alkaline waters of pH 7.5 to 9.5.[29]

Acute effects from silver in mammals are usually associated with intravenous administration. For example, silver nitrate has been used frequently since 1932 to produce acute pulmonary edema for study. Dogs injected with 0.5 cc of 10% AgNO$_3$/kg into the left ventricular wall or the pulmonary artery developed the edema, myocardial ischemia and lesion, hypertension, and swelling and necrosis of wall and endocardium. Genesis of pulmonary hypertension and edema by silver nitrate depends on its entering the pulmonary circuit, probably by stimulation of vagal terminations.[30/] Intravenous injections of silver nitrate in dogs produced hemodynamic disturbances resulting in pulmonary edema, with circulatory hypoxia causing death.[31/]

b. **Chronic**: The most important physiological effects of silver are those resulting from chronic exposure. Silver binds to proteins in mammalian plasma.[32/] Silver salts may alter membrane permeability. Erythrocytes in a 0.01 ppm silver solution have been shown to be permeable to potassium.[33/] At a silver ion concentration of 0.04 ppm, killifish show inhibited enzyme activity although they appear relatively healthy.[34/] Adult oysters and fish appear more resistant to elevated concentrations of silver than gametes, embryos, and fry.[29,35/]

Unlike mercury, silver is antagonistic to copper metabolism in chickens, cattle, and growing chickens.[36-38/] At 100 ppm in the diet, silver reduced growth in copper-deficient chicks, possibly by competing for a binding site on metallothionein.[39-41/]

Silver is also antagonistic to selenium and when fed in the diet will reduce the toxic effects associated with feeding abnormally high levels of selenium.[42-44/] Silver at 100 ppm in drinking water promoted liver necrosis characteristic of vitamin E and selenium deficiency in chicks.[45/] Silver is thought to modify selenium metabolism by a different mechanism than copper.[42/] Silver has an antagonistic effect on selenium and glutathione peroxidase in rat liver and erythrocytes.[43/] Ionic silver in the diet of vitamin E-deficient rats causes rapidly fatal hepatocellular necrosis and muscular dystrophy. Necrosis also occurred in the centrilobular area of the brain followed by necrosis of the nuclei, endoplasmic reticulum, and mitochondria.[46/]

Olcott suggests that chronic administration of silver salts in the diet of animals causes vascular hypertension.[9/] Rats given water containing 1,000 ppm silver salts had a higher incidence of hypertrophy of the left ventricle than did those receiving untreated water. No clinical symptoms of arteriosclerosis or other vascular lesions were observed; however, their life span was shortened.[47/]

Guyer and Mohs in 1933 and Walbaum in 1930 observed growth-promoting effects of silver in rodents.[48/] Although rats given subcutaneous injections of silver at 0.35 to 0.70 mg/100 g body weight showed no clinical symptoms of intoxication, they showed decreased threshold to the epileptogenic effect of electrical shock.[49] Rats administered 20 ppm silver in their drinking water showed increased DNA and RNA concentrations in the brain. After 12 months, however, DNA and RNA levels were reduced and brain dystrophy present. Other organs had different sensitivities to the effects of silver.[50]

Experiments with rabbits showed that silver-coated inert particles were phagocytized more slowly by alveolar macrophages than were carbon-coated particles.[51] Rabbits administered 0.25 and 0.025 mg silver per kg body weight showed histopathological changes in the vascular, nervous, and glial tissues of the encephalon and medulla. Conditioned reflexes and immunological activity were also impaired.[52] A silver protein (Protarg inhibited prostaglandin biosynthesis in bulls.[53]

It is thought that silver from silver iodide and other weather-modification agents is not likely to concentrate to harmful levels in either aquatic or terrestrial food chains.[28,54] (See Table II-11 on silver in waters.)

Silver is present in concentrations up to 16 ppm in the dry matter of marine and freshwater animals (see Table II-13). Silver has been detected in various cuts of beef, veal, pork, lamb, and mutton at levels of 0.004 to 0.024 ppm (see Table VIII-5).

c. Carcinogenic effects: Table VIII-6 summarizes the results of testing of silver for carcinogenic effects in mice and rats. Foil, platelets, and pellets made of silver or dental alloy when implanted under the skin of laboratory animals have caused sarcomas, malignant fibrosarcomas, fibromas, fibroadenomas, and invasions of muscle with connective tissue.[55-59] Silver may, however, act as a nonspecific irritant rather than as a specific carcinogen.[60] Intratumoral injections of colloidal silver also promoted cancer growth in rats, possibly by producing an area of lowered tissue resistance which allows resistant cancer cells to grow freely.[61]

2. Absorption, deposition, and excretion of silver:

a. Absorption and deposition: The hepatopancreas and nephridial organs of brachiopods, the mollusks, and arthropods, particularly Crustacea, accumulate heavy metals. The glandular tissue of the liver of fishes and all other vertebrates concentrates metals.[62] (See Table II-13.)

The Japanese eel, Anguilla japonica, and goldfish, Carassius auratus, accumulate silver selectively in the liver. The rate of silver uptake by these organisms was determined to be 1.2 to 4.2 x 10^{-7} mg/hr from a 0.74 ppm solution of radiosilver (^{110}Ag) sulfate.[63] Table VIII-7 summarizes tissue uptake data for other animals.

Marine animals accumulate silver in concentrations which are higher than their environment. Clams and scallops growing near municipal sewage sludge dumping sites accumulate higher concentrations of silver than do those growing where the concentrations of silver are lower.[64]

b. Excretion: Ligature and radioisotope tracing experiments using mice, rats, monkeys, and dogs have shown that silver is excreted through the bile and feces rather than the urine. The ratio of urinary-fecal excretion is 0.001 to 0.258.[9,11,13,65,66] Excretion of radiosilver (^{110}AgNO$_3$) was faster and a larger percentage of it was excreted when it was administered orally than when it was injected either intraperitoneally or intravenously. More than 90% of the carrier-free silver administered by any of these routes was excreted in the feces with at least 90% of the orally ingested silver not being absorbed.[13] Less than 0.1 to 0.2% of the carrier-free radiosilver administered intragastrically to rats by Cohen et al. was absorbed. Such results are inconclusive, however, because of the rapid elimination of carrier-free amounts.[67]

C. Plant Effects

1. Effects on microflora: Silver is toxic to bacteria and has been used as an antimicrobial in medicine and water purification. Reviews of the toxic effects of silver on bacteria and other microflora are found in References 68-70.

The heterotrophic activity of bacteria is reduced by 0.1 ppb silver ion.[71,72] The disinfectant action of silver is thought to result from metal-ion absorption coagulating the colloids of bacterial protoplasm.[68] Silver nitrate at a concentration 10 ppb killed 50% of the fungi Alternaria tenuis. The silver cations were assumed to form an unionized complex with surface ionogenic groups such as PO_4^{3-}, HS-, or CO_2H. Only osmium was more toxic to the fungus.[73] Some of the effects of silver on microflora are shown in Table VIII-8.

Russian scientists believe silver is the safest and longest lasting method for converting polluted waste into potable water on board orbiting space stations and spaceships. Water contaminated with 200 to 1,900 microbiological units of microorganisms usually is completely sterilized in 15 or 20 min with 100 to 200 ppb silver ion. After 24 to 72 hr, there is usually a complete absence of microorganisms.[74]

361

Silver may function as an algicide in swimming pools if chlorine, bromine, and iodine are not present. It prevents growth of the blue-green algae _Phormidium inundatum_, commonly found in swimming pools, at concentrations of 0.14 ppm silver nitrate or 0.08 ppm silver sulfate.[75] Silver and copper ion in conjunction proved to be a slightly more effective algicide than either ion alone when used against _Anabena flos-aqua_, _Anacystis_, and _Chlorella_. Silver ion in conjunction with copper ion was no more effective than copper ion alone against _Pediastrum_ or _Eudorina_.[76] Silver is less toxic to the green alga _Chlorella vulgaris_ than mercury but more toxic than copper, cadmium, chromium, nickel, lead, cobalt, or zinc.[77]

2. Effects on higher plants: All literature published prior to 1940 with regard to silver in relation to plants and plant disease control has been reviewed by Nielsen.[78] Silver is not a usual constituent of plants,[79] but Table II-12 lists the silver concentrations found in many plant species. Different plant communities do contain relatively constant amounts of silver.[54] Concentrators of silver include _Rosa kokanica_, _Lonceria_ spp., _Caulerpa prolifera_, _Clavulina cinerea_, _Spirea_, _Mentha_, yarrow, St. John's wort, _Ephedra gerardiana_, vetch (_Vicia_ spp.), _Dioscorea_ (roots only), and mushrooms.[80-83] Use of _Erigonium ovifolium_ (buckwheat family) led to discovery of several Montana silver deposits.[4] The difference between the maximum and minimum silver content in the plants studied by Horowitz et al. is a factor of 1,600.[82]

Marine and freshwater plants concentrate silver by a factor of 200. The silver concentrations of marine and freshwater plants, respectively, are approximately 0.0600 ppm and 0.0260 ppm.[84]

Radiosilver accumulates in the leaf margin of corn (_Zea mays_).[32] Silver is usually more concentrated in the seeds of flowering plants than in other parts of the plant. Whole wheat contains 0.4 ppm silver while wheat germ contains 0.8 ppm.[85] The ratio of silver to manganese varies with plant growth and development.[4]

Absorption of radiosilver by mint plants was slight and in a form not readily soluble in ethanol or methanol. The radiosilver present in the plant ash was almost completely extractable in hydrochloric acid.[4]

Toxic effects of silver on terrestrial plants are described in Table VIII-9. Bohn and Drzervina found that metallic silver stimulates root growth of watercress, onion, and other plants, but inhibits root growth of tobacco.[4]

Silver has lesser mutagenic effect on beet seedlings than tellurium, cadmium, or osmium but a greater mutagenic effect than titanium, tantalum, gold, palladium, and other metals.[81]

362

D. Enzyme Effects

Some effects of silver on enzymes have been mentioned in Section VIII.B.1.b.

Silver ions inhibit other enzymes such as α-chymotrypsin,[86,87] RNA polymerase,[88] tyrosinase,[89] glutamate dehydrogenase,[90] nicotinamide deamidase,[91] leucine aminopeptidase and ATPase (mast-cell enzymes),[92] isocitric dehydrogenase,[93] α-glucosidase (soil maltase),[94] fibrinolysin (plasmin),[95] yeast invertase (saccharase),[96] N-acetylhomocysteinyl ribonuclease,[97] cathepsin A,[98] trypsin (coinhibition with Pb^{2+}),[99] and glucose oxidase.[100] The inhibiting action of silver ions seems to be due to binding of sulfhydryl groups of some enzymes[19,37,90,101] but not in others.[95,96] In certain enzymes, binding is probably at a histidine imidazole group.[86,87,97] With glucose oxidase, silver ions compete with molecular oxygen as a hydrogen acceptor.[100]

The inhibition of tyrosinase, an enzyme involved in the series of reactions that converts tyrosine to melanin pigments, is accompanied by replacement of copper from the enzyme.[79,89] On the other hand, Buckley assumed the stain on the hands of a photoprocessor to be mostly melanin and supposed that the silver had reacted with the epidermal sulfhydryl groups to release inhibition of tyrosinase.[18] Furst states that when silver deposits in the skin, it displaces copper, releasing it to activate tyrosinase.[102]

Schroeder has concluded that silver concentrations in human tissues are so small that silver probably causes little, if any, inhibition in vivo.[79]

TABLE VIII-1

ACUTE TOXIC EFECTS OF SILVER ON HUMANS[2/]

How Administered	Dosage	Survival Time	Observed Effects	Remarks
i.v. Collargol	36 cc of 12% soln.	3-14 days	Purpura hemorrhagica on the 4th day. Death. Ag chiefly in the reticulo-endothelial system.	
i.v. Collargol	32 cc of 5% soln.	3-14 days	Extensive necrosis and hemorrhage of bone marrow, liver, and kidney.	
i.v. Collargol	To fill renal pelvis for X-ray study		Death. Severe hemorrhagic diathesis with parenchymatous hemorrhages in the stomach, intestines, and body cavities.	
i.v. Collargol	10 cc of 2% soln.	5 min	Cyanosis, coma; death due to pulmonary edema.	No Ag found in lungs.
Intravaginally	2 cc unknown concn. of AgNO$_3$		Death.	Abortion attempt. Death possibly not due to AgNO$_3$.
Oral	8 g AgNO$_3$ in soln.		Vomitus contained AgCl.	Patient recovered.
Oral	2-30 g AgNO$_3$	A few hr to a few days	Usually death at dosages > 10 g.	10 g is usually fatal, but 30 g has been survived.
Oral metallic Ag	50-260 g		Gastric fullness, anorexia, gastric pain, and/or diarrhea	

364

TABLE VIII-2

ARGYRIA

Observed Effect	Ag Compound	Exposure Conditions	Length of Exposure	Time Until Appearance of Argyria	Ag Intake or Total Dose	Ag Excretion	Remarks	Reference
Retention							Greatest in endothelial organs.	9
Argyria and other symptoms of Ag poisoning	Ag_2S, Ag_2SO_4, Ag_2O, $AgMnO_4$, $AgClO_4$, $AgCl$							103
Increased densities in lung X-rays	Ag particles	Silver polishers	Long periods				Ag impregnation of vascular elastic membranes	1
Localized argyria	Ag particles	Penetration of fine particles						1
Generalized argyria	Ag salts	Ingestion or inhalation of Ag salts						1
Argyrosis		$1\text{-}2$ mg Ag/m^3 in air during spraying operations in manufacturing Ag varnish and in silvering radio-tech. parts					11 were affected in upper respiratory passages. 9 in conjunctiva or cornea.	1
Generalized argyria, possibility of	Ag in air	Breathe 10 m^3 air/day; retention of 50% of Ag (assumed)	20 years		5-fold the recommended TLV, 0.05 mg/m^3, would lead to accumulation of 1.2 g Ag.		Hill and Pillsbury say 0.91-7.6 g Ag will cause argyria.	1, 2
Generalized argyria		Medication or industrial exposure			Lung and G.I. tract	Primarily in feces; only traces in urine.	Absorbed via G.I. tract or by dust inhalation.	9
Generalized argyria						Very slight, over 3 week-long periods.		9
Generalized argyria caused therapeutically					Food = 0.7 mg Ag/week	Urinary: -- Fecal: 1.3 to 2.3 mg/week	Possible desquamatization of Ag-pigmented alimentary tract cells.	9
Argyria - no recognizable health disturbances							Possible cause of kidney lesions with consequent dangers of arteriosclerosis and lung damage but not fibrosis.	9

365

TABLE VIII-2 (Concluded)

Observed Effect	Ag Compound	Exposure Conditions	Length of Exposure	Time Until Appearance of Argyria	Ag Intake or Total Dose	Ag Excretion	Remarks	Reference
Pulmonary argyria							Often have bronchitis and emphysema, but no cause-effect relationship has been established.	7
Lung pigmentation	Ag and Fe_2O_3	Worked as a silver finisher.					Due primarily to Fe, but Ag present.	104
Generalized argyria	$AgNO_3$	Administered orally to treat epilepsy and G.I. symptoms.	weeks to 20 years	E.g., 2 years after taking >600 g for 1.2 year	9 to > 1,000 g			2
Generalized argyria	Protargol	300-g soln. instilled into urethra daily	2 days	3 days				2
Generalized argyria	$AgNO_3$, stick	Local application for sore throat and tongue ulcers	0.5 to 20 years	E.g., 1 year (when used for 3 years)				2
Generalized argyria	Collargol	Administered orally to treat pulmonary tuberculosis	E.g., 5 years (260 g Ag)	1 year	50 to 530 g			2
Generalized argyria	Ag arsphenamine	i.v.	2 to 10 years	16 months to 9 years	6.3 to 53 g			2
Generalized argyria							201 cases from 1700 to 1939	2
Localized argyria							17 cases from 1700 to 1939	2
Argyrosis							57 cases from 1700 to 1939	2
Ind. argyrosis							12 cases from 1700 to 1939	2
Localized argyria of gums	Dental alloy	During preparation for a dental crown						105
Mottled pigmentation	AgC:CH	Explosion					Caused blue pigmentation	106

TABLE VIII-3

EFFECT OF SILVER ON AQUATIC ANIMALS

Organism	Developmental Stage	Ag Concentration and Form in Water[a]	Survival Time	Percent of Sample	Observed Effects	Remarks	References
Daphnia magna		0.0051 ppm Ag$^+$			Immobilization		107
Daphnia magna					Toxicity	Toxicities: Cu > Ag = Hg > Cd > Cr > Zn > Pb = Co	108 109
Daphnia		0.03 ppm Ag$^+$			Threshold toxicity		107
Microregma		0.03 ppm Ag$^+$			Threshold toxicity		107
Polycelis nigra (flatworm)		0.15 ppm Ag$^+$	4 days		Death	Temperature was 23 to 27°C.	107
Paracentrotus (Sea urchin)	eggs	0.01 to 0.1 ppm AgNO$_3$			Inhibited development	Ag toxicity 80x > Zn, 20x > Cu, 10x > Hg; adults not affected.	110 111
Taphius glabratus (snail)		0.05 to 0.1 ppm Ag$_2$SO$_4$			Distress	Inability to move, breathe, or feed.	26
Australorbis glabratus (snail)		0.05 to 0.1 ppm Ag$_2$SO$_4$			Distress	Inability to move, breathe, or feed.	27
Crassostrea virginica (American oyster)	embryo	0.0058 ppm AgNO$_3$		50	Failure to develop	Background concn. of Ag in seawater is 0.003 ppm	35
Crassostrea virginica	embryo	0.01 ppm AgNO$_3$		100	Lethal	Embryos may be more sensitive to Ag than are the larvae. Adults seem fairly resistant.	35
Guppies		0.0043 ppm AgNO$_3$		50	Lethal		112
Fundulus heteroclitus (Mummichog or killifish)	3.5 to 5 cm	0.04 ppm Ag$^+$ in seawater	96 hr	~50	Complete inhibition of xanthine oxidase	Three other liver enzymes, acid and alkaline phosphatase, and catalase were inhibited by at least 50%.	34
Eels	young	0.2 ppm AgNO$_3$	> 25 hr		Tolerated		29
Sticklebacks	large	0.1 ppm Ag$^+$	1 day		Death	Jones (1938, 1939).	29, 107
Sticklebacks	large	0.02 ppm Ag$^+$	2 days		Death	Jones (1938, 1939).	29, 107
Sticklebacks	large	0.01 ppm Ag$^+$	4 days		Death	Jones (1938, 1939).	29, 107
Sticklebacks	large	0.004 ppm Ag$^+$	7 days		Death	Jones (1938, 1939).	29, 107

367

TABLE VIII-3 (Concluded)

Organism	Developmental Stage	Ag Concentration and Form in Water [a]	Survival Time	Percent of Sample	Observed Effects	Remarks	References
Sticklebacks	large (30 to 50 mm)	0.003 ppm Ag^+	~ 10 days		Lethal concn. limit	Jones (1938, 1939).	29
Sticklebacks	small (18 to 20 mm)	0.003 ppm Ag^+	25 to 30 days		Lethal concn. limit	Jones (1938, 1939).	29
Sticklebacks		0.004 ppm Ag^+			Toxicity in soft water	Jones (1947).	110
Salmon (Chinook)	fry	0.044 ppm $AgNO_3$	48 hr		Definitely toxic	Ag^+, Cu^{2+}, and Hg^{2+} all highly toxic.	29
Salmon (Chinook)	fry	0.04 ppm $AgNO_3$	48 hr	some but not all	Death	In tap water.	112
Salmon (Chinook)	fry	0.44 ppm $AgNO_3$	48 hr		Decidedly toxic		112
Salmon (Chinook)	fry	0.033 ppm $AgNO_3$	48 hr		Survived		112
Lepomis macrochirus Rafinesque (Bluegill)	wt. 2.94 ± 0.97 g length 5.80 ± 0.63 in.	0.070 ppm Ag^+	Tolerated 6 months		Accumulated Ag in concentrations greater than in the water. E.g., 9 to 12x increase over controls. Gill Ag concn. 4, 20, and 120 times controls at 0.0009, 0.004, and 0.070 ppm Ag^+.	The tap water was moderately hard, 180 mg/ℓ (70% $CaCO_3$ and noncarbonate forms). pH 7.5, sulfate 133 mg/ℓ. Fish were acclimatized 5 months in the lab prior to the experiment. Controls had 0.0003 ppm Ag^+. Ag^+ uptake apparently via gills via active transport. Ag^+ depressed Zn levels in experimental animals.	110
Lepomis macrochirus Rafinesque (Bluegill)	wt. 2.94 ± 0.97 g length 5.80 ± 0.63 in.	0.007 ppm and 0.0009 ppm Ag^+	Same as controls		Same as controls		110
Micropterus salmoides, Lacepede (Largemouth Bass)	wt. 9.6 ± 2.3 g length 9.7 ± 0.7 in.	0.007 ppm and 0.0009 ppm Ag^+	Similar to controls		Slight growth suppression	Same as above.	110
Micropterus salmoides, Lacepede (Largemouth Bass)	Same as above.	0.070 ppm Ag^+	Toxic ≤ 24 hr		Dying fish appeared to have respiratory problems. Gills reddened. Body tremors. Erratic swimming. No mucus on gills.	Same as above.	110
Orizias latipes		0.2 ppm $AgNO_3$	> 25 hr		Tolerated		29

a/ 1 ppm Ag_2SO_4 = 0.7 ppm Ag^+, 1 ppm $AgNO_3$ = 0.6 ppm Ag^+.

TABLE VIII-4

EFFECT OF SILVER ON TERRESTRIAL ANIMALS

Organism	Developmental Stage	How Administered	Dosage	Survival Time	Percent of Sample	Observed Effects	Remarks	References
Nematode Pratylenchus penetrans			0.01-0.1 ppm			Toxic		113
Vertebrates and Invertebrates		i.v.				First: leg weakness, nervous dysfunction, loss of voluntary movement, convulsions, contractures, and paralysis. Secondly: respiratory embarrassment.		2
Various		i.v. Ag_2O	≤ 4 cc 1.52 g Ag_2O/ℓ t.i.d. for 3 weeks			No apparent toxicity.		2
Various		Instillation, externally, i.p., orally	Ag_2O soln. or 5% ointment			No toxic effects or argyrial pigmentation.		2
Cats, rabbits, guinea pigs, frogs, and pigeons		s.c. $Ag_2S_2O_3$	5 cc of 1% Ag hyposulfite soln.			Similar to above.	Results similar to strychnine.	2
Frog		i.v.				Convulsions before respiratory paralysis. Heart arrest in diastoles probably caused by paralysis of the exciting nerve supply.	Congestion and edema probably caused by paralysis of the central vasomotor system, particularly of the vasomotor pulmonary fibers aided by cardiac paralysis.	2
Chickens (White Plymouth Rock)	Young chicks	Ag_2SO_4 in feed	0-200 ppm			Growth suppression.	Adding Cu to diet prevented growth depression.	36
Chickens	Young chicks: Cu deficient	In feed	100 ppm			Reduced growth.	Diet deficient in Cu (Cu < 1 ppm, Zn ~ 25 ppm). Ag acts as a Cu antagonist.	39 41
Chickens	Young chicks	In feed	50 ppm			Increased mortality	Same as above.	41
Chickens	Young chicks	In feed	10 ppm			Reduced hemoglobin concentration and elastin content of aorta.	Same as above. Effects completely overcome by addition of Cu to feed.	41

369

TABLE VIII-4 (Continued)

Organism	Developmental Stage	How Administered	Dosage	Survival Time	Percent of Sample	Observed Effects	Remarks	References
Chickens	Chicks: Vitamin E-deficient	$AgNO_3$ in drinking water	1,500 ppm			Ag is a pro-exudative factor and synergizes with Se when methionine is limited. Growth suppression.	Ag is also a pro-hemorrhagic factor. Ag causes dietary stress.	44
Chickens	Baby chicks	Aerosol	0.4 mg Ag^+/min (200 ppm Ag^+ in H_2O) (max. 10 ppb in air)			Cured Salmonella pullorum-gallinarum and Escherichia coli infection.	No adverse effect on chicks. The bacteria developed resistance to the bactericide 2 to 3 times more slowly than to neomycin alone.	114
Mammals						Affected circulation in the bulbar vasomotor center with intial stimulation and increase of arterial pressure. Paralysis followed.		2
Rats		Injected Ag lactate containing 2Y pituitary extract	0.2 cc of 5% soln./200 g body wt.			Reduced the antidiuretic activity of the pituitary extract.	Action similar to Hg, Au, and Pd. Unlike that of Zn, Cd, and Ni.	115
Rats		s.c.	0.35 or 0.7 mg/100 g body wt.			Decreased threshold of electrical stimulation of epileptiform convulsions.	No clinical symptoms of intoxication.	49
Rats	Vitamin E-deficient	AgOAc in drinking water	1,500 ppm Ag^+	2-4 weeks		Liver necrosis and death in Vitamin E-deficient animals.	Effect prevented by 120 ppm D-α-tocopheryl acetate. Partially prevented by 1 ppm Se. Stress probably raises tocopherol requirement. Results inconsistent with Ag stress being a pro-oxidant effect.	116
Rats	3 months old	Electrolytic Ag^+ in drinking water	0.5 mg Ag^+/ℓ for 6 months			Slight stimulatory effect on the organism.		50
			2.0 mg Ag^+/ℓ for 12 months			Less pronounced effects than 20.0 mg/ℓ.		50
			20.0 mg Ag^+/ℓ for 6 months			After 6 months DNA and RNA concentrations in the brain increased. DNA and RNA decreases and dystrophy observed 12 months later.	Rat organs had different sensitivities to the chronic administration of Ag. Liver was less affected than the brain.	50

TABLE VIII-4 (Continued)

Organism	Developmental Stage	How Administered	Dosage	Survival Time	Percent of Sample	Observed Effects	Remarks	References
Rats	8.3% casein diet	In drinking water or diet	130-1,000 ppm			Liver necrosis which could be prevented by adding Vitamin E.	3 ppm cyanocobalamin and 0.05 ppm Se prevented necrosis at 130 ppm Ag. 1,000 ppm Ag not neutralized by 1 ppm Se.	44
Rats		2.0 ppm in Kata-dynized drinking water	0.050 mg/100 g body wt.			No abnormalities of internal organs. No granules in kidneys.	Equivalent to 37 mg/100 kg body wt.	68
Rats		O-Silver ointment and solutions				Little penetration compared with amount of Ag in normal skin.		68
Rats		Feeding Ag salts				Hypertrophy of right ventricle (presumably associated with Ag deposition in kidneys which thickens the basement membranes of the glomeruli).	Olcott believes the chronic feeding of Ag^+ causes vascular hypertension.	9 47 117
Rats		Fed $AgNO_3$ for long periods	0.1% $AgNO_3$ or AgCl in 1:300 soln. of $Na_2S_2O_3$			Not lethal. Intense pigmentation of many tissues.		68
Rats		Fed	6 mg/kg/day			At 12 weeks, kidney and liver impregnated. At 3 months, Ag content reduced. At 6 months, none in kidney, traces in liver.	NO_3^- from $AgNO_3$ caused nephrosis in argyrial rats.	68
Rats		$AgNO_3$ s.c. in tail or scalp				More $AgNO_3$ stored at site than with Ag lactate. Translocation from scalp slower than from tail.	Removal by liver and blood highest for soluble compounds.	68
Rats		s.c. injection $AgNO_3$	7 mg/kg body wt.			Affected testis histology and spermatogenesis. Peripheral tubules affected and some central tubules completely degenerated after 18 hr. Some tubules recover. Duct system seldom fully recovers.	Marked deformation of tubules at head of epididymis. Epithelial cells appeared swollen. Spermatogenesis active.	118
Rabbits		i.v.	50 cc daily of 0.25 g/1,000 cc colloidal Ag			Weight loss.		2
Rabbits		i.v.				Pulmonary edema.	No changes in heart.	2

371

TABLE VIII-4 (Continued)

Organism	Developmental Stage	How Administered	Dosage	Survival Time	Percent of Sample	Observed Effects	Remarks	References
Rabbits		i.v. Cryptargol	1-3 cc soln. contg. 0.1 g Ag/cc	4-48 hr		Congestion of kidneys, tubular swelling, and/or glomerular necrosis.		2
Rabbits		i.v. Cryptargol daily	0.6 cc soln. contg. 0.1 g Ag/cc			No albumin or casts in urine.	Administered for 71 days.	2
Rabbits		i.v. Ag arsphenamine (14.5% Ag)	66.7 mg/kg for 47 to 70 days. 10 mg/kg for 47 to 70 days			More Ag retained by animals losing weight. Most showed a gradual increase in hemoglobin and red blood cells. No toxic effects or discoloration.	Minimum dosage 277 mg in 47 days. Maximum dosage 2,363 mg in 70 days.	2
Rabbits		i.p. AgNO₃	20 mg/kg in neutral soln.	2 hr		Death in coma. Degenerative aspects and Ag granules in liver parenchyma and kidney tubules.	No abnormalities in heart, lungs, brain, or adrenals.	119
Rabbits		In drinking water	0.25 and 0.025 mg/kg/day for 11 months			Marked effect on immunological capacity. Histopathological changes of nervous, vascular, and glial tissues of the encephalon and medulla. Affected conditioned reflexes.	No effect on hemoglobin, RBC, differential WBC, proteinogenic function of liver or on serum SH groups.	52 120
Rabbits		In drinking water	0.0025 mg/kg body wt.			None	In maritime and other circumstances, Ag⁺ used for water preservation should not exceed 0.05 mg/ℓ which corresponds to ~ 0.0025 mg/kg body wt.	52
Rabbits		Urine-soaked paper pulp on abraded skin				No increase in Ag content of organs.	0-Silver paper for use in disposable diapers.	68
Guinea pig		2 ml i.p. AgNO₃	0.239 M AgNO₃	1-7 days		Death.		121
Guinea pig		i.v. daily for 2 months colloidal Ag	1 or 2 cc of 0.25 g/1,000 cc colloidal Ag soln.			No symptoms.		2

372

TABLE VIII-4 (Continued)

Organism	Developmental Stage	How Administered	Dosage	Survival Time	Percent of Sample	Observed Effects	Remarks	References
Guinea pig		$AgNO_3$ to 3.1 cm^2 skin	0.239 M aqueous soln. $AgNO_3$				Absorption rate = 157 mμM Ag/ cm^2/hr.	121
Guinea pig ear skin (cultured in vitro)		$AgNO_3$ in culture medium	1.25 mg/ml			23% respiratory inhibition.	After 24 hr.	122
			2.5 mg/ml			48% respiratory inhibition.		122
			5.0 mg/ml			54% respiratory inhibition.		122
			10.0 mg/ml			83% respiratory inhibition.		122
			8.7 mg/ml			50% respiratory inhibition.		122
		Ag 2,2-dinaphthyl-methanedisulfonate	0.054 mg/ml			50% respiratory inhibition.		122
		$AgNO_3$	3.16 mg/ml			50% respiratory inhibition.		122
Dogs		i.v. Ag albuminate	0.03 g	< 0.5 hr		Death.		2
Dogs		i.v. $Ag_2S_2O_3$	0.2 g in 60 cc H_2O			Death in convulsive seizures, pulmonary edema.	At lower dosages: anesthesia and paralysis of hind legs followed by increased bronchial secretion and asphyxial death.	2
Dogs		i.v. $AgNO_3$				Death due to mechanical asphyxia.		2
Dogs		i.v. $AgNO_3$	32 mg			Death.		2
Dogs		i.v. Argyrol	3 mg/kg	18 hr		Death despite regular respiration while in coma.		2
Dogs		i.v. Argyrol	4-5 mg/kg			Also had edema of lungs and intestinal hemorrhages.		2
Dogs		i.v. Colloidal Ag	100 mg			Hemolysis.		2
Dogs		$AgNO_3$ placed directly in stomach	2.3-2.6 g	A few days if vomiting is impeded.		Death if vomiting prevented.		2

373

TABLE VIII-4 (concluded)

Organism	Developmental Stage	How Administered	Dosage	Survival Time	Percent of Sample	Observed Effects	Remarks	References
Dogs		Fed AgNO$_3$	10 mg/day			Variable. Some animals: diarrhea, marasmus, and death. Corrosive effect on G.I. tract.		2
Dogs		Oral - daily AgNO$_3$	97 mg			Diarrhea. Appetite loss, drowsiness, and reduced urine volume with prolonged administration.		2
Dogs		i.v. Collargolum	500 mg	24 hr		Death, hemolysis, lung edema	A dog given 2,600 mg Collargol over 4 months in doses of 20 to 600 mg died after the last injection of 600 mg.	123
Dogs		i.v. Collargol	1,300-1,500 mg over 3-7 days			Tolerated.		123
Dogs		i.v. Collargol	200-300 mg			Well tolerated		123
Dogs		i.v. Collargolum (1% emulsion of Ag)	500 mg	12 hr		Pulmonary edema, anorexia, profound anemia, active hyperplastic bone marrow.	Also had weight loss and weakness.	9
Dogs		i.v. Collargolum (?)				Chronic effects: hyperplasia of bone marrow, anemia without leucocytosis or platelet deficiency		9
Dogs		i.v. colloidal Ag	200 cc daily of 0.25 g/1,000 cc colloidal Ag			Slight hypertension for 10 min after injections.		2
Horses		i.v. (?)	AgNO$_3$			Death, hemorrhage and thrombi of heart and kidneys.		2

TABLE VIII-5

SILVER IN MEATS

Type of Meat	Ag Content, ppm	Reference
Bovine	av. 0.013	124
Rib eye (choice)	0.007	125
Rib eye (good)	0.017	125
Rib eye (commercial)	0.020	125
Rib eye (utility)	0.024	125
Rib eye (canner)	0.010	125
Rib eye (cutter)	0.007	125
Rib eye (bull)	0.004	125
Veal round (200 lb)	0.017	124
Veal round (milk fed)	0.010	124
Porcine		
Loin (female)	0.007	124
Loin (male)	0.010	124
Ham (female)	0.009	124
Ham (male)	0.012	124
Ovine		
Leg of lamb	0.006	124
Leg of ewe	0.011	124

TABLE VIII-6

SILVER TESTED FOR CARCINOGENICITY[57,126-128]

Investigators	Animal	Strain or Type	Sex	Preparation and Dose	Site and Route	Animals with Tumors	Survival	Duration of Experiment
				Silver Nitrate				
Daels, 1923	Mice	-	-	Impregnated thread	Through skin	0	-	150 days
O'Connor, R. J., 1954	Mice	White	-	Fused crystals	Colonic mucosa, through anus	0[a]	50% survived operation	≤ 35 days
Frei, J. V., and Stephens, P., 1968	25 Mice	Swiss inbred, 6-10 weeks old	M	10% in distd. water, 2/week for ≤ 50 days	Top ears	0[b]		50 days
				Metallic Silver				
Hanzlik and Presho, 1923	2 Pigeons	-	-	0.6 and 1.6 g Ag granules/kg	Gizzard	0	-	88 days
McDonald, D. F., and Huffman, P. G., 1955	13 Rats	Long Evans	M		Implanted in bladder	0		8 weeks
Nothdurft, H., 1955	Mice			Disks 12 x 0.02 mm	Implanted 6 s.c. on back, 4 i.p. 2 s.c. on abdomen	1 Sarcoma		
Nothdurft, H., 1955	Rats	Wistar		Disks 17 x 0.02 mm	Implanted 6 s.c. on back, 4 i.p. 2 s.c. on abdomen	5 Sarcomas		
Nothdurft, H., 1956	84 Rats			17 mm disk implanted (8 per animal)	s.c.	65 Sarcomas		23 months
Oppenheimer, B. S., et al., 1956	25 Rats	Wistar	M	2 pieces of foil, 1.5 cm wide	Imbedded, s.c., abdominal wall	14 (32%) (fibrosarcomas at site of imbedding)		At least 625 days
Nothdurft, H., 1958	35 Rats	Wistar	M&F	Fragments 1 x 1 x 0.02 mm	s.c.	0	24 at 18th month	At least 29 months

a/ Induced necrosis; healing in 35 days.
b/ Induced 100% epithelial hyperplasia.

TABLE VIII-7

SILVER DISTRIBUTION IN ANIMAL TISSUES

Organism	Organ	Form of Ag	10 min	30 min	1 hr	3 hr	6 hr	24 hr	2 days	7 days	Dosage	Remarks	References
White mice	Blood	$110Ag^{125}I$	19.7%		13.5%	15.2%	44.3%	0	0	0	0.2 ml i.v. of 50-60 µg/ml in tail vein	Ag also found in lungs, kidneys, small intestine, intestine, bladder, muscle, testes, and brain.	66
	Liver		65.6%		48.3%	40.7%		30.9%	20.0%	10.1%			
	Spleen		0.35%		0.70%	0.60%		0	0	0			
	Stomach		0.51%		0.92%	1.25%		0	0	0			
	Thyroid				0.02%	0		0.01%	0	0			
	Bone		0.42%		0.31%	0.51%	0.93%	0	0	0			
	Total		86.58%		63.75%	58.32%	45.25%	30.91%	20.0%	10.1%			
White mice	Blood	$110Ag^{82}Br$		0.82%	1.12%			0.56%			0.2 ml i.v. of 50-60 µg/ml in tail vein	Results indicate Ag is released in an insoluble form and not as Ag^+. Radiosilver is slowly excreted through bile and urine.	66
	Liver			58.7%	63.6%			26.1%					
	Spleen			0.34%	0.18%			2.09%					
	Stomach			0.73%	0.57%			0.41%					
	Thyroid				-			-					
	Bone			0.21%	0.14%			0.45%					
	Total			60.80%	65.61%			23.61%					
Rats	Lungs	$110AgNO_3$ at pH 5.0 in 0.05 M acetate buffer				Found							66
	Kidneys					Found							
	Heart					Found							
	Pancreas					Found							
	Small intestine					Found							
	Large intestine					Found							
	Bladder					Found							
	Muscles					Found							
	Testes					Found							
	Brain					Found							
Rats	Blood	$AgNO_3$ and $^{64}Cu(NO_3)_2$ injected into in vivo ligated segments of the G.I. tract.									0.01 µmoles Cu^{2+} in 0.4 ml distd. H_2O with 1.5, 3.0, and 6.0 µmoles Ag^+	Ag had little effect on uptake of Cu except that a significantly greater proportion of Cu was deposited in the liver and significantly less retained by the blood in Ag-treated rats.	19
	Heart												
	Kidneys												
	Liver												
	Spleen												
Rodents (organs listed in order of decreasing Ag concentration)	Spleen > Liver > Bone marrow > Muscle > Skin	i.v. injection of colloidal Ag										Gammill (1950)	9
Cat	Inflamed tissue of brain	$111AgNO_3$										Accumulates in inflamed tissue not in healthy or necrotic areas.	68
Goldfish (Carassius auratus) and Japanese eel (Anguilla japonica)	Liver	$110m-110Ag$									0.74 ppm	Liver concentrates Ag much more than other tissues. Absorption via gills: $1.2-4.2 \times 10^{-7}$ mg/hr.	63

Note: the rat group with $110AgNO_3$ shows distribution "Found" at 2 hr.

Table VIII-8

EFFECT OF SILVER ON MICROFLORA

Organism	How Ag Administered	Ag Concentration	Observed Effect	Remarks	Reference
Yeast	In growth medium	0.22 ppm	Growth reduced 50%.	Molasses and malt wort in medium reduced the effect of Ag.	129
Yeast	In growth medium	0.4 ppm	Growth arrested.	Molasses and malt wort in medium reduced the effect of Ag.	129
Heterotrophic bacteria	In culture medium	0.001-0.01 ppm Ag_2SO_4	Erratic uptake of ^{14}C-glucose and reduced counts.	At 0.001 and 0.00001 ppm Ag, bacterial counts were unaffected within 0.5 hr of treatment.	72
Bacteria	Sterilizing dose	0.040 ppm $\longrightarrow$ 2.4 $\times 10^{14}$ Ag^+/ml	Sterilization.	1 Ag^+ ion will kill 1 bacterium.	68
Soil microorganisms				Toxicities: $Ag^+ > Hg^{2+} > Cd^{2+} > Ni^{2+} > Zr >$ $Tl^+ > Pb^{2+} > Be > Cr^{3+} > Ba^{2+} > Sr^{2+} > Li^+$	108
Microorganisms	In brewery and perfumery	$\geq$ 0.015 ppm	Prevents cloudiness; improves taste.	Affects acid-ester ratio of alcoholic liquids.	68
Aerobic microbes		ppb level	Toxic to some.	Ag and other metals may interfere with aerobic digestion.	130
Bacteria, yeasts and fungi	In H_2O substrate	0.001-1.200 ppm	Lethal.	Lethal time 2-24 hr.	131
Bacteria, yeasts and fungi	In fruit juices, must, bullion, serum, or vinegar	0.050-20 ppm	Lethal.	Lethal time 2-24 hr.	131
Water microorganisms	--	0.5-2.0 ppm	Complete sterilization.		132
Bacterium tabacum	As antimicrobial on tobacco seeds		Toxic.	Toxicity of Ag $\approx$ Hg. Commonly used tobacco seed treatment. Toxicity of Hg > Ag in proteinaceous compounds, but toxicity of Ag $\geq$ Hg in inorganic compounds. Toxicity positively correlated with solubility of compound.	78
Phycomycetes spp.			Toxic.		78
Ascomycetes spp.			Toxic.		78
Basidiomycetes spp.			Toxic.		78
Fungi imperfecti			Toxic.		78
Botrytis paeoniae			Toxic.		78
Pestalotia stellata			Toxic.		78
Uronyces caryophyllinus			Toxic.		78
Sclerotinio americana			Toxic.		78
Alternaria solani spores		100 ppm	Lethal.		78
Alternaria solani		12.5 ppm	Inhibition of spore generation.		78
Escherichia coli		0.006 ppm	Death in 2-24 hr.		107

TABLE VIII-8 (Concluded)

Organism	How Ag Administered	Ag Concentration	Observed Effect	Remarks	Reference
Pseudomonas aeruginosa	$AgNO_3$ compresses	0.5% $AgNO_3$	Control infection of burns.		122
Pseudomonas spp.		0.08 ppm $AgNO_3$	Prevented growth.		133
Ascularis teraptera (intestinal parasite)		100 ppm in tap water, 1.0 ppm in distilled water	Ovicidal within 24 hr.	Sometimes found in swimming pools. Ag^+ the most effective ovicide currently used. Sunlight and heat increase the ovicidal activity of Ag.	134
Enterobius vermicularis (intestinal parasite)		100 ppm in tap water, 1.0 ppm in distilled water	Ovicidal within 24 hr.		134
Salmonella pullorum-gallinarum (infected baby chicks)	In two 0.5-hr ionic aerosol treatments	0.4 mg Ag^+/min in 200 ppm Ag^+ in H_2O (max. 10 ppb in air)	Similar to neomycin. No observed side effects. No reoccurrence in 2 weeks.	Microbes developed resistance to Ag 2-3x more slowly than to neomycin alone.	114
Aspergillus spp.		0.5 ppm	Completely inhibited growth.		133
Candida utilis		0.09 ppm	Completely inhibited growth.		133
Escherichia coli	In culture medium	0.1-0.5 ppm	Complete sterilization.	Death after 1 hr.	132
Bacillus mesentericus spores	Katadynized quartz sand		Did not kill the spores.		68
Mycobacterium spp.		0.01 ppm	Completely inhibited growth.		133
Chlorella vulgaris (alga)	In liquid culture		Temporary increase in respiration.	Followed by prolonged respiratory inhibition.	136
Zooglea ramigira		10 ppm	Toxic.		136

379

TABLE VIII-9

EFFECT OF SILVER ON TERRESTRIAL PLANTS

Organism	Developmental Stage	How Administered	Dosage	Observed Effects	Remarks	Reference
Barley	Seeds	In water	Dilute $AgNO_3$ soln.	Toxic		78
Wheat	Seeds	In water	Dilute $AgNO_3$ soln.	Toxic		78
Peas	Seeds	In water	Dilute $AgNO_3$ soln.	Toxic	Due to seed coat permeability.	78
Cruciferae spp.	Seeds	In water	Dilute $AgNO_3$ soln.	Toxic		78
Wheat	Seedlings	In water	Various concns. Ag^+	Damaged		78
Lupine	Seedlings	In water	Various concns. Ag^+	Damaged		78
Lupine			4.9 ppm	Fatal		107
Peas	Seedlings	In water	Various concns. Ag^+	Damaged		78
Corn	Seedlings	In water	Various concns. Ag^+	Damaged		78
Maize			9.8 ppm	Fatal		107
Tomato	Seedlings	In water	> 20 ppm Ag	Seriously injured		78
Gypsophila	Seedlings	In water	> 20 ppm Ag	Seriously injured		78
Snapdragons	Seedlings	In water	> 20 ppm Ag	Seriously injured		78
Tomato	Young plants	Spray	100-1,000 ppm $AgNO_3$	Toxic	Wetting agents increased toxic effect of spray.	78
Bean	Young plants	Spray	100-1,000 ppm $AgNO_3$	Toxic		78
Apple	Mature trees	Spray	Inorganic Ag compd.	Russeting of fruit	Leaves appeared normal.	78

380

BIBLIOGRAPHY. SECTION VIII.

1. Committee on Threshold Limit Values, Documentation of the Threshold Limit Values for Substances in Workroom Air, 3rd ed., American Conference of Governmental Industrial Hygienists, Cincinnati, Ohio, 1971.

2. Hill, W. R., and D. M. Pillsbury, Argyria, the Pharmacology of Silver, The Williams and Wilkins Company, Baltimore, Maryland, 1939.

3. Cooper, C. F., and W. C. Jolly, Ecological Effects of Weather Modification: A Problem Analysis, School of Natural Resources, University of Michigan, Ann Arbor, Michigan, 1969.

4. Boyle, R. W., "Geochemistry of Silver and Its Deposits with Notes on Geochemical Prospecting for the Element," Geol. Surv. Can., Bull., No. 160, 1-264 (1968).

5. Wall, F. E., "Chapter 21. Bleaches, Hair Colorings, and Dye Removers" in Cosmetics: Science and Technology, E. Sagarin, Ed., Interscience Publishers, Inc., New York, New York, 1957, pp. 479-530.

6. Schwartz, L., L. Tulipan, and S. M. Peck, Occupational Diseases of the Skin, Lea and Febiger, Philadelphia, Pennsylvania, 1947.

7. Gafafer, W. M., Ed., Occupational Diseases, a Guide to Their Recognition, U.S. Department of Health, Education, and Welfare, Public Health Service, U.S. Government Printing Office, Washington, D.C., 1964.

8. Dreisbach, R. H., Handbook of Poisoning, 4th ed., Lange Medical Publications, Los Altos, California, 1963.

9. Browning, E., Toxicity of Industrial Metals, Butterworths, London, 1961, pp. 62-267.

10. Schroeder, H. A., Pollution, Profits and Progress, The Stephen Greene Press, Brattleboro, Vermont, 1971.

11. Anghileri, L. J., "In Vivo Breakdown of Insoluble Halides," Acta Isotop., 9(4), 347-356 (1969); Chem. Abstr., 74, 148 (1971).

12. Plaut, D., "Timely Topics in Clinical Chemistry: Toxicology and Trace Metals II," Am. J. Med. Technol., 35 (10), 652-658 (1969).

13. Furchner, J. E., C. R. Richmond, and G. A. Drake, "Comparative Metabolism of Radionuclides in Mammals. IV. Retention of Silver-110m in the Mouse, Rat, Monkey, and Dog," Health Phys., 15 (6), 505-514 (1968).

14. Sax, N. I., "Silver--Silver Thioarsenite," Dangerous Properties of Industrial Materials, 2nd ed., Reinhold Publishing Corporation, New York, New York, 1963, pp. 1174-1178.

15. Tipton, I. H., and M. J. Cook, "Trace Elements in Human Tissue. Part II. Adult Subjects from the United States," Health Phys., 9, 103-145 (1963).

16. Bala, Yu, V. M. Lifshits, S. A. Plotko, G. I. Aksenov, and L. M. Kopylov, "Age Level of Trace Elements in the Human Body," Tr., Voronezh. Gos. Med. Inst., 64, 37-44 (1969); Chem. Abstr., 13, 155 (1970).

17. Buckley, W. R., C. F. Oster, and D. W. Fassett, "Localized Argyria. II. Chemical Nature of the Silver Containing Particles," Arch. Dermatol., 92, 697-705 (1965).

18. Buckley, W. R., "Localized Argyria. I. Chemical Nature of the Silver Containing Particles," Arch. Dermatol., 88, 531-539 (1963).

19. Van Campen, D. R., "Effects of Zinc, Cadmium, Silver and Mercury on the Absorption and Distribution of Copper-64 in Rats," J. Nutr., 88 (1), 125-130 (1966).

20. Kehoe, R. A., J. Cholak, and R. V. Story, "A Spectrochemical Study of the Normal Ranges of Concentration of Certain Trace Metals in Biological Materials," J. Nutr., 19, 579-592 (1940).

21. Sunderman, F. W., Jr., "Atomic-Absorption Spectrometry of Trace Metals in Clinical Pathology," Human Pathol., 4 (4), 549-582 (1973).

22. Barsegyants, L. O., "Differentsirovaniye Vydelenii Chelovecheskogo Organizma putem Emissionnogo Spectral'nogo Analiza" ["Discrimination of Human Excretions by Emission Spectrography"], Sudebno-Med. Ekspertiza, Min. Zdravookhr. SSSR, 10 (4), 30-34 (1967); Chem. Abstr., 68, 5533 (1968).

23. Tipton, I. H., P. L. Stewart, and P. G. Martin, "Trace Elements in Diets and Excreta," Health Phys., 12 (12), 1683-1689 (1966).

24. Doudoroff, P., G. Leduc, and C. R. Schneider, "Acute Toxicity to Fish of Solutions Containing Complex Metal Cyanides, in Relation to Concentrations of Molecular Hydrocyanic Acid," Trans. Am. Fish. Soc., 95, 6-22 (1966).

25. Drzewina, A., and G. Bohn, "Action Antagoniste de l'Argent et de l'Etain Metalliques sur les Êtres Vivants" ["Antagonistic Action of Metallic Silver and Tin on Living Organisms"], Compt. Rend., 183, 571-572 (1926).

26. Harry, H. W., and D. V. Aldrich, "The Distress Syndrome in Taphius glabratus (Say) as a Reaction to Toxic Concentrations of Inorganic Ions," Malacologica, 1, 283-289 (1963).

27. Harry, H. W., and D. V. Aldrich, "The Ecology of Australorbis glabratus in Puerto Rico," Bull. World Health Organ., 18, 819-832 (1958).

28. Anonymous, Trace Elements in Water. A Bibliography, Office of Water Resources Research, U.S. Department of the Interior, PB 201 266, National Technical Information Service, Springfield, Virginia, 1971.

29. Doudoroff, P., and M. Katz, "Critical Review of Literature on the Toxicity of Industrial Wastes and Their Components to Fish. II. The Metals, as Salts," Sewage Ind. Wastes, 25, 802-839 (1953).

30. Sales Luis, A., and C. Silva Duarte, "Experimental Study on the Pathogenesis of Acute Pulmonary Edema. I. Pulmonary Edema Induced by Silver Nitrate," Mal. Cardiovasc., 1, 39-49 (1960); Chem. Abstr., 56, 10801g (1962).

31. Mazhbich, B. I., "Some Problems in Pathogenesis of Pulmonary Edema Provoked by Silver Nitrate. III. The Mechanism of Death of Experimental Animals," Byull. Eksptl. Biol. i Med., 50 (8), 70-75 (1960); Bull. Exptl. Biol. and Med., 50 (8), 821-824 (1961); Chem. Abstr., 55, 11657c (1961).

32. Bowen, H. J. M., Trace Elements in Biochemistry, Academic Press Inc., New York, New York, 1966.

33. Danielli, J. F., and J. T. Davies, "Reactions at Interfaces in Relation to Biological Problems," Advan. Enzymol., 11, 35-89 (1951).

34. Jackim, E., J. M. Hamlin, and S. Sonis, "Effects of Metal Poisoning on Five Liver Enzymes in the Killifish (Fundulus heteroclitus)," J. Fisheries Res. Board Can., 27, 383-390 (1970).

35. Calabrese, A., R. S. Collier, D. A. Nelson, and J. R. MacInnes, "The Toxicity of Heavy Metals to Embryos of the American Oyster Crassostrea virginica," Marine Biol., 18, 162-166 (1973).

36. Hill, C. B., B. Starcher, and G. Matrone, "Mercury and Silver Interrelationships with Copper," _J. Nutr._, 88, 107-110 (1964).

37. Evans, G. W., P. F. Majors, and W. E. Cornatzer, "Mechanism for Cadmium and Zinc Antagonism of Copper Metabolism," _Biochem. Biophys. Res. Commun._, 40 (5), 1142-1148 (1970).

38. O'Dell, B. L., and B. J. Campbell, "Chapter II. Trace Elements: Metabolism and Metabolite Function," in _Comprehensive Biochemistry, Vol. 21, Metabolism of Vitamins and Trace Elements_, M. Florkin, and E. H. Stotz, Eds., Elsevier Publishing Company, New York, New York, 1971, pp. 179-26

39. Davis, G. K., "'Competition Among Mineral Elements Relating to Absorption by Animals,' Geochemical Environment in Relation to Health and Disease, _Ann. N.Y. Acad. Sci._, 199, 62-69 (1972).

40. Underwood, E. J., _Trace Elements in Human and Animal Nutrition_, Academic Press, New York, New York, 1971.

41. Hill, C. H., and G. Matrone, "Chemical Parameters in the Study of In Vivo and In Vitro Interactions of Transition Elements," _Federation Proc._, 29 (4), 1474-1481 (1970).

42. Jensen, L. S., "Interactions of Silver and Copper with Selenium in Chicks Abstract No. 2738), _Federation Proc._, 33 (No. 3, Part 1), 694 (1974).

43. Swanson, A. B., P. A. Wagner, H. E. Ganther, and W. G. Hoekstra, "Antagonistic Effects of Silver and Tri-o-cresyl Phosphate on Selenium and Glutathione Peroxidase in Rat Liver and Erythrocytes" (Abstract No. 2733), _Federation Proc._, 33 (No. 3, Part 1), 693 (1974).

44. Bunyan, J., A. T. Diplock, M. A. Cawthorne, and J. Green, "Vitamin E and Stress. VIII. Nutritional Effects of Dietary Stress with Silver in Vitamin E-Deficient Chicks and Rats," _Brit. J. Nutr._, 22 (2), 165-182 (1968).

45. Ganther, H. E., P. A. Wagner, M. L. Sunde, and W. G. Hoekstra, "Protective Effects of Selenium Against Heavy Metal Toxicities," in _Trace Substances in Environmental Health. VI_, D. D. Hemphill, Ed., Proceedings of University of Missouri's 6th Annual Conference on Trace Substances in Environmental Health, June 13-15, 1972, Columbia, Missouri, 1973, pp. 247-252.

46. Grasso, P., R. Abraham, R. Hendy, A. T. Diplock, L. Goldberg, and J. Green, "The Role of Dietary Silver in the Production of Liver Necrosis in Vitamin E Deficient Rats," _Exptl. Mol. Pathol._, 11, 186-199 (1969).

47. Olcott, C. T., "Experimental Argyrosis. IV. Morphological Changes in the Experimental Animal," Am. J. Pathol., 24, 813-833 (1948).

48. Tietz, N. W., E. F. Hirsch, and B. Neyman, "Spectrographic Study of Trace Elements in Cancerous and Noncancerous Human Tissues," J. Am. Med. Assoc., 165, 2177-2187 (1957).

49. Fedotov, D. D., L. M. Dondysh, S. E. Petrenko, and L. V. Kochetkova, "Effect of Silver Ions on the Threshold of Electroconvulsions," Tr. Gos. Nauch.-Issled. Inst. Psikhiat., 52, 281-285 (1968); Chem. Abstr., 71, 185 (1969).

50. Kharchenko, P. D., G. D. Berdishev, P. Z. Stepanenko, and O. O. Velikoivanenko, "Zmina Vmistu Nukleinovikh Kislot u Golovnomu Mozku i Pechintsi Shchuriv pri Trivalomu Vvedenni Ioniv Sribla z Pitnoyu Vodoyu" ["Change in the Nucleic Acid Level in Rat Brain and Liver During Long-Term Introduction of Silver Ions with Drinking Water"], Fiziologichnii Zhurnal Akademii Nauk. Ukrains'koi RSR, 19, 362-368 (1973).

51. Camner, P., P.-A. Hellström, and M. Lundborg, "Coating 5 μ Particles with Carbon and Metals for Lung Clearance Studies," Arch. Environ. Health, 27 (5), 331-333 (1973).

52. Barkov, G. D., and L. I. El'piner, "O Neobkhodimosti Ogranicheniya Kolichestva Serebra v Pit'evoi Vode" ["The Need for Limiting the Silver Content of Drinking Water"], Gigiena i Sanit., 33 (6), 16-21 (1968).

53. Deby, C., Z. M. Bacq, and D. Simon, "In Vitro Inhibition of the Biosynthesis of a Prostaglandin by Gold and Silver," Biochem. Pharmacol., 22, 3141-3143 (1973).

54. Anonymous, "Silver Iodide from Cloud Seeding Posed No Ecological Threat," Chem. Eng. News, 52 (10), 14 (1974).

55. Williams, D. R., "Metals, Ligands, and Cancer," Chem. Rev., 72 (3), 203-213 (1972).

56. Becker, T., E. Margraf, H. Oswald, B. Schyra, and K. Winnefeld, "Behavior of Metallic Foreign Bodies in Animals," Wiss. Chir.-Tag. Deut. Demokrat. Repub., 6th, 2, 1722-1727 (1966 [pub. 1967]); Chem. Abstr., 70, 199 (1969).

57. Oppenheimer, B. S., E. T. Oppenheimer, I. Danishefsky, and A. P. Stout, "Carcinogenic Effect of Metals in Rodents," Cancer Res., 16, 439-441 (1956).

58. Fujita, S., "Silver-Palladium-Gold Alloys Carcinogenicity and Acid Muco-
    polysaccharides in the Induced Tumors," Shika Igaku, 34 (6), 918-932
    (1971); Chem. Abstr., 77, 110 (1972).

59. Habu, T., "Histopathological Effects of Silver-Palladium-Gold Alloy
    Implantation on the Oral Submucous Membranes and Other Organs,"
    Shika Igaku, 31 (1), 17-48 (1968); Chem. Abstr., 69, 8885 (1968).

60. Cannon, H. L., and H. C. Hopps, Eds., Environmental Geochemistry in
    Health and Disease, The Geological Society of America, Inc., Boulder,
    Colorado, 1971.

61. Guyer, M. F., and F. E. Mohs, "Rat Carcinoma and Injected Colloidal
    Platinum," Arch. Pathol., 15, 796-817 (1933).

62. Vinogradov, A. P., The Elementary Chemical Composition of Marine Organisms
    Sears Foundation for Marine Research, Yale University, New Haven,
    Connecticut, 1953.

63. Hibiya, T., and M. Oguri, "Gill Absorption and Tissue Distribution of
    Some Radionuclides (Cr-51, Hg-203, Zn-65 and Ag-110m. 110) in Fish,"
    Bull. Japan Soc. Sci. Fish., 27, 996-1000 (1961).

64. Anonymous, "EPA Finds Ocean Dumping Causing Build-Up of Metals in Some
    Maryland Shellfish," Toxic Mater. News, 2(3), 24 (1975).

65. Kalistratova, V. S., A. G. Kogan, and M. D. Kozlova, "Behavior of [111]Ag
    in Animals," Raspredel. Biol. Deistvie Radioaktiv Izotop., Sb. Statei,
    146-151 (1966); Chem. Abstr., 67, 4852-4853 (1967).

66. Anghileri, J., "In Vivo Breakdown of Insoluble Halides," Acta Isotop.,
    9 (4), 347-356 (1969).

67. Anonymous, Public Health Service Drinking Water Standards, HEW Publica-
    tion 956, U.S. Department of Health, Education, and Welfare, Washington,
    D.C., 1962.

68. Romans, I. B., "Chapter 24. Oligodynamic Metals," in Disinfection, Steri-
    lization, and Preservation, C. A. Lawrence and S. S. Block, Eds., Lea
    and Febiger, Philadelphia, Pennsylvania, 1968, pp. 372-400.

69. Romans, I. B., "Chapter 28. Silver Compounds," in Disinfection, Steri-
    lization, and Preservation, C. A. Lawrence and S. S. Block, Eds., Lea
    and Febiger, Philadelphia, Pennsylvania, 1968, pp. 469-475.

70. Woodward, R. L., "Review of the Bactericidal Effectiveness of Silver," J. Am. Water Works Assoc., 55, 881-886 (1963).

71. Albright, L. J., and E. M. Wilson, "Sublethal Effects of Several Metallic Salts--Organic Compounds Combinations Upon the Heterotrophic Microflora of a Natural Water," Water Res., 8, 101-105 (1974).

72. Albright, L. J., J. W. Wentworth, and E. M. Wilson, "Technique for Measuring Metallic Salt Effects Upon the Indigenous Heterotrophic Microflora of a Natural Water," Water Res., 6, 1589-1596 (1972).

73. Somers, E., "Plant Pathology: Fungitoxicity of Metal Ions," Nature, 184 (4684), 475-476 (1959).

74. Anonymous, "Silver Cleans Up Polluted Water," The Silver Institute Letter, 3 (7), 3 (1973).

75. Fitzgerald, G. P., Algicides, University of Wisconsin Water Resources Center, PB 198 130, National Technical Information Service, Springfield, Virginia, 1971.

76. Young, R. G., and D. J. Lisk, "Effect of Copper and Silver Ions on Algae," J. Water Pollution Control Federation, 44(8), 1643-1647 (1972).

77. Ishizaka, O., Y. Ito, and S. Yamamoto, "Determination of the Toxicity of Food Additives by Their Effects on the Life Cycle of Chlorella. I. Cultures and Method," Nagoya Shiritsu Daigaku Yakugakubu Kenkyu Nempo, 14, 66-78 (1966); Chem. Abstr., 68, 20598h (1968).

78. Nielsen, L. W., and L. M. Massey, "Chapter 17. Silver as a Fungicide," in Silver in Industry, L. Addicks, Ed., Reinhold Publishing Company, New York, New York, 1940.

79. Schroeder, H. A., "Possible Relationships Between Trace Metals and Chronic Diseases," in Metal-Binding in Medicine, M. J. Seven and L. A. Johnson, Eds., J. B. Lippincott Company, Philadelphia, Pennsylvania, 1960, pp. 59-67.

80. Flerova, T. P., and V. E. Flerov, "Experiment on Biochemical and Geobotanical Prospecting in the Dzungarian Ala Tau," Materialy po Geol. i Polezn. Iskop. Yuzhn. Kazakhstana (Alma-Ata: Akad. Nauk Kaz. SSR), Sb., 1964(2), 144-152 (1964); Chem. Abstr., 62, 1435e (1965).

81. Lück, H., and S. W. Souci, "Lebensmittel--Zusatzstoffe und Mutagene Wirkung. II. Mutagene Stoffe in unserer Nahrung, [Food Additives and Mutagenic Action. II. Mutagenic Materials in Our Foods"], Z. Lebensm.-Untersuch. u.-Forsch., 107, 236-256 (1958); Chem. Abstr., 52, 11302c (1958).

82. Horovitz, C. T., H. H. Schock, and L. A. Horovitz-Kisimova, "The Content of Scandium, Thorium, Silver, and Other Trace Elements in Different Plant Species," _Plant Soil_, 40, 397-403 (1974).

83. Dawson, R. F., "Basaltic Ash as an Agricultural Substratum in Guatemala," in _Trace Substances in Environmental Health - VIII_, D. D. Hemphill, Ed., Proceedings of University of Missouri's 8th Annual Conference on Trace Substances in Environmental Health, University of Missouri, Columbia, Missouri, June 11-13, 1974, pp. 115-118.

84. Chapman, W. H., H. L. Fisher, and M. W. Pratt, _Concentration Factors of Chemical Elements in Edible Aquatic Organisms_, UCRL-50564, Lawrence Livermore Laboratory, University of California, Livermore, California, 1968.

85. Kent-Jones, D. W., and A. J. Amos, _Modern Cereal Chemistry_, 5th ed., The Northern Publishing Company, Ltd., Liverpool, England, 1957.

86. Berezin, I. V., Kh. Vill, and K. Martinek, "Reversible Inactivation of α-Chymotrypsin Observed in the Case of Interaction of Cu^{2+} and Ag^{+} Metal Cations With the Imidazole Group of the Histidine Residue as the Active Center," _Dokl. Akad. Nauk SSSR_, 175 (1), 230-233 (1967); _Chem. Abstr._, 67, 7456 (1967).

87. Martinek, K., Kh. Vill, Z. A. Strel'tsova, and I. V. Berezin, "Structure of the α-Chymotrypsin Active Site as Revealed from a Kinetic Investigation of the Inhibitory Effect of Silver Ions," _Mol. Biol._, 3 (4), 554-565 (1969); _Chem. Abstr._, 71, 38 (1969).

88. Novello, F., and F. Stirpe, "Effects of Copper and Other Ions on the Ribonucleic Acid Polymerase Activity of Isolated Rat Liver Nuclei," _Biochem. J._, 111 (1), 115-119 (1969); _Chem. Abstr._, 70, 40 (1969).

89. Degawa, T., "The Inhibiting Effect of Heavy Metals on the Formation of Melanin," _Nippon Hifukagakki Zasshi_, 71, 651-669 (1961); _Chem. Abstr._, 61, 12261a (1964).

90. Rogers, K. S., "Protein Fluorescence and Inactivation of Glutamate Dehydrogenases During Treatment with Silver," _Enzymologica_, 36 (3), 153-160 (1969); _Chem. Abstr._, 70, 32 (1969).

91. Curti, B., and G. Porcellati, "Properties of Nicotinamide Deamidase of Pigeon Liver Extracts," _Giorn. Biochim._, 12 (1), 13-27 (1963); _Chem. Abstr._, 59, 663e (1963).

388

92. Keller, R., "The Histochemistry of the Esterase of Mast Cells," Schweiz. Med. Wochschr., 93, 1504-1505 (1963); Chem. Abstr., 62, 6881f (1965).

93. Kratochvil, B., S. L. Boyer, and G. P. Hicks, "Effects of Metals on the Activation and Inhibition of Isocitric Dehydrogenase," Anal. Chem., 39 (1), 45-51 (1967); Chem. Abstr., 66, 3323 (1967).

94. Kiss, I., and I. Péterfi, "Inhibiting the Activity of Soil Maltase," Pochvovedenie, 1960 (8), 84-86 (1960); Chem. Abstr., 55, 866i (1961).

95. Kowalski, E., Z. Latallo, and S. Niewiarowski, "Plasminogen and Plasmin. II. Influence of Metal Ions on Plasmin Activity," Acta Biochem. Polon., 3, 109-118 (1956); Chem. Abstr., 51, 10703c (1957).

96. Myrbäck, K., and E. Willstaedt, "Inhibition of Yeast Invertase (Saccharase) by Metal Ions," Arkiv Kemi, 11, 275-283 (1957); Chem. Abstr., 51, 16693e (1957).

97. Hough, D. W., and S. Shall, "Inhibition of Enzymically Active N-Acetyl-homocysteinyl Ribonuclease by Silver Ions," FEBS (Fed. Eur. Biochem. Soc.) Lett., 8 (5), 243-246 (1970); Chem. Abstr., 73, 35 (1970).

98. Misaka, E., and A. L. Tappel, "Inhibition Studies of Cathepsins A, B, C, and D from Rat Liver Lysosomes," Comp. Biochem. Physiol. B, 38 (4), 651-662 (1971); Chem. Abstr., 74, 51-52 (1971).

99. Berezin, I. V., Yu.V. Savin, and K. Martinek, "Two-Component Inhibition as a Method for Studying of Enzyme Active Center Flexibility," FEBS (Fed. Eur. Biochem. Soc.) Lett., 14 (3), 178-180 (1971); Chem. Abstr., 75, 53-54 (1971).

100. Nakamura, S., and Y. Ogura, "Mode of Inhibition of Glucose Oxidase by Metal Ions," J. Biochem. (Tokyo), 64 (4), 439-447 (1968); Chem. Abstr., 70, 34 (1969).

101. Christensen, G. M., "Effects of Metal Cations and Other Chemicals Upon the In Vitro Activity of Two Enzymes in the Blood Plasma of the White Sucker," Chem.-Biol. Interactions, 4 (5), 351-361 (1972).

102. Furst, A., The Chemistry of Chelation in Cancer, Charles C. Thomas, Springfield, Illinois, 1963.

103. Stecher, P. G., Ed., The Merck Index, 8th ed., Merck and Company, Inc., Rahway, New Jersey, 1968.

104. Johnstone, R. T., and S. E. Miller, <u>Occupational Diseases and Industrial Medicine</u>, W. B. Saunders Company, Philadelphia, Pennsylvania, 1960.

105. Burton, R. M., "The Case of the Mysterious Tattoo," <u>J. Dent. Child.</u>, <u>34</u>, 114 (1970).

106. Orentreich, N., and H. H. Pearlstein, "Traumatic Tattoo Due to Silver Salt," <u>Arch. Dermatol. (Chicago)</u>, <u>100</u>, 107-108 (1969).

107. Cooper, C. F., and W. C. Jolly, "Ecological Effects of Silver Iodide and Other Weather Modification Agents: A Review," <u>Water Resources Res.</u>, <u>6</u> (1), 88-98 (1970).

108. Lisk, D. J., "Trace Metals in Soils, Plants, and Animals," in <u>Advances in Agronomy</u>, Vol. 24, Academic Press, New York, New York, 1972, pp. 267-325.

109. Warnick, S. L., and H. L. Bell, "The Acute Toxicity of Some Heavy Metals to Different Species of Aquatic Insects," <u>J. Water Pollution Control Federation</u>, <u>41</u>, 280-284 (1969).

110. Coleman, R. L., and J. E. Cearley, "Silver Toxicity and Accumulation in Largemouth Bass and Bluegill," <u>Bull. Environ. Contamination Toxicol.</u>, <u>12</u> (1), 53-61 (1974).

111. Bradford, G. R., "Trace Elements in the Water Resources of California," <u>Hilgardia</u>, <u>41</u> (3), 45-53 (1971).

112. McKee, J. E., and H. W. Wolf, Eds., <u>Water Quality Criteria</u>, 2nd ed., Publication 3-A, California State Water Resources Control Board, 1963 (Reprint January 1973).

113. Pitcher, R. S., and D. G. McNamara, "Toxicity of Low Concentrations of Silver and Cupric Ions to 3 Species of Plant-Parasitic Nematodes," <u>Nematologica</u>, <u>18</u>, 385-390 (1972).

114. Anonymous, "Worldwide Silver Technology in New Publication," <u>The Silver Institute Letter</u>, <u>4</u> (5), 1-2 (1974).

115. Dodds, E. C. R. L. Noble, H. Rinderknecht, and P. C. Williams, "Prolongation of Action of the Pituitary Antidiuretic Substances and of Histamine by Metallic Salts," <u>Lancet</u>, <u>2</u>, 309-311 (1937).

116. Diplock, A. T., J. Green, J. Bunyan, D. McHale, and I. R. Muthy, "Vitamin E and Stress. III. The Metabolism of D-α-Tocopherol in the Rat Under Dietary Stress with Silver," <u>Brit. J. Nutr.</u>, <u>21</u> (1), 115-125 (1967).

117. Olcott, C. T., "Experimental Argyrosis. V. Hypertrophy of the Left Ventricle of the Heart in Rats Ingesting Silver Salts," Arch. Pathol. (Chicago), 49, 138-149 (1950).

118. Hoey, M. J., "The Effects of Metallic Salts on the Histology and Functioning of the Rat Testis," J. Reprod. Fert., 12 (3), 461-472 (1966).

119. La Torraca, F., "Reperti Anatomo-isto-patologici ed Istochimici nell' Intossicazione Acuta Sperimentale da Sali di Argento" ["Anatomic, Histopathological, and Histochemical Aspects of Acute Experimental Intoxication with Silver Salts"], Folia Med. (Naples), 45, 1065-1069 (1962); Chem. Abstr., 58, 11883f (1964).

120. Little, Arthur D., Inc., Water Quality Criteria Data Book, Vol. 2, Inorganic Chemical Pollution of Freshwater, Report for the U.S. Environmental Protection Agency, U.S. Government Printing Office, Washington, D.C., 1971.

121. Wahlberg, J. E., "Percutaneous Toxicity of Metal Compounds. A Comparative Investigation in Guinea Pigs," Arch. Environ. Health, 11 (2), 201-204 (1965).

122. Lawrence, J. C., "Effect of Silver Nitrate, Sulfamylon, and Other Antibacterial Agents on the Metabolism of Mammalian Skin," Proc. Int. Symp. Pharmacol. Treat. Burns, 1968, A Bertelli, Ed., Excerpta Med. Found., Amsterdam, Netherlands, 1969, pp. 234-241.

123. Shouse, S. S., and G. H. Whipple, "Effects of Intravenous Injection of Colloidal Silver on Haemopoietic System in Dogs," J. Exptl. Med., 53, 413-420 (1931).

124. Anonymous, Spectrographic Study of Meats for Mineral-Element Content, Final Report for National Livestock and Meat Board, Armour Research Foundation of Illinois Institute of Technology, Chicago, Illinois, 1952.

125. Mitteldorf, A. J., and D. O. Landon, "Spectrochemical Determination of the Mineral-Element Content of Beef," Anal. Chem., 24, 469-472 (1952).

126. Hartwell, J. L., Survey of Compounds Which Have Been Tested for Carcinogenic Activity, 2nd ed., Public Health Service Publication No. 149, Federal Security Agency, Public Health Service, U.S. Government Printing Office, Washington, D.C., 1951.

127. Thompson, John I. and Company, <u>Survey of Compounds Which Have Been Tested for Carcinogenic Activity, 1968-1969 Volume</u>, DHEW Publication No. (NIH) 72-35, Public Health Service Publication No. 149, U.S. Department of Health, Education, and Welfare, Washington, D.C., 1969.

128. Shubik, P., and J. L. Hartwell, <u>Survey of Compounds Which Have Been Tested for Carcinogenic Activity</u>, Supplement 2, Public Health Service Publication No. 149, U.S. Department of Health, Education, and Welfare, U.S. Government Printing Office, Washington, D.C., 1969.

129. White, J., "Inhibitory Effect of Common Elements Towards Yeast Growth," <u>J. Inst. Brewing</u>, <u>57</u> (<u>48</u>, new series), 175-179 (1951).

130. Lanford, C. E., "Trace Minerals Affect Stream Ecology," <u>Oil and Gas J.</u>, <u>67</u> (13), 82-84 (1969).

131. Goetz, A., R. L. Tracy, and F. S. Harris, Jr., "Chapter 16. The Oligo-dynamic Effect of Silver," in <u>Silver in Industry</u>, L. Addicks, Ed., Reinhold Publishing Company, New York, New York, 1940.

132. Monier-Williams, G. W., <u>Trace Elements in Food</u>, John Wiley and Sons, Inc., New York, New York, 1949, pp. 418-427.

133. Golubovich, V. N., "Toksicheskoe Deistvie Ionnogo Serebra na Pazlichnye Gruppy Mikroorganizmov" ["Toxic Effect of Ionic Silver on Various Group of Microorganisms"], <u>Mikrobiologiya</u>, <u>43</u>, 922-924 (1974).

134. Anonymous, <u>New Silver Technology. Silver Abstracts from the Current World Literature</u>, The Silver Institute, Washington, D.C., July 1974.

135. Hassall, K. A., "A Specific Effect of Copper on the Respiration of <u>Chlorella vulgaris</u>," <u>Nature</u>, <u>193</u>, 90 (1962).

136. Poon, C. P. C., and K. H. Bhayani, "Metal Toxicity to Sewage Organisms," <u>J. Sanit. Eng. Div., Am. Soc. Civil. Eng.</u>, <u>97</u> (SA2), 161-169 (1971).

IX. HUMAN HEALTH HAZARD FROM ENVIRONMENTAL FORMS OF SILVER

A. Silver Ingested From Sources Other Than Water

At present concentrations of silver found in the environment, there is little or no likelihood for acute poisoning of humans. The only proven effect of chronic exposure to silver in humans is argyria,[a] a cosmetic and psychological problem at its worst, which has been caused by occupational or therapeutic exposure to much larger amounts of silver than can be feasibly absorbed from environmental forms. Some cases of argyria have been caused by the use of silver hair dyes. No cases of argyria were ever attributed to the widespread use (in Europe) of silver to disinfect water, beverages, etc., or to its use in food-processing apparatus, dentistry, or tableware. Presumably, little of any metallic silver ingested is absorbed.

We have calculated, in Section VIII, that an average 150-lb human, taking in only environmental forms of silver, might contain about 32 mg in his body from all sources even though he ingests about 1 g of silver every 31 years through his diet alone. Even silver nitrate, when given orally, is retained by the body to the extent of less than 10%.[4] In rats, only 39% of an intramuscular dose of $^{110}AgNO_3$ was retained by the tissues.[5] Thus, if as much as 10% of ingested silver is absorbed, only about 4% is retained in the tissues. This agrees well with our calculation above for human tissue retention. However, one set of data indicated that a woman retained 16% of the dietary silver she ingested in a 1-month period.[6]

The average number of reported cases of generalized argyria in the period 1931 to 1939, when more people were exposed to therapeutic forms of silver than any other period, was only about nine per year. There were only 10 cases of occupational argyria or argyrosis reported in the same period. Obviously, there are large individual variations in silver absorption, retention, elimination, and/or susceptibility. Although intravenous administration of a total of 0.91 to 7.6 g (average 2.3 g) silver as silver arsphenamine for 2 to 9 years has caused argyria, hundreds of patients have received up to 1.7 g silver as silver arsphenamine without developing argyria.[3] Threshold limit values for silver and drinking water standards are based on the above data. These standards indicate that

---

[a] Silver has been shown to be antagonistic to selenium in rats and exacerbates symptoms of selenium and Vitamin E deficiencies, but the significance of this antagonism in human nutrition is unknown since a human requirement for selenium has not been established.[1,2]

393

silver ranks among the substances most hazardous to man, yet the only known consequence of these levels is argyria.

B. Silver From the Air

The American Conference of Governmental Industrial Hygienists states that "If one assumes a 20-year exposure, a 10 m^3/day respiratory volume, and a 50% body retention, a level of silver five-fold the recommended TLV[a] (0.05 mg/m^3) will result in an accumulation of 1.2 g or a probable borderline amount for the production of argyria."[8] The problem of how absorption of metallic silver from the lungs might parallel direct injection of silver compounds into the bloodstream was not dealt with.

More pertinent information with regard to a TLV for silver in air has been supplied by Fassett, who after observing silver workers for many years, believes that silver concentrations of 0.01 mg/m^3 in workroom air are unlikely to cause argyria. Jindrichova observed 12 cases of argyria resulting from exposure to workroom air concentrations of 1 to 2 mg/m^3.[8]

Maximum values reported for ambient air silver concentrations were 0.000175 mg/m^3 near a lead smelter, which was in the process of shutting down,[b] 0.000005 mg/m^3 in a highly industrialized urban area,[10] and 0.000001 mg/m^3 in a cloud-seeding target area.[11] The general population, therefore, is scarcely in danger of argyria from any of these sources.

C. Silver From Water

The U.S. Public Health Service Drinking Water Standards, 1962[12] set an upper limit for silver in drinking water at 0.05 mg/liter (50 ppb), citing that the need was due to intentional addition of silver to water for disinfection purposes. The drinking water standard was determined by use of the limit 1 g silver deposited in the integument and the assumption that

---

a/ The OSHA (Occupational Safety and Health Standards) standard for silver metal and soluble compounds is also 0.01 mg/m^3 for the 8-hr time-weighted average. Any employee's exposure in any 8-hr shift shall not exceed the 8-hr time-weighted average.[7]

b/ The minimum silver concentration in the emissions of that same sampling day was < 0.0000004 mg/m^3.

"all silver ingested is deposited in the integument." Thus, daily intake of 2 liters of water containing 10 ppb silver for a lifetime would result in ingestion of less than 1 g silver, and at 50 ppb silver, water could be ingested for 27 years without exceeding the 1-g limit.[a] The average concentration of silver in municipal water supplies is 8 ppb[15,16] and 2 liters of such drinking water per day would represent about 20 to 50% of the daily intake from food.

Other authorities have recommended higher silver concentrations for safely providing pure drinking waters: U.S. National Aeronautics and Space Administration (NASA), 100 ppb; Swiss health officials, 200 ppb; and German health officials, 100 ppb.[17] Russian scientists found that 100 and 200 ppb silver in the drinking water of animals did not accumulate in the tissues and did not produce any detrimental physiological changes.[18][b]

Silver in cooking water would tend to be complexed or adsorbed by foods, especially by sulfur-rich vegetables (the Brassicaceae).[12] Relatively little is known about absorption of metals bound to food or fiber.

Based on skin sorption studies, no significant amounts of silver are expected to be added to human intake via swimming pool waters treated with silver.[12]

The major human health hazard arising from silver-polluted water might be expected to be concentration of silver in food fishes, crustaceans, and mollusks.[c] Organisms serving as food for the higher aquatic species concentrate silver by a factor of about 200 (brown algae, 240; diatoms, 210). Other concentration factors in higher organisms of the food chain are mussels, 330; scallops, 2,300; oysters, 18,700; and North Sea marine organisms, average 22,000.[20] Thus, regular ingestion of fish, etc., from contaminated water might significantly increase silver dietary intake.

A consequence of silver in drinking water might be its rendering of iodine unavailable in regions that otherwise might have just enough

---

[a] It is interesting to note that the average silver concentration found in 32 cow's milk samples from various U.S. cities was 47 ppb.[13] However, the concentration found for cadmium was more than 10 times that reported in Reference 14.

[b] Earlier Russian workers had reported that chronic ingestion (11 months) by rabbits of silver ions in amounts comparable with that ingested at 0.05 ppm in drinking water lowered immunological activity (as measured by phagocytosis) and produced tissue changes.[19]

[c] Their population reduction by direct effects on reproduction or effects on their food supplies may also be important when world food supplies are considered.

iodine to prevent goiter. Elevated levels of silver are found in the water of endemic goiter regions such as the western slopes of the Colorado Rocky Mountains. However, studies with rats have not demonstrated that such a relationship exists.[21]

D. Silver From Soil

The organic and clay components of soil complex with and/or adsorb silver very strongly so that silver may move with the dust but will not leach significantly into waters. However, sewage-sludge-amended soils may have 10 times or more silver than normal and may increase human intake of silver by its incorporation into food crops in greater than normal amounts since silver uptake by plants appears to be directly related to its soil concentration.[20] No health problems have been attributed to silver intake from mushrooms, which concentrate silver. Addition of phosphate to the soil contaminated with silver reduces its plant availability.[22] It is likely that the silver content would be increased in the meat of animals pastured or fed grains raised on these soils.[a] At least one study, however, has indicated that the transfer of iron, copper, nickel, chromium, zinc, cadmium, and lead from sewage-sludge-amended soils to dairy or beef cattle milk or tissues is minimal.[14]

---

[a] If a 0.25-lb portion of meat contains 0.007 ppm (see Table VIII-5), the 0.0065 mg silver consumed would represent only about 1 to 2% of the low silver dietary intake reported by Tipton et al.[6]

BIBLIOGRAPHY. SECTION IX.

1. Wagner, P. A., W. G. Hoekstra, and H. E. Ganther, "Alleviation of Silver Toxicity by Selenite in the Rat in Relation to Tissue Glutathione Peroxidase," Proc. Soc. Exptl. Biol. Med., 148(4), 1106-1110 (1975).

2. Committee on Dietary Allowances and the Committee on Interpretation of the Recommended Dietary Allowances, Food and Nutrition Board, National Research Council, Recommended Dietary Allowances, 8th revised ed., National Academy of Sciences, Washington, D.C., 1974.

3. Hill, W. R., and D. M. Pillsbury, Argyria, the Pharmacology of Silver, The Williams and Wilkins Co., Baltimore, Maryland, 1939.

4. Furchner, J. E., C. R. Richmond, and G. A. Drake, "Comparative Metabolism of Radionuclides in Mammals. IV. Retention of Silver-110m in the Mouse, Rat, Monkey, and Dog," Health Phys., 15(6), 505-514 (1968).

5. Durbin, P. W., "Metabolic Characteristics within a Chemical Family," Health Phys., 2, 225-238 (1960).

6. Tipton, I. H., P. L. Stewart, and P. G. Martin, "Trace Elements in Diets and Excreta," Health Phys., 12(12), 1683-1689 (1966).

7. Department of Labor, Occupational Safety and Health Administration, "Occupational Safety and Health Standards. Rules and Regulations," Federal Register, 37(202) Part II, 22140-22142 (1972).

8. Committee on Threshold Limit Values, Documentation of the Threshold Limit Values for Substances in Workroom Air, 3rd ed., American Conference of Governmental Industrial Hygienists, Cincinnati, Ohio, 1971.

9. Wesolowski, J. J., W. John, and R. Kaifer, "Lead Source Identification by Multi-Element Analysis of Diurnal Samples of Ambient Air," in Trace Elements in the Environment, Advances in Chemistry Series 123, E. L. Kothny, Ed., American Chemical Society, Washington, D.C., 1973, pp. 1-16.

10. Harrison, P. R., K. A. Rahn, R. Dams, J. A. Robbins, J. W. Winchester, S. S. Brar, and D. M. Nelson, "Areawide Trace Metal Concentrations Measured by Multielement Neutron Activation Analysis. A One Day Study in Northwest Indiana," J. Air Pollution Control Assoc., 21 (9), 563-570 (1971).

11. Douglas, W. J., "Toxic Properties of Materials Used in Weather Modification," in Proceedings of the First National Conference on Weather Modification, American Meteorological Society, Boston, Massachusetts, 1968, pp. 351-360.

12. Anonymous, Public Health Service Drinking Water Standards, HEW Publication No. 956, U.S. Department of Health, Education, and Welfare, Washington, D.C., 1962.

13. Murthy, G. K., and U. Rhea, "Cadmium and Silver Content of Market Milk," J. Dairy Sci., 51, 610-612 (1968).

14. Nelmes, A. J., R. St. J. Buxton, F. A. Fairweather, and A. E. Martin, "The Implication of the Transfer of Trace Metals from Sewage Sludge to Man," in Trace Substances in Environmental Health - VIII, D. D. Hemphill, Ed., Proceedings of University of Missouri's 8th Annual Conference on Trace Substances in Environmental Health, University of Missouri, Columbia, Missouri, June 11-13, 1974, pp. 145-151.

15. Taylor, F. B., "Trace Elements and Compounds in Water," J. Am. Water Works Assoc., 63(11), 728-733 (1971).

16. McCabe, L. J., J. M. Symons, R. D. Lee, and G. G. Robeck, "Survey of Community Water Supply Systems," Am. Water Works Assoc. J., 62(11), 670-687 (1970).

17. Anonymous, "Silver Guards Good Health," The Silver Institute Letter, 5(5), 1-2 (1975).

18. Anonymous, "Silver Cleans Up Polluted Water," The Silver Institute Letter, 3(7), 3 (1973).

19. Barkov, G. D., and L. I. El'piner, "O Neobkhodimosti Ogranicheniya Kolichestva Serebra v Pit'evoi Vode" ("The Need for Limiting the Silver Content of Drinking Water"), Gigiena i Sanit., 33(6), 16-21 (1968).

20. Cooper, C. F., and W. C. Jolly, Ecological Effects of Weather Modification: A Problem Analysis, School of Natural Resources, University of Michigan, Ann Arbor, Michigan, 1969.

21. Boissevain, C. H., and W. F. Drea, "Relation Between the Occurrence of Endemic Goiter and the Presence of Traces of Silver and Barium in Drinking Water," Endocrinology, 26, 686-687 (1936).

22. Dawson, R. F., "Basaltic Ash as an Agricultural Substratum in Guatemala," in Trace Substances in Environmental Health - VIII, D. D. Hemphill, Ed., Proceedings of University of Missouri's 8th Annual Conference on Trace Substances in Environmental Health, University of Missouri, Columbia, Missouri, June 11-13, 1974, p. 24.

X. CONCLUSIONS AND RECOMMENDATIONS

A. Conclusions

   1. Magnitude of environmental losses: Attempts to estimate
annual environmental losses even after the probable sources have been identified are severely hampered by the wide variations in data for silver recycling and industrial sales, by the varying silver content in mill and
smelter feeds and emissions so that industry-wide generalizations can
scarcely be made, and by lack of much data where some evidence indicates
very large losses may be occurring.

   Thus, although Table X-1 summarizes the best estimates for known
losses, many shortcomings are readily apparent. For example, large atmospheric emissions are ascribed to iron and steelmaking, but there are few
reliable data on which to base an estimate for the losses to water and land
from these processes. Also, the magnitude of losses from smelting and refining and from cement manufacture have been estimated, but we have not
determined how much silver is lost to each medium. Other sources of possible large losses are mine drainage and leaching and blowing of tailings;
however, the silver concentrations in water and air resulting from these
sources do not appear to be of sufficient magnitude to pose a direct human
health hazard.

   The following losses to the environment are delineated in Table
X-1: 3.1 million troy ounces in mining and milling, 9.5 to 13.5 million
troy ounces in primary and secondary smelting and refining, 0.15 to 0.26
million troy ounces from fabrication operations, 39.1 million troy ounces
from use and disposal, and at least 26.8 to 28.2 million troy ounces from
inadvertent sources. However, the estimates for losses from iron and
steel making and from cement manufacture are very questionable because of
the paucity of reliable data. The assumed 9.1 to 10.6 million troy ounces
atmospheric silver emissions have yet to produce any reported ambient air
concentrations approaching the threshold limit value of 0.01 mg/m^3.

   The most likely losses that would enter the food chain are those
to surface waters (at least 4.73 million troy ounces from photography, mill
tailings, and electroplating) and those to agricultural land (perhaps as
much as 2.5 million troy ounces silver is found in sewage sludges used in
landspreading).

   2. Chemical forms of environmental losses: Forms of silver in
atmospheric emissions are probably silver sulfide, silver sulfate, silver
carbonate, silver halides, and metallic silver; only the sulfate is appreciably water-soluble.

The chief source of water pollution by silver is the 16 million troy ounces lost annually as silver thiosulfate complexes in developing solutions discarded directly to sewers by small photofinishers. Probably 75% of this silver is eventually trapped in the sewage sludge. Very minor amounts of silver cyanide are expected to be discharged to waters; after treatment at the source, the wastes usually contain silver hydroxide complexes and silver chloride. Silver in sewage-treatment-plant effluents may be associated with suspended particulates or present as the thiosulfate complex, colloidal silver chloride and sulfide, and soluble organic complexes. In natural waters, silver may be present in these forms and also adsorbed to plankton and present in the tissues of microorganisms. Silver on suspended matter (perhaps 30 to 70% in natural waters) and in colloidal forms ultimately settles out in the sediments as do insoluble silver salts. The average silver concentration found in 6.6% of U.S. surface waters was 2.6 ppb and in 956 drinking water-treatment-plant influents was 8 ppb (the sampling in the latter case was biased toward plants known to have high trace-metal levels). At the water-treatment plant, most of the silver is precipitated after lime treatment or adsorbed on the alum flocculent. Chlorination converts some silver to silver chloride or soluble silver chloride complex. Tapwater is sometimes found to contain higher silver concentrations than water-treatment-plant effluents although this is not readily explained by dissolution of plumbing materials.

Silver in soils is largely immobilized by precipitation as insoluble salts and by complexation and/or adsorption by organic matter, clays, and manganese and iron oxides. The most probable source of soil contamination by silver and one of the most likely points of entry into the food chain is the use of sewage sludge to fertilize cropland or sludge effluent for irrigation. However, after mixing the sludge with the soil, most of the silver is immobilized. Little is known about plant uptake of silver from such soils.

Silver occurring in foods, when due to contamination or direct treatment by silver during processing, may be ionic Ag^+ but more probably is complexed by the organic materials present, probably via sulfur linkages. The forms of silver incorporated in edible plant and animal tissues are most probably protein complexes with bonding by sulfide or amino acid residues.

3. <u>Human health hazards from environmental exposure to silver</u>: Present concentrations of silver found in the environment appear to offer little likelihood for acute or chronic poisoning of humans. The magnitude of the threshold limit value (0.01 mg/m^3) and the U.S. Public Health Service drinking-water standard for silver (50 ppb) misrepresent the relative danger from silver compared with known toxic materials.

The only proven effect of chronic exposure of silver in humans is argyria, a cosmetic and psychological problem at its worst, which has been caused almost exclusively by occupational or therapeutic exposure to much larger amounts of silver (minimum necessary absorption 0.91 g) than can be feasibly ingested or inhaled from environmental sources. There is apparently great individual variability in susceptibility to argyria, which is probably explained by the observed great variability in absorption and retention. Generally, less than 10% of ingested silver is absorbed[a/] and only about 3 to 10% of the amount absorbed is retained in the tissues.

Average daily intake from food and water is probably less than 0.1 mg. (Little ingested metallic silver, e.g., from deteriorating dental restorations, would be absorbed.) If as much as 20% of this intake is retained in the tissues, it would take over 124 years to accumulate sufficient silver to produce argyria in some individuals. Regular ingestion of foods originating from silver-contaminated waters or soils appear to pose no problem with respect to argyria at present. Sewage-sludge-amended soil may have 10 times or more silver than normal and silver may be incorporated into food crops in greater than normal amounts since its uptake by plants appears to be directly related to its soil concentration. No data were found to indicate whether animals pastured or fed grains raised on these soils may have increased silver content in their flesh and milk. However, the highest silver level reported in the soft parts of mollusks, known concentrators of silver, is only about 3 times the highest level reported for silver in beef. The intake of silver by the general public via the air is negligible compared with the intake from food and water.

4. <u>Effects on lower life forms</u>: The toxicity of silver to microorganisms and to aquatic species is well known. Concentrations as low as 0.004 ppm silver are toxic to some aquatic species (e.g., <u>Daphnia</u>, guppies, and stickleback). Silver affects aquatic species at many stages of development and affects behavior as well. American oyster embryos fail to develop at silver nitrate concentrations of 0.0058 ppm (0.0037 ppm silver) and are killed at 0.01 ppm (0.0064 ppm silver). Adult oysters and fish appear more resistant to elevated concentrations of silver than gametes, embryos, and fry. Silver may retard the growth of fish in fresh water; and at concentrations of 0.1 to 0.5 ppm in soft water, silver is definitely injurious. Thus, if 6.6% of U.S. surface waters have silver concentrations in the range 0.0001 to 0.038 ppm (average 0.0026 ppm), the silver contents of a few U.S. surface waters are obviously detrimental to some aqueous species.

---

a/ H. J. M. Bowen (<u>Trace Elements in Biochemistry</u>, 1966) has erroneously reported that more than 70% silver is absorbed, but the reference cited (<u>Biology Data Book</u>, 1964, pp. 192-196) states that silver absorption is less than 5%.

The effects of silver on birds and mammals have usually been studied with respect to acute toxicity; but among effects attributed to chronic exposure studies are lowered immunological activity, altered membrane permeability, enzyme inhibitions including antagonism to copper and selenium metabolism, vascular hypertension, and shortening of the life span. There is no evidence that terrestrial animals concentrate silver from environmental sources.

The toxicity of silver to lower plant life is comparable with that of the very toxic ions of mercury, copper, and cadmium. The inhibition of growth of algae, fungi, and bacteria by silver is detrimental when these plants serve as food for higher animals. The inhibition or retardation of bottom-sediment decomposition by silver may slow the rate at which essential nutrients are returned to the water. The toxicity of silver to anaerobic bacteria may be important in deoxygenated waters, in sewage treatment plants, and in naturally anaerobic sediments. Among edible plants that concentrate silver are _Mentha_, _Dioscorea_, and mushrooms.

B. Recommendations

The uptake of silver from sediments by organisms serving as food for fish should be determined since sediments are probably the ultimate "sink" for most silver reaching natural surface waters. Studies should be performed to determine the uptake of silver by food crops grown on sewage-sludge-amended soils and the uptake of silver by animals pastured on these soils or fed grains raised on them.

The variations in absorption and retention of silver from food and medicinals (especially since argyria has usually been produced therapeutically and since there is currently renewed interest in silver's medicinal uses) within a large human population should be determined so that better estimates of the public's tolerance to silver in the environment can be made.

Many more analyses for silver should be made of emissions from primary and secondary copper, lead, zinc, and silver smelters and refineries but especially of those from iron and steel making and cement manufacture, which have been implicated as major sources of atmospheric silver.

TABLE X-1

ANNUAL LOSSES OF SILVER TO THE ENVIRONMENT
(million troy ounces)

Loss Category	Air	Water	Water plus Land	Land	Total
Mining and Milling, Total	0.042	0.70		2.4[a]	3.1
Cyanidation		0.024			
Michigan Cu ore tailings				0.47	
Other Cu ore tailings				0.73	
Mo. Pb ore tailings				0.78	
Mine drainage		?			
Leaching of tailings		?			
Blowing of tailings	?				
Primary Smelting and Refining, Total	1.2–1.3?		4.2–4.35		5.5
Of Copper	0.35–0.48		0.22–0.35		0.70
Lead	0.07?		1.5		1.57
Zinc	> 0.06?			2.5[b]	2.56
Silver	0.7?				?
Secondary Smelting and Refining, Total	0.8		3.2–7.2		4–8
Of Precious-metal scrap					?
Of Copper scrap	?				?
Of Lead scrap	0.0002				
Fabrication, Total	0.097		0.05–0.16		0.15–0.26
Of sterling silver	0.0002				
Of medicinals and dental materials	0.0001				
Of electroplate	0.00025	0.03			

TABLE X-1 (Concluded)

Loss Category	Air	Water	Water plus Land	Land	Total
Fabrication, Total (continued)					
Of other coatings	0.01175				
Of silver compounds	0.00025				
Of photographic products	0.084				
Brazing	0.00015				
Use and Disposal, Total	0.92	4.0		34.2	39.1
Photography	0.07	4.0		12.0c/	
Brazing alloys	0.07?				
Cloud seeding	0.1				
Other uses	> 0.0003			22.2	
Urban refuse	0.68	?			
Inadvertent Sources, Total	6.0-7.4?		20.8?		> 26.8-28.2?
Iron production					
Sintering	0.03?				
Blast furnaces (5% scrap)	0.03?				
Steelmaking					
Open hearth furnaces (44% scrap)	0.36-1.8?				
Basic oxygen furnaces (29% scrap)	0.015?				
Electric arc furnaces (97% scrap)	0.40?				
Iron foundries (~ 88% scrap)	0.38?				
Cement manufacture	3.1?		15.1?d/		
Fossil fuels					
Petroleum (fuel oil + gasoline)	0.5				
Coal	1.24			5.7	
	9.1-10.6		69.6-73.6		78.7-84.2

a/ Tailings ponds.
b/ Residues probably held in inventory.
c/ Sewage sludge: lagooned, 3.2; landfilled, 6.3; land-spreading, 2.5 million troy ounces.
d/ Dry surface piles: 7.8 million troy ounces.

406

APPENDIX A

PHYSICAL PROPERTIES OF SILVER AND ITS ALLOYS

Of all the metals, silver has the highest electrical[a] and thermal conductivities and optical reflectivity. Its ductility and malleability are second only to those of gold. This low strength and high ductility of annealed fine silver indicate good deep-drawing characteristics. Silver's melting point, fixed at 960.8°C, is one of the six fundamental and fixed temperature points on the International Temperature Scale, while its boiling point has been estimated from 1950 to 2259°C.[1,2]

The silver volatilization rate is quite high at high temperatures and is greater under oxidizing gases than under reducing gases. Temperature-vapor pressure relationships for silver are given in Table A-1.

Cold-worked fine silver has an initial high rate of work hardening with an initial rapid increase in strength and decrease in ductility. Hardness also increases with cold working and deep drawing becomes more difficult. "High" fine silver will soften and recrystallize at ambient temperatures after cold working but commercial fine silver, which contains impurities, is not as prone to low-temperature recrystallization. Increasing cold work lowers the recrystallization temperature so that a rise in temperature during cold working may cause "self annealing." An annealing temperature of 300°C (572°F) is often used for 50% cold worked material.[2]

Numerous physical constants of pure silver are compiled in Table A-2. A comparison of certain physical properties of silver with those of silver electrical-contact alloys and of refractory and semirefractory materials, containing silver, are presented in Tables A-3, A-4, and A-5.

---

a/ Silver has the highest electrical conductivity when rated volumetrically. The volumetric electrical conductivities of copper, gold, aluminum, and iron are ~ 92, 66, 57, and 16%, respectively, that of silver. On a mass basis, the high density of silver (10.49 g/cm^2) changes the relation so that some lighter metals rate higher than silver. The relative conductivities on a mass basis are aluminum 100, copper 50, and silver 44.[1]

TABLE A-1

TEMPERATURE-VAPOR PRESSURE RELATIONS OF SILVER

T, °K	P, atm.	P, mm Hg	Reference
298.15	7.6×10^{-44}	5.8×10^{-41}	3
400	3.8×10^{-31}	2.9×10^{-28}	3
500	1.0×10^{-23}	7.6×10^{-21}	3
600	8.7×10^{-19}	6.6×10^{-16}	3
700	2.9×10^{-15}	2.2×10^{-12}	3
800	1.3×10^{-12}	9.9×10^{-10}	3
899	1.0×10^{-10}	7.6×10^{-8}	3
900	1.1×10^{-10}	8.4×10^{-8}	3
952	1.0×10^{-9}	7.6×10^{-7}	3
958	1.1×10^{-9}	8.3×10^{-7}	1
979	2.36×10^{-9}	1.8×10^{-6}	1
1000	5.92×10^{-9}	4.5×10^{-6}	3
1010	8.55×10^{-9}	6.5×10^{-6}	1
1015	1.0×10^{-8}	7.6×10^{-6}	3
1065	5.13×10^{-8}	3.9×10^{-5}	1
1085	8.15×10^{-8}	6.2×10^{-5}	1
1091	1.0×10^{-7}	7.6×10^{-5}	3
1100	1.26×10^{-7}	9.6×10^{-5}	3
1115	1.84×10^{-7}	1.4×10^{-4}	1
1123	2.36×10^{-7}	1.8×10^{-4}	1
1152	5.39×10^{-7}	4.1×10^{-4}	1
1179	1.0×10^{-6}	7.6×10^{-4}	3
1190	1.18×10^{-6}	9.0×10^{-4}	1
1200	1.59×10^{-6}	1.2×10^{-3}	3
1228	3.02×10^{-6}	2.3×10^{-3}	1
1234	3.46×10^{-6}	2.6×10^{-3}	3
1237	3.68×10^{-6}	2.8×10^{-3}	1
1265	8.55×10^{-6}	6.5×10^{-3}	1

T, °K	P, atm.	P, mm Hg	Reference
1287	1.0×10^{-5}	7.6×10^{-3}	3
1287	8.42×10^{-6}	6.4×10^{-3}	1
1300	1.28×10^{-5}	9.7×10^{-3}	3
1313	1.58×10^{-5}	1.20×10^{-2}	1
1315	2.28×10^{-5}	1.73×10^{-2}	1
1335	2.57×10^{-5}	1.96×10^{-2}	1
1349	3.28×10^{-5}	2.49×10^{-2}	1
1356	5.66×10^{-5}	4.30×10^{-2}	1
1374	7.24×10^{-5}	5.50×10^{-2}	1
1392	6.45×10^{-5}	4.90×10^{-2}	1
1393	6.85×10^{-5}	5.21×10^{-2}	1
1400	7.38×10^{-5}	5.61×10^{-2}	3
1402	8.68×10^{-5}	6.60×10^{-2}	1
1418	1.0×10^{-4}	7.6×10^{-2}	3
1467	2.91×10^{-4}	2.21×10^{-1}	1
1500	3.36×10^{-4}	2.55×10^{-1}	3
1503	3.29×10^{-4}	2.50×10^{-1}	1
1582	1.0×10^{-3}	7.6×10^{-1}	3
1600	1.25×10^{-3}	9.50×10^{-1}	3
1700	3.97×10^{-3}	3.02	3
1800	1.11×10^{-2}	8.44	3
1900	2.77×10^{-2}	21.05	3
2000	6.28×10^{-2}	47.73	3
2100	1.31×10^{-1}	99.56	3
2200	2.57×10^{-1}	195.32	3
2300	4.72×10^{-1}	358.72	3
2400	8.25×10^{-1}	627.0	3
2437	1.00	760	3
2500	1.35	1,026	3

PHYSICAL CONSTANTS OF SILVER

Property and Value	Remarks	Reference
Atomic Number - 47		4
Atomic Weight - 107.88		4
Melting Point - 960.5°C (1760.9°F)		4
Boiling Point - 1955°C (3551°F); 1950-2259°C		1,4
Density (20°C) - 10.49 g/cc (0.378 lb/cu in.)		4
Heat of Sublimation - ~ 65 kcal/mole		1
Latent Heat of Fusion - 24.3 cal/g		5
Latent Heat of Vaporization - 556 cal/g, 565 cal/g		1,4
Specific Heat - 0.0562 cal/g/°C, 0.0558 cal/g/°C; Ag vapor ~ 0.046 cal/g/°C; liq. Ag from m.p. to 1300°C, 0.0692 cal/g/°C		1,4,5
Thermal Conductivity (0°C) - 1.0 cal/cm²/cm/°C/sec		4
Thermal Expansion Coefficient - 1.9 x 10⁻⁵/°C (0-100°C); 10.9 x 10⁻⁶/°F		4,6
Electrical Resistivity - 1.5-1.59 microhm-cm (20°C); 1.62 microhm-cm		4,5
Crystal Structure - Face centered cubic		4,5
Thermal Neutron Capture Cross Section - 63 barns/atom; 60 barns/atom		4,6
Electrical Conductivity - 100-108.4% IACS; 106% IACS; 104% IACS		4,7,8
Magnetic Susceptibility - - 0.020 x 10⁻⁶ cgs	Slightly diamagnetic	1,4
Thermal emf versus Platinum - + 0.74 mV		6,7
Tensile Modulus of Elasticity (10⁶ psi) - 11; 10.5; 11.1		6,9,10
Hardness - 40 (cast, Brinell); 30 (Annealed, Rockwell 15T): 75 (Cold Worked, Rockwell 15T)	Hardness decreases with annealing temperature above 93°C	2,5,8
Tensile Strength, Annealed - 25,000 psi; 18,200 psi; 22,000 psi	Ultimate tensile strength decreases with increasing annealing temperature	2,6,8,9
Elastic or Young's modulus - 7.1 x 10¹¹ dynes/cm² (10.3 x 10⁶ lb/in.²) at 20°C	The modulus decreases with increasing temperature	2
Torsion, Shear, or Rigidity Modulus - 2.68 x 10¹¹ dynes/cm² (3.89 x 10⁶ lb/in.²) at 27°C	Hard-drawn wire has higher modulus at all temperatures	2
Temperautre coefficient of resistance - 0.00393/°C at 20°C	Coeff. decreases with increasing pressure and tension. Resistivity increases on melting and increases further with temperature rise.	1
Electronegativity Ag⁺¹ - 175 kcal/g-atom		11
Ionic potential, Z/r of Ag¹⁺ - 0.76		11

TABLE A-3

PHYSICAL PROPERTIES OF SILVER AND SOME ALLOYS

Material	*Specific Gravity or Density (troy oz/in²)	Tensile Strength, 1,000 psi		Electrical Conductivity % IACS[b]	Hardness (Rockwell 15T)		Elongation % in 2 in.		References
		Annealed	Cold Worked		Annealed	Cold Worked	Annealed	Cold Worked	
Fine Silver (99.9+% Ag)	*10.49 5.54	25 22 18.2	45 54 43 (hard)	104 106	30	75	55 48 54	5 2.5 6 (hard)	8, 9 6, 8 7, 9
Sterling Silver (92.5% Ag-7.5% Cu)	5.45	39 41	66 64 (hard)	88 85	65 65	81 83	35 26	5 4 (hard)	8 7, 8
Coin Silver (90.0% Ag-10.0% Cu)	5.43	42 40	65 (hard) 75	85 85	70 70	83 84	32 26	4 4 (hard)	8, 9 7, 8, 9
Alloy 1[a] (72.0% Ag-28.0% Cu)	5.24	53	80	84 87	79 77	85 84	20	5	8
Alloy 2[a] (75.0% Ag-24.5% Cu-0.5% Ni)	5.27	45	80	75	78	85	32	4	8
Alloy 3[a] (77.0% Ag-22.6% Cd-0.4% Ni)	5.43	35	68	31	50	85	55	4	8
Alloy 4[a] (86.8% Ag-5.5% Cd-0.2% Ni-7.5% Cu)	5.32	40	75	43	72	85	43	3	8
Alloy 5[a] (85.0% Ag-15.0% Cd)	5.36	28	58	35	51	83	55	5	8
Alloy 6[a] (99.55% Ag-0.25% Mg-0.20% Ni)	5.45	30	50	70	61	77	35	6	8
Alloy 7[a] (97.0% Ag-3.0% Pt)	5.56 5.55	25	47	45 50	45 48	77 78	37	3	8 7
Alloy 8[a] (90.0% Ag-10.0% Pd)	5.57 5.61	34	53	27 30	63 62	80 82	31	3	8
Alloy 9[a] (97.0% Ag-3.0% Pd)	5.55 5.55	27	48	58 60	45 48	77 80	37	3	8
Alloy 10[a] (99.0% Ag-3.0% Pd)	5.54	26	47	79	44	76	42	3	8
Alloy 11[a] (90.0% Ag-10.0% Au)	5.81	29	46	40	57	76	28	3	8
Alloy 12[a] (Ag-Cu-Cd-Au)	4.68	37	65	90	51	84	40	2	8

a/ Electrical contact materials
b/ IACS - International Annealed Copper Standard

TABLE A-4

PHYSICAL PROPERTIES OF SILVER SEMIREFRACTORY MATERIALS[8/]

Material	Density (troy oz/in²)	Ultimate Tensile Strength, psi Annealed	Cold Worked	Conductivity, % IACS	Hardness, Rockwell F Annealed	Cold Worked
97.5% Ag-2.5% CdO	5.39	16,000	25,000	88	22	70
95.0% Ag-5.0% CdO	5.35	16,000	25,000	84	32	76
90.0% Ag-10.0% CdO	5.16	16,000	-	75	42	84
86.7% Ag-13.3% CdO	5.31	29,000	-	68	48	84
85.0% Ag-15.0% CdO	5.28	30,000	-	65	50	85
95.0% Ag-5.0% Ni	5.49	24,000	-	95	32	84
90.0% Ag-10.0% Ni	5.44	25,000	-	87	35	89
85.0% Ag-15.0% Ni	5.28	27,000	-	80	40	93
70.0% Ag-30.0% Ni	5.02	-	-	55	42	87
60.0% Ag-40.0% Ni	5.06	35,000	60,000	44	-	92
40.0% Ag-60.0% Ni	4.69	-	-	25	42	97
99.75% Ag-0.25% C	5.48	25,000	37,000	103	45	73
99.50% Ag-0.50% C	5.43	24,500	36,500	102	44	72
99.25% Ag-0.75% C	5.38	24,000	35,800	100	39	70
99.0% Ag-1.0% C	5.33	23,500	35,000	99	36	69
98.5% Ag-1.5% C	5.29	22,000	33,500	97	33	66
98.0% Ag-2.0% C	5.04	-	-	77	-	-
95.0% Ag-5.0% C	4.57	-	-	55	-	25
90.0% Ag-10.0% C	3.32	-	-	35	-	3
88.0% Ag-2.0% C-10.0% Ni	4.94	-	70,000	70	26	64
99.34% Ag-0.41% MgO-0.25% NiO	5.47	31,000	39,500	70	-	97[b/]
90.0% Ag-10.0% Fe	5.40	-	-	90	48	81
50.0% Fe-25.0% Cu-25.0% Ag	4.49	-	-	21	84	94

413

TABLE A-5

PHYSICAL PROPERTIES OF SILVER REFRACTORY MATERIALS[8/]

Material	Density (g/cc)	Conductivity, % IACS	Hardness, Rockwell B
27.5% Ag-72.5% W	15.56	49	90
35.0% Ag-65.0% W	14.77	51	85
49.0% Ag-51.0% W	13.48	65	55
50.0% Ag-50.0% W	13.40	62	65
46.0% Ag-53.0% W-1.0% C	12.85	55	85
48.0% Ag-51.75% W-0.25% C	13.38	65	55
90.0% Ag-10.0% W	11.01	92	41 (hard)
65.0% Ag-35.0% WC	11.87	57	57
50.0% Ag-50.0% WC	12.37	47	91
40.0% Ag-60.0% WC	12.92	37	100
40.0% Ag-60.0% Mo	10.22	47	82
50.0% Ag-50.0% Mo	10.24	52	75

BIBLIOGRAPHY. APPENDIX A.

1. Butts, A., "Chapter 7. The Physical Properties of Silver," in <u>Silver.</u>
    <u>Economics, Metallurgy, and Use</u>, A. Butts and C. D. Coxe, Eds., D.
    Van Nostrand Co., Inc., Princeton, New Jersey, 1967, pp. 104-122.

2. Weglein, E. B., "Chapter 9. Mechanical Properties and Uses of Fine
    Silver," in <u>Silver. Economics, Metallurgy, and Use</u>, A. Butts and
    C. D. Coxe, Eds., D. Van Nostrand Co., Inc., Princeton, New Jersey,
    1967, pp. 137-152.

3. Hultgren, R., R. L. Orr, P. D. Anderson, and K. K. Kelley, <u>Selected</u>
    <u>Values of Thermodynamic Properties of Metals and Alloys</u>, John Wiley
    and Sons, Inc., New York, New York, 1963.

4. Anonymous, <u>High Purity Silver</u>, Atomergic Chemetals Co., Division of
    Gallard-Schlesinger Chemical Manufacturing Corp., Carle Place,
    Long Island, New York, 1968.

5. Doan, G. E., and E. M. Mahla, <u>The Principles of Physical Metallurgy</u>,
    2nd ed., McGraw-Hill Book Co., Inc., New York, New York, 1941.

6. Anonymous, "1974 Materials Selector," <u>Mater. Eng.</u>, <u>78</u>(4), 1-484 (1973).

7. Lyman, T., H. E. Boyer, P. M. Unterweiser, J. E. Foster, J. P. Hontas,
    and H. Lawton, Eds., <u>Metals Handbook</u>, <u>Vol. I, Properties and Selec-</u>
    <u>tions of Metals</u>, 8th ed., American Society for Metals, Novelty, Ohio,
    1961.

8. Larsen, E. I., and R. H. Imes, "Chapter 26. Electrical Contacts--
    Applications," in <u>Silver. Economics, Metallurgy, and Use</u>, A. Butts
    and C. D. Coxe, Eds., D. Van Nostrand Co., Inc., Princeton, New
    Jersey, 1967, pp. 372-385.

9. Anonymous, <u>Properties of Some Metals and Alloys</u>, The International
    Nickel Co., Inc., New York, New York, 1968.

10. Manzone, M. G., and J. Z. Briggs, <u>Mo. Less-Common Alloys of Molybdenum</u>,
    Climax Molybdenum Company, New York, New York, 1962.

11. Boyle, R. W., "Geochemistry of Silver and Its Deposits with Notes on
    Geochemical Prospecting for the Element," <u>Geol. Surv. Can., Bull.,</u>
    No. 160, 1-264 (1968).

APPENDIX B

CHEMISTRY OF SILVER

A. Oxidation States and Representative Compounds of Silver

1. **Oxidation states**: Although silver, copper, and gold have a single $\underline{s}$ electron outside a full $\underline{d}$ shell, there are few similarities in their chemistry. However, the metals all crystallize with the same face-centered cubic lattice, and Cu_2O and Ag_2O have the same body-centered cubic structure. The stability constant sequence for halo complexes of silver(I) and copper(I) is the reverse of that for many metals: $F > Cl > Br > I$. Silver(I) and copper(I) often form the same types of compounds.[1] Due to its electronic configuration, silver may be expected to have similarities in its chemical behavior with that of palladium or cadmium. Silver and palladium, however, do not seem to have any relationships in the natural environment; but silver and cadmium are associated in some kinds of deposits, and some silver minerals often have above-average cadmium contents.[2]

Silver exhibits oxidation states of +1, +2, and +3 with the +1 valence state, resulting from removal of the 5s electron, being the most stable and the only one possible in natural aqueous environments. The +2 and +3 states are unstable in aqueous environments, especially above 100°C. Since both of these higher states have oxidation potentials greater than that required for the oxidation of water, they are reduced to the monovalent state in aqueous solution.[2] None of the silver oxides, formed in basic solution, occurs in nature.

Latimer gives the potentials (volts) for the oxidation states of silver:

Acid solution

$$Ag \underset{-0.799}{\rule{3cm}{0.4pt}} Ag^+ \underset{-1.98}{\rule{3cm}{0.4pt}} Ag^{2+} \underset{\sim\,-2.1}{\rule{3cm}{0.4pt}} AgO^+$$

Basic solution

$$Ag \underset{-0.344}{\rule{3cm}{0.4pt}} Ag_2O \underset{-0.57}{\rule{3cm}{0.4pt}} AgO \underset{-0.74}{\rule{3cm}{0.4pt}} Ag_2O_3 \;^{[2]}$$

The argentous ion, Ag^{+1}, does not undergo any appreciable hydrolysis in aqueous solution and is considered to be a mild oxidizing agent. Of the halide salts of the Ag(I) ion, argentous fluoride, AgF, is the only one which is soluble in aqueous solution, not photosensitive, and does not occur naturally. In general the majority of the Ag(I) salts are relatively insoluble in aqueous solution; however, salts such as the nitrate, chlorate, and perchlorate are soluble in aqueous solution. The least soluble silver compound is Ag_2S, which is formed by the addition of sulfide ion or H_2S to solutions of silver(I) ions under slightly acidic, neutral, or slightly basic conditions.[2]

Silver readily forms compounds with sulfur, arsenic, antimony, selenium, and tellurium, many of these compounds being found as natural minerals.[2] Examples of such compounds may be found in Table II.1.

The atypical reactions of silver in basic solutions and in atmospheric oxygen, as compared with other heavy metals, has importance with respect to the silver species formed during various processing steps, such as furnacing and the oxidation of cyanide wastewater. The brown substance that forms when silver salts are treated with strong hydroxide solutions is probably hydrous argentous oxide rather than silver hydroxide.[2] But another source suggests that Ag_2O is present, in aqueous solution, as $AgOH$ and $Ag(OH)_2^-$ while still another suggests that AgO hydrolyzes to $Ag(OH)_2$ and $Ag(OH)_3^-$.[3,4] The K_{sp} (solubility product) of $AgOH$ is claimed to be 10^{-8}.[5]

If silver has been oxidized to Ag_2O by heating in air below 180°C, then at temperatures above 180°C, the Ag_2O decomposes to elemental silver and molecular oxygen.[6] Further discussions of metallic silver and of silver-oxygen reactions may be found in Section B of this appendix.

In monovalent compounds, silver is moderately ionized in crystals; however, silver(II) exhibits primarily covalent bonding in its compounds. The only known silver(II) salt is argentic fluoride, AgF_2. Alkaline oxidation of aqueous $Ag(I)$ solutions with nonreducing salts results in the formation of argentic oxide, AgO, which dissolves in acidic media at room temperature to give the $Ag(II)$ ion. In aqueous solution, the $Ag(II)$ ion produces $Ag(I)$ ions and O_2, particularily at elevated temperatures.[2]

Silver(III) oxide has been claimed to be formed during anodic oxidation of $Ag(I)$ solutions under alkaline conditions, whereas another source states that anodic oxidation of silver in 12$\underline{M}$ potassium hydroxide gives $Ag(III)$ as $Ag(OH)_4^-$.[1,2,4] The silver silicates $AgSiO_4$, $(Ag_2SiO_3)_n$, $(Ag_2Si_2O_5)_n$, and $AgAl_2[AlSi_3O_{10}](OH)_2$ have been prepared by treatment of alkali or alkaline-earth metal silicates with fused silver nitrate at about 300°C, but these silicates do not occur in nature.[2]

Several representative silver compounds are given in Table B-1 along with information regarding their physical and thermodynamic properties.

2. **Complexes**: Silver(I) usually forms either linear complexes, using sp bonding, or tetrahedral complexes with sp^3 bonding. Most stable Ag(I) complexes exist in the linear form L-Ag-L, where L = a ligand.[1] Silver(II) and -(III) form stable square planar complexes with dsp^2 bonding.[2]

Water-insoluble silver halides can be treated with excess halide ion to form water-soluble complexes; likewise, silver(I) sulfide can be dissolved in alkali sulfide solutions to form the soluble alkali silver sulfide complex ion.[2] Examples of soluble silver(I) complex ions are shown in Table B-2.

There are apparently a few silver chelate complexes, which are usually coordinated through oxygen and/or sulfur rather than through nitrogen.[2] However, silver binds oxygen only feebly.[1]

There are numerous silver(I) complexes, existing both in solution and in the solid state, containing π-bonding and non-π-bonding ligands. All olefins, particularly alkenes, and many aromatic compounds form complexes with the silver(I) ion; however, the ability of simple alkenes to form π-bonded complexes is much greater than that of the simple alkynes. An example of alkyne complex formation is the reversible reaction of a silver(I) solution with acetylene to produce a yellow-white precipitate or $AgC\mathbin{:}CAg$.[1] Silver (I) also forms σ-bonded complexes such as phenyl-silver.[7]

Many silver(II) complexes are known, such as $[Ag(py)_4]^{2+}$, $[Ag(dipy)_2]^{2+}$, and $[Ag(\underline{o}\text{-phen})_2]^{2+}$.[1] Table B-1 provides examples of Ag(III) complexes.

3. **Hazardous compounds**: Several silver compounds are potential explosion hazards; e.g., silver oxalate, which decomposes explosively when heated to elevated temperatures; silver acetylide ($AgC\mathbin{:}CAg$), which is sensitive to detonation on contact; and silver azide (AgN_3).[8]

Fulminating silver, which is believed to be either silver nitride (Ag_3N) or silver imide, may detonate spontaneously when silver oxide is heated with ammonia or when alkaline solutions of a silver amine complex are allowed to stand. The silver amine solutions can be rendered harmless by adding HCl.[8] Silver fulminate is very sensitive to explosion by friction or impact and is used in trick matches and cigars and in small noisemakers called torpedoes.[9]

Moistening mixtures of powdered magnesium and finely crushed silver nitrate produces a burst of flame with a dazzling flash. Sublimed arsenic, when triturated with excess silver nitrate, bursts into flames when shaken out onto paper, and silver cyanide pyrogenically decomposes to silver and cyanogen.[9/]

4. Isotopes: The stable isotopes of silver are $_{47}Ag^{107}$ and $_{47}Ag^{109}$ with relative abundances 57.35 and 48.65%, respectively. There are radioisotopes of silver with mass numbers 102, 103, 104, 105, 106, 107^m, 108, 109^m, 110, 110^m, 111, 111^m, 112, 113, 113^m, 114, 115, 115^m, 116, and 117. None of these isotopes occurs in nature since Ag^{110m} exhibits the longest half-life of 253 days. Ag^{110m} is a beta emitter and is the most suitable isotope for chemical tracer work.

In the fission of U^{235}, Ag^{107} is derived from Pd^{107} (half-life of 7.5 million years) and Ag^{109} is derived from Pd^{109} (half-life of 13.6 hr). The fission yields are 0.19% and 0.030% for the chains yeilding Pd^{107} and Pd^{109}, respectively. Thus, all rocks containing uranium contain silver.[2/]

B. Corrosion

1. General corrosion: Silver metal undergoes corrosive attack by numerous substances including sulfur and sulfur compounds (hydrogen sulfide, alkali sulfides and polysulfides, viscose, organic acids contaminated by sulfur, sulfur trioxide, and thiosulfate); hydrogen selenide and selenic acid; moist ammonia, ammonium hydroxide, and substituted derivatives; alkali cyanides and ferrocyanides; ferrous and ferric sulfates; concentrated oxidizing mineral acids (even dilute nitric acid); peroxides, persulfates, lead dioxide, commercial nitrogen tetroxide (an equilibrium mixture of NO_2 and N_2O_4); hydrohalic, halic, and hypohalic acids and their salts; halogen gases and their mixtures with water vapor; mercury and its salts; molten glass; carbon monoxide; acetylene; and aromatic aldehydes.[10-12/] A more detailed compilation of specific materials can be obtained from the cited references.

When silver is immersed in HCl or Cl$^-$ solutions, a AgCl film is formed that inhibits further corrosion. In a similar manner, halogen gases also form a silver halide film that inhibits further attack.[11/] In the presence of an oxidizing agent, however, HCl will corrode silver at elevated temperatures and chlorides in alcoholic solutions (e.g., antifreeze) will rapidly corrode silver solder.[12/] In the presence of O_2 or other oxidizing agents, ammonia and cyanides corrode silver due to the formation of complexes with the silver.[13/]

At high temperatures, several gases rapidly attack silver; e.g., sulfur-containing gases and fused alkali sulfides corrode silver at a

421

rapid rate. Ammonia attacks silver metal with the probable formation of silver nitrides. Carbon monoxide may attack silver at 300°C, while at temperatures above 500°C the metal is attacked by molten chlorides, fused sodium carbonate, and MoO_3-containing air.[14,15] At room temperature, SO_2 causes surface tarnishing of silver metal; however, at red heat, the corrosive attack is very strong and proceeds according to the reaction:

$$Ag + SO_2 \text{ (g)} \longrightarrow Ag_2S + Ag_2SO_4 \text{ [16]}$$

Tarnish is rarely an important cause of silver loss. Industrial tarnish removal may use dilute solutions of sodium or potassium cyanide. Other procedures that are used to prevent tarnish are:

1. Cathodic treatment in a solution of alkali chromate.

2. Cataphoretic deposition of oxides of aluminum, beryllium, thorium, and zirconium.

3. Lacquers.

4. Storing in antitarnish paper, which is impregnated with a chemical that reacts preferentially with H_2S, e.g., cupric or cadmium acetate.

5. Chemisorption of polar, long-chain aliphatic compounds containing sulfur at the active end of the molecule.[10]

Small amounts of H_2S (in the presence of moisture and O_2 or of O_3) cause tarnishing and darkening of silver with formation of Ag_2S and Ag_2O, respectively. Although the sulfide film decomposes at about 400°C, tarnished sterling silver cannot be cleaned by heating because of copper oxidation. Ag_2S tarnish on low voltage electrical contacts is troublesome. It is a semiconductor that produces electrical noise and may cause a 0.2 V drop; however, thin tarnish films of Ag_2S offer little electrical resistance. Silver and silver-rich alloys are acceptable as contact materials where the tarnish film is broken by pressure, rubbing, or arcing except as a contact material in voice transmission circuits. Tarnishing also diminishes silver's solderability.[10,12] Adding > 40% palladium produces alloys that will not tarnish in atmospheric environments.[13] However, most silver alloys are less corrosion resistant than pure silver.[11]

Reported corrosion of silver coins by poly(vinyl chloride) was due to their copper content. German investigators found that silver coins, kept in poly(vinyl chloride) foil, lost their gloss and eventually turned blue-green. Evidently, the coin copper was dissolved by stearic acid formed by the poly(vinyl chloride) HCl scavenger--Ca or Ba stearate.[17]

422

Austenitic stainless steels joined by the most popular brazing alloys (45% Ag-15% Cu-16% Zn-24% Cd and 50% Ag-15.5% Cu-16.5% Zn-18% Cd) produce seams that are rapidly corroded by salt spray. Nickel-free chromium steels should be brazed with 60% Ag-28% Cu-10% Sn-2% Ni to avoid crevice corrosion.[12]

Silver is cathodic to all metals except gold, the platinum-group metals, and mercury. Thus, silver in contact with any other clean metal is likely to cause galvanic corrosion of the base metals.[11] Ordinary silver plating leaves pinholes through which air and moisture can corrode the base metal. Since the potential difference will be small between silver and metals normally protected by a film such as aluminum, chromium, and stainless steel, any silver corrosion will be low.[10]

Silver is thermodynamically more stable than copper and mercury. Its equilibrium electrode potential, + 0.799 V, is much more positive than that of the hydrogen electrode and a little more negative than that of the oxygen electrode (+ 0.81 V) in natural environments. Silver will not dissolve by hydrogen depolarization (in nonoxidizing acids); but in aqueous corrosion media in the presence of oxygen, silver corrodes by oxygen depolarization.[13]

Because of its corrosion resistance, silver has been used industrially in handling HF, dilute HCl, phenol, fruit juices, essential oils, and many pharmaceuticals; in the synthesis of urea from NH_3 and CO_2; the production of Na phosphate salts; and high-temperature work with KOH and NaOH (provided nitrates are absent).[6] Silver linings (usually claddings) are used in steel apparatus,[11] and cadmium-free brazing alloys are preferred for food-handling appartus.[12] Cells comprising Ag/solid AgCl/seawater are used for cathodic protection in marine environments, e.g., of ship hulls.[6]

2. Reaction with oxygen: Uhlig's Corrosion Handbook stated in 1948 that, alone, oxygen corrodes silver only at high temperatures and pressures, e.g., 300°C and 15 atm; however, the 1966 translation of N. D. Tomashov's Theory of Corrosion and Protection of Metals states that silver can be oxidized by atmospheric oxygen at normal temperatures and that it becomes oxidation-resistant above 100 to 150°C at a partial oxygen pressure of 0.2 atm.[6,15]

U. R. Evans in The Corrosion and Oxidation of Metals, 1960, states that silver oxidizes when heated in air below 180°C, but above 180°C, the oxide decomposes:

$$2Ag_2O \rightleftharpoons 4Ag + O_2$$

At 180°C, the oxygen pressure is 0.2 atm; however, the reaction is not reversible upon cooling. At much higher temperatures, a two-dimensional film may exist.[6]

The heat of chemisorption of molecular oxygen by silver is large, and an ordered oxide surface structure has been detected by X-ray powder diffraction after heating silver powder at 300°C for 10 min in noncirculating air, although when sintering occurred "to a certain extent," the peaks vanished. The Ag-O could not be removed by heating silver in a reducing atmosphere.[18]

Metallic silver surfaces are used to catalyze the air oxidation of ethylene to ethylene oxide and CO to CO_2. Some workers have assumed the adsorbed species to be O_2 or atomic O. Recent work indicates that at 298°K, 0.02% of the adsorbed oxygen is present as O_2^-, the superoxide ion, which plays the major role in the oxidations. Stable Ag_2O layers were formed on metallic silver catalysts supported on Vycor quartz when the catalysts were treated at 298 to 333°K with oxygen at $\leq$ 0.6 Torr pressure.[19]

Atomic oxygen at 10^{-8} atm has been found to oxidize silver extensively at room temperature to 315°C, where no oxidation was detected with molecular oxygen at 40 μ pressure. Below 168°C, both AgO and Ag_2O formed; whereas above 168°C, only Ag_2O formed.

Oxygen diffuses more freely through solid silver than through any other metal.[20] At elevated temperatures, oxygen diffuses through commercial pure silver with the rate increasing rapidly above 400°C.[15]

Molten silver dissolves very large volumes of oxygen. In air at atmospheric pressure (under a partial pressure of about 0.2 atm oxygen) and slightly above its melting point, silver can dissolve about 10 times its volume of oxygen. Vigorous evolution of most of the dissolved oxygen just before solidification is called "spit."[6,20]

Solid silver can dissolve enough oxygen at high temperatures that it will become embrittled when heated in hydrogen above 500°C. The hydrogen diffuses through silver at elevated temperatures and reacts with any oxygen to cause the embrittlement and surface blisters.[15]

The solubility of oxygen in silver at 39 to 1,203 mm Hg oxygen pressure is closely proportional to the square root of the pressure, which supports the view that oxygen dissolves as atoms. Some research indicates that a silver-argentous oxide eutectic may form at high oxygen concentrations.[6,20]

C.   Environmental Chemistry of Silver

        Section II has indicated the extent of the natural distribution
of silver and the silver concentrations normally found. This section will
focus on the forms of silver in rocks, soils, other weathering products,
and natural waters and precipitates. Reactions whereby silver may be precipitated from natural waters and mobilized from or fixed in soils and
primary deposits in rocks are discussed.

        1.   Forms of silver in the natural environment: In rocks and
soils, silver occurs chiefly as a minor constituent of sulfide minerals,
complexed by humic components, or adsorbed to oxides of manganese and iron.
Weathered detritus of rocks that contain gold and silver are chiefly com-
posed of latenite with silver concentrating in native gold particles.

        Silver occurs in variable forms among minerals precipitated from
natural waters. In manganese oxides and certain limonites, silver may be
adsorbed or an integral part of the oxide complexes. Under strongly reducing conditions, silver may precipitate as the humate or sulfide.

        Silver may exist in natural waters as Ag^+, as soluble and col-
loidal complexes, or as an integral part of microorganisms and plants; and
silver is often transported in surface waters by adsorption to suspended
particulates. Sedimentation of silver-bearing organisms and particulates
tends to immobilize silver. Soluble species may be precipitated by the
presence of appropriate anions; by increasing the pH; by coagulation of
colloids; by adsorption by carbonaceous materials, metal hydroxides,clay,
etc.

        a.   Silver in rocks: In most igneous rocks, the bulk of
the silver is in the sulfides or in ferromagnesian minerals. There is
usually less than 5 ppm silver in pyrite and pyrrhotite from igneous rocks,
but the pyrite in silver-rich areas has greater than average amounts of
silver. The presence of silver in sedimentary manganese and iron ores is
due to the colloidal adsorption by oxide colloids and gels. Many sedimentary iron deposits also contain pyrite, which concentrates silver.[2/]

        In metamorphic rocks, silver occurs in the same minerals as
in igneous and sedimentary rocks (see Table II-3 for the form of silver in
various silver-bearing deposits)--pyrite, pyrrhotite, chalcopyrite, etc.--
and in the ferromagnesian minerals--principally biotite, pyroxenes, amphi-
bole, and magnetite (an iron ore).[2/]

        b.   Silver in soils: There are no major differences in the
silver content of soils from different rocks unless the rocks are silver-
bearing. Silver may occur in soils as native silver and as a constituent

of gold particles; silver-bearing lead minerals; heavy minerals (especially magnetite, pyrite, chalcopyrite, and sphalerite); particles of iron and manganese oxides and their coatings on sand and silt; and organic matter (so tightly bound to humic components that little can be removed except by ashing). It can also be a minor constituent of the clay fraction, although the mode of binding is uncertain. Some silver is adsorbed, but the rest is so tightly bound, perhaps by Ag^+ replacement of K^+ or Na^+, that it cannot be extracted. Silver orthophosphate might occur in some soils since it can be precipitated in the presence of soluble phosphates as well as arsenates, molybdates, tungstates, and chromates. Silver also occurs in the minerals jarosite and beudantite and in the saline soils of arid regions, as $AgCl$, $AgBr$, or AgI. There is probably some silver in the soil solution of all soils and in bacteria and other soil organisms.[2]

    c. <u>Silver in other weathering products</u>: In the weathered detritus of gold- and silver-bearing rocks and deposits, gold and silver concentrate in particles of native gold. These eluvial deposits, common in Brazil, the Guianas, Mexico, and elsewhere, are composed chiefly of laterite --a mixture of ferric oxides, hydrated ferric oxides, clay, and sand. Weathering of the material in eluvial deposits will further decompose, erode, transport, and redeposit this material. Gold-silver particles may be ground into flour or, in an aqueous environment, they may be recrystallized, partly dissolved, and the gold reprecipitated on the larger particles. Since silver is more soluble than gold, the particles become enriched in gold with increasing distance from the source.

    Frequently accompanying gold-silver placers are silicates, magnetite, ilmenite, monazite, garnet, zircon, pyrite, native bismuth, cassiterite, and cinnabar. Certain types of eluvial and alluvial fans contain oxidation products of lead-zinc-silver veins; however, the grade of the gravels, clays, etc., is rarely greater than 0.5 troy oz/ton (17 ppm silver).[2]

    d. <u>Silver in natural waters, natural precipitates, and</u> <u>suspensions</u>:

    (1) <u>Silver dissolved in water</u>: The average silver content for all fresh waters is 0.0002 ppm. Most silver in natural waters comes from silver in rocks, deposits, and their weathered products; smaller amounts are derived from industrial and domestic pollution. Nuclear explosions contribute minute amounts of Ag^{110m} to natural waters.[2]

    The silver content of spring waters is generally slightly higher than that of streams, rivers, or lake waters. Acid waters carry more silver than neutral and alkaline waters, but some hot springs are exceptions to this generalization. Waters high in chloride, sulfate, and bicarbonate are often enriched in silver. Chloride and thiosulfate complexes give silver mobility in natural aqueous environments because Ag^+ is not readily precipitated by the anions present (carbonate, phosphate, etc.). Some organic waters and waters high in dissolved iron and manganese also tend to have higher amounts of silver. Waters that leach silver-bearing deposits tend to carry 10 to 100 times more silver than normal natural water bodies; however, generalization fails where carbonate gangue accompanies the silver minerals. Silver is generally accompanied by copper, zinc, cadmium, vanadium, and uranium and, less commonly, by barium, titanium, tin, zirconium, molybdenum, arsenic, antimony, phosphorus, lead, gold, bismuth, nickel, cobalt, and tungsten.[2/]

In anaerobic environments, the presence of HS^- precludes the existence of free $\underline{d}^{10}$ metal cations, such as Ag^+, in concentrations greater than about 10^{-15} $\underline{M}$. The soluble thio complexes may occur at typical concentrations 10^{-7} to 10^{-8} $\underline{M}$, and colloidal metal sulfides may exist, at least temporarily. The solubility of Ag_2S ($K_{sp} = 10^{-50}$) in natural water is determined by the presence of the soluble species $AgSH$, $Ag(SH)_2^-$, and $Ag_2S_3H_2^{2-}$. The true solubility of Ag^+ under natural water conditions is $\geq 10^{-8}$ $\underline{M}$ [$\geq$ 1 ppb].[21/]

Ordinary concentrations of dissolved organic matter are 0.2 to 2 mg carbon/liter with up to 10 mg carbon/liter in polluted water; typically the concentration is $\leq 10^{-6}$ $\underline{M}$. The organic matter has little specificity and is satisfied with the calcium and magnesium ions present at much higher concentrations than Ag^+.[21/]

Kharkar et al. estimated that, in addition to the dissolved silver load of streams, 10% more soluble silver is added to the oceans as a result of desorption from particles in streams on contact with seawater. This desorption is caused by displacement of ions by magnesium and sodium ions.

Kharkar et al. found an average soluble silver content of 0.30 ppb in 10 U.S. rivers (range of average values: 0.17 to 0.55 ppb), the Amazon (0.23 ppb) and the Rhone (0.38 ppb). Montmorillonite and illite, under laboratory conditions resembling those in streams, adsorb 20 to 30% of silver present in solution. Silver in amounts 0.01 to 0.03 ppb was desorbed from the various river waters on contact with seawater.[22/]

Table B-3 lists the probable silver species dissolved in natural waters.

(2) Silver in natural precipitates[2/]: Natural precipitates from cold and hot springs and underground waters often contain small amounts of silver. In natural precipitates, silver is most often

427

found with copper, gold, zinc, lead, cadmium, zirconium, titanium, antimony, arsenic, barium, boron, phosphorus, and sulfur and less often with mercury, vanadium, uranium, thorium, tungsten, cobalts, nickel, molybdenum, bismuth, lithium, and tellurium. Some precipitates are enriched, especially those associated with silver deposits. Manganese oxides (wad) often concentrate silver, and certain varieties of limonite (an iron ore) carry large amounts of silver, especially if manganese oxides, phosphate, and arsenate are also present. In manganese oxides and limonites, silver may be adsorbed or an integral part of the oxide complexes. Silver in vein limonites occurs as native silver, secondary silver-bearing minerals, and probably sometimes as insoluble silver salts. If mixed with organic substances, the limonite's silver content is probably in the form of complex silver humates.

Calcareous, siliceous, limonitic, or ocherous precipitates from waters containing chloride ion, probably contain insoluble silver chloride. Barite and siliceous sinters contain silver in associated galena and other sulfides.

Humic complexes apparently are major concentrators of silver in some areas. Where decaying animal remains and vegetation are abundant, silver is usually precipitated as the humate or as a sulfide under strongly reducing conditions.[2/]

Table B-4 lists mechanisms by which the most probable silver species present in natural waters may be precipitated.

(3) _Silver in suspensions_; In 1967, Turekian and Scott reported the silver, chromium, molybdenum, nickel, cobalt, and manganese contents of suspended material in 18 U.S. rivers.[23/] The amount of silver carried varied from 1.0 ppm in a suspended load of 12 mg/liter in the Flint River of Georgia to a high of 15.00 ppm in a suspended load of 54 mg/liter in the Susquehanna River of Pennsylvania. (See Table 9 in Section II.)

The Mississippi River and those rivers west of it that drain into the Gulf of Mexico have higher suspended loads than do eastern rivers and have sediments rich in montmorillonite. The eastern rivers are characterized by higher concentrations of most elements; by larger proportions of kaolinite, illite, and aluminum-interlayered clay; and by sediments containing more carbon than the average for U.S. streams. Since the ion-exchange capacity of the clay fraction of eastern rivers is lower than that of central and western rivers, the major mode of transport cannot be simple cation exchange. If the transport mode is cation exchange, it would also be expected that fine fractions of sediments would contain higher contents of trace elements than the coarser fractions. This was not true for the Brazos River, which carried the highest sediment load of the 18 rivers studied.

Turekian and Scott suggested that the eastern rivers are carrying higher concentrations of trace elements due to "a greater amount of a trace-element rich soil component and industrial contamination in the eastern rivers."

In the main rivers of the U.S.S.R., silver was found in small amounts in suspensions as were molybdenum, lead, vanadium, manganese, cobalt, nickel, copper, and iron. Nickel and copper were also found to migrate in solution.[24]

It has been reported that Var River (Monaco) sediments take up Ag^+ very rapidly compared with zinc or cobalt ions. The suspended sediment in the river may vary as much as by 1,000 times the mean concentration while the concentration of a particular trace element is usually only 4 to 5 times the mean.[25]

2. <u>Mobilization and fixation of silver in primary silver deposits and soils</u>: Silver in mineral deposits may be mobilized by waters containing dissolved oxygen or carbon dioxide, excess halide ion, ferric sulfate, sulfuric acid, nitrate under oxidizing conditions, and thiosulfate. The presence of ferrous ion, sulfide minerals, and adsorptive species tend to immobilize silver.

Silver is mobilized from soils by an acidic environment, complexing ions, nitrates, ferric ions, and oxidation of humic complexes. An alkaline environment, potassium clay minerals, negatively charged hydrated iron and manganese oxides, organic matter, and appropriate precipitating anions tend to fix silver in the soil.

a. <u>Oxidation and secondary enrichment of silver deposits</u>: Meteoritic waters containing oxygen attack silver sulfides and sulfo salts to form relatively soluble silver sulfate. Silver bicarbonate and hydrogen sulfide are also formed from silver sulfides and sulfo salts by the action of waters containing dissolved carbon dioxide. When nitrate is present in oxidizing solutions, some silver may migrate as silver nitrate. If salt beds provide chloride ion, silver may form $AgCl_2^-$; however, the action of solutions containing Cl^-, Br^-, and I^- on primary silver-bearing minerals such as native silver, acanthite, and freibergite may precipitate AgCl, etc.[2]

Where pyrite is being oxidized and ferric sulfate is abundant, silver sulfate may form.

$$2Ag + Fe_2(SO_4)_3 \rightleftharpoons Ag_2SO_4 + 2FeSO_4$$

Sulfuric acid, which is formed by oxidation of pyrite and other sulfides, slowly dissolves acanthite, various other silver sulfides and sulfosalts, and native silver:

$$Ag_2S + H_2SO_4 \rightleftharpoons Ag_2SO_4 + H_2S$$

$$2Ag + 2H_2SO_4 \rightleftharpoons Ag_2SO_4 + 2H_2O + SO_2$$

H_2S inhibits the first reaction, but it may be oxidized to sulfur or sulfate by oxygen or ferric sulfate. In deposits containing iron sulfides, any ferrous ion from ferrous sulfate tends to precipitate silver, but sulfuric acid dissolves silver. When free oxygen is abundant, the oxidation of ferrous to ferric ion is rapid, but as solutions pass downward through a deposit, the oxidation potential decreases and the ferrous ion concentration increases so that silver precipitation occurs.[2]

Thiosulfate is formed in neutral and alkaline solutions during oxidation of sulfides:

$$S^{2-} \longrightarrow S_2O_3{}^{2-} \longrightarrow SO_3{}^{2-} \longrightarrow S_{2-6}O_6{}^{2-} \longrightarrow SO_4{}^{2-}$$

$$Ag^+ + 2S_2O_3{}^{2-} \rightleftharpoons [Ag(S_2O_3)_2]^{3-}$$

Binding of silver by the thiosulfate ion is catalyzed by cupric ion. In neutral and alkaline waters, the complex ion migrates as the sodium, potassium, calcium, etc., species.[2]

The solubility of silver carbonate is increased with increasing carbon dioxide concentration, probably due to the formation of silver bicarbonate.[2]

Native silver is precipitated from neutral and slightly acid solutions containing silver sulfate and presumably also silver carbonate and silver bicarbonate by numerous sulfide minerals such as chalcocite, niccolite, covellite, bornite, tennantite, alabandite, smaltite, marcasite, pyrrhotite, and chalcopyrite; quartz; mica; kaolinite; native copper; clay; etc. Mixtures of metallic sulfides and carbonates, various sulfides and sulfo salts and carbonaceous and graphitic substances also precipitate silver from dilute solutions. Cinnabar, stibnite, pyrite, galena, millerite, sphalerite, jamesonite, orpiment, and realgar cause little or no silver precipitation from dilute solutions.[2,26]

Silver sulfide sols are not significantly precipitated by sulfide ores; however, calcite and, presumably, other carbonates will coagulate the silver sulfide sols. Argillaceous materials, colloidal aluminosilicates, kaolinite, and carbonaceous matter probably also precipitate silver sols.[2]

430

Ideally, in oxidized silver deposits, silver halides will predominate if their formation is favored, native silver will occur in intermediate horizons, and acanthite and sulfosalts will occur at or near the water table. Among gold-silver deposits, the greatest enrichment of silver and gold as a result of oxidation occurs in deposits in which the various base-metal sulfides--pyrite, pyrrhotite, and arsenopyrite--are abundant.[2]

Almost all vein, porphyry, and other types of copper deposits contain small amounts of silver in, or associated with, the minerals chalcopyrite, bornite, enargite, and tetrahedrite. As copper deposits are oxidized, ferrous sulfate in the oxidizing solutions greatly inhibits the migration of silver and gold but does not affect copper sulfate in solution. Thus, silver is precipitated and copper is leached in the oxidized zones.

Chalcocite has such a marked precipitating effect on silver, that little silver as secondary minerals develops below chalcocite zones. The probable reaction is

$$Cu_2S + 2Ag_2SO_4 \rightleftharpoons 2CuSO_4 + Ag_2S + 2Ag$$

Silver may replace some copper in the lattice to give $(Cu,Ag)_2S$ or be bound as acanthite, stromeyerite, and native silver. Other silver sulfide and sulfo salts are rare in chalcocite zones.[2]

Various arsenates, limonite, wad, and secondary minerals of lead and other metals may be present in many copper sulfate, carbonate, chloride, and silicate ores and these may contain silver in their lattices or adsorbed to their surfaces.[2]

b. Mobility and fixation in soils[2]: All silver compounds are slightly soluble and are gradually removed from the soil. Thus, well-drained soils tend to have lower silver concentrations than poorly drained soils in the same area. Generalizations on the geochemistry of silver are permissible where elevations are subdued, but soils that tend to be disturbed by downhill migration cause mixing of materials.

The normal redox potentials (Eh) of soils have little direct effect on silver mobility, but the soil Eh is of major importance for the part it plays in the hydrolysis of iron and manganese, precipitation of their oxide hydrates, production of sulfide ion, and oxidation of organic material, all of which influence Ag^+ chemistry.

The sulfate, bicarbonate, and nitrate anions and various organic acids render silver relatively soluble, while phosphate, chloride, bromide, iodide, chromate, and arsenate anions precipitate silver and decrease its mobility.

Soil organisms that render nitrogen compounds soluble as nitrates would increase the mobility of silver. The organisms would break down organic complexes and liberate any complexed silver; however, if any H_2S or S^{2-} is produced by bacterial action on protein complexes in organic environments, silver's mobility would be reduced. In addition, complexing Ag^+ with thiosulfate or excess chloride ion to give $[Ag(S_2O_3)_2]^{3-}$, $[AgCl_2]^{2-}$, and $[AgCl_3]^{2-}$ mobilizes Ag^+.

Colloids of silver chloride, if they exist in nature, would be expected to increase silver's mobility. The silver halide complexes may carry either a positive or negative charge, and precipitation of these colloids would depend on the types of colloids and electrolytes present in the soil solutions. For example, positive colloidal ferric hydroxide would precipitate the negative halide colloids, and the positive halide colloids would be precipitated by negative manganese colloids.

Silver salts are normally more soluble and mobile in an acidic environment. Silver is relatively immobile in soils of pH > 4 because slight hydrolysis of Ag^+ occurs with decreasing acidity and acidic and basic salts may be precipitated. In an alkaline environment, Ag_2O or its hydrate is precipitated. However, these simple reactions seldom occur in any soil because iron, manganese, alumina, and organic matter modify the chemistry.

Where decreasing acidity and relatively high Eh prevail, ferrous iron is oxidized to the ferric state by the reversible reaction:

$$Fe^{2+} + Ag^+ \rightleftharpoons Ag^0 + Fe^{3+}$$

If the concentration of Fe^{2+} in solution is high, Ag^0 is precipitated. If the Fe^{3+} concentration is high, silver is kept soluble and mobile as Ag^+.

Analogously, in neutral and mildly alkaline soils:

$$2Ag^+ + Mn^{2+} + 4OH^- \rightleftharpoons 2Ag + MnO_2 + 2H_2O$$

Ferric ion undergoes hydrolysis and may precipitate as a basic salt or the oxide hydrate $FeO(OH) \cdot nH_2O$. Some soils of pH 3 to 5 contain the basic complex ferric sulfates beudantite and jarosite, which will scavenge and immobilize silver. The positively charged colloidal iron oxide hydrate attracts phosphate, arsenate, manganese dioxide, silica, humic colloids, etc., which may give the combined colloidal complex a negative charge. When this occurs, Ag^+ and other cations are adsorbed or coprecipitated on the negative

colloid. Negatively charged hydrated manganese oxides that precipitate with
decreasing acidity also adsorb and coprecipitate Ag^+.[2] Aged iron and manganese oxides are not good cation absorbers but fresh iron oxide (hydroxides)
forming in soil profiles or from the neutralization of acid industrial wastes
may account for much of the transport of metals in the suspended load of
streams.[23]

Potassium clay minerals, which are formed by basic hydrolysis
of alumina and are a complex series of hydroxides and aluminosilicates, may
also scavenge and immobilize Ag^+ because of the similarity of its size to
that of K^+. Organic matter, especially humic substances, also adsorbs and
perhaps chelates silver. Much silver is immobilized and enriched in soils
containing abundant organic matter, e.g., in peat, half-bog soils, and de-
composing organic debris in marshes. Decreasing the pH to 3.0 does not significantly decrease the silver content of humic components. However, as
humification proceeds, large coordinated humic groups, retaining much of
their silver, dissociate into a soluble (colloidal) form in the soil solutions which facilitates their removal by groundwaters. Humic complexes may
be oxidized and liberate any bound silver under a high oxidation potential;
however, any remaining humic complexes quickly tie up the silver again.
This repeated process eventually leads to the silver enrichment of organic
layers of soils and in peats.[2]

D. Alloys

1. Binary alloys: Phase diagrams are available for binary alloys
of silver with over 38 elements such as: magnesium, calcium, titanium,
chromium, manganese, nickel, palladium, copper, gold, zinc, cadmium, mercury, lead, tin, phosphorus, oxygen, and sulfur.   The extensive use of
silver brazing alloys for joining ferrous alloys is explained by the extremely limited solubility of iron, cobalt, nickel, vanadium, molybdenum,
and tungsten in liquid and solid silver and the absence of intermediate
phases between these metals and silver.

Most alloyed silver is produced in wrought form. Wrought single-
phase silver-cadmium alloys for electrical contacts are converted to two-
phase materials by internal oxidation of cadmium to cadmium oxide, which
is useful because of its nonwelding properties. The most important commercial silver-magnesium alloy, containing less than 0.25% magnesium, can
be hardened by internal oxidation of Mg to MgO.   Table B-5 shows some
of the binary alloy systems and their industrial uses.

Bimetal materials that cannot be produced by alloying can be
formed by powder metallurgical techniques. For example, sintered silver-
tungsten and silver-nickel products for electrical contact materials are

produced by powder metallurgy. Silver that has been infiltrated into sintered tungsten powder is used for contacts and for rocket-nozzle walls. Sintered silver-iron products containing 10 to 20% silver are produced by powder metallurgy and used for electrical contacts.[27]

    2. _Ternary and higher silver alloys_: The most attractive systems for developing ternary and higher silver alloys are silver-gold, silver-palladium, and silver-gold-palladium, which give solid solutions for all compositions. The next most attractive system is silver-copper.[27]

    Ternary alloys comprising silver and palladium with iron, chromium, cobalt, nickel, manganese, platinum, copper, and gold are known.[28] High-temperature brazing alloys containing silver comprise 52 to 95% silver in binary or ternary alloys with copper, palladium, nickel, and manganese.[29]

    Ternary alloys based on silver-gold contain nickel, platinum, or copper as their third element. The silver-gold-copper alloys are used as jewelry and dental solders. For example, the low-karat solder is 45% Au-30 to 35% Ag-15 to 20% Cu; general-purpose solder, 60% Au-12 to 22% Ag-12 to 22% Cu; and high-karat solder, 80% Au-3 to 8% Ag-8 to 12% Cu. All of these solders may have a few percent zinc and tin.

    Nickel, cadmium, indium, zinc, tin, and copper phosphide are added to silver-copper systems. An important family of industrial brazing alloys is based on 0 to 15% silver-40 to 60% copper-35 to 55% copper phosphide alloys. Silver-copper-indium and -tin alloys are used for brazing in the vacuum tube industry. Other ternary alloys are based on the interalloying of silver with zinc, cadmium, tin, indium, and mercury. Examples are silver-mercury-tin and silver-cadmium-indium, -tin, and -zinc. A few weight percent silver is also added to tin, tin-base, and lead alloys for use as soft solders.

    Up to 5 atom percent lithium is often added to silver brazing alloys as a wetting agent. Lithium is also often used as a deoxidizer for silver and silver alloy melts. Silver alloys containing 0.06 wt % lithium and 0.04 wt % silicon are used for vapor coating of reflectors used in some sealed-beam lamps. In silver-lithium-silicon alloys, silicon is used as a wetting agent. The use of 0.6% silicon to give an age-hardenable silver is not common.

    Titanium is added to silver brazing alloys as a wetting agent in materials designed for ceramic brazing. A commercial product for joining metals to ceramics comprises a titanium core surrounding by a silver-copper eutectic brazing alloy. A composite wire containing 3 to 8% titanium is most common.

Among the higher alloys are the typical colored golds, comprising 41.7 to 75.0% Au- 48.0 to 6% Cu-4.0 to 48.9% Au-0 to 9.0% Zn; gold-silver-copper-palladium-platinum-zinc dental casting alloys, containing 3 to 26% silver in yellow golds and 7 to 30% silver in white golds; and dental amalgam, having a nominal composition 33% Ag-52% Hg-12.5% Sn-2% Cu-0.5% Zn.

E. Analysis

The numerous analytical procedures suitable for analysis of silver in various sources are described in Table B-6.

F. The Photographic Process

The following discussion is adapted from the chapter "Silver in Photography" by E. A MacWilliam appearing in the 1967 treatise Silver. Economics, Metallurgy, and Use.[30/]

In the primary reaction of silver salts with light, the direct photometric yield (atoms released/quantum absorbed) seldom approaches unity. Silver salts undergo an unusual secondary amplification process called "development."

Certain mild reducing agents called "photographic developers" increase the rate of reduction to the metallic silver image manyfold if the silver salt crystals (grains) carry very small amounts of silver metal at the developer-crystal surface (perhaps as few as 5 silver atoms/10^{12} atoms in the whole crystal). The silver speck serves as a very effective catalyst for this reduction or "development," which may provide an amplification factor of $\geq 10^{11}$ to the effect produced by the original light exposure. These silver specks--the latent image centers--are formed during light exposure. During processing, the silver halide not developed is removed.

Most silver-containing photographic emulsions contain < 10 mole % I^- in the AgBr or silver chlorobromide lattice. Photographic emulsions are prepared by mixing a solution of a soluble silver salt, usually $AgNO_3$, with a soluble alkali metal halide, e.g. NaCl or KBr, in the presence of a colloidal substance to prevent immediate coalescence of the crystallites. By varying KBr solution concentrations, temperature, and silver halide composition, the grain size, size-frequency distribution, and sensitivity can be varied.

None of the silver halides is sensitive to light much beyond the blue region of the spectrum. Other substances adsorbed on the emulsion grains can absorb energy at longer wavelengths and transfer that energy to the silver halide grain. Spectral sensitizing dyes provide the color selectivity necessary for the functioning of color films.

In commercial emulsions, latent images are formed in the interior of the grains and do not catalyze development because the developer solution is unable to reach them. Dissolving the silver halide by adding the solvent, usually $Na_2S_2O_3$, to the developer solution uncovers these latent images. Alternatively, KI is added to the developer, which causes recrystallication of the silver halide grain and exposure of the internal latent image.

Development proceeds at the grain surface in most conventional photographic systems. In this type of "chemical development," silver ions from the crystal combine at the latent-image site with electrons from the developer molecule.

If there is a high level of silver solvent in the developer, "physical" development occurs, in which the silver halide is first dissolved and then the silver ions are reduced by the dissolved developer and separated from the solution as silver atoms. Particles, formed by separation on any available centers, are compact spheres.

In "solvent transfer developments," a receiving sheet, uniformly coated with very tiny nuclei, is brought in contact with an exposed photographic negative. A developer solution between the two containing a solvent for silver halide develops the exposed silver halide grains to a negative and dissolves the unexposed grains to produce a "phsyical" developer in that neighborhood. Rapid development of this dissolved silver onto the adjacent nuclei of the receiving sheet produces a positive image of the original scene. This system is used in the Apeco Company office copiers and in the Polaroid-Land camera.

The "fixing bath," which may contain any solvent for silver halide in neutral or acid solution, removes the undeveloped silver halide in order to stabilize the image. The most common fixing bath is $Na_2S_2O_3$, called "hypo." Concentrated KBr or KSCN solutions can also be used.

"Hypo" forms a series of soluble complex salts with silver ions. The most common is $Na_3Ag(S_2O_3)_2$, which can be washed from the film or paper with water. $(NH_4)_2S_2O_3$ is often used in rapid-acting fixing baths since it dissolves silver salts more rapidly than $Na_2S_2O_3$.

For reversal movie films and color reversal films, the negative silver is now discarded rather than the undeveloped silver halide. The silver image is oxidized to a soluble silver salt in a solution that does

not attack silver halide crystals. The residual silver halide is distributed as a positive with the smallest amount occurring where most exposure
was given and vice versa. Exposing the film to light and developing a
second time produces a positive silver image.

Color film senses the relative amounts of the three primary
colors, blue, green, and red, in the exposing light. One of three photo-
sensitive layers coated on the film records the amount of each color.
Spectral sensitizing dyes and a blue-absorbing filter achieve the selectivity. Development of the exposed film produces a silver image in one
or more layers depending on the light color.

To produce a positive image, the reversal procedure employs a
special developing agent that will produce the colored dye image. The
oxidized form of the special developing agent, which results from the
reaction between the developer and the developing silver halide, reacts
with a third substance, the "coupler," to form a dye. The coupler produces a dye that absorbs the color of light corresponding the the color
sensitivity of the particular recording layer where development occurs.

Use of Kodachrome or Ektachrome films produces a color positive
by a reversal process. Kodacolor negative film by direct color development produces a color negative.

In color development to produce either a negative or a positive,
the developed silver must be removed by oxidizing it to a salt that is
soluble or can be removed by fixing in hypo.

Reversal processing, involving the use of one or more silver
bleach baths, provides other uses for silver in photography. A yellow
filter, usually a dispersion of metallic silver, is required under the
blue-sensitive top layer in color films to prevent the underlying green-
and red-sensitized layers from also recording the blue light image. A
black and white reversal film may use an "antihalation undercoat" of blue-
black colloidal silver to prevent reflection of unabsorbed light, which
would produce halos around bright objects.

Developed images may be modified with "reducers," "intensifiers,"
or "toning solutions" to lighten dense negatives, to make thin negatives
more dense, or make the image color more blue or brown, respectively.

The fine silver filaments of the photographic image are stable
not only because of silver's inertness but also because the filaments produced by a normal photographic process have an adsorbed layer of silver
sulfide or silver-hypo complex.

TABLE B-1

PHYSICAL PROPERTIES OF SILVER COMPOUNDS

Compound Name	Oxidation State	M.P. (°C)	B.P. (°C)	Solubility	Color, Physical Form	ΔHc kcal/mole	Remarks	References
$K_6H[Ag(IO_6)_2]\cdot10H_2O$	III				Yellow or orange crystals		Diamagnetic. Prepared by oxidizing Ag_2O with boiling solution of KOH or NaOH with KIO_4.	1 31
$K_7[Ag(IO_6)_2]\cdot KOH\cdot8H_2O$	III				Yellow or orange crystals			
$K_6H[Ag(IO_6)_2]\cdot KOH\cdot8H_2O$	III				Yellow or orange crystals			
$Na_6K[Ag(IO_6)_2]\cdot NaOH\cdot H_2O$	III				Yellow or orange crystals			
$Na_7H_2[Ag(TeO_6)_2]\cdot14H_2O$	III				Yellow or orange		Diamagnetic.	1, 31
$Na_6H_3[Ag(TeO_6)_2]\cdot18H_2O$	III				Yellow or orange			
$KAgF_4$	III				Yellow		Diamagnetic. Extremely sensitive to moisture.	1 31
$CsAgF_4$	III				Yellow		Very stable.	1 31
Silver ethylenedibiguanide (edbg)$^{+3}$ complexes, e.g.,	III							
$[Ag(edbg)]_2(SO_4)_3\cdot7H_2O$					Red		Hydroxide. Prepared from sulfate.	1, 31
$[Ag(edbg)](OH)_3\cdot3H_2O$					Violet red			
Ag_2O_3	III				Black		Claimed by anodic oxidation Ag(I).	1, 32
$Ag(Ag_3O_4)_2NO_3$	III				Crystals with metallic luster. High c.d. gives prismatic needles. Low c.d. gives cubic octahedra.		Similar compounds reported in which the anion is ClO_4^- or F^-. Prepared by electrolysis of aqueous $AgNO_3$ with a Pt anode. Decomp. spontaneously to $AgNO_3$, AgO, and O_2.	33
AgO (or Ag_2O_2)	II (?) or more likely $Ag^I Ag^{III} O_2$	Decomp. > 100		Insoluble in H_2O. Forms Ag^{2+} in acid media. Dissolves in dil. alk. media without decompn.	Gray-black, cubic	-2.73, -2.769, -2.9, -6.0	Used as an oxidizing agent in anal. chemistry. Pptd. from alk. oxidn. of Ag(I) nonreducing salts.	1 32 33
AgF_2	II	690	Decomp. 700° under 1 atm of F_2		Dark brown crystalline solid (amorphous)	-83.0, -84.5	Strong oxidizing and fluorinating agent. True Ag(II) compd. Ferromagnetic at < 163°K. Unknown in nature.	1 2 32 33

438

TABLE B-1 (Continued)

Compound Name	Oxidation State	M.P. (°C)	B.P. (°C)	Solubility	Color, Physical Form	ΔHc kcal/mole	Remarks	References
[AgPy$_4$]$^{+2}$ (py = pyridyl)	II						Obtained as crystalline persulfates.	1
[Ag(dipy)$_2$]$^{+2}$ (dipy = 2,2'-dipyridyl)	II							
[Ag(o-phen)$_2$]$^{+2}$ (o-phen = 1,10-phenanthroline)								
[AgPy$_4$]S$_2$O$_8$	II						Ag(II) is also stabilized by complexing with tripyridyl and pyridine carboxylic acids.	33
AgO$_2$CCH$_3$ Silver acetate	I	Decomp.		1:100 in cold H$_2$O 1:35 in hot H$_2$O Very sol. in HNO$_3$	White plates			34 35
Ag$_2$C$_2$ Silver acetylide	I	Explodes		Insol. in H$_2$O	White ppt.		Severe explosion hazard when exposed to heat or shock.	1 35 36
Ag$_3$AsO$_4$ Silver orthoarsenate	I	Decomp.		Water soly. 8.5 x 10^{-4} g/100 cc (25°C) Sol. in NH$_4$OH, HNO$_3$, AcOH. K$_{sp}$ 10^{-21}	Cubic, dark-red crystals		Poisonous.	2 32 35 36
Ag$_3$AsO$_3$ Silver orthoarsenite	I	Decomp. 150°		Insol. in H$_2$O Sol. in NH$_4$OH	Yellow powder		Poisonous. Protect from light.	34, 35 36, 37
AgN$_3$ Silver azide	I	252	297	Insol. in H$_2$O Sol. in KCN, HNO$_3$, NH$_4$OH K$_{sp}$ 2.9 x 10^{-9}	White rhombic	88.9	Severe explosion hazard when exposed to heat or shock.	32 35 36
AgO$_2$C$_6$H$_5$ Silver benzoate	I			Sl. sol. in cold H$_2$O Sol. in hot H$_2$O	White powder			35 36
Ag$_2$B$_4$O$_7$ Silver tetraborate	I			Sl. sol. in cold H$_2$O	White crystal			35
AgBrO$_3$ Silver bromate	I	Decomp.		Sl. sol. in H$_2$O Sol. in NH$_4$OH Sl. sol. in HNO$_3$	White powder	-6.5	Poisonous. Protect from contact with organic matter.	32, 34 35, 36 37

439

TABLE B-1 (Continued)

Compound Name	Oxidation State	M.P. (°C)	B.P. (°C)	Solubility	Color, Physical Form	ΔHc kcal/mole	Remarks	References
AgBr Silver bromide	I	432	Decomp. > 1300 Decomp. > 500	Water soly. 1.3×10^{15} g/100 cc (25°C). Sl. sol. in NH$_4$OH. K$_{sp}$ 5.0 or 7.7×10^{-13}. Sol. in Na$_2$S$_2$O$_3$ or KCN soln.	Yellow powder	-23.7 -24.0	Protect from light. Poisonous.	2 32 34 35 37
Ag$_2$CO$_3$ Silver carbonate	I	Decomp. ≤ 218		Water soly. 3.2×10^{-3} g/100 cc (25°C). Sol. in HNO$_3$, NH$_4$OH, KCN. K$_{sp}$ = 6.15×10^{-12} (25°C)	Yellow powder	-121.0	Protect from light. Probably occurs in small amounts in some natural waters.	2, 5 32 34 35 36 37
AgClO$_3$ Silver chlorate	I	230	Decomp. 270	10 g/100 cc H$_2$O at 15°C. 50 g/100 cc H$_2$O at 80°C	White tetragonal crystals	-6		32 34 35 36
AgClO$_4$ Silver perchlorate	I	Decomp. 486		Very sol. in H$_2$O	White, deliquescent crystals	-7.5		32, 34 35, 36
AgCl Silver chloride	I	455	1550	Water soly. 1.8×10^{-4} g/100 cc at 25°C. Insol. HNO$_3$, dil. H$_2$SO$_4$. Sol. in NH$_4$OH, Na$_2$S$_2$O$_3$, KCN, Cl$^-$ solns, concd. HNO$_3$	White cubic crystal, often crystalline powder	-30.3	Protect from light. Very ductile. Can be rolled into large sheets. Ag halides form complex ions AgX$_2^-$ where X = Cl$^-$, Br$^-$, and I$^-$. Vapor pressure 1 mm at 912°C.	1 2 8 32 34 35 36 37
AgClO$_2$ Silver chlorite	I	Explodes at 105		Sl. sol. in H$_2$O	Yellow crystals	2.1		32, 34 35, 36
AgCrO$_4$ Silver chromate	I			Water soly. 2.5×10^{-3} g/100 cc (25°C). Sl. sol. in NH$_4$OH. Sol. KCN, HNO$_3$. K$_{sp}$ = 1.3 or 1.9×10^{-12}	Red monoclinic crystals	-174		2 32 34 35 36

TABLE B-1 (Continued)

Compound Name	Oxidation State	M.P. (°C)	B.P. (°C)	Solubility	Color, Physical Form	ΔHc kcal/mole	Remarks	References
$Ag_3C_6H_5O_7$ Silver citrate	I	Decomp.		Very sl. sol. in cold H_2O. Sl. sol. in hot H_2O. Sol. in HNO_3, NH_4OH, KCN.	White needlelike powder			34, 35
$Ag_2Cr_2O_7$ Silver dichromate	I	Decomp.		Insol. in H_2O. Sol. in HNO_3, NH_4OH, KCN	Dark red crystalline powder			34, 35, 36
AgOCN Silver cyanate	I	Decomp.		Sl. sol. in cold H_2O. Sol. in hot H_2O.	Colorless crystals			35, 36
AgCN Silver cyanide	I	Decomp. 320		Insol. in H_2O. Sol. in HNO_3, NH_4OH, KCN.	Colorless hexagonal crystals or powder	34.9	Poisonous. Protect from light.	32, 34, 35, 36, 37
$Ag_3Fe(CN)_6$ Silver ferricyanide	I			Insol. in H_2O. Sol. in NH_4OH.				35
$Ag_4Fe(CN)_2 \cdot H_2O$ Silver ferrocyanide	I			Insol. in H_2O. Sol. in KCN.	White			35
$Ag_3(GaF_6) \cdot 10H_2O$ Silver fluogallate	I			Very sol. in H_2O.	Colorless orthorhombic crystals			35, 36
AgF Silver fluoride	I	435	~1159	Sol. in H_2O.	Yellow cubic crystals	-48.5 -50	Hygroscopic. Protect from light. (UV radiation decomp. it to Ag_2F and F_2). Not photosensitive. Unknown in nature. Intermediate between metal and salt.	2, 8 31, 32 34, 35 36, 37
Ag_2F Disilver fluoride, Silver subfluoride	0, I	Decomp. 90		Hydrolyzes in H_2O to AgF and Ag.	Yellow or bronze crystalline. Hexagonal plates.		Stable in dry air or aromatic hydrocarbons. Prepared by electrolyzing satd. AgF.	7 31 35
$Ag_2SiF_6 \cdot 4H_2O$ Silver fluosilicate	I	> 100	Decomp.	Very sol. in H_2O.	Colorless crystals or white deliquescent powder			35, 36
$Ag_2C_2N_2O_2$ Silver fulminate	I	Explodes		Very sl. sol. in cold H_2O. Sol. in hot H_2O. Sol. in NH_4OH.	Small needles		Severe explosion hazard. When heated to decompn. temp., emits highly toxic fumes.	35, 36
$AgIO_3$ Silver iodate	I	> 200	Decomp.	Insol. in H_2O. Sol. in HNO_3, NH_4OH, KI $K_{sp} = 3.1 \times 10^{-8}$	Colorless, rhombic crystals	-41.8		32 35, 36

441

TABLE B-1 (Continued)

Compound Name	Oxidation State	M.P. (°C)	B.P. (°C)	Solubility	Color, Physical Form	ΔHc kcal/mole	Remarks	References
$AgIO_4$ Silver periodate	I	Decomp. 180		Sol. in HNO_3.	Yellow tetragonal crystals		Protect from light.	35
AgI Silver iodide (β)	I	558	1506	Water soly. 2.8×10^{-7} g/100 cc (25°C) Sol. in concd. HI, KI, NaI, etc. Sol. in $Na_2S_2O_3$ or KCN soln. $K_{sp} = 1.5 \times 10^{-16}$ (25°C)	Trimorphic: yellow α form—cubic, stable > 145.8°C; green-yellow hexagonal β form, stable <145.8°C; γ form "cold cubic" exists below 137°C.			2 8 34 35 36 37
AgI Silver iodide (α)	I	Changes to AgI(β) at 146°		Insol. in H_2O. Sol. in KCN, $Na_2S_2O_3$, KI. $K_{sp} = 8.7 \times 10^{-17}$	Yellow hexagonal	-14.9		32 35
Ag_2HgI_4 Silver iodomercurate (β)	I	Decomp. 158		Insol. in H_2O. Sol. in KI, KCN.	Red cubic			35
Ag_2HgI_4 Silver iodomercurate (α)	I	Changes to Ag_2HgI_4 (β) at 50.7°		Same as (β).	Yellow tetragonal			35
$Ag_2N_2O_2$ Silver hyponitrite	I	Decomp. 110		Very sl. sol. in H_2O.	Yellow crystals		Explodes at 302°C. Emits toxic oxides of nitrogen when heated to decompn.	34, 35 36
AgH_2PO_2 Silver hypophosphite	I				White crystals		Emits toxic fumes of phosphorus oxides when heated to decompn.	34
$AgC_3H_5O_3 \cdot H_2O$ Silver lactate	I			Sl. sol. in H_2O.	White or slightly gray crystalline powder			34, 35 36
$AgC_{12}H_{23}O_2$ Silver laurate	I	212.5		Insol. in H_2O.	White greasy powder			35
$AgC_5H_7O_3$ Silver levulinate	I			Sl. sol. in H_2O.	Leaf			35
$AgMnO_4$ Silver permanganate	I	Decomp.		Very sl. sol. in cold H_2O. Sl. sol. in hot H_2O.	Dark violet monoclinic crystals or powder		Protect from light.	34, 35 36, 37
Ag_2MoO_4 Silver molybdate	I	483		Sol. in HNO_3, KCN, NaOH; 0.00386 g/100 g H_2O (25°C)	White ppt., or pale yellow after fusion	-200.4 -216.6	Pptd. from Ag^+ solns. by adding MoO_4^{-2} or prepd. by fusing $AgNO_3$ with MoO_3 at 500 to 600°C.	38

TABLE B-1 (Continued)

Compound Name	Oxidation State	M.P. (°C)	B.P. (°C)	Solubility	Color, Physical Form	ΔHc kcal/mole	Remarks	References
$AgC_{14}H_{27}O_2$ Silver myristate	I	211		Insol. in H_2O.				35
$AgNO_3$ Silver nitrate	I	212	Decomp. 444	Water soly. 329 g/100 cc (25°C); 122 g/100 ml cold H_2O; 952 g/100 ml boiling H_2O. Sol. in NH_4OH. $K_{sp} = 1.2 \times 10^{-4}$ (25°C).	Colorless rhombic crystals	-29.8	Protect from light. Easily reduced to the metal by many organic compounds.	2, 8 32 34 35 36 37
$AgNO_2$ Silver nitrite	I	Decomp. 140		Very sl. sol. in cold H_2O. Sl. sol. in hot H_2O.	White rhombic crystals; 2 tautomeric forms	-10		2, 8, 32 34, 35 36, 37
Ag_3N Silver nitride	I				Colorless solid	61.0 63	Prepd. by treating $AgNO_3$ soln. with hydrazine or hydrazoic acid. Severe shock hazard. Highly explosive fulminating Ag, believed to be Ag_3N or Ag inide, may detonate when Ag_2O is heated with NH_3 or when Ag amine complexes are allowed to stand.	8 32 36
$Ag_2[Pt(NO_2)_4]$ Silver nitroplatinite	I	Decomp. 100		Sl. sol. in cold H_2O. Sol. in hot H_2O.	Yellow-brown monoclinic prisms			35
$Ag_2[FeNO(CN)_5]$ Silver nitroprusside	I			Insol. in H_2O. Sol. in NH_4OH.	Light pink		Highly toxic. Emits toxic fumes upon heating.	34 35,36
$Ag_2C_2O_4$ Silver oxalate	I	Explodes at 140		Insol. in H_2O. Sol. in NH_4OH, concd. HNO_3.	White, crystalline powder		When heated to decompn., emits highly toxic fumes.	34 35 36
Ag_2O Argentous oxide	I	Decomp. 300 (begins decomp. at 100° to Ag and O_2).		Water soly. 2.1×10^{-3} g/100 cc at 25°C. Sol. in NH_4OH, dil. HNO_3.	Brownish-black powder	-7.2 -7.4 (1000°K: -5.95)	Unknown in nature. Oxidizing agent. Forms when excess OH added to $AgNO_3$ soln. or when the metal is heated in the presence of O_2. Forms Ag_2S with S^{-2} and Ag_2CO_3 from atm. CO_2. Readily reduced to Ag by H_2. Solutions absorb CO_2 from the air to form Ag_2CO_3.	1 8 32 34 35 36
$AgC_{16}H_{31}O_2$ Silver palmitate	I	209		Insol. in H_2O.	White greasy powder			35

443

TABLE B-1 (Continued)

Compound Name	Oxidation State	M.P. (°C)	B.P. (°C)	Solubility	Color, Physical Form	ΔHc kcal/mole	Remarks	References
$HOC_6H_4SO_3Ag$ Silver phenolsulfonate (also silver sulfocarbolate)	I				White to faintly reddish crystals		When heated to decompn., emits highly toxic fumes.	36
$AgPO_3$ Silver metaphosphate	I	ca. 482		Insol. in H_2O. Sol. in HNO_3, NH_4OH.	White amorphous			35
Ag_3PO_4 Silver orthophosphate	I	849		Water soly. 6.5×10^{-4} g/100 cc (25°C) Sol. in NH_4OH, dil. HNO_3, $Na_2S_2O_3$. $K_{sp} = 10^{-16}$ to 10^{-21}	Yellow cubic crystals or powder		Protect from light.	2, 32, 34, 35, 36, 37
Ag_2HPO_4 Silver hydrogen orthophosphate	I	Decomp. 110			White trigonal crystals			35
$Ag_4P_2O_7$ Silver pyrophosphate	I	585			White			35
$AgC_3H_5O_2$ Silver propionate	I			Very sl. sol. in cold H_2O. Sl. sol. in hot H_2O.	White leaf or needles			35
$AgOC_6H_2(NO_2)_3 \cdot H_2O$ Silver picrate	I			Sl. sol. in H_2O.	Yellow crystal		Can be explosive.	34, 37
$AgReO_4$ Silver perrhenate	I			Sl. sol. in H_2O.	White crystals tetragonal or rhombic			35
$KAg(CN)_2$ Silver potassium cyanide	I			Sol. in H_2O. Insol. in acids.	White crystals, slight odor of HCN		Protect from light. Poisonous.	32, 36
$Ag(CN)_2^-$ (aq.)						64.3		37
$HC \equiv CCO_2Ag$ Silver propargylate	I				Crystals		Moderate explosion hazard.	36
$AgC_7H_5O_3$ Silver salicylate	I			Sl. sol. in H_2O.	White to reddish-white crystals			35
Ag_2SeO_4 Silver selenate	I			Very sl. sol. in H_2O. $K_{sp} \cong 4 \times 10^{-9}$	White orthorhombic crystals	-80		32, 34, 35, 36

444

TABLE B-1 (Continued)

Compound Name	Oxidation State	M.P. (°C)	B.P. (°C)	Solubility	Color, Physical Form	ΔHc kcal/mole	Remarks	References
Ag_2Se Silver selenide	I	880 (Decomp. > 300°C to form moss Ag)	Decomp.	Insol. in H_2O.	Cubic, thin gray plates	-11	Known as the mineral naumannite.	8, 32 34 35 36
Ag_2SeO_3 Silver selenite	I	Decomp.		Sl. sol. in cold H_2O. Sol. in hot H_2O, HNO_3. $K_{sp} = 2 \times 10^{-15}$	Needle-like crystals	-92		32 34 36
$Ag C_{18}H_{35}O_2$ Silver stearate	I	205		Insol. in H_2O.	White amorphous powder			35
Ag_2SO_4 Silver sulfate	I	652	Decomp. 1085	Water soly. 0.78 g/ 100 cc (25°C). Sol. in HNO_3, NH_4OH, concd. H_2SO_4. $K_{sp} = 1.24 \times 10^{-5}$ (25°C)	White rhombic crystals	-170.5	Protect from light. Its thermal stability permits direct oxidn. and recovery of Ag contained in sulfide minerals.	2, 8 34 35 36 37
$Ag_2S(\beta)$ Silver sulfide (Acanthite)	I	Transforms to argentite at 175°	Decomp.	Water soly. 1×10^{-16} g/100 cc (25°C) Sol. in HNO_3, KCN. Insol. in NH_4OH. $K_{sp} = 1.1 \times 10^{-49}$ (25°C)	Gray-black rhombic crystals	-7.6	All natural Ag_2S is acanthite. Very ductile. Can be cast and drawn into strips or wires.	2 32 34 35, 36
$Ag_2S(\alpha)$	I	845	Decomp.	Sol. in HNO_3, alk. KCN, concd. H_2SO_4. Insol. in H_2O. $K_{sp} = 6.8 \times 10^{-50}$ (25°C)	Black cubic	-7.01		2 8 34 35
Ag_2SO_3 Silver sulfite	I	Decomp. 100		Very sl. sol. in H_2O. Sol. in NH_4OH, KCN. $K_{sp} = 2 \times 10^{-14}$	White crystals	-116.0		32
$Ag_2C_4H_4O_6$ Silver d-tartrate	I	Decomp.		Very sl. sol. in H_2O. Sol. in NH_4OH, KCN.	White scales			35, 36
$Ag_2H_4TeO_6$ Silver orthotellurate, tetra-H	I	Decomp. > 200		Insol. in H_2O. Sol. in KCN, NH_4OH.	Straw yellow rhombic crystals			35
Ag_2Te Silver telluride	I	955		Insol. in H_2O. Sol. in KCN, NH_4OH.	Gray cubic crystals	-7.0 ~ -10.0	Mineral hessite.	8, 32 35

445

TABLE B-1 (Concluded)

Compound Name	Oxidation State	M.P. (°C)	B.P. (°C)	Solubility	Color, Physical Form	ΔHc kcal/mole	Remarks	References
Ag_2TeO_3 Silver tellurite	I		250 (black) 450 (pale yellow)	Insol. in H_2O. Sol. in KCN, NH_4OH.	Yellow-white precipitate			35
$AgClN_4$ Silver tetrazol	I				Solid		Severe shock hazard.	36
$AgSbS_3$ Silver thioantimonite	I	486		Insol. in H_2O. Sol. in HNO_3.	Red, trigonal crystals			35
$AgAsS_3$ Silver thioarsenite	I	490		Insol. in H_2O. Sol. in HNO_3.	Scarlet red trigonal crystals			35
AgSCN Silver thiocyanate	I	Decomp.		Insol. in H_2O. Sol. in NH_4OH. $K_{sp} = 1.0 \times 10^{-12}$	Colorless crystals	21.0		32 35
$Ag_2S_2O_6 \cdot 2H_2O$ Silver dithionate	I				Rhombic crystals			35
$Ag_2S_2O_3$ Silver thiosulfate	I	Decomp.		Sl. sol. in H_2O. Sol. in $Na_2S_2O_3$, NH_4OH.	White crystals		Dissolves in excess thiosulfate to give variety of complexes.	8 35
$[Ag(S_2O_3)_2]^{3-}$ (aq.)						-285.5	At low $S_2O_3^{2-}$ concns., the chief species is $[Ag_2(S_2O_3)_2]^{2-}$. At high $S_2O_3^{2-}$ concns., species such as $[Ag_2(S_2O_3)_3]^{10-}$ may be present.	2
Ag_2WO_4 Silver tungstate	I	Decomp.		Insol. in H_2O. Sol. in KCN, NH_4OH, HNO_3. $K_{sp} \cong 10^{-13}$	Pale yellow crystals			32 35
$[Ag(NH_3)_2]ReO_4$ Diamminesilver perrhenate	I			Insol. in H_2O. Sol. in concd. NH_4OH.	Colorless monoclinic crystals			35

446

TABLE B-2

SOLUBLE COMPLEX IONS[1,2]

Species	Stability	Remarks
$[AgCl_2]^-$ $[AgCl_3]^{2-}$ $[AgCl_4]^{3-}$	Stable in acid and mildly alkaline media. Some stable at high temperatures.	
$[Ag(CN)_2]^-$		
$[AgSO_4]^-$		
$[Ag(S_2O_3)_2]^{3-}$	Stable in alkaline and neutral solutions. Decomposes in acid to give S, Ag_2S, and some Ag_2SO_4.	Can be reduced by strong reducing agents to Ag_2S.
Ag_3Cl^{2+} Ag_2Cl^+		Evidence given by soly. of AgCl in $AgNO_3$ solns.
$Ag(NH_3)_2^+$		AgI is only sparingly sol. in NH_3.

TABLE B-3

FORMS OF SILVER IN NATURAL WATERS[2,21]

Form	Formula	Remarks
True Solution:		
Ag Ion	Ag^+ dissolved with HCO_3^-, HSO_4^-, or NO_3^-	
Halide Complex Ions	$[AgCl_2]^-$, $[AgCl_3]^{2-}$, or $[AgCl_4]^{3-}$	Where waters or vapors charged with KCl, NaCl, HCl, etc., easily dissociated. Could complex with Br or I.
Ammonia Complex	$[Ag(NH_3)_2]^+$	Occurs in areas of maximum biological activity.
Thionate or Polythionate	$[Ag(S_2O_3)_2]^{3-}$	Soluble in alkaline and neutral solution.
Inorganic Ion Pairs	E.g., AgSH	Found in cold waters.
Sulfide and Polysulfide Complexes	AgS^-, $[Ag(S_4)_2]^{3-}$, $[AgS_5S_4]^{3-}$, and $[Ag(HS)S_4]^{2-}$	Hot springs and waters highly charged with H_2S. Could occur with Te, Se, As, or Sb as double complexes.
Organic Complexes, Chelates	E.g., AgO_2CR, AgSR, acetates, tartrate, etc.	No data on their occurrence.
Dialyzable and/or Membrane Filterable:		
Silver Species Bound to High-mol.-wt. Organic Material	Ag complexes with lipids, humic acid polymers, polysaccharides	
Filterable:		
Colloidal Compounds	AgCl, AgBr, Ag_2S, Ag_2Te, Ag_2Se, Ag_3SbS_3, Ag_3AgS_3, etc.	No data on their occurrence in nature, but expected in normal surface waters where electrolytes and oxidizing sulfide not present.
Species Sorted on Colloids	Perhaps $Ag_x(OH)_y$, Ag_2CO_3, Ag_2S, etc., on clays, FeOOH, or Mn(IV) oxides	
Aerosols	$Ag_2O \cdot nH_2O$, Ag_2S, etc.	Expected in volcanic emanations and steam-impregnated rocks.
Humic Colloids		Occur in natural waters and underground streams.
Adsorbed to Suspended Particles		
As an Integral Part of Microorganisms and Plants		Plankton adsorbs silver strongly.
Elemental Ag Colloids		May be possible in nature, especially in the oxidizing waters of sulfide deposits.

TABLE B-4

MECHANISMS OF PRECIPITATION OF SILVER FROM NATURAL WATERS AND VAPORS[2]

Mechanisms	Remarks Where Likely to Occur
1. Precipitation as the Halide	Probably operative in the oxidized zones of Ag deposits in arid regions.
2. Precipitation as Insoluble Phosphate, Chromate, or Arsenate	Not observed in nature.
3. Precipitation as Sulfide in the Presence of H_2S or S^{2-}	Rocks formed in a reducing environment.
4. Precipitation Due to Decomposition of Soluble Chloride Complexes Caused by Reduced Cl^- Concentration	Decreased CO_2 could also cause breakdown of HCO_3^-.
5. Precipitation Due to Increased pH When Present as Ag^+ Ion	pH of hydrolosis is 7.8 to 8.0.[a] Relatively insoluble in basic solutions unless complexed with ammonia or some other agent.
6. Precipitation as Ag_2S Due to Decomposition of $Ag(S_2O_3)_2$ 3- or AgS^-	As a result of an increase in soln. acidity or redn. by carbonaceous matter.
7. Changes in Oxidation-Reduction Potential	Decreased redox potential increases concentration of Fe^{+2} and shifts Fe^{+2} + $Ag^+ \rightleftharpoons Ag + Fe^{+3}$ to the right. In alkaline solutions, Ag^+ may be precipitated according to the reaction: $2Ag^+ + Mn^{2+} + 4OH^- \rightleftharpoons 2Ag + MnO_2 + 2H_2O$. Oxidation-reduction reactions precipitate silver in the sea, fresh water, manganese, bogs, iron bogs, and oxidation zones of silver deposits.
8. Adsorption Processes, Sometimes in Conjunction with Hydrolytic Reactions or Oxidation-Reduction Reactions	Adsorption by humic compounds, coalified wood in sandstones, coal, and carbonaceous sediments. Ag may be adsorbed and precipitated by inorganic colloids, hydroxides, gels, etc., including clay minerals, collophane, aluminum hydroxide, and silt of all types.
9. Precipitation in Jarosites by Adsorption or Copptn.	
10. Precipitation Due to Evaporation of Solutions	
11. Sublimation	Mainly in volcanic and fumarolic processes.
12. Precipitation Due to Decreased Temperatures or Pressure on Gases or Solutions	Probably operative during formation of primary Ag deposits.
13. Decrease in H_2S, S^{2-}, or CO_2 Concentrations	Where Ag as $AgHCO_3$, $AgSH$, etc.
14. Coagulation of Colloids	Colloidal compounds of Ag and organic colloids with adsorbed Ag may precipitate by various mechanisms such as altered pH, precipitation by electrolytes, and others. The effect of these in formation of primary veins is uncertain, but much silver is probably precipitated from fresh and seawaters by colloidal processes.

a/ The world average pH of rivers is ~6.5.[25]

TABLE B-4 (Concluded)

Remarks
Where Likely to Occur

Mechanisms	Remarks / Where Likely to Occur
15. Oxidation of Organic (Humic) Complexes	Humic compounds decomp. to CO_2 and H_2O, liberating any adsorbed or complexed silver.
16. Sedimentation of Silver-Bearing Particulate Matter	Acts in all sedimentary basins. The silver is then incorporated in the sediments.
17. Death and Sedimentation of Silver-Bearing Plants and Animals	Plankton strongly adsorbs silver and other organisms incorporate it. The H_2S produced by decomposition ppts. silver.
18. Precipitating Action of Organisms	Certain algal species are thought to precipitate silver in thermal waters. Some bacteria and fungi may also be important in precipitating silver from natural waters.

450

BINARY SILVER ALLOY SYSTEMS[27/]

System	Composition	Use	Remarks
Silver-aluminum	Ag-Al eutectic and some Ag-rich Al alloys.	Brazing.	No industrially important alloys.
Silver-beryllium			No industrially important alloys. If brittle intermetallic phases form when joining Be with Ag brazing alloys or in high-temp. services, the brazed joints will degrade.
Silver-calcium		Have been used in past as Raney-type Ag catalyst in which Ca is leached out.	No industrially important binary alloys.
Silver-cadmium	Ag-< 14% Cd; ~ 95% Cd-Ag	Electrical contacts, brazing, neutron adsorbers for regulating nuclear reactor power levels.	Addn. of in improved the alloy's hot-water resistance and structural strength. Contact materials transformed into two-phase materials by internal oxidn. of Cd to CdO.
Silver-copper	90% Ag-10% Cu	Coin silver, slip rings and commutator bars in manuf. of electronic app.	Best combination of strength, hardness, and elec. properties of any Ag alloy.
	80% Ag-20% Cu	Elec. contacts. European tableware. Face pieces of trimetal half dollars minted after 1965.	
	21.5% Ag-78.5% Cu	Center of above coins.	
	72% Ag-28% Cu (eutectic)	Brazing in vacuum tube industry. Basis for Ag-Cu-Zn and Ag-Cu-Zn-Cd brazing alloys. Spring contacts in electronic app.	
	50-99.8% Ag-Cu	Elec. contacts and brazing.	
Silver-germanium	Ag-Ge		No industrially important alloys.
Silver-mercury	Ag-Hg	Dental amalgam.	
Silver-lithium	Ag-Li	Sometimes for brazing.	
Silver-magnesium	< 0.25% Mg-Ag	Elec. devices, esp. spring members in relays.	Most important Mg-Ag alloy. Hardened by internal oxidn. of Mg to MgO. Grain growth during oxidn. restricted by adding < 0.25% Ni.
	1.7% Mg-Ag	Secondary emitter in vacuum tubes for TV cameras.	
Silver-manganese	85% Ag-15% Mn	One of the first high-temp. brazing alloys (World War II).	Largely superseded by Ni-base brazing alloys. Still used when Ag-base alloy desirable but where Ag-Cu-Zn-Cd alloys lack the required high-temp. strength.
Silver-nickel	Ag-Ni	Brazing.	
Silver-palladium	90% Ag-10% Pd	High-temp. brazing.	See also the palladium technical report of this series.
	40% Ag-60% Pd	Elec. relays in telephone app., potentiometers, etc.	

451

TABLE B-6

ANALYTICAL METHODS FOR DETERMINING SILVER

Type of Method	Description	Application	Remarks	Ref.
Gravimetric	Pptn. and weighing of an insol. Ag salt, preferably AgCl. 2-Thio-5-keto-4-carbethoxy-1:3-dihydropyrimidine ppts. in acid soln. (purple ppt.) only with Ag. (Another anal. involves prior extn. of the Ag dithizone complex in an org. solvent and pptn. as AgCl.)	Recommended for most industrial alloys and products.	Not recommended for detg. Ag in alloys contg. > 90% Ag	39
		Food.		40
Titrimetric				
Gay-Lussac	Acid soln. of Ag$^+$ titrated with strong Br$^-$, I$^-$, or Cl$^-$ almost to equivalence point. Titration finished with weaker soln. of precipitant to the point at which no Ag halide ppt. is formed on addn. of precipitant.	Detg. Ag in coinage and other high-Ag alloys.		39
Volhard	Based on insolv. of AgSCN and the intense ferric thiocyanate color formed by the reaction of excess SCN$^-$ with an Fe salt added as the internal indicator.			39
Mohr's method	AgNO$_3$ used as titrant in a soln. contg. excess halide. A sol. chromate serves as internal indicator.	Limited use in detg. Ag or anions that form Ag salts of solubilities less than that of Ag chromate.		39
Combination of Gay-Lussac and Volhard	As in the parent methods, the simultaneous use of stds. or alloys of a compn. approxi-mating that of the samples is required.		Avoids tedium of Gay-Lussac end point detn.	39
Fire assay	A Pb-Ag alloy is formed by fusing the sample with a flux, generally a mixt. of Na or K carbonates and borates, litharge sand, possibly salt, and a carbonaceous rcdg. agent. The Pb-Ag alloy that seps. from the slag is remelted in an oxidizing atm. on a porous cup called a cupel. The Pb and re-tained base metal as the oxides are absorbed by the cupel. The Ag is recovered as a bead remaining on the cupel surface.	Alloys, metallurgical by-products, scrap, ores	Most commonly used method for detg. Ag.	39

452

B-6 (Continued)

Type of Method	Description	Application	Remarks	Ref.
Methods involving complexes	Ag measured indirectly in acid soln. by measuring the amt. of Ni displaced from its CN^- complex.			39
	Ag can be detd. in ammoniacal nitrate solns. by complexing with EDTA as the titrant with dimethyl yellow and thymolphthaloxone as indicators.			
	Ag as a complex cyanide can be pptd. as Ag_2S by treating with org. or inorg. sulfides. The Ag_2S is dissolved in acid and detd. by the Gay-Lussac, Volhard, or potentiometric methods.		Cyanides can also be decompd. by wet oxidn. and the Ag detd. directly.	39
Potentiometric	Method using KI as the titrant with Ag-calomel electrodes and a KNO_3 bridge. Org. substances are wet oxidized and the halides are decompd. by acid.	Detg. Ag in film, photog. paper, and waste products of the photog. industry.		39
	Method similar to above using Br^- as titrant; uses EDTA to complex interfering metals.	Detg. Ag in coinage alloys, refined Ag, and other Ag alloys.		39
	A glass electrode with $MgCl_2$ as titrant can be used to det. potentiometric end points in the titration of $AgNO_3$.			39
	Ascorbic acid suggested as titrant. Ag is reduced to the metal and is detd. potentiometrically.	To det. Ag in photog. developing and wash solns. and in coinage.		39
Voltammetric				
Polarographic	Determines Ag-EDTA complex, Ag^+ in alkali nitrates and perchlorates (supporting electrolyte), or $KAg(CN)_2$ without excess CN^- or other supporting electrolytes. Ag can be detd. as the complex iodide formed by evapg. an aqua regia soln. with hydriodic acid.		No methods for detg. Ag in trace concns. Potential almost completely indistinguishable from that of Hg.	41 39

Type of Method	Description	Application	Remarks	Ref.
Anodic stripping		Used by Eisner and Mark (1970) to analyze Ag in rain and snow. Their technique used a wax-impregnated pyrolytic graphite electrode.	Sensitivity $\geq 4 \times 10^{-11}$M. Only voltammetric methods and ion-selective electrodes are adequate in sensitivity to analyze metals in water to $\leq$ mg/ℓ levels.	42
Ion-selective electrodes	Measures ion activity (ionic strength). Any complexed metal is unmeasured.		Ag electrode com. available. Sensitivity ≥ 0.01 mg/ℓ.	42
Electrometric	Ag detd. by deposition as metal on cathodes from either an ammoniacal or an acid nitrate soln. The coulombs expended are a measure of the Ag content of the electrolyte because of the high electrode efficiency of the nitrate soln.			39
Chromatographic	One method used a cation-exchange resin to remove Ag from an EDTA soln. of Ni and Ag. Another method removed both Ag and Cd on a cation-exchange resin; elution with different concns. of HNO_3 sepd. Ag and Cd.		Academic interest only	39
Radiometric				
Neutron activation analysis	Sample irradiated for 10 sec in a neutron flux and the radiation at 0.66 Mev of ^{110m}Ag is measured.	Detg. trace amts. of Ag in Pb. Similar method used for seawater.	Many problems assocd. with water anal.	42
			Half life of ^{110m}Ag is 253 days.	39
γ-ray spectrometry	^{108}Ag [half-life 2.3 min.], γ-ray energy 0.63 mev. Detected concn. 1.2 ppm. [Detection limit 0.0003 μg.]	Ores, galenas, blendes, Al, Pt sponge, plants.	Sensitivity of radioactivation 0.0055 μg/ml.	41
				41

Type of Method	Description	Application	Remarks	Ref.
Spectrophotometric or spectrographic methods	Emission measured by a photo-cell receiver. Emission spectrum recorded on a plate.			41
Spectral methods based on complexes formed with dithizone (diphenylthiocarbazone) or p-dimethylaminobenzylidenerhodanine, absorbing at 500 mμ and 495 mμ, resp. Also colorimetric detn. as colloidal Ag.	Ag dithizonate in 0.5 N acid is extd. with an org. solvent. The rhodanine complex is a violet colloidal ppt. in 0.05 N HNO_3.	Ores, etc. Food anal.	Sensitivities of the dithizone and rhodanine complexes are 1 to 5 μg/20 ml ext. and 0.5 μg/ml, resp.	41 40
	Ammoniacal Ag soln. reduced by Na hyposulfite in the presence of gelatin to form a clear yellow soln. of colloidal Ag.	Food anal.		40
Flame spectrography and spectrometry	Acetylene-air flame spectrography with 0.5 to 5.0 μg/ml in solns. feeding the flame. H_2-O_2 flame with direct measurement of the emissions-- 0.4 to 4.0 μg Ag/ml.	Detg. Ag in biol. materials, sulfides, metals, alloys, and slags.	Ag present in "natural" samples in such small amts. that flame photometry cannot be used directly after mineralization and solubilization of the sample.	41
Arc spectrography				
Qualitative	Identification of Ag based on the presence of several characteristic lines in the sample's spectrum. Most suitable excitation: a dc arc with cathodic or anodic excitation (high-purity carbon or graphite electrodes).	Soils ≥ 1 ppm Plant ash > 1 ppm $CaCO_3$ > 2 ppm (3280.7 Å)	Sample must be homogeneous. All matter that would form volatile products must be removed.	41
Semi-quant. anal.	Approx. concn. assessed by comparing line intensity with that of the same line in a std. sample of similar compn.	Soils, minerals, Pb- and Sn-base alloys, natural waters. Control quality of pure Ag.	Possible to estimate only within a factor of 10 or to within 30 to 50%.	41
Quant. anal.	Based on detn. of ratio between intensities of two characteristic lines of Ag and of an element present in the sample that is chosen as the internal std. Samples, except for metals and	Rocks, minerals, plants, soils, petroleum, petroleum ash, lubricating oils, carbon of various origins, waters, vegetable ash, tissues, blood, plasma, urinary calculi, beverages, metals		41

Type of Method	Description	Application	Remarks	Ref.
	alloys, are used as a nonconducting powder, which is mixed with C powder and placed in the crater of a graphite, C, or metal electrode. Spectral excitation by cathode layer, d.c. arc, a.c. arc, or interrupted arc excitation.	after sepn. by pptn., Mg and its alloys, Cr, Pb, purified Sn, Bi, Pt, Ga.		
Spark spectrography		Chosen method for many years for analyzing metals and alloys. Main advantage--can analyze aq. seawater solns., too. Semiconductors. Plants (sensitivity after sepn. 0.1 ppm). Soils, rocks, and ores (sensitivity after sepn. 1 ppm).	Elec. spark less sensitive than elec. arc. Trace metals must be sepd. for Ag anal.	41
Porous electrode				41
Rotating electrode		Petroleum products, gasolines, and oils (sensitivity 0.1 ppm).		41
Direct-reading spectrophotometry.	Excitation by arc or spark. Requires internal std. photocell detector.	Anal. of Ag in Cu, Mg, Pb, Sn.	Limited to concns. 0.001-1% in ores, metals, alloys.	41
Molecular fluorescence spectrometry	Three fluorescence reagents for detg. Ag.		Limit of detection 0.01-0.004 mg/l.	42
Atomic absorption spectroscopy	Flame or thermal atomization. (Only 1 element can be analyzed for each sample volatilized.)	Important for measuring metals in water. Ag could not be sepd. from the volatilization of the major salts in anal. of seawater. Used to det. Ag in PbS, Ag ores, and concs.	Conventional sensitivity 0.030 µg/ml. Carbon rod atomizer 1.2 picograms. Ta ribbon/inert gas 50 picograms.	42 39
Atomic fluorescence spectroscopy		Not well developed for water anal.	Detection levels for Ag in picograms	
Atomic emission spectroscopy	Flame or plasma excitation.	Not used much for water anal.	Sensitivity for most metals 10^{-8} to 10^{-12} g.	42

Type of Method	Description	Application	Remarks	Ref.
Emission spectroscopy	Samples must be concd. Excitation by d.c. arc, spark, or plasma torches. Detn. of Ag in nonmetallic samples requires a flux contg. Fe sulfate; the Fe serves as an internal std.	For example, detg. Ag in pig Pb and in Al.	Detection limits 0.1 to 50 $\mu g/l$.	42 39
X-Ray emission spectroscopy.	Excitation by electrons, x-rays, or radioisotope sources. For sensitivities < few mg/l, sample must be concd.			41
X-Ray fluorescence spectrography	Secondary emissions of the sample are compared with those of stds. of known compn.	Ag alloys; detg. small amts. of Cu, Pb, and Fe in fine Ag; detg. Ag in Pb.		39 43
Mass spectrometry	Spark source		Detection limits 0.1-0.01 nanograms.	42
Nephelometric	Trace amts. of Ag^+ in acid solns. detd. by adding Cl^- or Br^-. Opalescence compared with that of stds.	Also used for trace halide detns.		39
Fluorimetric	Similar to above. AgCl or AgBr produced absorb colored ions. For example, AgCl and fluorescein in excess $AgNO_3$ give a pinkish color that turns to yellow with excess Cl^-.			39
Liq. Extraction	Ag dithizonate in strong H_2SO_4 solns. extd. by benzine. Exts. washed with ammonia water and centrifuged; intensity of the Ag complex measured. Ag can be extd. almost specifically from fairly strong HNO_3 soln. by tri-isooctyl or tri-$\underline{n}$-butyl thiophosphate in CCl_4. $PhNO_2$ is quite specific as a solvent for the species formed between Ag and 1,10-phenanthroline with bromopyrogallol.	Detg. Ag in Pb, Cu, and Au concs.		39

457

BIBLIOGRAPHY. APPENDIX B.

1. Cotton, F. A.,and G.Wilkinson, <u>Advanced Inorganic Chemistry. A Compre-</u>
   <u>hensive Text</u>, Interscience Publishers, A Division of John Wiley and
   Sons, USA, 1962.

2. Boyle, R. W., "Geochemistry of Silver and Its Deposits with Notes on
   Geochemical Prospecting for the Element," <u>Geol. Surv. Can., Bull.</u>,
   No. 160, 1-264 (1968).

3. Feitknecht, W., and P. Schindler, "Solubility Constants of Metal
   Hydroxide Salts in Aqueous Solution," <u>Pure and Applied Chemistry</u>,
   $\underset{\sim}{6}$, 125-199 (1963).

4. Mesmer, R. E., and C. F. Baes, Jr., <u>The Hydrolysis of Cations. A</u>
   <u>Critical Review of Hydrolytic Species and Their Stability Constants</u>
   <u>in Aqueous Solution</u>, Part III, Oak Ridge National Laboratory, Oak
   Ridge, Tennessee, (U.S. Government Printing Office: 1974-748-189/78),
   1974.

5. Lisk, D. J., "Trace Metals in Soils, Plants, and Animals" in <u>Advances</u>
   <u>in Agronomy</u>, Vol. 24, Academic Press, New York, New York, 1972,
   pp. 267-325.

6. Evans, U. R., <u>The Corrosion and Oxidation of Metals: Scientific</u>
   <u>Principles and Practical Applications</u>, Edward Arnold (Publishers),
   Ltd., London, 1960.

7. Anonymous, <u>New Silver Technology. Silver Abstracts from the Current</u>
   <u>World Literature</u>, The Silver Institute, Washington, D.C., April 1974.

8. Tischer, T. H., "Silver Compounds" in the <u>Kirk-Othmer Encyclopedia of</u>
   <u>Chemical Technology</u>, Vol. 18, 2nd completely revised ed., Interscience
   Publishers, Division of John Wiley and Sons, Inc., New York, New York,
   1969, pp. 295-309.

9. Ellern, H., <u>Military and Civilian Pyrotechnics</u>, Chemical Publishing
   Company, Inc., New York, New York, 1968.

10. Butts, A., "Chapter 8. The Chemical Properties of Silver" in <u>Silver</u>
    <u>Economics, Metallurgy, and Use</u>, A. Butts and C. D. Coxe, Eds.,
    D. Van Nostrand Company, Inc., Princeton, New Jersey, 1967,
    pp. 123-136.

11. Leach, R. H., "Corrosion in Liquid Media, the Atmosphere, and Gases. Silver and Silver Alloys" in The Corrosion Handbook, H. H. Uhlig, Ed., John Wiley and Sons, Inc., New York, New York, 1948, pp. 314-320.

12. Vines, R. F., "Chapter 22. Noble Metals" in Corrosion Resistance of Metals and Alloys, 2nd ed., F. L. LaQue and H. R. Copson, Eds., American Chemical Society Monograph No. 158, Reinhold Publishing Corporation, New York, New York, 1963, pp. 601-622.

13. Tomashov, N. D., Theory of Corrosion and Protection of Metals. The Science of Corrosion, translated and edited by B. H. Tytell, I. Geld, and H. S. Preiser, The MacMillan Company, New York, New York, 1966.

14. Hauffe, K., Oxidation of Metals (based on the German ed. of Oxydation von Metallen und Metallegierungen), Plenum Press, New York, New York, 1965.

15. Leach, R. H., "High-Temperature Corrosion. Silver" in The Corrosion Handbook, H. H. Uhlig, Ed., John Wiley and Sons, Inc., New York, New York, 1948, pp. 718-720.

16. Butts, A., and J. M. Thomas, "Chapter 15. Corrosion Resistance of Silver and Silver Alloys" in Silver in Industry, L. Addicks, Ed., Reinhold Publishing Company, New York, New York, 1940.

17. Groll, P., and L. Stieglitz, "Die Korrosive Wirkung von Kunststoff-Folien (PVC) auf Silbermünzen" (The Corrosive Effect of Plastic Foils (PVC) on Silver Coins"), Z. Anal. Chem., 267(3), 189-191 (1973).

18. Guiot, J. M., "Interaction of Oxygen with Palladium Powder," J. Appl. Physics, 39(7), 3509-3511 (1968).

19. Clarkson, R. B., and A. C. Cirillo, Jr., "The Formation and Reactivity of Oxygen as O_2^- on Supported Silver Catalytic Surfaces," J. Catalysis, 33(3), 392-401 (1974).

20. Chaston, J. C., "Chapter 20. Oxygen in Silver" in Silver. Economics, Metallurgy, and Use, A. Butts and C. D. Coxe, Eds., D. Van Nostrand Company, Inc., Princeton, New Jersey, 1967, pp. 304-309.

21. Stumm, W., and H. Bilinski, "Trace Metals in Natural Waters; Difficulties of Interpretation Arising from Our Ignorance on Their Speciation" in Advances in Water Pollution Research, Proceedings of the Sixth International Conference held in Jerusalem, June 18-23, 1972, S. H. Jenkins, Ed., Pergamon Press, New York, New York, 1973, pp. 39-52.

22. Kharkar, K., K. Turekian, and K. Bertine, "Stream Supply of Dissolved Ag, Mo, Sb, Se, Cr, Co, Rb, and Cs to the Oceans," Geochim. Cosmochim. Acta, 32, 285-298 (1968).

23. Turekian, K. K., and M. R. Scott, "Concentrations of Cr, Ag, Mo, Ni, Co, and Mn in Suspended Material in Streams," Environ. Sci. Technol., 1, 940-942 (1967).

24. Konovalov, G. S., A. A. Ivanova, and T. Kh. Kolesnikov, "Trace and Rare Elements Dissolved in Water and Present in Suspended Substances of the Main Rivers of the USSR," Geokhim. Osad. Porod, 72-89 (1968); Chem. Abstr., 71, 222 (1969) from Ref. Zh. Geol., V, Abstr. No. 11V016 (1968).

25. Murray, C. N., and L. Murray, "Adsorption-Desorption Equilibria of Some Radionuclides in Sediment-Fresh-Water and Sediment-Seawater Systems" in Proceedings of Radioactive Contamination of the Marine Environment Symposium, Intern. Atomic Energy Agency, Seattle, Washington, 1973, pp. 105-124.

26. Clarke, F. W., The Data of Geochemistry, Bulletin 770, 5th ed., U. S. Geological Survey, Department of the Interior, Washington, D.C., 1924.

27. McDonald, A. S., B. R. Price, and G. H. Sistare, "Chapter 18. Alloying Behavior of Silver and Its Principal Alloys" in Silver. Economics, Metallurgy, and Use, A. Butts and C. D. Coxe, Eds., D. Van Nostrand Company, Inc., Princeton, New Jersey, 1967, pp. 235-271.

28. McDonald, A. S., B. R. Price, and G. H. Sistare, "Chapter 19. Ternary and Higher-Order Alloys of Silver" in Silver. Economics, Metallurgy, and Use, A. Butts, and C. D. Coxe, Eds., D. Van Nostrand Company, Inc., Princeton, New Jersey, 1967, pp. 272-303.

29. Rhys, D. W., and W. Betteridge, "Brazing for Elevated Temperature Service," Metal Ind., 101(2), 2-4, 27-30, 45-46 (1962).

30. MacWilliam, E. A., "Chapter 14. Silver in Photography" in Silver. Economics, Metallurgy, and Use, A. Butts and C. D. Coxe, Eds., D. Van Nostrand Company, Inc., Princeton, New Jersey, 1967, pp. 200-217.

31. Kleinberg, J., W. J. Argersinger, Jr., and E. Griswold, Inorganic Chemistry, D. C. Heath and Company, Boston, Massachusetts, 1960.

32. Gedansky, L. M., and L. G. Hepler, "Thermochemistry of Silver and Its Compounds," Engelhard Ind. Tech. Bull., 9(4), 117-128 (1969).

33. McMillan, J. A., "Higher Oxidation States of Silver," _Chem. Revs._, _62_(1), 65-80 (1962).

34. Stecher, P. G., Ed., _The Merck Index_, 8th ed., Merck and Company, Inc., Rahway, New Jersey, 1968.

35. Weast, R. C., Ed., _Handbook of Chemistry and Physics_, 50th ed., Chemical Rubber Publishing Company, Cleveland, Ohio, 1969-1970.

36. Sax, N. I., "Silver-Silver Thioarsenite," _Dangerous Properties of Industrial Materials_, 2nd ed., Reinhold Publishing Corporation, New York, New York, 1963, pp. 1174-1178.

37. Rose, A., and E. Rose, _The Condensed Chemical Dictionary_, 7th ed., Reinhold Publishing Corporation, New York, New York, 1966.

38. Anonymous, "Properties of the Simple Molybdates," _Molybdenum Chemicals, Chemical Data Series_, Bulletin Cdb-4, Climax Molybdenum Company, New York, New York, 1962.

39. Donahue, G. F., "Chapter 28. The Analytical Chemistry of Silver" in _Silver. Economics, Metallurgy, and Use_, A. Butts and C. D. Coxe, Eds., D. Van Nostrand Company, Inc., Princeton, New Jersey, 1967, pp. 409-417.

40. Monier-Williams, G. W., _Trace Elements in Food_, John Wiley and Sons, Inc., New York, New York, 1949, pp. 418-427.

41. Pinta, M., _Detection and Determination of Trace Elements_, Distributor Daniel Davey and Company, Inc., New York, New York, 1966. Translated from French by Miriam Bivas and edited by IPST, Israel Program for Scientific Translations, Jerusalem, 1966.

42. Minear, R. A., and B. B. Murray, "Methods of Trace Metals Analysis in Aquatic Systems" in _Trace Metals and Metal-Organic Interactions in Natural Waters_, P. C. Singer, Ed., Ann Arbor Science Publishers, Inc., Ann Arbor, Michigan, 1973.

43. De Neef, J., F. Adams, and J. Hoste, "Radioisotopic X-Ray Analysis. Part II. The Determination of Silver, Tin and Antimony in Lead," _Anal. Chim. Acta_, _62_, 71-77 (1972).

466

production 2, 81, 99, 104, 105, 127
mirrors 218, 219
mobilization and fixation of silver in primary silver deposits and soils 429-433
mucous membrane antiseptics and germicides 264, 265

natural sources 1, 11-15, 18, 19, 20-34, 80-92, 103-105

office-copying systems 231
oil shales, silver content 16, 17, 62
oils (refined)
  catalyst, silver in refining 215
  content, of silver 63, 335, 336, 406
open hearth steelmaking 318, 319, 335-337, 406
ores, silver 2, 11, 73, 80 82-85, 137-139, 429-431
ores, silver containing 1, 2, 11, 16, 18, 19, 25-30, 73, 80-92, 116, 118-120, 129, 137-139, 429-431
oxidation catalysts 213-215, 253
oxidation states 418, 419, 438-446
oxygen, reactions of silver with 423, 424

petrochemicals 215, 216, 258
petroleum refining
  refined oils 63
  silver as catalyst 215, 256
  silver content and location 62
photographic process 435-437
photography
  import-export 229-231
  loss of silver to environment 310, 311, 324, 406
  process 435-437

silver content of film 188
silver in 5, 77, 108, 109, 124, 125, 132, 402
silver recovery from waste 167-174
uses 204
physical constants of silver 411
physical properties of silver and its alloys 408-414
physical properties of silver compounds 438-446
plants, silver
  effects on higher plants 362, 380
  effects on microflora 361, 362, 378, 379
  in 1, 8, 15, 50-53, 404
pollution 4-8, 12-15
  (see water, air, soil)
polymerization catalyst 215, 257
precipitates (natural) 13, 14, 427, 428, 449, 450
precipitation in silver recovery 168
primary sources of domestic silver
  mines 74, 75, 82-92
  ores 73, 79-81, 86-88
process and laboratory equipment 220, 273
production, silver
  by district and area 82-85, 182, 183
  by state and source 81
  methods 139-187, 199-203
  milling 179, 180, 291-297
  mines 87, 88, 104, 105, 114-119
  producers 99, 228
  U.S. 126-128
  world 110
proprietary compounds, silver 260-263

toxicity 4, 6-8, 353, 355, 356,
       358-360, 361, 362, 364,
       367-374, 378-380, 402-404
toxicity (animals)
  acute 355, 358, 359
  chronic 356, 359, 360
toxicity (humans) 6-8, 353,
       355, 356, 364

urban water supplies 14, 15,
       47-49, 272, 394-396
uses of silver 4, 199-276, 406
  (see consumption of silver)

vacuum coatings 212
vinyl polymerization 215

wastewater treatment practices
       15, 167-170, 189
water, natural
  forms of silver in 448
  mechanism of silver precipi-
       tation 449, 450
  suspended particles 45, 426-
       429
  U.S. 13, 41-44
water pollution 5, 13-15, 324-
       326, 394-396, 403
water, silver dissolved in 426,
       427
weather modification 4, 12,
       220-225, 274
world statistics 98, 102

zinc 2, 3, 5, 81-87, 91, 117,
       118, 129, 139, 158-160,
       227, 304-306, 405
zinc circuit 158-160